Dracula's Literary Ancestors Revealed

Vampire Grooms and Spectre Brides

The Marriage of French
and British Gothic Literature

1789-1897

Tyler R. Tichelaar, PhD

Author of

The Gothic Wanderer: From Transgression to Redemption

Marquette Fiction

Vampire Grooms and Spectre Brides:
The Marriage of French and British Gothic Literature, 1789-1897

Copyright © 2023 by Tyler R. Tichelaar

All rights reserved. No part of this book may be used or reproduced by any means, graphic, electronic, or mechanical, including photocopying, recording, taping, or by any information storage retrieval system without the written permission of the publisher except in the case of brief quotations embodied in critical articles and reviews. Inquiries should be addressed to:

Marquette Fiction
1202 Pine Street
Marquette, MI 49855
www.MarquetteFiction.com

All efforts have been made to source properly all quotations.

ISBN-13: 978-0-9962400-9-3 (hardcover)

ISBN-13: 978-0-9962400-8-6 (paperback)

ISBN-13: 979-8-9872692-0-6 (eBook)

Library of Congress Control Number: 2022921439

Printed in the United States of America

Cover Art: Inna Vjuzhanina, www.InnaVjuzhanina.com

Cover Design and Interior Layout: Larry Alexander, Superior Book Productions

Publication managed by Superior Book Productions, www.SuperiorBookProductions.com

"This is, moreover, the tendency of our age, and the law of radiance of the French Revolution; books must cease to be exclusively French, Italian, German, Spanish, or English, and become European, I say more, human, if they are to correspond to the enlargement of civilization."

— Victor Hugo,
Letter to M. Daelli, publisher of the
Italian translation of *Les Misérables*,
October 18, 1862

Contents

A Note on the Text i
Introduction iii
Chapter 1: Vampire Invasion 1
   Mrs. Radcliffe and the Gothic Novel 2
   Sir Walter Scott and the Historical Novel 10
   John Polidori's *The Vampyre* 17
   Conclusion 27
Chapter 2: Historicizing the Gothic and Gothicizing History 29
   Sir Walter Scott's *Ivanhoe* 30
   Victor Hugo's *Notre-Dame de Paris* 35
   William Harrison Ainsworth's Early Gothic Novels 50
     *Rookwoo*d 51
     The Tower of London 57
Chapter 3: City Mysteries 71
   Eugène Sue's *The Mysteries of Paris* 72
   Paul Féval's *Les Mystères de Londres* 80
   George W. M. Reynolds' *The Mysteries of London* 92
   Alexandre Dumas' *The Count of Monte Cristo* 105
   Conclusion 116
Chapter 4: Wandering Jews 119
   The Wandering Jew's Origins 120
   Matthew Lewis' *The Monk* 123
   William Harrison Ainsworth's "The Spectre Bride" 128
   George Croly's *Salathiel* 131
   Edgar Quinet's *Ahasvérus* 152
   Eugène Sue's *The Wandering Jew* 161
   Sue's *The Mysteries of the People* and Reynolds'
     The Mysteries of the Court of London 177
   Alexandre Dumas' *Isaac Laquedem* 179
   Paul Féval's *The Wandering Jew's Daughter* 188
   Conclusion 192
Chapter 5: Secret Societies 193
   Sir Walter Scott's *Anne of Geierstein* 197
   George W. M. Reynolds' *Faust* 207
   George W. M. Reynolds' *Wagner, the Wehr-Wolf* 211
   Bram Stoker's *Powers of Darkness* (The Swedish *Dracula*) 221

Chapter 6: The French Revolution Revised 237
  Edward Bulwer-Lytton's *Zanoni* 238
  Alexandre Dumas' Marie Antoinette Novels 249
    Joseph Balsamo 254
    The Mesmerist's Victim 261
    The Queen's Necklace 262
    The Storming of the Bastille 263
    The Hero of the People 265
    The Royal Life Guard 268
    The Countess de Charny 268
  Dumas' *Le Chevalier de Maison-Rouge* and Dickens'
    A Tale of Two Cities 270
  Other Sources for *A Tale of Two Cities* 276
  Rosicrucian Immortality and Christian Redemption in
    A Tale of Two Cities 283
  Conclusion 300
Chapter 7: The Road to *Dracula* 301
  Polidori's *The Vampyre* and Its Imitators 302
    Cyprien Bérard's *Lord Ruthwen ou les vampires* 304
    Charles Nodier's *The Vampire* 308
    J. R. Planché's *The Vampire and Der Vampyr* 310
    Alexandre Dumas' *The Vampire* 315
    Dion Boucicault's *The Vampire and The Phantom* 319
    Jules Dornay's *Douglas Le Vampire* 322
    Gilbert and Sullivan's *Ruddigore* 325
  Other Vampire Texts Between *The Vampyre* and *Dracula* 329
    Uriah Derick D'Arcy's "The Black Vampyre" 330
    Étienne-Léon de Lamothe-Langon's *The Virgin Vampire* 334
    Elizabeth Caroline Grey's "The Skeleton Count, or
      The Vampire Mistress" 343
    Théophile Gautier's "Clarimonde" 346
    Alexandre Dumas' *The Thousand and One Ghosts* 350
    George W. M. Reynolds' *The Necromancer* 354
    Angelo de Sorr's *The Vampires of London* 358
    Pierre-Alexis Ponson du Terrail's Vampire Novels 363
      The Vampire and the Devil's Son 364
      The Immortal Woman 366
    Léon Gozlan's *The Vampire of the Val-de-Grâce* 369
    Paul Féval's Vampire Novels 373
      The Vampire Countess 373

  Knightshade 376
  Vampire City 377
 Joseph Sheridan Le Fanu's *Carmilla* 383
 Marie Nizet's *Captain Vampire* 388
 Anonymous' *The Vampire: or, Detective Brand's Greatest Case* 394
 Jules Verne's *The Carpathian Castle* 397
 Florence Marryat's *The Blood of the Vampire* 403
 Vampire Short Stories 408
  Karl von Wachsmann's "The Mysterious Stranger" 408
  William Gilbert's "The Last Lords of Gardonal" 413
  Guy de Maupassant's "The Horla" 413
  Julian Hawthorne's "Ken's Mystery" 415
  Eric Stenbock's "The Sad Story of a Vampire" 417
  Mary E. Braddon's "Good Lady Ducayne" 420
 Bram Stoker's *Dracula* 421
Afterword 457
Acknowledgments 461
Bibliography 463
Endnotes 487
Index 503
About the Author 517
Books by Tyler R. Tichelaar 519

A Note on the Text

I HAVE OPTED THROUGHOUT THIS BOOK to provide both French and English titles for works originally written in French upon first reference and then have used the English title after that for ease of reading for those not proficient in French. One exception is I have retained the French title of Paul Féval's *Les Mystères de Londres* to prevent it being confused with George W. M. Reynolds' *The Mysteries of London*. Also, some English titles are not literal translations from the French; for example, *Notre-Dame de Paris* is commonly translated into English as *The Hunchback of Notre-Dame*. In such cases, I have noted the name changes.

I have relied upon ebook editions for many of the main texts. This decision has its advantages and disadvantages. The disadvantage is that not all ebooks incorporate page numbers. When this was the case, I have only been able to reference the chapter from which a quote was taken. I trust readers will still be able to find the passages easily. In my opinion, ebooks are the new best friend of the scholar because they are easily searchable and allow the copying and pasting of text to ensure no errors are made in retyping. Anyone who wants to find a quoted passage can easily do so with an ebook. I wish ebooks had existed when I wrote my first Gothic study, *The Gothic Wanderer: From Transgression to Redemption*, because it would have saved me countless hours trying to find a passage I had handwritten in a notebook and then forgotten to write the page number beside. Ebooks also allow for searches to find key words of interest. Plus, they take up less space, are more environmentally friendly, and cost less. I encourage academics to embrace ebooks.

I have used both endnotes and footnotes. Endnotes solely list sources of information and can be ignored by the reader unless the reader wishes to know the source. I have avoided using Ibid. and listed the full source for each item because in ebooks the endnotes may come up as showing just the individual note, so it is not always easy to see the notes that come before it. Footnotes do contain additional information about the text, and I encourage readers to read them.

Introduction

"his trousers here, his towels there, and his
French novels everywhere."

— Wilkie Collins, *The Moonstone*

THE ABOVE QUOTE FROM WILKIE COLLINS' 1868 masterpiece[1] testifies that young gentlemen in England at the time were reading French novels, and yet the influence of French literature has been all but ignored by most scholars of British Gothic literature. This omission is surprising given that French novels were read in England by a wide audience in the nineteenth century as British literature of the period itself testifies. Besides the reference in Collins' *The Moonstone*, in Anthony Trollope's *The Small House at Allington* (1864), we are told of the Earl de Courcy that "He always breakfasted alone, and after breakfast found in a French novel and a cigar what solace those innocent recreations were still able to afford him."[2] In the last chapter of *Barchester Towers* (1857), Trollope references three contemporary French authors as he attempts to complete his story, "What novelist, what Fielding, what Scott, what George Sand, or Sue, or Dumas can impart an interest to the last chapter of his fictitious history?"[3] Mary E. Braddon, best remembered for *Lady Audley's Secret* (1862), writes in her short story "Good Lady Ducayne" (1896) of a young companion paid to read to the title character, but because the companion's French is not good, the French maid instead reads French works to Lady Ducayne: "When she is tired of my reading she orders Francine, her maid, to read a French novel to her, and I hear her chuckle and groan now and then, as if she were more interested in those books than in Dickens or Scott."[4] Furthermore, in *Lady Audley's Secret*, the lawyer Robert Audley is emphatically associated with reading French novels to the point of neglecting his work, and in William Makepeace Thackeray's *Pendennis* (1848-50), a student's quarters are described as, "While there was quite an infantine law library clad in skins of fresh new born calf, there was a tolerably large collection of classical books which he could not read, and of English and French works of poetry and fiction which he read a great deal too much."[5]

Countless books have been written on nineteenth-century British Gothic literature, including my previous book *The Gothic Wanderer: From Transgression to Redemption*. Possibly, books have also been written on nineteenth-century French Gothic literature that are not accessible to an English-speaking audience since they were written in French, although the study of the Gothic does not yet seem to have become popular among academics in France.[6] Even some significant nineteenth-century French Gothic novels have not been translated into English, and some of those that have been translated have suffered from being abridged. As a result, many students of the Gothic, myself included until recently, have been unfamiliar with the incredible influence that French and British Gothic novelists of this period had upon one another.

In scholarly works, if influence between French and British literature is mentioned, it is usually done so in passing and rarely detailed. To the best of my knowledge, no one to date has written a full study of how British and French Gothic texts influenced each other. The most thorough study I have found of English literature's influence on French novels has been Eric Partridge's *The French Romantics' Knowledge of English Literature*, which was published in 1924, and as thorough as it is, it only briefly mentions a few Gothic novels and quotes extensively in French, which makes it inaccessible to many readers. M. G. Devonshire's *The English Novel in France* (1929) similarly extensively discusses how English literature influenced French literature from 1830-70, but also makes little mention of Gothic fiction beyond Radcliffe and Lewis. Neither Partridge nor Devonshire mention Polidori or vampire fiction at all. Many other critics have discussed the specific influence of an individual work upon an author or work, but none have broadly discussed such influences upon the Gothic novel throughout the nineteenth century.

A misconception also appears to exist that British Victorians did not read French literature, thinking it too risqué. The above examples prove that is largely untrue. While some Victorians did hold that viewpoint, the extent of it has been heavily exaggerated. In his Preface to *The Modern Literature of France* (1839), George W. M. Reynolds, one of the most prolific British Victorian Gothic novelists, addressed this issue by stating that the journals of the day expressed as much dislike for anything French as they did during the Napoleonic Wars. He also disputed an article written three years earlier in the *Quarterly Review* that suggested the 1830 insurrection in France resulted from "the depraved taste of the nation with regard to literature, a proposition no less ridiculous than unfounded."[7] He goes on to argue that the divorce, licentiousness, and murders that take place in France cannot be attributed to its literature and that the British are just as guilty if not more so of such behaviors. Then he argues that the sense of freedom that resulted from the 1830 revolution is precisely what has led to an increase of high quality literature in France.* Consequently, his study reviews only French literature written after 1830. Most remarkably, with every author Reynolds discusses, he translates passages from works not yet known in England as examples of the French authors' writing styles.

---

*One of the giants of French Romanticism, Charles Nodier, would agree with him on this point. In his essay "Du fantastique en littérature" in the *Revue de Paris* in 1830, Nodier argued that: "the fantastique requires a virginal imagination and beliefs that secondary literatures lack, and which are only reproduced therein following revolutions whose passage renews everything." (Quoted in Stableford, "Introduction," *Weird Fiction in France*, p. 6.)

Despite Reynolds' arguments and efforts, it is hard to know how many people listened to him. While some prejudice toward French literature doubtless remained, Juliette Atkinson has revealed in her 2013 article "The London Library and the Circulation of French Fiction in the 1840s" that circulation records from the London Library and other British libraries prove early British Victorians were reading French literature. Furthermore, Alexander Hugh Jordan, in an article discussing the influence of Carlyle upon Eugène Sue, remarks:

> As Juliette Atkinson has recently noted, the assumption that the Victorians rejected contemporary French literature as "immoral" has proven stubbornly persistent, despite overwhelming evidence to the contrary (391-93). In fact, the productions of leading French novelists met with a wide-ranging and enthusiastic response in Britain, not least through the medium of English translations. For instance, between 1842 and 1847, no less than seven of George Sand's novels made their way to Britain (Bensimon 200-01). Moreover, thanks to the endeavours of Berry Palmer Chevasco [in *Mysterymania*], we now possess a near-exhaustive study of the British reception of Eugène Sue, and particularly of his *Mystères de Paris*. As Chevasco points out, in 1844 and 1845 alone, thirteen separate editions of Sue's novels appeared in Britain (80).[8]

Consequently, a convincing argument can be made not only that the British read French literature, but that British authors were influenced by their French contemporaries and vice versa. In fact, the influence of British authors on French authors is better documented, at least among studies written in English. Literary historian Maurice Lévy has documented more than one hundred English Gothic novels translated into French by the 1820s.[9] Regardless, much work remains to be done to understand the influences that extended in both directions among British and

French Gothic novelists from the time of the French Revolution through the nineteenth century.

Vampire Grooms and Spectre Brides: The Marriage of French and British Gothic Literature seeks to help fill the void of documenting the influence that both nations' Gothic literature had upon one another. While no study can fully display the depth of influence individual works had upon each other, I hope this book will inspire a revision of Gothic studies with the understanding that there is no isolated British or French Gothic tradition, but rather a tradition that crosses national boundaries. I am also fully aware that the French and British novels I will discuss influenced other nations' literatures and were influenced by them. For example, it is well known that German Gothic works had a significant influence upon British and French Gothic works, especially in the days of the Gothic's infancy. However, to create a manageable survey, I will focus, with a few exceptions, on British and French texts.

The title of this book reflects the frequent attempts by male vampire characters, usually based upon John Polidori's vampire Lord Ruthven, to force a woman to marry him so she can become his victim. William H. Ainsworth's short story "The Spectre Bride" is also referenced in the title. It refers to a bride who, surprisingly, is not supernatural but forced to marry a supernatural being. The word "marriage" in this book's subtitle is perfect to describe the relationship between French and British Gothic because it goes beyond the idea of simple influence to a partnership. I believe in many cases the French and British Gothic writers were conscious that they were writing within the same Gothic tradition and being influenced by one another's work. Proof of that influence will be provided in every chapter of this book and, hopefully, readers will be convinced by the book's conclusion of my argument for this incredible shared influence that crossed national and language barriers.

Before diving further into our subject, it is best to define a few terms. By French Gothic, I am referring specifically to novels, plays, and short stories written within the boundaries of France. Similarly, by British, I mean works produced within Great Britain. I have chosen not to use the term English because it is less encompassing and could refer solely to England, while British would include works produced in Ireland, Scotland, Wales, and England. I have also opted to use British rather than English so it is not confused with works written in English by people outside of Great Britain, such as in the United States, Canada, New Zealand, or Australia. Only works produced within the national boundaries of Great Britain and France between 1789 and 1897 will be discussed in detail, with the exception of two American vampire works and the Swedish translation of *Dracula*.

Secondly, by using the term Gothic, I am referring to texts that include supernatural beings and occurrences, also known as the masculine Gothic, which includes works by Matthew Lewis, Alexandre Dumas, Bram Stoker, and others. I am also referring to texts where supernatural beings or events are believed to be occurring, even though they turn out to have rational explanations; this school is known as the feminine Gothic and is represented primarily by the novels of Mrs. Radcliffe, although male authors like Pierre-Alexis Ponson du Terrail and Jules Verne also fit into this category.* By Gothic, I am also referring to works that are devoid of anything supernatural but still have a Gothic atmosphere, specifically crime-related novels, which arose out of the "mystery" aspect of earlier Gothic literature. Such works include the city mysteries novels of Eugène Sue, Paul Féval, and George W. M. Reynolds.

The bulk of the works discussed in this book belong to what I consider the Second Golden Age of the Gothic. As is well known, the Gothic novel began with Horace Walpole's *The Castle of Otranto*, published in 1764, but its Golden Age really began in the 1790s when the terrors of the French Revolution resulted

---

* The terms masculine and feminine Gothic were first coined by Kate Ellis in *The Contested Castle: Gothic Novels and the Subversion of Domestic Ideology* (1989).

in a flood of Gothic novels that reflected people's fears played out in a fictional form and set in the past because the present horrors were too terrifying to contemplate. This period ranges roughly from 1789-1820 and includes the works of Mrs. Radcliffe, Matthew Lewis, Mary Shelley's *Frankenstein* (1818), and Charles Maturin's *Melmoth the Wanderer* (1820). The Second Gothic Golden Age began about a dozen years later. The year 1818 is a key year for the Gothic because two Gothic parody novels, Jane Austen's *Northanger Abbey* and Thomas Love Peacock's *Nightmare Abbey*, were published that year, announcing if not causing the Gothic's death knell for the next decade. Parodies are always a sign that genres are popular but have also begun to decline in quality or influence.

The Gothic craze fell off in the 1820s with few notable works. Not until Victor Hugo published *Notre-Dame de Paris* in 1831 (translated into English in 1833 by Frederic Shoberl as *The Hunchback of Notre-Dame*) and William Harrison Ainsworth published *Rookwood* in 1834 did the Gothic regain its popularity. This Second Gothic Golden Age would run through the 1850s, at which time crime fiction, the child of the Gothic, superseded it in popularity along with sensational Victorian novels. However, the Gothic would remain popular throughout the nineteenth century, and following the 1897 publication of *Dracula*, and the subsequent film versions of that novel that made horror a staple of modern cinema, the Gothic has become immortal in a way many of its characters who sought the elixir of life never could have foreseen.

This Second Gothic Golden Age is when the influences of French and British Gothic literature were strongest upon each other, and it is that mutual influence I wish to highlight in this book. The nineteenth century was a period when authors in France and Great Britain largely spoke each other's language and read each other's books, often in their original language, but also in translation. Today, I suspect people are less bilingual than they were then. As an American, I studied French in school, but I cannot speak it fluently or even read it without it being a somewhat painstaking task. I suspect many literary scholars (despite most PhD programs requiring one or two foreign languages) and most general readers would say the same. Consequently, we must rely upon translations and the decisions of publishers and translators about which works will be translated. I hope *Vampire Grooms and Spectre Brides* will bring attention to the incredible influence that British and French authors of this period had upon each other. This literary marriage has long been overlooked largely because of translation barriers, so I wish my work to inspire further scholarship and interest.

I also hope this book will bring more attention to many significant writers of nineteenth-century Gothic literature who have largely been ignored until recent years. While Charles Dickens, Victor Hugo, and Alexandre Dumas are, if not household names, known by most lovers of books, authors like George W. M. Reynolds, William Harrison Ainsworth, Eugène Sue, and Paul Féval are unknown to most readers. These authors were in many ways just as remarkable as their better-known contemporaries. In fact, Reynolds and Ainsworth's novels are said to have outsold those of Dickens, and as much as I love Dickens, both Reynolds and Ainsworth, in my opinion, surpassed Dickens in their plotting and pacing skills, if not in their character development or overall philosophical outlook. Similarly, the imaginations of the French authors of this period knew no bounds and their fantastic works deserve to be read today. Reading Sue's *The Wandering Jew* or Féval's *Vampire City* are incredible treats more readers should experience.

Nineteenth-century French and British Gothic is as capable today of teaching and entertaining us as it was for its original readers, for the twenty-first century is for us just as traumatic and terrorizing, if in different ways, as the nineteenth century was for our ancestors. By exploring such fears and the works they inspired, not only do we better understand Gothic literature, but we better understand the tastes, concerns, hopes, and dreams of our nineteenth-century ancestors, and in understanding them, we can understand more about ourselves because we are living their legacy.

Tyler R. Tichelaar
Marquette, Michigan
Halloween 2022

Chapter 1

Vampire Invasion

Mrs. Radcliffe, Sir Walter Scott, and John Polidori

"Valancourt, and who was he? cry the young people. Valancourt, my dears, was the hero of one of the most famous romances which ever was published in this country. The beauty and elegance of Valancourt made your young grandmammas' gentle hearts to beat with respectful sympathy. He and his glory have passed away."

— William Makepeace Thackeray, *Roundabout Paper* no. xxiv (1860), referencing the hero of Mrs. Radcliffe's *The Mysteries of Udolpho*

THE YEAR IS 1820. A vampire is about to invade France. He is Lord Ruthven, the villain of John William Polidori's 1819 novella *The Vampyre*. Polidori's story has already achieved great fame and created controversy in England, both because it has been wrongly attributed in print to Lord Byron and because Lord Ruthven has been rumored to be a depiction of Lord Byron. *The Vampyre* was not the first work to insinuate that Lord Byron had vampiric tendencies; that honor goes to Lady Caroline Lamb's 1816 novel *Glenarvon*. Lamb, who had suffered a tumultuous love affair with Byron, had gotten her revenge by writing the novel. Polidori was possibly seeking to do the same after spending a likely unpleasant time as Byron's physician, although given that the story was apparently published without Polidori's permission, he may have only wished for private, not public, revenge.[1]

The story of how *The Vampyre* came to be a written has been told repeatedly. During the cold summer of 1816, Percy and Mary Shelley and Mary's stepsister Claire Clairmont visited Lord Byron where he had rented a villa on Lake Geneva. Byron was accompanied by his physician, Polidori. To entertain themselves, the party read a book of ghost stories, which inspired them to write their own stories. Percy Shelley appears not to have succeeded in writing anything and Lord Byron only wrote a fragment, but Mary Shelley produced *Frankenstein* and Polidori wrote *The Vampyre*.

Ironically, the book of ghost stories the party read that summer, *Fantasmagoriana*, was a French translation of a German book. The book had already been translated into English in 1813 under the title *Tales of the Dead*, but the party read the French translation. Consequently, *The Vampyre*, an English story that would heavily influence French Gothic literature, was itself inspired by the French translation of a German work.

While *The Vampyre* is not well known today due to its being overshadowed by the success of Bram Stoker's *Dracula*, it was the first vampire novel and created an intense sensation in its own day, arguably becoming even more popular in France than in England. I will go into greater detail later about the influence of *The Vampyre* on French and British literature, but first, let us explore how some earlier British works helped to pave the way in France for a thirst for all things Gothic.

Mrs. Radcliffe and the Gothic Novel

The Gothic craze in France was first fueled by the novels of Ann Radcliffe, popularly known as Mrs. Radcliffe, in the 1790s. Mrs. Radcliffe's works were quickly translated from English into French. It is unlikely anyone reading this book does not know

Mrs. Radcliffe's name and at least one of her works. While she is not a household name today, anyone who is a devoted student of the Gothic will have read them. I will not detail them here since they have been widely discussed elsewhere, including in my book *The Gothic Wanderer*. A few details will suffice to testify to Mrs. Radcliffe's popularity in Britain, France, and indeed, across Europe.

Mrs. Radcliffe's first two novels, *The Castles of Athlin and Dunbayne* (1789) and *A Sicilian Romance* (1790), were both published anonymously. Both are somewhat immature works, but they reflect the development of the Gothic mode in her writing, to be fully realized in the three masterpieces that followed. *The Romance of the Forest* (1791) is the first novel she published under her name and the first to contain a charismatic and sinister villain, the Marquis de Montalt. The novel was so popular that Mrs. Radcliffe was made the unprecedented offer of 500 pounds to publish her next book, *The Mysteries of Udolpho* (1794), and then 800 pounds for *The Italian, or the Confessional of the Black Penitents* (1797).[2] *The Mysteries of Udolpho*, with its archetypal villain Montoni, became a bestseller that led to a flood of imitations, including Matthew Lewis' *The Monk* (1795). Mrs. Radcliffe, who did not approve of either Lewis' pretense of the supernatural as real—she always explained away anything thought supernatural in her works—or of his novel's excessive immorality, wrote *The Italian* in response. Regardless, Lewis' novel was as popular as Mrs. Radcliffe's works, and both would influence French Gothic literature. Mrs. Radcliffe and Matthew Lewis would remain the most popular British novelists until Sir Walter Scott's popularity superseded theirs.

Part of the reason for Mrs. Radcliffe's popularity in France may be that two of her finest novels, *The Romance of the Forest* and *The Mysteries of Udolpho*, are largely set there, even though the authoress never visited that country. However, the Gothic thrills and chills she created in her stories and their popularity in Great Britain were, no doubt, the primary reasons they were translated and became popular abroad. *The Mysteries of Udolpho*, Mrs. Radcliffe's most popular novel, went through numerous editions and translations in the late eighteenth and nineteenth centuries. As Bonamy Dobrée notes, "For some years after its publication in 1794—one may hazard fifty years—*The Mysteries of Udolpho* was a 'must', or in the phrase of today, 'required reading', for anybody who had any pretence at all to being a person of education, or culture, or even of popular reading habits."[3] Bonamy summarizes the novel's printing history as: "Twice printed in 1794, again in 1795, 1800, 1803; in Mrs. Barbauld's collection in 1810, and Scott's in 1821. There were other editions before that of 1832, notably two printings in 1823. Even after 1860 editions appeared—in 1870, 1877, 1882, 1891, &c.: it was translated into French in 1808, and again reprinted in 1864, 1869, and 1874."[4*] These numbers may actually be understated. In the prologue to his novel *Le Ville Vampire* (*Vampire City*) (1875), Paul Féval, in discussing the "illustrious" Mrs. Radcliffe's popularity in France, states:

> I do not use the word illustrious lightly and I am prepared to defend it against any claim of exaggeration. The fame of Anne [sic] Radcliffe was worldwide at one time, and her dark tales obtained a height of fashionability that our most successful contemporaries have been unable to equal. It was said that she cast her spell on cottage and country house alike. *The Mysteries of Udolpho* went through two hundred editions in England. In France the book was translated several times over, and one of those versions was reprinted forty times in Paris. Nor was it a brief infatuation; by now the fever has calmed somewhat, but *The Mysteries of Udolpho* and *The Confessional of the Black Penitents* still terrify thousands of young imaginations everywhere.[5]

Féval may have been exaggerating a bit to create new interest in Mrs. Radcliffe, whom he makes the heroine of *Vampire City*, as

---

* For a discussion of Mrs. Radcliffe's translations in French, see Terry Hale's chapter "Translations in Distress" in *European Gothic*.

we will explore in Chapter 7, but this remark and the fact that Radcliffe would be his novel's protagonist testify to her extreme popularity in France.

Madame de Staël knew she could refer to Udolpho and her readers would understand the reference. The artist Gavarni looked for Mrs. Radcliffe's novels at a reading room as a boy, and Jean-Edme Paccard used one of Mrs. Radcliffe's romantic phrases for an epigraph to his novel *Le Chateau de Luc* (1819). Many other examples exist of authors and poets who knew Mrs. Radcliffe and Lewis' novels.[6] Their works were popular enough even to inspire drama. The humorist Henri Monnier saw *Montoni*, or *Les Mystères d'Udolphe* revived at the Theatre Doyen about 1820, and in 1840 a farce titled *Les Mystères d'Udolphe* was played at the Follies-Dramatiques. Fontan closely imitated Lewis' novel in a five-act melodrama titled *Le Moine* in 1831.[7] In fact, *The Monk* remained popular enough that French film adaptations of it were made in 1972 and 2013, both titled *Le Moine*.

While Mrs. Radcliffe's French settings may have helped to popularize her novels in France, she was not necessarily complimentary to that country. She chose France, as well as Italy, because they were Catholic countries—allowing for monks, cloisters, and Catholic superstition to be depicted in her plots—which contrasted with the perceived more rational Protestant England. Scholars have long debated whether Mrs. Radcliffe was anti-Catholic. Either way, she was not above taking advantage of how the Catholic Church could itself be an instrument of terror, especially in terms of the Italian Inquisition in *The Italian*. She is kinder to Catholicism in *The Mysteries of Udolpho*, but in either case, she depicts Catholicism as a religion of superstition and repression. The Gothic novel has long been understood by literary scholars, and likely was by its 1790s audience, as a veiled commentary on the excesses of the French Revolution and the fear that overthrowing monarchy and patriarchy was a transgression or rebellion against God Himself. However, Mrs. Radcliffe's novels also show the injustices that the nobility and

Church were able to inflict upon people, making the revolution justifiable.*

The French, of course, were aware of these injustices—the very reason so many of them were in the process of overthrowing the monarchy and rejecting the Catholic Church in the years Mrs. Radcliffe was writing. The terror Adeline experiences in *The Romance of the Forest* when a marquis tries to force her to be his mistress, even though he is already married, would have resonated with a French audience appalled by the oppression of the French nobility. Furthermore, French readers had already developed an appetite for tales of such cruelty from reading the works of the Marquis de Sade, whose stories were not supernatural but full of incidents of sexual abuse, torture, and deviance. While Radcliffe probably did not read Sade herself, she benefited from this situation, adding supernatural terrors to a thirst for violence in literature to create an even more intense experience for readers.

Mrs. Radcliffe influenced many French Gothic writers, including many much earlier than Paul Féval. Her earliest influence in France is often cited to be upon the Marquis de Sade, although this is unlikely since his major novels slightly predate hers. Sade is often referred to as a Gothic writer, but in the literary criticism he wrote, he strived to prevent his fiction from being labeled Gothic since his works take place in a realistic, non-supernatural world. Regardless, Sade's novels are full of Gothic elements, particularly imprisonment of and violence toward women. His works, therefore, are close cousins to the Gothic if not Gothic themselves. His most famous novel, *Justine* (1787, revised 1791), anticipates many of Radcliffe's themes.

While Sade's major works were published before those of Radcliffe and Lewis, we know he read their books. Furthermore, it is believed the third revision of Justine in 1797 may have been influenced by his reading of *The Monk*.[8] In "An Essay on Novels"

---

* For a more detailed discussion of how the French Revolution influenced Gothic novels of the 1790s and beyond, see "Chapter 1: The Gothic Wanderer's Origins in the French Revolution" in my book *The Gothic Wanderer*.

published in 1800 in *The Crimes of Love*, Sade writes that the Gothic novel is a predictable result of the French Revolution, which had rightfully caused Gothic novelists to "look to hell for help in composing their alluring novels."[9] He held Lewis and Radcliffe high above the other Gothic writers, but stated *The Monk* was "superior in every respect to the strange outpourings of the brilliant imagination of Mrs. Radcliffe."[10] Still, he acknowledged both works had their faults, saying, "the author of *The Monk* was no more successful in overcoming them than Mrs. Radcliffe. For an unavoidable choice had to be made: either to develop the supernatural and risk forfeiting the reader's credulity, or to explain nothing and fall into the most ludicrous implausibility."[11]

That Sade praised Lewis' work the most is perhaps because Lewis' depiction of the monk Ambrosio's sacrificing his humanity to gratify his insatiable sexual appetite most closely reflects similar themes in Sade's own works.[12] Lewis read Sade (Lewis was proficient in French, even translating the French opera *Felix*),[13] but it is debatable to what degree he was influenced by Sade,[14*] while it is unlikely the respectable Mrs. Radcliffe would have read works deemed so scandalous. That said, Sade was read by English readers to a greater degree than has been acknowledged in the past. George W. M. Reynolds clearly read him since he references Sade in *The Modern Literature of France* (1839), saying Sade's novel *Justine* is "too licentious to be noticed at length," and is "a work, the tendency of which has been vituperated and condemned as pernicious in the extreme;—but a work which, we are fain to confess, tells a tale that is, alas! too true."[15†]

Even if she did not influence Sade, Mrs. Radcliffe soon had her imitators in France just like she did in Great Britain. In 1816,

---

* For a discussion on Sade's evolution as a Gothic writer and more on his influence on Lewis, see Angela Wright's chapter "European Disruptions of the Idealized Woman" in *European Gothic*.

† For more about the popularity of the Marquis de Sade in England and his influence on Reynolds' fiction, see Will McMorran's "The Marquis de Sade in English, 1800-1850" in *The Modern Language Review*, 112.3 (2017): 549-66.

Étienne-Léon de Lamothe-Langon published *L'Hermite de la tombe mystérieuse* (*The Mysterious Hermit of the Tomb*) under Mrs. Radcliffe's name. However, it is a tale of medieval chivalry that makes no real effort to imitate Mrs. Radcliffe's plots or style.[16] Regardless, the author pretends to be the translator of the work, claiming he received it in manuscript form from a relative of Mrs. Radcliffe. Such attempts to capitalize on Mrs. Radcliffe's fame were not uncommon among writers and publishers in England,* but Lamothe-Langon's claim is the only one I know of in France.

George W. M. Reynolds also argues for the influence of Radcliffe, as well as Lewis and Maturin, on French authors. He places Frédéric Soulié (1800-1847) in their school, saying Soulié has regenerated that school of horror which had nearly exploded a dozen years ago.[17] Reynolds singles out Soulié's *Les Deux Cadavres* (*The Two Cadavers*, 1832) as "the most extraordinary creation of the brain that was ever yet, in the guise of a historical tale, presented to the world."[18] The novel is set in the days of Cromwell in England and is filled with madness, plague, murders, riots, duels, deaths, and skeletons. Twenty-first century French literary historians Jean-Marc and Randy Lofficier claim the Gothic novel hit its peak in France with the publication of another novel by Soulié, *Les Mémoires du Diable* (*The Devil's Memoirs*), published in 1838. In it, Soulié combined the style of the Gothic with the passion of Sade to create a series of crimes, murders, and adulterous and incestuous liaisons that take place under the eye of a dandified Satan. In fact, the reading of Sade's *Justine* is used as a form of

---

* For example, *Manfrone, or The One-Handed Monk* (1809) is clearly a Gothic novel inspired by Mrs. Radcliffe's works. The alleged author is a Mary Anne Radcliffe. Scholars have been unable to determine if Mary Anne Radcliffe was a real person. A Mary Ann Radcliffe wrote *The Female Advocate, or An Attempt to Recover the Rights of Women from Male Usurpation* (1799), but she does not seem to have written Gothic novels and does not spell Ann with an e. The author of *Manfrone* may have coincidentally had the same name as the author of *The Female Advocate*, or the author or publisher may have been playing on the name of Ann Radcliffe as a marketing tool to trick readers into buying *Manfrone* under the belief it was by Mrs. Radcliffe. (Townshend 291)

torture in the novel.¹⁹ Unfortunately, Soulié's novels have rarely been translated into English, so we will have to take Reynolds' word for the influence of England's great Gothic novelists upon it. Reynolds also lists Paul de Kock's novel *La Barbier de Paris* as being "somewhat in the Radcliffe style."²⁰

Mrs. Radcliffe's works were also admired by French novelists Honoré de Balzac (1799-1850), Victor Hugo (1802-1885), and Alexandre Dumas (1802-1870). Among Balzac's early pen names is "Horace de St Aubin," which may have been derived from Horace Walpole's name and that of Emily St. Aubert, the heroine of *The Mysteries of Udolpho*.²¹* Balzac's supernatural novel *L'Héritière de Birague* (1822) follows the tradition of Radcliffe's style but also parodies it.²² In fact, Reynolds states that Balzac surpasses Radcliffe:

> The fatiguing delineations of scenery and costume, which are read in the romances of Ann Radcliffe, weary the mind, cloy the appetite, and encourage the approach of slumber; but, though De Balzac frequently descends to the most minute details, he is never tedious nor tiresome.²³

Unfortunately, Balzac's novel has not been translated into English and has received little attention from Balzac scholars so I cannot discuss it here. However, the use of the Gothic in Hugo's *Notre-Dame de Paris* and in several works by Dumas reflects Mrs. Radcliffe's influence. We will look later at several examples of the Gothic in Dumas, but two works I will not discuss that Mrs. Radcliffe likely influenced were Dumas' *Le Château d'Eppstein* (*The Castle of Eppstein; the Spectre Mother*) (1844) and *Le Trou de l'enfer* (*The Mouth of Hell*) (1851).²⁴†

---

* If the name is derived from Radcliffe's heroine, it is odd that Balzac changed the name to St. Aubin, yet curiously, in Chapter 11 of *Northanger Abbey*, Jane Austen has Catherine Morland refer to the death of St. Aubin in *The Mysteries of Udolpho*, a mistake for St. Aubert.

† For a discussion of *The Castle of Eppstein*, see my blog: https://thegothicwanderer.wordpress.com/2022/10/20/alexandre-dumas-castle-eppstein-a-mix-of-drama-and-radcliffean-romance/

Sir Walter Scott and the Historical Novel

Sir Walter Scott, along with Mrs. Radcliffe and John Polidori, is one of the other three major British literary influences on nineteenth-century French Gothic. Scott was himself a fan of Mrs. Radcliffe and influenced by her. In fact, his publisher James Ballantyne complained that Scott was imitating Mrs. Radcliffe when he wrote *Woodstock* (1826) through the alleged haunting of Woodstock Manor; Scott, however, disagreed, saying unlike Mrs. Radcliffe, his aim was not to scare the reader but to show the effect of supernatural terror upon his characters.[25] That said, no one can deny Scott was very familiar with Radcliffe's work. She is one of the authors Scott discusses in *Lives of the Novelists* (1821-4), a book he developed from a series of essays about various novelists for new editions of their works. Radcliffe's influence is apparent in numerous of his novels, none of which is truly Gothic, but many of them contain Gothic elements. I have chosen both *Ivanhoe* (1819) and *Anne of Geierstein* (1829) to discuss later for their Gothic elements. The former is probably Scott's best-known work today while the latter is lesser-known but his most Gothic novel.

While Gothic elements exist in many of Scott's novels, his fictional treatment of history is what made him so popular. Prior to Scott, the historical novel was only loosely based in history and more aligned with romance. Scott was the first to make a true effort to be historically accurate in depicting events and manners of a specific time period. Early examples of historical fiction in British literature include Sophia Lee's *The Recess* (1783-5) and Jane Porter's *The Scottish Chiefs* (1809), both of which are more aligned with romance than historical fiction. France may even hold the claim to the first historical novel with Madame de Lafayette's *La Princesse de Clèves* (1678). However, it was Sir Walter Scott's *Waverley* (1814) that put the historical novel center stage.

Scott's novels were not Gothic, although at times he used Gothic elements. They were not Romantic in the sense that there are no Gothic wanderer figures,* no Byronic heroes, no satanic pacts, and no Ancient Mariners struggling with transgression and redemption. Instead, in the historical novel Scott took medieval through eighteenth-century settings and created around them realistic narratives grounded in history.

Today, it is hard to conceive of the incredible influence Sir Walter Scott had not only on British but all European and American fiction. Already a popular poet, Scott chose to publish his first novel *Waverley* (1814) and its successors anonymously, but the secret of his authorship was well-known. *Waverley*'s tremendous success set off a demand for more historical fiction, resulting in Scott penning more than thirty historical novels before his death in 1832 and countless other authors imitating him.

A short list of testaments to Scott's popularity includes American author James Fenimore Cooper who was inspired by Scott's historical fiction about Scotland to write his own historical fiction set in the American colonies, as well as modeling his literary career on the belief he could be as financially successful as the author of *Waverley*.[26] Cooper would also use Gothic elements in his works. Some of the other authors influenced by Scott will be explored in this book.

In Europe, Scott's fame was widespread. In Denmark, Hans Christian Andersen wrote two plays based on *The Bride of Lammermoor* and *Kenilworth*.[27] In the Netherlands, novelist Multatuli (Edward Douwes Dekker) referred to Scott's writing style as justification for his long drawn-out place descriptions in Chapter 13 of his novel *Max Havelaar* (1860).[28] In Great Britain, Scott was so famous that he invited parody by William Makepeace Thackeray in *Rebecca and Rowena* (1850), a send-up of *Ivanhoe*.

---

* A Gothic wanderer is typically a character who has committed some form of transgression and feels guilt or angst. Often Gothic wanderers seek redemption. At the very least, they feel displaced or like an outcast. Characters who fall under this category include Frankenstein's Monster, Heathcliff, and Varney the Vampire. For more details about the Gothic wanderer figure and its relationship to Byronic heroes, Romantic wanderers, and other characters, see my book *The Gothic Wanderer: From Transgression to Redemption*.

In the United States, countless places were also named for Scott's works. In New York, the town of *Waverly* was named for Scott's first novel, though one of the e's was intentionally dropped.[29] In Milwaukee, Wisconsin, three streets were named for Scott's novels: Woodstock Place, Kenilworth Place, Ivanhoe Place, and a fourth Windsor Place because Windsor Castle was a significant location in *The Heart of Midlothian*.[30] In Minnesota, the town of Ivanhoe was named for his most famous book and the streets named after the characters in that novel.

In the Southern United States, Scott's depictions of chivalry inspired a feudal system holding onto the past. Mark Twain took several gibes at Scott, stating in *Life on the Mississippi* (1883) that Scott "had so large a hand in making Southern character, as it existed before the" American Civil War that he was "in great measure responsible for the war." He goes on to coin the term "Sir Walter Scott disease," which he blames for the South's lack of advancement. Twain also targeted Scott in *The Adventures of Huckleberry Finn* (1884), where a sinking boat is named the *Walter Scott*, and in *A Connecticut Yankee in King Arthur's Court* (1889), the main character, Hank Morgan, repeatedly utters "great Scott" as an oath reflecting the popularity of medieval themes in Scott's work as well as the medieval world to which Morgan has traveled back in time.[31]

Yet Scott also gained great reverence during his lifetime and after. The Sir Walter Scott Monument in Edinburgh, built from 1832 to 1844, was the first public monument erected to an author. Glasgow soon followed in 1838 with a monument of its own, and in New York City's Central Park, another statue of Scott exists.[32] Numerous masonic lodges were named after Scott or his novels. Even Karl Marx read Scott.[33] And most importantly for our purposes, in France, *Quentin Durward* (1823) took the country by storm, being the only one of Scott's historical novels to be set in that country. Scott's novels would create a thirst for historical fiction in France and influence numerous French authors, including Victor Hugo and Alexandre Dumas, as we will see in later chapters.

Scott was celebrated when he traveled to France in 1826. He and his daughter saw an operatic version of *Ivanhoe* at the Odéon.[34] He was welcomed to Paris by women who gave him a bouquet. He visited the Princess Galitzin, and the artist Madame de Mirbel nearly kneeled to get permission to paint him. He dined with the British Ambassador Lord Granville and befriended the American novelist James Fenimore Cooper. On the night before Scott left France, the Princess Galitzin held a soirée in which a "a whole covey of Princesses of Russia [were] arrayed in tartan!"[35] Scott's popularity in France would not wane after he left France or, indeed, this world.

What was it about Scott that so appealed to the French? Largely, his popularity in France can be attributed to the time period. Scott wrote in the years directly after the fall of Napoleon, a time when the monarchy had been restored and the French were returning to the traditions they had cast off during the French Revolution. Scott offered the French a model for writing about history, and they used that model to begin recreating their national past in their plays and novels.[36] Scott also taught the French about the true expression of manners and, according to French Romantic Charles Nodier, relieved them from the monotonous intrigues of the salon and boudoir.[37] Such works of intrigue, for example Pierre Ambroise François Choderlos de Laclos' *Les Liaisons Dangereuses* (1782), had become the focus of French literature in recent years.

The majority of the French read Scott in translation, and despite Scott trying to keep his authorship a secret, French publishers produced his books under his own name. And those books sold rapidly. The first novel published in its entirety in France was *Guy Mannering* in 1816.[38] By 1820, nine novels had been translated, and by 1824, sales were estimated at 200,000 copies. Those translated by Auguste Defauconpret, Scott's most accurate translator during this period, ran to nearly 1.5 million volumes shortly after 1830 and to 2 million by 1840.[39]

Among Scott's more celebrated French admirers during this time were Charles Nodier, Augustin Thierry, Victor Hugo, Alexandre Dumas, and Honoré de Balzac. *Quentin Durward* (translated 1823) would be the most influential of the novels because it helped to reawaken the taste for French history and for Louis XI in particular. Hugo praised the novel's well-knit plot and historical accuracy, and he was impressed by the "genius" who could so accurately capture the spirit of a past age.[40] Many of the novels, including *Quentin Durward*, were also adapted for the French stage.[41] For example, Dumas adapted *Ivanhoe* into a three-act melodrama and also planned to collaborate on a version of *Old Mortality*, though he never did, and he freely borrowed scenes from Scott's novels as inspiration for scenes in other plays, as well as the inspiration for writing his own historical novels, as we will later explore.[42] The influence of Scott's novels extended beyond literature and the theatre to music, painting, costumes, interior decoration, and fancy dress balls—the Duchesse de Berry gave several balls with costumes based on characters from the Waverley Novels.[43]

By the late 1820s, Balzac was inspired by Scott to write *Le Dernier Chouan* (1829), a historical novel set during the 1799 post-war uprising in Fougères. Balzac was such an avid reader of Scott that in *The Human Comedy*, Balzac's collection of ninety-one linked novels and stories, seventeen of the Waverley Novels are referenced. Balzac's letters show that he thought of Scott as his great literary rival because they both wrote on historical themes.[44] Scholar Donald Haggis states of this influence:

> Balzac, like Scott at his best, succeeds in creating what may be termed an organic relation between a historical situation that he presents and the fortunes of a fictional character (or of a group of characters). By showing the impact of a historical situation or of historical events in the lives of the ordinary folk who are his fictional characters the novelist shows us what history means. This is what Scott did in *Waverley*...Edward Waverley is brought to

understand the reality that underlies the glamour of the Jacobite cause.[45]

Haggis goes on to explain that he has borrowed the term "organic relation" from Hungarian literary critic Georg Lukacs, who says one of the weaknesses of Prosper Mérimée's *Chronique du Reègne de Charles IX* is that "there is no really organic link between the great historical event which Mérimée wishes to portray—the night of St Bartholomew—and the private destinies of the principal heroes."[46] Scott and Balzac, however, make such links clear in their works.

Haggis also discusses a review Balzac wrote of Eugène Sue's novel *Jean Cavalier* (1840) in *Revue Parisienne*, in which he compares Sue's novel to those of Scott with Scott being deemed superior. Balzac believes Scott's great originality was to convey history through what his fictional characters say and do and what happens to them. He does not need to give a long resume of historical events like Sue does before the story begins.[47] Similarly, in *The Achievement of Walter Scott*, A. O. J. Cockshut comments on a passage from *Old Mortality*, "Scott has no need here of a historical analysis because he is able as a simple storyteller describing what people did and thought to imply all that a longer historical digression could give."[48]

Praise for Scott was profuse both in words and through imitation. Dumas turned from imitating Scott in his plays to doing so in his historical novels. No French author shares to such a degree Scott's appreciation of adventure as does Dumas.[49] Charles Nodier, who praised Scott as an interpreter of the Middle Ages, would soon delve into the past in his own works.[50] Hugo would claim that Scott created a "new alliance" between history and romance that perfected the form of the novel.[51] Hugo would become known as the "most illustrious imitator" of Scott. Hugo's *Notre-Dame de Paris* (1831) marks what scholar E. Preston Dargan called "the most brilliant French attempt to superimpose a synthetic *Waverley Novel* upon a ground-plan of one's own gifts." Although Hugo's novel is weak on basic history and psychology, it is a "sumptuous restoration of the Gothic and the picturesque."[52] While Hugo's novel is clearly influenced by Scott, I would argue it is very much a blending of both Scott and Radcliffe's influence. I will analyze *Notre-Dame de Paris* as both a Gothic and historical novel in more detail in the next chapter.

Unfortunately, not all of Scott's imitators and successors would be wise enough to step away from historical analysis. Certainly, Leo Tolstoy, a Russian imitator, loves his long historical digressions in *War and Peace*. In France, Dumas kept historical commentary to the minimum, but Victor Hugo had no qualms about devoting an entire chapter to the history of Notre-Dame, while letting his plot wait. We will observe how both Dumas and Hugo would blend Gothic and historical fiction in their own works, following Scott's example, in upcoming chapters.

Despite his great popularity, Scott did have his detractors in France. In 1832, Stendhal said Scott had perhaps 200 imitators in France, but by 1834, imitations seemed to be on the wane. Furthermore, most of the imitators were writing historical fiction set in the Middle Ages and modeled on *Ivanhoe* and *Quentin Durward*.[53] Hugo's *Notre-Dame de Paris* would be one such imitation, but few of the imitators were of Scott or Hugo's caliber so their works soon grew tedious for the reading public. As early as 1825, the journal *La Pandore* warned French authors "Guard against germanisms and anglicisms. To imitate, copy slavishly, parody Shakespeare, Schiller, Scott and Byron, is not originality. To change one's master is not to become free."[54] Madame de Genlis in her *Mémoires* published the same year said that she found the Waverley novels boring and without imagination, interest, or any striking passages. Théophile Gautier in 1836 in *Le Chronique de Paris* would go so far as to say:

> Walter Scott is dead; God forgive him! But he has introduced into the world and made fashionable the most detestable kind of literary composition it is possible to invent; the name has in itself something deformed and monstrous that manifests from what antipathetic union it

was born: the historical novel, or in other words the false truth and the true lie.[55]

In 1829, theatre critic Charles Magnin, after seeing Dumas' *Henri III et sa cour*, cried, "God be praised! There's a drama that is imitated from neither Walter Scott nor Cooper."[56] Regardless, Dumas was a great fan of Scott and probably more influenced by British literature in his dramas than in his novels.[57] About 1824, when Dumas began reading good literature, he started with the works of Cooper and Scott, and in *Mes Mémoires*, he stated that *Ivanhoe* opened his eyes to new horizons. He even went so far as to be extra-kind to English people to help repay the debt he felt he owed to Scott and Shakespeare.[58] In *Souvenirs de 1830 à 1842*, Dumas remarked "The analysis of Walter Scott has made me understand the novel from a point of view different from that which prevails in this country; the same fidelity for manners and customs, of character and costume, with a livelier dialogue and more realistic passions, seemed to meet our requirements."[59] Dumas went so far as to see himself as a successor to Scott who also improved upon him, once stating to a friend, "Scott painted localities, characters, customs and manners: it was necessary to take the novel from his hands, as Raphael carried on from Perugini, and add a vivid treatment of the passions."[60]

We will look more closely at Scott's novels and influence in the chapters that follow, but first, let us return to France's vampire invasion.

John Polidori's *The Vampyre*

Now we turn to the third major British literary influence upon nineteenth-century French Gothic literature—John Polidori's *The Vampyre*. This novella was the work that first popularized the vampire in fiction. As previously noted, Polidori may have been inspired by Lady Caroline Lamb's *Glenarvon* (1816), the first novel to suggest the possibility of depicting vampires in fiction. Lamb does not have a vampire in her novel, but the title character is a depiction of Lord Byron with metaphorical vampiric qualities. Byron had been Lamb's lover, and the novel was her revenge upon him.* Polidori borrowed the name Ruthven from Lamb's novel, in which Glenarvon is a descendant of John de Ruthven, who "drank hot blood from the skull of his enemy,"[61] thus equating the family with vampirism.

Polidori's depiction of Lord Byron as a vampire probably resulted from the personal animosity that existed between the two of them, including heated verbal exchanges that resulted in Byron discharging Polidori from his employment. In revenge, Polidori named his vampire Lord Ruthven so readers would identify the vampire with Lamb's *Glenarvon*. Like Glenarvon, Lord Ruthven has the typical traits of a Byronic hero because he is an exile with a mysterious background.[62] Ruthven's exile is based upon Byron's own position as a social outcast after 1816, due to his wife learning of his homosexual or incestuous activities. Finding himself being spit upon in the streets, Byron felt it would be more tolerable to travel on the continent than remain in his native land.[63] He began his restless continental tour in 1816, hiring Polidori as his physician. Polidori, therefore, witnessed Byron's wanderings, which would come to embody both the wanderings of the Byronic hero and the literary vampire.

According to literary scholar Mario Praz, the vampire would have never become a famous figure in literature if not for the figure of the Byronic hero and the belief that Byron had written Polidori's story.[64] The story was first published anonymously in the April 1819 issue of *The New Monthly Magazine* and soon reprinted, again anonymously, by Sherwood, Neely & Jones. By then, a rumor had spread that it was written by Lord Byron, so Henry Colburn issued a pirated version with Byron's name on it. A French translation by Henry Faber, also credited to Byron, was published by the end of the year by *Chaumerot jeune*. That

---

* I have discussed *Glenarvon* at length in *The Gothic Wanderer*. I omit discussion of it here since it did not have a major influence on the vampire novels that succeeded Polidori's work.

translation was reprinted in a set of Byron's *Oeuvres complètes* published by Pierre-François Ladvocat in 1820.[65]

Byron had actually written an unfinished story in which the main character Augustus Darvell dies. Byron was likely planning to have Darvell come back to life as a vampire but never finished it. Polidori probably stole Byron's idea, but rather than charge Polidori with plagiarism, Byron hastened to deny that *The Vampyre* was his work, stating, "If the book is clever it would be base to deprive the real writer—whoever he may be—of his honours;—and if stupid—I desire the responsibility of nobody's dullness but my own."[66] Ironically, Johann Wolfgang von Goethe declared *The Vampyre* was the best work Byron ever wrote.[67] The true author of the story was rapidly revealed to be Byron's one-time friend Polidori, with whom he had fallen out. Whether Ladvocat knew Polidori was the author when he included the translation in his *Oeuvres complètes* is unclear, but he certainly knew it by the time the sequel he commissioned, Cyprien Bérard's *Lord Ruthwen ou les vampires*, was delivered as acknowledged in the book's notes.[68]

While Byron's presumed authorship of *The Vampyre* cannot be underestimated as a cause for the story's popularity, neither should Polidori's creativity be ignored. I will summarize the plot later in Chapter 7, but for now it's important to note that, according to Polidori's biographer D. L. Macdonald, Polidori made four significant innovations to the vampire figure in his work that established its popularity and future influence on Gothic literature.

1. Polidori makes his vampire not merely a spirit or a reanimated corpse but a being who is able to function in the daily world, whereas earlier folklore had been ambiguous about whether vampires could only be nocturnal.
2. Polidori makes Lord Ruthwen an aristocrat. Before Polidori's tale, there were no aristocratic vampires, although aristocrats, in their treatment of the lower classes, were often depicted satirically as vampires.

3. Polidori's vampire is a traveler, which makes him a continual threat because he can travel anywhere.
4. Polidori's vampire is a seducer (thus satirizing Lord Byron). Before, vampires only preyed upon their friends or family members, but now the vampire could attack anyone, making him a greater threat to society.[69]

I would add a fifth innovation in making the vampire a metaphor for capitalism. *The Vampyre* uses the gambling motif to comment upon how capitalism can drain one's wealth as a vampire drains a person's blood.* Polidori chose to make Lord Ruthven an aristocrat to draw upon the idea of the aristocracy's economic exploitation and political oppression of the lower classes. Lord Ruthven purposely gambles to make the poor lose and the rich win so the status quo will be maintained, which includes Ruthven's own aristocratic position of power. Consequently, Lord Ruthven becomes not only a satire of Lord Byron but a symbol of a mythologized upper class. While the aristocracy is interested in ancestral blood lines, Ruthven is interested in blood, and like the declining aristocracy, he needs new blood (and money) to revitalize himself.[70]

Polidori's decision to make his vampire a seducer is partially to satirize Byron's notorious sexual escapades, but it also derives from the conventional sexual fear and anxiety expressed in Gothic novels. The vampire's seduction of family members is suggestive of incest in later Gothic novels, but Polidori's decision that his vampire may attack anyone makes the vampire all the more frightening because the disease of vampirism cannot be contained but can spread to anyone like a fatal venereal disease.[71] Polidori links Ruthven's aristocratic and gambler roles to that of seducer because Ruthven chooses only morally superior women to victimize. These women reside upon "the pinnacle of unsullied virtue" from which he seeks to hurl them "down to the lowest

---

* For a discussion of gambling as a form of transgression in Gothic novels see "Chapter V: Gambling as Gothic Transgression" in my book *The Gothic Wanderer*.

abyss of infamy and degradation."[72] Similarly, Ruthven seeks to destroy those who gamble by lowering their social positions. Ruthven's degradation of others is a means to protect his own isolated position of aristocratic power. In addition, Ruthven seeks out those with latent internal weaknesses, bringing these repressed tendencies into action so they are displayed to the world, thus making Ruthven the "catalyst" of others' destructions.[73]

Polidori's innovations of the vampire included not only new attributes but a complex blending of the vampire character with many of the stock motifs of the Gothic wanderer figure. Polidori borrows from the Rosicrucian and Wandering Jew motifs by giving Ruthven's eyes hypnotic powers. In addition, like the Rosicrucian and the Wandering Jew, Ruthven as a vampire has a prolonged lifespan, which he achieves by sucking blood from young women; blood is forbidden for consumption in the Bible, so the vampire's blood drinking is a transgression against the laws of God and nature.[74]

Polidori may have also drawn upon Masonic ideas, which were sometimes linked with Rosicrucianism because Masons had to take secret oaths.[75] In *The Vampyre*, a secret oath occurs when Aubrey swears to Lord Ruthven that he will not reveal the crimes Ruthven has committed for one year. This oath is similar to those in other Gothic novels, which were linked to popular beliefs that secret societies had conspired to cause the French Revolution.[76] Polidori, himself, would have been familiar with such oaths because he joined a British sect of the Freemasons, despite being Catholic; the Catholic Church excommunicated its members who joined such organizations.[77] Although British freemasonry was considered respectable and apolitical in the nineteenth century, the secrecy of such groups made them suspect.[78] The use of such oaths in a novel, therefore, added to its suspense.

Most importantly, *The Vampyre* inspired all future fictional depictions of vampires by establishing the elements of the vampire character. While Lord Ruthven's lack of remorse notably places him more closely in the Byronic hero tradition than that of the Gothic wanderer, a figure usually filled with angst over his past transgressions, Polidori's nineteenth-century successors would adapt the vampire for their own purposes, a trend that has continued down to the present-day in books and films.

A complete survey of vampire literature inspired by Polidori's work is beyond the limits of this—and possibly any—book, but numerous nineteenth-century works that I will explore in Chapter 7 borrowed from the story, using Lord Ruthven in some form as a character, and many more vampire characters, not as closely linked to Lord Ruthven, were also created. Polidori even considered writing a sequel to *The Vampyre*, but his life was cut short in 1821 before he could.[79]

Kevin Dodd has provided one of the most complete discussion of the many works influenced by Polidori's story in his two-part article, "Plot Variations in the Nineteenth-Century Story of Lord Ruthven" published in *Journal of Vampire Studies*. The list that follows is adapted from Dodd's article with the exception of two items, Eugène Scribe and Mélesville's *Le Vampire* and Gilbert and Sullivan's operetta *Ruddigore*. Dodd leaves comical works out of his discussion, and both these works, while referencing characters named Ruthven, turn out not to have true vampires in them. Because Dodd summarizes the plots of all the works and discusses important elements in the development of vampire characters, I will only highlight the most important elements of each play or novel and recommend Dodd's excellent essay for readers who want more information. The list shows the wide-ranging influence of Polidori's story, encompassing not only British and French but also American and German works. Those works with bolded titles below will be explored in more detail in Chapter 7.

1. **1819 "The Black Vampyre: A Legend of St. Domingo" by Uriah Derick D'Arcy (American)**—This short story or novella was the first comedic vampire story. It is a parody of Polidori's story, introducing a "negro" or

mulatto "black" vampire to offset the "White Vampyre" in Polidori's story.

2. **1820 *Lord Ruthwen ou les vampires* by Cyprien Bérard (French)**—Written as a sequel to Polidori's story, it ends with Lord Ruthwen dying when a stake is driven through his heart. What makes it significant is it helped to determine many tropes that would recur in future vampire tales.

3. **1820 *Le Vampire* by Charles Nodier, Pierre-Frédéric-Adolphe Carmouche, and Achille De Jouffroy (French)**—This play was the first adaptation to the stage of Polidori's story. It was incredibly popular, and unlike D'Arcy and Bérard's works, it closely resembles Polidori's story and plot, but with some variations. The vampire's revival by moonlight exists in this story like it does in Polidori's. Most notably, the vampire is not a stranger but an acquaintance of someone in the family that he torments. This work would become the primary influence on all the stories that followed, making Polidori's story an indirect influence.

4. **1820 *The Vampire, or The Bride of the Isles* by J. R. Planché (English)**—This play was the first English adaptation of Nodier, Carmouche, and Jouffroy's play. Variations to their play that were introduced were that the vampire has stronger mesmeric effects than in earlier versions and the vampire also begins to be sympathetic.

5. 1820 *The Vampire* by W. T. Moncrieff (English)—This was the second English adaptation of Nodier, Carmouche, and Jouffroy's play. Here the vampire is also sympathetic. It is also suggested he must marry before he can partake of his victim, although that is not the case at the end of the story.

6. 1820? *The Bride of the Isles* by Anonymous (English)—This was an anonymous adaptation of Planché's play, misattributed to Lord Byron, like Polidori's original story. In fact, the title page had "Lord Byron" as its byline.

7. 1821 *Le Vampire* by Eugène Scribe and Mélesville (French)—This work has a character believed dead who reappears having adopted the name of Lord Ruthven. It is rumored he's a vampire, but it turns out not to be true and concludes with a song about how various people in society—soldiers, bureaucrats, and actors among them—may be metaphorical vampires. Called a vaudeville, it was apparently intended to be a spoof on the more serious vampire plays.
8. 1821 *Der Vampyr* by Heinrich Ludwig Ritter (German)—This was a German adaptation of Nodier, Carmouche, and Jouffroy's play, but it took substantial liberties with the storyline, especially in terms of religion.
9. 1828 *Der Vampyr*, composer Heinrich Marschner, libretto Wilhelm August Wohlbrück (German)—This is the first of two operas based on Ritter's adaptation.
10. 1828 *Der Vampyr*, composer Peter Joseph von Lindpaintner, libretto Cäsar Max Heigel (German)—This is the second opera based on Ritter's adaptation.
11. **1829 *Der Vampyr* by J. R. Planché (English)**—Planché, who had already adapted Nodier's play into English, now freely translated Marschner and Wohlbrück's opera into English, but kept the German title. In this version, the vampire takes a month to travel across the Carpathian Mountains, where later, Bram Stoker will place Dracula's castle. This is probably the first reference to the Carpathians in vampire fiction.
12. 1838 "Der Vampyr" by Johann Peter Lyser (German)—Lyser was the pseudonym of Ludwig Peter August Burmeister. He authored this story as part of his larger collection *Abendländische Tausend und eine Nacht, oder Die schönstein Mährchen und Sagen aller europäischen Völker*, a fifteen-volume work. Among the story's interesting elements is the idea that vampires must take oaths each

Walpurgis Night to kill an innocent girl and drink her blood before the moon's next cycle. Stoker would later reference Walpurgis in *Dracula*.

13. 1845 *The Last of the Vampires* by Smyth Upton (American)—Yet another variation, in which the main character, Baron von Oberfels, is the last vampire. He has made a Faustian pact with the devil for perpetual youth. In exchange, every tenth year a young female is to be sacrificed to his master. Faustian pacts will be common in many Gothic novels to come. For example, in George W. M. Reynolds' *The Necromancer* (1851-2), Lord Danvers is granted life extension, but in return, he must, over the course of 150 years, convince six women to elope and marry him, thus allowing Satan to take their souls. Notably, Reynolds would also write *Faust: A Romance of the Secret Tribunals* (1847) drawing on the Faust legend.

14. **1851** *Le Vampire, drame fantastique en cinq actes, en dix tableaux* **by Alexandre Dumas and Auguste Maquet (French)**—The most complex variation, this five-act play is probably the finest version of the Lord Ruthven stories.

15. **1852** *The Vampire, a Phantasm Related in Three Dramas* **by Dion Boucicault (English)**—This production has a structure identical to that of Dumas and Maquet's play. Significantly, the vampire is named Alan Raby but goes by the name of Gervase Rookwood. (*Rookwood* was a popular 1834 novel by William Harrison Ainsworth that we will explore in Chapter 2. The name may be in homage to Ainsworth.) Also significant is that the vampire's first victim is named Lucy; perhaps Stoker borrowed this character's name for that of Lucy Westenra in *Dracula*. Also interesting is that the vampire is attached to a single family over generations.

16. **1856** *The Phantom; A Drama, in Two Acts* **by Dion Boucicault (English, first performed in Philadelphia)**—

This is a rewrite of Boucicault's *The Vampire*, the first act following Dumas and Maquet's play, while the second act jumps ahead sixty years.

17. 1859 *Ruthven* by Augustus Harris (English)—Harris reworked Dumas and Maquet's play for an English audience. Here, for the first time, a cross worn around the neck is used to protect the victim from the vampire, although crosses were used in Gothic literature to fight evil prior to this, such as in Reynolds' novel *The Necromancer* (1851-2).

18. **1861 *Le Vampire du Val-de-Grace* by Léon Gozlan (French)**—This novel contains only a subplot that relates to the Ruthven storyline. However, the novel will be explored in full in Chapter 7.

19. **1865 *Douglas le Vampire* by Jules Dornay (French)**— Here, the vampire can only revive himself three times, yet if he feeds on a virgin's blood, he can have eternal life. Unfortunately for the vampire, the victim for the first time fights back, not succeeding in killing the vampire but delaying his attack long enough that he cannot feed on her before dawn.

20. **1887 *Ruddigore; or The Witch's Curse*, composer Arthur Sullivan, libretto W. S. Gilbert (English)**—In this comic operetta, the main character, Sir Ruthven Murgatroyd, disguises himself as Robin Oakapple, a young farmer. The play parodies many works including Marschner's *Der Vampyr*, in which Lord Ruthven must abduct and sacrifice three maidens or die. In *Ruddigore*, neither Sir Ruthven, nor anyone else, is a vampire, but he is haunted by his ancestors, including the first baronet who persecuted and burned witches. The family curse requires that the baronet commit a crime every day, and Sir Ruthven is ordered by his deceased uncle to carry off a maid that day or perish. Of course, being a comic operetta, the play has a happy ending.

While it is obvious that Lord Ruthven had become a figure of fun by the late nineteenth century, he had inspired numerous authors beyond those listed above to create their own vampire characters, who were not named Ruthven or did not have plots directly based on the Ruthven story, while still retaining many of the vampire elements the story introduced. We will examine many of these works, British, French, and even American, in Chapter 7.

Conclusion

The Gothic novels of Mrs. Radcliffe, the historical fiction of Sir Walter Scott, and John Polidori's novella *The Vampyre* created the perfect trifecta to allow French literature to have a Gothic Golden Age of its own and to influence a Second Gothic Golden Age in Great Britain. Throughout this period, French Gothic fiction would influence British Gothic fiction, and that British Gothic fiction would often then influence new French Gothic fiction. In the chapters that follow, we will explore the many forms of these shared influences in fiction in terms of historical treatments and the creation of Wandering Jews, city mysteries novels, secret societies, and ultimately, the legion of vampires that are Dracula's literary ancestors. The English Channel could not contain the horror but rather allowed for easy travel from France to England and back again for both authors and books, creating a richer Gothic tradition than most scholars and readers have acknowledged or even realized existed.

Chapter 2

Historicizing the Gothic and Gothicizing History

Sir Walter Scott, Victor Hugo, and William Harrison Ainsworth

> "[H]istory is but a tiresome thing in itself; it becomes more agreeable the more romance is mixed up with it."
> — W. H. Ainsworth, *Crotchet Castle*

From its beginning, the Gothic had always tried to be pseudo-historical, setting its novels in the past. For example, *The Castle of Otranto* (1764) is vaguely set during the Crusades, and *The Mysteries of Udolpho* (1794) begins in 1584. However, critics have long read the latter and most Gothic novels of the 1790s as a response to the French Revolution, a commentary on current events veiled by being set in a different time. That historical setting changed by the second decade of the nineteenth century. Mary Shelley's *Frankenstein* (1818) was set in modern-day Europe as was Polidori's *The Vampyre* (1819). Such works testified that Gothic horror was not a thing of the past but also existed in the modern world; regardless, many authors were becoming more focused on creating realistic historical fiction than simply using the world as a setting for romance. While Gothic authors belong more strictly to the field of romance than historical fiction, plenty of crossover had occurred by the early to mid-nineteenth century. The question then is whether the Gothic novelists of this period historicized the Gothic or Gothicized history? In truth, they did a little of both.

Sir Walter Scott, as we have seen, was the leader in creating historical fiction in this time, and yet even he was not above using Gothic elements in his novels. He never delved into the supernatural as a reality in his storylines, but he frequently played with Gothic themes. I will discuss *Ivanhoe* here as his best-known work to illustrate how he used Gothic themes in a novel that is predominantly historical fiction. Later in Chapter 5, I will discuss his most Gothic novel, *Anne of Geierstein*.

Sir Walter Scott's *Ivanhoe*

Ivanhoe (1819) is filled with Gothic elements, despite being devoid of supernatural events or characters. Scott draws upon the legend of the Wandering Jew, which we will explore in detail in Chapter 4, but briefly, the legend is that the Wandering Jew was a shoemaker whom Christ passed by on his way to his crucifixion. The Wandering Jew refused to let Christ rest on a stool in front of his home, so Christ cursed him to wander the earth until his Second Coming. This legend became a metaphor for the wandering Jewish people who were exiled from their homeland and believed cursed because of their role in Christ's death.

Scott depicts not a mythical but a real Jew, Isaac, and his daughter, Rebecca. Rebecca is the first literal Wandering Jewess in British literature, but Fanny Burney's *The Wanderer, or Female Difficulties* (1814) may have been an influence upon her creation. We do not know if Scott read Burney's novel, but he certainly was familiar with her other works, even seeking out a meeting with Burney.[1] In *The Wanderer*, Burney's heroine is known as Ellis until her real name, Juliet, is revealed at the end. Ellis is not Jewish, but because she keeps her identity a secret and wanders about England trying to find forms of employment, she is depicted as being mysterious and even is referred to as "A Wandering Jewess" at one point in the novel.* Therefore, I would not be surprised if Scott's concept of Rebecca was in some degree influenced by Burney's novel.

Scott's depiction of Rebecca as a sympathetic Jewish character may seem revolutionary, but he was also preempted by Maria Edgeworth, who in *Harrington* (1817) created a sympathetic portrait of Jews after a reader complained to her about anti-Semitic depictions in earlier novels. Scott was a fan and friend of Edgeworth, who visited him in Scotland. He was heavily influenced by her regional fiction set in Ireland and adapted her methods to write regional novels set in Scotland. Therefore, it wouldn't be surprising if *Harrington* influenced *Ivanhoe*. That said, Edgeworth's novel is completely realistic and set in the modern day. Scott's novel is also realistic, but he sprinkles supernatural and Gothic images throughout and sets it in twelfth-century England.

Ivanhoe makes use of the Wandering Jew theme from the beginning. Ivanhoe is disguised as a pilgrim from the Holy Land who is wandering through the countryside when he meets up with Isaac of York. Through the combination of these two characters, we have a Wandering Jew reference early on. Other Gothic elements borrowed here are that Isaac, as a usurer, is accused of "sucking the blood"[2] of his victims to become fat as a spider—a vampire image, and a surprising one since *The Vampyre* was published the same year, but *The Vampyre* appeared in April and Scott's novel was not published until December so an influence is possible. However, the use of the term "vampire" was not uncommon at the time in references to finance and usury, and the Marquis de Sade used the term earlier in *Justine* (1791). Furthermore, Scott was familiar with Coleridge's poem "Christabel" (1816), in which the character Geraldine is believed by many critics to have been a vampire. Ivanhoe, in disguise, also has a mysterious origin like the Wandering Jew since his identity

---

* I discuss the Gothic elements in Burney's *The Wanderer* at length in *The Gothic Wanderer*.

is not known—this is typical of heroes in literature and especially supernatural beings.

Later, Scott reverses the Wandering Jew imagery when Front-de-Boeuf holds Isaac as his prisoner. We are told that Front-de-Boeuf fixes his eye on Isaac as if to paralyze him with his glance, a trait the Wandering Jew usually has. Isaac's fear of Front-de-Boeuf makes him unable to move.

Rebecca, Isaac's daughter, has the most Wandering Jew characteristics of anyone in the novel. She is a healer with knowledge beyond most people. This knowledge makes people think she is a witch, ultimately leading to her nearly being burned at the stake, but she is more closely akin to Rosicrucian Gothic wanderer figures who have knowledge beyond most people. She claims her secrets date back to the time of King Solomon, and when Ivanhoe is wounded, she says she can heal him in eight days when it would normally take thirty. Later, Rebecca takes on the angst of a Gothic wanderer figure in the unrequited love she feels for Ivanhoe. Many female characters of this period are also Gothic wanderers in their unrequited love, including Lady Olivia in Samuel Richardson's *Sir Charles Grandison* (1753-4), Elinor in Burney's *The Wanderer* (1814), and Joanna, Countess of Mar in Jane Porter's *The Scottish Chiefs* (1809). Finally, Rebecca ends up before an inquisition and is almost burnt for witchcraft. This scene reflects many inquisition scenes in other Gothic novels, including Mrs. Radcliffe's *The Italian* (1797) and the slightly later *Melmoth the Wanderer* (1820) by Charles Maturin.

Personally, I find Ulrica to be the most fascinating Gothic wanderer in the novel. She is a Saxon maiden who was forced to marry the Norman lord Front-de-Boeuf, and consequently, is filled with guilt and angst. She compares herself to the fiends in hell who may feel remorse but not repentance. When Ivanhoe's father Cedric reminds her of what she was before her marriage and how the Normans have badly used her, she decides upon revenge via death. She mocks her husband by pretending to be supernatural. As Front-de-Boeuf is dying, he hears an unearthly voice telling him to think on his sins, the worst of which was the murder of his father, a sin he thought hidden within his own breast. After Front-de-Boeuf's death, Ulrica burns down the castle, dying in the flames.

Scott is not above poking fun at the Gothic in the novel. Athelstane, heir to the Saxon kingdom that has been usurped by the Normans, ends up being wounded while trying to rescue Rebecca, mistaking her for Rowena. He is believed dead, so a group of monks decide to hold his funeral quickly, placing him in the coffin when he is still alive, to collect the funeral money. When he emerges from the coffin, it is as if he has been resurrected. This is a play both on Christ's resurrection and the vampire figure rising from the grave. It is also a humorous moment in the novel. Other than being extremely strong, Athelstane has nothing heroic or supernatural about him; he is a bit of an oaf and more interested in filling his stomach than loving the Saxon heiress Rowena or regaining his ancestors' crown.

I have always felt *Ivanhoe* misnamed since the title character is not much of a hero; for a good part of the novel, he lies wounded and unable to do much of anything. The novel's real hero turns out to be King Richard. Like Ivanhoe, he is incognito in the beginning, disguised as the Black Knight, and he displays great physical strength. Ultimately, all the major acts of heroism fall to him. He frees the Saxon and Jewish characters, including Ivanhoe, when they are taken prisoner, and in the end, he saves England from the treachery of his brother, Prince John. Richard even heals the bad feelings of the Saxons toward the Normans, making Cedric and Athelstane relinquish their efforts to restore a Saxon king to the English throne. In my opinion, King Richard, as depicted in this novel, may be our first real superhero figure, leading gradually to Superman and Batman.

A later novel, James Malcolm Rymer's *The Black Monk* (1844-5), which is far more Gothic than *Ivanhoe*, would use King Richard in a similar way, having him return to England incognito.* Rymer's reuse of this plot device speaks to *Ivanhoe*'s great popularity and influence in its own day and beyond.

In the end, of course, Ivanhoe and Rowena marry, despite Rebecca's love for him. Rebecca then visits Rowena to tell her she and her father are going to Granada where her father is in high favor with the king there and where, presumably, as Jews, they will be safer. She says she cannot remain in England because it is a "land of war and blood" where Israel cannot "hope to rest during her wanderings."[3]

And so, in the end, Rebecca and her father continue to embody the Wandering Jew figure, having to wander from England now to Granada, and who knows where beyond that.

Perhaps what is most remarkable about Scott's use of the Gothic in the novel is that he evokes sympathy for his Wandering Jew figures and by extension the Jewish people.

Countless critics have written about *Ivanhoe*'s historical elements, so I will only briefly touch on it as history. What stands out is how Scott creates a land filled with division—Normans versus conquered Saxons—and then throws in Jewish characters to show how they are outcasts regardless of whether the Normans or Saxons are in power. He recreates an England that few in his day would bother to think about as a period of divisiveness. He allows Robin Hood to enter the novel, thus playing on well-loved English legends to play up the popular element, but at the heart of the novel is a searing discussion about discrimination. Scott knew his treatment of Rebecca was not solely about a fictional Jewess in King Richard's time. It was a cry for tolerance and humanity for all in his own time. Scott's novel uses a plot, characters, and historical setting to do what literature should do—change the world for the better. Scott's finest successors would take up the torch of tolerance as well as the historical fiction torch, as we

---

* For more on *The Black Monk*, see my blog post: https://thegothicwanderer. wordpress.com/2016/06/08/the-black-monk-gothic-wanderers-and-the-early-comic-book-superhero/

will see to different degrees in Hugo's *Notre-Dame de Paris* and Ainsworth's *The Tower of London*.

Victor Hugo's *Notre-Dame de Paris*

Victor Hugo was interested in the Gothic from early in his career, and he was also a reader of Sir Walter Scott. His first novel, *Han d'Islande* (1823), published anonymously, featured a dwarf as its main character. Dwarfmania was then at its height in literature.[4] Among other works, Sir Walter Scott had published *The Black Dwarf* (1816). Although Gothic, *Han d'Islande* was instantly compared to the works of Scott. *The Literary Gazette* in London, reviewing the French edition, noted that it imitated Sir Walter Scott, but called it the "barbarous fantasies of a sick mind." It also may have been inspired by the work of Charles Nodier, one of the first French Romantics.[5] When the English edition, *Hans of Iceland*, appeared in 1825, illustrated by George Cruikshank, it was greatly abridged and aimed at juvenile readers. In time, the book became popular enough to be translated into English twenty-three times, twice under the title *The Demon Dwarf*.[6]

Notre-Dame de Paris (1831), however, would forever give Hugo a place in the history of Gothic and historical fiction. According to George W. M. Reynolds in *The Modern Literature of France* (1839), *Notre-Dame de Paris* was the only work in which Hugo "ably competed with the great Northern writer [Scott] now no more."[7] Reynolds noted the difference between how the two authors treated the medieval period in their works, by stating, "The knights of Scott are the creations of a benevolent and kind imagination; those of Victor Hugo are the offspring of uncompromising and stubborn truth."[8] Comparing *Ivanhoe* to *Notre-Dame de Paris* and Ivanhoe to Phoebus makes Reynolds' statement very accurate.

Today, *Notre-Dame de Paris* is better known to English readers as *The Hunchback of Notre-Dame*, the title chosen by Frederic Shoberl for his 1833 translation into English. It is a curious book that can't quite decide if it's a novel, an exposé on fifteenth-century Paris, or a treatise on medieval architecture. For the modern reader, the result is some impatience, some boredom, and often much to be surprised by because it is a work people assume they know something about, but it ranges far from most of the extra-textual materials—films, comic books, etc.—it influenced. Hugo's story has been bastardized, romanticized, and deeply changed in most of the versions, including giving it a happy ending in which Esmeralda and Phoebus ride off together into the sunset. Hugo's version is far darker, and perhaps not to twenty-first-century readers' tastes, but its Gothic elements and existential philosophy make it a major work in the Gothic tradition. In fact, it is the first major French Gothic work of the nineteenth century, excepting the French versions of Polidori's Lord Ruthven that were popular in the 1820s. While *The Vampyre* does not seem to have influenced the novel, the influences of Mrs. Radcliffe and Sir Walter Scott are apparent throughout.

We know Hugo read Radcliffe because he references her in *Les Misérables*, when he states: "at night there would be people looting isolated houses in deserted corners of Paris (here, you could detect the imagination of the police at work, that Ann Radcliffe element in the government)."[9] The immediate influence of Radcliffe on Hugo stems from his use of Gothic architecture by setting the novel in the medieval cathedral of Notre-Dame, and perhaps more specifically, in his depiction of Frollo, who may be seen as the literary child of the monk Schedoni in Radcliffe's *The Italian*. Schedoni nearly murders his daughter, not knowing her true identity, while Quasimodo intentionally murders his foster father Frollo. Lewis' *The Monk* was also regarded as a source. A critic in the *R. Britannique* in 1839 remarked that Claude Frollo was just a pale copy of the original Ambrosio.[10]

Scott's influence was noted immediately by readers and reviewers. One critic described the depiction of Louis XI in the novel as "le Louis XI de *Quentin Durward*."[11] The anonymous reviewer of the August 25, 1833 review in *The Examiner* states:

> The *Notre-Dame* of Victor Hugo must take rank with the best romances by the Author of *Waverley*. If it fall short in copiousness and variety of incident and adventure, it transcends on the other hand in vigour, animation, familiarity with the age. The reader of this book will never stop to admire the antiquarian lore of the author; it seems as if we were but listening to his reminiscences of the time of Louis XI. To put old Paris before our eyes appears to be rather an act of memory than an act of study, and he sets it forth with a freshness which sparkles in the fancy. 'Tis centuries since, but the scene has the vividness of the present sunshine. *Notre-Dame* abounds with characters any one of which would have served to carry on the interest of a modern novel. La Esmeralda, a gipsy dancing girl, will remind the reader of the Fenella of Scott [a female dwarf in *Peveril of the Peak* (1823)], but there is the difference between them of a being of warm blood, and the plastered gew-gaw figure on the top of a Twelfth cake. La Esmeralda has all the reality that Fenella wants.[12]

George W. M. Reynolds also believed some aspects of the novel surpassed the work of Scott:

> Again, it is in this book that we meet with the knight of the olden time—the savage, brutal, lustful, and selfish warrior—instead of the gentle, the courtly, the protecting, and the noble-minded hero whom Walter Scott so erroneously represented as the boast of those ages: here we have him in his true colours, divested of his disguise, and presented to us in all the nakedness of truth.[13]

Twentieth-century critic E. Preston Dargan saw at least six obvious influences of Scott upon the novel. In fact, he sees influence from so many of Scott's novels in different aspects of *Notre-Dame de Paris* that it is worth quoting his discussion in full here:

There are a half-a-dozen aspects in which this novel shows an assiduous reading of Sir Walter. Even Maigron admits that the general intention (not altogether fulfilled in the execution) was equally excellent and Scottian with reference to characters: individuals should be made representative of their period and raised to the level of general types—as Scott had done with Cedric and others in *Ivanhoe*. (Hugo had praised *Ivanhoe*; and had used in *Hernani* the device of the returning pilgrim, incognito in his sweetheart's home.) And just as Scott was "made for *Ivanhoe*," so Hugo was made for this Gothic subject, with the Cathedral dominant over "tout ce qui attire l'ceil et le retient, costumes barioles, armures luisantes...." The author of *Eviradnus* could soon proceed alone on the picturesque medieval highway; but it was Walter Scott who first led his feet to that favorite road. In the second place, the descriptions, though longer than in Scott, are of the same general kind: e.g., the Cathedral, the Palais de Justice, the Louvre, the king's room in the Bastille, even to the torture-chamber where Esmeralda suffers. The "Gothic" note is present in many of these, while the author's intention is evidently to stress customs and institutions under Louis XI. The episodical appearance of that monarch is linked with the wide revival of interest in his personality, which Scott had resuscitated [in *Quentin Durward*]. Delavigne and Balzac offer other examples. In connection with the latter, we shall go more fully into the role of Louis, whether in history or fiction. Hugo's portrait of the king is quite in the Romantic tradition. (The chapters on Louis were added in the edition of 1832.) Among the features similar to those in *Quentin* are: his cunning, his cruelty, his piercing look, his oaths, his anxiety about his health, his shabby dress, and the greasy hat, with its little leaden figures of saints. The extraordinary prayer to Our Lady, with its bribes and its bargaining, which Hugo puts in the mouth of Louis, is at least as close to the prayer in

Quentin as to the originals in the chronicles. In either novel a good deal is made of the wooden cages in which Louis had treacherous churchmen confined. Hugo refers several times to Cardinal Balue. He brings on the stage the familiar retinue, headed by Coictier, Tristan, and Olivier, that "terrible Figaro." The election of the Pope of Fools, with its travesty of religious rites and its depiction of a motley, turbulent, and free-spoken crowd, has certainly its parallel in *The Abbot*, chapter 14. But I am more impressed by the resemblance of the Kingdom of Cant (Cour des Miracles) to that other sanctuary of Whitefriars in [*The Fortunes of*] *Nigel*. In either instance, we find ourselves in a place apart, a rascals' Paradise with its own jurisdiction and its own governor. This "duke" performs, or would perform, unseemly marriages. No officers of the law dare enter either domain, which has its own code, its own argot, and its special brands of villainy. The passion of Claude Frollo for Esmeralda recalls the similar one of Brian de Bois-Guilbert for Rebecca, who likewise was condemned as a sorceress. In each case the lover is forced into the position of being officially the opponent of the girl whom he adores to the point of obsession. Consequently, he tries vainly to persuade her to flee with him to some spot beyond the pale. Conflicting passions and the tempest of emotion are nearly the end of Frollo as they are quite the end of de Bois-Guilbert. Without going so far as to say with a Quarterly Reviewer that *Notre-Dame* resembles a *Waverley Novel* about as much as Guse Gibbie resembles Lord Evandale, it is not difficult to discern in Hugo a lack of balance and a pronounced leaning to the grotesque which Scott rarely showed. Edmond Bire points out another difference inherent in the two opposed conceptions of Romanticism: that while Quentin and his creator are endowed with brave hearts, Hugo and Frollo and the rest are haunted by a gloomy fatalism.[14]

All these similarities are not surprising given how *Notre-Dame de Paris* came to be written. Hugo was hired in November 1828 to write a two-volume novel in the style of Sir Walter Scott. In 1823, he had favorably reviewed *Quentin Durward*.[15] Scott's influence is obvious in the historical elements of *Notre-Dame de Paris*, and yet, at the end of his life, Hugo denied ever writing a historical novel. That is not to say he disowned the book, but that he did not see it as historical. This is surprising given the novel's many historical elements and Hugo's great efforts to create an appropriate atmosphere for the book's time and setting; regardless, he obviously saw the Gothic and Romantic elements of the novel as more important than the historical ones. According to Alban Krailsheimer, one of the novel's many translators, while Hugo was generally appreciative of Scott's work, as his review of *Quentin Durward* shows, "Hugo regretted the absence of a truly epic dimension, a broadly sweeping view which would give the narrative some deeper meaning."[16] This is a fair criticism of Scott's work. Scott recreates historical periods and people, but he seldom guides us in what wisdom or understanding we are to learn from the events and periods he depicts. *Notre-Dame de Paris* is far clearer in its themes and overall lessons or purpose, while still requiring the reader to interpret. Hugo does not simply tell us what to think.

Notre-Dame de Paris' most overwhelming Gothic element is the cathedral itself. The cathedral is like a book to be read, the equivalent of the discovered manuscript in earlier Gothic novels, such as the manuscript the heroine Adeline discovers in Mrs. Radcliffe's *The Romance of the Forest* that reveals secrets from the past. Hugo wrote the novel largely to create interest in the cathedral to encourage its restoration. He definitely had an interest in preserving the monuments of the past, perhaps influenced by his experience in 1825 when he was named the official poet of the coronation of Charles X at Reims Cathedral. That cathedral received little respect at the coronation. Medieval sculptures protruding from the building were lopped off by masons to prevent them from falling on the king. Hugo picked up a stone head of Christ, chiseled off the face of his own church.[17]

Throughout *Notre-Dame de Paris*, Hugo highlights the importance of preserving architecture and even discusses how the printing press has killed it.[18] He argues that the great buildings of the past, especially cathedrals, were the books of their days because they told stories, made statements, and generally educated the population in religion, politics, and history.

The novel begins with Hugo claiming to have discovered an inscription in the cathedral, a Greek word, which later was removed. The inscription is Hugo's fictional invention, but is used to create a feeling of authenticity for his tale. Later, we learn Claude Frollo incised the word on the wall with a pair of compasses.[19] This word is 'ANÁΓKH, and it appears to mean fate, compulsion, or determinism in the novel. While Christianity teaches that humans have free will, all the characters play out their natural propensities, unable to resist their passions or desires, which ultimately leads to their destruction. We see this in how Frollo's obsession with Esmeralda undoes his reason; we see it in how despite Frollo's efforts to raise his younger brother Jehan in a moral way, Jehan becomes a wastrel; we see it in how Esmeralda's passion for Phoebus causes her stupidly to reveal her hiding place, thus leading to her execution; and we see it in Quasimodo, whose love for Esmeralda causes him to kill Frollo, the only one who loves him, and then to end his own life by burying himself in the tomb with Esmeralda, a love that remains unrequited. Indeed, not one character in the novel has their love returned, although most of the characters do love someone. Ultimately, while the novel can be described as Gothic, historical, and Romantic, it is also a precursor to the Naturalist movement of writers like Émile Zola and even to the existentialism of authors like Jean-Paul Sartre.

But the novel's role as Gothic literature is what most interests us here. A closer study of the three main characters—Claude Frollo, Esmeralda, and Quasimodo—illuminates the way Hugo effectively uses Gothic elements to create his dramatic and existential tale. Existential because, in the end, one has to wonder if the novel has any meaning other than to show the inability of the characters to create any sort of meaning for themselves because they live in a world that, despite their religious beliefs, is devoid of any supernatural forces, benevolent or sinister.

Claude Frollo

Despite English translations of the novel being titled *The Hunchback of Notre-Dame*, a more accurate title might be *The Archdeacon of Notre-Dame* because the novel's events are set in motion by Claude Frollo, Notre-Dame's archdeacon.

Frollo embodies many aspects of the Gothic wanderer figure. Indeed, all three of the best-known characters in the novel, Frollo, Esmeralda the gypsy, and Quasimodo the hunchback, are Gothic wanderers. Because Frollo is our villain, however, he is the truest Gothic wanderer. He is strict in his religious beliefs, and yet incapable of overcoming his baser nature. Hugo develops Frollo's character early on through sharing what the people of Paris say about Frollo, expressing their beliefs that he is a sorcerer. While in time we learn he is not a sorcerer, Frollo is obsessed with alchemy, which was aligned with sorcery in the medieval mind. Among Hugo's inspirations for the novel was Henri Sauval (1623-76), whose *Histoire et recherches des antiquités de la ville de Paris* was published in 1724. Sauval mentions the statues and figures in Notre-Dame and other buildings that alchemists associate with the mystery of finding the legendary philosopher's stone that can turn lead into gold. Frollo longs to discover the secret of the philosopher's stone. In Gothic fiction, this secret is believed to be known by the Rosicrucians, but Hugo surprisingly does not reference the Rosicrucians, even though their legendary founder, Christian Rosencreutz, was said to live in the fifteenth century, the time of *Notre-Dame de Paris*.*

---

* For more on Rosicrucianism in Gothic fiction, see *The Gothic Wanderer*,

Frollo, rather than looking for an actual stone, is obsessed with the gold of sunbeams, in which he believes lies the secret of transmutation. The desire for the philosopher's stone was considered a transgression against God. It was forbidden knowledge because the one who possessed the stone could make gold, which could upset nations' economies and allow him to enrich himself to the point of becoming a world leader.* Consequently, Frollo is committing a transgression through his alchemy pursuits. He is so gung-ho in these efforts that he goes to the home of the deceased medieval alchemist Nicolas Flamel. There he occupies himself in:

> turning over the earth in the two cellars whose buttresses had been daubed with countless verses and hieroglyphs by Nicolas Flamel himself. Flamel was supposed to have buried the philosophers' stone in these cellars and the alchemists for two hundred years, from Magistri to Father Pacifique, did not cease from tossing the soil about until the house, so roughly excavated and ransacked, finally turned to dust beneath their feet."[20]

Frollo's quest for forbidden knowledge eventually reaches the ear of King Louis XI who comes to him in secret; together, they debate astrology and medicine versus alchemy. The king thinks Frollo mad, but being in need of money, he wants the philosopher's stone, so they frequently discuss it. Frollo tells Louis XI "to make gold is to be god. That is the only science."[21]

Frollo's quest for forbidden knowledge soon takes a new turn when he begins to lust over Esmeralda. This desire represents another form of the quest for forbidden knowledge because Frollo, as a clergyman, has taken a vow of chastity, making the knowledge of sex forbidden to him.

Chapter IV: The Rosicrucian Gothic Wanderer. I will also investigate Rosicrucianism more in Chapter 6 of this book when I discuss Edward Bulwer-Lytton's *Zanoni* (1842).

* Such is the situation in William Godwin's novel *St. Leon* (1799) when the title character acquires possession of the philosopher's stone. I discuss *St. Leon* in *The Gothic Wanderer*, Chapter IV.

I will pass over the details of Frollo's attempts to deride and also seduce Esmeralda, but it's important to note that his love for Esmeralda adds to the supernatural element of his character. Eventually, he looks into his soul and comes to realize the relationship between love and hate. He blames his position in society for turning his love into hate.

> As he thus delved into his soul, when he saw what spacious provision nature had made in it for passions, he laughed all the more bitterly. He stirred up all the hatred, all the malice in his innermost heart, and recognized, with the cool eye of a physician examining a patient, that this hatred and malice was nothing but vitiated love; that love, source of every human virtue, could, in a priest's heart, turn into something horrible, and that a man constituted like him, by becoming a priest became a devil. Then he gave a dreadful laugh, and suddenly paled again as he contemplated the most sinister aspect of his fatal passion, of that corrosive, poisonous, hateful, implacable love whose only outcome had been the gallows for one of them, hell for the other: she condemned, he damned.[22]

The reader almost feels sorry for Frollo at this point. Had Frollo not taken his unnatural vow of chastity, he could have married and had release from his lust. Had he sought after good things rather than the philosopher's stone, he might not have isolated himself from humanity. Now his love for Esmeralda has made him into a devil, a type of supernatural being. Esmeralda recognizes this when he visits her in her cell, calling him a "monster."

In response, he begs for mercy.

> 'Mercy! mercy!' murmured the priest, pressing his lips to her shoulders.
>
> She seized his bald head in both hands by his remaining hair, and strove to ward off his kisses as if they had been bites.

'Mercy!' the wretched man repeated. 'If you knew what my love for you is like! It's fire, molten lead, thousands of knives in my heart!'

And he held her arms still with superhuman strength. Distraught, she said: 'Let me go, or I'll spit in your face!'

He let her go: 'Degrade me, hit me, be vicious! Do whatever you like! But mercy! love me!'[23]

In this scene, Esmeralda has Frollo under her spell as if she is the one with the supernatural power and he must beg mercy from her, and yet, she calls him a monster, and she avoids his kisses as if they are bites. Just a few lines later, she even calls him a "vampire."* He meanwhile holds her with superhuman strength—an attribute Quasimodo also shares.

Later, in one of the novel's most vividly Gothic scenes, Pierre Gringoire (Esmeralda's playwright husband) and Frollo try to rescue Esmeralda from being burned as a witch by escaping on a boat. Frollo is disguised by a hood and long robe, causing Esmeralda not to recognize him. Frollo's figure rowing the boat fills her with fear: "He could be dimly seen in the bows of the boat, like a spectre in the dark. His hood, still lowered, had the effect of a kind of mask, and each time he opened his arms as he rowed, with the wide black sleeves hanging down, they looked like two huge batwings."[24] Readers of classical literature will recall Charon, who ferries the dead to Hades. Readers of Gothic literature will think of the Phantom of the Opera, ferrying Christine to his underground cavern. (Indeed, Gaston Leroux's *Phantom of the Opera* (1910) has many parallels to *Notre-Dame de Paris*.) The description of bat wings also stirs up images of the vampire.

Frollo's final Gothic wanderer aspect is that he bears a version of the mark of Cain. In the Bible, God curses Cain by placing a mark on his forehead after he murders his brother. In Gothic literature, the Wandering Jew has a mark on his forehead for

---

* Notably, Hugo wrote "un vampire." It is not a loose translation.

his transgression in refusing to let Christ rest on the way to Calvary. However, Frollo's version of the mark of Cain is largely undeserved. Krailsheimer says, "Frollo, now raving mad and made more so by the news of Jehan's death, indirectly caused by his rejection of his brother, has to bear the mark of Cain to add to all his other crimes."[25] (Jehan is a drunkard, and Frollo has simply refused to give him more money to support his dysfunctional behavior—what we would call "tough love" today.) Later, Jehan joins the attack on the cathedral to rescue Esmeralda. Quasimodo mistakes the attack as an attempt to capture and kill her, so he ends up killing Jehan in the melee that follows. Eventually, Frollo learns of his brother's death, but he does not know Quasimodo murdered Jehan.

Frollo plants the mark of Cain upon his own forehead during a soliloquy after learning of Jehan's death:

> He fell silent for a moment, then went on, as though talking to himself, in a loud voice: 'Cain, what have you done with your brother?' There was another silence, then he continued: 'What have I done with him, Lord? I took him in, I brought him up, I fed him, I loved him, I idolized him, and I killed him! Yes, Lord, they have just now dashed his head before my eyes against the stones of your house, and it is because of me, because of this woman, because of her....'[26]

After Frollo is seen to die at Quasimodo's hands, Hugo states:

> Many rumours went round concerning this incident. There was no doubt in people's minds that the day had come when, in accordance with their pact, Quasimodo, that is the devil, was to carry off Claude Frollo, that is the sorcerer. It was supposed that he had shattered the body as he took the soul, as monkeys break the shell to eat the nut.
>
> That is why the archdeacon was not interred in consecrated ground.[27]

This is the final suggestion of Frollo's supernatural nature and again links him to vampires because he cannot rest in consecrated ground. He will remain a Gothic wanderer even in death.

Esmeralda

Esmeralda is also a Gothic wanderer. As a gypsy, she is an outcast of society. The Parisians go so far as to make her into a nonhuman, believing she is a "supernatural" creature and Gringoire compares her to a salamander, a nymph, and a goddess.[28*] Unknown to herself, Esmeralda is even an outcast among the outcasts, for she is not really a gypsy but a French child stolen from its mother.

In Book VIII, Chapter 3, Esmeralda is referred to as a "vampire" because she is a gypsy and consequently must be a child-stealer. Krailsheimer translates the French as vampire but the word is actually "stryga" in Hugo's French, which can also mean witch. In Albanian folklore, it is a vampiric witch that sucks the blood of children.[29]

Ironically, Esmeralda is cursed by her own biological mother, who not knowing her true identity calls her a child-stealer because she is a gypsy. Once their relationship is revealed, the mother tries to hide Esmeralda when she is being pursued by those intent on killing her. Esmeralda, however, believes she hears the voice of Phoebus, the man she loves, so she calls out his name, revealing her location to her pursuers, thus leading to her capture and death. Esmeralda's inability to overcome her passion for Phoebus, who is anything but a hero, and nothing more than a womanizer, brings about her downfall. While her love for Phoebus is not described as lust in the way Frollo's love for her is described, it amounts to the same—both Esmeralda and Frollo bring about their own downfall because of their inability to control their human desires.

---

* In French, "c'est une salamandre, c'est une nymphe, c'est une déesse."

Quasimodo

Quasimodo, like Esmeralda, is another outcast, not because of his race but because of his deformity. Later, we will learn he is a gypsy child, traded like a halfling child, for a white child, which also implies a supernatural element, since halflings were the children of fairies traded for white children. He is also described as the child of a "sow" and a "Jew,"[30] making him animal as well as human, and even by being part-Jew he is not quite human because in the Middle Ages, Jews were believed to have horns and be akin to the devil.[31]

Later, Quasimodo displays supernatural powers, not through use of magic but through his superhuman abilities. Besides his incredible strength, he is very nimble and can climb up the cathedral's façade.[32] The modern reader cannot fail to see the resemblance to Spiderman, while the Gothic enthusiast will recall how Count Dracula climbs up the exterior wall of his castle. In fact, we have here the seeds of future superhero characters embedded in the Gothic.

That Quasimodo was adopted by Frollo, who is believed to be a sorcerer, also adds to his supernatural abilities. The people of Paris spread tales that he must serve Frollo for a set number of years, and then he will be given a soul, in a sort of reverse Faustian contract.

Hugo describes how the people of Paris view Quasimodo and Frollo's relationship:

> We must say, however, that the sciences of Egypt, necromancy, magic, even of the whitest and most innocent kind, had no enemy more relentless, no one who denounced them more inexorably to the officiality of Notre-Dame. Whether this was from genuine horror or the play-acting of the thief shouting: 'Stop thief!', it did not prevent the archdeacon being regarded by the learned heads in the chapter as a soul who had ventured into the antechamber of hell, lost in the caverns of the Kabbala,

groping in the darkness of the occult sciences. The people made no mistake about it either; for anyone with a little sense Quasimodo was the demon, Claude Frollo the sorcerer. It was obvious that the bell-ringer had to serve the archdeacon for a given time, at the end of which he would carry off his soul by way of payment.[33]

In short, Frollo is viewed as Faust to Quasimodo's Mephistopheles.

Frollo and Quasimodo do have a bond, but it is not supernatural. Quasimodo reverences Frollo for how he saved him. However, their respect or love for one another is unable to withstand the love or lust they both feel for Esmeralda. Indeed, Hugo's text becomes oedipal here. Quasimodo seeks to kill his father-figure to be with the woman his father desires, although calling Esmeralda a mother figure would be going too far. In the end, this love of Esmeralda is destructive for both of them. After Quasimodo sends Frollo to his death, he cries out, "Oh! all I have loved!"[34] because he realizes he has now lost everyone who mattered to him.

In the end, Quasimodo makes his way to the sepulcher where Esmeralda is buried, and there he wraps his fingers around hers and gives up his life so he can spend eternity with her. Dead, Esmeralda never knows of the sacrifice he makes for her.

Existential Ending

In the end, love is unrequited for all the characters, and all the characters have let their love or lust lead to their committing actions that have brought about their deaths.

Hugo has painted a fatalistic world. There is no free will for the characters because they are unable to stop themselves from acting as they do. Instead, we might call *Notre-Dame de Paris* an early example of both naturalism and existentialism.

While earlier Gothic novels, even while often deriding Catholicism, worked within a Christian structure where the good are rewarded and the bad punished, to describe anyone in *Notre-Dame de Paris* as good or bad would be far too simplistic. Even Frollo, the novel's villain if there is one, had kind intentions in raising his brother after their parents died, and in caring for Quasimodo when no one else would, but his good intentions are brushed aside when lust consumes him. Despite the setting in Notre-Dame, there is little about God in this novel. As Krailsheimer says, "The most notable omission from the book is Christianity."[35]

William Harrison Ainsworth's Early Gothic Novels

William Harrison Ainsworth was one of the most popular authors of his day, though his name is largely forgotten now. Not only was he a friend of Charles Dickens, but his novels outsold those of Dickens and he helped Dickens to make early connections in the literary world. Ainsworth was also a pivotal author in the revival of Gothic literature in England in the 1830s and 1840s. He was heavily influenced by Mrs. Radcliffe and her imitators, but also by Sir Walter Scott and Victor Hugo.

Ainsworth's first novel, *Sir John Chiverton* (1826), was a mixture of Gothic and historical fiction, often said to be written in the style of Scott, and Scott himself read it and wrote about it in some articles.[36] However, there is little of Scott's style in the novel and other than it being set two centuries earlier, nothing of real historical interest about it. It more closely reflects the style of Mrs. Radcliffe. The title character wishes to gain control of the family property left to his sister and tries to thwart her relationship with her lover. He also pretends his sister is mad and tells his prospective bride's father that he will inherit his sister's property. The story ends tragically with few plot twists but plenty of conniving that backfires on the nefarious characters. Ainsworth all but disowned the novel in later life, yet his biographer, Stephen Carver, argues that while *Sir John Chiverton* was lacking in construction, it may be:

The first example in nineteenth-century literature of the struggle to establish a new form of English Gothic, which could escape the established European, medieval and Catholic cliches of the eighteenth-century genre while also taking it back from the model of the historical novel left by Scott.[37]

Ainsworth's second novel, *Rookwood*, published eight years later, would establish him as the major English Gothic novelist of his day or at least for the next decade. In this discussion of Ainsworth, I will focus on how *Rookwood* borrowed from and revolutionized the Gothic tradition and then how Ainsworth's novel *The Tower of London* borrowed from Hugo's *Notre-Dame de Paris* and Scott's novels to create a Gothicized version of English history.

Rookwood

Rookwood took the literary world by storm when it was published in 1834. Although few read it today, its influence can be seen in much better-known works of literature. Ainsworth's goal was to write a Gothic novel in the style of Walpole and Radcliffe, but at the same time, he was heavily influenced by the rise of the historical novel, particularly by Sir Walter Scott, so he set the novel in England in the reign of George II in 1737. This decision was also partly determined by his long-time interest in the famous highwayman Dick Turpin. Turpin is a main character in the novel. His role reflects the influence of the Newgate novels of the time, which focused upon criminals.

Anne Williams, in *Art of Darkness: The Poetics of Gothic*, has said "Gothic plots are family plots; Gothic romance is family."[38] Nothing could be truer of *Rookwood*, which has one of the most complex family inheritance storylines of any novel ever written.

The novel opens at the manor of Rookwood Place. Sir Piers Rookwood has recently died after the bough of an ancient tree was found on the ground. Family legend says a death always follows the dropping of a bough from the tree. Sir Piers' son, Ranulph, is believed to be the true heir to Rookwood Place, but then Peter Bradley, the estate's keeper, reveals to his grandson Luke Bradley that he is Sir Piers' legitimate and oldest son. Sir Piers had secretly married Peter's daughter. Peter brings Luke into the family vault to show him his mother's body and even the hand bearing the wedding ring. In a grotesque moment, Luke takes his mother's hand and ring as proof of his legitimate birth. Not surprisingly, we also learn Luke's parents were married by a Jesuit priest, Father Checkley. The Gothic loved to pick on Catholics, and the Jesuits were frequently manipulative plotters in Gothic storylines, as I will explore more in Chapter 4 in discussing Eugène Sue's *The Wandering Jew* (1846). *Rookwood* may be the first novel to use Jesuits in a Gothic plot.

Peter now plots to marry Luke to his cousin Eleanor Mowbray, the daughter of Sir Piers' sister. To complicate matters, Luke's cousin Ranulph is in love with Eleanor, and Luke is not interested in Eleanor because he is in love with a young gypsy, Sybil Lovel. Luke was raised by gypsies, so he and Sybil have known each other since childhood. Despite Luke's feelings for Sybil, his grandfather insists he marry Eleanor, and Luke finally agrees to the marriage. Eleanor is completely clueless about these plans. She is under the belief she will marry Ranulph.

Eleanor now travels to Rookwood Place with her mother to attend Sir Piers' funeral. However, the carriage is waylaid and she and her mother find themselves among the gypsies. The highwayman Dick Turpin intercedes to help Luke marry Eleanor. The gypsies have other plans, however, and at the ceremony, Luke is fooled into marrying Sybil. Once married, Sybil, realizing Luke does not love her, kills herself. Sybil's grandmother then takes revenge by giving Luke a poisoned lock of Sybil's hair, which eventually results in Luke's death.

After Luke's death, Peter Bradley reveals that he is really Alan Rookwood, the brother of Reginald Rookwood, the father of Piers. (This makes the family tree extremely complicated since

Luke's parents were first cousins and he also has attempted to marry his first cousin.) Ranulph's mother, Maud, who has also been scheming for her son, now finds herself accidentally locked inside the family tomb with Peter/Alan. In one of the novel's most terrifying moments, Maud and Alan realize they will die before they are ever found. In the end, Ranulph and Eleanor, the only surviving members of the family, marry.

The plot is more complicated than my summary, and it includes Dick Turpin being chased by the law in a scene that goes on for many chapters and was said to thrill contemporary readers. The modern reader, by contrast, wonders why Dick is even in the novel and just wants to get back to the dysfunctional family plot.

Today, the novel would win no awards for subtlety or even style, but it is a rousing good story overall. It is sensational and at times gory—who would want to carry around their dead mother's hand? It is also amoral. The reader is not clear for whom to cheer. At times, it seems like Ainsworth is on Luke's side as the rightful heir, but Stephen Carver, in his article "The Design of Romance: Rookwood, Scott, and the Gothic," argues that Luke's fatal flaw is his lust for power, property, and revenge for his mother's wrongs, which is why he fails in the end.[39] Furthermore, Luke is driven on by his grandfather's own desire for revenge upon the family—his own family.

As stated earlier, Ainsworth's goal was to write a novel like those of Mrs. Radcliffe. In *Rookwood*'s 1849 preface, he states:

> I resolved to attempt a story in the bygone style of Mrs. Radcliffe,—which had always inexpressible charms for me,—substituting an old English squire, an old English manorial residence, and an old English highwayman, for the Italian marchese, the castle, and the brigand of the great mistress of Romance.

Ainsworth succeeded in his goal, bringing the Gothic to England, though a century before his own time. Like Mrs.

Radcliffe, he also shied away from any actual supernatural events in the novel, even when the characters think supernatural occurrences are happening. To some degree, the characters' foolishness of believing in the supernatural is reflected in the family curses and legends and their contradicting curses and legends. Like Mrs. Radcliffe, Ainsworth also sprinkles poetry throughout the novel, most of it in the form of songs, many of them about highwaymen, and most of questionable merit—Mrs. Radcliffe was no great poet herself. The songs tend to delay the action for the modern reader, but they have some charm and add to the style Ainsworth seeks to copy.

Sir Walter Scott's influence is prevalent in the novel's historical setting in England. *Rookwood* is one of the first Gothic novels to be set in England rather than abroad. Ainsworth is less interested, however, in the historical drama of the period that Scott tried to depict in his own works. Stephen Carver argues that Scott's poetry was a greater influence on Ainsworth than his fiction.[40]

The influence of *Notre-Dame de Paris* is also felt here, although not to the degree it would be in Ainsworth's later novels. Hugo's novel had been translated into English in 1833, so Ainsworth may have read it before writing or at least completing *Rookwood*. In the novel's 1849 preface, Ainsworth references Hugo along with several other authors, stating:

> The chief object I had in view in making the present essay was to see how far the infusion of a warmer and more genial current into the veins of old Romance would succeed in reviving her fluttering and feeble pulses. The attempt has succeeded beyond my most sanguine expectation. Romance, if I am not mistaken, is destined shortly to undergo an important change. Modified by the German and French writers—by Hoffman, Tieck, Hugo, Dumas, Balzac, and Paul Lecroix (le Bibliophile Jacob)— the structure commenced in our own land by Horace Walpole, Monk Lewis, Mrs. Radcliffe, and Maturin, but left imperfect and inharmonious, requires, now that the

rubbish which choked up its approach is removed, only the hand of the skilful architect to its entire renovation and perfection.

In other words, Ainsworth acknowledges how French and German authors have improved upon English Gothic, and now it is time for him and other English writers to embrace those improvements. Noteworthy in this passage is the absence of Scott's name among the English writers of "romance," a term more akin to the Gothic than Scott's historical fiction. Of course, we cannot assume all the writers Ainsworth lists were influences upon him or *Rookwood* since the preface was written fifteen years after *Rookwood* was published and Dumas, for example, did not begin writing novels until a couple of years after *Rookwood* appeared. However, Hugo's influence seems highly likely, especially since after *Rookwood* was published, Ainsworth was praised in advertisements for the book as "The English Victor Hugo,"[41] a testament both to him and to the popularity of Hugo in Great Britain. In fact, Ainsworth quoted from Hugo's play *Marie Tudor* (1833) for the epigraph to Chapter 5 of *Rookwood*.

While the comparison to Hugo may be general because Ainsworth had written a popular Gothic and historical novel like Hugo, the influence seems more apparent in the work's lack of a clear moral, just as *Notre-Dame de Paris* presents an existential or amoral viewpoint. Certainly, Ranulph seems no more moral than Luke, and Luke has more reason than Ranulph to behave in dastardly ways because he has been cheated from his inheritance. None of the characters are overly moral, but Luke's failure does appear to be rooted in his lust for property, as Carver suggests. As in *Notre-Dame de Paris*, we are left with bodies littering the novel's pages, and most of the characters die because of their inability to control their passions. Scholar Heather Glen states that Dick Turpin, Luke, and the protagonists of other Newgate novels seem driven to break the law to right the injustices of society,[42] and Luke here believes himself wronged so he is trying to right that wrong. This position of the hero in these novels also makes him an outcast in society, a type of Gothic wanderer, who is not a transgressor, but rather feels society has transgressed against him, and consequently, he must transgress against society to right the first transgression.

Rookwood's influence would be considerable. One has to wonder if the revenge theme played into the creation of Féval's Rio Santo in *Les Mystères de Londres* (1845) and Dumas' Edmond Dantès in *The Count of Monte Cristo* (1844-6). In both novels, the protagonist seeks revenge after being wronged, carrying it on far more intelligently and successfully than Luke does, and at least in Dantès' case displaying some moral scruples in the end. We will look at both novels in more detail in Chapter 3.

Rookwood definitely influenced the works of Charlotte and Emily Brontë. Heather Glen has analyzed the influence of *Rookwood* on Charlotte Brontë's *Tales of Angria*, stating that the character of Henry Hastings in the stories is an ironic treatment of *Rookwood*.[43] In my opinion, *Jane Eyre* also well may have been influenced by *Rookwood*. The gypsies who are primary characters in *Rookwood* may have inspired Mr. Rochester dressing up as a gypsy in *Jane Eyre*. Notably, Brontë has Jane Eyre call this supposed gypsy a "Sybil," which is the name of the primary gypsy character in *Rookwood*. Of course, the name is also appropriate since a sybil can foresee the future and Brontë's fake gypsy claims to be a fortune teller. Furthermore, while Sybil in *Rookwood* does not appear to be prophetic, the novel itself contains several prophecies, one of which Sybil helps to fulfill.

An influence on *Wuthering Heights* is also probable. The complicated family relationships of *Rookwood* all relate to a family fight over who will inherit the property. It is interesting that Luke has to prove himself the legitimate heir. Scholars of *Wuthering Heights* have often speculated whether Heathcliff may be Mr. Earnshaw's bastard child. Heathcliff is referred to as a "gipsy" six times in the novel because his origins are unknown. Luke was himself raised by the gypsies. Like Luke, Heathcliff tries to gain control of the family property. Heathcliff succeeds where Luke fails, yet in the end, Heathcliff dies and the property returns to the only two remaining descendants of the Earnshaws and Lintons. Similarly, in *Rookwood*, the only remaining family members inherit the property. Emily Brontë may have had *Rookwood* in the back of her mind as she wrote, simplifying her family plot while whitewashing the taint of illegitimacy so that Heathcliff's illegitimacy only exists if one reads between the lines.

While *Rookwood* has been almost forgotten today, it is a notable link in the chain of British Gothic literature between Radcliffe and Scott and later writers like Dickens, George W. M. Reynolds, and the Brontës. It also shows how Radcliffe and Scott's influence on Hugo led to Hugo's influence on Ainsworth, which would be even greater in *The Tower of London* (1840).

The Tower of London

In Frances Hodgson Burnett's novel *Little Lord Fauntleroy* (1886), the title character's good friend, the American shopkeeper Mr. Hobbs, expresses his dislike of the English. When Mr. Hobbs learns Fauntleroy is grandson to an English earl and going to live in England, he decides he wants to learn more about England so he purchases a book about it. The book turns out to be Ainsworth's *The Tower of London*. While reading it, Mr. Hobbs and his friend Dick develop some strange ideas about the English, as Burnett illustrates:

> So the clerk sold him a book called "The Tower of London," written by Mr. Harrison Ainsworth, and he carried it home.
>
> When Dick came they began to read it. It was a very wonderful and exciting book, and the scene was laid in the reign of the famous English queen who is called by some people Bloody Mary. And as Mr. Hobbs heard of Queen Mary's deeds and the habit she had of chopping people's heads off, putting them to the torture, and burning them alive, he became very much excited. He took his pipe out

of his mouth and stared at Dick, and at last he was obliged to mop the perspiration from his brow with his red pocket handkerchief.

"Why, he ain't safe!" he said. "He ain't safe! If the women folks can sit up on their thrones an' give the word for things like that to be done, who's to know what's happening to him this very minute? He's no more safe than nothing! Just let a woman like that get mad, an' no one's safe!"

"Well," said Dick, though he looked rather anxious himself; "ye see this 'ere un isn't the one that's bossin' things now. I know her name's Victory, an' this un here in the book, her name's Mary."

"So it is," said Mr. Hobbs, still mopping his forehead; "so it is. An' the newspapers are not sayin' anything about any racks, thumb-screws, or stake-burnin's,—but still it doesn't seem as if 't was safe for him over there with those queer folks! Why, they tell me they don't keep the Fourth o' July!"[44]

Burnett's mention of *The Tower of London* in *Little Lord Fauntleroy*, published nearly half a century after Ainsworth's novel, shows how popular the work was throughout the nineteenth century. In fact, the novel was taught to British schoolchildren as late as the 1950s and seen as a source of reference about the Tower because of its historical accuracy.[45]

While *The Tower of London*'s Gothic and historical elements have roots in Radcliffe and Scott, here the influence of Hugo is more strongly felt. Earlier, I mentioned that Ainsworth uses a passage from Hugo's *Marie Tudor* in *Rookwood*. That play, published in 1833, to my knowledge was not translated or performed in Britain before *Rookwood* was published. This suggests Ainsworth read Hugo in French. He was definitely familiar with both the language and the literature of France. His own publication, *Ainsworth's Magazine*, would be the first to serialize *The Count of Monte Cristo* in English.[46] Later in life, Ainsworth would translate *Le Combat de Treste*, a French medieval ballad from 1351 about the Breton War of Succession under the title *The Combat of the Thirty*.[47]

Consequently, Ainsworth probably read *Marie Tudor* in French and was inspired to write his own work set during the reign of Mary I, resulting in *The Tower of London*, a novel about Lady Jane Grey's imprisonment in the Tower by Queen Mary. By comparison, Hugo's play is about the rise, fall, and execution of Fabiano Fabiani, a fictional character who is a favorite of Queen Mary. Eventually, Fabiani is imprisoned in the Tower, and despite wanting to spare his life, Mary is unable to do so. Both Hugo's play and Ainsworth's novel are set in 1553 and also feature Simon Renard, the Spanish ambassador, as a character, but there is little other similarity between the works.

A more notable influence on *The Tower of London* is *Notre-Dame de Paris*. Hugo used France's famous cathedral to tell a Gothic story set in a building with Gothic architecture. Ainsworth adopted this idea to tell a similarly Gothic story in England's famous Tower of London, which Ainsworth depicts as the most terrifying historical building in England because of the many executions and mysteries associated with it. Although the Tower is of Norman rather than Gothic architecture, it provides plenty of Gothic atmosphere for a novel.

Ainsworth's debt to Hugo is apparent throughout the novel, beginning with the Preface, in which he states:

> It has been, for years, the cherished wish of the writer of the following pages, to make the Tower of London—the proudest monument of antiquity, considered with reference to its historical associations, which this country or any other possesses,—the groundwork of a Romance; and it was no slight satisfaction to him, that circumstances, at length, enabled him to carry into effect his favourite project, in conjunction with the inimitable Artist, whose designs accompany the work.

Ainsworth goes on to discuss how he wanted the illustrations, by George Cruikshank, to depict every aspect of the Tower. Consequently, the illustrations are numerous—forty engravings and fifty-eight woodcuts. The engravings depict moments from the story while the woodcuts show off architectural features related to the Tower.[48] Ainsworth tried to work every place in the Tower into the novel, stating:

> Desirous of exhibiting the Tower in its triple light of a palace, a prison, and a fortress, the Author has shaped his story with reference to that end; and he has also endeavoured to contrive such a series of incidents as should naturally introduce every reflect of the old pile—its towers, chapels, halls, chambers, gateways, arches, and draw-bridges—so that no part of it should remain unillustrated.[49]

Areas both open and closed to the public at the time of the novel's publication were depicted. However, Ainsworth felt the entire Tower should be open to the public, stating:

> It is piteous to see what havoc has already been made by alterations and repairs. The palace is gone—so are many of the towers—and unless the progress of destruction is arrested, the demolition of others will follow. Let us attempt to preserve what remains.[50]

Furthermore, Ainsworth says that while the tower cannot be restored to its "pristine" condition, efforts can be made to prevent further destruction and allow access to the public. These arguments are in line with those of Hugo whose own complaints about the state of Notre-Dame de Paris led to its receiving better care. *The Tower of London*'s tremendous sales inspired thousands of visitors to seek out the places depicted by Ainsworth and Cruikshank, which fueled restoration of the Tower as one of the first Victorian museums and a patriotic symbol for the English. This "psycho-geography" turned national landmarks into Gothic castles for Ainsworth's readers, including not just the Tower of London but St. Paul's Cathedral and Windsor Castle, both of which were the subjects of later novels.⁵¹ According to literary critic George Worth:

> Ainsworth seems constantly to be trying to remind his readers, living in an age of urbanization and industrialization in which historic old landmarks were being swept away or defaced or 'restored' beyond recognition, that they had a heritage, one very large vested in physical structures of one kind or another, and that the heritage [...] might soon be gone beyond recall.⁵²

While Ainsworth chooses a different type of story for his tale, it is even more based in history than Hugo's. Hugo's novel is set in the past but predominantly fictional, not depicting any key moments in the cathedral or France's history. Ainsworth's story is based on a pivotal moment in England's history when Catholicism and Protestantism vied for control of England in the persons of Lady Jane Grey and her cousin Queen Mary I. The novel begins with the accession of Lady Jane Grey to the throne of England in 1553. It follows the events of her nine-day reign, depicts her overthrow, and then explores the early days of Queen Mary's reign, ending with Jane's execution. This was a pivotal time in English history since whoever held the crown determined the nation's religion.

Both Hugo and Ainsworth use their novels for criticism of the Catholic Church or at least some of its clergy. Some critics have argued that Ainsworth is not anti-Catholic nor anti-clerical, but if that is true, one has to wonder why he did not choose to set his Gothic novel during another time in the Tower of London's history. After all, Mary I's reign reflected the worst time of Catholic abuse in England. Certainly, a story based on the alleged murders in the Tower of the young princes Edward V and the Duke of York by their uncle Richard III would lend itself well to a Gothic tale. However, Ainsworth chose a conflict over religion, and while perhaps subtle, the result is a novel that appears anti-Catholic like so many other Gothic novels, including *Notre-Dame de Paris*.

Just like Hugo does for Notre-Dame de Paris, Ainsworth makes the Tower a character in its own right and a metaphor for the nation's history. Both authors treat their monuments as a "book of stone." Hugo states:

> In fact, from the origin of things up to the fifteenth century of the Christian era inclusive, architecture was the great book of mankind, the principal expression of man at his different stages of development, whether as strength or as intelligence.[53]

Consequently, the cathedral is a book to be read that tells the cathedral and nation's history. By comparison, Ainsworth writes:

> "There you behold the Tower of London," said Winwike, pointing downwards.
>
> "And there I read the history of England," replied Renard.
>
> "If it is written in those towers it is a dark and bloody history," replied the warder — "and yet your worship says truly. The building on which we stand, and those around us, are the best chronicles of our country.[54]

To discuss the entire plot of *The Tower of London* would only confuse the reader. I will instead highlight some of the key moments that are Gothic, reflect Hugo's influence, and reflect the subtle anti-Catholicism the novel employs. However, in terms of anti-Catholicism, it is worth noting that while Lady Jane Grey is the novel's Protestant hero, Ainsworth simultaneously wrote *Guy Fawkes; or, The Gunpowder Treason*, which has a Catholic hero.[55] Furthermore, it is hard not to argue that the atrocities committed during Bloody Mary's reign were enough to make anyone anti-Catholic, and because they are historical, Ainsworth is not unfair to the Catholic Church in his depictions of them. Ainsworth's biographer Stephen Carver notes that claims that Ainsworth was anti-Catholic come from misreading *The Tower of London*. *Guy Fawkes* could be argued as pro-Catholic given that Ainsworth shows the Gunpowder Plot was an act of "justified desperation rather than Jesuit-funded terrorism."[56] In fact, Ainsworth showed affection for Jacobites in other novels that created a belief he was himself Catholic.[57] Therefore, while interpreting *The Tower of London* as anti-Catholic may not be unwarranted, Ainsworth was not himself anti-Catholic. Furthermore, in the preface to *Guy Fawkes*, Ainsworth states "One doctrine I have endeavoured to enforce throughout – TOLERATION."[58]

According to scholar George Worth, while Ainsworth disagreed with Catholicism, he felt it was part of England's history and should be described neutrally. In depicting Queen Mary, he emphasized ways she was a decent queen, and while some Catholics in the novel try to use Mary to promote Catholicism in a fanatical way, Ainsworth also introduces Cardinal Pole as a voice of moderation.[59] Ultimately, the novel may be read as not so much against Catholicism as for England and its national identity as a Protestant nation at the historical moment when that identity was most threatened.

While Ainsworth's basic plot is based in history and relatively accurate, he does take literary license to enhance the plot. He also employs numerous historical personages as his main characters, notably Lady Jane Grey; her husband Guildford Dudley; Guildford's father, John Dudley, Duke of Northumberland; and Queen Mary. Simon Renard, the Spanish ambassador, plots against Lady Jane becoming queen from the novel's opening when Jane first enters the Tower to claim the throne. Renard not only wants the Catholic Mary on the throne, but he wants to marry her to Philip of Spain to ensure England stays Catholic and under Spanish power.

Carver notes that Ainsworth's willingness to take license with history results from his decision to approach it differently from Sir Walter Scott. Ainsworth, as John Moore puts it, presents "history in gorgeous Technicolour," thereby endorsing the character Lady Clarinda's assertion in Ainsworth's novel *Crotchet Castle* that "history is but a tiresome thing in itself; it becomes more agreeable the more romance is mixed up with it." Rather than the mediocre fictional heroes that frequented Scott's novels, Ainsworth used the kings, queens, and outlaws of England as his protagonists.[60]

In some ways, the novel is a regression in Gothic literature, going back before the treatment of history by Scott to earlier, more Gothic treatments of history like Sophia Lee's *The Recess* (1783-5), in which Mary, Queen of Scots has two illegitimate daughters who are the heroines. Still, *The Recess* is more far-fetched in its treatment of history than Ainsworth's work because Ainsworth had predecessors like Scott to imitate. While Ainsworth takes some historical license—for example, Guildford Dudley was imprisoned at the time of Wyatt's rebellion, yet Ainsworth has him freed so he can partake in it—the major events of Queen Jane's reign and the early events of Queen Mary's reign are depicted with accuracy, even if with colorful atmosphere.

From the book's opening, we know we are not just reading history but a Gothic novel. Lady Jane Grey is in a procession to the Tower of London where she will be crowned queen. During the procession, she is warned by an old woman, Gunnora Braose, not to enter the Tower because if she does she will never know happiness. "Go not to the Tower. Danger lurks therein."[61] Gunnora, who seems to be inspired by Shakespeare's Margaret of Anjou, repeatedly appears in the novel to prophesy doom. Eventually, we learn that she had poisoned Edward VI at the behest of Lady Jane's father-in-law, the Duke of Northumberland, but only so she could use it against the duke in revenge for how he murdered her lord, John Seymour, the late king's uncle. Gunnora and her grandson, Gilbert, are Catholics opposed to Jane's rule, so they welcome Mary's return.

The novel introduces us to several other nonhistorical characters. Among them are three giants, Magog, Gog, and Og, and a dwarf named Xit, who all reside at the Tower. The giants are all about eight-feet tall and the bastard sons of Henry VIII. Ainsworth introduces them for comic effect, especially in terms of their romantic relationships. However, their deformity, in terms of their size and great strength, calls to mind Quasimodo, who was also a guardian of his own respective ancient monument. The dwarf Xit also may be Hugo-inspired since Ainsworth could have read Hugo's *Hans of Iceland*, also illustrated by Cruikshank.[62]

Other characters in *The Tower of London* include Cuthbert Cholmondeley, a young courtier in the service of Guildford Dudley, and the young maiden he loves, Cicely, who serves Lady Jane. Cuthbert runs afoul of the jailor Nightgall, who wishes to marry Cicely, resulting in several Gothic moments in the Tower's dungeons where Nightgall eventually holds Cuthbert captive. While imprisoned, Cuthbert meets Alexia, an insane woman who appears mysteriously and cries because her child has been taken from her. In time, Cicely is revealed to be Alexia's child; her parentage has been kept a secret, and her parents were imprisoned because they were Catholics who had opposed Henry VIII. In the end, Cicely refuses to convert back to her parents' faith but stays a true Protestant and marries Cuthbert, while the evil jailor Nightgall meets his death in a dramatic fall from a tower.

The novel is full of political plots and secrets revealed. The Spanish ambassador Renard is the novel's chief villain, which is not surprising since his name means "fox." Renard continually plots to overthrow Lady Jane, then plots to keep Queen Mary from marrying her distant cousin, Edward Courtenay, in favor of the Spanish ruler Philip. Eventually, Renard's evil actions are revealed, but as history tells us, Mary married Philip regardless.

Dramatic moments include the last-minute conversion of the Duke of Northumberland to Catholicism with the belief, planted by Renard, that Mary will pardon him for his treason. Rather than be pardoned, Northumberland is beheaded and his head held up for all to behold the fate of traitors. The illustration by Cruikshank is significant because it recalls images of guillotined heads held up for all to see during the French Revolution.

The Tower of London is depicted with countless secret passages to add to the Gothic atmosphere. For example, in Part I, Chapter 3, the following discourse occurs:

> "You are acquainted, no doubt, with the secret passages of the White Tower, friend?" asked Renard.
>
> "With all of them," rejoined Nightgall. "I know every subterranean communication—every labyrinth—every hidden recess within the walls of the fortress, and there are many such—and can conduct you wherever you desire."

Nightgall is secretly in Renard's employ and able to hide secrets and people away from the world in the Tower's clandestine places. While Ainsworth wished to depict all aspects of the Tower in the novel, its role as a prison stands out the most, given that many of the characters are imprisoned at some point in the novel. Later when Renard is imprisoned, he remarks that not a chamber in the White Tower does not have a secret passage, and he knows them all from his friendship with Nightgall.

In depicting these prisons, Ainsworth is drawing upon English history and an English building, but he could have also been inspired by past Gothic novels with prison scenes, including Maturin's *Melmoth the Wanderer* (1820) and Mrs. Radcliffe's *The Italian* (1797), which respectively contain scenes of people imprisoned by the Spanish and Italian Inquisitions. He may have also had the Bastille in mind. This perhaps implied connection may have inspired the prison scenes of later novels set during the French Revolution, such as Bulwer-Lytton's *Zanoni*, Dumas' Marie Antoinette novels, and Dickens' *A Tale of Two Cities*, all works I will explore in Chapter 6. One also can't help thinking of the prison in *The Count of Monte Cristo*, which I will discuss in Chapter 3.

Certainly, the threat of the Spanish Inquisition pervades the novel. We are shown scenes of torture in the Tower committed especially by Nightgall and under the hand of Queen Mary, who seeks to restore the Catholic faith. In fact, the Tower becomes a

Catholic bastion in the novel. In Part II, Chapter 8, we are told, "Mary still continued to hold her court within the Tower. Various reasons were assigned for this choice of residence; but her real motive was that her plans for the restoration of the Catholic religion could be more securely concerted within the walls of the fortress than elsewhere." The Tower is where the Protestants who commit treason are held, tortured, and coerced, or at least beseeched, to convert to the Catholic faith. Edward Underhill, after his failed attempt to assassinate Mary, is burned at the stake on Tower Green after he refuses to convert, which is described as "a horrible sight."[63] The battle over the succession to the throne is not really over who is the rightful or legitimate heir but over religion, Jane representing the Protestant faction and Mary the Catholic faction. When Sir Thomas Wyat* begins his rebellion, he tries to persuade the people to follow him by warning them that the wrongs of the Spanish Inquisition will come to England if Mary marries Philip.

> "Fellow-countrymen," he shouted, "I am your friend, not your enemy. I would deliver you from thraldom and oppression. You ought rather to aid than oppose me. You are upholding Spain—and the inquisition—while I am fighting for England and liberty."
>
> These few words, vociferated while he made a desperate stand against his opponents, turned the tide of affairs. In vain the royalist leaders shouted "Down with the rebels! the queen!—the queen!" They were answered by deafening cries of "A Wyat! a Wyat! No Philip of Spain—no Popish supremacy—no inquisition!"[64]

Similar cries are heard more than once in the novel.

In accordance with history, Wyat's rebellion fails. He is captured and tortured. We see his mangled body in Part II, Chapter 34 when he tries to claim Princess Elizabeth was part of his plot and she confronts him for lying. Then Wyat blames

---

* The name is usually spelled Wyatt but Ainsworth dropped the second T.

Renard for bringing him to this state, stating "You, who have deceived the queen—deceived me—and would deceive the devil your master, if you could—you urged me to it—you—ha! ha!" Wyat's words suggest Renard is the true villain, the servant of the devil. Courtenay then begs Mary to forgive Elizabeth and also blames Renard, saying, "I beseech your highness not to let the words of that false and crafty Spaniard weigh against your sister. From his perfidious counsels all these disasters have originated." The use of "crafty" here suggests the craftiness of a fox but also recalls the serpent who counseled Eve to eat the apple, once more equating Renard, and Catholic Spain by association, with Satan.

Elizabeth is allowed to live, but Jane and Guilford Dudley are not so fortunate. Mary offers them their lives if they will convert to Catholicism, but both refuse. Guildford inscribes Jane's name twice on his prison wall—recalling the inscription Hugo claims he saw inscribed in Notre-Dame, and once again suggesting the Tower is a book to be read. Then Guildford is taken to the scaffold and killed. When Jane goes to the scaffold, she passes her husband's dead body being carried away. She dies a martyr's death, stating that her punishment is the result of her own sins in neglecting God's Word. Her final words recall the final words of Christ, "Lord, into thy hands I commend my spirit!"[65] Her death is a testament to her faith in the Protestant religion, making her the novel's Christ figure, the opposite of Simon Renard as the Satan figure. If Ainsworth is not anti-Catholic, one cannot help feeling the novel is after such a scene. That said, it can be read less on a religious than nationalist level since the characters are all motivated to fight for what they believe is best for England, whether or not that be Spanish domination. As most readers will know, Mary's reign only lasted for five years before she died and Elizabeth I succeeded to the throne, thus ensuring England's Protestant identity, which has remained ever since, despite other Catholic threats to it.

The Tower of London would have a tremendous influence on how the Tower was perceived by generations to come, although the public imagination focused primarily on its more Gothic elements. It became seen as a site of torture, imprisonment, and hauntings. The novel's influence can be seen decades and even a century later in the passage quoted above from *Little Lord Fauntleroy* and in the horror films *Tower of London* (1939) and *Tower of London* (1962), both of which focused not on the Tudor period like Ainsworth's novel but on the alleged murder by Richard III of his nephews in the Bloody Tower. The films starred Boris Karloff and Vincent Price respectively, both known for their roles in horror films. Even with the focus being on a different period than in Ainsworth's story, it is unlikely the films would have been made if Ainsworth had not transformed the Tower into a Gothic edifice in the public imagination. The novel also helped set the stage for the reimagining of other places as Gothic, moving from the historic to the modern and mundane, as we will see in our next chapter.

Chapter 3
City Mysteries
Eugène Sue, Paul Féval, George W. M. Reynolds, and Alexandre Dumas

> "Virtue often trips and falls over the
> sharp edge of poverty."
>
> — Eugène Sue

As French and English authors began to create more historically accurate and focused Gothic novels, they also began to have less qualms about depicting the contemporary horrors around them. While the French Revolution's atrocities would resound throughout the nineteenth century, no longer did Gothic novelists feel the need to write novels set in the Middle Ages or the Renaissance as veiled treatments of historical events. In Chapter 6, I will explore the French Revolution depicted in all its bloody horror in Gothic and historical novels, but it was long in the past by the mid-nineteenth century. What was not past was the rise of urban crime in major cities like Paris and London, as well as the displacement so many felt as industrialization led to increased numbers of people leaving their ancestral lands to move to the cities. The resulting difficulties of urban life were perfect fodder to fuel urban Gothic novels, and so the city mysteries genre was born.

The genre began with Eugène Sue's *The Mysteries of Paris*, one of the most widely read novels of the nineteenth century. Today, few people outside of literary scholars know this work, yet its popularity and influence were so significant that Eugène Sue deserves to be as well known today as Alexandre Dumas and Victor Hugo.

In this chapter, I will explore how Sue's novel influenced literature in both Britain and France, specifically two novels both titled *The Mysteries of London*, one by French author Paul Féval and one by English author George W. M. Reynolds, as well as Alexandre Dumas' *The Count of Monte Cristo*. *The Mysteries of Paris* is the direct ancestor of crime fiction and lives on through its influence, directly or indirectly, in novels by Charles Dickens, Arthur Conan Doyle, Agatha Christie, and many another detective or mystery novel.

Eugène Sue's *The Mysteries of Paris*

While *The Mysteries of Paris* would spawn a series of city mysteries novels, Mrs. Radcliffe was the first to use the word "mysteries" in a novel title. Consequently, she introduced a detective element into the genre in the sense that a need exists to reveal the secrets or mysteries of a specific geographic location. Whether or not Eugène Sue consciously chose his novel's title as a tribute to Radcliffe, *The Mysteries of Paris* owes an enormous debt to her, and like that work, it would spawn countless imitations.

Sue was also obviously influenced by the novels of Sir Walter Scott and Polidori's *The Vampyre* as evidenced by references in *The Mysteries of Paris*. One character has *Ivanhoe* read to him.[1] Another character is named Dr. Polidori and described as "Sinister" with a "nose, hooked like an eagle's beak,"[2] which may reflect vampiric tendencies, as well as Jewish origins, even though he is Italian. Sue was also influenced by Dickens' early novels that depicted the wrongs of society against the poor. Dickens' novels were translated into French, often in pirated editions, within a year of publication in England.[3] Unlike Scott and Radcliffe, Dickens was not extremely popular in France, at least in the 1840s, because his novels were considered works of realism and the French were still under the spell of Romanticism.[4] Furthermore, realistic depictions of low life and poverty were considered dangerous literary productions often related to political unrest.[5] Sue, who would become a socialist by the time he finished writing *The Mysteries of Paris*, was obviously influenced by Dickens' themes in his desire to help the poor, even increasing the melodramatic element in his own work.[6] Finally, Sue may have been inspired by the phrase "the mysteries of London" in a book that was probably *The Mysteries of Old St. Paul's* (1841) by Richard Thompson, which itself was a poor imitation of Ainsworth's *Old Saint Paul's*.[7] While *The Mysteries of Paris* was influenced by British literature, it would have a far greater influence of its own not only on British but world literature.

Sue's literary career began with writing nautical fiction. American author James Fenimore Cooper had pioneered this genre beginning with *The Pilot* (1824), and British author Captain Marryat had made it even more popular beginning with *The Naval Officer* (1829). Cooper was extremely popular in France and paved the way for Marryat's popularity there. Then Sue jumped onboard and rode the nautical wave, beginning with *Kernock le Pirate* in 1830.[8] However, his early novels are all but forgotten today. He is best remembered for *The Mysteries of Paris*, followed by his later works *The Wandering Jew* and the nineteen-volume series *The Mysteries of the People*, both of which I will discuss in Chapter 4.

The Mysteries of Paris was serialized in France in 150 parts in *Journal des débats* from June 19, 1842 to October 15, 1843.[9] According to critic Peter Brooks, it was "the runaway bestseller of nineteenth-century France, possibly the greatest bestseller of all time."[10] Brooks adds that it's hard to know how many people were familiar with it since the circulation numbers do not include how it was read aloud in village cafés, workshops, and offices throughout France, making it "a truly national experience."[11] The novel was as popular in England as in France, leading to at least seven different translations between 1843 and 1873.[12] The greatest testament to its popularity was that it spawned an entire genre of city mysteries novels, in both the nineteenth and twentieth centuries. Besides both versions of *The Mysteries of London* by Féval and Reynolds, other city mysteries would include *Les Mystères de Marseille* (1867) by Émile Zola, *Les Mystères de Lyon* (1933) by Jean de La Hire, *I misteri di Napoli* (1869-70) by Francesco Mastriani, *Les Nouveaux Mystères de Paris* (1954-9) by Léo Malet, *Die Mysterien von Berlin* (1844) by August Brass, *Die Geheimnisse von Hamburg* (1845) by Johann Wilhelm Christern, *De Verborgenheden van Amsterdam* (1844) by L. van Eikenhorst, *Mistérios de Lisboa* (1854) by Camilo Castelo Branco, *The Quaker City, or The Monks of Monk Hall: a Romance of Philadelphia Life, Mystery and Crime* (1844) by George Lippard, *The Mysteries and Miseries of New York* (1848) by Ned Buntline, and most recently, *The Mysteries of Pittsburgh* (1988) by Michael Chabon.[13]

The French version of Wikipedia adds to this list by stating:

> It was indeed Eugène Sue who began a "wave of soap opera writers," which was followed by Féval, then other more "minor" authors, with titles such as: *The Mysteries of the Bastille*, *The Little Mysteries of Paris*, *The Mysteries of Russia*, *The Mysteries of Brussels*, *The True Mysteries of Paris*, *The Mysteries of the Grand Opera*, etc. A variation of this model was to replace the one-on-all "mysteries," for example: *Beggars of Paris* (Clémence Robert), *Viveurs de Paris* (Montépin), *Victims of Paris* (Claretie), *Slaves of Paris* (Gaboriau), *Attic of Paris* (Zaccone), *Puritans of Paris* (Bocage), and *New Mysteries of Paris* (Scholl). It should be noted that the titles of the novels refer to major cities around the world. Thus we find *Mysteries of Buenos Aires*.[14]

It is truly difficult to conceive of such popularity today, especially since countless lawsuits would have been filed for plagiarism or copyright infringement if someone tried to capitalize in such a way upon a contemporary author's success.

In this discussion, I will focus primarily on the Gothic elements in *The Mysteries of Paris* and its role as one of the first novels about urban crime. Ultimately, the novel turns out to be less about crime than the redemption of criminals, which closely aligns it to Gothic themes of transgression and redemption, unlike a novel like Charles Dickens' *Oliver Twist* (1838) where none of the criminals are redeemed.

The novel's main character is Rodolphe. He is considered by many critics as the first modern superhero in literature because of his great strength, his being a master of disguise, and his being a vigilante avenger.[15] We first meet him on the streets of Paris when a male criminal, known as Slasher (Le Chourineur), hits a young prostitute named Songbird (La Goualeuse). Although the novel is not overly explicit about Songbird's past, she is clearly a prostitute at only seventeen years of age. Rodolphe stops the attack and gives Slasher a good thrashing. Slasher, who claims to be the second strongest man in Paris, is amazed to have been beaten by Rodolphe. In admiration, Slasher immediately befriends Rodolphe and the three go to a tavern to dine.

The plot is too complex to summarize from there—most editions of the novel run more than 1,300 pages—but to make a long story short, Rodolphe helps Slasher become a decent citizen and lead a moral life. He also helps Songbird by sending her to a farm where she can live virtuously.

As the story develops, the reader picks up on hints that Rodolphe is not the common man he pretends. He turns out to be the Prince of Gerolstein, Gerolstein being a fictional principality in Germany. More importantly, he is someone set on doing good. He also has a sidekick, Murph, who is an English knight and aids him in his efforts. Several scholars have compared Rodolphe to Batman. (Murph, although in the Robin role, seems to me to be more like Batman's butler, Alfred.) Such a comparison feels like a bit of a stretch, but the seeds of the superhero figure are there. Rodolphe does not go out and physically fight crime; he simply helps people when necessary. That said, while Batman may have his Batcave, Batmobile, costume, and other fancy gadgets, Rodolphe is the more interesting character because he is more human, and more Gothic. Most versions of the Batman story show Bruce Wayne witnessing his parents' murder by a criminal, which inspires him to fight crime. Rodolphe has a different motive. He is filled with guilt from having once raised his sword to his father in anger; consequently, he feels he deserves punishment and wishes to redeem himself. Batman is not a conflicted soul to the same extent, which makes Rodolphe more human and more endearing, at least to this reader.

At the novel's heart is the cause of Rodolphe and his father's argument. His father had disapproved of Rodolphe's marriage to the Countess MacGregor. Rodolphe only married her because she was pregnant, and she was supported in convincing Rodolphe to marry her by the sinister Dr. Polidori, whom Rodolphe also believes responsible for his mother's death. After their marriage, the countess told Rodolphe their daughter had died, when in truth, she had given the child into the care of dishonest people who told her falsely that the child had died. They had actually sold the child. After their child's believed death, Rodolphe divorced the countess, who never loved him but only sought to wear a crown. Throughout the novel, while Rodolphe is in Paris, she searches for him, trying to regain him as her husband to fulfill her ambitions. While trying to win back Rodolphe's affections, she begins to suspect he is in love with Songbird, so she arranges to have the girl murdered. At the last minute, she learns Songbird is her daughter who was sold. The countess plans to reveal this secret to Rodolphe so he will remarry her, but it is too late for her to enjoy her triumph—by this point, she is dying, and when she and Rodolphe do remarry, it is only to legitimize their daughter.

Rodolphe aids many other characters throughout the novel against wicked men and women. He continually rewards the virtuous and metes out punishment or justice (depending on how you want to view justice) to various characters. At one point, he blinds a criminal rather than kill him, believing it will cause the criminal to become self-reflective and repent for his crimes. This punishment is extreme and doesn't really work to save the criminal's soul, but most of Rodolphe's other good deeds end up benefiting their recipients. In all these cases, he is something of a vigilante, seeking his own form of justice.

Despite all Rodolphe's efforts to redeem himself by helping others, he ends up being punished for his crime through his daughter. Once Rodolphe and Songbird realize they are father and daughter, they enjoy great but temporary happiness. Songbird returns with Rodolphe to Gerolstein, where she is a princess. However, she hates keeping up the charade that she is a virtuous, innocent girl who has always lived with her mother until her father brought her home to Gerolstein. When she receives a marriage proposal from an eligible young prince, she refuses him, feeling she cannot be cleansed of her sin—the prostitution she partook in out of desperation. To redeem herself, she decides to become a nun. Because of how others view her as virtuous and because she is now the Princess Amelie, it is decided she will take her cousin's position as abbess on the day she becomes a nun. However, she does not feel worthy of this honor. Soon after, she dies, needing to free herself from her sin. Rodolphe is grief-stricken, but he feels her death is just punishment for his own crimes and that it finally expiates his sins. One cannot help comparing Songbird's death to that of Samuel Richardson's heroine in *Clarissa* (1748-9). Clarissa had to die because she was raped and death was the only way she could prove her virtue. Songbird dies to atone for her past as a prostitute, a past for which she is really not at fault. Her death washes away her sin.

Although *The Mysteries of Paris* is not a true Gothic novel—even the crime-ridden streets of Paris lack the Gothic atmosphere Dickens might have created—the Gothic theme of guilt and redemption is strong throughout Sue's story. So also is the Gothic family plot that includes the revelation of long-kept secrets as evidenced by Rodolphe discovering Songbird is his daughter. Several other characters besides Rodolphe undergo spiritual transformation and redemption as they struggle to become better. Slasher dies trying to save Rodolphe from an assassination attempt, which he also sees as expiation for his sins—because he has killed, so he must be killed. (He gained his nickname because he had worked as a butcher, and in a moment of madness, he slashed a man.)

Because the novel was serialized, Sue constantly received feedback from readers as he wrote. By the time the novel was finished, his constant speeches about how social structures needed to be put in place to relieve poverty and thus prevent crime led him to meeting and speaking with many people and, ultimately, becoming a socialist. While critics have focused on the novel's socialist perspective, in my opinion, *The Mysteries of Paris* is far less a socialist work than a Christian one. Sue's intention is to help the poor, to see them as his brothers and sisters, and to persuade his readers to help them. That is not socialism. That is Christianity, pure and simple, and it is beautiful, if dark, in the way Sue treats it. Unfortunately, his Christian characters do not get rewarded or they enjoy their rewards only briefly in this life. But no matter; they cannot completely wash away their sins or forget their pain while on earth. Only God can wash away their sins, so they must die to enter eternal life.

The novel is very powerful, and it certainly helped inspire Hugo's *Les Misérables* in its own depiction of criminals forced by society to commit their crimes, such as Jean Valjean stealing to feed his family and Fantine becoming a prostitute to feed her child. Surprisingly, prostitution was not only legal in France during this period, but parents could register their daughters as prostitutes to earn extra income for the family.[16]

Besides influencing future crime fiction, *The Mysteries of Paris* was a grandfather to the superhero genre. Rodolphe has extreme, almost superhuman strength. In *Les Misérables*, Jean Valjean will also be marvelously physically strong. Supernatural abilities often attributed to supernatural and Gothic characters eventually led to the development of redemptive Gothic transgressors in literature and then superheroes who had supernatural abilities and even dressed with Gothic capes—think of Superman with his great strength—after all Rodolphe is described as having "muscles of steel"[17] while Superman is known as "the man of steel." Both critics Umberto Eco and Charles Bernheimer see Rodolphe as a proto-Superman.[18] Think also of Batman, who has links to vampires through his bat connection. Rather than being criminals and transgressors, superheroes seek to be benefactors to humanity. Also noteworthy is that Rodolphe has a pseudo-supernatural ability to mesmerize or hypnotize people—an attribute of the Wandering Jew, which was then passed to vampire figures. Sue tells us:

> Certain gazes have an irresistible magnetic power.... Rodolphe was gifted with this terrifying, fixed, and piercing gaze. Those who were caught in its power could not evade it. This gaze would obsess and overpower them. They could feel it almost physically, and in spite of themselves, it held them. They could not look away.[19]

Rodolphe, therefore, is one of the first characters in literature to be a force of good, yet share the same supernatural-type abilities of supernatural villains. Consequently, a direct line exists from Rodolphe to Tarzan to Superman and Batman.*

A fuller discussion of how the Gothic developed the superhero is beyond the limits of this book, so I will turn now to more immediate influences that *The Mysteries of Paris* had upon nineteenth-century Gothic literature. Each of the three novels discussed below is a remarkable work in itself, but in this reader's opinion, none of them quite achieve the greatness of *The Mysteries of Paris* because they lack the overall greater Christian or benevolent viewpoint that raises *The Mysteries of Paris* above sensationalism and melodrama to a level perhaps only Hugo would again achieve in *Les Misérables*.

---

* For more on the evolution of the superhero from Gothic literature, see my book *The Gothic Wanderer*, Chapter 11: Modern Interpretations from Wanderer to Superhero.

Paul Féval's *Les Mystères de Londres*

Paul Féval, wishing to capitalize upon the popularity of Sue's novel, serialized *Les Mystères de Londres* from December 20, 1842 to December 12, 1844 in *Le Courrier Français* and published it in 1844 in eleven volumes, each of which ran nearly 400 pages.[20] The novel catapulted Féval to fame in France, although not in Great Britain, partly because by the time it was translated into English, British author George W. M. Reynolds had already begun serializing his own version, also named *The Mysteries of London*, in England.

Interestingly, since Féval set his novel in England, he chose to link himself to a popular British author of the time. His pseudonym Sir Francis Trollop was a play on the name of Frances Trollope (1779-1863), a writer of Gothic fiction quite popular in France, although today she is best remembered as the mother of Victorian novelist Anthony Trollope (1815-1882). Féval's use of Trollope's name suggests he was trying to trick readers into thinking his novel was by her and originally written in English to lend authenticity to its setting, all of which would have helped his book sales. He may also have been trying to hide his identity in case of any repercussions from Sue for stealing his ideas. Féval's efforts to pretend to be an English author are apparent from his referring to "our" last war with the French and "our talented countryman and brother writer Mr. Charles Dickens."[21] However, Stephen Knight notes that Féval's efforts to pretend to be an English narrator fail because in other places he says so many bad things about the English, who are his main character's enemies; these contradictions ultimately make the narrator unreliable.[22]

Although *Les Mystères de Londres* contains a somewhat convoluted plot with criminal characters, it is not focused on social criticism to the degree that Sue's novel is. However, it does criticize the British Empire and the atrocities of colonialism. Its protagonist is also an anti-hero fighting against those injustices.

Unfortunately, when the novel was finally translated into English in 1847 by R. Stephenson, it was heavily abridged. It also did not list the author at all, not even as Sir Francis Trollop. Both the original novel and the English translation are divided into four sections, but the original novel in French runs around 4,000 pages (large print) in eleven volumes. Stephenson's translation is 512 large print pages in one volume. Reading Stephenson's translation is somewhat frustrating since most of the huge cast of characters are never fully developed, making it hard to remember who each one is. At other times, sections are clearly missing from the text since characters suddenly find themselves in situations that are not explained. In the absence of a complete translation, however, readers of English must settle for Stephenson's translation, which is not even currently in print but can be found online.* The novel's failure to be popular with the British reading public means it has not been translated since 1847. However, a renewed interest in Féval's novels and in French Gothic literature makes me hopeful a complete modern English translation will soon result. For the remainder of this discussion, I will rely upon the abridged English translation by Stephenson.

As previously stated, the novel's failure to gain popularity in England was largely due to it being overshadowed by Reynolds' *The Mysteries of London*, which was serialized from 1844-5 and soon followed by Reynolds' second most popular work, *The Mysteries of the Court of London* (1848-55). However, a more significant reason has to be the novel's subject matter and criticism of the British Empire. Perhaps worst of all, its main character is a rebellious Irishman. Furthermore, while the novel is set in the 1830s, its references to starving Irishmen may not have

---

* A complete translation was made in the United States, but I have been unable to access a copy of it. Stephen Knight in *The Mysteries of the Cities* uses this translation when discussing the novel and does not seem to be aware of the Stephenson translation. In this chapter, I have referenced Knight's discussion of the American translation to fill in some gaps the abridged Stephenson translation leaves confusing, such as the origin of Rio Santo's scar.

been taken well given the ongoing Great Famine (1845-52) that was devastating Ireland and for which the British government was being heavily criticized. Féval must have struck an unhappy chord with British readers, even though he published the novel in France a year before the famine began. Regardless, the poverty in Ireland was already extreme before the famine. In fact, as Féval stated later in a memoir, he visited London to do research for the novel and met Daniel O'Connell (1775-1847), the acknowledged political leader of the Irish Catholics at the time, from whom he garnered details of Ireland's plight.[23] The novel's failure to be popular in England was probably partially due to the way it raised legitimate concerns over the mistreatment of the Irish. The English weren't likely to take kindly to a Frenchman criticizing them, and even though Stephenson's translation does not name the author, it does state it was translated from the French.

The novel does not reveal that the main character is Irish until about four-fifths of the way into the convoluted story, but for the sake of clarity, I will give his backstory upfront. I will not summarize the entire plot since it is too complicated to detail clearly, but I will discuss the highlights, especially in terms of how they relate to the Gothic tradition.

Our main character and hero/villain, depending on which perspective you want to take, is the Marquis de Rio Santo, a Portuguese nobleman, who has arrived in London and quickly become popular among the upper class. At first, it is rumored he will marry the Countess of Derby, and she "compromises" herself for him, but then he switches his affections to the beautiful Mary Trevor. Mary is already in love with Frank Percival, but while Percival is traveling, Rio Santo swoops in to steal Mary's affections. Such behavior recalls Lord Ruthven who preys upon upper class women of impeccable virtue.

Who is this mysterious and apparently immoral marquis? Eventually, we learn he is really Fergus O'Brian, an Irishman. When Fergus was eighteen, his parents, poor tenant farmers, were driven off their land by a Protestant British landlord. The family moved to London to make a living. Then one day Fergus' sister went out and never returned. In time, it is learned she lost her virtue to another man. Fergus' parents died of grief over his sister's fate, and Fergus never saw his sister again except once when he saw her riding in a grand equipage, presumably with the man who had made her his mistress. Fergus vows war on England for how his family has been treated.

In time, Fergus befriends a Scottish man, Angus Macfarlane, and falls in love with Angus' sister, also named Mary. Fergus and Mary become engaged, but when the Earl of White Manor tries to gain Mary's affection, it results in Fergus and the Earl fighting a duel. The Earl is wounded and Fergus is arrested, sentenced, and placed on a prison ship headed for the New World. Fortunately, he manages to escape with some companions and they seize a navy ship. In the fighting, Fergus is wounded on his forehead and ever after bears a scar there that is only noticeable in certain lights.[24] The scar, a symbolic mark of Cain, makes him a literary descendant of the biblical Cain and the Wandering Jew. Now even more intent on revenge against the British, he becomes a pirate and embarks on a series of adventures abroad that include visiting various parts of the British Empire and seeing how the natives are oppressed by the British. In time, Fergus makes his fortune, befriends the Portuguese royal family, and is made a marquis for his services to the crown.

Fergus now returns to London as the Marquis de Rio Santo, a title he has earned, but which also helps to hide his true identity as an Irishman. He enters the highest circles of English society with the intent to get close to the king to assassinate him. At the same time, he is busy gathering men from throughout Ireland and the entire British Empire to come to England to overthrow the government. These men, known as the Gentlemen of the Night, work secretly to bring about a revolution. Among the men is Angus. However, Angus' brother, Macnab, seeks to betray them, so Rio Santo finds it necessary to murder Macnab. Macnab's son Stephen witnesses the murder, and while unable to stop the murderer, he sees a scar on Rio Santo's forehead that he remembers, later allowing him to identify Rio Santo and bring about his downfall.

Meanwhile, Rio Santo continues to plot his desired revolution against the British government. Over many years, he has studied well the tactics needed for his plan to succeed. He has even managed to hold an interview with Napoleon on St. Helena to get advice. We are told during this meeting that "Fergus had imbibed, during four hours, the treasures of the most noble, the most enlightened and the boldest mind, which has perhaps ever dazzled the world."[25] As Stephen Knight points out, this meeting with Napoleon allowed French readers to view Rio Santo's revenge on the English as a replay of the Napoleonic Wars with Napoleon's blessing.[26]

While in London, Rio Santo is involved in various intrigues and complications until the day comes to overthrow the government, assassinate King William IV, and blow up the Bank of England. Throughout, he believes he is performing a heroic act, stating that his "crime" will be "the murder of an empire, and the salvation of one half of the world."[27] While these grandiose plans may seem solely the work of fiction, they built upon plausible fears by the English at the time. Contemporary French author Flora Tristan wrote in *Promenades dans Londres* (1840) that there were at least 200,000 Irish living in London at the time, which could make such a coup believable.[28]

True salvation is the work of Christ, so Rio Santo becomes a type of Antichrist here in his effort to provide salvation to the oppressed, especially since he is also equated with Satan. Like Satan, his sin is pride, and "Pride goes before the fall." Rio Santo is overly proud in thinking he can overthrow the British government. The Satan comparison is made at the moment when he feels certain victory will be his.

> And then, when he arranged upon the table all these letters, which, in mute concert, appeared to promise him success and victory, a feeling of intense pride pervaded

his heart. His noble features were illuminated by a look of omnipotent power. He felt himself like the rebellious archangel, capable of storming heaven itself.[29]

Although the passage is subtle, it implies Rio Santo's pride will be his downfall. However, his actual downfall results from Stephen identifying him by the scar on his forehead.

The next use of biblical symbolism occurs after Angus turns on Rio Santo, falsely believing he has been involved in the abduction of Angus' daughters, Clara and Anna. This belief leads to Angus betraying Rio Santo by warning the British government of his plans. After he has already betrayed his friend, unknown yet to Rio Santo, Angus meets with Rio Santo and, on parting, kisses his cheek, then pulls back, realizing what he has done, and screams, "Judas! Judas!"[30] In the gospels, Judas betrays Christ by kissing him on the cheek to signal to the soldiers whom to arrest. Now Angus takes on the role of Judas, thus again equating Rio Santo with Christ. However, in the gospels, this betrayal leads to Christ's arrest and death, and then his resurrection. Christ's death is his sacrifice to save mankind. The events that follow do not work out so nobly for Rio Santo.

Rio Santo sets off in his carriage to join the rest of the men descending upon London from all corners of the globe to overthrow the British government. However, he is stopped in the streets by the police. Stephen, the son of Macnab whom Rio Santo murdered, witnesses the melee that follows. In his vexation, Rio Santo's forehead becomes purple so that his scar stands out. Stephen then recognizes his father's murderer and assists in arresting him.

Rio Santo now goes to trial. He is found guilty of killing Macnab, belonging to an illegal association, and being an accomplice in an attempt to pillage the Bank of England during the insurrection. He is sentenced to hang at Newgate, but he says he'll never be hanged. Clara, Stephen's cousin and Angus' daughter, who has secretly loved Rio Santo all along, helps him to escape on a horse. They ride until she is so exhausted they have to stop. Hallucinating, Clara takes Rio Santo's pistol and accidentally shoots him, thus fulfilling the laird's prophecy that the only man who loved him would betray him and the only woman who could respect him would kill him.[31] (Again, the abridged translation fails here since this prophecy was never mentioned earlier.)

Just before Rio Santo dies, Mary Macfarlane—the woman he loved but who, for reasons never explained, married his rival, the Earl of White Manor after Fergus was sent off on the prison ship—now finds him. She kneels and prays beside him. In depicting Rio Santo's death, Féval again draws upon Gothic elements. Rio Santo's behavior as a nobleman who seduces women equates him with vampire figures like Polidori's Lord Ruthven. Now Féval draws upon the vampire figure again by having Rio Santo die in the moonlight. In Gothic literature, vampires are frequently revived by moonlight (see Chapter 7), so I kept waiting for Rio Santo to be revealed to be a vampire, but that does not happen; Féval avoids the supernatural as being real. Instead, as Rio Santo dies, he smiles—a sign that he is at peace.

> The moon had ascended to such a height, that its rays fell full upon the features of the dead.
>
> The mouth appeared to have closed with a serene smile—that dreaming, happy smile, so full of mysterious joys, which so often played upon the lips of the Marquis de Rio Santo, when he withdrew his thoughts from the world around him, and communed with himself.[32]

We are told that the moonlight, breeze, splendors of the night, and Mary kneeling over him and praying all mean "no death bed scene could be more tranquil or more beautiful."[33]

Similarly, after Count Dracula is killed, a look of peace comes over his face, showing his relief after being freed of his vampirism.

> It was like a miracle; but before our very eyes, and almost in the drawing of a breath, the whole body crumbled into dust and passed from our sight.

I shall be glad as long as I live that even in that moment of the final dissolution, there was in the face a look of peace, such as I never could have imagined might have rested there.[34]

The similarity of these passages makes me think Stoker could have been influenced by Féval's novel. This single similarity may not be a convincing enough argument for influence, but given that Stoker was Irish and Féval's novel was about an Irish freedom fighter, I would not be surprised if Stoker were interested in reading it, either in Stephenson's translation or possibly in the original French since it is believed Stoker could read French, as I will discuss in Chapter 7. Furthermore, it seems likely that Stoker knew Féval's vampire novels (also discussed in Chapter 7), so he may have sought out other works by the author. That Rio Santo is Irish, a nobleman, and wishes to overthrow the British Empire is not so dissimilar from Irish author Stoker creating a nobleman in *Dracula* who also wishes to conquer England.

While Rio Santo is the most interesting character in *Les Mystères de Londres*, Féval plays with Gothic elements in other ways in the novel. The character of Susannah is interesting because she is a Jewess who finds herself orphaned as a young woman. She has a significant role to play in the novel. Like Rebecca from *Ivanhoe*, she ends up being unable to marry the man she loves, although it is not her religion but her parentage that ultimately stands in the way. Susannah is the daughter of Ishmael Spencer, a Jew who was hanged for his crimes. She never knew her mother, but after her father's death, she meets Brian de Lancaster, whom she has long been in love with. When Susannah tells Brian her story, they both come to believe Ishmael is not her real father. By the end of the novel, we learn Susannah's parents are the Earl of White Manor and Mary Macfarlane. At the time Susannah was conceived, it was rumored Fergus had escaped from the prison ship, returned to London, and was secretly meeting with Mary, which makes the Earl of White Manor suspect Susannah is Fergus' child. These rumors are not true, but they result in the earl selling Susannah, while still a baby, to Ishmael. Once Brian de Lancaster learns this, he reveals the truth to Susannah, meaning they can never be together since he is her uncle.

Ishmael Spencer is one of the novel's worst villains. He is interesting from a Gothic perspective because he has almost supernatural qualities. Although hanged, he seemingly returns from the dead. In actuality, he explains there is nothing so wonderful about his being alive:

> Doctor Moore came to see me in prison and at the lower part of my throat made an incision, which he supported by means of a quill. They gave this operation a very extraordinary name—pharygotomy, I believe. When the cord was drawn tight around my neck, I breathed below the rope, through the incision, as I have mentioned.[35]

Ishmael was able to cheat the gallows and escape from both death and the law. He changed his name and masqueraded as Tyrell, a blind man, as well as Sir Edward Mackenzie, a member of society.

Nor is Ishmael the only character who resurrects himself. Angus also seemingly comes back to life. Rio Santo finds Angus lying dead in his apartments, only for him to revive later. This theme of resurrection was common in Gothic literature, especially in relation to vampires who are revived by moonlight. However, while resurrection is usually associated with Christ's resurrection, it also relates to resurrection men in the Victorian period, men who would dig up bodies from graves to sell to doctors for medical experiments. In *Frankenstein*, Victor Frankenstein famously assembles dead body parts for experiments. In *A Tale of Two Cities*, Jerry Cruncher is a resurrection man, and in Reynolds' *The Mysteries of London*, Anthony Tidkins wins the prize for the most horrid resurrection man. Here, Féval does not use the term "resurrection man," but he has a similar character in Bishop the burker. A burker, like a resurrection man, provided bodies to medical students for experimentation. The term burker was coined as a result of a series of sixteen murders by Burke and Hare, two men who sought to fill the need for medical corpses by killing people and selling the bodies. These murders took place in Edinburgh, Scotland, over a ten-month period in 1828. Ironically, after Burke was hanged for murder, his corpse was dissected. Today, his skeleton is on display at the Anatomical Museum of Edinburgh Medical School.[36] In the novel, Bishop is obviously committing a crime, and yet his work is so well known that when Anna and Clara are kidnapped, Stephen goes to visit Bishop to see if the girls' bodies are among his victims.

Overall, while not truly a Gothic novel, Féval's *Les Mystères de Londres* plays with Gothic themes and creates a compelling, if somewhat convoluted story. Although largely forgotten today, the novel had a significant impact on Gothic literature, especially upon *The Count of Monte Cristo,* as will be discussed later in this chapter, and possibly on *Dracula*.

Needless to say, Féval was furious when, as his novel's serialization was coming to an end, George W. M. Reynolds began publishing in England his own book titled *The Mysteries of London*. Féval apparently had no qualms about having stolen Sue's idea to write his book, but Reynolds' use of the same title was an especially low move. One might argue that Reynolds, in England, did not know about the French novel and simply was, like Féval, capitalizing upon the success of Sue's novel, but as we will see, Reynolds was very knowledgeable about contemporary French literature, and he had absolutely no qualms about stealing ideas from any author, including not only Féval and Sue, but also Dickens.

Féval's novel was popular in France, and when a three-volume edition was published in 1848 by M. Lévy, it may have inspired Féval to write his play, *Les Mystères de Londres, ou les Gentilhommes de la Nuit* (*The Mysteries of London, or The Gentlemen of the Night*) to capitalize on its popularity. The play was performed December 28, 1848 to February 11, 1849 at the Théâtre Historique in Paris.[37] Unfortunately, for theatre-goers who didn't read the novel, it was likely more confusing than Stephenson's abridged version. The storyline is severely simplified. The two noteworthy elements of the play are that Rio Santo meets with Daniel O'Connell, who advocates for peace, not violence, and that it has a happy ending. At the end of the play, when Rio Santo is ready to have the Gentlemen of the Night make their move to overthrow the British government, he receives news that O'Connell has just died and the Irish leader's last wish for peace makes Rio Santo decide not to act. He then declares his love for Susannah and the play ends happily. The ending is anticlimactic compared to that of the novel. Plus, while the play's setting is said to be the 1830s, O'Connell did not die until 1847, so his death is anachronistic. Furthermore, O'Connell is not a character in the novel at all, but his death after the novel was published must have made Féval feel he could use him as a character in the play.

Later, Féval would incorporate the Gentlemen of the Night secret organization into his *Les Habits Noirs* (*The Black Coats*) series of seven novels (1863-75). The Black Coats are an international criminal organization. In the fourth novel, *La Rue de Jerusalem* (*Jerusalem Street*), Féval began to provide a backstory to the series, linking it not only to *Les Mystères de Londres*, but three earlier novels *Bel Demonio* (1850), *Les Compagnons du Silence* (1857), and *Jean Diable* (1863).[38]

Féval would return to Irish themes again in *Le Quittance de Minuit* (*The Midnight Rent*) published in 1846. It consists of two volumes, the first titled *L'Héritière*, the second *La Galerie du Géant*. The story tells of a poor family, the MacDiarmids, who are descendants of the ancient kings of Ireland. Their father is a proud supporter of Daniel O'Connell, who was a pacifist. However, the eight sons go against their father's advice and join a secret organization that fights against the English presence in Ireland through violence. The novel depicts the tragedy that ensues as family members die, one after another, while pursued by British forces. The novel also reflects the troubles of the great famine and the early upheavals of the Irish independence movements.[39]

Unfortunately, but perhaps not surprisingly, *The Midnight Rent* has not been translated into English.

Besides *Les Mystères de Londres* influencing works by Reynolds and Dumas, as we will see below, it also seemed to inspire Ponson du Terrail, another French Gothic author whose vampire novels we will look at in Chapter 7. However, Ponson du Terrail is best known for his Rocambole series of novels. Rocambole is considered by many critics as the first modern literary superhero.[40] One novel in that series is titled *Les Misères de Londres* (*The Miseries of London*, 1867-8), clearly playing off Féval's title, and it also has Irish themes.[41]

Finally, I suspect *Les Mystères de Londres* influenced Jules Verne's depiction of Captain Nemo, the mysterious captain of the *Nautilus* in *Twenty Thousand Leagues Under the Sea* (1870). Verne is rather vague about Nemo's background in the novel, but in Chapter 57 of *The Mysterious Island* (1875), we learn Nemo's entire history, including that he is the Indian Prince Dakkar who fought in a rebellion against the British Empire and whose family was killed by the British. Dakkar/Nemo is less bent upon revenge on the British than simply seeking to avoid humanity by living under the sea, but he shares Rio Santo's hatred for the British Empire. In the *Nautilus*, he has a portrait gallery of famous men who worked to liberate their countries or enslaved peoples, including George Washington, John Brown, and Daniel O'Connell, the last of which may reflect a connection to Féval's novel. Captain Nemo also has incredible wealth that he acquires from sunken ships, a factor that might also reflect the influence of Rio Santo or the Count of Monte Cristo. Not surprisingly, when Verne's novels were first translated and published in Great Britain, references to the portrait gallery in *Twenty Thousand Leagues Under the Sea* and Captain Nemo's anti-imperialist sentiments in *The Mysterious Island* were often removed.[42]

Although largely forgotten today, Féval's novel lives on in the many popular works it influenced.

George W. M. Reynolds' *The Mysteries of London*

How does one even begin to write about George W. M. Reynolds' mammoth classic *The Mysteries of London*? The Valancourt Books edition, published in two volumes in 2013 and 2015, runs 2,296 pages. It is almost impossible to describe it fully, yet it deserves far more attention than it has received to date by scholars. Extremely popular in its day, it likely had a greater impact on Victorian and Gothic fiction than is currently understood. Like Ainsworth, Reynolds is said to have outsold Dickens, yet few remember his name today.

Part of the novel's obscurity may be due to Reynolds' bad reputation. His literary piracy made him unliked by his fellow authors. While not a plagiarist who directly stole passages from other authors, he certainly borrowed and capitalized on their ideas. He had already been doing so for years before he borrowed Sue's city mysteries concept. *The Mysteries of London* may also be overlooked today because past literary critics could not believe such popular serialized fiction was literature worth exploring; plus, the book's sheer size is off-putting for study.

Regardless, Reynolds is a pivotal figure in the interplay of French and British Gothic literature, and a brief overview of his life will help to explain why. Born in 1814, Reynolds attended the Royal Military College at Sandhurst with the intention of a career in the British Army. However, his father died in 1822 and after his mother died in early 1830, he quit the military and used his inheritance to devote himself to literature, although the amount of his inheritance has been disputed by biographers and he does not seem to have received it until well into his twenties.[43] After leaving Sandhurst in 1830, at the young age of sixteen, Reynolds traveled a great deal, especially in France where he became a naturalized citizen. Biographer Dick Collins claims Reynolds remained in London and was part of radical circles, not arriving in Paris until 1835, though some sources claim he was there as early as 1830.[44] The later date may be more likely since his first book *The Errors of the Christian Religion Exposed* was published in London in 1832. In Paris, he worked at a bookstore named Librairie des Etrangers.[45] He also began an English daily newspaper, but when that venture failed, he returned to England in 1836.[46]

However long Reynolds was in France, his time abroad allowed him to become highly knowledgeable about France and French literature. In England, he assumed the editorship of *The Monthly Magazine* between 1837 and 1838 and wrote articles under the pseudonym, Parisianus—a play on Paris. By this point, he was also writing novels and nonfiction. As previously noted, his interest in French literature is reflected in his book of literary criticism, *The Modern Literature of France* (1839), which focused on French works published after 1830. In it, Reynolds discusses numerous authors, including George Sand, Honoré de Balzac, Eugène Sue, Frédéric Soulié, Alphonse de Lamartine, Alexandre Dumas, Auguste Ricard, Prosper Mérimée, Paul de Kock, Victor Hugo, and Charles Nodier—and he provides an excerpt from a work by each. He apparently did his own translating of the extracts since he says he won't provide an extract of Merimée's novel *Mateo Falcone* because it is already well known in English, suggesting it was already translated. Reynolds would only give transcripts from works not translated.[47] Furthermore, Reynolds gives examples of Hugo's poetry that he must have translated because he states:

> We know how grievously the original must suffer in the judgment of the public by the translation; we feel that it is not just towards the poet himself, to solicit a favourable opinion through such a faulty and deficient medium; but at the same time we have the consoling conviction that we have adhered as closely to the original as the difference of versification, idiom, and thought, existing between the two languages, would permit.[48]

The same year, he published *The French Self Instructor*, a language course.⁴⁹

French influences can be seen in many of Reynolds' novels. His first novel, with an English theme but written in France, was *The Youthful Impostor* (1835), the story of which he partially borrowed from Dumas' play *Angèline*, which he likely saw performed in Paris in 1833 or 1834.⁵⁰ He later updated and republished it as *The Parricide* (1847).* Next followed *The Baroness* (1837), which was serialized in *The Monthly Magazine* under the pseudonym Parisianus. Then came *Pickwick Abroad* (1837-8), an unauthorized sequel to Charles Dickens' bestselling *The Pickwick Papers*, in which the members of the Pickwick Club go to France. Critic Stephen Knight argues that Reynolds uses the novel to show France is not only different from but more admirable than England.⁵¹ In my opinion, Reynolds improves on Dickens by creating a much tighter plot than Dickens' rambling novel provided.† Reynolds would borrow from Dickens again with *Pickwick Married* (1841) and *Master Timothy's Bookcase* (1841-2), a play on Dickens' *Master Humphrey's Clock*.‡ In *Robert Macaire* (1839), Reynolds created adventures in England for the popular bandit of French literature.§

However, it was *The Mysteries of London*, beginning in 1844, for which Reynolds is chiefly remembered. Because of the novel's mammoth size, I will focus solely on some plot highlights and the novel's Gothic elements.

The Mysteries of London opens with a young man in a bad neighborhood who ducks into an old building when he finds

---

* See my blog: https://thegothicwanderer.wordpress.com/2022/08/05/the-feminist-she-fiend-of-victorian-literature-george-w-m-reynolds-the-parricide/
† See my blog: https://thegothicwanderer.wordpress.com/2018/09/05/pickwick-and-literary-piracy-dickens-vs-reynolds/
‡ See my blog: https://thegothicwanderer.wordpress.com/2021/05/02/master-timothys-bookcase-george-w-m-reynolds-improvement-on-dickens/
§ See my blog: https://thegothicwanderer.wordpress.com/2021/07/23/robert-macaire-reformed-gothic-transgressor/

himself fearing for his safety. Inside, he overhears criminals plotting to rob the Markham house; then he is captured by the criminals and thrown through a trap door, which the criminals do not realize leads to another outlet. The young man escapes and warns the Markhams of the plot without revealing his identity. Later, we learn this young man is really a woman, Eliza Sydney, who is passing herself off as her deceased brother to gain the inheritance supposed to be left to him, but which she cannot inherit. Poor Eliza is being tricked into this deception by another who hopes to profit by it. Eventually, when it's time to collect the inheritance, her identity is revealed and she's sent to prison for her deceit. After being released from prison, she makes some better acquaintances, which allows her to be introduced into high society in Italy. There the Grand Duke of Castelcicala falls in love with and marries her.

The other major plot concerns the Markhams, whom Eliza had warned of the impending robbery. When the father dies, his two sons, Eugene and Richard, make a pact that they will each make their own way in the world and then meet after twelve years on a given date in 1843. The novel then follows Richard Markham through his ups and downs. All the while, Richard wonders how Eugene is faring. Richard befriends some gentlemen who turn out to be swindlers. He ends up going to prison for forgery, although he is innocent of the accusation. Numerous plots surround Richard until he falls in love with the beautiful Isabella. In time, Richard learns Isabella's father is not only a count but the nephew of the Grand Duke of Castelcicala, who has married Eliza. When the Grand Duke refuses to allow his country to become a republic, he is overthrown. Richard is involved in the revolution and helps to establish Eliza's father, by now his father-in-law, on the throne. Consequently, Richard becomes a prince and a hero.

Despite his successes, Richard is continually pursued by the criminal Anthony Tidkins, also known as the Resurrection Man because he digs up corpses and sells them to scientists. Tidkins has his reasons for hating Richard and is continually trying to kill him. In the final scene, after Tidkins has been murdered by another criminal, Crankey Jem, the agreed-upon meeting date in 1843 arrives and Richard reunites with his brother Eugene.

Eugene, meanwhile, has been living under two different identities, first as Montague and then as Greenwood. During the years separated from his brother, Eugene commits numerous white-collar crimes, including embezzlement, forgery, counterfeiting, and fake stock speculations. He also debauches several women, including Ellen Monroe, the daughter of Richard's legal guardian during his youth. Eugene's rise to wealth happens simultaneously with Richard being cast into poverty and prison, but then everything changes; while Richard becomes a hero and a prince, Eugene becomes impoverished.

Finally, Eugene goes to keep the appointment in 1843 with his brother. However, on the way, a man Eugene has cheated assaults him, so he dies from his injuries soon after meeting his brother. Richard and all those Eugene has wronged assure him he is forgiven. He dies in peace, a true redeemed Gothic wanderer, in a scene reminiscent of how Rio Santo dies at the end of Féval's *Les Mystères de Londres*.

Anthony Tidkins, the Resurrection Man, is the other great Gothic wanderer in the novel; however, he fails to find or even seek redemption. A hardened criminal, Tidkins never feels remorse for his crimes. Regardless, he is a true Gothic wanderer because of his backstory. We are told how he initially tried to be honest, but a miserable childhood and then feeling all of society was against him because of his past caused him to become so angry that he decided to be a true criminal.

Resurrection men were a historical fact in Victorian England, so it is not surprising they should appear in many literary works. Nevertheless, one has to believe Anthony Tidkins was in the back of Dickens' mind when he created Jerry Cruncher in *A Tale of Two Cities* (1859) and Robert Louis Stevenson may have been inspired by him in writing his short story "The Body Snatcher"

(1884), although it is also possible Stevenson was influenced by Féval's novel. Stevenson's characters are said to have been based on criminals who worked for the real-life surgeon Robert Knox, to whom the murderers Burke and Hare delivered bodies for study.[52] One of the criminals in Stevenson's story is named Macfarlane, the name of a character in Féval's novel, which makes it likely Stevenson read Féval, at least in translation. Since Reynolds' novel was far more popular, however, Stevenson may have drawn upon both books.

Another significant character in *The Mysteries of London* is one of the Resurrection Man's cronies, "the old hag." Her name is never given, but she continually helps to lead women into ruin. When Ellen Monroe is desperate for money, she goes to the hag, who leads her to a painter, then a sculptor, then a theatre manager, and, eventually, to Greenwood (Eugene Markham). Each new employer brings Ellen one step closer to debauchery; first, Ellen agrees to disrobe to be painted or sculpted nude, and finally, she sells her body to Greenwood.

In time, the hag does feel some guilt over the women she has wronged, especially Harriet Wilmot, who turns out to have had a child, Katherine Wilmot, with Richard and Eugene's father. Richard plays benefactor to Katherine before learning she is his half-sister. In the end, the Resurrection Man robs and beats the hag, who dies from her injuries. As the hag dies, Ellen forgives her. The hag, therefore, is another Gothic wanderer who is redeemed because of her remorse.

Reynolds likely borrowed the scenes between Ellen and the hag from French author Jules Janin's story "The Orphan," which Reynolds excerpted in *The Modern Literature of France*. In this story, a poor girl seeks aid from an old hag who has her sell her hair and then profits from the sale enough to buy new shoes while the girl wears old shoes. When the girl again needs money, the old hag helps her to sell her tooth, and with her share of that money, the hag buys a shawl while the orphan's shoulders are bare. The hag even gets the girl to sell her blood. The story ends by Janin detailing the rest of the sales made:

> It was my design, when I commenced this sad history, to narrate to you, circumstantially, all the partial sales of this forlorn girl. All of her body she sold—all save that only which so many of her sex sell—her virtue! The hapless girl, after having sold her vein to a student, sold her head to a painter. She sate for a subject in a city of the plague—so pale was she! Then they put rouge upon her,—and she may be seen to-day amongst the saints, in the Church of Saint-Estephe, and in the Cathedral of Antwerp. She sold her neck to a modeller; and the plaster, unskilfully applied, took away for ever the down of the peach. Her shoulder and her foot she sold to a statuary—the bosses of her head to a craniologist—and her hours of slumber to a disciple of Mesmer. She sold her dreams to a cook, who speculated in the Lottery—and her entire body to the Gymnast Dramatize theatre, as a figurine. Had she been in London, she would have sold her corpse to a surgeon; but we live in a land were [sic] corpses are abundant and fetch nothing![53]

Clearly, Reynolds borrowed this French tale to create that of Ellen and the hag in *The Mysteries of London*. Another obvious borrowing from a French author is when the character Lascelles saves Rainford from death by hanging when he has a throat tube inserted so he can breathe. As previously noted, this same device is used by Ishmael Spencer in Féval's *Les Mystères de Londres*.

Numerous crimes occur throughout *The Mysteries of London*, but perhaps the most fascinating criminal plot concerns Lydia Hutchinson. Lydia finds a teaching position in a boarding school for young ladies, where she befriends one of the pupils, Adeline. Adeline gets Lydia to act as her chaperone, but Adeline is less innocent than Lydia and leads them both into disgrace when they begin having sexual relations with a couple of young men. Adeline becomes pregnant and gives birth to a stillborn child in the school, which Lydia passes off as her own to protect Adeline. Because of her disgrace, Lydia loses her position at the school and then sinks further and further into degradation. She continually asks Adeline for help, but soon Adeline ends their acquaintance.

Through a series of twists and turns, Lydia gets a position as lady's maid to Adeline after Adeline marries and becomes Lady Ravensworth. Lydia is now in a position to blackmail Adeline; she has gone from virtue to vice and now becomes a terrible taskmaster to Adeline. Finally, Adeline can bear the abuse no longer and hires the Resurrection Man to murder Lydia. After the murder, Adeline is haunted by her crime and tries to redeem herself by being charitable. The Resurrection Man, meanwhile, has no remorse. He has buried Lydia's body, but when it suits him, he digs it up and threatens to blackmail Adeline with it. When he shows Lydia's corpse to Adeline, she is so overcome with horror and guilt that she bursts a blood vessel and dies.

While *The Mysteries of London* contains no supernatural elements, other than a rumor that Ravensworth Hall is haunted, it has plenty of Gothic guilt and redemption, villains, and mysterious and horrid haunts in London and its surroundings. It is the epitome of urban Gothic and would set the stage for the Gothic atmosphere used in many other Victorian novels, especially those with depictions of London, including Dickens' *Bleak House* (1853) and *Our Mutual Friend* (1865). Sensationalism permeates the entire novel and doubtless helped to create the sensation novel genre, which included such works as Wilkie Collins' *The Woman in White* (1860), Mrs. Henry Wood's *East Lynne* (1861), and Mary Elizabeth Braddon's *Lady Audley's Secret* (1862).

Many other Gothic themes and elements fill the pages of *The Mysteries of London*, from gambling to family secrets concerning illegitimate children and mysterious parentages. However, the redemption theme is at the heart of understanding the novel's criminal psychology. While Reynolds creates some truly despicable and horrible villains—the Resurrection Man, the old hag, Lady Ravensworth, and Eugene Markham—in almost every case, we see the characters struggling with their consciences.

They often are placed in situations that make it almost impossible for them not to commit more crimes. Reynolds uses the Gothic technique of telling stories within stories so the criminals can tell their histories, which makes the reader feel sympathy for them. Their miserable childhoods reveal what leads people to a life of crime, even when they would rather walk the straight and narrow path.

Reynolds is nothing if not charitable toward his criminals. He is not as effective in his arguments for reform as Eugène Sue since his first purpose appears to be to sensationalize the story so the book will sell well, yet his heart appears to be in the right place. Richard Markham is cast in the same mold as Sue's Rodolphe, and though not a prince, he eventually becomes one. Like Rodolphe, we find Richard on the city streets helping the poor. He is the benefactor to several characters, mostly women, and does get at least one criminal, Talbot, to reform. Plus, Richard's brother Eugene, the worst of the upper-class criminals, is allowed a long and moving death scene of reconciliation with his brother and the chance to receive forgiveness from those he has wronged.

The need for redemption by many of the characters also reflects a larger need for reform and redemption on a national level, which links the novel to Sue and Féval's works as a way to criticize the government. While Reynolds allows Richard Markham to become a prince on the level of Rodolphe in Sue's novel, more significant is the novel's depiction of the need for a true republic. That so much crime exists in the novel reflects the British government's failure to take care of its people. Consequently, Reynolds uses contemporary events and fictionalizes them to promote the need for national reform. He does this by creating the fictional duchy of Castelcicala in Italy and shows how its refusal to become a republic results in a coup. This fictional revolution reflects the historical efforts for Italian unification at the time Reynolds was writing. In 1844, for example, the Bandiera brothers made a failed attempt in Calabria to overthrow the government to help the cause of unification. The event was well-known in Britain because it was believed Lord Aberdeen had been involved in tampering with the brothers' correspondence and giving information to the Austro-Hungarian and Bourbon governments, which stopped the coup.[54] No doubt, Reynolds took inspiration from this event. But while the event is set in Italy, one can't help feeling the coup is a warning to Britain that it also needs to reform. Notably, the capital city of the fictional dukedom Reynolds creates is named Montoni, a name no doubt taken from the villain of Mrs. Radcliffe's *The Mysteries of Udolpho*.

Reynolds makes his social commentary about Britain clearer in another scene. A young criminal, Henry Holford, breaks into Buckingham Palace, planning to help the Resurrection Man to rob it. Holford hides under a sofa where he is able to witness Queen Victoria and Prince Albert's courtship. Reynolds makes the point that Victoria is a young, innocent queen and completely ignorant of the poverty and desperate situations of so many of her people. Holford becomes so enamored with the palace and the queen that he continually sneaks in to spy on the couple until Prince Albert spots him. Holford escapes and dares not reenter the palace, but he decides he will become famous by assassinating Prince Albert. Holford shoots at the prince while Albert and Victoria are in their carriage. (Historically, by the time Reynolds' novel was published, four assassination attempts had already been made against Queen Victoria when she and Albert were in their carriage. There would be eight total.[55]) When the attempt fails, Holford is sentenced to spending the rest of his life in an insane asylum. These chapters are very daring because, unlike most Gothic novels that had previously been set in the past, Reynolds is setting his in the present, and both fictionalizing and criticizing the royal family. We are left with a Queen Victoria who is a type of Marie Antoinette, popularly believed to have been clueless about the poverty in France. The implication is that a revolution could soon occur in England like it has in France and currently is in Italy.

Reynolds' Epilogue sums up his purposes in writing the novel. Despite all its violence and sensationalism, he argues the work has had a moral purpose:

> Kind Reader, who have borne with me so long—one word to thee.
>
> If amongst the circle of thy friends, there be any who express an aversion to peruse this work,—fearful from its title or from fugitive report that the mind will be shocked more than it can be improved, or the blush of shame excited on the cheek oftener than the tear of sympathy will be drawn from the eye;—if, in a word, a false fastidiousness should prejudge, from its own suppositions or from misrepresentations made to it by others, a book by means of which we have sought to convey many an useful moral and lash many a flagrant abuse,—do you, kind reader, oppose that prejudice, and exclaim—"Peruse ere you condemn!"
>
> For if, on the one side, we have raked amidst the filth and loathsomeness of society,—have we not, on the other, devoted adequate attention to its bright and glorious phases?
>
> In exposing the hideous deformity of vice, have we not studied to develop the witching beauty of virtue?
>
> Have we not taught, in fine, how the example and the philanthropy of one good man can *"save more souls and redeem more sinners than all the Bishops that ever wore lawn-sleeves?"*
>
> If, then, the preceding pages be calculated to engender one useful thought—awaken one beneficial sentiment,—the work is not without its value.
>
> If there be any merit in honesty of purpose and integrity of aim,—then is that merit ours.
>
> And if, in addition to considerations of this nature, we may presume that so long as we are enabled to afford

entertainment, our labours will be rewarded by the approval of the immense audience to whom we address ourselves,—we may with confidence invite attention to a SECOND SERIES of "THE MYSTERIES OF LONDON."[56]

Reynolds would go on not only to write a second series of *The Mysteries of London* (1846-8) but three series of *The Mysteries of the Court of London*. He would also write three of the greatest Gothic novels of the nineteenth century, *Faust: A Romance of the Secret Tribunals* (1845-6), *Wagner, the Wehr-Wolf* (1846-7), and *The Necromancer* (1851-2), although they are all but forgotten today. I will discuss the first two of these masterpieces in Chapter 5 and *The Necromancer*, because it is closely related to the Lord Ruthven stories, in Chapter 7.

In my opinion, Reynolds is the most fascinating and important Victorian novelist who is no longer read. Fortunately, a revival of interest in his works has begun in recent years. A few scholarly books have appeared on his works and an international George W. M. Reynolds Society has been established.* While Reynolds may not be as great an author as Dickens or Anthony Trollope, he is the equal of Ainsworth, Bulwer-Lytton, and perhaps even Sue and Dumas. He is a master at creating compelling plotlines and pacing his stories—the latter being something Dickens does not always succeed at. However, Reynolds fails in not providing us with internal monologues to make his characters live. Even his most guilt-ridden characters do not make the reader truly feel their guilt and agony in the way Trollope or Hugo can do over their characters' far lesser crimes. But Reynolds was also not writing for lovers of fine literature, but a lower and middle-class audience that wanted cheap thrills and a sensational storyline. That he tried to infuse some morality into his stories shows he not only knew his audience but also the power of the pen to bring about change. In that respect, Reynolds was like Dickens, although Dickens would have disliked the comparison. He despised Reynolds for capitalizing upon and stealing his characters to write

* Visit https://gwmreynoldssociety.com/. Accessed November 7, 2021.

unauthorized sequels and said Reynolds' periodicals pandered "to the lowest passions of the lowest natures—whose existence is a national reproach."[57]

Whatever Reynolds' faults, Dickens must have also been envious of Reynolds' popularity. Nor do I doubt that Dickens, as a shrewd businessman, would have read his competition's works and tried to learn from them, though not letting that influence show as blatantly as Reynolds did. Consequently, Jerry Cruncher, the resurrection man in *A Tale of Two Cities*, may well be a literary descendant of Anthony Tidkins. Stephen Knight suggests Dickens also drew upon the character of Reynolds' reformed villain convict Crankey Jem in depicting Magwitch in *Great Expectations*.[58] Knight further notes that the structure of the city mysteries novels with their multiple plots and "startling disparity and underlying connections" are features that also mark *Bleak House*. Dickens may have learned to create such structure from Reynolds, who is the greater structuralist. Ann Humpherys commends the "brilliant narrative structure" in Reynolds' works and E. F. Bleiler, who was extremely knowledgeable about nineteenth-century crime writing, thought Reynolds had "one of the most remarkable structural abilities in English letters."[59] Reynolds may have also influenced Thackeray, who wrote under Reynolds when Reynolds was editor of the *Paris Literary Gazette*,[60] in creating his contrasting good and bad characters Amelia Sedley and Becky Sharp in *Vanity Fair* (1847) since Richard and Eugene Markham were such contrasting characters prior.[61]

Despite the popularity of *The Mysteries of London* and its influence, the dislike of Reynolds by his contemporaries ensured his obscurity while writers like Dickens were remembered. Even Sue suffered by association with Reynolds in England, resulting in *The Mysteries of Paris* failing to be taken seriously or become a household name in England compared to works by Sue's contemporaries Dumas and Hugo. Furthermore, by association Reynolds may have hurt the cause of French literature in England, which is ironic given that he wrote *The Modern Literature of France* to reduce prejudice against it.⁶²

Alexandre Dumas' *The Count of Monte Cristo*

Although *The Count of Monte Cristo* (*Le Comte de Monte-Cristo*) does not follow the title pattern popularized by Sue's *The Mysteries of Paris*, it was nevertheless influenced by it. Dumas' publishers urged him to write a book that would capitalize on the runaway success of Sue's novel. At the time, Dumas had been working on a series of newspaper articles about historical tourism in Paris and believed he could turn them into a successful melodramatic novel.⁶³

Dumas may, according to researcher Félicité de Rivasson, have also been inspired by Féval's *Les Mystères de Londres*, particularly the character of Rio Santo, to create his own nobleman bent on revenge.⁶⁴ This suggestion seems very likely since Féval's novel concluded serialization in December 1844 and *The Count of Monte Cristo* was serialized in the *Journal des Débats* in eighteen installments from August 1844 to January 1846. Thus, the timeline, though perhaps slightly overlapping, is feasible for Féval's novel to be a major influence on Dumas' masterpiece. In addition, Féval's earlier novel *Le Loup Blanc* (*The White Wolf*, 1843) may have been an influence on *The Count of Monte Cristo*. In that novel, the main character is a Robin Hood type who hides under a wolf's mask to protect his secret identity.⁶⁵

Before serialization ended, *The Count of Monte Cristo* would appear in an eighteen-volume edition published by Pétion (1845-6). It was also quickly translated into English, first appearing in *Ainsworth's Magazine*.⁶⁶ Unfortunately, most English translations have been subpar and heavily abridged, resulting in *The Count of Monte Cristo* often being dismissed as an adventure novel or even a children's novel. The first time I read the novel, I found it incredibly dull. I do not know which translation I read, but the novel was reduced to half its length. The complete novel runs to

464,234 words or about 1,300 pages. Like many other translated novels of the period, the charm of the original language was missing in the translation, including any attempt to reproduce the slang; word choices were censored, as were parts of the plot to make it palatable to a rigid British Victorian audience. Fortunately, the recent Robin Buss translation has revealed for readers of English a greater understanding of the title character, whose real name is Edmond Dantès, and his intense desire for revenge in the novel. Past translations and also film versions that offer a happy ending—much like revised endings for *Notre-Dame de Paris*—fail to present the novel as Dumas envisioned it. Readers who think they know the story will be surprised if they read Buss' translation, for they will discover *The Count of Monte Cristo* is not simply an adventure story, but an excellent psychological study of revenge, guilt, and redemption—all elements that place it firmly within the framework of the Gothic novel, even though it lacks supernatural elements.

As usual, to summarize the plot of such a long novel would make it incomprehensible, so I will focus on the novel's Gothic elements and its place in the history of Gothic literature. Most readers know the basic story. Edmond Dantès, a sailor, is wrongfully accused of plotting to help restore the former French emperor, Napoleon. This happens because the ship Dantès works on landed at Elba where Napoleon is in exile. (The Napoleon connection is a sign Dumas may have been influenced by Féval's *Les Mystères de Londres* since Rio Santo meets Napoleon.) On the way home, the ship's captain, Leclère, dies, but not before he charges Dantès to deliver a package to General Bertrand (exiled with Napoleon) and a letter from Elba to an unknown man in Paris. Dantès is unaware of what the package contains, but others soon learn he has incriminating evidence on him. Dantès has four primary foes who accuse him of treason without his knowledge: his shipmate Danglars; Fernand Mondego, who is in love with Dantès' fiancée Mércèdes; Caderousse, an unscrupulous neighbor who dislikes Dantès; and Villefort, a magistrate who wants to protect his good name by protecting his father, who could be incriminated by the packet Dantès has brought back.

Never learning what he is accused of, Dantès is sentenced to prison in the Chateau d'If, an island fortress off the coast of Marseille. He will remain there for fourteen years. The novel's Gothic moments begin with these prison scenes, which recall those in other Gothic novels where characters are often unjustly imprisoned or held against their will.

In prison, Dantès meets fellow prisoner Abbé Faria when Faria digs a tunnel that leads to Dantès' cell. Together, the men plan to escape. Faria is both a Gothic and historical character, being based on Portuguese cleric Jose Custodia de Faria, an eccentric figure in Paris in the early nineteenth century who was known for his experiments with hypnotism and magnetism. Faria was a student of Swedenborg and Mesmer and lectured on hypnotism.[67] Hypnotism/magnetism are frequent themes in Gothic literature—the Wandering Jew, George du Maurier's Svengali in *Trilby* (1894), and Dracula all have hypnotic eyes. In the novel, Faria draws geometric lines in his cell, which cause his keepers to think him mad, although they also realize he has knowledge beyond most men. They never realize he is planning his escape. In his extreme knowledge, Faria reflects the Gothic Rosicrucian figure, who usually works for mankind's wellbeing and has two great gifts, the secret of life extension and the philosopher's stone that turns lead into gold.* Faria reflects the Rosicrucian gift of life extension since although he has had several strokes, he has a "life-giving draught," a sort of elixir of life, that restores him to health. And while Faria does not possess the philosopher's stone, he knows the location of a great treasure that Cesare Borgia hid on the isle of Monte Cristo. Faria gives Dantès a paper written in "Gothic characters" that reveals the treasure's hiding place.[68] This paper is equivalent to the found manuscript in many Gothic novels that reveals secrets of the

---

* Rosicrucians will be explored in more detail in Chapters 5 and 6. See also my book *The Gothic Wander*.

past. Besides working with Dantès to escape, Faria also educates Dantès, including teaching him several languages, which allows Dantès to hide his true identity as needed once he escapes.

Faria dies before they can escape, but his death becomes the very means for Dantès to get away. After hiding himself in the body bag intended for Faria, Dantès is flung into the sea. Managing to escape the body bag, he is rescued by pirates, and eventually gets to Monte Cristo where he finds the treasure. Dantès' escape is a type of resurrection since he disguises himself as Faria's corpse and then returns to life. He has been buried alive, not literally but through his imprisonment, and now he has resurrected. In rising from the dead, Dantès is both a vampire figure and a Christ figure (a dichotomy we previously saw with Rio Santo in Féval's novel), but as the novel progresses, he transforms from the former to the latter role.

Dantès then masquerades as the Count of Monte Cristo and begins his revenge. Dantès' imprisonment lasts fourteen years, which recalls the length of time the biblical Jacob labored to wed his beloved Rachel, but there will be no wedding for Dantès. Upon returning to Marseille, he learns that Mércèdes has married his enemy Fernand Mondego, who has now become the Count de Morcerf. Dumas may have borrowed this plot twist from Féval as well since Rio Santo finds that the woman he loves, Mary Macfarlane, has married his enemy, the Earl of White Manor, after he was sent off on a prison ship, just as Dantès was sent to prison.

Another Gothic element is how Dantès learns to communicate with the sailors and pirates who rescue him. They communicate through signs much like the freemasons. The freemasons were often associated with conspiracy theories and were claimed to have done everything from building the Tower of Babel to causing the French Revolution. That Dantès works with them shows he is himself a manipulator of politics and economies. Indeed, the Rosicrucians' possession of the philosopher's stone was seen as a transgression against God, as evidenced in novels like William Godwin's *St. Leon* (1799), because it allowed them to manipulate national and world economies.* Dantès has a similar power through his incredible wealth, although he only uses it to orchestrate his enemies' downfall. He is referenced by another character as being like Cagliostro and the Comte de Saint-Germain, saying he has the wit of one and the philosopher's stone of the other. Cagliostro was an Italian adventurer with an interest in the occult, including alchemy.† Saint-Germain was of unknown birth but became a nobleman and philosopher with an interest in alchemy; he claimed to be 500 years old to deflect inquiries into his origins.

Dantès is equated with several other historical and mythical figures. Soon after his return to civilization, he calls himself Sinbad the Sailor after the character in *The Arabian Nights*. The Gothic frequently used *The Arabian Nights'* technique of stories within stories, although Dumas does not use that framework, but the novel's many subplots serve a similar purpose. The Sinbad metaphor applies to all the "wandering" Dantès does in his early years as he sets into motion the elements for his revenge. The wandering aligns him with other Gothic wanderer figures who are usually transgressors, most notably the Wandering Jew, while the traveling that helps him prepare for revenge also parallels that of Féval's Rio Santo. Dantès is also linked to *The Arabian Nights* by being called an Ali Baba because he finds the treasure in a secret cave.

Most in line with the Gothic tradition is how Dantès is likened to a Byronic vampire. When he arrives in Paris, he is described by other characters as being a type of Byronic hero, specifically Manfred,[69] and like Byron's heroes, he is described as having the gift of spellbinding others[70]—another reference to hypnotism. Later, he is described as having a hand as icy as a corpse,[71] and he is equated with Lord Ruthven, the hero of Polidori's *The Vampyre*:

---

* See my discussion of *St. Leon* in *The Gothic Wanderer: From Transgression to Redemption*, particularly in Chapters III-V.

† Cagliostro is a character in Dumas' Marie Antoinette novels, which will be explored in Chapter 6.

'Well, then,' Franz asked the countess, who had decided to take another look at him [Dantès], 'what do you think of that man?'

'He looks to me like Lord Ruthwen in flesh and blood.'

Franz was struck by this new association with Byron. If any man could make one believe in vampires, this was he.[72]

Dantès also has an air of immortality about him. Vampires are typically immortal or at least have extended lives as the living dead. Dantès is described by other characters as "ageless"[73]—suggesting he shares the Rosicrucian gift of life-extension or perhaps the long life of a vampire. One scene that may well have inspired Bram Stoker in writing *Dracula* occurs in Chapter 31 when Franz visits the Count of Monte Cristo and is served hashish. He falls asleep and dreams of making love to three female statues in the count's residence who represent the courtesans Phryne, Cleopatra, and Messalina. This erotic scene brings to mind the sexual dreams Jonathan Harker has when visited by the female vampires in Dracula's castle.

The novel's resurrection theme continues when Dantès learns from Bertucci, his Corsican servant, how he had once broken into a home owned by Villefort and discovered Villefort burying a treasure. Bertucci attacked Villefort to get the treasure, only to discover the box contained a child whose umbilical cord was wrapped around its neck; Bertucci believes Villefort thought the child dead and was burying it—trying to hide that the child ever existed since it was also illegitimate—but Bertucci realizes the child is alive and rescues it. The child has then literally risen from the grave. The child grows up to be named Benedetto. He is a malevolent being, and in time, Dantès hires him to help in his revenge. Later, Dantès will reveal the secret of this child's burial when he invites Villefort and his mistress, mother of the child, to the house where the child was buried, and which Dantès has now purchased for himself. He frightens his guests by saying the house is haunted by ghosts and then recounts the story of the child's burial without revealing the players' names.

As the novel continues, Dantès wreaks havoc upon his enemies while his true identity remains unknown to them. He enjoys promoting his mysteriousness, telling Villefort he's one of the superior angelic beings and his kingdom is great because he's cosmopolitan—no one can claim to know his birthplace and only God knows when he will die. Because he's cosmopolitan, he has no national scruples.[74] These references again make him akin to the Wandering Jew, cursed by God to wander the earth for who knows how long—but who also works to reduce his curse by serving God's purposes.

Faust is also part of Dantès' characterization. Dantès says that, like everyone else, Satan has tempted him;[75] here he takes on the role of Christ, offered great wealth if he will worship Satan. This biblical scene is the original offer of a Faustian pact, which is a common theme in Gothic literature, but Christ refused to make the pact, and so does Dantès. He claims he resisted this temptation by becoming an agent of Providence, punishing and rewarding according to God's will. He is viewed as one of God's angels by the Morel family, to whom he is a benefactor. Monsieur Morel had owned the ship Dantès had sailed upon and was the only one who tried to help Dantès when he was unjustly accused.

Dantès is also a master of disguise. He claims as his close associates the Abbé Busani and Lord Wilmore of England, who now hates him after some nasty business happened between them in India. In truth, they are not Dantès' associates but people he masquerades as. He does so especially when Villefort makes inquiries of both to find out the truth about the count. Of course, in both roles Dantès feeds Villefort incredible stories. One is that the Count of Monte Cristo bought a house to open up a lunatic asylum—perhaps another suggestion that seeped into Bram Stoker's brain in writing *Dracula*. After all, Dracula is also a count and buys a house near a lunatic asylum where he manipulates the lunatic Renfield.

The Wandering Jew theme in *The Count of Monte Cristo* may have been suggested to Dumas partly because of his source material. The novel is based on the true-life story of François Picaud, who was a shoemaker. Dumas found the story in Jacques Peuchet's *Police dévoilée: Mémoires historiques tirés des archives de Paris...* (1838), a collection of anecdotes from the Paris police archives. While Picaud's story shares many similarities to that of Dantès, Dumas made some changes such as shifting Dantès' origins from Paris to Marseille. Picaud's origins are interesting since the Wandering Jew is typically portrayed as a shoemaker who refused to let Christ rest outside his door on the way to Calvary; as a result, Christ cursed him to wander the earth until his return. The shoemaker theme relates to wandering since shoes are needed for long journeys. The novel or Dumas' sources may have also influenced Dickens' *A Tale of Two Cities* (1859) since Dr. Manette, when imprisoned in the Bastille, takes up shoemaking. Manette also ceaselessly wanders about his rooms at night. Manette's imprisonment in the Bastille also recalls Dantès' long imprisonment, including that he was wrongly accused. Just as Dantès seems to return to life, so Dickens used the resurrection theme to have Dr. Manette reclaimed to life and have Jerry Cruncher be a resurrection man.

Gambling is another Gothic theme in *The Count of Monte Cristo*. Madame Danglars is a great gambler who over time loses much of her husband's fortune. Gambling is not limited to gaming, however; the count purposely uses the new telegraph system to create false rumors that affect the buying and selling of stocks, which leads to Danglars' financial ruin. Gambling was seen as a transgression against God in Gothic literature because people tried to use gambling to achieve great wealth and improve their social and financial statuses. This transgression was linked to the philosopher's stone that could manipulate world economies by manufacturing wealth.*

---

* For more on gambling as a Gothic transgression, see *The Gothic Wanderer*.

The novel's debt to Sue's *The Mysteries of Paris* is reflected in much of the story being set in Paris. Furthermore, that Dumas took the frame of his story from Peuchet's *Police dévoilée* suggests he was trying to create an urban crime story to ride Sue's coattails. Paris is where the count secretly enacts most of his revenge, thereby creating many mysteries that his victims do not understand. At the same time, Dantès often chooses to be benevolent like Sue's Prince Rodolphe. Rodolphe disguises himself as a common worker to go out among the people, like Haroun al-Rashid—another tie to *The Arabian Nights*—to find people deserving of his benevolence. However, while Sue's prince aids convicts to help reform them, Dantès only aids criminals so they will help him achieve his revenge. These criminals also end up punished in various ways, despite their roles in bringing about the count's form of justice.

Although Dantès believes he is the hand of Providence, at the novel's end, he realizes the full extent of the misery he has inflicted upon his enemies. Then he begins to question the justice of his actions. After Dantès' actions have directly or indirectly led to almost everyone in Villefort's family dying, Villefort understands he has been unjust toward his own wife, who has poisoned some of the family. He says she caught the disease of crime from him like it was the plague. He decides they will leave France together to wander the earth—another play on the Wandering Jew theme. However, Villefort arrives home to find it is too late—his wife has already killed herself. At this point, Dantès reveals who he is to Villefort, and having pity on him, tells Villefort he has paid his debt and he is satisfied. It's too late, however, because Villefort then goes mad. Dantès rushes from the house in horror, fearing he has gone too far in his revenge.

Dantès is now filled with doubt and despair. He meets Mércèdes one last time—she long ago realized who he was, and she begged him to spare her son when the two dueled—film versions often make the son Dantès' son, but Dumas did not go that far. After Mércèdes' husband Fernand commits suicide,

Dantès realizes he has impoverished Mércèdes and her son. He now parts from her, but he makes sure she and her son are provided for.

Reexamining his life, Dantès returns to the Chateau d'If, where he had been imprisoned, and there he hears from the guard the history of the abbé and the escaped prisoner—the guard does not realize he is repeating Dantès' own story to him. Dantès now asks God to take away his doubt that he has been acting as God's agent in carrying out his revenge. When the guard gives Dantès the Abbé Faria's manuscript of the history of the Italian monarchy, Dantès notices the book's epitaph, "'You will pull the dragon's teeth and trample the lions underfoot,' said the Lord." He takes this as a sign that he has done the right thing in bringing about justice.[76]

In the novel's final chapter, Dantès completes his transformation from a resurrected vampire into a resurrected Christ figure. Throughout the novel, while he has wreaked revenge on his enemies, he has also spared the good, especially those of the second generation who were not responsible for their fathers' sins. By not punishing sins to the third and fourth generation like the Old Testament God of the Hebrews, Dantès also acts like a Christ figure who forgives sins. Among the second generation is Valentine, Villefort's daughter. When Villefort's wife (Valentine's stepmother) was poisoning members of the family so that her son could become sole heir, Dantès manipulated events so that when Valentine's life was in jeopardy, it would only appear she had died. Dantès does not reveal his secret even to Valentine's lover, Max Morel. Now in the novel's final scene, he brings Max to the isle of Monte Cristo, where Max expects the count will help him carry out his suicide because he is so grief-stricken over Valentine's death. Instead, Max finds Valentine there, alive and well, like "the daughter of Jairus" raised from the dead by Christ.[77] One can't help thinking of Romeo and Juliet in this scene since Valentine had to take a potion to appear dead and Max has contemplated suicide, but unlike in Shakespeare, life and happiness are restored for Dumas' lovers.

While films and other adaptations have treated *The Count of Monte Cristo* as a great adventure novel, it is more akin to Shakespearean and other Renaissance revenge tragedies. The novel may well have brought the revenge theme strongly back into literature in a way it had not known since the Renaissance, though again in this respect, it owed a debt to Féval's *Les Mystères de Londres*. Regardless, *The Count of Monte Cristo* may be a source for the large number of revenge-themed novels that followed in the nineteenth century.

The first such novel is Emily Brontë's *Wuthering Heights* (1847). The novel's main character, Heathcliff, like *The Count of Monte Cristo*, is bent upon revenge. Heathcliff also has a great deal of mystery about his origins, how he gained his wealth, and what he did in the years he was absent from Wuthering Heights. While no evidence exists that Brontë read *The Count of Monte Cristo*, it seems very likely since several translations were available in England beginning in 1845, and Brontë could also read French and had lived in Belgium in 1842 where she and her sister Charlotte went to improve their French. Critic Robert Stowell has also suggested Brontë read Dumas, pointing out similarities between the novels, but ultimately, there is no hard evidence.[78]

Revenge is also a key theme in American novelist Lew Wallace's *Ben-Hur* (1880) as is redemption. Wallace scholars are well aware of Dumas' influence on *Ben-Hur*. According to Wikipedia:

> *Ben-Hur* was also inspired in part by Wallace's love of romantic novels, including those written by Sir Walter Scott and Jane Porter, and *The Count of Monte Cristo* (1846) by Alexandre Dumas, père. The Dumas novel was based on the memoirs of an early 19th-century French shoemaker who was unjustly imprisoned and spent the rest of his life seeking revenge. Wallace could relate to the character's isolation of imprisonment. He explained in his

autobiography that, while he was writing *Ben-Hur*, "the Count of Monte Cristo in his dungeon of stone was not more lost to the world."[79]

The Count of Monte Cristo likely also influenced Lew Wallace's later work, *The Prince of India* (1893), its title character being the Wandering Jew. Dantès' cosmopolitan nature may have inspired the Wandering Jew's own cosmopolitan existence in the novel as he masquerades as an Indian prince when he goes to Constantinople at the time of its fall in 1453.

Victor Hugo was also clearly influenced by the revenge theme, though, as Brian Stableford notes, he chose to reverse it when he created Jean Valjean in *Les Misérables*, a novel also predominantly set in Paris. Jean Valjean has as much reason as Rio Santo or Edmond Dantès to want to avenge himself on his enemies, yet he chooses the path of forgiveness.[80] Hugo's is a Christian message more in line with Sue's work than that of Féval or Dumas.

Also, as noted above, I suspect an influence on *A Tale of Two Cities* and *Dracula*. In addition, *The Count of Monte Cristo* brings to mind the financier Melmotte in Anthony Trollope's *The Way We Live Now* (1872) and Jay Gatsby in F. Scott Fitzgerald's *The Great Gatsby* (1925). Melmotte and Gatsby both have enormous wealth and mysterious backgrounds. *The Count of Monte Cristo*'s incredible influence on both Gothic and realistic fiction cannot be overstated.

The Count of Monte Cristo is a masterpiece of Gothic fiction and arguably Dumas' greatest work. Nor is it Dumas' only Gothic work. We will explore several more in Chapters 4, 6, and 7.

Conclusion

The city mysteries genre took the Gothic out of medieval Gothic castles, abbeys, and forests and placed it in the middle of contemporary urban settings. Suddenly, novels reflected the Gothic world that readers were living in. These Gothic works provided a more immediate vehicle for social criticism and highlighted the need for social changes, particularly to help the poor and oppressed. They reflected socialist ideas (Sue), democratic ideals (Reynolds), and revolutionary needs (Féval), as well as how individuals sometimes had to take action to protect themselves and bring about vigilante justice (Dumas, Sue, and Féval) when society and its institutions failed to protect the rights of the individual.

Often, city mysteries novels also contained an undertone of distrust of the government and those in power and a fear that powerful and invisible forces might be manipulating events, leaving the individual at the mercy of invisible forces—the Count of Monte Cristo and Rio Santo both inspire such fear through the events they manipulate. Such fears resulted in conspiracy theories and a belief in the existence of powerful secret societies, as we will explore in more detail in Chapter 5.

Chapter 4

Wandering Jews

Matthew Lewis, William Harrison Ainsworth, George Croly, Edgar Quinet, Eugène Sue, Alexandre Dumas, and Paul Féval

> "Time is like the Wandering Jew.
> It moves on and on...."
>
> — Paul Féval, *The Wandering Jew's Daughter*

WE NOW TURN TO THE WANDERING JEW, perhaps the most significant figure to influence Gothic Wanderer characters and a direct literary ancestor of Dracula and his vampiric descendants. The Wandering Jew was a malleable figure that lent itself to explorations of themes ranging from transgression and redemption to history and the overall human condition. Although originally a symbol of the Jews being cursed for their role in Christ's crucifixion, the Wandering Jew evolved into a metaphor for all humans, particularly the oppressed, as we will see in the works discussed below.

Ultimately, the figure reflects the human condition, the extended toil of humanity upon the earth and the ceaseless questioning of when that toil will end and humanity may return to God. At the same time, it is a distinctly Christian legend working within a Christian understanding of the universe. Although extremely popular throughout the nineteenth century, its stereotypes of the Jewish race, the archaic contention that the Jews are to be blamed for Christ's death, and the atrocities of the

Holocaust have caused the Wandering Jew to fall out of popular culture. Regardless, the figure is significant for an understanding of Gothic literature's origins and evolution.

I will begin with a brief overview of the development of the Wandering Jew legend before Gothic novelists adapted it. Then I will discuss treatments of the Wandering Jew in British and French literature. In my previous book *The Gothic Wanderer*, I also devoted a chapter to characters based on the Wandering Jew in British Gothic literature, so I will refer the reader to that book if they wish to understand the British texts in more detail. Here, with the exception of Matthew Lewis' *The Monk*, I will not repeat discussions of British texts treated in *The Gothic Wanderer* and instead will focus on France's own rich literary tradition of the Wandering Jew.

The Wandering Jew's Origins

The legend of the Wandering Jew began as a symbol of the Jewish people who had become wanderers and outcasts among the world's settled nations. In 70 AD, the Jews unsuccessfully rebelled against Rome, leading to Rome punishing them by dispersing them from their homeland and selling thousands of them into slavery. This dispersion resulted in the Jewish people migrating all over the known world and becoming residents in every European country.

Because Christians blamed the Jews for Christ's crucifixion, wherever the Jewish people settled, they were mistreated and sometimes forbidden to reside in certain countries. Even when they did settle in a country, political changes often resulted in later forced migration elsewhere. During the Middle Ages, one of the harshest penalties imposed upon Jewish people was a prohibition against owning property. This situation added to their wandering patterns. Because they needed a source of income they could not achieve by living off the land, some Jews capitalized on Christianity's prohibition against usury by becoming moneylenders, thereby developing great wealth. Consequently, the Jewish people had two primary stereotypes attached to them: they were wanderers, and they were greedy people, constantly grasping for money by loaning it out and collecting interest.

Europeans who were jealous of the Jews' wealth spread fabulous derogatory tales about them, including that Jews had hidden and heavily guarded treasures, Jews possessed the evil eye by which they could curse and destroy people, and Jews had horns or tails and emitted foul odors of brimstone and sulphur, which suggested their alliance with Satan. Jews were even accused of draining blood from Christians to use for sorcery practices.[1] Particularly in times of social upheaval or economic crisis, such stories were circulated to encourage anti-Semitism and legitimize removal of Jews by forced emigration or even extermination.

From all this anti-Semitism rose the medieval legend of the Wandering Jew. In most versions of the legend, the Wandering Jew was a shoemaker named Ahasuerus who refused to allow Christ to rest on His way to the cross. Christ punished Ahasuerus by forcing him to wander the earth without rest or the release of death until Christ's return on Judgment Day. Usually, this cursed condition is interpreted to mean that Christ will eventually redeem Ahasuerus, who will have atoned for his sins by his prolonged wandering.[2]

As he wandered the globe, the Wandering Jew allegedly made remarkable appearances without explanation at the sites of great historical events such as the sack of Rome, the Crusades, and decisive Napoleonic battles; these appearances suggested that the Jew had supernatural powers that allowed him to appear wherever and whenever he chose.[3] The Jew's constant wandering is enhanced by his fear that Christians will learn who he is; he must continually move from place to place before his true identity is revealed and he is mistreated.

Because Christ is usually portrayed as loving and forgiving, it is odd that a story would have developed of his uttering such a terrible curse against the Wandering Jew for such a minor unkindness. Scholar Isaac-Edersheim offers the explanation that the Wandering Jew should not be understood as merely an individual sinner, but as a force in opposition to Christ, a type of superhuman figure who must be defeated.[4] While numerous other psychological and historical explanations have been offered for the Wandering Jew legend, Gothic novelists chose to represent him as a transgressor, and therefore, a force in opposition to Christ. At the same time, the Wandering Jew appeals to readers' psyches because everyone feels a bit of wanderlust and also shares the common human fear of becoming an outcast.[5]

The Gothic uses wandering as a metaphor for guilt, despair, and displacement, and the Wandering Jew became the perfect vehicle for depicting such emotions. The Wandering Jew feels great guilt over his transgression, a guilt that becomes nearly unbearable because of his extended life. He frequently yearns to escape from his punishment by committing suicide, yet he is unable to accomplish such a deed because he cannot die until Christ's return: If the Jew tries to drown himself, the sea pulls away, refusing him entrance; if he tries to jump into a volcano, he is spit out alive; and in battle, no man is able to harm him, so his prolonged life becomes only prolonged misery.

Isaac-Edersheim remarks that the Jew's prolonged life symbolizes the human repressed desire not to die,[6] but ultimately, this desire is rejected when life-extension is fully considered. Gothic scholar Marie Roberts observes that the legend becomes a lesson about man's moral responsibility to reconcile himself to death, for not only is death inevitable, but the reverse would be far worse.[7] Not to die is worse than death if you see everyone you love die around you, leaving you alone.

The Wandering Jew was only a minor figure in British literature before his adaptation by Gothic novelists. The first recorded reference in England of the legend was in 1228 in the chronicle of St. Alban's monastery, *Flowers of History* by Roger of Wendover.[8] The most notable medieval depiction is in Geoffrey

Chaucer's late fourteenth century "The Pardoner's Tale" in which an old man must wander the earth until he can find someone willing to exchange youth for his old age.

The Wandering Jew's popularity in literature increased during the seventeenth century. He was given the name Ahasuerus in an anonymous German pamphlet of 1602 entitled *Kurtze Beschreibung und Erzehlung von einem juden mit Namen Ahasverus*.[9] Ahasuerus would become the favored name for the Jew, although Matthew Paris also wrote a story in the seventeenth century in which he named the Jew Cartaphilus.[10] During the seventeenth century, the Wandering Jew also became credited with healing powers attributed to the Rosicrucians, as stated in Peck's *History of Stamford* and Aubrey's *Miscellanies*.[11] Later, the legend of the Wandering Jew and the Rosicrucians would become blended together in Gothic literature. Other notable treatments of the Wandering Jew prior to the Gothic novel occur in late eighteenth-century German literature. Goethe wrote a fragmented tale either simultaneously with or directly after his famous *The Sorrows of Young Werther* (1774), but it was not published until 1836.[12] Christian Schubart also wrote a fragment published in 1783 called *Der Ewige Jude*.[13] Finally, Reichard's *Der Ewige Jude* (1785) ambitiously chronicled the Jew's entire wanderings throughout history.[14] None of these early treatments, however, popularized the Jew or were of significant influence to the Gothic tradition. Matthew Lewis' *The Monk* (1795) is primarily responsible for the Wandering Jew becoming an important Gothic figure.

Matthew Lewis' *The Monk*

Matthew Lewis was the first to use the Wandering Jew as a character in a Gothic novel. His portrayal was so popular that it resulted in numerous adaptations where Gothic novelists created characters based on the Wandering Jew, as well as the Romantic poets making the Wandering Jew a frequent figure in their poetry. While Lewis' depiction of the Wandering Jew owes a debt to Schubart's depiction, it is primarily his own imaginative version.[15] Lewis was responsible for first depicting the Wandering Jew with a burning cross upon his forehead, a characteristic that later became a standard feature of the Jew's appearance.[16]

While the link between the Wandering Jew and the biblical Cain may have already existed, Lewis' burning cross recalled the mark placed on Cain after he murdered his brother. A tradition existed that Cain's mark was shaped like a cross, so Lewis similarly chose to make the Jew's mark exist in the form of a cross to symbolize the Jew's rejection of Christianity.[17]

The Jew's link to Cain was relevant because Cain was already understood to be a wandering outcast while Abel was commonly interpreted as a character similar to Christ; Cain's murder of Abel was compatible with the Wandering Jew's crime of denying Christ a place to rest because the Jewish people were blamed for murdering Christ. Like the Wandering Jew, Cain is also traditionally a wanderer. Following the murder of Abel, God tells Cain: "You shall become a restless wanderer on the earth." Cain fears the hatred of other men, however, so God declares that no one is allowed to kill Cain, and to prevent against accidents, "the Lord put a mark on Cain, lest anyone should kill him at sight" (Genesis 4:12-15). Similarly, the mark on the Wandering Jew's forehead reveals his identity.

In *The Monk*, the Wandering Jew only makes a brief appearance, but it is a stunning one. The Jew appears to exorcise the Bleeding Nun so she will no longer haunt Raymond. Raymond describes the Jew's appearance as follows:

> He was a Man of majestic presence: His countenance was strongly marked and his eyes were large, black, and sparkling: Yet there was a something in his look, which the moment that I saw him, inspired me with a secret awe, not to say horror. He was drest plainly, his hair was unpowdered, and a band of black velvet which encircled his fore-head, spread over his features an additional gloom. His countenance wore the marks of profound

melancholy; his step was slow, and his manner grave, stately, and solemn.[18]

Raymond does not recognize the Wandering Jew until the Jew describes his situation:

> "Fate obliges me to be constantly in movement: I am not permitted to pass more than a fortnight in the same place. I have no Friend in the world, and from the restlessness of my destiny I never can acquire one. Fain would I lay down my miserable life, for I envy those who enjoy the quiet of the Grave: But Death eludes me, and flies from my embrace. In vain do I throw myself in the way of danger. I plunge into the Ocean; The Waves throw me back with abhorrence upon the shore: I rush into fire; The flames recoil at my approach: I oppose myself to the fury of Banditti; Their swords become blunted, and break against my breast: The hungry Tiger shudders at my approach, and the Alligator flies from a Monster more horrible than itself. God has set his seal upon me, and all his Creatures respect this fatal mark!"
>
> He put his hand to the velvet, which was bound round his fore-head. There was in his eyes an expression of fury, despair, and malevolence, that struck horror to my very soul. An involuntary convulsion made me shudder. The Stranger perceived it.
>
> "Such is the curse imposed on me," he continued: "I am doomed to inspire all who look on me with terror and detestation. You already feel the influence of the charm, and with every succeeding moment will feel it more. I will not add to your sufferings by my presence...."[19]

The burning cross on his forehead is so frightening that the Wandering Jew refuses to reveal it to Raymond. Later, however, the Wandering Jew demands that the Bleeding Nun tell him how her soul may find peace. When she is reluctant to tell, he reveals to her the burning cross, which compels her to answer. During this scene, Raymond had been instructed not to look on the cross, but now he cannot resist:

> He [the Wandering Jew] spoke in a commanding tone, and drew the sable band from his fore-head. In spite of his injunctions to the contrary, Curiosity would not suffer me to keep my eyes off his face: I raised them, and beheld a burning Cross impressed upon his brow. For the horror with which this object inspired me I cannot account, but I never felt its equal! My senses left me for some moments; A mysterious dread overcame my courage, and had not the Exorciser caught my hand, I should have fallen out of the Circle.
>
> When I recovered myself, I perceived that the burning Cross had produced an effect no less violent upon the Spectre. Her countenance expressed reverence, and horror, and her visionary limbs were shaken by fear.[20]

The Bleeding Nun's fear forces her to reveal her history of murder and that she will not rest until her bones are reburied at her ancestral castle. She has haunted Raymond because he is a relative whose duty it is to provide her with a proper burial. While the Wandering Jew is heroic because he provides a way for the Bleeding Nun to rest, he remains unable to achieve a similar rest for himself. Upon bidding Raymond farewell, he remarks, "Youth, farewell! May the Ghost of your Relation enjoy that rest in the Tomb, which the Almighty's vengeance has denied to me for ever!"[21]

Critic William Day remarks that this scene between the Wandering Jew and the Bleeding Nun is created merely for its sensational effect, rather than to show any serious encounter between the spiritual worlds of good and evil or those of the supernatural and the physical.[22] Nevertheless, the enormous popularity of this scene influenced the creation of numerous Romantic poems that found an element of spiritual truth in

Lewis' creation. The Wandering Jew's kindness, despite his cruel fate, evokes the reader's sympathy. While the Jew has committed a transgression, his centuries of eternal wandering seem an intense punishment for denying Christ rest, especially when compared to the Bleeding Nun's much shorter punishment for her more severe crime of murder. Yet the scene must be read metaphorically, with the understanding that the Jew's crime serves as a symbol for the entire Jewish race's rejection of Christ as Son of God, whereas the Bleeding Nun's crime is an individual murder of a sole human.

Christianity states that the only way to salvation is to believe that Christ is the Son of God, so while even murder can be forgiven, denial of Christ is an unpardonable sin. Lewis' depiction of the Wandering Jew, however, grants the Jew the reader's sympathy. The scene was so popular that George K. Anderson notes at least half-a-dozen French plays based on the story between 1798 and 1835, not counting ballets.[23] Consequently, it is not surprising that some of the most significant novelistic treatments of the legend in the nineteenth century would be by French authors. Lewis' successors would build upon the Wandering Jew's psychological implications as well as create characters based upon him who are sympathetic transgressors who feel remorse for their crimes.

Among the characters based on the Wandering Jew are the titular characters in Coleridge's "The Rime of the Ancient Mariner" (1798), William Godwin's *St. Leon* (1799), and Charles Maturin's *Melmoth the Wanderer* (1820). It is possible that even Mrs. Radcliffe was influenced by the scene since her evil monk Schedoni was created in response to Lewis' novel; like Lewis' Wandering Jew, Schedoni has penetrating eyes: "his eyes were so piercing, that they seemed to penetrate, at a single glance, into the hearts of men, and to read their most secret thoughts; few persons could support their scrutiny, or even endure to meet them twice."[24]

However, it would be more than thirty years before a British novelist chose to devote an entire book to the Wandering Jew, and then the French would embrace the figure and develop him more fully than the British, as the rest of this chapter will explore.

William Harrison Ainsworth's "The Spectre Bride"

William Harrison Ainsworth's short story "The Spectre Bride" (1821) was published when he was only sixteen, but it already showed the promise of the incredible novels to come. Ainsworth's biographer Stephen Carver suggests that the story's title reflects the influence of Washington Irving's 1819 story "The Specter Bridegroom," a comedy in which the protagonists are destined to be together but something keeps them apart, causing the suitor to have to pretend he is a ghost.[25] Ainsworth's title is a bit misleading since although the story is about a bride, it is not the story of a man marrying a ghost, as might be expected. Rather, she is the bride of a spectre figure who eventually reveals himself to be the Wandering Jew.

The story begins like it is yet another version of the Lord Ruthven story since the female main character weds a mysterious man. The scene opens with the heroine, Clotilde, celebrating her birthday in her father's castle. A stranger arrives and joins the party, and soon he has won her heart. All goes well for a time until one day Clotilde's father is found dead and the stranger has disappeared. The reader realizes the stranger likely killed Clotilde's father, but Clotilde only knows she loves the stranger and now misses him. Eventually, the stranger returns, saying he has traveled all over and seen many women, but Clotilde is the one he loves. After she professes her love to him, he tries to dissuade her from being with him by stating:

> leave me—forget me—avoid me for ever—or your eternal ruin must ensue. I am a thing abandoned of God and man—and did you but see the scared heart that scarcely beats within this moving mass of deformity, you would flee me, as you would an adder in your path. Here is my heart, love, feel how cold it is; there is no pulse that betrays

its emotion; for all is chilled and dead as the friends I once knew.²⁶

When Clotilde is not dissuaded, he asks her to swear an oath that she will love him. If ever there was a dramatic oath in Gothic literature, it is this one:

> He then desired her to kneel, and holding his right hand in a menacing attitude towards heaven, and throwing back his dark raven locks, exclaimed in a strain of bitter imprecation with the ghastly smile of an incarnate fiend, 'May the curses of an offended God,' he cried, 'haunt thee, cling to thee for ever in the tempest and in the calm, in the day and in the night, in sickness and in sorrow, in life and in death, shouldst thou swerve from the promise thou hast here made to be mine. May the dark spirits of the damned howl in thine ears the accursed chorus of fiends— may the air rack thy bosom with the quenchless flames of hell! May thy soul be as the lazar-house of corruption, where the ghost of departed pleasure sits enshrined, as in a grave: where the hundred-headed worm never dies where the fire is never extinguished. May a spirit of evil lord it over thy brow, and proclaim, as thou passest by, "THIS IS THE ABANDONED OF GOD AND MAN;" may fearful spectres haunt thee in the night season; may thy dearest friends drop day by day into the grave, and curse thee with their dying breath: may all that is most horrible in human nature, more solemn than language can frame, or lips can utter, may this, and more than this, be thy eternal portion, shouldst thou violate the oath that thou has taken.' He ceased—hardly knowing what she did, the terrified girl acceded to the awful adjuration, and promised eternal fidelity to him who was henceforth to be her lord.²⁷

After making the vow, Clotilde goes to bed with the intention of marrying the stranger the next day. That night, she is visited by the ghost of her father who warns her that she will also soon be a ghost, yet she goes through with the marriage the next day. Once married by a priest, her husband now reveals his true identity:

> Spouse of the spirit of darkness, a few moments are yet thine; that thou may'st know to whom thou hast consigned thyself. I am the undying spirit of the wretch who curst his Saviour on the cross. He looked at me in the closing hour of his existence, and that look hath not yet passed away, for I am curst above all on earth. I am eternally condemned to hell and I must cater for my master's taste till the world is parched as is a scroll, and the heavens and the earth have passed away. I am he of whom thou may'st have read, and of whose feats thou may'st have heard. A million souls has my master condemned me to ensnare, and then my penance is accomplished, and I may know the repose of the grave. Thou art the thousandth soul that I have damned.[28]

Although Clotilde's new spouse to this point in the story appears to be like a vampire, he turns out to be the Wandering Jew. Ainsworth has given his own twist to the legend since this Jew has cursed his Savior while on the cross rather than refusing to let him rest while on the way to the crucifixion. Furthermore, the Jew is clearly working for Satan to destroy other souls, something not in any other version of the legend, but which will be common in the Lord Ruthven vampire stories.

Clotilde's husband now casts her into the pit of hell, but he makes certain to tell her he is not to blame for his actions, stating, "not mine is the crime, but the religion that thou professest; for is it not said that there is a fire of eternity prepared for the souls of the wicked; and hast not thou incurred its torments?"[29]

As Clotilde falls into the burning pit, ten thousand voices cry, "'Spirit of evil! here indeed is an eternity of torments prepared for thee; for here the worm never dies, and the fire is never quenched."[30]

The ending is somewhat obscure for it seems unlikely the voices are addressing Clotilde; more likely they are telling the Wandering Jew he will end up in hell, despite God's promise to free him from his extended life once he collects a million souls. After all, the repose of the grave he has been promised is nothing but death, and with death comes the afterlife, which no doubt will be hell for him.

Ainsworth's completely evil Wandering Jew helps to create a stunning short work, but as novelists adapted the Wandering Jew to longer works, they would evolve him into a character of greater sympathy as we will see throughout the rest of this chapter. Later, in Chapter 7, we will encounter more supernatural characters who must win over a certain number of souls for Satan, but rather than be versions of the Wandering Jew, they will usually be vampires.

George Croly's *Salathiel*

Reverend George Croly's novel *Salathiel* is all but forgotten today, yet it holds an important place in Gothic literary history for how it helped to evolve the Wandering Jew figure and for being a possible source for *Dracula*. It also holds a significant, but usually overlooked place in the development of historical fiction and biblical fiction.

The novel was first published anonymously in three volumes in 1828 under the title *Salathiel. A story of the Past, the Present, and the Future*. A new edition in 1855 changed the title to *Salathiel the Immortal*. By 1901, it was titled *Tarry Thou Till I Come or Salathiel, the Wandering Jew*.[31]

George Croly (1780-1860) was an Irish Anglican clergyman who eventually moved to London. He also traveled in France and would be well known for his poem "Paris in 1815." Later, he would write the novel *Marston* (1845) concerning the Napoleonic Wars, but *Salathiel* was his best-known work. It is also his most Gothic because of its supernatural theme, even though it lacks a Gothic atmosphere.

As critic Albert Power observes, Croly departs from usual versions of the Wandering Jew legend by making the Jew not a shoemaker nor a known biblical character like Pontius Pilate or John the Evangelist, but a Jewish priest who helps to raise the rabble that calls for Christ's crucifixion.[32] For this action, Christ tells Salathiel, "Tarry thou, until I come."[33] The novel opens with these words. Salathiel is recalling hearing them and how they resonated with him. Instantly, he understands how his words have tormented Christ and he fears his future as someone unable to die until Christ's return. The Preface states the novel is written by the Wandering Jew and the first-person narration provides us with an inside look into Salathiel's story.

Salathiel was the first novel in English or French completely dedicated to the theme of the Wandering Jew, and one would expect it to tell his whole history, but Croly does not seem to know what to do with Salathiel once he becomes immortal; at times, the reader wonders if Croly has even forgotten that his title character is immortal. Rather than depicting the Wandering Jew over the course of centuries, Croly focuses on a period of time covering what would be the normal lifespan for the character, depicting his life throughout the Battle of Masada and the destruction of Jerusalem in 70 AD, at which time Salathiel is unlikely to be older than in his sixties.

Like most Gothic novels, *Salathiel* has a fairly complicated plot. A large cast of mostly undeveloped characters is presented whom the reader is expected to remember whenever they serendipitously or coincidentally reappear. First, we receive a description of Jerusalem during the crucifixion. Once Christ utters the condemnatory words, Salathiel flees the city in terror. He returns in time to experience fire and earthquakes and then darkness descend over the city. When he enters the Temple, the high priest is frozen in terror. Finally, the earth opens and swallows Salathiel and his family. All this is the result of God's displeasure over Christ's death, as the gospels depict, although the novel makes the events more dramatic.

Salathiel wakes to find his relatives have rescued him and his family and taken them to Samaria. In the days that follow, Salathiel is depressed about the curse upon him, but he keeps it from his family. Eventually, his brother-in-law Eleazar notes the "gloom that sits eternally on your forehead,"[34] but he cannot get answers from Salathiel about the reasons for it. This gloom signifies that Salathiel is marked like Cain to wander the earth, even though the novel never depicts an actual scar or mark on his forehead.

Early on, Salathiel meets another immortal. The man approaches him and asks if he is like him. This man is of incredible strength and beauty, and he tells Salathiel nothing can hurt him. He claims, "I could outstrip that whirlwind;—I could plunge unhurt into the depths of that sea;—I could ascend that mountain, swifter than the eagle;—I could ride that thundercloud." Salathiel feels of this man that "Conscious mastery was in all about him. I should not have felt surprise, to see him spring up into the clouds!"[35] And in near despair, he asks the man to give him the same kind of power, but then the man reveals that in life he had been "Epiphany." Salathiel jumps back in horror, exclaiming, "You, Antiochus! the tyrant—the persecutor—the spoiler—the accursed of Israel!"[36] Salathiel informs the reader that this man is one of the evil spirits of the dead that in recent years had been reappearing on earth and haunting the land of Judea. The reference is to Antiochus IV Epiphanes, a Greek Hellenistic King who ruled the Seleucid Empire from 175-164 BC. He was deeply reviled by the Jewish people for such acts as defiling the temple by placing a pig in it, which led to the Maccabean revolt. Before Salathiel manages to escape his presence, Epiphany warns him that a worse conqueror than he will come to Jerusalem.

After Epiphany's appearance, the novel becomes very historical and lacks any more supernatural elements until its end. Salathiel raises a family with his wife Miriam. Early on, they have an infant son who gets lost during a chaotic moment, but not surprisingly, he will reappear as a grown man before the story is over. Salathiel also has two daughters. The novel details the events leading to the Jews fortifying themselves at Masada against the Romans, their eventual defeat by the Romans, and the Romans' destruction of Jerusalem. Throughout, Salathiel finds himself in many situations where he is imprisoned, involved in espionage, and continually escaping from danger.

Because he repeatedly survives these desperate situations, Salathiel is accused of sorcery a couple of times. Surprisingly, given that he must be well into his sixties by the time of Masada, no one ever remarks upon his youthful appearance, but he is charged with making an evil compact with the devil as the reason for why he was able to take the fortress of Masada.

> You are charged with unutterable acts. Your abandonment of the priesthood; sights seen in your deserted chambers, which not even the most daring would venture to inhabit; your escape from dangers, that must have extinguished any other human being, have bred fatal rumours. It has been said, that you worshipped in the bowels of the mountain of Masada, where the magic fire burns eternally before the image of the Evil One; nay, that you even conquered the fortress, impregnable as it was to man, by a horrid compact; and that the raising of your standard was the declared sign of that compact, dreadfully to be repaid by you and yours![37]

Although no evidence exists to support these charges, Salathiel is imprisoned, but he manages to escape. In fact, he makes more than one escape in the novel; he even manages to join up with some pirates for a while, making the book read like an adventure novel.

In the end, however, the Romans destroy Jerusalem. Croly then returns to supernatural themes. The novel also appears to become anti-Jewish at this point. In Chapter 47, angels from heaven descend upon the battlefield and attack not the Romans but the Jews, suggesting they are no longer the chosen people, presumably because they denied Christ like Salathiel did.

One of the most interesting moments in the novel occurs soon after in Chapter 48. After the battle, Salathiel is reunited with his family, from whom he has long been separated. It turns out his family had been on a ship that he and the pirates had attacked. His wife describes how they had seen a figure of a man on a burning ship during this event.

> "The blazing ship came towards us with terrific rapidity. As it approached, the figure of a man was seen on the deck, standing unhurt in the midst of the burning. The Syrian pilot, hitherto the boldest of our crew; at this sight, cast the elm from his hands in despair, and tore his beard, exclaiming that we were undone. To our questions, he would give no other answer than by pointing to the solitary being, who stood calmly in the centre of conflagration, more like a demon than a man.
>
> "I proposed that we should make some effort, to rescue this unfortunate man. But, the pilot, horror-struck at the thought, then gave up the tale, that it cost him agonies, even to utter. He told us, that the being whom our frantic compassion would attempt to save, was an accursed thing; that, for some crime, too inexpiable to allow of his remaining among creatures capable of hope, he was cast out from men, stricken into the nature of the condemned spirits, and sentenced to rove the ocean in fire, ever burning and never consumed!"
>
> I felt every word, as if that fire were devouring my flesh. The sense of what I was, and what I must be, was poison. My head swam; mortal pain overwhelmed me. And this abhorred thing I was; this sentenced and fearful wretch I was, covered with wrath and shame, this exile from human nature, I was; and I heard my sentence pronounced, and my existence declared hideous, by the lips, on which I hung for confidence and consolation against the world.

> Flinging my robe over my face, to hide its writhings, I seemed to listen; but my ears refused to hear. In my perturbation, I once thought of boldly avowing the truth, and thus freeing myself from the pang of perpetual concealment. But, the offence and the retribution were too real and too deadly, to be disclosed, without destroying the last chance of happiness to those innocent sufferers. I mastered the convulsion, and again bent my ear.[38]

The scene is significant in the novel because it makes Salathiel recall the horror of what he has become and how men perceive him because of his curse. It is also an interesting moment because it seems to play off the Flying Dutchman, another Gothic wanderer figure.

The Flying Dutchman's legend dates to the late eighteenth century, and it developed through several references in print from 1790 onward, including the notes to Sir Walter Scott's 1812 poem "Rokeby," in which Scott first equated the ship with a pirate ship. Coleridge had drawn upon the legend in creating the image of the Ancient Mariner, just as he had drawn upon the Wandering Jew legend. In 1821, a story in *Blackwood's Edinburgh Magazine* introduced the name Captain Hendrick Van der Decken for the ship's captain.[39] In 1826, Edmund Fitzball's play *The Flying Dutchman; or the Phantom Ship: a Nautical Drama, in three acts* was first performed. Croly was likely familiar with some of these works and planted the image into the novel. Notably, Victorian novelist Captain Frederick Marryat would later write *The Phantom Ship* in 1839, a truly fine Gothic novel that also draws upon the Flying Dutchman and Wandering Jew themes. Later, Richard Wagner's opera *The Flying Dutchman* (1843) would forever popularize the figure.

As the novel comes to a conclusion, Salathiel is tempted by a minstrel who is really a diviner. The minstrel says if Salathiel pledges himself to him, he will make Salathiel into the prophesied Messiah, the deliverer of his people, able to save them from the Romans. When Salathiel asks what oath he must make, the man whispers the required words (not shared with the reader) and Salathiel draws back in horror.[40] He is unwilling to commit such a crime even to save his people.

Salathiel has a few more adventures before Jerusalem falls to the Romans. Then more horror erupts as nature reacts to Jerusalem's destruction.

> On one night, that fatal night! no man laid his head upon his pillow. Heaven and earth were in conflict. Meteors burned above us; the ground shook under our feet: the volcano blazed: the wind burst forth in irresistible blasts, and swept the living and the dead, in whirlwinds, far into the desert.[41]

Salathiel leads a small group of surviving Jews from the city, but the group soon realizes it is their time to die. They have a vision of a Temple in the clouds and the guardian angels of the city marching into it, as if to say they are abandoning the holy city. Here Croly may be drawing upon stories such as that of the Fall of Constantinople, when it is said that the light that burned in Hagia Sophia was seen ascending into heaven the day before the city fell.[42]

In the morning, Salathiel wakes to find all the Jews are dead but him. Then Epiphany, the immortal he met early on, appears and speaks to him.

> "I told you," said he, with a sudden return to calmness, "that this day would come; and to tell you so, required no spirit of prophecy. There is a time for all things; long-suffering, among the rest; and your countrymen had long ago come to that time. But, one grand hope was still to be given; they cast it from them! Ages on ages shall pass, before they learn the loftiness of that hope, or fulfil the punishment of that rejection. Yet, in the fullness of time, shall the light break in upon their darkness. They shall ask, Why are we the despised, the branded, the trampled, the abjured, of all nations? Why are the barbarian and the

civilised, alike our oppressors? Why do contending faiths join in crushing us alone? Why do realms, distant as the ends of the earth, and diverse as day and night—alike those who have heard our history, and those who have never heard of us, but as the sad sojourners of the earth—unite in one cry of scorn? And what is the universal voice of nature, but the voice of the King of nature?"

I listened in reverence, to language that pierced my heart with an intense power of truth, yet with a pang that made me writhe. I longed, yet dreaded, to hear again the searching and lofty accents of this being of unwilling wisdom. "Man of terrible knowledge," said I, "canst thou tell, for what crime this judgment shall come?"

His mighty brow was stooped in awe, and his features quivered, as he slowly spoke.—"Their crime? There is no name for it. The spirits of Heaven weep, when they think of it. The spirits of the abyss tremble.—Man alone, the man of Judea alone, could commit that horror of horrors."

He paused, and prostrated himself, at the words; then rising, rapidly uttered—"Judge of the crime by its punishment. From the beginning Israel was stubborn, and his stubbornness brought him to sorrow. He rebelled, and he was warned by the captivity of a monarch, or the slaughter of a tribe.—He sinned more deeply, for he was the slave of impurity; then was his kingdom divided; yet a few years saw him powerful once more.—He sinned more deeply still; for he sought the worship of idols. Then came his deeper punishment, in the fall of his throne, and the long captivity of his people. But, even Babylon sent back the forgiven.

"Happy, I say to you, happy will be the hour for Israel—for mankind—for creation, when he shall take into his hand the records of his fathers, and, in tears, ask—What is that greater crime than rebellion? than blasphemy? than impurity? than idolatry? which, not seventy years, nor a thousand years, of sorrow have seen forgiven; which has prolonged his woe into the old age of the world—which threatens him with a chain, not to be broken, but by the thunder-stroke that breaks up the universe!"

"And still," said I, trembling, before the living oracle—"still is there hope?"[43]

Croly does not say it straightforwardly, but the Jews' obvious crime here has been to reject Christ. Still, Epiphany says there is hope. Then he picks up Salathiel and carries him to a battlement from which to observe safely. As Salathiel sees the Temple destroyed by the Romans, he expects his own death will finally come, but again he hears the voice saying, "Tarry thou, till I come!"[44]

The novel concludes with Salathiel telling us:

> Here I pause. I had undergone that portion of my unhappy career, which was to be passed among my people. My life, as father, husband, and citizen was at an end. Thenceforth I was to be a solitary being. The ties of society were to be cut from me. I was to see wondrous things, and do wondrous things; to see, and to share, in the rise and fall of empires; to let loose, and ride on, the torrent of mighty changes; to command those elements of passion and folly which shake the world.—To see all die, and yet to live.
>
> I have still the strangest, and the stateliest, of all histories to tell.[45]

One wishes Salathiel had told more, but given that the novel is nearly 500 pages, and that Croly is long-winded in telling the story and he fails to develop any of the characters except Salathiel, we can be grateful he did not write sequels. That said, this passage is quoted from the 1855 edition published by Henry Colburn's successors. The 1901 edition published by Funk & Wagnalls has a more detailed conclusion that elaborates upon Salathiel's further adventures:

> Here I pause. I had undergone that portion of my unhappy career which was to be passed among my people. My life as father, husband, and citizen was at an end. Thenceforth I was to be a solitary being.
>
> My fate had yet scarcely fallen upon me, but I was now to feel it in the disruption of every gentler tie that held me to life. I was to make my couch with the savage, the outcast, and the slave. I was to see the ruin of the mighty and the overthrow of empires. Yet in the tumult that changed the face of the world, I was still to live and be unchanged. Every sterner passion that disturbs our nature was to reign in successive tyranny over my soul. And fearfully was the decree fulfilled.
>
> In revenge for the fall of Jerusalem, I traversed the globe to seek out an enemy of Rome. I found in the northern snows a man of blood; I stirred up the soul of Alaric and led him to the rock of Rome. In revenge for the insults heaped on the Jew by the dotards and dastards of the city of Constantine, I sought out an instrument of compendious ruin: I found him in the Arabian sands, and poured ambition into the soul of the enthusiast of Mecca. In revenge for the pollution of the ruins of the Temple, I roused the iron tribes of the West, and at the head of the crusaders expelled the Saracens. I fed full on the revenge, and I felt the misery of revenge!
>
> A passion for the mysteries of nature seized me. I toiled with the alchemist; I wore away years in perplexities of the schoolmen; and I felt the guilt and emptiness of unlawful knowledge.
>
> A passion for human fame seized me. I drew my sword in the Italian wars—triumphed—was a monarch—and learned to curse the hour when I first dreamed of fame!

A passion for gold seized me. I felt the gnawing of avarice—the last infirmity of the fallen mind. Wealth came, to my wish and to my torment. In the midst of royal treasures I was poorer than the poorest. Days and nights of misery were the gift of avarice. I felt within me the undying worm. In my passion I longed for regions where the hand of man had never rifled the mine. I found a bold Genoese, and led him to the discovery of a new world. With its metals I inundated the old, and to my own misery added the misery of two hemispheres!

But the circle of the passions, a circle of fire, was not to surround my fated steps forever. Calmer and nobler aspirations were to rise in my melancholy heart. I saw the birth of true science, true liberty, and true wisdom. I lived with Petrarch, among his glorious relics of the genius of Greece and Rome. I stood enraptured beside the easel of Angelo and Raphael. I conversed with the merchant kings of the Mediterranean. I stood at Mentz beside the wonder-working machine that makes knowledge imperishable and sends it with winged speed through the earth. At the pulpit of the mighty man of Wittenberg I knelt; Israelite as I was, and am, I did voluntary homage to the mind of Luther!

But I must close these thoughts, as wandering as the steps of my pilgrimage. I have more to tell—strange, magnificent, and sad.

But I must wait the impulse of my heart. Or, can the happy and the high-born, treading upon roses, have an ear for the story of the Exile, whose path has for a thousand years been in the brier and the thorn![46]

I have been unable to consult the original 1828 publication so I do not know if Croly or one of his editors cut down the novel's final paragraphs for the 1855 edition or if Croly expanded the conclusion for a later edition. Certainly, a scholarly edition of the novel is desperately needed to resolve such discrepancies in the text.

The novel has its shortcomings, but regardless, it seems remarkable that Croly was able to create such a historical novel and bring the events, if not the people, of first century Judah to life. For the most part, the novel is historically accurate, other than one lapse where a character claims to have served with Mark Antony,[47] which would have been impossible given that the novel takes place circa 70 AD and Antony died in 30 BC, which would make the warrior who served under him well over 100 if he had been even a teenager when Antony died.

Although all but forgotten today, *Salathiel* was quite popular in its day as its reprintings testify. As historical fiction, it is in many ways the equal of Scott's novels. Furthermore, it may be the first novel to depict the biblical era, which probably accounts for a large part of the charm it held for a contemporary audience. Still, the supernatural image of the Wandering Jew was the novel's primary attraction. Critic Albert Power succinctly sums up the novel's faults and strengths:

> *Salathiel* can claim no great favour on the bare head *alone* of its blown bloody recitals of the conflict between Israel and Rome in the decades after the crucifixion of Christ. In Croly's tempestuous three-tome text there is much abundance of such stuff, a tendency to pile incident on incident in a manner that motors story but shores up a buttress against the higher originality which points at genius. Yet that is not all that is to it: for there resides in this novel narrative power of great strength and depth, and a scope for out-of-the-body visions both vast-reaching and sublime, the whole tinctured with a recurrent *motif* of the dark theme which is as choice wine to throats choked by butter-bland dullness in fiction.[48]

I would agree wholeheartedly with this assessment. As a historical novel, *Salathiel* is not a monumental work, although obviously influenced by Sir Walter Scott and deserving recognition for trying to capture a place and time far removed from Scott's much more recent historical settings. But its history pales beside the supernatural theme of the Wandering Jew, and while it is the first novel wholly devoted to that figure, one can only wish Croly had done more to focus on the Wandering Jew's curse and immortality and less on the details of Jewish history. Today, it is difficult for modern readers to understand the fascination Sir Walter Scott's novels held for his contemporary readers since their pacing is much slower than the action-packed and far less descriptive works of today, and the same can be said of *Salathiel*, but the patient reader will find much to admire about it. It also holds up favorably beside the works of Croly's contemporaries.

Salathiel is often compared to *Melmoth the Wanderer* (1820) by Croly's fellow Irish Anglican clergyman, Charles Maturin.* The comparison is based on both works containing an immortal protagonist. While most critics have favored *Melmoth the Wanderer* over *Salathiel*, due to the difficulty of acquiring these texts until recent decades, I suspect many critics have not read both works but relied on others' judgments. While *Melmoth the Wanderer* succeeds in being more Gothic than *Salathiel*, it also has its fair share of tedium. I would agree with Powers' assessment:

> Though penned a mere eight years after *Melmoth the Wanderer*, and to some extent treating of a similar theme, *Salathiel* shews none of the weighty doom-laden turgesence [sic], the frenzied rhapsodic excoriations, which are the pride of Charles Robert Maturin's tormented creation, but for readers of flagging vigour at once their challenge and their chastisement.[49]

---

* I have discussed *Melmoth the Wanderer* at length in *The Gothic Wanderer*, particularly in Chapters II-IV. Therefore, I have not discussed *Melmoth's* influence on French literature here, but it is worth noting that Balzac wrote a sequel titled *Melmoth Reconciled*. For more on *Melmoth the Wanderer's* influence on French literature, see *European Gothic* edited by Avril Horner, which contains several essays on the topic.

Furthermore, George K. Anderson, in his exhaustive study *The Legend of the Wandering Jew*, compares *Salathiel* to *Melmoth the Wanderer*, stating that the latter is "Less successful than *Salathiel*, as a piece of literature" and noting that the resemblances between Melmoth and Ahasuerus are not many and that other nineteenth-century novels also tried to combine the legends of Faust and the Wandering Jew and "seldom very attractively."[50]

In recent years, *Salathiel* has gained new interest because it has been proposed as a possible source for *Dracula*. The suggestion, put forth by Paul Murray in his biography *From the Shadow of Dracula: A Life of Bram Stoker*,[51] is based on a passage in Stoker's book *Famous Impostors* (1910), in which he discusses the Wandering Jew and remarks that his father knew George Croly. Stoker states:

> A century and a half later—1828—was published a much more pretentious work on the same theme. This was a novel written by Rev. George Croly. It was called: "Salathiel: a Story of the Past, the Present, the Future." It was published anonymously and had an immediate and lasting success. It was founded on historical lines, the author manifestly benefiting by the hints afforded by the work of that consummate liar (in a historical sense) Westphalus—or his informant. Croly was a strange man with a somewhat abnormal faculty of abstraction. I used to hear of him from my father who was a friend of his about a hundred years ago. Being of gentle nature he did not wish to cause any pain or concern to his family or dependents; but at the same time he, as a writer, had to guard himself against interruption and consequent digression of his thoughts during the times he set apart for imaginative work. So he devised a scheme which might often be put in practice with advantage by others similarly employed. When settling down to a spell of such work—which as every creative writer knows involves periods of mental abstraction though of bodily restlessness—he would stick

an adhesive wafer on his forehead. The rule of the house was that when he might be adorned in this wise no one was to speak to him, or even notice him, except under special necessity. The great vogue of Salathiel lasted some ten or more years, when the torch of the Wandering Jew was lighted by Eugène Sue the French novelist who had just completed in the Debats his story "Les Mysteres de Paris." As its successor he chose the theme adopted by Croly, and the new novel Le Juif—Errant ran with overwhelming success in the Constitutionnel.[52]

We will look at Stoker's further remarks on Sue's novel later in this chapter. Stoker's anecdote about Croly is interesting, especially in relation to the wafer on the forehead—one can't help thinking of the Wandering Jew's cross on his forehead, itself a version of the mark of Cain. It is almost as if Croly felt the curse was upon him when he was compelled to write—a feeling many a writer can relate to. Stoker makes no statement here that Croly's novel influenced him, yet the anecdote will recall to readers of *Dracula* the wafer Professor Van Helsing applies to Mina's forehead that leaves a burn mark, another version of the mark of Cain. The scene in *Dracula* begins with Van Helsing speaking:

> "Then it is well. Now, Madam Mina, you are in any case quite safe here until the sunset. And before then we shall return…if…We shall return! But before we go let me see you armed against personal attack. I have myself, since you came down, prepared your chamber by the placing of things of which we know, so that He may not enter. Now let me guard yourself. On your forehead I touch this piece of Sacred Wafer in the name of the Father, the Son, and…"
>
> There was a fearful scream which almost froze our hearts to hear. As he had placed the Wafer on Mina's forehead, it had seared it…had burned into the flesh as though it had been a piece of whitehot metal. My poor

darling's brain had told her the significance of the fact as quickly as her nerves received the pain of it, and the two so overwhelmed her that her overwrought nature had its voice in that dreadful scream. But the words to her thought came quickly. The echo of the scream had not ceased to ring on the air when there came the reaction, and she sank on her knees on the floor in an agony of abasement. Pulling her beautiful hair over her face, as the leper of old his mantle, she wailed out:—

"Unclean! Unclean! Even the Almighty shuns my polluted flesh! I must bear this mark of shame upon my forehead until the Judgement Day."[53]

Coincidence or influence? Since *Dracula* is the first vampire novel in which the Eucharistic host is used to ward off a vampire, I think Croly's influence here is plausible, even if Stoker does not admit to any influence.

Power, in assessing Murray's suggestion of *Salathiel*'s influence on *Dracula*, contends:

In the absence of evidence of textual linkage or vouched accreditation, such possibility must rest in speculation. But it is a fascinating hypothesis even so, and arguably not implausible. Both novels have a principal character whose sole and unusual name, in three syllables, the stress falling on the first, forms the title of the book; in each the character is doomed to unwanted immortality by reason of great sin; each is a doughty warrior of unchallengeable valour; each is denied the luxury of rest in the tomb—though the tomb is where Dracula spends, and Salathiel is afeared that he *will* spend, much time.[54]

Stoker's statement that *Salathiel* had a "lasting success" reflects that the novel remained popular throughout the nineteenth century, and if Stoker did not claim to be influenced by it, another major author of the late nineteenth century was willing to acknowledge *Salathiel*'s influence on his work.

In the 1901 edition of *Salathiel*, an "introductory Letter" was included by the publisher from Lew Wallace, the author of *Ben-Hur: A Tale of the Christ* (1880), the most popular novel published in The United States since *Uncle Tom's Cabin* (1852). *Ben-Hur*'s bestseller status would not be surpassed until the publication of *Gone With the Wind* in 1936.[55] The 1901 publisher included the introductory letter because of Wallace's status and his testimony to the influence *Salathiel* had upon *Ben-Hur*. As Power notes, the result is that *Salathiel* has been relegated ever since to the status of "an ur-text to Wallace's more famous, though not necessarily better novel."[56] Certainly, no work of literary genius deserves to be remembered solely for its influence, but that influence is also in itself a testament to *Salathiel*'s mesmeric power for the readers of its time. Because of its interest, I have quoted the letter in full.

INTRODUCTORY LETTER
**From General Lewis Wallace
(Author of "Ben Hur")**

CRAWFORDSVILLE, IND., *September 1, 1900.*

GENTLEMEN: I have learned that you have in mind the issuance of a new edition of Croly's story of "The Wandering Jew." Perhaps you will lend a willing ear to a suggestion or two, so much is the book in my love.

In my judgment, the six greatest English novels are "Ivanhoe," "The Last of the Barons," "The Tale of Two Cities," "Jane Eyre," "Hypatia," and this romance of Croly's. If Shakespeare had never been born; if Milton, Byron, and Tennyson were singers to be, and Bacon, Darwin, and Ruskin unknown; if there had been no British dramatists, no British historians, no works in British libraries significant of British science and philosophy, no alcoves glutted with bookish remains of British moralists and preachers, still the six works named would of themselves suffice to constitute a British literature.

This is bold, I know: bold in assertion, and even bolder in the lift of Croly's story from the ground to a place in the upper sky. Can I justify the classification? Certainly, if only your patience and my time permitted.

Here, to begin, is a broad adverse generality,—the very worst of possible arguments against the book is, that of the five great classics with which I have thrust it into association, it is the least known to-day by the general public. Yet the admission is not in the least decisive of merits; in inquisitorial phrase it serves merely to put objections to question.

It is a religious novel, says one, sneering. That used to be urged against the "Pilgrim's Progress"; yet the Pilgrim goes marching on, and I fancy his progress will stop only when the world stops. And how is it that of late years, at least, several novels religious in tone and spirit have been more than well received? Indeed, is it not a fact that some of them have attained extraordinary popularity, thus gainsaying the narrow Puritanism which less than a century ago put the novel under ban, regardless of kind and excellence?

Another objection. The style is somewhat too exalted; and then the critic makes haste to stretch the alleged defect to the author's want of art. Now, I would not like to be dogmatic or unkind, but such points certainly disclose a lamentable comprehension. Why, coiled up in that objection lie the very excellencies of the book. How, pray, could exaltation be avoided? Who does not know that in description the sublime always imposes its own laws? Imagine, if you can, the commonplace used by a narrator struggling to convey an idea of the tremendous in a hurricane at sea.

And as to a want of art, I would like to say mildly that the absence of art in the book is its main charm. Any, the slightest show of premeditation or design would have been gross treason to nature. Does a woman, struck to the heart, utter her grief by measure as a singer sings or a poet writes? And how is it with a man in rage or pain? Yet, verily, there was never a woman or a man in speech so impelled by a sting of soul as Salathiel.

Passing, now, the matter of criticism and mere negative dealing, I choose to be affirmative. Salathiel, the subject of the book, was a Jew, and in rank a Prince of the Tribe of Naphtali. In the persecution of Christ, his arrest, his trial, his scourging, Salathiel was the leading insatiate; and such, doubtless, he would have continued down to the last minute of the third hour of the Crucifixion but that the victim stopped him. At what stage of the awful crime the stoppage took place, the author leaves to inference; but how the incident befell and its almost inconceivable effect upon Salathiel, no man should again try to describe. This is from Croly, his words:

"But in the moment of exultation I was stricken. He who had refused an hour of life to the victim was, in terrible retribution, condemned to know the misery of life interminable. I heard through all the voices of Jerusalem—I should have heard through all the thunders of heaven—the calm, low voice, 'Tarry thou till I come!'"

Such the retribution; now the effect.

"I felt my fate at once! I sprang away through the shouting hosts as if the avenging angel waved his sword above my head. Wild songs, furious execrations, the uproar of myriads stirred to the heights of passion, filled the air; still, through all, I heard the pursuing sentence, 'Tarry thou till I come,' and felt it to be the sentence of incurable agony! I was never to know the shelter of the grave!"

And then follow five paragraphs, each beginning with the same words uttered, as I imagine, in the tone of a shriek of anguish, "Immortality on earth!" And of those paragraphs, regarded as a dissection of the moral part of a man by virtue of which he is susceptible of infinite happiness or infinite misery, I say that for completeness and eloquence they are without parallel in the language. Nor is that all. In those paragraphs, one reading will find the definition of a punishment which in subtlety, in torture, and in duration is as far out of range of human origin as in execution it is out of range of human power. Yet more. Instantly with the comprehension of the punishment defined, the immeasurable difference between the agonies of death on a cross, though of days in duration, and the agonies of immortal life under curse on earth, becomes discernible. In that difference there is a divine thought in anger, an avenging impulse. The superiority in misery of the punishment of Salathiel, its term of sentence, its depth of suffering, its superhuman passion of vengeance, seem impossible to the all-patient Christ; and while we are considering its possibility, the book carries us to the question, Is there a wandering Jew?

I think so. Let smile now who will; yet, as I see, a whole race is the multiple of the man, just as the man is the incarnation of the race. Israel, the plural, merges in Salathiel, the singular, insomuch that to think of the one is to think of the other. In this instance, also, the similitudes become creative, and life, nature, history, and doom, sinking the race, make room for the wandering Jew.

Not only do I think there is a wandering Jew, but I know him intimately. To Croly he was a young man, a warrior; to me, he came an old man, a philosopher. Croly beheld him irate, passionate, vengeful. I saw him wiser by many hundreds of years, and repentant, and trying vainly to bring about a brotherhood of man by preaching the unity of God. With Croly, he was the Prince of Naphtali; with me, he was the Prince of India.

Returning now—with such a subject, dealt with so magnificently, I can not see how the great reading public in America can be indifferent to a new edition of Croly's romance. Only take us into your faith, gentlemen, and see to it that the issue be worthy the theme. Be even luxurious with it; give it fine paper, wide margins, large type, and choice binding; and, if Gustave Doré were living, I would further beg you to have the edition illustrated by him.

Very respectfully,

Lewis Wallace

The publishers took Wallace's advice and had their edition illustrated, as they state in the "Publisher's Note." Also notable is that Wallace's list of greatest novels are all historical fiction, save for *Jane Eyre*, and Charles Kingsley's *Hypatia* is also set in ancient times. Furthermore, while the publishers choose to list Wallace as the author of *Ben-Hur*, and this letter has resulted in *Salathiel* being seen as an influence on that famous novel, Wallace himself references his own novel *The Prince of India* (1893), which was about the Wandering Jew during the Fall of Constantinople. Obviously, *Salathiel* influenced both works. *Ben-Hur*, like *Salathiel*, is set in biblical times and also explores an encounter by its main character with Christ. However, *The Prince of India* is specifically about the Wandering Jew, and while *Salathiel* depicts the Fall of Jerusalem, Wallace's novel depicts the Fall of Constantinople. George K. Anderson, in his survey of the Wandering Jew, calls *The Prince of India* a "worthy representative of what we may call the Croly tradition or the Destruction-of-Jerusalem motif." Today, *The Prince of India* is just as forgotten as *Salathiel*. In truth, the Wandering Jew figure is itself forgotten and none of the novels discussed in this chapter are any longer read except by Gothic scholars and enthusiasts. That said, Wallace's novel is a significant treatment of the Wandering Jew and the last major one in the nineteenth century, unless one counts *Dracula*, which draws upon the Wandering Jew figure, as we will explore in Chapter 7.

In my book *The Gothic Wanderer*, I dismissed *Salathiel* and *The Prince of India* as of little interest to students of the Gothic because they treated the Wandering Jew theme more as history than Gothic literature. At the time, it had been a decade since I had read *The Prince of India* and while I had enjoyed it, I scarcely remembered it, plus I was writing about the British Gothic tradition and it was by an American author. As for *Salathiel*, I could not gain access to a copy of it in the days before online bookstores and ebooks made so many forgotten and obscure texts accessible, so hopefully I have righted that wrong in this book. While *Salathiel* may pale beside some of the successive Wandering Jew novels we will explore, it set the stage for all later tales of the Wandering Jew and deserves more attention than it has received. *The Prince of India* is also a remarkable novel in many ways, but given that it is an American work and did not appear until 1893, I will omit further discussion of it since our focus is on the mutual influence of French and British Gothic texts.

Edgar Quinet's *Ahasvérus*

Before *Salathiel* was even published, in France, Edgar Quinet (1803-1875) was busy creating his own version of The Wandering Jew legend. In fact, the legend was well known in France long before Matthew Lewis and his British successors wrote their versions of the story, so their influence is not completely singular. French ballads and other works about the legend had been produced since the early seventeenth century, but the French Romanticists were the ones who popularized the legend in the early nineteenth century in theatrical melodramas.[57]

Then Quinet, a French historian, intellectual, and author, produced the first full-length prose works on the subject. Quinet's interest in the Wandering Jew, however, was not as a means to create Gothic fiction but to explore larger questions about history and humanity's place within it. In 1823, five years before *Salathiel* was published, Quinet published his first book, *Tablettes du juif errant* (*Tablets of the Wandering Jew*), which symbolized the progress of humanity.[58] He would then expand on that theme to create *Ahasvérus* (1834), a long prose poem about the Wandering Jew.

Ahasvérus is unlike any other fictional treatments of the Wandering Jew. While it is unlikely Quinet read Croly's book and was influenced by it, Quinet's book would influence Eugène Sue's *The Wandering Jew*, which would be the most popular nineteenth-century treatment of the figure, so it is worth discussing here. Notably, *Ahasvérus* was not translated into English until 2013 as *Ahasuerus* by Brian Stableford. Therefore, it is not probable it influenced treatments of the Wandering Jew in English such as Lew Wallace's *The Prince of India* or influenced Bram Stoker who, consciously or not, drew on elements of the Wandering Jew in the creation of *Dracula*.

Ahasvérus is written in a play format with each speaker's name presented before their speech. While the Wandering Jew, named Ahasuerus, is the main character, he is only on stage for a few extended scenes. The rest of the play is filled with various other creatures or objects that speak, including angels, the Ocean, ancient cities, and historical and fictional people. The closest comparable work in English is Percy Bysshe Shelley's *Prometheus Unbound* (1820), although *Ahasvérus*' visionary style also reminds one of William Blake's poetry. In French, the work closest to it may be Jean-Baptiste Cousin de Grainville's 1805 novel *Le Dernier Homme* (*The Last Man*), which depicts the end of humanity and the world. That work, though a prose poem, was really the rough draft for an epic poem Cousin de Grainville intended to write, but he died before completing it.* Frankly,

---

* For more on *Le Dernier Homme*, visit my blog: https://thegothicwanderer. wordpress.com/2017/05/16/the-last-man-cousin-de-grainvilles-dernier-le-homme-and-mary-shelley/

while Quinet's treatment of the Wandering Jew is interesting, the other characters' speeches, while poetical, tend to be boring and do little to advance the story. When the Wandering Jew is not in a scene, the reader quickly loses interest.

Ahasvérus does not cover just the Wandering Jew's life, but the entire history of the world from creation to the Last Judgment. It begins with God destroying the old world, which has lasted 3,500 years, and then creating a new one. Then it passes through history to arrive, a quarter of the way through the work, at Ahasuerus being cursed by Christ to wander. When the scene opens, Ahasuerus has gone outside of his family's house—he is the oldest son in the family and is not married—to watch Christ pass by on his way to Golgotha. I will quote the scene to provide an example of Quinet's style.

> AHASUERUS
>
> As he [Christ] comes closer, his aureole shines more brightly than that of a prophet elect; that's another one of his magic spells.
>
> CHRIST
>
> Is that you, Ahasuerus?
>
> AHASUERUS
>
> I don't know you.
>
> CHRIST
>
> I'm thirsty; give me a little water from your well.
>
> AHASUERUS
>
> My well is empty.
>
> CHRIST
>
> Take your cup to it; you'll find it full.
>
> AHASUERUS
>
> It's broken.
>
> CHRIST
>
> Help me to carry my cross along this hard road.

AHASUERUS

I'm not your cross-bearer; summon a gryphon from the desert.

CHRIST

Let me sit down on your bench at the door of your house.

AHASUERUS

My bench is full; there's no room for anyone.

CHRIST

On your threshold, then?

AHASUERUS

It's empty, and the door is bolted shut.

CHRIST

Touch it with your finger, and you'll be able to go in to fetch a stool.

AHASUERUS

Be on your way.

CHRIST

If you wanted, your bench might become a golden stool at the door of my father's house.

AHASUERUS

Go wherever you wish, blasphemer. You're already withering my vine and my fig-tree. Don't lean on the rail of my stairway; it would crumble on hearing you speak. You want to bewitch me.

CHRIST

I wanted to save you.

AHASUERUS

Get out of my shadow, fortune-teller. Your road is before you. Walk on, walk on.

CHRIST

Why do you say that, Ahasuerus? It's you who will walk, until the last judgment, for more than a thousand years. Go get your sandals and your traveling clothes. Everywhere you pass, people will call you the Wandering Jew. It's you who will find neither a seat on which to sit down nor a mountain spring to slake your thirst. In my stead, you will bear the burden that I shall quit upon the cross. For your thirst, you will drink what I leave in the bottom of my chalice. Others will take my tunic; you will inherit my eternal dolor. Hyssop will sprout on your traveler's staff, absinthe will grow in your water-skin; despair will squeeze your loins in your leather belt. You will be the man who never dies. Your age will be mine. To see you pass, the eagles will perch on the edge of the aerie. The little birds will hide under the crests of rocks. The stars will lean over on their clouds to hear your tears fall, one drop at a time, into the abyss.

I am going to Golgotha; you will walk from one ruin to the next, one kingdom to the next, without ever attaining your Calvary. You will break your stairway under your feet, and you will no longer be able to come back down. The gates of cities will say to you: "Go further, my bench is worn out;" and the river where you want to sit down will say: "Go further, go further on, all the way to the sea; my bank is my own and full of brambles;" and the sea too will say: "Go further, go further on, are you not the eternal voyager who goes from one people to the next, century after century, drinking his tears from his cup, who does not sleep by day or by night, neither on silk nor on stone, and who cannot go back along the path he has followed?"

The gryphons will sit down, the sphinxes will sleep, but you will have neither seat not [sic] slumber. It is you who will go to ask for me in one temple after another, without ever encountering me. It's you who will cry: "Where is he?" until the dead show you the way to the last judgment. When you see me again, my eyes will be ablaze; my finger with rise up beneath my robe to summon you to the valley of Jehosophat.

Christ now continues on, as does the crowd. Ahasuerus tries to reenter his home, but Saint Michael appears to tell him he cannot live there any longer. Michael allows Ahasuerus to say goodbye to his family and then his wanderings begin.[59] Feeling his punishment unfair, Ahasuerus asks, "Is there not another God somewhere better than the God of Judea?"[60] This is just the beginning of the book's continual questioning of whether God is truly fair.

As the story continues, we meet Rachel, an angel who was thrown out of heaven for feeling pity for Ahasuerus. Once on earth, she forgets her former angelic status. Eventually, she meets Ahasuerus and they fall in love. When another character asks Rachel about her lover, fearing he's a heretic who doesn't go to church, Rachel says he sobs when he sees a crucifix. Rachel is warned that he may be a prince just wanting to use her as his plaything.[61] Rachel, however, loves Ahasuerus and in time agrees to marry him, though she has a temporary recall of memory where she seems to remember who he is and calls him a deceiver and a demon of hell pretending to be something else. Despite this outburst, she goes through with the marriage.

Rachel and Ahasuerus are married by Pope Gregory in a cathedral, but during the ceremony, Ahasuerus is unable to reveal his name. Then an image of Christ in a stained-glass window speaks, revealing Ahasuerus' identity.[62]

Once married, Ahasuerus tells Rachel that no one believes in Christ or God any longer, but she continues to pray for him. Other characters talk about how God is dead. Throughout all the couple's wanderings, we are given a sense of time passing, with references to historical people and events such as King Arthur, Charlemagne, and the French Revolution.

As the story draws to an end, all the dead assemble in the Valley of Jehosophat to be judged by God. Those to be judged include cities like Rome, the People of the Middle Ages, the Arabs, and kings. Finally, when everyone and everything else has been judged, Ahasuerus' turn comes. God is then surprisingly merciful to him. While God plans to destroy the current world, he chooses to allow Ahasuerus to live, not as a punishment but to become the "second Adam" for his new world. God then decides it's time to retire, so Ahasuerus will lead humanity in a new world without God. God explains to Christ:

> Ahasuerus is the eternal man. All the others resemble him. Your judgment of him will serve for them all. Now, our work is finished, and the mystery also. Our city is closed. Tomorrow, we shall create other worlds. Until that time, let's both go and rest under a tree in our forest, in our eternity.[63]

However, it is not to be; in the Epilogue, Eternity arrives and burns Christ and God in their sepulcher, then swallows up the earth, extinguishing everything.

In truth, *Ahasvérus* is a very strange work. The most interesting aspect of it, other than the treatment of the Wandering Jew, is its criticism of God. And yet it ends with a medieval statement, "Here ends the mystery of Ahasuerus. Pray for the man who wrote it." This need for the author's own redemption or forgiveness of sins flies in the face of the idea that God is unfair or unjust and that redemption is not needed, at least not from a God who may not exist.

The poem has been hailed as a work of genius by some critics while others have found it odd, challenging, and heretical. Brian Stableford, in his introduction to the English translation, finds it surprising the work was not translated into English previously, but if it had been at the time, it might have risked prosecution under English law on a charge of blasphemous libel like Shelley's *Prometheus Unbound*. Its overall purpose was less to tell a story than to present ideas about history. The characters are undeveloped and merely personifications of ideas or talking heads allowed to express their ideas without any real storyline.

Ultimately, what is most significant about *Ahasvérus* is its treatment of religion and God and their role in history. While Croly's version of the Wandering Jew seems to support Christian belief since Christ is real in the storyline and the Jews are clearly punished for rejecting him, Quinet also uses the Wandering Jew to reflect God's injustice by meting out a punishment more extreme than the Jew's crime deserves. Quinet was not wholly antireligious; he believed Christianity and religion in general were part of the story of human progress, but he also saw their flaws. Stableford sums up this situation well in his introduction while placing the book in the context of its time period:

> Although he was not unsympathetic to the historical role played by religions, which he considered to be vitally important to social evolution, Quinet's hostility to certain aspects of Catholic faith won him even more enemies than his political radicalism; *Ahasvérus* can easily be read as an atheistic and explicitly anti-Christian work, although that is probably not the right way to read it, and the apologetic ambiguity with which it is carefully dressed is genuinely representative of a theological uncertainty on Quinet's part. Anyone inclined to suspect the work of anti-Christian inclinations would not, however, have been reassured by the author's subsequent exploits as a polemicist, and there must have been a temptation to tar him with the same brush as Alphonse de Lamartine and Victor Hugo, both of whom eventually took skepticism to the extreme of producing literary works explicitly sympathetic to Satan's rebellion against divine authority, in *La Chute d'un ange* [*The Fall of an Angel*] (1838) and *La Fin de Satan* [*The End of Satan*] (incomplete; written 1854-62; published 1886) respectively.

Indeed, even before Darwin's theories of evolution led many to a crisis of faith, the nineteenth century was a time of increasing skepticism, atheism, and criticism of religion, continuing, in this respect, the work of the French Revolution. Ultimately, *Ahasvérus'* greatest value was in furthering such questioning of religion.

While Eugène Sue was influenced by *Ahasvérus*, one of Quinet's later books would be even more inspirational for him. In 1842, Quinet published *Génie des religion* (*The Genius of Religions*), in which he showed sympathy to all religions without supporting one over the others. That same year, he became the Chair of Southern Literature at the Collège de France, but neglecting his proper subject of study at the university, with his friend Jules Michelet, he embarked on a violent polemic with the Jesuits in a series of lectures. The lectures were incorporated into *Des Jésuites* (1843), co-signed with Michelet. When Quinet refused to return to his proper subject, the government put an end to his lectures and he was dismissed from the college for, among other reasons, his attacks on the Roman Catholic Church and his belief that religion is a determining force in societies.[64]

Quinet's lectures against the Jesuits would inspire Sue in writing *The Wandering Jew*. Like Quinet's Ahasuerus, Sue's Wandering Jew is largely symbolic, and Sue also took up the thesis of Quinet and Michelet's *Des Jésuites* to make the Jesuits the villains of his novel.[65] Stableford sums up *Ahasvérus'* influence by stating:

> Although neither Sue nor Dumas copies anything directly from Quinet's particular version of the legend, there can be little doubt that both writers had its symbolism and its radicalism in mind in planning their own alternative versions. The third member of the great triumvirate of mid-century feuilletonists,* Paul Féval, added his own version to the canon in *La Fille du juif errant* (1864), and although he did not copy anything directly from Quinet either, he too was aware of his work—he was later to pen

---

* Feuilletons were parts of newspapers—supplements—devoted to literature, literary criticism, art, gossip, and other non-political news. They typically contained serialized novels. Feuilletonists were the writers of novels serialized in the feuilleton section of a newspaper.

a fervent rebuttal of Quinet and Michelet's *Des Jésuites* — and probably intended his own repentant version of the accursed wanderer partly as an ideological reply to Quinet.[66]

So, while *Ahasvérus* has been all but forgotten today, Quinet did plant some seeds for future depictions of the Wandering Jew and he also furthered discussion about religion's role in history. Those seeds continue to flourish today through other authors' works. While *Ahasvérus* is my least favorite work depicting the Wandering Jew, George K. Anderson called it "Probably the masterpiece of French literature dealing with the Wandering Jew — certainly of all the writings about him in the first half of the nineteenth century."[67] High praise indeed.

Eugène Sue's *The Wandering Jew*

Of all the nineteenth-century works about the Wandering Jew, Eugène Sue's mammoth novel is recognized by most critics as the finest and it certainly was the most popular in its day. *Le Juif errant* (*The Wandering Jew*) was serially published in the *Constitutionnel* in 1844-5, reputedly increasing the paper's circulation from somewhere between 3,600 and 6,000 subscribers to 20,000 or 25,000.* It was then published in book form in 1845 as eleven volumes. It was also translated and published in British journals as each installment appeared and then published in book form throughout Europe in 1845.[68] Most editions of the novel run 1,400-1,500 pages. Considering the novel's incredible length, the plot is relatively simple compared to other long novels of the period, notably the city mysteries novels.

Despite the novel's title, the Wandering Jew's role is minimal in the work, which is one reason George K. Anderson complains that it does the legend a "disservice" because it makes the title misleading.[69] That is an odd charge from Anderson considering

---
* Two sources, Berry Palmer and Brian Stableford, provide different circulation numbers, which accounts for the wide range here.

the same could be said of *Ahasvérus*, which Anderson considers a masterpiece. Anderson also notes that in an unpublished review of the novel, Edgar Allan Poe shared those feelings, remarking that the novel's essential weakness was that Sue did not use the Wandering Jew to further the plot.[70] Regardless, the novel was enormously popular and a true page-turner.

The story opens with the Wandering Jew and a woman crying out to each other across the Bering Strait because they cannot cross it to be together. The woman is the biblical Hérodiade (Herodias), responsible for encouraging her daughter Salome to ask for John the Baptist's head. Numerous critics, including George K. Anderson, have repeatedly and incorrectly stated she is the Wandering Jew's sister, but the novel makes it clear the two characters are not related. The Wandering Jew's name is not given, but he is described as an artisan and cursed to wander the earth for how he mistreated Christ. He does not bear an actual cross on his forehead, but we are told "his eyebrows, uniting in the midst, extended from one temple to the other, like a fatal mark on his forehead."[71] Furthermore, "the seven nails in the sole of the man's shoe form a cross."[72] This focus on his shoes reflects the Wandering Jew's traditional role as a shoemaker, and by extension, for Sue's purposes, a poor member of the working class. His crime of refusing Christ a place to rest is justified by his poverty, as he tells Herodias in recounting his story:

> "Oh, cursed, cursed be the day, when, as I bent over my work, sullen with hate and despair, because, in spite of my incessant labor, I and mine wanted for everything, the Saviour passed before my door.
>
> "Reviled, insulted, covered with blows, hardly able to sustain the weight of his heavy cross, He asked me to let Him rest a moment on my stone bench. The sweat poured from His forehead, His feet were bleeding, He was well-nigh sinking with fatigue, and He said to me, in a mild, heart piercing voice: 'I suffer!' 'And I too suffer,' I replied, as with harsh anger I pushed Him from the place; 'I suffer,

and no one comes to help me! I find no pity, and will give none. Go on! go on!' Then, with a deep sigh of pain, He answered, and spake this sentence: 'Verily, thou shalt go on till the day of thy redemption, for so wills the Father which art in heaven!'[73]

The reader may miss this point, but here Sue equates the Jew with the working class to show his sympathy for the poor in the novel, a theme he also presented in *The Mysteries of Paris* and which permeates *The Wandering Jew*, culminating in the final scene when the Jew suggests the redemption of the working class will soon come.

Herodias is also forced to wander the earth and referred to as a "Wandering Jewess."[74] The Wandering Jew is committed to looking after the descendants of his sister, and Herodias is aiding him in that work. Despite their close connection of both being cursed with an extended life, they are only allowed to meet occasionally, hence their despair in the opening scene when the Bering Strait prevents their being together at such an appointed time.

To complicate matters, the Wandering Jew spreads cholera wherever he journeys. Not until 1854 would it be understood that cholera was spread through fecal contamination.[75] Consequently, when cholera hit Paris in 1832, the year the novel is set, its origins were mysterious, thereby allowing Sue to imagine it resulting from the Wandering Jew's entering the city. The historical outbreak began in March and extended through September, killing 18,000 people in Paris, including the prime minister, Casimir Périer, and the former Napoleonic hero, General Maximilien Lamarque, whose funeral procession on June 5 set off the rebellion planned by Republican secret societies as Victor Hugo depicts in *Les Misérables*.[76] *The Wandering Jew* ends on June 1, just days before the rebellion.

The novel's plot centers on the Rennepont family, the last descendants of the Wandering Jew's sister. Marius de Rennepont was a Huguenot persecuted under Louis XIV by the Jesuits in

1682. He was a man of great wealth with several family members whose descendants he chooses for his eventual heirs. He had bronze medals made that he distributed to his family members. The medals remind their descendants to meet on February 13, 1832 in Paris at his house at rue Saint-François No. 3. Marius then leaves his small fortune of 150,000 francs in the hands of a Jewish banker, and that fortune eventually grows under the supervision of the banker's son and grandson to 212,175,000 francs by the year 1832.

The novel opens as the meeting date approaches. The reader is introduced to the seven surviving Rennepont family members who are eligible to partake in the inheritance, although they are unaware of the reasons they are to meet at the house. The Wandering Jew and Herodias, unknown to the family members, are watching over them to help them reach Paris. In one extreme case, one of the family members, a priest named Gabriel, is nearly crucified by Native Americans in North America, but Herodias shows up to save him. Gabriel then sets out for Paris, while other family members travel from as far away as India and Siberia. The family is spread out because in 1685, Louis XIV had revoked the Edict of Nantes, forcing Protestants to leave France, although some of the family members again reside in France at the time the novel opens. The plot revolves around the efforts of the Jesuits to stop the members of the Rennepont family from reaching the house so the Jesuits can claim the fortune for themselves.

The seven Rennepont descendants are:

1. Gabriel Rennepont, a Jesuit missionary in America, who encounters no obstacles because the Jesuits want him to collect the fortune since he has already sworn to deliver all worldly goods to the Jesuits. Notably, Gabriel is described as having a "bright red scar" on his forehead.[77] His cousins, Rose and Simon, see him in a vision as an angel. These details connect him to the supernatural, the Wandering Jew, and the working class.

2. Rose Simon, daughter of Marshal Simon, who served under Napoleon. She is an heir through her mother.
3. Blanche Simon, Rose's twin sister.
4. Djalma, a prince of India, who is also an heir through his mother's line.
5. Jacques Rennepont, a Parisian workman.
6. François Hardy, a progressive factory owner in Paris.
7. Adrienne de Cardoville, an independently wealthy young woman living in Paris.

The novel's villains are:

1. Abbé d'Aigrigny, a former marquis and soldier under Napoleon who turned traitor and is now a Jesuit leader.
2. Rodin, secretary to d'Aigrigny, and eventually mastermind of the plot.*
3. The Princess de Dizier, former mistress of d'Aigrigny and aunt to Adrienne de Cardoville.
4. Dr. Baleinier, an adept at drugging people and carrying them off to places of confinement.

This Jesuit coalition works to ensure only Gabriel Rennepont will appear on the prescribed day to inherit the Rennepont fortune so he can surrender it to the Society of Jesus. To stop the rest of the Renneponts from appearing on the prescribed date, these villains confine Adrienne in an insane asylum, kidnap Rose and Blanche and hold them prisoners in a convent, drug and kidnap Prince Djalma, lure Hardy to central France so he cannot be at the meeting, and have Jacques thrown into debtor's prison.

---

* Sue's Rodin may have been inspired by a surgeon named Rodin in the Marquis de Sade's *Justine*. He is vampiric in his erotic pleasure over performing surgery in a time without anesthesia and the flowing of blood (Stuart 29). Priests like Radcliffe's Schedoni, Lewis' Ambrosio, and Hugo's Frollo are also notably vampiric in their sexual lusts (Stuart 27). Therefore, Rodin, the novel's greatest villain, has vampiric tendencies based in his character name and occupation.

Finally, February 13 arrives and Rodin, d'Aigrigny, and Gabriel go to the Rennepont mansion to collect the fortune, even though Gabriel, who is now having doubts about remaining a Jesuit, does not know the reason for the visit there. Up to this point, the novel has been intricately plotted and suspenseful, but its serialization was so popular that Sue, probably at the request of his publishers, decided not to end the novel with this meeting. Therefore, he has Herodias mysteriously appear at the house. Gabriel recognizes her as the woman who saved him in North America. She pulls out a codicil to the will that requires the heirs to meet again on June 1, thus allowing the novel to continue past what has now become its halfway mark.

This surprise event outrages the Jesuits and causes d'Aigrigny to surrender his role as head of the plot and allow Rodin to take over. Rodin believes he can ensure the Jesuits still inherit, but he also becomes paranoid about how the other Catholic Church leaders treat him. The Wandering Jew now enters Paris, forced against his will by a whirlwind, and begins to spread cholera. When Rodin becomes sick from cholera and nearly dies, he initially believes someone from Rome has poisoned him. However, he recovers and then decides to use cholera to destroy the Rennepont family. In time, he succeeds in causing Jacques, Rose, and Blanche to be placed in situations where cholera kills them.

Rodin also manages to dispatch the other members of the family. After his factory burns, Hardy takes refuge among the Jesuits, who convince him to enter their order, thus making him surrender any claims to earthly wealth.

Meanwhile, Adrienne has become aware of the plots, but she is no match for Rodin. She and Djalma have fallen in love, but Djalma, being from India, is a "savage" with savage passions. The Jesuits manipulate him into believing Adrienne loves another and seemingly confirm it when Rodin arranges for him to see a woman who resembles Adrienne with her lover. (Rodin later says this idea was inspired by the famous scandal over Marie

Antoinette's necklace, a scandal we will revisit in Chapter 6 when we discuss Dumas' Marie Antoinette novels.) In a rage, Djalma murders the fake Adrienne and her alleged lover. Then Djalma takes poison. Adrienne finds Djalma dying, learns what he has done, and also takes poison so they die together in "voluptuous agony" on May 30.[78]

Gabriel previously agreed to give anything he inherited to the Jesuits. By this point in the novel, he has left the Jesuit order, but he is too much a man of his word to go back on his actions. Now the only living heir, he surrenders the fortune to the Jesuits. Therefore, Rodin shows up on the prescribed date of June 1 with death certificates for all the Rennepont family and Gabriel's agreement to surrender his claim. Rodin then plans to claim the fortune for the Society of Jesus.

However, Samuel, the Jewish guardian of the house and fortune, has been busy secretly bringing the Renneponts' corpses to the house. When Rodin arrives, Samuel reveals the corpses on display to show that he knows how Rodin has brought about their deaths. At Gabriel's command, Samuel then burns the fortune. Throughout this meeting, Rodin feels strange but believes he is just excited about obtaining the inheritance. However, it turns out the Society of Jesuits has poisoned him; the holy water he dipped his finger in when he attended chapel that morning was poisoned. The poisoner is Faringhea, a Thug from Java who previously tried to kill Djalma. Faringhea is now working for the Society of Jesus, having forsaken his old master, the vengeful god Bowanee. He declares he prefers the Jesuits because "Bowanee makes corpses which rot in the ground. The Society makes corpses which walk about."[79]

The novel ends with a two-chapter epilogue. The first chapter depicts a happy domestic scene among characters who have helped the Rennepont family, including Gabriel. The second chapter depicts the Wandering Jew and Herodias, now turned old whereas before they appeared young. They know death approaches as a sign now that they have been forgiven for their transgressions and they hope their Divine Redemption will be extended to all those who suffer on the earth. The conclusion's philosophy feels a bit forced, but the suggestion is that the Wandering Jew, being an artisan, is a member of the working class and his sufferings have somehow led to redemption for the poor and working class so the day of their emancipation is approaching.

The Wandering Jew's closing words express this belief:

> Henceforth I will only shed tears of pride and glory for those of my race, who have died the martyrs of humanity, sacrificed by humanity's eternal enemies—for the true ancestors of the sacrilegious wretches, who blaspheme the name of Jesus by giving it to their Company, were the false Scribes and Pharisees, whom the Saviour cursed!—Yes! glory to the descendants of my family, who have been the last martyrs offered up by the accomplices of all slavery and all despotism, the pitiless enemies of those who wish to think, and not to suffer in silence—of those that would feign enjoy, as children of heaven, the gifts which the Creator has bestowed upon all the human family. Yes, the day approaches—the end of the reign of our modern Pharisees—the false priests, who lend their sacrilegious aid to the merciless selfishness of the strong against the weak, by daring to maintain in the face of the exhaustless treasures of the creation, that God has made man for tears, and sorrow, and suffering—the false priests, who are the agents of all oppression, and would bow to the earth, in brutish and hopeless humiliation, the brow of every creature. No, no! let man lift his head proudly! God made him to be noble and intelligent free and happy.[80]

The novel's ending feels a bit forced in this regard. Despite their efforts to protect the Rennepont family, the Wandering Jew and Herodias failed to do so, though they did prevent the Jesuits from obtaining the inheritance. But because the Renneponts are now dead, the work of these near-immortals appears finished and they are able to die. The moral falls somewhat flat, although it may have resonated with readers at the time. Sue has several other preachy moments in the novel where he digresses into discussions about the wrongs committed by the Jesuits and the situation of the poor, although the digressions are usually only a few pages long and do not distract much from the text—certainly not to the extent of Victor Hugo's digressions in *Notre-Dame de Paris* and *Les Misérables*. However, the reader who has read 1,400 pages may feel disappointed that no one inherits the fortune, and the second half of the novel does feel unnecessarily drawn out, many of the chapters doing little to advance the plot since Sue was obviously running out of steam while trying to please his readers and publisher.

Despite *The Wandering Jew*'s faults—it is an inferior work to *The Mysteries of Paris*—it was immensely popular. Perhaps more importantly from Sue's perspective, it would influence legislation on the Jesuits and create Jesuitphobia among people.[81] Nor did Sue hold back in his depiction of the Jesuits' nefariousness. Here is a passage from the novel describing how they spy upon people:

> When we read, in the rules of the order of the Jesuits, under the title De formula scribendi (Institut. 2, 11, p. 125, 129), the development of the 8th part of the constitutions, we are appalled by the number of letters, narratives, registers, and writings of all kinds, preserved in the archives of the society. It is a police infinitely more exact and better informed than has ever been that of any state. Even the government of Venice found itself surpassed by the Jesuits: when it drove them out in 1606, it seized all their papers, and reproached them for their great and laborious curiosity. This police, this secret inquisition, carried to such a degree of perfection, may give some idea of the strength of a government, so well-informed so persevering in its projects, so powerful by its unity, and, as the constitutions have it, by the union of its members. It is not hard to understand, what immense force must

belong to the heads of this society, and how the general of the Jesuits could say to the Duke de Brissac: "From this room, your grace, I govern not only Paris, but China—not only China, but the whole world—and all without any one knowing how it is done:" (Constitution of the Jesuits, edited by Paulin, Paris, 1843.)[82]

Sue is so adamant in his desire to discredit the Jesuits that he provides his sources for such statements. In the novel, Rodin is the worst Jesuit of all, and consequently, he is described in an almost supernatural manner:

> About fifty years of age, he wore an old, shabby, olive greatcoat, with a greasy collar, a snuff-powdered cotton handkerchief for a cravat, and waistcoat and trousers of threadbare black cloth. His feet, buried in loose varnished shoes, rested on a petty piece of green baize upon the red, polished floor. His gray hair lay flat on his temples, and encircled his bald forehead; his eyebrows were scarcely marked; his upper eyelid, flabby and overhanging, like the membrane which shades the eyes of reptiles, half concealed his small, sharp, black eye. His thin lips, absolutely colorless, were hardly distinguishable from the wan hue of his lean visage, with its pointed nose and chin; and this livid mask (deprived as it were of lips) appeared only the more singular, from its maintaining a death-like immobility. Had it not been for the rapid movement of his fingers, as, bending over the desk, he scratched along with his pen, M. Rodin might have been mistaken for a corpse. By the aid of a cipher (or secret alphabet) placed before him he was copying certain passages from a long sheet full of writing, in a manner quite unintelligible to those who did not possess the key to the system. Whilst the darkness of the day increased the gloom of the large, cold, naked-looking apartment, there was something awful in the chilling aspect of this man, tracing his mysterious characters in the midst of profound silence.[83]

Rodin appears to be practically a living corpse, which speaks to Faringhea's statement earlier about how the Jesuits create living corpses. His writing in a secret language also equates him with mysticism and secret societies, much like the Abbé Faria in *The Count of Monte Cristo*, as we saw in Chapter 3. Later, when Rodin is restored after nearly dying of cholera, we are told "the monster felt that he was becoming once more strong and powerful, and he seemed conscious the evils that his fatal resurrection was to cause."[84] Rodin's resurrection links him to vampires here as does the sense that he is a living corpse. In fact, we are told that anyone who follows the Jesuits is led into "corpse-like obedience."[85] This includes Hardy, who once converted reads passages from Thomas à Kempis' religious classic, *The Imitation of Christ*, a book Sue claims contains "not enough merely to plunge the soul of the victim into incurable despair, but also to reduce him to the corpse-like obedience required by the Society of Jesus. In that awful book may be found a thousand terrors to operate on weak minds, a thousand slavish maxims to chain and degrade the pusillanimous soul."[86] This statement, while seemingly a gibe at the Jesuits, is especially harsh since *The Imitation of Christ* is a classic of Christian literature admired by Catholics and Protestants alike, yet Sue feels it only enslaves the working class to religion.

The Jesuitphobia that resulted from the novel is understandable given that Sue creates paranoia in readers that the Jesuits may be spying on them, again providing support for his statements:

> Every day, the General receives a host of reports, which serve to check one another. In the central house, at Rome, are immense registers, in which are inscribed the names of all the Jesuits, of their adherents, and of all the considerable persons, whether friends or enemies, with whom they have any connection. In these registers are reported, without alteration, hatred or passion the facts relating to the life of each individual. It is the most gigantic biographical

> collection that has ever been formed. The frailties of a woman, the secret errors of a statesman, are chronicled in this book with the same cold impartiality. Drawn up for the purpose of being useful, these biographies are necessarily exact. When the Jesuits wish to influence an individual, they have but to turn to this book, and they know immediately his life, his character, his parts, his faults, his projects, his family, his friends, his most sacred ties. Conceive, what a superior facility of action this immense police-register, which includes the whole world, must give to any one society! It is not lightly that I speak of these registers; I have my facts from a person who has seen this collection, and who is perfectly well acquainted with the Jesuits. Here then, is matter to reflect on for all those families, who admit freely into their houses the members of a community that carries its biographical researches to such a point. (Libri, Member of the Institute. Letters on the Clergy.)[87]

While the novel is obviously anti-Catholic, such statements make the anti-Catholicism seem justified and turn the Catholic Church into a secret society conspiring against mankind in the style of secret societies common in Gothic novels (see Chapter 5). In addition, Sue provides footnotes referring to works about the Jesuits, including Quinet's work, to provide further credibility to his statements.

Perhaps the most damning statement against the Jesuits comes in Marius de Rennepont's will. He accuses the Jesuits of hiding behind their missionary work as a cover for their nefarious schemes:

> Thus, the missions have thrown a scanty but pure and generous light on the darkness of this Company of Jesus—founded with the detestable and impious aim of destroying, by a homicidal education, all will, thought, liberty, and intelligence, in the people, so as to deliver them, trembling, superstitious, brutal, and helpless, to the

despotism of kings, governed in their turn by confessors belonging to the Society.[88]

Therefore, the Jesuits are the enemies of the common people, the working class. Worse, their evil practices are possible because no one believes in such conspiracies. When Adrienne is first confronted with the idea that the Jesuits are a secret society, she laughs, saying the Jesuits while "frightful historical personages" now "have no existence, except in books."[89]

Sue's novel is clearly socialist, perhaps more so than *The Mysteries of Paris*. The novel also does less to model Christianity than the earlier work, but perhaps more to model socialism. That said, Karl Marx, who lived in Paris when the novel was serialized, felt the need to respond to its popularity in a series of essays which became part of his book *The Holy Family* (1845). Marx disputes Sue's belief that ignorance prevents the rich from aiding the poor and casts doubt on the genuineness of the author's socialism.[90] He even calls Sue "a sentimental middle-class social fantasizer,"[91] a dismissive statement that perhaps is understandable given that Sue was born to a wealthy family. Sue surrendered his real name Marie Joseph for Eugène Sue, a name taken from his godfather Prince Eugène Beaucharnais, while his godmother was Josephine Bonaparte. He spent money freely, modeling his life after that of Lord Byron; only after he lost his mistress and fortune did he choose to write about the miseries of modern life.[92] This sarcastic view, however, does not diminish the incredible accomplishment he achieved in writing his novels.

The Wandering Jew remained extremely popular throughout the nineteenth century. One of its first major influences was inspiring an opera, *Le Juif errant* by Fromental Halévy in 1852 with libretto by Eugène Scribe and Jules-Henri Vernoy de Saint-Georges. The opera was only loosely based on the novel, and while it has scenes set in Paris, it is also set in 1190, opens in Amsterdam, and includes scenes in Constantinople. Furthermore, one of the characters is named Irène. The Constantinople setting would later be used by Lew Wallace in *The Prince of India*, in which one of the characters is also named Irène, so it is possible Wallace knew the opera as he did *Salathiel* and Sue's novel. In the opera, Irène is the daughter of Baudoin, the former emperor of the East, and she is a descendant of the Wandering Jew.[93] Although praised more for its dazzling sets than its storyline, the opera was popular enough to result in a *Wandering Jew Mazurka*, a *Wandering Jew Waltz*, and a *Wandering Jew Polka*.[94]

Part of *The Wandering Jew*'s popularity was also due to the character of Prince Djalma. In truth, Djalma is one of Sue's poorest creations, a blatantly racist stereotype who is repeatedly referred to as a "savage" and said to be very passionate. Yet, just as Djalma charmed Adrienne in the novel, he charmed female readers as testified to in the classic Dutch novel *Max Havelaar* (1860), where we are told:

> The lady of the house had read the novel by Eugène Sue which briefly caused such a stir, and every time she looked at Saijah she thought of Prince Djalma. The young girls, likewise, understood better than before why the Javanese painter Raden Saleh had met with such enthusiasm in Paris.[95]

While this exotic orientalism is offensive today, I suspect Djalma, being a prince from India, also inspired the title of Lew Wallace's novel *The Prince of India*.

Perhaps the novel's most significant influence, however, was upon Bram Stoker, who devoted a chapter to the topic of the Wandering Jew in *Famous Impostors* (1910), as we previously saw. Besides referencing Croly's *Salathiel*, Stoker praises Sue's novel, saying:

> Sue was what in modern slang is called "up to date." He knew every trick and dodge of the world of advertisement, and in conjunction with his editor, Dr. Veron, he used them all. But he had good wares to exploit. His novels are really excellent, though the changes in social life and in religious, political and artistic matters, which took place

between 1844 and 1910, make some things in them seem out of date. His great imagination, and his firm and rapid grasp of salient facts susceptible of being advantageously used in narrative, pointed out to him a fresh road. It was not sufficient to the hour and place that Cartaphilus—or Joseph—or Ahasuerus, or Salathiel or whatever he might be called—should purge his sin by his personal sufferings alone. In the legend, up to then accepted, he had long ago repented; so to increase the poignancy of his sufferings, Sue took from the experience of his own time a means of embittering the very inmost soul of such an one. He must be made to feel that his existence is a curse not only to himself but to all the world. To this end he attached to the Wanderer the obligation of carrying a fell disease. The quick brain of the great feuilletonist seized the dramatic moment for utilising the occasion. A dozen years before, the frightful spread of the cholera, which had once again wrought havoc, woke the whole world to new terror. Some one of uneasy mind who found diversion in obscure comparisons, noted from the records of the disease that its moving showed the same progress in a given direction as a man's walking.

A hint was sufficient for the public who eagerly seized the idea that the Wandering Jew had, from the first recorded appearance of the cholera, been the fated carrier of that dreaded pestilence. The idea seemed to be a dramatic inspiration and had prehensile grasp. Great as had been the success of the *Mysteries of Paris*, that of *The Wandering Jew* surpassed it, and for half a century the new novel kept vividly before its readers the old tradition, and so brought it down to the present.[96]

Scholars have long suggested that the character of Dracula was partly influenced by depictions of the Wandering Jew or similar figures on the stage. In fact, Hal Caine, to whom Stoker dedicated *Dracula*, also was called upon to write plays for

Irving and stated, "I remember that most of our subjects dealt with the supernatural, and that the Wandering Jew, the Flying Dutchman and the Demon Lover were themes around which our imagination[s] constantly revolved."[97] Consequently, Stoker must have constantly been thinking of the Wandering Jew figure and especially his depiction in Sue's novel, so it is not surprising if the novel influenced *Dracula*. That Adrienne is confined to an insane asylum also might have influenced the depiction of Renfield in an asylum in *Dracula*. It is well known that Wilkie Collins' *The Woman in White* was also an influence on *Dracula*; Collins' novel also contains a woman unjustly locked away in an insane asylum. While that plot is often equated with how the novelist Edward Bulwer-Lytton put his wife Rosina in an insane asylum, and other sources are frequently cited,[98] it would not be surprising if Collins read *The Wandering Jew* and was inspired by it in creating the plot in his novel to have Sir Percival Glyde and Count Fosco try to obtain control of Lady Laura's marital settlement.*

Although few people read *The Wandering Jew* today, its influence remains far-reaching. Furthermore, its use of the Wandering Jew as a metaphor for the working class and by extension the human race in all its toil and tribulation transformed the figure from a racial stereotype into a type of everyman we can all relate to.

---

* Asylum literature actually had a long tradition in France. According to Brian Stableford:

> Although highly controversial, and dismissed as charlatanry by an investigative commission set up by Louis XVI before the Revolution, the Mesmeric school of medicine remained popular in France, becoming intricately confused with therapeutic hypnotism, and with proto-psychological investigations of somnambulism and dreaming. France was home to many pioneering investigations and attempted analyses of mental disorders, and its asylums, including Charenton, Bicêtre and the Salpêtrière, became important locations of empirical research and attempted psychotherapies. That research prompted intense interest on the part of many littérateurs, and "asylum manuscripts" became a prolific subgenre. (Stableford, "Introduction," *Weird Fiction in France*, p. 19-20.)

Sue's *The Mysteries of the People* and Reynolds' *The Mysteries of the Court of London*

A brief digression from our topic of the Wandering Jew is worthwhile here to note Sue's later influence upon Reynolds and how Sue reused characters from *The Mysteries of Paris* and *The Wandering Jew* in his later works.

Soon after completing *The Wandering Jew,* Sue would begin his longest series, *The Mysteries of the People* (1849-1856), consisting of nineteen individual but related novels. Sue was probably influenced by Scott's *Ivanhoe* in depicting a society divided into the conquerors and the conquered, or the rulers and the proletariat. While Scott depicted Saxons and Normans, Sue depicts Gauls and Franks throughout French history.

The series tells the story of a family of Gauls, beginning at the time Julius Caesar conquers Gaul. Sue carries the family through the withdrawal of the Romans, the conquest of Gaul by the Franks, the Middle Ages and Renaissance, and finally to the French Revolution and the 1848 Revolution. The main family are the descendants of Joel, a Gaul chief. They record their family history in what become the novels that make up the series. Each novel highlights one or more significant moments in France's history.

In the sixteenth book, *The Pocket Bible or Christian the Printer*, it is revealed that the family, now named LeBrenn, is related to the Duke of Gerolstein, a family that shares its French roots. Later, a member of the LeBrenn family marries a Rennepont. This Gerolstein family is related to Rodolphe, the hero of *The Mysteries of Paris*, and the Renneponts are the main family in *The Wandering Jew*, so Sue creates intertextual connections between his three greatest works. In the same volume, he documents the Protestant Reformation and the creation of the Society of Jesus/Jesuits, thus providing additional background to the plot in *The Wandering Jew*. He even goes so far as to have his character Christian think Christianity itself is false, although he sides with the Protestant

Reformation because of its enlightened beliefs that men should be free to worship as they choose as opposed to being controlled by the Catholic Church.

The eighteenth novel in *The Mysteries of the People*, titled *The Sword of Honor*, would be most closely tied to *The Wandering Jew* and *The Mysteries of Paris*. In that novel, we are introduced to Samuel and Bathsheba, the Jewish couple guarding the Rennepont treasure, although they have a minor role in the novel. Franz, Prince of Gerolstein, presumably father or grandfather to Rodolphe in *The Mysteries of Paris*, makes an appearance, and most notably, the villain Rodin appears as a young child during the French Revolution; here he is not above biting people to further the Jesuits' nefarious schemes. Surprisingly, *The Mysteries of the People* is devoid of any Gothic atmosphere or other Gothic elements, unless one counts anti-Catholicism, but its connections to Sue's earlier novels shows how much he lived with his characters, always keeping them in his mind even after finishing his novels. His characters were real to him and his powerful imagination makes them real to those who still read his works. Like the Wandering Jew himself, they linger on.

One final noteworthy aspect of Sue's *The Mysteries of the People* is that it is clearly revisionist history, based in Sue's socialism. Sue rejects notions that the Romans and even the Franks were noble, but represents them merely as the oppressors of the original Gauls. Because the novels have been largely ignored in English, their influence upon George W. M. Reynolds has gone unnoticed. *The Mysteries of the People* was not translated into English until the early twentieth century, but I have no doubt Reynolds would have read them in French. Reynolds was writing *The Mysteries of the Court of London* simultaneously from 1848-1855 and he also provides revisionist history in it, not holding back his dislike of George III, his children, or any monarchs. As the critic Antony Taylor has stated:

> For G.W.M. Reynolds, the British aristocracy was tainted, bearing the historical stain of the Norman

Conquest and carrying inherited predispositions towards tyranny that bent the British constitution to their will. *Reynolds's Newspaper* remarked: 'The Norman freebooters indeed elaborated a system of government so ingeniously compounded of violence and cunning, that to this day the mass of the people groan under it, while taught to believe they are in the enjoyment of a "glorious constitution" that is the envy and admiration of the whole world.' Unpicking the history of aristocracy for most radicals meant revealing a history of avarice and self-interest….

Maintaining their [the aristocracy's] power and position meant expanding their imperial interests. In the eyes of Reynolds and other radicals, the impulse here was towards fresh Norman Conquests in the wider world that would augment the wealth and station of Britain's traditional ruling elite and ensure that England 'is never without some little or contemptible war upon her hands.' On this basis the history of empire and the history of Britain's aristocracy at home were inextricably intertwined. From the early 1850s exposures of the imperial misdeeds of a transplanted British aristocracy littered the pages of *Reynolds's Newspaper*.[99]

In short, for Reynolds, the Normans were just as much the oppressors of the Anglo-Saxons as for Sue the Franks were the oppressors of the Gauls. While Scott's *Ivanhoe* might also be a source for this concept, more work needs to be done on how *The Mysteries of the People* may have influenced Reynolds' work. Such a discussion is beyond our focus here, however, so we will return to the Wandering Jew.

Alexandre Dumas' *Isaac Laquedem*

Alexandre Dumas' *Isaac Laquedem* (1852-3) was the next major work about the Wandering Jew. Although Dumas named the Jew Isaac Laquedem rather than Ahasuerus, the book is clearly influenced by Sue and Quinet's works. Unfortunately, Dumas never finished the novel because he ran afoul of the Second Empire's censors,[100] but because the novel was serialized from the beginning, the forty-two chapters he did complete were popular. Dumas intended to resume the novel at a favorable time, which might have happened in 1871 once Napoleon III was removed from office following France's defeat in the Franco-Prussian War, but Dumas died during the war on December 5, 1870.[101] According to scholar Arthur F. Davidson, the fragment of *Isaac Laquedem* that we have is a mere two volumes of the projected twelve. Had Dumas written all twelve, it would have made his other completed works look like child's play since the fragment itself is about 190,000 words, meaning it would have run more than a million words in its entirety. By comparison, *The Count of Monte Cristo* runs to 464,234 words or 1,300 pages.

Isaac Laquedem has only been completely translated into English once by Frank W. Reed in 1953. That translation is long out of print and difficult to find. Recently, a new translation has been begun by Paul Terence Matthias Jackson for Noumena Press, but that translation, intended to be completed in 2020, was delayed and at the time of this book's printing only the "Prologue" has been released. This prologue is really the first six of the novel's forty-two chapters. It is referred to as the prologue in this new translation because it describes the Wandering Jew traveling to Rome to meet Pope Paul II in 1469 and ends with him beginning to tell his story to the pope. The entire novel is available in the original French at the Dumas Society's website, www.dumaspere.com, so I used Google Translate to read it in English.

The first six chapters (prologue) offer a good build-up to the story and show the extent to which Dumas was writing his most historically detailed novel. As the Wandering Jew, simply referred to as "the traveler," traverses the Appian Way, the reader is inundated with numerous details about ancient Rome and the Roman Empire. The Jew, although keeping to himself, has to make his way through or past three fortresses, and at each one when he interacts with people, he displays his extreme knowledge of the past. At the first fortress, he reveals to a member of the Orsini family where a treasure was buried in the fortress. At the second fortress, he is unable to pay the amount demanded for passage, so he offers to pay his debt with an archery lesson for the English archers at the fortress. He impresses the other archers with his skill. Then he declares he knows of a better bow and asks them to lift up a slab of stone at the fortress. When the other men are physically unable to do so, the "superhuman"[102] lifts it himself and reveals the bow that belonged to the Emperor Maximin. He uses the bow to show further his prowess in archery. Awed by his skill, the men wish him on his way and he asks them to pray for him. At the third fortress, not wanting to lose more time, for it is Maundy Thursday and he hopes to make it to St. Peter's Square in time for the pope's annual blessing, he tries to skirt around the fortress. The guards, upset that he does not pay the toll or respond to their cries, shoot arrows at him, but he brushes the arrows off and is unharmed. All these incidents make it clear to the reader that the traveler, who has not yet been named, has knowledge of the past, superhuman physical abilities, and is charmed from being able to be killed.

Once in Rome, the traveler makes his way to St. Peter's Square where he hears the pope bless the 300,000 Christians present. Then he manages to become one of the thirteen pilgrims whose feet the pope will wash. However, when Pope Paul II goes to wash his feet, the traveler exclaims that he does not deserve it from a saint. When Paul then asks what he wants, the traveler begs him to hear his confession. Paul agrees and asks him to go to the Venetian Palace where he will meet with him in private.

During the meeting, the traveler explains to the pope how he wishes to be pardoned, but he fears God cannot pardon Satan. The pope replies that Satan was not repentant, but if the traveler is, he can be pardoned. The traveler then reveals the "fiery mark" on his brow and the pope, in shock, asks if he is Cain.[103] The traveler says that Cain was killed by Lamech, but he is not so fortunate because he cannot die. He then describes how he has outlived his loved ones, seen the Roman Empire fall, and traveled around the world trying to find ways to kill himself, including throwing himself into a volcano and swallowing poison, but nothing kills him. Finally, he reveals he is the Wandering Jew, the one on whom God takes vengeance "on behalf of humankind."[104] The pope then agrees to hear his story and see if he can serve as "the intermediary between offender and judge, between offence and pardon."[105]

Surprisingly, although the Jew is now telling his story, the novel remains in third person. We are plunged into three chapters detailing the history of Jerusalem. Then in Chapter 10, we find Jesus' apostles preparing for the Last Supper, which leads to the entire life story of Jesus. Dumas retells the gospels without making them novelistic, reiterating the main stories with a few interesting additions such as relying on apocrypha to describe miracles Jesus performed as a child. Notably, Jesus is described as blond, blue-eyed, and with a beard tinged with red, reflecting Dumas' reliance on popular European images of Jesus rather than the historical reality of someone born in the Middle East. The next major addition to Jesus' story is in Chapter 16 where the Virgin Mary expresses her concern about Jesus' future. Also, in Chapter 18 when Jesus is praying in Gethsemane, he is presented with three hours of temptation from Satan, who shows him the future, including how all the apostles will meet their deaths and the wars of Christianity. Regardless, Jesus still chooses to go through with his crucifixion.

Jesus is taken prisoner and put on trial, again following the gospel stories, but in Chapter 23, Dumas finally reintroduces Isaac Laquedem at the trial where he demands Jesus perform a test. Isaac holds out a staff and tells Jesus to try to get past him; with little effort, Jesus pushes Isaac back, causing Isaac to declare Jesus is a wizard. The trial then concludes and Jesus is condemned to crucifixion. In Chapter 26, Isaac and his family are watching the procession as Jesus makes his way to the place of crucifixion. Jesus stops to ask Isaac for water and is refused. Next, he asks to sit on the family's bench and is again refused. Finally, Jesus asks to sit on the threshold. When Isaac refuses a third time, Jesus curses him, telling him he can have a last meal with his family, but then his wandering will begin. Jesus then goes on to Golgotha, with the enlistment of Simon the Cyrene to carry his cross. At Golgotha, soldiers with "frizzy" hair like that of "negroes" appear like "demons" in the "infernal work." This remark is surprisingly racist given that Dumas was himself part-African. Christ is then crucified and dies.

In Chapter 28, we return to Isaac eating with his family when the angel Eloha appears at the door and tells him it's time to leave. Isaac refuses to go but finds himself forced to depart by powers beyond his control. Eloha places his sword on Isaac's forehead, giving him the mark of Cain so he will be recognized as a brother of the first murderer. As Isaac leaves his house, the sky grows dark and an earthquake occurs. An invisible hand pushes Isaac to Golgotha where he sees Christ dying on the cross. Isaac exclaims, "Either you are man, or you are God; If you are a man, I will easily overcome you...if you are God, I will fight against you, for your curse has made you my equal: whoever is immortal is God!"

In Chapter 29, the resurrection is recounted as told in the gospels. Then in Chapter 30, Isaac Laquedem's story takes over the narrative. Dumas here jumps ahead twenty-some years and eventually we learn Nero is now emperor. Isaac has been wandering all this time, including to Egypt where he saw the Sphinx, as we will later be told. He has now arrived in Greece to find Apollonius of Tyana, a historical philosopher and reputed sorcerer. Apollonius already knows who Isaac is when he arrives and agrees to help him. A chain of events leads to them traveling to speak to Canidia, a famous witch in Roman history.

In Chapter 38, Isaac asks Canidia where the Fates live, how to reach them, and how to get the thread of life from them for a person who has already died. Canidia is unable to answer the question, so she calls on Erichto, a legendary Thessalian witch, but Erichto also cannot answer and says to ask Medea. Medea, famous for aiding Jason and the Argonauts and later for murdering her children, says if she knew the answer to his question, she would have brought her children back to life. She recommends Isaac find Prometheus and ask him. Isaac thought Prometheus was freed by Hercules, but Medea replies that while Hercules killed the vulture that ate Prometheus' liver, he was unable to break his chains. The journey to Prometheus in the Caucasus would be arduous except that Canidia has used her powers to make the Sphinx leave Egypt to be with her. The Sphinx agrees to carry Isaac to Prometheus.

Once Isaac meets Prometheus, they share their stories. After hearing of the god Jesus who resurrected himself, Prometheus believes he is no longer subject to Jupiter's punishment and feels himself dying. Isaac agrees to create a fire to kill Prometheus, and in exchange for this mercy killing, Prometheus tells him how to get to the Fates. After a few more adventures, in Chapter 41, Isaac meets the Fates. When they wonder how he survived the many dangers in the tunnel he had to pass through to reach them, he tells them he is immortal and shares his name with them. They then confirm who he is by looking at the thread of his life and seeing he is immortal, but they don't understand how. When he tells them of Jesus, they realize their power and that of the old world is fading away. Isaac then asks them for the threads of Cleopatra's life. They surrender them to him, saying it does not matter now that their time is passed. As Isaac leaves, they disappear and the cave closes.

Isaac now flies on the Sphinx to Egypt where he enters Cleopatra's tomb. He finds her body, attaches the threads of her life back together, and watches her body revive. She is momentarily confused, but then she remembers the events leading to her death. Isaac explains to her that she has been dead a hundred years. He then shares his story and tells her that to accomplish anything, there must be a "duality of genius," so he has chosen her to be his helper. She agrees to help if it means she will always be beautiful, which he affirms she will be. He then tells her they are going to Rome where Nero is now emperor. There they will assume new names, she as Poppea and he as Tigellin. (Poppea would marry Nero and Tigellin would be his cruel friend.) Here Dumas left off writing the novel.

Isaac Laquedem is certainly one of the strangest novels ever written, but the censors' disapproval of it is somewhat surprising. Napoleon III's government did not like Dumas' republicanism, but there is nothing about republicanism in the novel. However, Dumas' depiction of the Roman Empire was seen as a message against imperialism and the French Empire. Furthermore, Dumas' treatment of religion was considered as bordering on blasphemy.[106] While Dumas' retelling of Christ's story is fairly orthodox, when Isaac enters the cave to see the Fates, he travels down into the depths of the earth where he finds embedded in the walls the history of the earth, including animals from various ages before humanity existed, and animals that are missing links from one species to another. This clearly references the nineteenth-century discoveries about evolution that were in conflict with Christianity, and although Dumas tries to reconcile Christianity and evolution by saying the five ages Isaac sees are the five days of the creation, thus revealing "The Genesis of Moses," conservative Christians likely found such references upsetting. Furthermore, this scene would have been in the last issue of the serialized novel before it was censored.

As George K. Anderson states, "The novel is assuredly one of the master fabricator's less inspired works."[107] Modern readers would likely find the novel tedious because of the excessive historical detail. For example, as Isaac travels with Apollonius through Greece, Apollonius tells him the history of every place they pass, which leads to retellings of tales of Greek mythology. The reader who knows the Bible, Greek mythology, and basic world history will be tempted to skim through the long historical digressions that make even Victor Hugo's famous digressions look tame. Nevertheless, Dumas writes in a poetic and epic prose style that moves swiftly so that readers feel like all the history of the world is rapidly passing before their eyes. One can't help feeling Dumas is simply trying to show off his own learning. In a letter dated March 16, 1852, in which Dumas first proposed the novel to the publisher Anténor Joly, he describes his vision for the book:

> How about an immense 8-volume novel of the Country which would begin with Jesus Christ and which would end with the last man of creation, giving five different novels, one under Nero, one under Charlemagne, one under Charles IX, one under Napoleon, one l'Avenir [the future]?
>
> I intended to write this novel entirely composed in my head for a review, since the feuilleton cuts too much interest, but by making longer feuilletons, we would achieve the same result [...]
>
> The main heroes are the Wandering Jew, Jesus Christ, Cleopatra, the Fates, Prometheus, Nero, Poppea, Narcissus, Octavia, Charlemagne, Roland, Vitikind, Velléda, Pope Gregory VII, King Charles IX, Catherine de Medici, Cardinal of Lorraine, Napoleon, Marie-Louise, Talleyrand, the Messiah and the Angel of the Chalice.
>
> This sounds crazy to you, but ask Alexandre [Alexandre Dumas fils] who knows the book from cover to cover what he thinks about it.[108]

While this plan is highly ambitious, it is less "crazy" than visionary. That said, the novel does tend to bore at times, a point the Dumas Society agrees with, stating on its website of *Isaac Laquedem*:

> It is true that Alexandre Dumas has not accustomed us to this kind of work and that this novel can disconcert lovers of *The Three Musketeers*. No doubt this is why publishers are in no hurry to bring it out again, and this novel is undoubtedly among the least easy to find.[109]

Isaac Laquedem is a far cry from *The Three Musketeers* or even *The Count of Monte Cristo*, yet it contains many Gothic elements in its themes of revolution, transgression, and redemption, and in the monster-like creatures from Greek mythology that make appearances. Had it been published in English in the nineteenth century, it likely would have been heavily abridged. That said, it offers a side of Dumas not seen in his other works—a broad, sweeping vision of history more akin to that of Edgar Quinet and perhaps George Croly than of Eugène Sue in its treatment of the Wandering Jew. The Wandering Jew becomes human history in Dumas' work, something that Sue also states, saying the Jew and his family are the human race, but Dumas takes the idea to a whole new level. Dumas is also creating what might be considered one of the first fantasy novels in the way he blends history with mythology, both Christian and pagan, to create a truly fantastic world where it seems anything is possible. That said, Sue may have influenced the novel's historical approach through his *The Mysteries of the People* series, which he was halfway through writing by the time *Isaac Laquedem* began appearing, and which covered nearly 1,900 years of French history.

Biographer Arthur F. Davidson, in *Alexandre Dumas: His Life and Works*, says of *Isaac Laquedem*:

> It was as well, perhaps, that the Government should intervene to prevent the sacred drama of the Passion from being presented to the Parisian public in the same style as the story of the Musketeers, since the thing was bound to move scoffing in some and pain in others. But there is no doubting the good faith of Dumas himself: irreverence and inexpediency were as far from his view as the opposite qualities they connote. In all sincerity he had set himself to explain and adorn the mysteries of religion for the benefit of the man in the street; and this ingenuousness of treatment is only less astonishing than the magnitude of conception. What the future course of *Isaac Laquedem* would have been is but guess work. It is said—and is likely enough—that

the author meant to have represented the Pope as securing for the criminal a conditional pardon—the condition being that he should still wander, but henceforth as the apostle of good, not of evil. In that case we can see how, after the interview with Paul II, the story would have started off again with the wide vista of the modern world before it, affording opportunities without end for the activity of the regenerate Jew. As it stands *Isaac Laquedem* is an inchoate epic of the human race, which can only be criticized by large marks of exclamation.[110]

Davidson, who wrote in 1902, may have shared some of the censoring government's concerns about the novel's presentation of Christianity, but the novel had already moved well past its presentation of Christ by the time it was censored. As previously stated, the censorship reasons had more to do with a belief the novel was too pro-Republican once Louis Napoleon had established himself as Emperor Napoleon III.[111]

In today's age when fantasy novels and historical fiction are so popular, it is a shame we do not know more about Dumas' plans for the novel's completion. *Isaac Laquedem* may have remained an odd work, but it would have been a new kind of masterpiece, a true *sui generis*, and who knows what influence it might have had, if finished, on not just Gothic literature but historical and fantasy fiction. In short, fragmented as it is, Dumas appears to have been the author with the greatest vision for how the Wandering Jew might be used in literature. Sadly, that vision was never fully realized.

Paul Féval's *The Wandering Jew's Daughter*

Just as stories of Lord Ruthven eventually received comical treatment, so the Wandering Jew suffered the same affliction. However, being satirized or parodied is also a sign of a work's popularity. Paul Féval began writing *La Fille du Juif Errant* (*The Wandering Jew's Daughter*) in 1864 and completed it in its final form in 1878. Personally, I find it a rather disappointing novel because Féval failed to take his subject seriously. Regardless, it is noteworthy for anticipating future fantasy and Gothic literature in its depiction of multiple immortals who have battled each other over the centuries. Brian Stableford, the novel's translator into English, states that it "anticipates later developments in popular fiction, featuring an invulnerable but flawed hero who stops bullets and blades with his body and gives succor to the wounded. The book adds another item to an already-extensive catalogue of Féval's anticipations of modern mythology."[112] The novel, in truth, is more akin to the *Highlander* film franchise and other Hollywood treatments of immortals than to the nineteenth-century tradition of the Wandering Jew. Still, most readers of popular modern fantasy would probably find this novel almost unreadable. Even the battle between immortals that ensues is disappointing and more a mockery than what we would expect from a good adventure novel.

The story is a hodgepodge of confusion. The novel opens by introducing us to a young boy, Vicomte Paul, and his parents. With them lives Lotte, the Wandering Jew's daughter, although how she came to live with them is never explained, and it is only surmised that she is the Wandering Jew's daughter because the little girl does not seem to age. When Paul's house catches fire, he is rescued but the girl disappears. Then Paul's father suddenly changes in his demeanor because his body has been taken over by Ozer, one of the Wandering Jews.

Yes, the novel has more than one Wandering Jew. Lotte's father, Ahasuerus, also known as Isaac Laquedem, is the most traditional Wandering Jew in the novel. But a whole household of immortals live in Paris at the House of Jews. Ironically, many of them are not even Jewish. They represent a slew of biblical characters, including Holofernes; Lot's daughters; Barabbas' niece; the brothers Korah, Dathan, and Abiram; Madam Potiphar; Caiaphas' valet; the Pharisee Nathan who let merchants into the Temple; and Ozer, the Roman soldier who gave Christ a sponge to drink from during the Crucifixion. Féval is parodying Sue and Dumas by using the names of both of their Wandering Jews for his hero/good guy Wandering Jew. (He also references Apollonius of Tyana who appeared in Dumas' *Isaac Laquedem*, and Joseph Balsamo, a historical figure of note during the French Revolution whom we will meet in Dumas' Marie Antoinette novels in Chapter 6.)

All of Féval's Wandering Jews have been cursed with extended lives, and some have various other gifts or supernatural powers. None of them are developed other than Ozer, who has the ability to possess people's bodies so he can keep changing his appearance and retain his youth. At the novel's end, we learn that Paul's father was possessed by Ozer during the fire, which explains his behavioral change. Ozer is the only true villain of the novel, but the other Wandering Jews support him in his battle against Ahasuerus/Isaac Laquedem whom they view as a traitor because he has repented for his mistreatment of Christ.

After Lotte's disappearance following the fire, years pass and Paul grows up. Then as a young man, he meets the grown-up Lotte. Of course, the two fall in love, but before they can be together, Ahasuerus must wreak his vengeance on Ozer. Because Ahasuerus has repented for his sins, his curse is to be lifted, but the other immortals have not repented. Ahasuerus battles Ozer to prevent him from taking another soul, and he ends up killing him. He also kills as many of the other characters in the House of Jews as he can. Here's a little taste of Féval's mockery of this battle of the immortals: "All these murders passed unnoticed, by courtesy of the civil war. Besides, every one of these brave Israelites had already been broken on the wheel, hung, executed by firing-squad and guillotined several times over, at various times. All of them are in the best of health as we inscribe these lines."[113] Humorous as this statement is, other parts of the novel fall flat in their attempts to mock the Wandering Jew theme, so that the novel is more like watching *Dracula, Dead and Loving It* than Francis Ford Coppola's *Bram Stoker's Dracula*. Of course, humor has its place, but great Gothic and Romantic literature can move the soul in a way such parodying cannot, and the novels Féval is mocking are, in my opinion, far superior to his own.

The Wandering Jew's Daughter can be read as a response to the many treatments of the Wandering Jew already discussed. Brian Stableford points out that neither Sue nor Dumas were devout men, so they used the Wandering Jew in a heretical way; by comparison, Féval was devout, which affected his strategy.[114] Despite Féval's devotion, however, his mockery of the legend comes off as more heretical than anything Sue and Dumas wrote, though Sue's anti-Catholicism, of course, made the establishment consider him unorthodox. Stableford also says the novel was a political response. It is set against the 1830 revolution (as referenced in the quote above as a "civil war"), and the novel makes many historical and political references to the period, but the result is that it is dated and of little interest to the modern reader unfamiliar with French political history, which is doubtless why the novel is little known today. The reader tends to grow tired of the novel's politics as something to be waded through while still hoping some sort of real plot will evolve, only to be disappointed when it does not.

Féval's style does not help matters. The novel is written in a slap-dash, fragmented format. The chapters are extremely short—eighty-two chapters in just 170 pages—and they are choppy, plus the scenes jump about without adequate transitions. Féval begins by focusing on Paul and Lotte as children, and it feels like he is writing a children's book, which was his initial goal with the first version of the novel, but no child could read this book today.[115] The novel ends with Paul and Lotte together, and a strange, confusing image that Lotte has been split in two so she can be with both Paul and her father—sadly, this conclusion is not really comprehensible, though it is uncertain if it were meant to be.

Ultimately, it is not surprising that Stableford's 2005 translation for Black Coat Press was the first and only one in English. Regardless, *The Wandering Jew's Daughter* is an important book for understanding how the Wandering Jew evolved into other immortal characters who, in turn, led to much of the fantasy and superhero fiction we have today. Fortunately, Féval's other Gothic novels are of more merit.

Conclusion

The Wandering Jew has disappeared as a popular figure in the twenty-first century. Largely, this lack of popularity is due to it no longer being a politically correct figure because it has long been seen as a metaphor for the Jewish race forced to wander after rejecting Christ. Even the Catholic Church has now apologized for its mistreatment of the Jewish people over the centuries, and while antisemitism still exists, it is no longer considered acceptable in mainstream media.

Regardless, the Wandering Jew lives on in numerous other literary characters, including vampires, superheroes, and other immortals. Relieved of its ethnic name, the figure transcends boundaries of race and time to reflect the toil of all humanity and the passage of time. As I grow older, I personally feel more and more like the Wandering Jew, watching the world I knew as a child disappear and all those I love dying off, leaving me alone to wander through life and wondering why so many ill events must be part of my and all of humanity's fate. Certainly, there are times when we all feel our life must be cursed and ask God why. I suspect a little of the Wandering Jew lives in all of us.

Chapter 5
Secret Societies
Sir Walter Scott, George W. M. Reynolds, and Bram Stoker

"Everywhere the artery was throbbing. Like those membranes that result from certain inflammations and develop in the human body, the network of secret societies began to spread all over the country."

— Victor Hugo, *Les Misérables*

AFTER THE USE OF THE SUPERNATURAL, conspiracy theories and secret societies might be the most popular element in Gothic fiction. Conspiracies committed by secret societies are closely aligned to other Gothic themes because these organizations are viewed as transgressive, trying to overturn a natural and patriarchal order or government believed to be ordained by God. Fear of secret societies or organizations conspiring against the government or the common people has probably existed since the dawn of civilization, and it continues today in modern politics in many forms. The depiction of secret societies and conspiracy theories in Gothic literature became popular as a result of the French Revolution. The revolution was such a dramatic and unbelievable overthrow of the status quo that it easily lent itself to theories that unknown groups and powers were manipulating events behind the scenes.

The era of the French Revolution and the decades that followed was also a time when the legitimacy of monarchy and the forms of government that replaced it were questioned. The legitimacy of religious and social institutions, and the entire social order, were also questioned, especially because they were viewed as oppressive to the lower classes.

Gothic literature provided some comfort or at least a place for discussion of and a way of coping with the social upheaval of the French Revolution and other events by creating fabulous explanations and theories for why those events happened. In *Mythology of the Secret Societies*, J. M. Roberts discusses how conspiracy theories were popular at the time because they attempted "to impose some sort of order on the bewildering changes which suddenly showered upon Europe with the Revolution and its aftermath."[1] Roberts argues that Christians particularly found such theories comforting.

> Educated and conservative men raised in the tradition of Christianity, with its stress on individual responsibility and the independence of the will, found conspiracy theories plausible as an explanation of such changes: it must have come about, they thought, because somebody planned it so.[2]

The most popular conspiracy theories were linked to such secret societies as the Freemasons, Illuminati, and Rosicrucians. Both the Illuminati and the Rosicrucians were sworn to work for the increase of human knowledge and the betterment of humanity.[3] Beliefs arose that these groups had secretly organized the French Revolution and were controlling its events. Such theories claimed authenticity through the symbols of the French Revolution. For example, alleged evidence that the Freemasons had caused the Revolution existed in the fact that Dr. Guillotine was himself a Freemason, and the triangular shape of the guillotine's blade was a Freemason symbol.[4]

While Gothic novels reflected these conspiracy theories, they condemned characters who acted as potential conspirators. Rosicrucians were frequently depicted in Gothic novels because the secrets they possessed—the philosopher's stone and the elixir of life—could threaten the social order. The elixir provided the Rosicrucian with longevity so he had more time to manipulate events toward achieving his political purposes, while the philosopher's stone, which turned lead into gold, allowed him to create great wealth, thereby granting him power over nations' economies.

Another common Gothic feature was the swearing of secret oaths, which reflected the membership oaths of secret societies believed to have caused the French Revolution.[5] D. L. Macdonald has traced such oaths in several Gothic novels where characters swear not to reveal some form of secret knowledge. In Mrs. Radcliffe's *The Mysteries of Udolpho* (1794), Emily St. Aubert swears to her father that she will destroy certain papers without reading them. Emily is unaware that these papers hold family secrets, the knowledge of which could only benefit her. In Polidori's *The Vampyre* (1819), a secret oath occurs when Aubrey swears to Lord Ruthven that he will not reveal for one year the crimes that Ruthven has committed. In Maturin's *Melmoth the Wanderer* (1820), the title character asks an English clergyman to conceal the fact of his death. In Rymer's *Varney the Vampire* (1847), a sexton swears not to reveal that Varney is a vampire, while Varney remarks that the sexton need make no oath for he will remain silent out of fear for his life. In Stoker's *Dracula* (1897), Lucy makes Mina promise not to tell her mother about her sleepwalking. Renfield is also sworn to secrecy so he cannot reveal Dracula's plans to the male protagonists. Finally, Mina forces her friends to swear that they will not tell her their plans for Dracula's destruction so she cannot be forced to impart them to Dracula.[6]

The Gothic frequently depicted conspiracies as resulting in disastrous events the conspirators could no longer control. In *Frankenstein* (1818), Victor believes his ability to restore life will make him a benefactor to humanity, but he is unable to control the Monster he brings to life. Critic Ronald Paulson suggests that the Monster is representative of the Jacobins whose behavior grew out of control during the French Revolution.[7] Similarly, critic Jane

Blumberg remarks that the Monster is composed of various body parts that reflect the atrocities of the French Revolution that were committed in an attempt to regenerate humanity.[8] Blumberg concludes that the Frankenstein Monster is "the dark, destructive and unrestrained manifestation of the Revolution ('more or less than man'), which, had it not been abandoned by educators and guides, might have been the savior of mankind."[9]

The need to find an explanation and source for the French Revolution's events reflected a Christian belief that history evolves according to God's divine plan. Interpretations of the French Revolution as a transgression against God caused both the Romantic poets and the Gothic novelists to turn to Milton's *Paradise Lost* (1667) to support their beliefs for or against the legitimacy of transgression. The Romantic poets would interpret *Paradise Lost* as a justification of rebellion against tyrannical forms of authority. The Gothic novelists, however, were divided upon transgression's legitimacy. These differing viewpoints resulted in two distinct forms of Gothic and the creation of the Gothic wanderer figure. I have discussed these theories and the use of *Paradise Lost* in Gothic literature, as well as *Frankenstein* and several other Gothic novels in relation to these ideas, in *The Gothic Wanderer*, and I invite readers to look there if they want more information on these topics.

Here I wish to discuss a few Gothic novels that are less well-known but provide significant treatments of secret societies and conspiracy theories. We have already met several secret societies in earlier chapters. In Chapter 3, we saw how the Marquis de Rio Santo's Gentlemen of the Night failed in their efforts to overthrow the British Government in Paul Féval's *Les Mystères de Londres*. In Chapter 4, we saw how Eugène Sue treated the Jesuits as a secret society willing to kidnap, deceive, and murder to get its hands on a fortune in *The Wandering Jew*. In Chapter 6, we will look at Gothic novels set during the French Revolution. There we will meet Rosicrucians in Bulwer-Lytton's novel *Zanoni*, see how Dickens used Rosicrucian elements in *A Tale of Two Cities*, and meet an international secret society behind the Revolution in Dumas' *Marie Antoinette* novels.

In this chapter, I will not discuss any French Gothic novels, although as just made clear, secret societies abound in them. Here, I have chosen to focus on three British novels that deserve far more attention than they have received and all of which depict secret societies. The first is Sir Walter Scott's most Gothic novel, *Anne of Geierstein*. The other two are among the greatest Gothic novels ever written that hardly anyone reads anymore: George W. M. Reynolds' *Faust: A Romance of the Secret Tribunals* and its sequel or spin-off, *Wagner the Wehr-Wolf*. It is hard to understand how these fabulously plotted novels have fallen into obscurity, so I hope this discussion will create new interest in them. Finally, I will discuss a British novel that has Swedish connections— the newly discovered *Powers of Darkness*. Currently, critics are divided on whether this novel is an early version of *Dracula* that was published in Sweden, or a rewrite of *Dracula* by a Swedish author, or a mix of both. Either way, it contains one of the most dramatic and extensive treatments of a secret society in Gothic literature—and one completely absent from the final version of *Dracula* that was published in Great Britain. The result of these explorations will be a better understanding of the role secret societies play in Gothic literature and also how conspiracy theories arise from basic human fears during times of change and social upheaval, fears no different two centuries ago than today as recently revealed by the coronavirus pandemic and the social and political upheavals in the United States and other countries in the early 2020s.

Sir Walter Scott's *Anne of Geierstein*

Anne of Geierstein (1829) is Sir Walter Scott's most Gothic novel and probably the last true masterpiece he wrote. It was well-received upon publication and holds up remarkably well today. Despite Scott's typical slow-pacing, the novel contains a plethora of dramatic scenes that keep the reader interested and often in suspense, creating an overall powerful impression. Although not central to the plot, a secret society, the Holy Vehme, is featured in a key scene and referenced in other places. It was based on a proto-vigilante tribunal system in Westphalia that operated often in secret from the thirteenth through sixteenth centuries and possibly as late as the eighteenth.[10] I will first discuss the overall plot and Gothic elements of *Anne of Geierstein* and then focus specifically on Scott's depiction of the Holy Vehme.

The story begins with an English merchant named Philipson and his son Arthur traveling through Switzerland in the 1470s. When Arthur takes a path that results in his nearly falling off a cliff, he finds himself perched in a tree with a ravine below him that he dare not try to cross. Enter Anne, our heroine, who, as nimble as a mountain goat, jumps across to the tree and convinces Arthur he can jump back. Realizing how easy the jump is, Arthur feels a bit silly; after all, the reader will soon learn Arthur is a brave knight and he and his father are traveling in disguise.

The Philipsons continue their journey with the party of Anne's uncle, Arnold Biederman. Anne is under her uncle's protection. As they travel, the Philipsons learn that Arnold is the rightful heir to the nearby castle of Geierstein, but he has given up his title to his brother, Albert of Arnheim. Albert will prove to be the novel's villain. Of course, Arthur falls in love with Anne during the journey.

But Arthur and his father have their own concerns. Arthur's father is really the Earl of Oxford, and they are on a mission to ask the Duke of Burgundy to enlist in the Lancastrian cause during the English Wars of the Roses. This mission will lead them to Anjou where Margaret, the rightful Queen of England, is in exile now that her husband Henry VI and her son Edward have both died. She lives at her father's court in misery while her father tries to distract her with frivolous entertainments.

The novel's Gothic moments are frequent throughout, the first being Arthur's fear when faced with jumping over the ravine.

Switzerland's sublime mountainous landscape had already become popular as a setting in such Gothic novels as Radcliffe's *The Romance of the Forest* (1791) and Shelley's *Frankenstein* (1818), but Scott capitalizes on the landscape to a greater degree than either of those novels to create moments of fear and awe in his characters and readers.

Secret societies are introduced into the novel in relation to Anne's family. According to the family legend Anne tells Arthur, her grandfather, Herman, Baron of Arnheim, had once taken a stranger, a Persian named Dannischemend, into his castle to give him protection. Although Dannischemend told Herman he would only live for a year and a day, he begged the baron to protect him for the remainder of his life. Herman agreed in exchange that Dannischemend teach him the secrets of the Sacred Fire, a society to which the Persian belonged. Dannischemend agreed to do so, but when the year came to an end, he asked that his daughter be given shelter in the castle, and in exchange, she would also teach secrets to the baron. However, Dannischemend warned Herman not to fall in love with her. Despite this warning, they fell in love, were married, and had a daughter. At the child's christening, Herman accidentally let a drop or two of holy water fall on his bride, who immediately turned to ash. This story recalls that of the French medieval fairy Melusine and many other fairy-type characters who were pagan and unable to be baptized or to live as Christians. Although Arthur later hears the truth of what happened to Anne's grandmother and knows he should dismiss this story as false, his next encounter with Anne makes him wonder whether there may be some truth to Anne having a supernatural parentage.

As the novel progresses, the Gothic themes continue. Arthur eventually finds himself imprisoned in a castle. His belief in Anne's supernatural parentage is reinforced when she and another woman appear through inexplicable means as if they were elemental spirits. Arthur cannot understand how these women entered the prison, and being under a vow, Anne cannot speak to him, which adds to the mystery. Of course, Anne leads Arthur out of the prison to safety, and in time, she explains how she was able to enter the prison, thus explaining away the supernatural.

Perhaps the most stunning Gothic moment in the novel is when Arthur's father rents a room in an inn. As he is lying in bed, he finds himself suddenly strapped to the bed as a prisoner. The bed is then lowered through the floor into a mysterious subterranean chamber where he becomes the prisoner of the Holy Vehme, a secret organization that has taken upon itself to judge men for their crimes. The Holy Vehme is also known as the Initiated, the Wise Men, and the Secret Tribunal. Dressed as monks, the members of the Holy Vehme interrogate Philipson in a manner that recalls scenes of the Inquisition in Radcliffe's *The Italian* (1797) and Maturin's *Melmoth the Wanderer* (1820). Although accused of slandering the Holy Vehme, Philipson is finally set free.

Scott now begins to cast aside the love story and focus on Arthur and his father's mission. They travel to Anjou to meet Margaret and her father, King René. These scenes are some of the most powerful in the novel as we are introduced to King René, who engages in merriment, and Queen Margaret, who is grieving her losses. Margaret, unable to enjoy her father's frolicsome ways, does not live in his castle but at the nearby monastery. In a dramatic scene, Arthur meets with Margaret at the monastery to tell her what progress has been made in negotiating with the King of Burgundy to aid the Lancastrian cause. Margaret is willing to make sure Burgundy gets the province of Provence from her father in exchange for his aid, though her father is less willing to agree to this deal. Margaret and Arthur meet on a parapet where Arthur finds her seated with her disheveled hair tossing about in the wind. She is described as noble and beautiful, yet having ghastly and wasted features. Arthur feels terror over being on the parapet because a storm is approaching, and he beseeches her to go inside, but she refuses because monks and walls have ears and she does not want their discussion overheard.

Margaret tells Arthur that a cavern exists beneath the monastery where in pagan days people went to consult an oracle. The voice of the oracle, known as Lou Garagoule, comes up from the cavern to answer people's questions. Roman generals once consulted the oracle, but Margaret finds it deaf to her inquiries. The scene reflects the former queen's desperation in seeking supernatural aid. It recalls Gothic wanderer figures willing to sell their souls to the devil to achieve what they desire, including forbidden knowledge of the future. Margaret, in her desperate and bereaved state, certainly wins the prize as the most extreme Gothic wanderer in the novel. Unfortunately, soon after Arthur's meeting with Margaret, she dies.

The novel seems to lose its intensity after Margaret's death. During the scenes in Anjou, Anne has been absent for about a third of the novel. Toward the end, some battles are fought before all is resolved; then Arthur and Anne marry and the happy ending comes about. We are told the newlyweds live in Switzerland for a while until Henry VII gains the throne of England. Then they go to live in England where Anne becomes an ornament of Henry VII's court.

Sir Walter Scott, though the father of the historical novel, takes many liberties with history in *Anne of Geierstein*, which makes it more akin to Gothic romance and Mrs. Radcliffe's novels than many of his other historical works. Scott's use of history here is more for his own narrative purposes; he does not let the facts shape his narrative as in other works. Today, no self-respecting historical novelist would so deviate from history as to have Margaret die in 1476 when she did not actually die until 1482, or to have King René outlive her when he actually died in 1480. Worse, while the Earl of Oxford did historically support the Lancastrian cause, he never had a son named Arthur, meaning our hero and heroine are completely fictional.

Regardless, Scott's portraits of his characters are remarkable, and his depiction of Margaret of Anjou easily rivals that of Shakespeare in the *Henry VI* plays. Scott also knows how to take a fascinating moment in history and make it come alive in complex ways as reflected in his depiction of the court of Burgundy, the court of King René, and the various political situations. Scott may not always be historically accurate, but he inspires the reader to want to learn more about the history behind his novels. Furthermore, his characters' pathos and their broken hearts directly result from some of history's most tragic moments, making the moments real for the reader in a way historical nonfiction rarely achieves.

All that said, Scott's treatment of the Holy Vehme is odd because it does not end up being overly integral to the plot. It is included to add Gothic thrills to the narrative, but because the accusation made against Philipson that he has spoken ill of the Holy Vehme turns out to be untrue, he is freed. The Holy Vehme is not involved in the novel further and overall is unimportant to the plot. Regardless, that a secret society is on the watch is one of those fears that creates paranoia and succeeds in making the reader uncomfortable even after all the characters' other troubles are resolved.

The chapters concerning the Holy Vehme occur in Volume II, Chapters 6-8.[*] The scenes begin when Philipson and Arthur decide to split up and take different routes to Burgundy after Anne, in disguise, warns them that their guide, Brother Bartholomew, cannot be trusted. Philipson continues with Bartholomew while Arthur takes a different route, but Bartholomew is sent off when a Black Priest joins Philipson. The Black Priest leads Philipson to the inn. There he awakes in the night to find his bed being lowered through the floor. He arrives in a subterranean chamber, and before he can escape the bed, two men on either side grab and tie his arms. He then hears chanting, like that of mourners

---

[*] Chapters 18-20 in editions that number the chapters consecutively without volume breaks.

at a funeral, and realizes he must be in the presence of the Holy Vehme, which is known by a few names. Scott depicts the scene as follows:

> The nature of the verses soon led Philipson to comprehend that he was in presence of the Initiated, or the Wise Men; names which were applied to the celebrated Judges of the Secret Tribunal, which continued at that period to subsist in Swabia, Franconia, and other districts of the east of Germany, which was called, perhaps from the frightful and frequent occurrence of executions by command of those invisible judges, the Red Land. Philipson had often heard that the seat of a Free Count, or chief of the Secret Tribunal, was secretly instituted even on the left bank of the Rhine, and that it maintained itself in Alsace, with the usual tenacity of those secret societies, though Duke Charles of Burgundy had expressed a desire to discover and discourage its influence so far as was possible, without exposing himself to danger from the thousands of poniards which that mysterious tribunal could put in activity against his own life;—an awful means of defence, which for a long time rendered it extremely hazardous for the sovereigns of Germany, and even the Emperors themselves, to put down by authority those singular associations.
>
> So soon as this explanation flashed on the mind of Philipson, it gave some clue to the character and condition of the Black Priest of St. Paul's. Supposing him to be a president, or chief official of the secret association, there was little wonder that he should confide so much in the inviolability of his terrible office as to propose vindicating the execution of De Hagenbach; that his presence should surprise Bartholomew, whom he had power to have judged and executed upon the spot; and that his mere appearance at supper on the preceding evening should

have appalled the guests; for though everything about the institution, its proceedings and its officers, was preserved in as much obscurity as is now practised in free-masonry, yet the secret was not so absolutely well kept as to prevent certain individuals from being guessed or hinted at as men initiated and intrusted with high authority by the Vehme-gericht, or tribunal of the bounds. When such suspicion attached to an individual, his secret power, and supposed acquaintance with all guilt, however secret, which was committed within the society in which he was conversant, made him at once the dread and hatred of every one who looked on him; and he enjoyed a high degree of personal respect, on the same terms on which it would have been yielded to a powerful enchanter, or a dreaded genie. In conversing with such a person, it was especially necessary to abstain from all questions alluding, however remotely, to the office which he bore in the Secret Tribunal; and, indeed, to testify the least curiosity upon a subject so solemn and mysterious was sure to occasion some misfortune to the inquisitive person.

All these things rushed at once upon the mind of the Englishman, who felt that he had fallen into the hands of an unsparing tribunal, whose proceedings were so much dreaded by those who resided within the circle of their power, that the friendless stranger must stand a poor chance of receiving justice at their hands, whatever might be his consciousness of innocence. While Philipson made this melancholy reflection, he resolved, at the same time, not to forsake his own cause, but defend himself as he best might; conscious as he was that these terrible and irresponsible judges were nevertheless governed by certain rules of right and wrong, which formed a check on the rigours of their extraordinary code.[11]

Eventually, all the members of the Holy Vehme assemble and then as a group repeat their oath.

"I swear by the Holy Trinity, to aid and co-operate, without relaxation, in the things belonging to the Holy Vehme, to defend its doctrines and institutions against father and mother, brother and sister, wife and children; against fire, water, earth, and air; against all that the sun enlightens; against all that the dew moistens; against all created things of heaven and earth, or the waters under the earth; and I swear to give information to this holy judicature, of all that I know to be true, or hear repeated by credible testimony, which, by the rules of the Holy Vehme, is deserving of animadversion or punishment; and that I will not cloak, cover, or conceal, such my knowledge, neither for love, friendship, or family affection, nor for gold, silver, or precious stones; neither will I associate with such as are under the sentence of this Sacred Tribunal, by hinting to a culprit his danger, or advising him to escape, or aiding and supplying him with counsel, or means to that effect; neither will I relieve such culprit with fire, clothes, food, or shelter, though my father should require from me a cup of water in the heat of summer noon, or my brother should request to sit by my fire in the bitterest cold night of winter: And further, I vow and promise to honour this holy association, and do its behests speedily, faithfully, and firmly, in preference to those of any other tribunal whatsoever—so help me God, and His holy Evangelists."[12]

After the oath, Philipson is brought forth, dragged by six attendants on the bed toward the altar. He is ordered to arise but can only sit up in the bed. The Judge, who turns out to be the Black Priest, then interrogates him about his identity and history and accuses him of entering in disguise the "Sacred Territory, which is called the Red Land" and of having spoken of "the Holy Tribunal in terms of hatred and contempt, and declared that were he Duke of Burgundy, he would not permit it to extend itself from Westphalia, or Swabia, into his dominions."[13] He is also accused of using his influence with the Duke to make him prohibit meetings of the Holy Vehme. Philipson explains that he did say such things when pressed to respond by others about questions concerning the Holy Vehme, but he said them outside of the tribunal's jurisdiction. After deliberation, it is decided to release him, but with a warning:

> "Child of the cord," said the presiding Judge, "thou hast heard thy sentence of acquittal. But, as thou desirest to sleep in an unbloody grave, let me warn thee, that the secrets of this night shall remain with thee, as a secret not to be communicated to father nor mother, to spouse, son, or daughter; neither to be spoken aloud nor whispered; to be told in words or written in characters; to be carved or to be painted, or to be otherwise communicated, either directly or by parable and emblem. Obey this behest, and thy life is in surety. Let thy heart then rejoice within thee, but let it rejoice with trembling. Never more let thy vanity persuade thee that thou art secure from the servants and Judges of the Holy Vehme. Though a thousand leagues lie between thee and the Red Land, and thou speakest in that where our power is not known; though thou shouldst be sheltered by thy native island, and defended by thy kindred ocean, yet, even there, I warn thee to cross thyself when thou dost so much as think of the Holy and Invisible Tribunal, and to retain thy thoughts within thine own bosom; for the Avenger may be beside thee, and thou mayst die in thy folly. Go hence, be wise, and let the fear of the Holy Vehme never pass from before thine eyes."[14]

Acquitted, Philipson now is forced to lie back down on the bed. Then it is repositioned so it can be raised back up to his room in the inn. He gladly departs the inn the next morning.

Later in the novel, it is revealed that the Black Priest was actually Anne's father, Albert of Arnheim, who has been manipulating some of the events in his own interest and continues to do so, although not to an extent that is dangerous to the other characters; therefore, the Vehme's role in the novel turns out to be fairly minor. Still, this scene is the novel's most memorable and terrifying moment and reflects the early nineteenth-century paranoia regarding secret societies, despite its medieval setting.

Although all but forgotten today, *Anne of Geierstein* was quite popular in Scott's day. Furthermore, his treatment of the Holy Vehme likely inspired George W. M. Reynolds' treatment of the Holy Vehme in his novel *Faust: A Romance of the Secret Tribunals*, which we will now explore.

George W. M. Reynolds' *Faust*

Faust: A Romance of the Secret Tribunals (1845-6) was the first of three incredible Gothic novels George W. M. Reynolds wrote. It was serialized in *The London Journal* from October 4, 1845 to September 26, 1846.[15] Unlike Reynolds' *The Mysteries of London*, it contains supernatural elements. Reynolds' other supernatural Gothic novels are *Faust*'s sequel *Wagner the Wehr-Wolf* (1846-7), which will be discussed later in this chapter, and *The Necromancer* (1851-2), to be discussed in Chapter 7. Of the three, *Faust* is the most loosely-plotted and least thrilling, yet there is plenty to enjoy in it, including Reynolds' treatment of the Holy Vehme, or simply "Vehm," as Reynolds spells it.

Readers might assume they know the story of Faust* from reading Christopher Marlowe's play *The Tragical History of the Life and Death of Dr. Faustus* (published circa 1604) or Goethe's two-part closet drama *Faust* (published 1808 and 1832). However, Reynolds expands on the story, adding extensively to the storyline to take the reader on a journey through much of Central and Eastern Europe, including Germany, Italy, and Turkey.

Because the novel's storyline is complicated, I will only discuss highlights of the main plots and focus on the secret society aspect.

---

* The Faust legend is actually based on the historical person Johann Georg Faust (1466/80-1540), a German alchemist, astrologer, and magician. Little is known of him that can be historically verified, and he has been mostly forgotten in the wake of the legends of his pact with Satan.

Basically, like in Reynolds' *The Mysteries of London*, we have two opposing main characters representing evil (Faust) and good (Otto). As expected, Faust is the villain because he sells his soul to the devil. Reynolds, however, qualifies this transgression by having Faust forced to do so to save the woman he loves.

The novel begins at the end of the fifteenth century when Faust, a common man, is in love with Therese, the daughter of a baron. Therese's father refuses to let her marry Faust and even throws Faust in prison to keep him away from his daughter. The devil appears to Faust and proposes a deal in which he helps Faust win Therese and also acquire great power and riches for twenty-four years; in exchange, at the end of that time, Faust's soul will belong to him, as well as that of his firstborn child. Faust agrees to the deal. He then passes himself off as a young nobleman and saves Therese from being abducted, leading to her father giving them permission to marry. Faust adopts the title of Count of Aurana and weds Therese. Happiness seems imminent for the couple—except that Faust relents on his willingness to let Satan have his child's soul.

Fortunately, Faust's friend, an archduke, has a wife who becomes pregnant at the same time as Therese. Therese gives birth to a boy and the archduke's wife gives birth to a girl, but before either mother knows the sex of her child, Faust convinces his mistress, Ida, to switch the babies, thinking that will protect his son.

We could almost sympathize with Faust in wanting to protect his child, but he does so through deceit. His moral depravity is clear in that he takes Ida for a mistress soon after his marriage. Meanwhile Ida's brother, Otto, the novel's hero, learns of the affair and tries to defend his sister's honor. Faust agrees to do what is right by Ida, but he is already married, so he arranges a marriage for her with Baron Czernin.

Meanwhile, Otto, through a series of accidents while traveling, ends up imprisoned inside a mountain by the Vehm. Eventually, the Vehm release Otto, but not before he learns that the true Baron

Czernin is also imprisoned there, while his sister's husband is an impostor. By helping the baron escape, Otto ends up on the Vehm's blacklist.

At this point, the plots become convoluted and I suspect Reynolds was running out of ideas to keep the serialized novel going, so he takes us to the Vatican and introduces us to Pope Alexander VI and his children, Caesar* and Lucrezia Borgia. Otto will unwillingly become involved with the Borgias in an attempt to protect himself from the Vehm. Meanwhile, Lucrezia becomes attracted to him, but he is so repelled by her reputation that he spurns her, causing her to vow revenge.

The novel now jumps ahead to when Faust's twenty-four-year pact with Satan is coming to an end. By then, Faust's son and adopted daughter have grown up, fallen in love with each other, and wish to be married. Faust is against the marriage because he believes if he enters a church to attend the ceremony, he will instantly become the devil's before his time is up. Finally, he confesses the secret of his satanic pact to Otto. Otto tries to get Faust to pray, but Faust fears Satan will only come for him if he tries. Faust says Otto can do nothing to save him, but he can save his son. If Otto will travel to Mt. Ararat and retrieve a piece of wood from Noah's Ark, which his son can wear about his person, then Satan will be unable to take his son. Otto agrees to this quest, one of the more fascinating events in the novel, and is able to retrieve a piece of the sacred wood.

On his way home from Mt. Ararat, Otto is shipwrecked and finds himself on an island where Lucrezia Borgia resides. She is now married to her third husband, the Duke of Ferrara. Still bent on revenge, Lucrezia has Otto cast into "The Iron Coffin"—a dungeon that has walls and a roof that over several days slowly move inward until the prisoner is crushed to death. Otto is terrified he will lose his life, but on the day before he will be completely crushed, Lucrezia comes to ask for his love. When he again refuses on moral principles, she condemns him to death,

---

* Caesar is Reynolds' spelling. The correct spelling is Cesare.

but moments later, her husband the duke, having learned of her schemes, rescues Otto and places Lucrezia in the coffin to die.

Otto now returns to Faust with the talisman from Noah's Ark to save his son. Faust's final day then arrives. When Satan comes to claim him, Faust begs for his life. Satan tells him if he had listened to Otto and prayed, he might have still saved his soul, but now it is too late. The novel concludes when Satan and Faust travel to Mt. Vesuvius. There Satan pushes Faust into the volcano, which is an entrance to hell.

The plot is far more complicated than I have detailed here. It is filled with evil priests, plenty of court intrigue, and the secret tribunal of the Vehm. The Vehm's role in the novel leads to several plot twists and may have been inspired by Scott's work, but it fails to be as dramatic as in *Anne of Geierstein*—the Borgias steal the show instead. Reynolds tries to be historical, setting the novel in the 1490s to early 1500s, and he constantly provides dates for the events. He documents the plague that swept Vienna, and he even provides footnotes stating when he altered events and dates for his own purposes. Lucrezia's death is wholly fictional and created for dramatic effect. She actually died following an illness after childbirth.

Amazingly, Reynolds brings all his various plots together to complete them, though some more successfully than others. But what is most fascinating about the end is that Faust fails to achieve the redemption he seeks. Although not always acting morally, most of Faust's devious actions are carried out to save the woman he loves or his child. He only turned to the devil out of desperation, and the devil, never one to play fair, always goes to extremes to make Faust's crimes worse. For example, when Faust begs the devil to create a distraction so his son and adopted daughter will forget their love for each other, the devil creates the plague—an extreme solution Faust would not have desired.

Faust's plummeting into the mouth of Mt. Vesuvius is also fascinating since one of Reynolds' fellow writers of penny dreadfuls, James Malcolm Rymer, depicts Varney the Vampire trying to destroy himself by plummeting into a volcano, but the volcano always spits Varney out, refusing to let him lose his existence, though in the end he also dies by jumping into Mt. Vesuvius. *Varney the Vampire*'s serialization of 1845-7 overlapped with that of *Faust*, and it reflects the first time a Gothic wanderer achieves true redemption.* Reynolds wasn't ready to give his anti-hero that relief. A few years later, as we saw in Chapter 4, Dumas would describe Isaac Laquedem unsuccessfully trying to kill himself by plunging into a volcano.

With *Faust*, Reynolds showed himself able to take readers on a fantastic roller-coaster ride through a Gothic version of history. He lets us journey through half of Europe and meet the most notorious people from the period when the novel is set. Indeed, Lucrezia Borgia supersedes her already bad reputation in the novel to become one of the greatest female villains in Gothic fiction. Yet as Gothic and dramatic as *Faust* is, in *Wagner the Wehr-Wolf*, Reynolds would surpass himself.

George W. M. Reynolds' *Wagner, the Wehr-Wolf*

Wagner, the Wehr-Wolf, a sequel to *Faust: A Romance of the Secret Tribunals*, was serialized in *Reynolds's Miscellany* from November 6, 1846 to July 24, 1847.[16] The serialization began just six weeks after *Faust* had ended, and in between, Reynolds began the serialization for the second series of *The Mysteries of London*. He was always prolific, and he was always willing to capitalize on the popularity of others' works. The title *Wagner, the Wehr-Wolf* likely owes its alliteration and inspiration to *Varney the Vampire*, which began serialization a year earlier.

Wagner, the Wehr-Wolf, even more so than *Faust*, is full of plot twists. Lovers of Gothic literature will delight in the remarkable coincidences, family secrets, mysterious manuscript, bloody deeds, and supernatural events. The setting, other than the brief prologue that takes place in Germany, is primarily Florence,

---

* I have discussed *Varney the Vampire* at length in *The Gothic Wanderer*.

Italy, in the 1520s, with some scenes on a deserted island and in Constantinople. Despite a large cast of characters, only Wagner and Nisida really stand out. I will focus on them and the novel's main plot, while including a few comments about minor characters and subplots to highlight the Gothic elements that add to the novel's fascination. Most significantly for this discussion, Reynolds includes another secret society in the novel—the Rosicrucians, and their founder, Christian Rosencreutz (Reynolds uses the Italian name Christianus Rosencrux but often shortens the first name to Christian), plays a significant role in the plot.

When the novel opens, Wagner is a ninety-five-year-old grandfather who fears he has been abandoned by his granddaughter and left alone in their forest home. He is visited by a mysterious stranger, whom we later learn is Faust—although it is not clear if this is the Faust of the last novel. Faust gives Wagner the gift of youth in exchange for traveling with him for a year and a half. But there is one other condition linked to his achieving youth—Wagner will become a werewolf for twenty-four hours once a month. Wagner agrees to the terms and drinks from a vial to achieve the transformation. This detail is interesting because most werewolf stories show the transformation happening from being bitten by the werewolf. However, the vial is a type of elixir of life that restores youth and gives extended life; notably, the Rosicrucians were said to have two primary secrets: the elixir of life and the philosopher's stone that turns lead into gold. While Faust, who gives this gift to Wagner, is not a Rosicrucian, we will encounter Rosicrucians later in the novel.

Following the prologue, Faust does not appear in the book again. Instead, the narrative jumps ahead several years, and we learn that after Wagner completed the prescribed eighteen months of traveling with Faust, Faust passed away.

However, Wagner's affiliation with Faust has not yet ended. Satan now appears to tempt Wagner to seal a pact with him like the one he had with Faust. By this point, Wagner is tormented by his werewolfism and longs to be freed from it, but Satan says he must sell his soul to him in exchange for freedom from the werewolf transformation plus to receive additional power. Wagner refuses to agree to this, and at the moments when he is most tempted, he manages to send off Satan with a crucifix.

Some of the novel's best passages are the descriptions of Wagner as a werewolf. For example, his transformation in Chapter 12 results in extreme violence:

> In the midst of a wood of evergreens on the banks of the Arno, a man—young, handsome, and splendidly attired—has thrown himself upon the ground, where he writhes like a stricken serpent, in horrible convulsions.
>
> He is the prey of a demoniac excitement: an appalling consternation is on him—madness is in his brain—his mind is on fire.
>
> Lightnings appear to gleam from his eyes, as if his soul were dismayed, and withering within his breast.
>
> "Oh! no—no!" he cries with a piercing shriek, as if wrestling madly, furiously, but vainly against some unseen fiend that holds him in his grasp.
>
> And the wood echoes to that terrible wail; and the startled bird flies fluttering from its bough.
>
> But, lo! what awful change is taking place in the form of that doomed being? His handsome countenance elongates into one of savage and brute-like shape; the rich garments which he wears become a rough, shaggy, and wiry skin; his body loses its human contours, his arms and limbs take another form; and, with a frantic howl of misery, to which the woods give horribly faithful reverberations, and, with a rush like a hurling wind, the wretch starts wildly away, no longer a man, but a monstrous wolf!
>
> On, on he goes: the wood is cleared—the open country is gained. Tree, hedge, and isolated cottage appear but dim points in the landscape—a moment seen, the next left behind; the very hills appear to leap after each other.

A cemetery stands in the monster's way, but he turns not aside—through the sacred inclosure—on, on he goes. There are situated many tombs, stretching up the slope of a gentle acclivity, from the dark soil of which the white monuments stand forth with white and ghastly gleaming, and on the summit of the hill is the church of St. Benedict the Blessed.

From the summit of the ivy-grown tower the very rooks, in the midst of their cawing, are scared away by the furious rush and the wild howl with which the Wehr-Wolf thunders over the hallowed ground.

At the same instant a train of monks appear round the angle of the church—for there is a funeral at that hour; and their torches flaring with the breeze that is now springing up, cast an awful and almost magical light on the dark gray walls of the edifice, the strange effect being enhanced by the prismatic reflection of the lurid blaze from the stained glass of the oriel window.

The solemn spectacle seemed to madden the Wehr-Wolf. His speed increased—he dashed through the funeral train—appalling cries of terror and alarm burst from the lips of the holy fathers—and the solemn procession was thrown into confusion. The coffin-bearers dropped their burden, and the corpse rolled out upon the ground, its decomposing countenance seeming horrible by the glare of the torch-light.

The monk who walked nearest the head of the coffin was thrown down by the violence with which the ferocious monster cleared its passage; and the venerable father—on whose brow sat the snow of eighty winters—fell with his head against a monument, and his brains were dashed out.

Wagner continually commits manslaughter (it's not exactly intentional murder) in his werewolf state, although the novel only shows us his transformation on a few occasions. Nevertheless, his situation is not hopeless, nor is he unredeemable.

But before discussing Wagner's redemption, let us look at the novel's other remarkable main character. If ever there was a villainess, it is Nisida. I wonder if Reynolds got her name from Dumas' *Celebrated Crimes* (1839-41), which includes a story titled "Nisida." The Nisida was a prison on an island off the coast of Naples that was known for its cruelty. Such a name is then fitting for Reynolds' villainess. When we are first introduced to Nisida, it is believed she is deaf and dumb, but it is soon revealed she fakes these disabilities as a way to spy upon others. She is also not above cross-dressing. And certainly not above committing murder to get her way.

Early in the novel, this "noble" woman meets Wagner and they fall in love. However, Nisida eventually suspects Wagner is having an affair with Agnes. Agnes is Wagner's granddaughter whom he feared had deserted him in the forest. After much persuading by Wagner that he is her grandfather despite his youthful appearance, Agnes comes to live with him. Nisida, not knowing their true relationship, but knowing Agnes is her father's former mistress, naturally thinks Wagner is cheating on her. When Nisida murders Agnes, Wagner is arrested for the crime. Wagner is unable to explain his true relationship with Agnes since he knows no one will believe him, so he is imprisoned. Nisida then cross-dresses to visit Wagner in prison.

Eventually, Wagner escapes from prison, and after a series of events, he and Nisida end up shipwrecked on a deserted island. (Interestingly, a volcanic island off the coast of Italy is also named Nisida, which may have given Reynolds the idea for his character's name and temper.) Only on the island does Nisida reveal to Wagner that she can hear and speak.

Wagner and Nisida enjoy a sort of island paradise experience that recalls both the Garden of Eden and the island scenes between Immalee and Melmoth in *Melmoth the Wanderer*, only here it is the male, not the female, who is innocent and has a tempter.

Critic Louis James has also suggested this scene is reminiscent of the Haidée episode in Canto 2 of Byron's *Don Juan*.[17] Such a source would not be surprising given that Reynolds published his own sequel in verse to *Don Juan* in 1843. During this time, Nisida feels overcome by Wagner's beauty "so joyful, too, was she in the possession of one whose masculine beauty was almost superhumanly great."[18]

However, Nisida soon grows bored on the island. She is unhappy that Wagner leaves her once a month without explanation. (He doesn't want her to know he transforms into a werewolf.) Nisida longs to return to Italy to look after her brother whom she knows is in love with Flora, her maid—a relationship she is not happy about.

Satan appears on the island to tempt Wagner, but he rejects Satan's overtures. Satan then turns to tempting Nisida—rather like Satan tempting Eve in the Garden of Eden. He tells Nisida that Wagner has the power to leave the island but refuses to share this power with her. (Wagner does not have this power, but he would if he sold his soul to Satan.) Satan urges Nisida to demand Wagner transport them from the island, and if Wagner refuses, to question why he leaves her each month. Despite Nisida's questions, however, Wagner does not reveal his secret.

Eventually, a boat arrives. Nisida returns to the mainland, but Wagner stays behind, not wanting to live among humans because he might harm them when he is a werewolf. Nisida promises to return to Wagner once she takes care of her brother Francisco. While she is away, Wagner despairs of ever being freed from his werewolfism. Then he has a dream in which an angel tells him he has done much already to atone for his sins by resisting Nisida and Satan's temptations. Wagner is led to find a boat, which the angel tells him to take to Sicily. There he will meet a 162-year-old man who can help him. This aspect of the story recalls Acts 9 when Christ tells Paul to go to Ananias to cure him of his blindness.

Wagner cannot understand how a man can be so old, but he goes to Sicily where he inquires of an innkeeper about the whereabouts of such a man. The innkeeper remarks that he has heard a ridiculous legend about the Rosicrucians and their legendary founder, Christianus Rosencrux, who would be 162 years old if the legends are true since it is now the year 1521 and he was said to have been born in 1359. The man describes Christianus as follows:

> the fabled philosopher was a monk, and a very wise as well as a very good man. I am only telling you the most generally received legend, mind, and would not have you think that I believe it myself. So this Rosencrux, finding that his cloistral existence was inconvenient for the prosecution of his studies, traveled into the East, and spent many years in acquiring the knowledge handed down to the wise men of those climes by the ancient Magi and Chaldeans. He visited Egypt, and learnt many wonderful secrets by studying the hieroglyphics on the Egyptian pyramids. I forget how long he remained in the East; but it is said that he visited every place of interest in the Holy Land, and received heavenly inspirations on the spot where our Saviour was crucified. On his return to Europe, he saw full well that if he revealed all his knowledge at once, he would be put to death by the inquisition as a wizard, and the world would lose the benefit of all the learning he had acquired. So says the legend; and it goes on to recite that Christianus Rosencrux then founded the order of the Rosy Cross, which was nothing more or less than a brotherhood of wise men whom he initiated in all his secrets, with the intention that they should reveal from time to time small portions thereof, and thus give to the world by very slow degrees that immense amount of knowledge which he supposed would have stupefied and astounded everybody if made public all at once.[19]

Wagner soon realizes it must be Rosencrux whom he seeks, and that night, a mysterious stranger comes to him and leads him to Rosencrux. Wagner is surprised that the mysterious stranger knows he seeks Christian Rosencrux, but the stranger explains that the Rosicrucians are the servants of the angels who show them in visions what they must do to fulfill God's will, and so he has come to bring Wagner to Rosencrux.

Rosencrux, however, doesn't really do much for Wagner except point him toward the next part of his journey. He tells him to go to Florence to meet Nisida, and he says Wagner will be released from his werewolf curse when he sees two innocent people's skeletons hanging from the same beam.

How the novel leads to this conclusion is convoluted, but after a series of events, Wagner sees the skeletons and falls dead at the sight. We then learn the skeletons are tied to a secret that has been Nisida's primary motivation for all her actions, including a promise to her mother to protect her brother's inheritance. She confesses everything to her brother Francisco and his new bride Flora before she becomes ill. Francisco thanks her for all she has done for him. Christianus Rosencrux then appears to act as her confessor. After Nisida dies, Rosencrux tells Flora and Francisco that Nisida is forgiven and can rest in peace.

The redemption theme here is strange since Gothic novels to this point almost always depicted transgressors as receiving damnation, as did Faust in Reynolds' earlier novel. However, Reynolds allows the horrible villainess Nisida to be forgiven. Reynolds may have been inspired by *Varney the Vampire*, one of the first novels to depict a repentant and redeemed Gothic transgressor,* but while Varney's remorse and repentance are believable, neither Wagner nor Nisida do anything to gain forgiveness—no acts of kindness required—just repentance at the last moment. While Wagner committed murder as a werewolf, it might be argued he cannot be blamed for what happens to him during his transformed moments. However, Nisida has cruelly

---

* I have been unable to locate the date *Varney the Vampire*'s serialization ended, but it was definitely in 1847 and probably prior to the end of *Wagner the Wehr-Wolf*'s serialization on July 24, 1847 since the book version of *Varney the Vampire* was published in September 1847.

and intentionally murdered, and her justifications for her crimes make her sound more psychotic than deserving of forgiveness; she even states in the case of killing a woman named Margaretha that the woman got what she deserved. Still, for Reynolds, repentance is enough, even if you are a liar and a murderer.

Religion's role in the novel is interesting in terms of this redemption. Both Nisida and Wagner seek redemption and die as Christians. But Reynolds is not as kind to non-Christians. For example, Alessandro, the brother of Flora, Nisida's maid, early in the novel travels to Constantinople to serve in Florence's embassy. There he meets the beautiful Aisca, who tempts him to convert to Islam in exchange for enjoying her company. After he does so, he is promoted until he becomes grand vizier to Sultan Solyman the Magnificent, who turns out to be Aisca's brother. Aisca's tempting of Alessandro recalls Eve tempting Adam—it is a woman who turns a man to sin, just as we saw how Nisida tempted Wagner. For Reynolds, this conversion to another religion serves as a serious transgression.

The other temptation and the only real sin Alessandro (who becomes Ibrahim upon conversion) commits is that he falls in love with a beautiful young woman, Calanthe, and commits adultery with her. When Aisca's mother finds out about his betrayal, she has Calanthe drowned. Then Alessandro is warned that any woman he seeks to be with other than Aisca will meet the same fate. At the end of the novel, Calanthe's brother, Demetrius, murders Alessandro in revenge for his sister's death. It's not clear whether Demetrius thinks Alessandro is the murderer, or just the one who stole his sister's virtue. In any case, Alessandro's crimes are minor compared to the multiple murders Nisida commits, yet Alessandro does not receive redemption.

While the novel appears to be anti-Muslim for how it treats Alessandro, it is not anti-Semitic. Isaachar, a Jew, finds himself imprisoned by the Inquisition, but he is defended by a marquis (himself an adulterer) and rescued. Isaachar only survives two years after the torture he experienced in the Inquisition's prison.

When he dies, he leaves all his fortune to the marquis. (Christian male adulterers apparently get rewarded for being kind to Jews.) Before his death, Isaachar gives some fine speeches in defense of the Jewish people, as does the marquis. Reynolds is clearly not against the Jews and saves his preaching for pointing out the Inquisition's cruelty—if anything, Reynolds is anti-Catholic, as is typical of Gothic novels.

One final interesting aspect of this novel is the treatment of the Inquisition and the inclusion of female torture. Earlier novels that feature the Inquisition, notably *Melmoth the Wanderer*, depict male torture and are masochistic in their tone, but *Wagner the Wehr-Wolf* includes a convent where the women are forced to become nuns and those who attempt to escape are whipped. While Flora manages to avoid punishment when she is imprisoned in the convent, Giulia (the marquis' lover who is unfaithful to her husband), is not so fortunate, and later when she is tried before the Inquisition, her husband, the Count of Arestino, arranges for her torture and takes great delight in watching her suffer and die. (Fortunately, the marquis then kills him.) In a true double-standard, Reynolds' female adulterers are punished while his male adulterers (provided they are Christian, not Muslim) are rewarded.

In the end, *Wagner the Wehr-Wolf* is one of the most violent and disturbing, yet compelling Gothic novels ever written. The pacing and plotting never lags. The only criticism of its plot really must be that the werewolf scenes are minimal. While it feels more like a 1790s Gothic novel than one from the 1840s, Reynolds' incredible popularity in his day makes one wonder why it has not become one of the better-known Victorian Gothic novels. It certainly goes to more extremes than Reynolds' contemporaries were willing to do, and for that reason, it might be dismissed as not serious literature, but its themes of religion and gender deserve further study.

As for secret societies, I cannot imagine any Gothic novelist but Reynolds being so brash as to depict Christian Rosencreutz as a character in his novel.

Bram Stoker's *Powers of Darkness* (The Swedish *Dracula*)

I will discuss *Dracula* in depth at the end of Chapter 7 on vampire literature. However, I wish to discuss here the recently discovered Swedish translation of *Dracula* known as *Mörkrets Makter* (*Powers of Darkness*). This translation is vastly different from *Dracula*, and places Dracula, called Count Draculitz in this version, at the head of an international secret society and conspiracy to overthrow world governments, a marked contrast to *Dracula*, in which the Count acts alone other than with the help of a few gypsies who serve him. While *Powers of Darkness* may be outside the realm of French and British Gothic influence, I feel its recent discovery and use of secret societies warrants its placement here.

Before discussing the secret society in *Powers of Darkness*, some discussion is needed to understand how this version of *Dracula* is so different and why Stoker may have rewritten it. More questions than answers still surround this most fascinating literary mystery. Scholars have known for years that the translation of *Dracula* published in Iceland, known as *Makt Myrkranna*, contained an introduction by Bram Stoker, although no one understood why Stoker would write one solely for that edition. More recently, it was discovered that the Icelandic translation was not a direct translation of *Dracula* but considerably shorter and drastically different. This discovery led to a translation by Hans Corneel de Roos of *Makt Myrkranna* into English in 2014 as *Powers of Darkness*. Soon after the translation's publication, Swedish fantasy specialist Rickard Berghorn revealed the Swedish version of *Dracula* was also vastly different and it became clear the Icelandic version was based on an abridged version of the Swedish translation. In 2022, the Swedish translation, titled *Mörkrets Makter*, which also translates to *Powers of Darkness* in English, was translated into English.

This is not the place to discuss at length the differences between *Dracula* and the Swedish *Powers of Darkness*, but I'll list a few key points so readers can understand how extensive the differences are. In *Powers of Darkness*, Mina and Jonathan are named Wilma and Thomas and Dracula is always referred to as Draculitz with the exception of a chant uttered in the novel that uses the name Dracula. Numerous characters in *Powers of Darkness* are not in *Dracula*, including Arthur Holmwood's sister Mary, her husband the Romanian Prince Elemar Koromeszo, and a beautiful lady living in Draculitz's castle. Nor are there three female vampires in the castle, so there is no scene where the Count gives them a baby to satiate their bloodthirst. Two additional characters are the detectives, Barrington Jones and Tellet, who aid Wilma in searching for Thomas Harker when he disappears. Rather than being pursued to Romania, Draculitz is found and killed in a villa in Hampstead. Both Dr. Seward and Arthur Holmwood die by the novel's end. Dracula does not seduce Mina/Wilma, the Harkers have no son named Quincey, and Quincey Morris does not die or even have a hand in killing the Count. Perhaps most fascinating for our discussion here is that Draculitz is the head of an international secret society apparently set on overturning world governments to create a new government of "The Chosen."

How can we account for these changes? In my opinion, four possibilities exist, some being more likely than others.

1. *Powers of Darkness* reflects an earlier draft of *Dracula*. There are several reasons to think this is the case. In the introduction to the Icelandic *Powers of Darkness*, Hans Corneel de Roos, who discovered the Icelandic translation, notes that it contains at least seven items referenced in Stoker's notes for *Dracula* that did not end up in the final version. For example, in *Dracula*, the Count has no housekeeper, but Stoker's notes state that he has one, and he does in *Powers of Darkness*.[20] While the Swedish translator might have freely rewritten *Dracula* to suit his fancy, it is unlikely he would have had access to Stoker's notes and incorporated them in his rewrite.

2. The Swedish translator simply chose to rewrite *Dracula* to suit his own fancy. In this case, we might say he was plagiarizing *Dracula* to create his own novel, or perhaps writing fan fiction to revise the novel to suit him. Given the similarities to Stoker's notes for *Dracula*, however, I think it unlikely he rewrote without some knowledge of earlier drafts.

3. The Swedish translator made some minor rewrites to an early version of *Dracula* that he translated. This seems the most likely possibility because *Dracula* was published in 1897 in England, yet *Powers of Darkness* has references that date after that, such as a reference to the Orléanist Conspiracy of 1898.[21]

4. Stoker himself rewrote the novel after its publication in England and sent that revision to Sweden for publication. Why he would do so is unclear, and no evidence or notes exist that he did this. Therefore, I think it unlikely that *Powers of Darkness* is a later rather than earlier version by Stoker.

We may never know the truth about *Powers of Darkness* unless lost manuscripts of earlier versions of *Dracula* surface. It also remains a mystery how an earlier version of Stoker's manuscript could get to Sweden to be published. Equally surprising is that *Powers of Darkness* is a completely developed and polished novel that in many ways is as good and in some ways even better than *Dracula*. It far exceeds any of Stoker's other novels. If this is an earlier version, though, we have to wonder why Stoker chose to rewrite it to become the *Dracula* we know today. I think if *Powers of Darkness* reflects any earlier version, Stoker rewrote it because of the racism and bestiality displayed in it as I have discussed in my essay "Romania and Racism in the Swedish *Dracula*," which was published in the 2022 English translation of the Swedish *Powers of Darkness* edited by Will Trimble. Ultimately, I think Stoker may have feared *Powers of Darkness* would be too scary or indecent for his British audience, so he chose to censor and rewrite himself.

Why was *Powers of Darkness* too scary? Among other reasons, because Draculitz is the head of a secret society bent on world domination. In truth, I don't think there is a more powerful and frightening depiction of a secret society in Gothic literature than that depicted in *Powers of Darkness*.

The powerful characterization of this secret society may in part be due to Stoker belonging to an occult society, the Hermetic Order of the Golden Dawn. This organization existed only from 1887 to 1903, but at some point during that short time, Bram Stoker was a member.[22] The order was founded by Freemasons and based on Cipher Manuscripts that date to the early nineteenth century but contained older wisdom from previous magical traditions, including Rosicrucianism.[23] While the society's secrets are beyond this book's scope, they were interesting enough to attract about a hundred male and female members; several prominent writers of the time belonged, including Arthur Conan Doyle, William Butler Yeats, and Bram Stoker. Little is known about Stoker's involvement in the organization. His biographers rarely mention it, and given that it was a secret order, he would not have written directly about it. Still, some scholars have found traces of the society's mystical beliefs in Stoker's writings.[24] I suspect his membership in the Golden Dawn inspired his depiction of a secret society in *Powers of Darkness*, even if the novel's secret society is far more extreme in its mission than that of most.

In *Powers of Darkness*, those who belong to the secret society are known as the "Chosen Ones" and they are all, whether they know it or not, the followers of Count Draculitz. The secret society's existence first becomes known to readers in a shocking scene not included in *Dracula*. Thomas Harker writes in his journal entry for May 21 of how he is imprisoned in Castle Draculitz. While looking for a way to escape, he comes upon a large underground cavern. There, while hiding behind a pillar, he witnesses a shocking scene.

A group of about fifty men and women are assembled. They are all half-naked from the waist up, and many appear to be bestial, apelike creatures. Harker realizes the more human ones resemble those represented in the castle's portrait gallery, and he assumes they are Dracula's relatives. He hypothesizes that the beasts and humans must represent different sides of Dracula's family. The group appears to be involved in some sort of religious ceremony.

Harker then notices a platform with an altar on it, and in front of the altar is an elongated black marble block. Six hideous figures sit below it who are described in animalistic terms. Behind the altar is a large painting of such a "grossly indecent nature" that Harker refuses to describe it, but he says similar images exist in Indian temples. The group sings in a language Harker doesn't understand, but at the end of the singing is the word "Dracula." After the music and the sound of trumpets, a tall older man enters. He wears a fiery red cloak with a sparkling green brooch shaped like a snake. A gold headband features a similar snake. He holds a black staff and is accompanied by a wolf. Harker recognizes him as Count Draculitz.

Next, a greenish-white glow appears and takes the shape of a colossal face above the altar. Harker describes it as "half human, half animal, and at the same time seemed like Evil personified."[25]

A captive young woman is now brought forward and laid on the altar. One of the hideous creatures comes forward and bites her neck, drawing blood. The Count next steps forward, dips his hands in the blood, and scatters it upon the crowd, causing the participants to go mad in a sort of orgy. Harker, having seen enough, now retreats. He does not understand what he has witnessed, but he feels he has stood at the edge of hell and seen the devils at their work.

This repellent scene suggests Draculitz has a large number of followers to carry out his bidding and that he may himself be subject to a higher evil, such as Satan, who may be represented by the face above the altar that appears to be "Evil personified."

As the novel progresses, Harker escapes from the castle and Draculitz makes his way to England where he moves into several properties, including Carfax, strategically planting his coffins in various locations. Carfax is next-door to Dr. Seward's sanitarium, so the doctor is able to see the many visitors going there. Eventually, Dr. Seward is called upon by his new neighbors to treat a woman at Carfax who has become ill. While he protests that he is a psychiatrist, not a medical doctor, he goes to her aid. This strange foreign woman, over a series of visits, soon places Seward under a spell that makes him attracted and eventually submissive to her. The woman appears to be a type of vampire or enchantress. Her dress is decorated with spiders, and Seward comes to feel he has become wrapped up in her web. The other visitors to Carfax become friendly with Seward after he first treats the woman, so they invite him to stay for a ceremony.

Seward comes to realize the house is the meeting place for a secret society composed of people who believe themselves the "Chosen Ones." This term now becomes clear after having been already referenced a couple of times earlier in the novel. While still at Castle Draculitz, Harker had stumbled upon some of the Count's correspondence, written in French by a man well known in political circles. One letter's content makes Harker suspect the scene he has witnessed in the underground cavern is tied to a greater conspiracy by the Count. Although the letter is full of obscure allusions, it ends with the words:

> All preparations for the great catastrophe are in full swing. Our holy cause wins new followers daily. Everyone feels that Mankind's Chosen Ones have suffered for too long under the unbearable compulsion imposed on them by a narrow-minded and despicable numerical majority. We have outgrown this servile mentality and will soon be ready to proclaim the great liberating message of Jokala-Adonai.
>
> The world belongs to the Strong![26]

Before Dr. Seward goes to Carfax, he also records in his notes on August 22 that his patient Renfield is speaking to him with obscure allusions, claiming he is "one of the Chosen." Once at Carfax, Seward begins to realize the people at the meetings also believe themselves to be the Chosen. Before one of the ceremonies, Seward also meets "the master," the Marquis de Caraman-Rubiano, who in time will be revealed to be none other than Count Draculitz, although he now appears young compared to when Harker saw him in Transylvania.

During a ceremony, the lights suddenly go out and a strange scent fills the air. Seward is drugged by the perfume, which causes him to hallucinate. He feels himself flying over London until he arrives at the grave of Lucy Western (not Westenra as in *Dracula*). He had been in love with Lucy, but she had married his friend Lord Godalming, only to die strangely. Lucy's coffin remains unsealed because she lays in a sort of coma that causes Lord Godalming to refuse to believe she is dead; consequently, she is able to prey on her victims as a vampire. During his hallucination, Seward kisses Lucy and she kisses him back. She wraps her arms around him and says his blood is in her veins (from the blood transfusion he gave her earlier), which is what called him to her. He wakes from the hallucination to find the other members of the secret society excited about their own drugged experiences, but Seward says he feels like an animal in an experiment.

When Seward leaves Carfax to walk home, he is joined by Signor Leonardi, a hunchbacked musician who has befriended him and assumes Seward is already one of the Chosen Ones. Leonardi is enthusiastic about what they have just experienced and talks at length about it, thus giving Seward insight into the secret society's beliefs. Leonardi remarks:

> A world-historical evening, you could even call it. You have not lived in vain when you have experienced something like this! You feel as if you have been brought up on a high mountain and caught a glimpse across the border—the border, you see, which separates the new

world from the old! It is uplifting, my dear Doctor! You can feel yourself growing, growing to the same level as the stars, as you begin to grasp the powers that the human spirit carries within—carried for so long without realizing it—and what a transformation the world will undergo, once we learn how to fully use these powers!"[27]

Leonardi then states that the Countess, Seward's patient, who had a key role in the evening's experience, is a clairvoyant. She is said to be descended from the Pharaohs, and the ancient Egyptian mysteries have secretly been preserved in her family for two thousand years. She can even defy the law of gravity by ascending three feet off the floor. While Seward is amazed by these comments, Leonardi insists they are true and that the society's members wish to subject her powers to scientific criticism to prove their truth and spread the knowledge of these powers to wider circles. That said, he realizes the masses will never completely understand these mysteries.

Leonardi's remarks now turn into what some of the novel's critics have described as Social Darwinism, a belief that certain people and races are superior to others. Leonardi explains to Dr. Seward:

"…The general public is so ignorant, and so skeptical precisely because of their ignorance. We need the eyes and pens of scientists to spread the knowledge of these grand truths in wider circles. Admittedly, for the most part of the great, undeveloped public, the innermost core will always remain hidden! But precisely because of this the masses must learn to revere the chosen ones, the initiated, who master these secret powers and therefore are also the only ones who have the right to rule the world. This reverence, my best Doctor, that was a natural instinct to the good people of lost times and constituted their strength and greatness; it has, as you know, disappeared under the influence of the unnatural notions of equality which, like some insidious disease, have attacked the people of today—"

"Unnatural?" I repeated in surprise.

"Yes, I said 'unnatural.' Do you find that expression too strong, dear friend? A scientist like you should, however, realize its justification. Where, other than in this preconceived, degenerate modern society, do you find elsewhere in nature something corresponding to the concept of equality, which gives the physically or intellectually inferior, the being of a lower degree of development, the same rights as the most gifted among his kind? Nowhere—you must admit it! I could give examples, but there are too many. The law of nature is that the masses exist only for the sake of the most highly developed individuals. Only when the world realizes this again will humanity again witness great achievements, such as those we marvel at when we see them preserved from ancient times. The pyramids of Egypt, the wonderful temples of India and Central America testify to civilizations infinitely superior to those which people now, in their ignorance, boast about! Ah! this so-called statutory, democratic state of society, in which every natural slave considers himself entitled to think and judge, to have the same right to live and in the same manner as the most highly developed— what a ridiculous, regrettably ridiculous and contemptible outlook, my dear Doctor!"

He paused for a moment and then resumed:

"Indeed it is a most curious psychological study to observe how these Christian ideas and societal ideals eventually succeeded in penetrating and poisoning humanity and retarding its development for almost two millennia! And even more interesting to now see how they disintegrate through the very effects of the concept they have created themselves—it is truly a *Nemesis Divina*. It is

Christianity that has made the mob a factor that must be taken into account—preaching the equal rights of all, both from a social and a moral point of view. The ancient world knew better than that! They had their holy, privileged castes, who alone had access to the highest mysteries. The masses followed their commandments with blind reverence and left both thinking and ruling to the rulers. Nowadays everyone considers themselves entitled to form an opinion, to have a conviction, and what is the result? Atheism in the religious realm, anarchy in the political realm—this is the masses' concept of freedom! And in their blind stupidity, they do not even understand that the liberation from the ideas of Christianity, which they regard as progress, is in fact their own death sentence. For with the end of Christianity falls all this false humanity, which has cherished and nurtured the weak—those who really exist to perish, all this so-called human love, which has only burdened mankind with an incredible number of incompetent individuals! Yes, it is ridiculous enough—but for us, Doctor, for those of us who hope for and strive for the new world order, for us the two ultimate antipodes—atheism and Catholicism—are definitely our best allies. They both work in our favor, albeit in different ways! Isn't that right? One is continuously undermining the Christian ideals of society, without realizing how much else will fall with them, and the other is doing everything to retain or return the masses to that belief in authority that puts all power in the hands of a few. It is enormously interesting, my dear friend, enormously interesting for those who have learned to understand what forces are actually working beneath the surface!"

Leonardi certainly has a plethora of anti-democratic and unorthodox ideas. Given that we know Stoker read Sue's *The Wandering Jew*, the concept here that Catholicism keeps the masses submissive may have been derived from that novel's anti-Jesuit depictions. Later, Leonardi visits Seward's asylum and tries to convince Seward that he should quit trying to treat his patients for madness and instead let them follow their inclinations; this freedom will create a new breed of humans, one that prevents the plague of conventionalism. Leonardi remarks that Renfield's feeding flies to spiders illustrates how the lower orders should serve the higher orders, the "superman" of the future. "The strongest are destined to rule the world, and so they shall! The weak? They only exist to be used. They are flies and spiders, created to be eaten!"[28]

Soon after, Seward discovers he is one of the flies after the Countess kisses him and he cuts his neck on her spider clasp. He faints, and the Countess likely sucks his blood while he is unconscious. He wakes to have her tell him he is a child who must now obey. Before Seward knows it, his insane asylum has been taken over by members of the secret society and he is kept as a patient/prisoner there.

Meanwhile, Van Helsing and the detectives, Barrington Jones and Tellet, find Draculitz's coffins, defile them, and kill the Count at another property of his, a villa in Hampstead, thus ending th threat of his world domination. But it is too late for Seward. While Quincey Morris manages to help Seward escape from the asylum, Seward dies soon after, and the asylum burns to the ground. Soon all traces of Draculitz and his nefarious schemes have vanished from London. In the novel's Afterword, Thomas Harker tells us:

> So, I have learned that a certain Marquis de Caraman-Rubiano, who, like a new Cagliostro,* had played a prominent role in certain elite and diplomatic circles the past few months, has suddenly disappeared without a trace. He was rarely seen in public and was little known

---

* As previously noted, Cagliostro, also known as Joseph Balsamo, was an Italian-born, self-proclaimed magician who pretended to have lived for centuries and made his way to Paris just prior to the French Revolution. Stoker wrote about him in *Famous Impostors*. Cagliostro is a major character in Dumas' Marie Antoinette novels as we will see in Chapter 6.

outside of these circles, but there was no doubt that he had a powerful, pervasive, and mysterious influence within them. His mysterious disappearance coincided perfectly with the eternally memorable day when a few brave men dared to visit Count Mavros Draculitz from Transylvania in his newly built villa near Hampstead—and also met him there. A few days after this incident—and after Barrington Jones had secretly handed certain papers over to the State Department, which had come into his possession under strange circumstances—the beautiful Madame de Saint-Amand, one of society's and the diplomatic corps' brightest stars, committed suicide; several other previously highly trusted diplomatic agents were suddenly and without any explanation recalled by their respective governments. There was talk of secret arrests, house searches, blood-curdling revelations, and much more—but the true contents of the documents that Barrington Jones took from Count Draculitz's writing room on that fine December day have never been known. This entire matter is, and will probably forever remain, shrouded in mysterious and impenetrable secrecy as far as the general public is concerned.[29]

That *Powers of Darkness* depicts Draculitz as the leader of an international conspiracy makes the novel in many ways more frightening than *Dracula* because it suggests that not only does an external supernatural threat exist, but it infiltrates many nations' governments. Stoker may have revised the novel into the *Dracula* we know today because he decided this world-domination threat may have been going too far for his British readers. In that case, Count Dracula is really a toned down version of Count Draculitz, making him simply a vampire and not someone working directly for Satan or some mysterious and unknown supernatural being. Perhaps most frightening for the modern reader is that *Powers of Darkness* seems to reflect the attitudes that led to the rise of Nazi Germany and Adolf Hitler's belief in a master race.

The Social Darwinism beliefs of the "Chosen Ones" in the novel are surprising since Draculitz's followers include bestial creatures who seem to serve as a not-so-subtle metaphor for the inferiority of Romanians and other Eastern Europeans. Yet Rickard Berghorn, who helped bring the Swedish version to light, notes that by the 1890s, the *völkisch* movement had emerged as a major force in Germany and some of its leaders were already advocating killing the mentally and physically disabled because they threatened the purity of the *Herrenvolk* ("master race").[30] Even this idea is at odds with the novel, given that Leonardi suggests the insane may be among the Chosen. Certainly, the novel deconstructs itself in many ways that may have caused Stoker to feel it was too loose and unfocused, another reason for rewriting it, if he did so.

I have written elsewhere* about how *Dracula* reflects a fear of reverse colonization—the fear that people from the colonies or the East (Romania was not technically a British colony but treated like one) would immigrate to Britain and lead to its denigration. This fear is reflected in numerous other novels of the time besides *Dracula*, such as H. Rider Haggard's *She* (1887) and Joseph Conrad's *Heart of Darkness* (1903). *Powers of Darkness* is interesting in this regard because it includes a secret society that is intended to help bring about the destruction of Great Britain— something we also saw in Paul Féval's *Les Mystères de Londres*.

I suspect Féval's novel may be an overlooked ur-text for *Dracula*, and that possibility is even greater if *Powers of Darkness* is itself an early version of Stoker's novel. While, as previously noted, *Les Mystères de Londres* was not popular in England, because Féval also wrote vampire novels, I think it likely Stoker would have been aware of it. Possibly Stoker read the abridged 1847 English translation, but it's also possible he read the full American translation or the original French version, in which case,

---

* See my discussion of Imperial Gothicism in *The Gothic Wanderer*, p. 247-9, and my article in the English translation of the Swedish *Powers of Darkness* edited by Will Trimble.

more work needs to be done to explore the possible influence. I contend that many of these French Gothic novels, especially the vampire texts we will explore in Chapter 7, influenced Stoker. Stoker is believed to have had a reading knowledge of French, and we know he could converse in it at least enough to be understood as I'll discuss more in Chapter 7. Therefore, it is not far-fetched that Stoker may have known Féval's novel.

Similarities definitely exist between *Les Mystères de Londres* and *Powers of Darkness*. Stoker, being Irish, may have identified to some degree with Féval's antihero, Fergus O'Brian. As I described in Chapter 3, Fergus seeks revenge after an English landlord throws his family off their land and an English nobleman abducts his sister in London. Fergus wins the favor of the Portuguese royal family and is made the Marquis de Rio Santo. He then returns to London under this new identity and becomes the toast of London society. While Rio Santo debauches upper-class women, he also plots to overthrow the British government. He has traveled extensively and seen firsthand how the British Empire oppresses its foreign subjects, and he enlists many of the oppressed in his cause. His secret revolutionary society becomes known as the Gentlemen of the Night. This secret organization's members all descend upon London on an appointed day intending to assassinate King William IV and blow up the Bank of England.

Similarly, in *Powers of Darkness*, Count Draculitz comes to London where he masquerades as the Marquis de Caraman-Rubiano. The marquis collects around him a group of people known as the Chosen Ones who plan to take over the world's government. In both novels, the marquis fails in his goal. Today's reader may feel some sympathy for the Irish Marquis de Rio Santo, for he is fighting a just cause to end oppression, despite his questionable methods. Regardless, Féval's novel may have failed to gain popularity among the English reading public of his day because it depicted a threat against the British government and there was a general dislike of the Irish. Stoker, as an Irishman and supporter of Home Rule for Ireland,[31] may have seen Rio Santo's cause more favorably than English readers. While Stoker was against violence and disliked the Fenians who sought to create an Irish republic, believing instead that Home Rule should come about through ameliorative means,[32] he was still Irish and would have felt some sympathy for Rio Santo's cause.

Furthermore, Stoker may have been fascinated by Rio Santo's vampire-like qualities. While Rio Santo is not a supernatural being, he is repeatedly described in supernatural terms. He claims his "crime" will be "the murder of an empire, and the salvation of one half of the world,"[33] which makes him a savior and equates him with Christ, although his methods might render him, like Count Draculitz, closer to an Antichrist. Rio Santo also has a scar on his forehead that reflects the mark of Cain as one cursed by God, not dissimilar to Mina Harker's scar. Rio Santo's death scene in the moonlight recalls how vampires in early nineteenth-century works, beginning with Lord Ruthven in Polidori's *The Vampyre* (1819), were revived by moonlight. Finally, like Dracula, Rio Santo is described as finding peace in death.

While Féval's novel may have influenced *Powers of Darkness*, if the novel is an early version of *Dracula*, Stoker perhaps decided Count Draculitz's attempted conquest of England as part of an international plot was too much for readers to stomach, especially when the Count was associated with perceived inferior races from Eastern Europe. While the Count is defeated in both *Powers of Darkness* and *Dracula*, he is a far greater threat in *Powers of Darkness* because of his many foreign and diplomatic connections. Stoker may have rewritten the novel so Dracula would act alone, and he removed traces of bestiality from the storyline, reducing the threat of racially inferior and less evolved foreigners. Consequently, *Dracula* may be a toned-down version of Stoker's initial vision.

The jury is still out on the extent to which *Powers of Darkness* is Stoker's own work or that of its Swedish translator. That said, the inclusion of a secret society in *Powers of Darkness* only helps to place *Dracula* more firmly within the Gothic tradition, a tradition Stoker knew well.

We are not done, however, with secret societies. As mentioned at the beginning of this chapter, they were often cited as being the impetus behind the French Revolution. In the next chapter, we will explore how Edward Bulwer-Lytton, Alexandre Dumas, and Charles Dickens placed secret societies at the very heart of their retellings of the French Revolution.

Chapter 6

The French Revolution Revised

Bulwer-Lytton, Dumas, and Dickens

"The shops are closed,—the people are gorged with gore, and will lap no more."

— Edward Bulwer-Lytton, *Zanoni*

AND SO WE COME TO THE FRENCH REVOLUTION. It didn't birth the Gothic genre, but it helped to shape it into what it is today. As early as 1794, Thomas James Mathias, in *The Pursuits of Literature: A Satirical Poem in Four Dialogues*, associated the Gothic with the French Revolution.[1] In the 1790s, Gothic novels were written largely as metaphors for the concerns that arose from the French Revolution, but by the mid-nineteenth century, the revolution's horrors were distant enough and the genre of historical fiction had developed enough that the French Revolution could be at the center of a Gothic novel.

In this chapter, we will look at Gothic novels with French Revolution settings. Edward Bulwer-Lytton's occult novel *Zanoni* (1842) leads the list. It likely was read by Alexandre Dumas who created what may still be the most thorough treatment of the French Revolution in fiction in his eight Marie Antoinette novels (1845-55). And then there is *A Tale of Two Cities* (1859) by Charles Dickens, the most famous novel ever written about the

French Revolution. It is well known that Dickens was inspired by *Zanoni* in writing the novel, but the influence of Dumas' novels on Dickens has been mostly overlooked. I will explore how these three authors used Gothic elements to depict the horrors of the French Revolution as well as how they incorporated secret societies into their plots to reflect the conspiracy theories that circulated about the French Revolution. I have discussed *Zanoni* and *A Tale of Two Cities* at length in *The Gothic Wanderer*, but some of it will bear repeating here since Bulwer-Lytton's influence on Dumas and Dumas' influence on Dickens were not previously explored. I will also briefly mention other possible British and French influences on *A Tale of Two Cities*, including the city mysteries novels and Sue's *The Mysteries of the People*.

Edward Bulwer-Lytton's *Zanoni*

Today, the name of Edward Bulwer-Lytton (1803-1873) is synonymous with bad writing. However, in his day he was considered one of the greatest English authors. While his style may not be to everyone's taste, his importance in the history of the novel cannot be underestimated. He was a significant contributor to the silver fork and Newgate novels of the 1830s and 1840s, and with the publication of *Zanoni* in 1842, he made a great contribution not only to Gothic literature but to occultist history since the novel would inspire the Theosophy movement.

Bulwer-Lytton was knowledgeable about French literature and had an influence upon it. In 1836, at the age of thirty-three, he traveled extensively in France for several months.[2] His novels were frequently translated into French; for example, *Paul Clifford* (1830) was included in Baudry's European Library, published in Paris in 1838.[3] A French translation of *Zanoni* was made by Adele Sobry in 1842, the same year the novel was published in England.[4] Later, M. Sheldon, under the direction of P. Lorain, published it in Paris in the *Bibliotheque des Meilleurs Romans Etrangers* (Library of the Best Strange Romances).[5] In 1839, Bulwer-Lytton wrote a play about Cardinal Richelieu. His interest in France extended to the end of his life, as evidenced by his 1873 work *The Parisians*. Bulwer-Lytton also befriended the French author and occultist Éliphas Lévi Zahed (1810-1875), whom he assisted in magical evocations. Zahed has been said to be the model for the magus character in Bulwer-Lytton's *The Haunted and the Haunters* (1859).[6]

It is no surprise then that Bulwer-Lytton turned to the French Revolution as the setting for *Zanoni*, which would include occultist philosophies and Gothic elements. Like many a Gothic novel, *Zanoni* is claimed to be based on a mysterious manuscript. Bulwer-Lytton says he received the manuscript from the character of Glyndon when he was dying. Glyndon wanted his writing to be preserved for posterity. The manuscript is Glyndon's history of the title character Zanoni and Glyndon's involvement with him. It is written in a hieroglyphic cipher and accompanied by a dictionary to the hieroglyphics. Bulwer-Lytton claimed that he only translated a small portion of the manuscript, which he published as *Zicci* (1838). The public's interest in *Zicci* encouraged him to toil further so the entire manuscript was translated and could appear as *Zanoni*.[7]

Despite such Gothic elements as the supernatural and the found manuscript device, *Zanoni* was a dramatic departure from earlier Gothic novels where transgressors who sought occult or forbidden knowledge were punished. Bulwer-Lytton, who claimed to be a Rosicrucian,* redeemed the Rosicrucians from earlier negative depictions such as in William Godwin's *St. Leon* (1799) where the main character achieves the Rosicrucian secrets of extended life and the philosopher's stone only to have them lead to tragedy for him and his family. Similarly, in *Melmoth the*

---

* A lot of ink has been spilled on whether or not Bulwer-Lytton was a Rosicrucian. He made obscure statements to hint that he was but claimed he could say no more from fear of revealing the society's secrets; however, his ignorance when questioned by others on Rosicrucian topics suggests he may not have been a member. For more, see Marie Roberts' discussion in her chapter on Bulwer-Lytton in *Gothic Immortals: The Fiction of the Brotherhood of the Rosy Cross*.

Wanderer, Melmoth has an extended life but is cursed.* In *Zanoni*, the Rosicrucian characters are truly wise and use their knowledge and powers only for good, making them more like supermen than transgressive Gothic wanderers. *Zanoni* is original to the Gothic tradition because it rejects earlier depictions of the Rosicrucian as a transgressor against God who seeks autonomy in the form of earthly immortality. The novel vindicates Rosicrucianism by presenting it as beneficial to those who are trained to use its secrets wisely.

Zanoni's ending is also an affirmation of Christianity. Bulwer-Lytton rejected the Gothic depictions of Rosicrucians as opponents to Christianity; he wrote *Zanoni* to express the true tenets of Rosicrucianism that were in agreement with Christianity as reflected in the society's symbolic name, which means Rosy Cross. The novel's immortal characters are true Christians in their practice and belief, despite their contact with the supernatural and their extended lives. As the immortal character Mejnour states regarding Christianity, "Knowledge and atheism are incompatible. To know nature is to know that there must be a God!"[8]

Zanoni also differs from earlier Rosicrucian novels because it is not a tale about the quest for the elixir of life or the philosopher's stone. The title character is already an immortal who possesses great knowledge and belongs to a mystical society even older than the Rosicrucians. Zanoni opens the eyes of the other characters to hidden knowledge, provided they are prepared to receive the knowledge. The novel argues that the air is filled with invisible intelligences whose deeds influence human actions; some of these intelligences are hostile while others are benevolent to humanity. The novel also borders on being scientific, arguing certain plants can prevent the body's natural decay so that extended life can be achieved naturally rather than supernaturally.[9] Bulwer-Lytton's theories on the increased lifespan of humanity recall those of

---

* As previously noted, I have discussed *St. Leon* and *Melmoth the Wanderer* at length in *The Gothic Wanderer*.

William Godwin, as expressed in *St. Leon*. Godwin also believed that the human lifespan would gradually increase by natural processes. The character Mejnour, who has lived even longer than Zanoni, explains that the purpose of his mystical sect is to use its knowledge about Nature to create a dominant race who will be the true lords of the earth:

> a race that may proceed, in their deathless destinies, from stage to stage of celestial glory, and rank at last amongst the nearest ministrants and agents gathered round the Throne of Thrones? What matter a thousand victims for one convert to our band?[10]

Mejnour's statement is somewhat elitist; he is determined only the most deserving will be part of this race, but similarly, Christianity only allows for the most deserving to enter heaven. By creating immortal characters who are satisfied with their state and seek to bring about a superior order of humans, Bulwer-Lytton is refusing to degrade Rosicrucianism by creating selfish characters whose sole purpose is to manipulate a fabulous plot. Compared to Godwin's selfish St. Leon, who discovers that immortality is a curse, Zanoni and Mejnour are types of supermen who embody the virtues to which all people should aspire. Bulwer-Lytton rejects completely the earlier Rosicrucian novel plot and instead creates a tale inspired by his own interests and knowledge of Rosicrucianism and its metaphysical mysteries.

Zanoni's interest in spirituality makes it both a Rosicrucian and a Christian novel. At the novel's opening, Glyndon tells Bulwer-Lytton that the Rosicrucians are true Christians: "no monastic order is more severe in the practice of moral precepts, or more ardent in Christian faith."[11] Glyndon himself has matured beyond the foolish character depicted in the main story of the novel because he has spent the past fifty years not seeking occult knowledge, but living as a devout Christian.[12] Glyndon began as a typical Gothic wanderer who desired forbidden knowledge, but he eventually learned that man's true mission upon earth is to work for the benefit of others. This Christian perspective makes *Zanoni* deviate from a typical Gothic plot to emphasize that the Rosicrucian novel need not be simply a fantastic adventure story; it can be a medium for studying metaphysical questions. Critic James L. Campbell argues that *Zanoni* should not even be considered a "Rosicrucian romance" but rather a parable based upon occult concepts of the Chaldeans and Platonists.[13] In fact, the novel does not contain an actual Rosicrucian character. The two immortal characters, Zanoni and Mejnour, are members of a much older cult from which the Rosicrucians are a later branch. The characters' only connection to Rosicrucianism is that Zanoni and Mejnour are willing to make Glyndon their pupil because one of his ancestors had been an alchemist and possibly a Rosicrucian, and they consider Rosicrucianism a junior branch of knowledge compared to their society.[14]

Glyndon is the only true Gothic wanderer in the novel. While Zanoni and Mejnour are immortals, they are not transgressors and do not consider their immortality a form of suffering. Instead, they view extended life as a blessing that gives them time to use their knowledge for humanity's benefit (the goal of Rosicrucianism as declared in its original manifestoes of 1614-5 titled *Fama Fraternitas* and *Confessio Fraternitas*). Zanoni and Mejnour make Glyndon their pupil, believing because he has a Rosicrucian ancestor, he has qualities that will benefit their sect. Mejnour takes Glyndon to his castle and begins to teach him the elementary knowledge of his mysterious order. Glyndon, however, hungers for the greater knowledge he is not yet advanced enough to receive. This desire for forbidden knowledge leads Glyndon to a transgression that makes him a typical Gothic wanderer.

Early in his studies, Glyndon is warned by Mejnour that certain knowledge is fruitless to seek: "Not in the knowledge of things without, but in the perfections of the soul within, lies the empire of man aspiring to be more than men."[15] Mejnour further informs Glyndon: "thy first task must be to withdraw all thought, feeling, sympathy from others. The elementary stage of knowledge is to make self, and self alone, thy study and thy world."[16] Mejnour trains Glyndon with the intent that Glyndon will discover his true nature and learn self-control rather than selfishness so he will be prepared to use wisely the more advanced knowledge he will eventually receive.

Despite these warnings, Glyndon succumbs to his curiosity and seeks out the knowledge he is temporarily forbidden. When Mejnour goes on a journey, Glyndon is free to give into temptation by drinking the elixir of life. Mejnour had warned Glyndon he must slowly build up a tolerance to the elixir by first splashing it on his face and smelling it. Glyndon, however, greedily imbibes the mysterious liquid, then instantly sees apparitions he longs to join, but they float away from him. He is next confronted by the apparition of a reptilian creature in what is the novel's most Gothic scene. Glyndon is so frightened by this creature that "All fancies, the most grotesque, of Monk or Painter in the early North, would have failed to give to the visage of imp or fiend that aspect of deadly malignity which spoke to the shuddering nature in those eyes alone."[17] The creature's eyes have a "burning glare so intense, so livid, yet so living, had in it something that was almost human in its passion of hate and mockery."[18] When the creature speaks, it causes Glyndon's hair to stand erect while "his soul rather than his ear comprehended the words it said."[19] The creature states:

> "Thou hast entered the immeasurable region. I am the Dweller of the Threshold. What wouldst thou with me? Silent? Dost thou fear me? Am I not thy beloved? Is it not for me that thou hast rendered up the delights of thy race? Wouldst thou be wise? Mine is the wisdom of the countless ages. Kiss me, my mortal lover." And the Horror crawled near and nearer to him; it crept to his side, its breath breathed upon his cheek! With a sharp cry he fell to the earth insensible, and knew no more.[20]

Glyndon wakes to find himself in bed. Mejnour then informs him that because he succumbed to temptation, he is dismissed from further training. Plus, because he drank the elixir, he will have to battle continually with the demon, although the powers of the elixir may allow him to shine in the world of men. Glyndon's situation parallels that of Adam and Eve in tasting forbidden knowledge; he is thrust from a type of Eden where he could have become one with the immortals. The possibility that he may shine, however, suggests a hope for the future similar to God's promise to Adam and Eve that humanity will eventually be redeemed.

Before leaving the castle, Glyndon again encounters the Being, described as the "presence of the Nameless."[21] This time, Glyndon tries to overcome his fear:

> With a violent effort that convulsed his whole being, and bathed his body in the sweat of agony, the young man mastered his horror. He strode towards the Phantom; he endured its eyes; he accosted it with a steady voice; he demanded its purpose and defied its power.
>
> And then, as a wind from a channel, was heard its voice. What it said, what revealed, it is forbidden the lips to repeat, the hand to record. Nothing save the subtle life that yet animated the frame, to which the inhalations of the elixir had given vigour and energy beyond the strength of the strongest, could have survived that awful hour. Better to wake in the catacombs and see the buried rise from their cerements, and hear the ghouls, in their horrid orgies, amongst the festering ghastliness of corruption, than to front those features when the veil was lifted, and listen to that whispered voice![22]

Despite his bravery in facing the creature, Glyndon now flees from Mejnour's castle. Nevertheless, he cannot erase from his memory either the demon or its words; by drinking the elixir, Glyndon has allowed the demon to enter inside him, just as Milton's Satan feels hell burn within him because of his transgression.

Glyndon continues to have demonic visions throughout the remainder of the novel, but he eventually comes to terms with them. Toward the novel's end, Zanoni explains to Glyndon that wherever men labor and aspire "everywhere cowers and darkens the Unutterable Horror. But there where thou hast ventured, alone is the phantom visible; and never will it cease to haunt, till thou canst pass to the Infinite, as the seraph, or return to the Familiar, as a child!"[23] This passage reflects Bulwer-Lytton's drawing upon the Romantic myth of consciousness: Glyndon's transgression places him in the stage of experience; unable to return to the innocence of childhood, Glyndon must learn how to achieve the "philosophic mind" that brings wise innocence. Glyndon tells Zanoni that he tries to resist the Specter by clinging to Virtue, which has made the Specter become faint. Zanoni replies that Resolve is the beginning of success in overcoming the terror and mystery of the Specter, so Glyndon can rejoice because eventually his exorcism will be complete.[24]

Bulwer-Lytton's use of the Specter, or Dweller of the Threshold, is a rejection of Gothic manifestations of the supernatural to show that humanity's true horrors are psychological and it is with our inner selves that we must wrestle. At the beginning of Glyndon's training, Mejnour had warned Glyndon he must overcome his true nature. Now Glyndon has finally succeeded by seeking virtue over his natural selfishness and the other inner demons that controlled him. Glyndon has achieved redemption as a Gothic wanderer.

While Glyndon is a more traditional Gothic wanderer because of his transgression and redemption, Zanoni is the most original wanderer figure and the one who learns the greatest lesson. Zanoni is never completely definable as a Gothic wanderer because, despite his immortality, he is neither a transgressor nor the victim of transgression. Plus, Zanoni is already immortal at the novel's beginning when he falls in love with the singer Viola.

Zanoni and Viola marry and find happiness together by living solitary lives on an island, thus recreating an Eden where innocence can exist. Critic Robert Lee Wolff notes that Zanoni and Viola's life on an island is similar to how Maturin's Melmoth finds Immalee on an island.[25] Bulwer-Lytton intentionally borrowed from *Melmoth the Wanderer* in creating Zanoni and Viola's relationship, but he also radically changes the relationship. Melmoth selfishly sought a partner to ease the burden of his cursed, prolonged existence. His selfishness resulted in his marriage to Immalee, followed by Immalee's imprisonment for allegedly engaging in occult behavior by marrying Melmoth. Consequently, both Immalee and her child die in the prisons of the Spanish Inquisition.

Bulwer-Lytton adapts Maturin's love story by making Zanoni immortal, but not cursed like Melmoth. Zanoni seeks Viola as his partner out of love and a desire to confer immortality upon her so their bond can never be broken by her death. To obtain immortality for Viola and their child, Zanoni must go to the supernatural being, the Dweller of the Threshold, also known as Adon-ai. Because Adon-ai is the Hebrew word for God, we can assume Zanoni is a Christian and disciple of God. The Dweller of the Threshold agrees to Zanoni's request, but he also demands a price in return, not yet stating what that price will be.[26]

Zanoni and his family now move to Paris where they witness the events of the French Revolution. During the Reign of Terror, Zanoni finds himself deeply interested in the people who die at the guillotine. In a letter to Mejnour, he theorizes that death can be good because he sees many people die to save a loved one. The novel's Christian theme is clearly expressed in Zanoni's description of these people's courage.

> Because such hearts live in some more abstract and holier life than their own. But to live forever upon this earth is to live in nothing diviner than ourselves. Yes, even amidst this gory butcherdom, God, the Everlasting, vindicates to man the sanctity of His servant, Death![27]

Even Death can be benevolent because it brings people to God. Zanoni's reflections upon death foreshadow the novel's stunning climax.

Nicot, an enemy of Glyndon and Zanoni, now betrays them to Robespierre. Zanoni escapes arrest, but Glyndon, Viola, and her and Zanoni's child are cast into prison. Zanoni manages to help Glyndon escape, but he is unable to rescue Viola, who is sentenced to death at the guillotine. Desperate to save his wife and child, Zanoni seeks help from the Dweller of the Threshold. The Dweller informs Zanoni that Viola and the child can be rescued if Zanoni takes their place because it is written that a sacrifice can always save. Whether the Dweller himself demands this sacrifice is unclear, but he also comforts Zanoni by telling him not to worry about Viola and the child after his death. The Dweller says Zanoni could not care for them any better than God now will:

> what, with all thy wisdom and thy starry secrets, with all thy empire of the past, and thy visions of the future,— what art thou to the All-Directing and Omniscient? Canst thou yet imagine that thy presence on earth can give to the hearts thou lovest the shelter which the humblest take from the wings of the Presence that lives in Heaven? Fear not thou for their future. Whether thou live or die, their future is the care of the Most High! In the dungeon and on the scaffold looks everlasting the Eye of HIM, tenderer than thou to love, wiser than thou to guide, mightier than thou to save![28]

Zanoni now turns himself over to the French government and dies at the guillotine in place of Viola and their child. In the end, Zanoni's supernatural immortality is both powerless and ultimately meaningless compared to his sacrifice of love that results in eternal life in heaven. However, while Zanoni's sacrifice is admirable, the reader feels unsatisfied when Viola dies of grief while yet in prison. Consequently, Zanoni has failed to save his wife, although Viola's death expresses the power of her love for him. Her death allows her to share in Zanoni's heavenly life as she had previously shared in his earthly immortality.

Despite Zanoni and Viola's deaths, the novel ends upon a note of hope, for the child left behind in prison is pitied by a woman who decides to care for him. The novel concludes with a priest remarking to the woman, "THE FATHERLESS ARE THE CARE OF GOD!"[29] The conclusion of *Zanoni*, therefore, effectively revises the end of *Melmoth the Wanderer* where Melmoth's selfishness results in the death of his wife and child. While Viola still dies, Zanoni is selfless, and their child remains alive as a symbol of hope. The orphaned child will have God as its father.

According to critic David Punter, the lessons of sacrifice and self-control that Zanoni and Glyndon respectively learn emphasize the novel's theme that people who receive special gifts must be responsible by using those gifts for the betterment of humanity.[30] Bulwer-Lytton vindicates Rosicrucianism by showing it is a force for good. At the same time, he agrees with his Gothic predecessors that earthly immortality is undesirable when compared to immortality in heaven. Marie Roberts suggests that Zanoni's death liberates him into true immortality and he ascends to heaven in a Dantean vision of the apocalypse.[31] Zanoni's death is also symbolic as a political and religious statement against political visionaries like the atheistic Robespierre, whose downfall occurs the day after Zanoni's death.[32] Consequently, Zanoni serves as the Christ-like sacrifice that frees France from its terror, as Christ freed humanity from its sins.

Zanoni was largely condemned by the critics as unreadable, but Bulwer-Lytton always felt it was his best novel. Harriet Martineau was so impressed with the novel that she told Bulwer-Lytton that even if only one person read *Zanoni* for every hundred who had read *St. Leon*, he should feel rewarded for working out such a sacred philosophy.[33] Martineau's enthusiasm for the novel extended to her writing a key to its philosophical meanings, which Bulwer-Lytton printed in subsequent editions. Martineau and

Thomas Carlyle were among the novel's few recorded enthusiastic readers. However, Bulwer-Lytton was extremely popular in his day, so the novel was soon translated into French, and as we will see, it seems likely it was read by Alexandre Dumas, who would embark on writing his own novels of the French Revolution soon after. Furthermore, *Zanoni* had a significant impact on Dickens in writing *A Tale of Two Cities,* and I believe Dumas' novels also influenced Dickens so that *Zanoni* may have both directly and indirectly inspired Dickens.

Alexandre Dumas' Marie Antoinette Novels

While I have not found proof that Alexandre Dumas read *Zanoni* or any of Bulwer-Lytton's works, given that Bulwer-Lytton was extremely popular in his time, it is unlikely Dumas was unaware of his work. Eric Partridge, in his exhaustive study of English literature's influence on French Romanticism, states that by the 1840s, Bulwer-Lytton's place as a popular author in France was secure.[34] M. G. Devonshire in *The English Novel in France, 1830-1870* has provided extensive critical commentary upon Bulwer-Lytton's novels by the French, but surprisingly, only remarks that *Zanoni* did not receive much criticism.[35] Still, it is unlikely Dumas did not know of and read Bulwer-Lytton's work, given both authors were friendly with Dickens. In fact, today Bulwer-Lytton is probably best known for writing "It was a dark and stormy night," the opening sentence of his 1830 novel *Pelham*. While the sentence has become synonymous with how to write a bad novel, it really is a strong opening sentence. Some English editions of Dumas' *The Three Musketeers* (1846) have translated that novel's opening sentence, "*C'etait une nuit orageuse et sombre,*" as "It was a dark and stormy night."[36] This suggests Dumas may have borrowed the line from Bulwer-Lytton or the translators could not resist using the famous line in their translations. I personally think it likely Dumas knew *Zanoni* because he names a character Zannone, and he makes several

Rosicrucian references in his Marie Antoinette novels, although, of course, he could have gotten knowledge of Rosicrucianism from other sources, including Hugo's *Notre-Dame de Paris*.

Dumas also was influenced by Sir Walter Scott, as we have previously seen, even adapting some of Scott's novels into plays. However, while both authors wrote historical novels, Dumas realized serializing his novels required a different approach from that of Scott. Biographer Michael Ross sums up the difference between Scott and Dumas' writing as follows:

> Dumas had given a great deal of thought to the serial form. Although he admired Walter Scott immensely, he realised that the Scottish writer would be incapable of writing a serial. Scott established his characters from the first page, by indulging in long descriptions of their peculiarities; but in a serial, which must hold its readers' attention from the very first lines, the author cannot permit himself a long-drawn-out beginning, and Dumas, capitalising on this, jumps immediately into dialogue and action. In practically every one of his many novels he supplies his readers in his opening paragraph with time, date and place. In a serial, Dumas realized, an author has no right ever to be boring.[37]

Dumas' understanding of the importance of starting in the middle of the action was revolutionary and is the advice most teachers of fiction writing will give today. Dumas' pacing, character development, and dialogue all help to keep the reader interested from page to page in a way Scott and other authors of the period could not always achieve. Certainly, if readers find Dumas boring, the fault largely lies with Victorian English translations that fail to capture his playful use of slang and the vivacity of his style.

By the time Dumas turned his pen to the French Revolution, he had already successfully written several historical novels, and since he was French and the son of a general of Napoleon, he probably would have written about the French Revolution whether or not he ever read *Zanoni*. That said, his interest in the supernatural influenced how he decided to treat the revolution, and that influence may have been inspired by *Zanoni*, as well as Thomas Carlyle's *The French Revolution: A History* (1837). Carlyle's book was an influence upon both Bulwer-Lytton and Dickens, and it is well-known that Carlyle loaned Dickens many books on the French Revolution when Dickens wrote *A Tale of Two Cities*.*

The central character of Dumas' Marie Antoinette novels is not the queen but Cagliostro, a historical person whose full name was Count Alessandro di Cagliostro (1743-1795). Cagliostro was actually the alias of Giuseppe Balsamo, known in France as Joseph Balsamo. He was an occultist who claimed he had magical powers. By Dumas' day, Cagliostro's reputation had greatly disintegrated, especially after Thomas Carlyle, in *The French Revolution*, referred to him as the "prophetic Quack of Quacks,"[38] but Dumas chose to treat Cagliostro's magical powers seriously, attributing to him some legitimate supernatural powers that make the novels into romances as much as historical fiction. In his first appearance in the series, the character is known as Joseph Balsamo, but he later returns as Cagliostro, and then yet again as Baron Zannone, a banker with great wealth. Given the similarity to the name Zanoni and that Bulwer-Lytton's character has great wealth, Zannone, who does not seem to be a historical person, may be a type of tribute by Dumas to Bulwer-Lytton's character.

Dumas' biographer Arthur F. Davidson suggests Dumas' interest in the occult influenced the writing of the Marie Antoinette novels:

> the *Mémoires d'un Médecin* series opens with the five volumes called *Joseph Balsamo*, chiefly concerned with the doings of that remarkable impostor—the "arch-quack" of Carlyle's pages. The phenomena of occultism had always fascinated Dumas: he dabbled, at

---

* I have discussed at length Carlyle's *Sartor Resartus* (1834) and *The French Revolution* (1837) and their influence on Bulwer-Lytton, Dickens, and Gothic literature in *The Gothic Wanderer*.

different times, in palmistry, phrenology, clairvoyance, spiritualism; especially he was attracted by that form of mesmeric development which is nowadays called hypnotism. To test the reality of this power he made several experiments at the time when he was writing *Joseph Balsamo*, and with considerable success, though he admits that the subjects he operated on were always persons peculiarly liable to such influence—young girls or impressionable women. The conclusion he arrived at was this: "I believe that by the help of magnetism a bad man might do much harm, I doubt that a good man could do much good...I consider that magnetism is an amusement but not yet a science." In the story of *Joseph Balsamo* the possibilities of magnetism are stretched to the uttermost demands of fiction. The "arch-quack" is seen with all his quackeries; only, he is a quack who believes in himself and in his mission to regenerate humanity by breaking up the existing order of things. As the head of a widespread society of Nihilists, whose motto is L.P.D. (lilia pedibus destrue), he directs the undermining of society's foundations: he pulls the strings with which the puppets are made to dance.[39]

Joseph Balsamo is the series' most interesting Gothic character, even lending his name to the first book. The series is known as the Marie Antoinette novels because they center around the ill-fated Queen of France and a group of fictional characters involved in bringing about her downfall, including Joseph Balsamo. Depending on who is making the list and how the novels are divided, there are usually seven or eight titles, although some lists only include five because several have been published together. Rather than get into the differentiations of various editions and the abridged or complete versions, for our purposes here, I will discuss the important Gothic elements in the novel title by title, using the following list:[40]

1. *Joseph Balsamo* (*Mémoires d'un médecin: Joseph Balsamo*, 1846–8) (a.k.a. *Memoirs of a Physician, Cagliostro, Madame Dubarry, The Countess Dubarry*, or *The Elixir of Life*). *Joseph Balsamo* is usually published in two volumes in English translations: Vol 1. *Joseph Balsamo* and Vol 2. *Memoirs of a Physician*. The long unabridged version includes the contents of book two, *Andrée de Taverney*. The short, abridged versions usually divide *Balsamo* and *Andrée de Taverney* as completely different books.
2. *Andrée de Taverney*, or *The Mesmerist's Victim*
3. *The Queen's Necklace* (*Le Collier de la Reine*, 1849–50), first serialized in *La Presse*.[41]
4. *Ange Pitou* (1853) (a.k.a. *Storming the Bastille* or *Six Years Later*). Long unabridged versions of this book sometimes include book five. Many short versions treat *The Hero of the People* as a separate volume.
5. *The Hero of the People*
6. *The Royal Life Guard* or *The Flight of the Royal Family*
7. *The Countess de Charny* (*La Comtesse de Charny*, 1853–5). Long unabridged versions include the contents of book six, but many short versions leave *The Royal Life Guard* as a separate volume.
8. *Le Chevalier de Maison-Rouge* (1845) (aka *The Knight of the Red House*, or *The Knight of Maison-Rouge*)

As can be seen from this list, it is easy to be confused about which novels to read and in which order. Notably, Dumas wrote the last novel in the series, *Le Chevalier de Maison-Rouge* first, and it contains none of the main characters from the other seven, save Marie Antoinette, so it is not really part of the proper Marie Antoinette series, although Dumas himself suggested it was such at the end of *The Countess de Charny*, as I will examine below. Let us now turn to analyzing how Dumas used supernatural elements in the novels to place them within the Gothic tradition.

Joseph Balsamo

The first of the Marie Antoinette novels opens with the meeting of a secret society, named the LPD. It stands for the Latin phrase *Lilia Pedibus Destrue*, meaning "Let's trample the lily," a reference to a desire to overthrow the French monarchy since the lily or fleur-de-lys is the French monarchy's symbol.[42] Beyond overthrowing the French monarchy, the society's greater goal is to bring about the advancement of mankind by manipulating political events. The members of the LPD come from various nations. The society's president is Emanuel Swedenborg, who represents Sweden. Other members include John Paul Jones, who represents the new republic of the United States of America, and the novel's title character, Joseph Balsamo, who is Italian but there to work for France. Balsamo shares with the group his occultist upbringing and past, which is shrouded in the mists of time:

> "The sources of great rivers are sacred, therefore unknown. Like the Nile, the Ganges, the Amazon, I know to what I tend, not whence I come. All that I can reveal is that, when the eyes of my spirit first opened to comprehend external things, I was in Medina, the holy city, playing in the gardens of the Mufti Salaaym. He was a venerable man, kind as a father to me, yet not my father, for though he looked on me with love, he spoke to me with respect. Thrice a day he left me, and then came another old man, whose name I may pronounce with gratitude, yet with fear. He was called Althotas, and him the seven great spirits had taught all that the angels know, to comprehend God. He was my tutor, my master, my friend—a friend to be venerated indeed, for his age was double that of most among you."
>
> His solemn tone, his majestic deportment, deeply impressed the assembly. They seemed trembling with anxiety to hear more.

He continued, "When I reached my fifteenth year I was initiated into the mysteries of nature. I knew botany, but not as one of your learned men who has acquired only the knowledge of the plants of his own corner of the world. To me were known the sixty thousand families of plants of the whole earth. My master, pressing his hands on my forehead, made a ray of celestial light descend on my soul. Then could I perceive beneath the seas the wondrous vegetations which are tossed by the waves, in the giant branches of which are cradled monsters unknown to the eye of man.

"All tongues, living and dead, I knew. I could speak every language spoken from the Dardanelles to the Straits of Magellan. I could read the dark hieroglyphics on those granite books, the pyramids. From Sanchoniathon to Socrates, from Moses to Jerome, from Zoroaster to Agrippa, all human knowledge was mine.

"Medicine I studied, not only in Hippocrates, in Galen, and in Averrhoes, but in that great teacher, Nature. I penetrated the secrets of the Copts and the Druses. I gathered up the seeds of destruction and of scarcity. When the simoom or the hurricane swept over my head, I threw to it one of those seeds which its breath bore on, carrying death or life to whomsoever I had condemned or blessed.

"During these studies, I reached my twentieth year. Then my master sought me one day in a grove, to which I had retired from the heat of the day. His face was at the same moment grave and smiling. He held a little vial in his hand. 'Acharat,' he said, 'I have told thee that nothing is born, nothing dies in the world, that the cradle and the coffin are twins, that man wants only to see into past existences to be equal to the gods, and that when that power shall be acquired by him, he will be as immortal as they. Behold! I have found the beverage which will dispel his darkness, thinking that I had found that which destroys death. Acharat, I drank of it yesterday. See, the vial is not full. Drink thou the rest today.

"I had entire confidence in my venerable master, yet my hand trembled as it touched the vial which he offered me, as Adam's might have done when Eve presented him with the apple.

"'Drink!' he said, smiling.

"I drank.

"Then he placed his hands on my head, as he always did when he would make light penetrate to my soul.

"'Sleep!' he said.

"Immediately I slept, and I dreamed that I was lying on a pile of sandal-wood and aloes. An angel, passing by on the behests of the Highest from the east to the west, touched the pile with the tip of his wing, and it kindled into flame. Yet I, far from being afraid, far from dreading the fire, lay voluptuously in the midst of it, like the phoenix, drawing in new life from the source of all life.

"Then my material frame vanished away and my soul only remained. It preserved the form of my body, but transparent, impalpable, it was lighter than the atmosphere in which we live, and it rose above it. Then, like Pythagoras, who remembered that in a former state he had been at the siege of Troy, I remembered the past. I had experienced thirty-two existences, and I recalled them all. I saw ages pass before me like a train of aged men in procession. I beheld myself under the different names which I had borne from the day of my first birth to that of my last death. You know, brethren—and it is an essential article of our faith—that souls, those countless emanations of the Deity, fill the air, and are formed into numerous hierarchies, descending from the sublime to the base, and the man who, at the moment of his birth, inhales one of those pre-existing souls, gives it up at his death, that it may enter on a new course of transformations."

He said this in a tone so expressive of conviction, and his look had something so sublime, that the assembly interrupted him by a murmur of admiration.

"When I awoke," continued the illuminated, "I felt that I was more than man—that I was almost divine. Then I resolved to dedicate not only my present existence but all my future ones, to the happiness of man.

"The next day, as if he had guessed my thoughts, Althotas said to me, 'My son, twenty years ago thy mother expired in giving birth to thee. Since that time, invincible obstacles have prevented thy illustrious father revealing himself to thee. We shall travel. We shall meet thy father. He will embrace thee, but thou wilt not know him.'

"Thus, in me, as in one of the elect, all was mysterious—past, present, future.

"I bid adieu to the Mufti Salaaym, who blessed me and loaded me with presents, and we joined a caravan going to Suez.

"Pardon me, sirs, if I give way for a moment to emotion, as I recall that one day a venerable man embraced me. A strange thrill ran through me as I felt his heartbeat against mine.

"He was the Cheriffe of Mecca, a great and illustrious prince, who had seen a hundred battles, and at the raising of his hand three millions of men bent their heads before him. Althotas turned away to hide his feelings, perhaps not to betray a secret, and we continued our road.

"We went into the heart of Asia. We ascended the Tigris. We visited Palmyra, Damascus, Smyrna, Constantinople, Vienna, Berlin, Dresden, Moscow, Stockholm, Petersburg, New York, Buenos Ayres, the Cape of Good Hope, and Aden. Then, being near the point at which we had set out, we proceeded into Abyssinia, descended the Nile, sailed to Rhodes, and lastly to Malta. Before landing, a vessel came out to meet us, bringing two knights of the order. They saluted me and embraced Althotas, and conducted us in a sort of triumph to the palace of the grandmaster, Pinto.

"Now, you will ask me, sirs, how it came that the Mussulman Acharat was received with honour by those who have vowed the extermination of the infidels. Althotas, a Catholic, and himself a Knight of Malta had always spoken to me of one only God, omnipotent, universal, who, by the aid of angels, his ministers, made the world a harmonious whole, and to this whole, he gave the great name of Cosmos. I was, then, not a Mussulman but a theosophist.

"My journeyings ended, but in truth, all that I had seen had awakened in me no astonishment, because for me there was nothing new under the sun, and in my preceding thirty-two existences I had visited the cities before, through which I had lately passed. All that struck me was some change in their inhabitants. Now I would hover over events and watch the progress of man. I saw that all minds tend onward and that this tendency leads to liberty. I saw that prophets had been raised up from time to time to aid the wavering advances of the human race and that men, half-blind from their cradle, make but one step towards the light in a century. Centuries are the days of nations.

"'Then,' said I to myself, 'so much has not been revealed to me that it should remain buried in my soul. In vain does the mountain contain veins of gold, in vain does the ocean hide its pearls, for the persevering miner penetrates to the bowels of the mountain, the diver descends to the depths of the ocean, but better than the mountain or the ocean, let me be like the sun, shedding blessings on the whole earth.'

"You understand, then, that it is not to go through some masonic ceremonies I have come from the East. I have come to say to you, brethren, take the wings and the eyes of the eagle. Rise above the world, and cast your eyes over its kingdoms.

"Nations form but one vast body. Men, though born at different periods, in different ranks, arrive all in turn at that goal to reach which they were created. They are continually advancing, though seemingly stationary, and if they appear to retreat a step from time to time, it is but to collect strength for a bound which shall carry them over some obstacle in their way.

"France is the advance guard of nations. Put a torch in her hand, and though it kindle a wide-spreading flame, it will be salutary, for it will enlighten the world.

"The representative of France is not here. It may be that he has recoiled at the task imposed on him. Well, then, we must have a man who will not shrink from it. I will go to France."

The council decides that despite the hope for change that the future Louis XVI and Marie Antoinette's upcoming marriage holds, Cagliostro will spend twenty years attempting to regenerate France and bring about a second golden age of man, but this work cannot happen until the monarchy is dead.

The story now shifts to young Gilbert, a servant to the Baron de Taverney. He is reading Jean Jacques Rousseau's *Le Contrat Social* when he meets "Baron" Joseph Balsamo and brings him to the Taverney chateau. There Balsamo surprises his hosts because despite appearing to be about age thirty, he speaks of events he witnessed that happened thirty years ago. Balsamo remarks that he was forty-one at the time of the events, but he is not the same man now.

That night, Balsamo enters the bedroom of Andrée de Taverney,* the baron's daughter, and paralyzes her. Gilbert is

---

* Some translations spell her name as Andrea. I have retained that spelling in the passages quoted from such translations.

spying on him and sees this happen. Balsamo next prophesies to the family that Marie Antoinette will visit them, and his prediction comes true. When Marie Antoinette arrives, Balsamo makes a table magically appear so the family can host her. He reveals his powers by whispering into Marie Antoinette's ear that he knows her secret that she altered her mother's letters to Madame Pompadour. When she asks him about her future, at first he refuses to tell her, and then when he does tell her, she faints. The future queen leaves, promising to show favor to the baron's children when they come to court.

Soon after, Gilbert follows Andrée de Taverney to court. Then we meet Madame du Barry,* whom Balsamo helps to get presented at court, even though she is a mistress to the king and not considered respectable.

We learn Balsamo has a wife, Lorenza, whom he raised from being "buried alive" and in a paralyzed state, suggesting he has the power to resurrect people. He also claims he is a man who can make gold, which hints that he can manipulate economies, but the remark also relates to the philosopher's stone that could turn lead into gold. Balsamo practiced his magical arts with Lorenza and Altothas. Altothas is trying to discover the elixir of life that Balsamo seeks so he can bring about human perfection. Altothas and Balsamo soon come to odds, however. Altothas is not above killing a child to get its life blood for his elixir experiments. This links him to racist stereotypes of Jews killing children. At the same time, Altothas thinks Balsamo's efforts to create freedom and equality are foolish because he says a Caesar or Cromwell will rise up and take power from the people regardless (perhaps a reference to Robespierre or Napoleon).

Meanwhile, Gilbert has met Rousseau and is now studying with him. The novel ends when Gilbert comes close to death while trying to rescue Andrée from a mob that nearly crushes

---

* Some translations write Dubarry, DuBarry, or Du Barry. I have opted for du Barry throughout to be consistent and because it appears to be Dumas' preference in his original French texts.

her in 1770 during the dauphin and Marie Antoinette's wedding celebrations. Gilbert manages to get Andrée to Balsamo, who is able to convey her to safety.

One problem with the Marie Antoinette novels is they are rather incoherent in how they treat the supernatural themes. We are given moments when Balsamo seems to be working for a purpose for mankind's betterment, yet nothing he attempts ever quite comes to fruition. The Rosicrucian scenes seem to result in little being achieved. The relationship between Balsamo and Altothas may have been inspired by that of Zanoni and Mejnour in Bulwer-Lytton's novel, although Bulwer-Lytton's characters are never in such extreme conflict. Of course, Balsamo is also inspired by the historical Cagliostro, who becomes even more mysterious as the series continues.

The Mesmerist's Victim

The second Marie Antoinette novel begins with Andrée describing her rescue by Balsamo, whom she describes as "supernatural." She claims his gaze attracted her, pulling her to him so she could be saved. She is now at court where she quickly becomes Marie Antoinette's favorite.

Meanwhile, Lorenza refuses to be a true wife to Balsamo. She is afraid of him because he studies the black arts. When she threatens to kill herself, he tells her he will only revive her.

The Countess du Barry comes to Balsamo for an elixir that will relieve Louis XV of his boredom so he can be happy, a change that will be attributed to her being his mistress.

Balsamo claims he is three thousand years old. He says he has a bodiless voice that reveals secrets to him. He uses Lorenza as his instrument for communicating with the voice. Among other things, she can read other people's letters from a distance.

Rousseau visits the LPD secret society, of which Marat and Balsamo are members. After hearing out the society's members, Rousseau refuses to join. Marat says a machine is needed to bring death without pain—a hint that the guillotine will soon be invented.

Balsamo puts Andrée in a trance to learn what Lorenza is doing. He then reconciles with Lorenza, saying he'll love her and use Andrée rather than her for his purposes. However, Altothas soon after murders Lorenza for her virgin blood.

Meanwhile, while Andrée is in a trance, Gilbert takes advantage of her. Gilbert later proposes to her, but she refuses him, though eventually she will give birth to his child.

The novel clearly expands on Balsamo's sorcerer-like powers while moving slowly toward the events that will cause the French Revolution. The use of the second sight—the ability to see what others are doing from a distance—is particularly interesting here. Dumas had used it previously in *Urbain Grandier* (1841), in which a brother in a trance can see events at a distance, and again in *The Corsican Brothers* (1844) in which conjoined twins separated at birth are so connected that each can sense when his twin is in danger, and when one dies, his astral body appears to the other.[43] Dumas would use the second sight again in *The Hero of the People*, as we will see below.

The Queen's Necklace

The Queen's Necklace is the most famous Marie Antoinette novel, yet it makes little sense if read outside the larger series. The story begins at a party where Balsamo, now calling himself Cagliostro and pretending to be a different person, claims to be the oldest person present. He has wine that he says he bottled himself 120 years ago, and he claims that he served Cleopatra. He says the Countess du Barry is youthful because she took the elixir his friend Joseph Balsamo gave her. He adds that Balsamo disappeared two or three years before when he was in Ohio and planning to cross the Rocky Mountains. Cagliostro then gives Baron Taverney some elixir, which makes him feel youthful for a short time. Cagliostro admits he is not immortal but has simply learned how to avoid danger. He also says he cannot change the future, but he can foretell it. He then predicts the deaths of everyone at the party, including du Barry, who will die on the scaffold, as will Louis XVI.

As the novel continues, Marie Antoinette finds herself compromised in the scandal over the famous diamond necklace. She little realizes Cagliostro is orchestrating events throughout the novel to ruin her reputation in the newspapers; he also manipulates the various characters to disgrace the queen through the necklace affair. Of additional interest is the character Olivia who is arrested for impersonating the queen; she is part of Cagliostro's ploy to ruin the queen's reputation. This impersonation/substitution of one person for another is significant since Dumas previously used it in *Le Chevalier de Maison-Rouge*, as discussed below. Also significant is that Andrée Taverney marries Count Charny, which will be relevant in upcoming novels. By the novel's end, Cagliostro's role in the diamond necklace scandal is revealed and he is banished from France.

The Storming of the Bastille

This novel opens with Gilbert leaving his and Andrée's son, Sebastian, with a farmer who will raise him. Sebastian grows up as the schoolmate of Ange Pitou, the title character of the later novel in the series, *The Hero of the People*. Meanwhile, Gilbert travels to the United States, where he writes a book about the freedom of men before he returns to France. Upon his return, he calls himself Dr. Gilbert and travels to Paris.

By now, Ange has grown up. He is nearly arrested for possessing Dr. Gilbert's book, which has been censored. Ange decides to go to Paris, accompanied by Farmer Billet, to find Sebastian Gilbert, who is attending school there. They learn Dr. Gilbert has been arrested and imprisoned in the Bastille. Dumas now stops the narrative to describe what it meant to be locked up in the Bastille:

> The King was accounted too good to order people to be beheaded; but he sent people into the Bastile.* Once there a man was forgotten, isolated, sequestered, buried alive, annihilated. He stayed there till the monarch remembered him, and kings have so many new matters to think of that they often forget the old ones.[44]

This passage is significant because of the "buried alive" wording used. Dickens would use the same wording in *A Tale of Two Cities* to refer to Dr. Manette when he is imprisoned in the Bastille: "To be buried alive for eighteen years!"[45] In fact, Dickens considered naming his novel *Buried Alive*.[46]

Ange Pitou and Farmer Billet free Gilbert from the Bastille through violence. Gilbert is here described as age thirty-five and:

> Pale without sickliness, with black hair and steady though animated eyes, one could tell that he, like his teacher Balsamo-Cagliostro, was endowed with the power of magnetism. As he could now mesmerize Andrea, he could mentally master most men.[47]

This statement is surprising given that Gilbert has been imprisoned for a week—why didn't he mesmerize the jailor to set him free? However, Gilbert is working with Cagliostro to bring about the French Revolution, so he apparently felt his imprisonment important to trigger the storming of the Bastille which would start the revolution.

During the attack on the Bastille, Gilbert requests that any documents found be preserved:

> "Friends," he said, "in the name of history, who will find the condemnation of tyranny in these papers, cease such devastation, I entreat you. Demolish the Bastile, stone by stone, till not a trace remains, but respect documents and books, for the light of the future is in them."
>
> The multitude had scarce heard the rebuke than its high intelligence gauged he was correct.

---

* Throughout the novel, Dumas spells Bastille with only one l.

"The doctor is right," cried a hundred voices; "no more spoiling. Let us take these papers to the City Hall."

A fireman who had brought a small hand-engine into the fort, with half a dozen comrades, directed the horse-butt at the fire which was about to repeat a conflagration of books like that of Alexandria, and they put it out.[48]

This moment is significant because the documents are used later to condemn the people who tried to condemn those in the Bastille. Dickens would use a similar tactic in *A Tale of Two Cities*—Dr. Manette's document that condemns the Evremonde family will be found by Defarge and preserved later to be used against Charles Darnay as a member of the Evremonde family.

However, when people's heads begin being put on pikes, Dr. Gilbert begins to feel disillusioned about the violence that is part of the process Cagliostro envisions for the evolution of liberty.

Dr. Gilbert now goes to Louis XVI to get answers about why he was imprisoned. He learns that Andrée Taverney, the woman he loved, ravished, and had a child with, and who is now the Countess de Charny, ordered his arrest. Meanwhile, the king pardons Gilbert and makes him the court physician. We also learn Marie Antoinette is in love with the Count de Charny, and she convinced Andrée to marry him to keep the king from suspecting.

As court physician, Gilbert is influential enough to convince the king to go to Paris to become a constitutional monarch, thus peacefully bringing about the revolution. The novel ends with Versailles being attacked. The royal family is brought to Paris where they become prisoners of the people. Farmer Billet now wants to return home, but Gilbert persuades him to remain to continue the work of establishing the new order.

The Hero of the People

Early in this novel, Dr. Gilbert is with Marie Antoinette when they see Cagliostro disguised as a gunsmith. Gilbert reunites with

Cagliostro, who has been imprisoned by the pope but escaped and faked his death.* Balsamo/Cagliostro is now masquerading as Baron Zannone, a Genoese banker.† Unlike Cagliostro, Zannone is not a historical personage. Instead, I suspect Dumas chose the name for its similarity to Zanoni. Barone Zannone has great wealth much like Zanoni does in Bulwer-Lytton's novel.

Zannone predicts the Marquis Favras will be hanged, even though nobles are not being hanged but guillotined. That the prediction comes true attests to Zannone's supernatural powers.

Sebastian Gilbert is reunited with his mother, now Countess de Charny, but when her husband arrives, she hides Sebastian so her husband will not know of his existence. As the novel progresses, Andrée and the Count de Charny, who arranged their marriage to keep Louis XVI from being suspicious about Charny and Marie Antoinette's affair, grow to love each other, but they do not reveal their feelings to each other. After Charny leaves, Andrée goes to where Sebastian was hiding, only to find he is gone and Gilbert has taken his place.

Gilbert now hypnotizes Andrée to learn where Sebastian went. This scene is surprising since Andrée doesn't know where Sebastian is, but in a trance, she is able to see things beyond human ability. It is a similar kind of second sight that Balsamo was able to create when he put his wife Lorenza in a trance in *The Mesmerist's Victim*. Andrée realizes Sebastian has had an accident and been rescued by a "vampire" doctor. Dumas, or the translator, calls this a "second-sight vision."[49] As previously noted, Dumas loved to use "second sight" or what today we could call "remote viewing" as a plot device. His use of the second sight is interesting in this scene because it is similar to how, in *Dracula*, Mina Harker, after drinking blood from Dracula's breast, develops the second sight, which allows her to tell the protagonists how to locate

---
* The historical Cagliostro had gone to Italy where he was betrayed in 1789 to the Inquisition for trying to found a Masonic lodge in Rome. He died in prison in 1795.
† Dumas first spells the name Zanone but then switches to Zannone.

Dracula. Perhaps Stoker read this novel or other works by Dumas that used the second sight. He certainly knew Dion Boucicault's play of *The Corsican Brothers*, which Sir Henry Irving, Stoker's employer, performed in.

Gilbert searches for Sebastian, who turns out to be with Jean-Paul Marat, who is the "vampire" doctor. Years before, Marat had healed Gilbert when he first came to Paris and was the pupil of Rousseau. Marat shares with Gilbert that he is composing an enormous body of writing and has made a pact with death that he may live ten years without needing to sleep so he may complete the work. Marat is described from Gilbert's perspective as follows: "The vain creature was transformed under Gilbert's eyes: his eyes became bloodshot; his yellow skin shone with sweat; the monster became great in his hideousness as another is grand in his beauty."[50]

Meanwhile, Baron Zannone has infiltrated his way to the king, who is now borrowing money from him. In Chapter 21, at a meeting with the Invisible Brotherhood, he says he's a Rosicrucian and they are 60,000 strong in France. Although Cagliostro had previously stated that he lost the ability to turn lead into gold when Altothas died, he must have regained it to create such vast wealth to loan to the king.

Zannone also foretells to Gilbert the coming of Napoleon and the French Empire. Later, Zannone tells one of the characters how he knew Oedipus as a boy at one royal court and as a man at another. By the end of the novel, Favras has died at the guillotine as Zannone predicted.

As the monarchy comes closer to destruction, the novel ends by asking:

> What mysterious enemy pursued him [Mirabeau, a French Revolution leader and supporter of constitutional monarchy], or rather pursued the monarchy like a hellhound? This is what we shall learn, with many another secret which none but Cagliostro the superhuman might divine.[51]

The Royal Life Guard

The Royal Life Guard opens with Dr. Gilbert being a friend to Mirabeau because he wants to preserve the king as head of state, but Cagliostro warns Dr. Gilbert that Marie Antoinette is merely cajoling him and that the French royalty are doomed.

Dr. Gilbert gives Mirabeau some of the elixir of life he got from Cagliostro to preserve Mirabeau, but it turns out Cagliostro gave Dr. Gilbert only a mixture of hemp, so Mirabeau dies.

Charny dies, but not before he and Andrée confess their love for one another.

The royal family tries but fails to flee from France. Marie Antoinette, who has long believed Cagliostro dead, feels haunted when she sees him in the crowd in Chapter 22. He saves her from a mob, but only because he still needs her to ensure the monarchy is forever destroyed. Later, in Chapter 27, Marie Antoinette sees Cagliostro at a play and feels his mesmeric power:

> Once her eyes were fastened on his, she could not turn hers aloof, for he exercised the fascination of the serpent on the bird.
>
> The play commenced and she managed to tear her gaze aloof for a time, but ever and anon it had to go back again, from the potent magnetism. It was fatal possession, as by a nightmare.[52]

The Countess de Charny

In the final novel that belongs to the true Marie Antoinette series, Cagliostro continues to torture the queen. In Chapter 6 when she sees a man in the crowd and asks what he holds, Cagliostro appears at her side to tell her it is the axe that killed King Charles I of England. Dr. Gilbert advises Marie Antoinette to escape, but instead, she wants to crush the rebellion.

In Chapter 22, Cagliostro reminds Dr. Gilbert that he had told him if the royal family remained in power in France, he would bring on the revolution. He remarks that Marat and Robespierre are not villains but "mere instruments" like Attila who came to scourge and reform a corrupt Rome. The affairs of France are the affairs of the world, and Altothas had calculated how much blood must be shed to bring about a free world.

Gilbert votes in the assembly against the king's death, believing it will destroy the revolution, but Louis XVI goes to the guillotine regardless.

The novel ends with Andrée dying. Once she is dead, Gilbert, Sebastian, and Farmer Billet decide to leave France for America. What becomes of Cagliostro is not told, but the novel ends by telling us the next book will discuss how Sebastian will fly to arms to avenge his mother's death. This statement is strange given that Dumas tells the reader the story continues in *Le Chevalier de Maison-Rouge*, which chronologically comes next in terms of the events of the French Revolution, but was written before Dumas envisioned this larger series so it contains none of the main fictional characters. Only Marie Antoinette is in it since it is the novel that details her death.

Before discussing *Le Chevalier de Maison-Rouge*, it is worth noting here that Dumas' sprawling seven-novel Marie Antoinette series is full of intrigue, but Cagliostro is the main character of interest because he is the primary manipulator of the French Revolution. Dumas capitalized to a far greater degree than Bulwer-Lytton on conspiracy theories that the French Revolution had been manipulated by secret societies, while Dickens would shy away from conspiracy theories and any sense of supernatural powers or secret societies at work. Dumas' work is entertaining but somewhat unsatisfactory since we never learn what became of Cagliostro or if his goals were successfully completed. Part of the problem is history itself since, as Cagliostro predicts, the revolution led to the rise and fall of Napoleon and then the restoration of the French monarchy. Dumas could not rewrite history to allow Cagliostro to succeed in bringing about his idyllic society—he ultimately has to fail. Even as Dumas wrote these novels in the 1840s and 1850s, France was far from the idyllic society Cagliostro hoped for. In fact, halfway through writing the series, Dumas went into exile to flee Louis-Napoleon's regime.

Despite its loose baggy monster feel, the Marie Antoinette novels are the most thorough treatment of the French Revolution in nineteenth-century fiction. The Rosicrucian elements Dumas used to develop the character of Balsamo/Cagliostro/Zannone may well have been inspired by the title character of *Zanoni*. Both characters claim to be of ancient age, both have supernatural powers and occult knowledge, both belong to secret societies, both have enormous wealth, and of course, both find themselves mixed up in the events of the French Revolution, although with different results.

Dumas' novels also likely influenced *A Tale of Two Cities*, but it is *Le Chevalier de Maison-Rouge*, which is only loosely tied to the other Marie Antoinette novels, that probably had the greatest influence on Dickens. In the next section, I will discuss the two novels together.

Dumas' *Le Chevalier de Maison-Rouge* and Dickens' *A Tale of Two Cities*

Le Chevalier de Maison-Rouge (*The Knight of the Red House*) was written and published a year before Dumas wrote *Joseph Balsamo*, the first of the Marie Antoinette novels. It is only loosely tied to the other novels because the title character, the chevalier, is Philippe de Taverney, brother of Andrée de Charny. Philippe is the mastermind behind the plot to save Marie Antoinette from the guillotine, although he is not a main character in the novel. Marie Antoinette is the only other character from the series of novels named for her.

Although not one of Dumas' better-known works, *Le Chevalier de Maison-Rouge* is significant in its own right and for being a probable influence on *A Tale of Two Cities*. Most Dickens scholars have ignored it as a source for Dickens' novel, perhaps because the length of the Marie Antoinette novels and the confusion over how many books there are can be off-putting. Furthermore, Dumas' use of the supernatural may have made his novels seem irrelevant since Dickens' novel is realistic fiction, despite some Gothic elements. However, *Le Chevalier de Maison-Rouge* has too many similarities to *A Tale of Two Cities* to be simply coincidental. After I discovered these similarities myself, I was happy to find critic Richard Maxwell agrees with me as I will explore below.

An influence of Dumas upon Dickens is not at all unlikely. Dickens was a Francophile who often holidayed in France. In 1846, when he delivered a speech in Paris—in French no less—he called the French "the first people in the universe."[53] When he visited his friend William Macready in Paris in 1846, Macready introduced him to his own Parisian friends, Théophile Gautier, Louis Blanc, Victor Hugo, and Alexandre Dumas.[54] Macready, Dickens, and Dumas would sit in Dumas' box at the theatre to see his play *Christine* performed.[55] Dickens would also meet Eugène Scribe, François-René de Chateaubriand, and Eugène Sue.[56]

Later, Dickens would spend three months in Paris while working on *Dombey and Son* from November 1846 to February 1847. During that time, he and John Forster did extensive sightseeing, including seeing a melodrama called *The French Revolution* at the Cirque filled with battles and mob scenes that Dickens said was "positively awful,"[57] but regardless, it may have inspired an interest in the subject for his future book. By this point, Dickens spoke French fluently, but with a heavy English accent. He and Forster socialized with many theatrical and literary celebrities. They supped with Dumas and Eugène Sue, met Gautier, and saw a lot of Scribe. Dickens renewed an acquaintance with Lamartine and visited Chateaubriand. For Dickens, however, the greatest author he met was Victor Hugo, whose apartment was crammed with furniture, tapestries, and other objects that made Dickens refer to it as "like an old curiosity shop."[58] Upon another visit in 1863, Dickens met Paul Féval whom he called "a capital fellow."[59] While meeting authors is clearly not the same as reading their books, it is unlikely Dickens was not familiar with many of their works, including those of Dumas.

I will now discuss *Le Chevalier de Maison-Rouge*, stopping as needed to highlight similarities to *A Tale of Two Cities*, which I assume most readers will know. As mentioned above, *Le Chevalier de Maison-Rouge* was written before the Marie Antoinette novels, but Dumas tried to connect it to them as part of the series by stating at the end of *The Countess de Charny*:

> Let us turn from these truly happy ones, in the peaceful country, to the bereaved widow of Louis XVI. In her lonesome jail she mourns over the loss of all—husband, lover, friend. What can replace a Charny or an Andrea? She thinks there is no champion of the blood of either, for she knows not that Cagliostro's surmise was not baseless. When the son of Andrea shall know how his mother fell, he will fly to arms to avenge that loss and to spite her foes, who are also the queen's! We shall trace his gallant, and desperate attempts to rescue the royal captive in the pages of the conclusion of this series, entitled: "The Knight of Redcastle: or, The Captivity of Marie Antoinette."[60]

Perhaps Dumas intended to go back and rewrite the novel, but to my knowledge he did not. Sebastian Gilbert does not revenge his mother's death and is not even in the novel. Curiously, a Gilbert appears in the novel as one of Marie Antoinette's jailors. However, he only makes minor appearances in Chapters 34-52, and he in no way resembles Dr. Gilbert or Sebastian. Rather, this jailor Gilbert is based on the historical Jean Gilbert, who was involved in a plot to free the queen, but then turned against the conspirators, either from fear or a desire for more money.[61]

The novel opens after Louis XVI's death. The main character, Maurice Lindey, is a young man who tries to assist an old woman when she has been stopped by the police for being out at night without a pass. She turns out to be a beautiful young woman in disguise named Genevieve, and Maurice immediately falls in love with her. However, he will eventually learn she is married to a man named Dixmer and involved in a Royalist plot to help Marie Antoinette escape from prison. Also involved in the plot is the eponymous character, the mysterious Knight of the Maison-Rouge, the mastermind behind the plot. The novel is based on the events of the "affair of the carnation" in which the Marquis Alexandre Gonsse de Rougeville attempted to communicate with Marie Antoinette by hiding a message in a carnation's petals. Dumas actually titled the work *Le Chevalier de Rougeville*, but changed the title after the Marquis de Rougeville's son complained.[62]

I will not elaborate on the entire plot, but it is worth noting that its overall tone is different from that of the Marie Antoinette novels and any trace of the supernatural is absent from it. However, some plot elements are similar to those of *A Tale of Two Cities*.

The first and probably weakest similarity in arguing an influence exists is that both novels have main characters who are in love with married women. Maurice Lindey loves Genevieve, who is married to Dixmer. Sidney Carton loves Lucie Manette, who ends up marrying Charles Darnay. However, the way the love triangles play out is vastly different. Carton sacrifices himself to take Darnay's place at the guillotine, allowing Darnay and Lucie to preserve their marital union. Lucie is never in love with Carton and always faithful to Darnay. By contrast, Genevieve knows her husband is a villain, and she plans to run away with Maurice. When Dixmer discovers their plans, he arranges to put Genevieve in prison. Dixmer calls Maurice an adulterer, but Maurice says he is no better, having purposely used Maurice for his own purposes. Eventually, the two men fight a duel. Maurice slices off Dixmer's hand, but Dixmer's death results when he impales himself on his sword. Maurice then retrieves a pass to the prison from Dixmer's wallet so he can get inside to see Genevieve. The significance of this pass will be made clear when I discuss the third similarity between the novels.

The second similarity is the references to knitting in both novels. That women knitted at the trials of prisoners sentenced to the guillotine is a historical fact and also referenced in Carlyle's *The French Revolution*. Carlyle writes, "for there are Citoyennes too, thick crowded in the galleries here. Citoyennes who bring their seam with them, or their knitting-needles; and shriek or knit as the case needs; famed Tricoteuses, Patriot Knitters."[63] In *Le Chevalier de Maison-Rouge*, a character comments about women knitting during the trials of prisoners being sent to the guillotine:

> Morand elaborated a theory about women in politics, starting with Théroigne de Méricourt, the heroine of the tenth of August, and ending with Madame Roland, that soul of the Gironde. In passing, he said what he thought of the tricoteuses—those bloodthirsty crones who did their knitting at the foot of the guillotine. His words made Maurice smile despite the cruel derision of these female patriots, later given the hideous name of guillotine-lickers.[64]

Later, the knitting women are referenced again:

> The mob in the galleries was in a ferocious mood that day, the kind of mood that excites the severity of the jurors: placed under the immediate surveillance of the *tricoteuses*—knitting away—and the working class faubouriens from the suburbs, jurors hold up better, sticking to their guns like actors redoubling their efforts before a hostile audience.[65]

A reader familiar with *A Tale of Two Cities* cannot help but read these passages and think of Madame Defarge knitting the names of the enemies of the Republic.

The third and most notable similarity between the two novels is the use of doubles or lookalikes. Dumas uses this device in two ways. First, in Chapter 51, Genevieve is put on trial for her involvement in the plot to free Marie Antoinette. She is ultimately condemned to the guillotine because she admits she knelt before the queen and begged her to change clothes with her so she could die in her place. She did so under the persuasion of her husband, Dixmer, as his revenge for learning she has become Maurice's lover. In fact, Gilbert testifies against Genevieve as having seen her kneel in this way before the queen, thus helping to bring about rather than prevent her death.

The more notable attempt by characters to switch places occurs after Dixmer dies and Maurice has obtained the pass from his wallet to get into the prison. The pass is written for a "citizen," not a "citizeness,"[66] so Maurice, who had considered dying in Genevieve's place, realizes Genevieve cannot use the pass to escape. Maurice decides to die with Genevieve, so he gives the pass to his friend Lorin so he can escape. After much cajoling, Lorin takes the pass and leaves the prison. Maurice is relieved when the guards tear up the pass after Lorin leaves so he cannot return. However, Lorin agreed to leave only so he could kill Dixmer, not knowing he is already dead. When Lorin learns Dixmer is dead, he assumes Dixmer killed himself to atone for his crimes. Lorin returns to the prison where Maurice hints to him the truth about Dixmer's death.

The time comes to go to the guillotine, but there are fifteen prisoners now and only fourteen are condemned. Maurice again tries to get Lorin to leave, but when he refuses, all three go to the guillotine. Genevieve dies first, then Maurice, and finally Lorin. The closing sentence of the novel says, "With that the head of the generous young man fell next to the heads of Maurice and Geneviève!"[67] Lorin is far from a Sidney Carton—there's no great death speech about what a good thing he's doing—and yet, here we have a kindhearted man willing to die with his friends since he cannot die for them.

In the later play version, Lorin succeeds in taking the lovers' place, thus facilitating their escape while he dies at the guillotine.[68] The play was first performed at the Théâtre-Historique on August 3, 1847. A book edition of the play soon followed.[69] Then the play was adapted into English by Dion Boucicault.[*] Titled *Geneviève;*

---

[*] Notably, the year prior Boucicault had produced his play of Dumas' *The Corsican Brothers*.

or *the Reign of Terror*, it was produced in England in 1853, with Benjamin Webster (1797-1882) starring as the self-sacrificing Lorin.[70] Dickens knew Webster because he had played John Peerybingle in his own dramatization of his novella *The Cricket on the Hearth*.[71] Dickens also likely knew the play based on Dumas' novel either by seeing it performed or reading it. He may even have read the novel. Certainly, he had plenty of possible sources for the victim substitution plot in *A Tale of Two Cities*.

Of course, Zanoni's sacrificial death at the guillotine was also an influence on Dickens' decision to have Sidney Carton sacrifice himself. Since the seed of such a martyrdom is here in Dumas' novel, perhaps Dumas borrowed from Bulwer-Lytton, and Dickens borrowed from both.

I believe enough evidence exists to argue that this last novel, if not all of Alexandre Dumas' Marie Antoinette novels, is a probable missing link between the novels of Bulwer-Lytton and Charles Dickens. It once again testifies to how British and French nineteenth-century Gothic authors influenced and were influenced by each other.

In the end, Dickens' novel became the most famous and was appreciated in France. In 1872 in *Le Correspondant*, French critic Andre Joubert wrote of *A Tale of Two Cities* (published in France under the title *Paris et Londres en 1793*) that he preferred Dickens' historical novels to Scott's and he admired *A Tale of Two Cities* without reserve for its drama and impressive realism that surpassed anything Dumas had written about the French Revolution. He only wished Dickens had not pleaded so strongly for the demagogical ideas of the Revolution.[72]

Other Sources for *A Tale of Two Cities*

While Bulwer-Lytton and Dumas' works are the two primary Gothic sources for *A Tale of Two Cities*, plenty of other works inspired the novel. It is well known Carlyle's *The French Revolution* was an influence, but Eugène Sue as a source has been largely overlooked. Sue and Dickens were acquainted from at least 1845. According to critic Alexander Hugh Jordan, Dickens and Sue became acquainted through their connections to Carlyle. Jordan states:

> Alongside his admiration for Carlyle, Dickens also held Eugène Sue in high regard. In October 1845, both Dickens and Sue were invited to a meeting of the Manchester Athenaeum. Unable to attend, Sue charged Dickens with conveying his apologies, and Dickens duly informed the organisers that "M. Eugène Sue has begged me to write to you, and acknowledge with many heartfelt thanks the receipt of your flattering invitation" (17 Oct. 1845, qtd. in Chevasco 156). And, two years later, in the winter of 1847, Dickens and Forster visited Paris, where, as Forster recalled, "we supped…with Eugène Sue" (Forster 2: 331). Also worthy of mention is the fact that Dickens and Forster had acquired their letter of introduction to Sue from the Count d'Orsay, another member of Carlyle's circle (Chevasco 156).[73]

Dickens may have been influenced by the city mysteries genre in choosing the title *A Tale of Two Cities*, which might as well have been titled *The Mysteries of Paris and London*. Mysteries abound in both cities in the novel. While most are set in Paris and center around how the Evremonde brothers imprisoned Dr. Manette to keep their secret safe, in London, Lucie has grown up not even knowing her father is alive. His existence is a mystery to her, as are the horrors of his past once she is reunited with him. The Defarges' reasons for wanting to bring about the revolution are also a mystery to the reader until Dr. Manette's manuscript is found and their connections to his story revealed. Richard Maxwell points out that the characters themselves are mysteries to one another and themselves, Lucie and her father being mysteries to each other, and Carton a mystery to everyone. Similarly, Jerry Cruncher's occupation as a resurrection man is a mystery to his son and Mr. Lorry. Only when the characters go to Paris do all these mysteries come to light.[74]

One possible influence Dickens would have hated to own was Reynolds' *The Mysteries of London*. Richard Maxwell notes that Jerry Cruncher is "the least terrifying Resurrection Man in literature, especially with the most notorious practitioner of the trade in mid Victorian literature, G. W. M. Reynolds' Anthony Tidkins."[75] If Jerry Cruncher was not inspired by Anthony Tidkins, perhaps he was inspired by the resurrection man in Féval's *Les Mystères de Londres*. In either case, Dickens was clearly influenced by the city mysteries genre at large, and his later novels like *Bleak House* and *Our Mutual Friend*, which focus on crime, wickedness, and mysteries in London, would not have had such Gothic atmospheres if not for Sue, Reynolds, and Féval's earlier works.

Of course, Mrs. Radcliffe's *The Mysteries of Udolpho* may have inspired the use of "mystery" in the city mysteries genre, but Mrs. Radcliffe may also have influenced Dickens with the found manuscript device. Found manuscripts are a staple of Gothic literature, but specifically in Radcliffe's *The Romance of the Forest*, Adeline finds a manuscript in an abbey written by someone who was a prisoner there. Similarly, Dr. Manette writes his manuscript while a prisoner in the Bastille.

Dickens also drew upon the historical record with Dr. Manette's manuscript. In *The Bastille: A History of a Symbol of Despotism and Freedom*, German cultural historians Hans-Jürgen Lüsebrink and Rolf Reichardt discuss how a group of widely read memoirs by former prisoners created a myth of the Bastille as a place of unjust imprisonment of people who were usually of noble birth or had a promising career, but who were imprisoned due to conspiracies against them. The prisoners were arrested with blank warrants. They were tortured, and they inscribed their names on the walls of their prisons. Then they heroically escaped or were secretly released. Such themes were frequently used by Dumas in his fiction.[76] Both *The Man in the Iron Mask* and *The Count of Monte Cristo* come to mind, as well as Dr. Gilbert being imprisoned in *The Storming of the Bastille*. Dickens draws upon this same theme of imprisonment and prisoners writing memoirs. Both his and Dumas' treatments of the Bastille make it a symbol in the same way Hugo and Ainsworth transformed Notre-Dame de Paris and the Tower of London into symbolic Gothic structures. Carlyle also referenced manuscripts in the Bastille in relation to Louis XVI, which I'll discuss in the next section.

Among Dickens' numerous other sources for the Bastille and French Revolution, according to Maxwell, were Mercier's writings of Paris in the eighteenth century, Dumas' *Le Vicomte de Bragelonne* with its depiction of the Man in the Iron Mask, John Frederick Smith's *The Substance and the Shadow*, from which Dickens may have borrowed the character of La Vengeance[*] and some of the elements that inspired Madame Defarge, and Albert Smith's *The Marchioness of Brinvilliers*, which may have given him knowledge of the "North Tower" where Dr. Manette is imprisoned. Finally, he used the memoirs of Linguet, who was imprisoned there in the eighteenth century.[77]

For the droit du seigneur theme—the right of the lord to have his way with the women on his property—which results in the death of Madame Defarge's sister by the Evremondes, Dickens borrowed from *The Iron Trevet, or Jocelyn the Champion*, the fourteenth book in Eugène Sue's *The Mysteries of the People* series and G. P. R. James' *The Jacquereie, or the Lady and the Page* (1842).[78]

As for Dr. Manette's shoemaking, in *Le Chevalier de Maison-Rouge*, Simon, a former shoemaker and historical person, is given a free hand in dealing with the dauphin, teaching him to sing insulting songs about his mother and compelling him to make shoes. The shoemaking may be a coincidence here with Dr. Manette, but Richard Maxwell argues that for Dr. Manette, shoemaking is a way to express or cope with anger, so after the doctor first leaves the prison, Defarge fetches the shoemaking equipment for him to use in the inn until Mr. Lorry and

---

[*] But see below my discussion of Dickens' The Vengeance as inspired by Sue.

Lucie come to fetch him. Dr. Manette finds himself indulging in compulsive shoemaking much like Madame Defarge compulsively knits as an expression of anger and desire for revenge.[79] Dr. Manette also reverts to his shoemaking and has a mental lapse when he is parted from Lucie for the first time since his imprisonment because she goes on her honeymoon. This happens after Darnay confesses to Dr. Manette that he is the son of one of the Evremonde brothers who imprisoned Dr. Manette, so the marriage may trigger him to revert to his past compulsive coping mechanisms.

In addition, while Bulwer-Lytton and Dumas' novels may have influenced the theme of doubles and prisoner substitution, other possible sources exist. Dickens had recently acted in Wilkie Collins' play *The Frozen Deep* in which one character acts as a double for another.[80] In *The French Revolution*, Carlyle also mentions the historical case of last-minute victim substitution, in which General Loiserolles dies for his son.[81] Critic Richard Maxwell suggests that in 1857 when Dickens was working with Wilkie Collins on *The Frozen Deep*, actor Benjamin Webster may have read to him the yet unpublished and unperformed script of *The Dead Heart* by Irish playwright Watt Philips. Webster had bought the rights to that play, which also contains a victim-substitution plot and has been suggested as a source for *A Tale of Two Cities*.[82]

Finally, we cannot overlook that Dickens may have borrowed from Eugène Sue's own novel about the French Revolution, *The Sword of Honor*, the eighteenth novel in his nineteen-novel series, *The Mysteries of the People*. Sue's novel is realistic, not Gothic at all, in its depiction of the Revolution, but one character seems likely to have been borrowed by Dickens. In *A Tale of Two Cities*, one of Madame Defarge's closest companions during the revolution is known as "The Vengeance." We are first introduced to her when she is knitting beside Madame Defarge. "One of her sisterhood knitted beside her. The short, rather plump wife of a starved grocer, and the mother of two children withal, this lieutenant had already earned the complimentary name of The Vengeance."[83] She frequently accompanies Madame Defarge, but does not when Madame Defarge goes to visit the Darnays at the end of the novel and discovers their escape. Had The Vengeance been with her, Madame Defarge may not have died at the hand of Miss Pross. As Carton, believed to be Darnay, is executed, The Vengeance wonders where her friend Madame Defarge is, regretting she will miss the execution. The Vengeance even makes it into Carton's famous final speech when he says, "I see Barsad, and Cly, Defarge, The Vengeance, the Juryman, the Judge, long ranks of the new oppressors who have risen on the destruction of the old, perishing by this retributive instrument, before it shall cease out of its present use."[84]

While a relatively minor character, The Vengeance reveals that Dickens read Sue's novel since it also contains a character who is equated with vengeance. In Sue's novel, the vengeful character is Victoria, a daughter of the house of Lebrenn, Sue's proletariat family who are the heroes of the series. Victoria is named for an ancestor who appears in the fifth book in the series who was a great warrior queen of the Gauls. Her story also closely resembles that of Madame Defarge's sister, who was abducted by the Evremonde brothers and raped. Victoria was kidnapped as a child and given to Louis XV as a sex toy. When he tired of her, she was sent to work in a house of prostitution. During this time, hatred grew in her for the nobility and the church. And after she was found and restored to her family, and her father published her story, he was sent to the Bastille as a prisoner. For that reason she wants vengeance, stating:

> all created and matured in me that craving for vengeance, or rather for reprisals, which now possesses me. I long to serve that vengeance, at the cost of my life, if need be. That is why I have consented to this initiation, the hour of which is now approached. Vengeance will be but justice, and I wish it to be implacable.[85]

Victoria's story closely resembles that of Madame Defarge and Dr. Manette. Madame Defarge's sister becomes the sex toy of the Evremonde brothers. To keep Dr. Manette silent when he is called upon to try to save the girl and the brother who died trying to protect her honor, Dr. Manette is imprisoned in the Bastille. However, there he writes his manuscript that will later reveal the Evremondes' crimes, just as Victoria's father goes to the Bastille, although with the reverse that it is after he published his manuscript, not before.

Victoria wants vengeance just like Madame Defarge and her friend, The Vengeance, do, and like the latter, she comes to personify Vengeance in the novel. When the revolution erupts, Franz, Prince of Gerolstein, tells Victoria she may have to restrain herself from vengeance if peaceful means can be used in the revolution, but if the people are not listened to, he tells her:

> "It will be the unchaining of popular passions. No bridle can hold them. The justice of God will pass over a terror-stricken world. Then, in the midst of that tempest which shall overturn thrones and altars—then, Victoria, you shall appear, terrible as the Goddess of Vengeance, striking with her broad sword the old world, condemned in the name of the good of the peoples."
>
> "Oh, my life, my whole life for one hour of such vengeance!" cried the young woman, palpitating in wild exaltation. "Aye, let my life be a hundred times more miserable, more abject, more horrible than that which a King put upon me—I shall live it twice over in order to assist in the hour of this vengeance. A day, an hour of reprisals, for my life of misery!"
>
> "Come then, Victoria, you shall be ours as we shall be yours, in life, in death, in triumph, in vengeance!"[86]

Like Madame Defarge, in the end, Victoria also has a violent death, dying of wounds received in fighting for liberty for the French people. However, the reader is sympathetic to Victoria, while Madame Defarge and The Vengeance are seen as villains in *A Tale of Two Cities*, even if their desire for vengeance is righteous.

Sue may have influenced another Victorian British novelist in his character of the Vengeance. In John Frederick Smith's *The Substance and the Shadow* (1858), also about the French Revolution, is another character named Vengeance. Critic Harland S. Nelson has argued that Smith's Vengeance is the source for Dickens' character, and certainly, there are some parallels between the novels as he illustrates.[87] To some degree, I feel these are coincidences, but it can't be denied that Smith depicts his Vengeance waiting alone at the scaffold. Dickens has The Vengeance as one of a group of women knitting at the guillotine. However, she is notably alone in the novel in the sense that she is upset that Madame Defarge does not arrive in time to see Sidney Carton, believed to be Darnay, die. If Dickens was influenced by Smith's novel, I believe it was in this scene. I also think it likely Smith read Sue's novel and was inspired by it, though his Vengeance is very different from Sue's. Still, Smith's Vengeance finds herself imprisoned in the Bastille for many years. Sue's Vengeance does not end up in the Bastille but her father does. In Smith's novel, Vengeance takes her name after learning an old man in the Bastille calls himself Destiny. This old man, according to Nelson, might be a source for Dr. Manette.

Whether consciously or not, Dickens may have read both Sue and Smith's novels and then rearranged the characters and scenes a bit for his own purposes. That is not to say Dickens was not original in creating his novel. Smith was a writer of popular penny dreadful fiction, so Dickens would not have wanted to admit an influence from such a writer, but regardless, I believe he drew from Sue and Smith and who knows what other sources that have not yet been identified.

Rosicrucian Immortality and Christian Redemption in *A Tale of Two Cities*

While critics have acknowledged that Zanoni's sacrifice inspired Sidney Carton's, they have overlooked Dickens' borrowing of Bulwer-Lytton's Rosicrucian theme to create in Sidney Carton an immortal Gothic wanderer figure who reverses the curse of damnation, exchanging it for eternal life in heaven.

A Tale of Two Cities is less a novel about the French Revolution than the tale of a group of English characters whose love and lives are threatened by the revolution, thus making the revolution itself subservient to plot mechanics. The revolution becomes the vehicle that motivates the characters' actions, which, in turn, lead to Carton's sacrifice and Christian redemption.

While the French Revolution was far enough in the past that few of Dickens' readers would remember it, Dickens reminds his readers that human nature, and its desires and fears, remains the same, so the past and the present have many similarities. Readers, therefore, should find something relevant to their own lives in his historical tale. Dickens breaks down the gap between the past and present by creating an opening that reflects his story's timelessness.

> It was the best of times, it was the worst of times, it was the age of wisdom, it was the age of foolishness, it was the epoch of belief, it was the epoch of incredulity, it was the season of Light, it was the season of Darkness, it was the spring of hope, it was the winter of despair, we had everything before us, we had nothing before us, we were all going direct to Heaven, we were all going direct the other way — in short, the period was so far like the present period, that some of its noisiest authorities insisted on its being received, for good or for evil, in the superlative degree of comparison only.[88]

This sense of timelessness also prepares the way for Dickens' Christian theme and biblical symbolism. In *"Noah's Arkitecture": A Study of Dickens's Mythology*, Bert G. Hornback has exhaustively recorded Dickens' recurring use of biblical symbols in his novels. Hornback argues that this usage reflects Dickens' continual questioning of human civilization's progress and his theories of historical evolution. Dickens' novels symbolically begin in the mythic times of Genesis, especially the Creation, Garden of Eden, and the Flood, and from there, they either evolve into order or move backward, progressing toward or returning to an idyllic world.[89] Dickens' use of the Edenic myth places him, like Carlyle and his Gothic predecessors, among those Gothic novelists who wish to revise *Paradise Lost*;* Dickens creates his own revision of Milton's epic by blending the Gothic and grotesque with biblical mythology to emphasize the need for human redemption and the importance of cultivating one's spirituality in a fallen world. The opening of *A Tale of Two Cities* uses this biblical mythology by comparing Light and Dark, which reflects Genesis and the times of Chaos and creation, suggesting that both the years 1775 and 1859 are such times of new beginnings as well as endings.[90] Hornback argues that Dickens' use of the myth "is to collapse all time into the crisis of the historical present."[91]

Similarly, David Marcus suggests that the opening of *A Tale of Two Cities* is intended to confuse the reader, making time impossible to define just as it is impossible for people to understand the times in which they live.[92] Dickens believes that all time periods are similar, whether it's the creation of the world, pre-French Revolution, or the mid-Victorian age because they are all confusing to those living within those periods. Consequently, while Dickens sets the novel during the French Revolution, the setting becomes symbolic and universal because the novel's events could happen anywhere at any time under the right conditions. George Lukacs concludes from this setting that the French Revolution becomes merely a "Romantic background" and the characters are historically displaced as a result.[93] Hornback, in agreement, believes that because the biblical images collapse time, the characters' stories could easily have been told without the French Revolution as the setting.[94]

---

* For an extensive discussion of the influence of *Paradise Lost* on Gothic literature, see *The Gothic Wanderer*.

More important than the novel's historical background is its typical Gothic emphasis upon the sanctity of the family and the need to preserve it. For Dickens, the family is where morals are learned and character is formed. Familial love rather than revolution is more productive in bringing about individual reform and redemption. Dickens uses the family as a place where reform occurs. The novel opens with an attempt to repair the broken Manette family. Lucie travels to France to meet and care for her father who has just been released from the Bastille. Dr. Manette is mentally wandering, but Lucie restores his mind and health by establishing a home for him. As the novel progresses, more broken families are introduced: the Evremondes, the Defarges, and the solitary Sidney Carton, who is without a family but reforms from his despair and alcoholism when he becomes an honorary member of the Darnay family and achieves a sense of belonging. The novel's broken English families become restored and strengthened, while the broken French families serve as a contrast to emphasize the disaster that results when the bonds of familial love are violated by society or a family member. The novel's three Gothic wanderers—Dr. Manette, Charles Darnay, and Sidney Carton—become the central focus within these families. A brief overview of each character's role as a Gothic wanderer will clarify how they all relate to the novel's emphasis on the family.

Dr. Manette, the first Gothic wanderer introduced, is a victim of the aristocratic and patriarchal system of pre-revolutionary France. He is imprisoned because of his knowledge regarding a crime of rape and murder committed by the aristocratic Evremonde family. Because of their social status, the Evremondes are powerful enough to lock Dr. Manette in the Bastille so he cannot reveal their crimes. Dr. Manette's imprisonment is typical of the confinements of victims in Gothic novels, and the horror of his imprisonment ultimately results in his madness. Dickens describes Dr. Manette's incarceration as being "buried alive" because he is locked in his cell without access to the outside world or other prisoners. Dickens characterizes the Bastille as a Gothic prison, exaggerating the horrors that would have been faced by its prisoners to make Dr. Manette's situation all the more sensational and Gothic. Critic Shawn Lyons points out that by the reign of Louis XVI, the Bastille's dungeons were no longer used. Furthermore, the Bastille had better government funds than other prisons in France because it frequently held important political prisoners. Because of their political influence, these prisoners could often bribe their jailors to bring them luxuries. Lyons suggests, therefore, that Dr. Manette could have had books or other intellectual pursuits in prison, rather than becoming a shoemaker.[95]

However, Dickens intentionally depicts Dr. Manette in prison as a shoemaker to link him with the Wandering Jew. Dickens also makes Dr. Manette a shoemaker to show the severe mental degradation that prison has upon him. Like Milton's Satan who has hell within him, Dr. Manette is never free from his memories of prison, even when he is physically free. The torture of being in prison becomes manifested in his worst moments when he reverts to his former occupation of making shoes. Dickens borrows from Mercier's *Tableau de Paris* the story of an old man who, when freed from imprisonment in the Bastille, recreated his cell in a room of his house; similarly after he is freed, Dr. Manette continues to make shoes in his own home when his madness comes upon him.[96] At such times, he also wanders back and forth in his room, trying to shake off his madness like the Wandering Jew who continually wanders from place to place to hide his identity and escape persecution. Dr. Manette is further linked to the Wandering Jew when he is described as "a famished traveller, wearied out by lonely wandering in a wilderness,"[97] suggestive of the biblical Hebrews' wanderings in the wilderness, and the Wandering Jew as symbol of the Jewish race.

Dr. Manette also metaphorically shares the Wandering Jew's extended life because he was practically dead while in prison and now he has been "recalled to life" and moves about like a supernatural being, as if he "were a Spirit moving among mortals."⁹⁸ We are even told that Dr. Manette "never spoke, without first wandering in this manner, and forgetting to speak."⁹⁹ He remains displaced even after his release, trying to adjust to a normal life, but often relapsing to his old state. The housekeeper, Mrs. Pross, describes his state as:

> his mind is walking up and down, walking up and down, in his old prison. She [Lucie] hurries to him, and they go on together, walking up and down, walking up and down until he is composed. But he never says a word of the true reason of his restlessness…they go walking up and down, walking up and down together, till her love and company have brought him to himself.¹⁰⁰

For Dickens, love is what ultimately restores and redeems the Gothic wanderer. For Dr. Manette, Lucie's love restores him to the fullest extent possible after his horrible experience.

Another source for Dr. Manette's imprisonment in the Bastille is the historical imprisonment there of Louis XVI as described in Carlyle's *French Revolution*. Carlyle wrote that when the Bastille was attacked and searched, "its paper archives shall fly white. Old secrets come to view; and long-buried Despair finds voice."¹⁰¹ Carlyle records that among the papers discovered was a secret document concealed in the wall of the Tuilleries by Louis XVI with the aid of a locksmith. The discovery of this document was responsible for finally condemning the king to death. Similarly, the discovery of a document written by Dr. Manette will condemn his son-in-law, Charles Darnay.

Dr. Manette is also connected to Louis XVI because during his imprisonment, Louis XVI would pretend he was a locksmith as a form of escapism from his imprisonment. Louis XVI actually learned the trade of locksmith from the man who helped him conceal his secret papers.¹⁰² Dickens uses this historical detail but changes Dr. Manette's occupation from locksmith to shoemaker to enhance the Gothic wanderer theme. Dickens also uses the

Gothic discovered manuscript device, which reveals not only a history of family transgression, but the relationships between most of the main characters, thus showing once more that Gothic plots are family plots.

Dr. Manette becomes a prisoner in the Bastille, and hence a Gothic wanderer, because he has unwillingly acquired forbidden knowledge about the Evremondes, and they punish him for possessing that knowledge. As recorded in the manuscript, the Evremonde brothers, Darnay's father and uncle, raped Madame Defarge's sister and murdered her brother. Dr. Manette was called upon to treat the wounded from this conflict, but his knowledge of the event results in the Evremondes imprisoning him.

Both during his imprisonment and after his release, like other Gothic wanderers, Dr. Manette takes on supernatural characteristics. When he is first seen by Mr. Lorry, he looks almost like a ghost. Mr. Lorry, in his role to bring Dr. Manette back to London, is described as being "on his way to dig some one out of a grave."[103] In his dreams, Mr. Lorry sees numerous prisoners' faces, all of which are the faces of Dr. Manette, with "sunken cheek, cadaverous colour, emaciated hands and figures"[104] and with a "ghostly face."[105] These descriptions suggest Dr. Manette has been dead or buried alive, and now he has been "recalled to life,"[106] a phrase borrowed from *Paradise Lost* and spoken by Adam in reference to the human race's future redemption by Christ's sacrifice "yet recall'd/To life prolong'd and promis'd Race."[107] Dr. Manette's release from prison becomes another example of Dickens' use of the biblical myths of Creation and the Deluge, all myths of death and regeneration that foreshadow Christ's resurrection.[108] Dickens ties this biblical resurrection to the Gothic tradition by suggesting Dr. Manette is a reversal of Christ's resurrection, being almost more like a vampire or the living dead who returns to life pale or bloodless.

Released from his physical imprisonment, Dr. Manette eventually realizes he can use his suffering to benefit others. Once the French Revolution breaks out, Dr. Manette's reputation as a former prisoner of the Bastille makes him almost a superhero to the French people. Consequently, he is able to use his popularity to persuade the courts to free Darnay. Dr. Manette now realizes that the evil he suffered has brought about some good.

> the Doctor felt, now, that his suffering was strength and power. For the first time he felt that in that sharp fire, he had slowly forged the iron which could break the prison door of his daughter's husband, and deliver him. "It all tended to a good end, my friend: it was not mere waste and ruin. As my beloved child was helpful in restoring me to myself, I will be helpful now in restoring the dearest part of herself to her; by the aid of Heaven I will do it!" Thus, Doctor Manette.[109]

By saving Darnay, Dr. Manette takes on the role of Christ, his suffering having become the sacrifice that redeems Darnay. Furthermore, Dickens transforms his Gothic wanderer into an Everyman figure, for the name Manette suggests Mankind, while the feminine ending of the name incorporates women as well as men into this role. Dr. Manette's sufferings are representative of the sufferings everyone must undergo to be able to empathize with others and help them in their tribulations. In the novel's Preface, Dickens himself attested to this truth by realizing his own experiences made him able to depict sympathetically the novel's events: "I have so far verified what is done and suffered in these pages, as that I have certainly done and suffered it all myself."[110]

Charles Darnay is the novel's second Gothic wanderer. He is a son and nephew to the Evremonde brothers who imprisoned Dr. Manette. Although innocent of committing crimes against the French people, Darnay is cursed because of his family's crimes, making him the victim of patriarchy despite his position as the family heir. Darnay tried to escape his cursed family background by rejecting his aristocratic connections, changing his name from Evremonde to Darnay, and moving to England. Nevertheless, his family background continues to haunt him. The name Evremonde, like Manette, is intended as a universal symbol. Michael Goldberg argues that Evremonde is a combination of the English word "every" with the French "tout le monde" meaning "all the world." This combination results in a French word that would be equivalent to the English "Everyman."[111] Consequently, the evils of the Evremonde family become the evils of all humanity; therefore, Carton's sacrificial death to compensate for the evils of the Darnay/Evremonde family is equivalent to Christ's death to wash away the sins of Everyman/mankind.

Dickens further expands upon the Everyman theme by connecting the Evremonde family with Gothic immortality because of the curse placed upon the family. Critics have overlooked the significance of this curse, which provides a literary link between the Evremonde family and the Wandering Jew, the curse of Cain, and the Rosicrucians. Dr. Manette records that the young man whom he medically assisted placed the curse upon the Evremonde brothers after he had fought for the honor of his violated sister. Darnay's father, by his aristocratic position, views the rape as his "droit du seigneur," while the girl's brother views the rape as a transgression against his family. Dr. Manette records that before dying, the young man cursed the Evremonde family.

> "'Marquis,' said the boy, turned to him with his eyes opened wide, and his right hand raised, 'in the days when all these things are to be answered for, I summon you and yours, to the last of your bad race, to answer for them. I mark this cross of blood upon you, as a sign that I do it. In the days when all these things are to be answered for, I summon your brother, the worst of the bad race, to answer for them separately. I mark this cross of blood upon him, as a sign that I do it.'
>
> "Twice, he put his hand to the wound in his breast, and with his forefinger drew a cross in the air. He stood for an

instant with the finger yet raised, and, as it dropped, he dropped with it, and I laid him down dead.[112]

The cross placed upon the Evremonde brothers is a cross of blood to symbolize the murder they have committed. The cross is equivalent to the mark of Cain. As noted earlier, the mark of Cain was transferred in literature to the Wandering Jew, who is usually depicted with a burning cross upon his forehead. Later in his narrative, Dr. Manette emphasizes the fatal result of this curse upon the Evremonde family.

> I believe that the mark of the red cross is fatal to them, and that they have no part in His mercies. And them and their descendants, to the last of their race, I, Alexandre Manette, unhappy prisoner, do this last night of the year 1767, in my unbearable agony, denounce to the times when all these things shall be answered for. I denounce them to Heaven and to earth.[113]

Dr. Manette defines the curse as extending to all the Evremondes' descendants, just as Cain's descendants were traditionally believed to be cursed by God until Judgment Day, and as the Wandering Jew, representative of the Jewish race, is traditionally depicted as cursed to wander the earth until Christ's Second Coming. While the color of the Wandering Jew's cross is not described, Dickens has the Evremonde family cursed with a cross of blood. While a red cross, symbolic of blood, may seem an obvious choice, it is used here to emphasize the novel's immortality theme by connecting the curse's cross with Rosicrucianism, whose symbol is a rose and a cross, and whose name means the Rosy Cross, suggestive that the cross is red.

Evidence that Dickens was aware of the Rosicrucian implications of a red cross can be derived from his use of similar symbols in *The Mystery of Edwin Drood* where Hyrom Grewgious has in his rooms a doorway with tiles containing symbols of the Freemasons and the Rosicrucians.[114] The Freemasons themselves have been associated with the Rosicrucians in their origins.[115]

Furthermore, because Dickens borrows the idea of Sidney Carton's sacrifice from Bulwer-Lytton's *Zanoni*, the Rosicrucian connection seems even more likely. As a friend of Bulwer-Lytton, Dickens would have been aware of Rosicrucian societies and perhaps even been knowledgeable about them.

As a member of the eternally cursed Evremonde family, Darnay is a Gothic wanderer who represents how the sins of the father are visited upon the child. Repulsed by his family's crimes, Darnay rejects his ancestry and his place of power in the patriarchal system. This rejection results in his feeling guilty as if he had committed parricide, for his uncle, the patriarchal head of the aristocratic family, is murdered immediately after Darnay rejects the Evremondes.[116]

Darnay's rejection of his family is his own attempt to redeem himself from the family curse. The new surname he chooses means "mender,"[117] suggestive of his attempt to make peace between his past and his new life with a different name and in a different country, as well as to compensate for the previous crimes of his family. When the French Revolution erupts, Darnay feels he should return to France to aid his countrymen and help prevent too much bloodshed. When he learns one of his former servants has been imprisoned, Darnay attempts to play the Christ-like role of savior by returning to France to try to gain his servant's freedom. Ironically, while Darnay succeeds in rescuing his servant, he finds himself imprisoned.

Dickens' emphasis on the importance of family bonds is evidenced by Dr. Manette now journeying to France to rescue Darnay. Dr. Manette has long since accepted that his son-in-law is a member of the Evremonde family that oppressed him; both Darnay and Dr. Manette have forgotten the crimes of the past because they realize love and family sanctity are more important. Dr. Manette fails to save Darnay, however, because the document Dr. Manette hid in the Bastille is discovered and it condemns all the Evremondes and their descendants, which includes Darnay (and Dr. Manette's own granddaughter). Dickens uses the manuscript to endanger the family unit, then chooses a non-family member, Sidney Carton, to make the ultimate sacrifice that preserves the family. While Dickens may have borrowed the final scene of sacrifice at the guillotine from *Zanoni*, he rejects the death of one of the married couple in favor of a non-family member so the sanctity of the family unit can remain unbroken.

Sidney Carton's sacrifice makes him the novel's only character who successfully fulfills the role of savior. First, however, Carton plays the role of Gothic wanderer to become the most successful example in the Victorian period of how a Gothic wanderer can redeem himself by rejecting selfishness for self-sacrifice.

Carton's role as Gothic wanderer is apparent from his first introduction to the reader as one who has no interest in life, suffers from despair, and consequently, like Dr. Manette, may be described as one of the living dead. Although still a young man, Carton feels his life is wasted; he knows he could be ambitious and achieve great deeds, but lacking the motivation and purpose, he despairs of ever accomplishing anything of importance. The most moving depiction of Carton's despair occurs early in the novel after he assists in freeing Darnay from charges of treason as a spy because of how the resemble each other. Following the trial, Carton works late into the night, then returns home to feel overwhelmed by despair.

> Waste forces within him, and a desert all around, this man stood still on his way across a silent terrace, and saw for a moment, lying in the wilderness before him, a mirage of honourable ambition, self-denial, and perseverance. In the fair city of this vision, there were airy galleries from which the loves and graces looked upon him, gardens in which the fruits of life hung ripening, waters of Hope that sparkled in his sight. A moment, and it was gone. Climbing to a high chamber in a well of houses, he threw himself down in his clothes on a neglected bed, and its pillow was wet with wasted tears.

> Sadly, sadly, the sun rose; it rose upon no sadder sight than the man of good abilities and good emotions, incapable of their directed exercise, incapable of his own help and his own happiness, sensible of the blight on him, and resigning himself to let it eat him away.[118]

Carton, unable to battle against despair, finds it easier to let it destroy him. His vision of a fair city and gardens suggests a desire to create a paradise or Eden for himself, but he despairs of ever accomplishing such a goal. His despair is especially bitter for he has just met and fallen in love with Lucie Manette. Carton realizes that by saving Darnay, he has preserved his rival for Lucie's love; he immediately comes to hate Darnay for being preferred by Lucie. Eventually, no longer able to hide his emotions, Carton professes his love to Lucie.

During the conversation with Lucie, Carton characterizes himself in words typical of the Gothic wanderer figure. He remarks, "I am like one who died young,"[119] suggesting that like Dr. Manette, he has died, but his body unnaturally lives on. In response, Lucie asks "can I not save you, Mr. Carton? Can I not recal [sic] you—forgive me again!—to a better course?"[120] Lucie's use of the word "recall" suggests that she would recall Carton to life as she has done for her father, but Carton believes her concern and pity are insufficient to cure him; only her love could recall him to life. He then tells Lucie, "For you, and for any dear to you, I would do anything.... I would embrace any sacrifice for you and for those dear to you.... [T]hink now and then that there is a man who would give his life, to keep a life you love beside you!"[121] Unknown to himself, Carton has just spoken his own death sentence, but he has also begun his redemption by his willingness to sacrifice himself for one he loves, rather than focusing upon himself by demanding that love. Love is always the redeemer in Dickens' novels. Before Carton had been indifferent to life, but once he begins to love, according to David Marcus, "he finally emerges from the self-imposed prison of indifference" to be "recalled to life."[122]

Carton proves the strength of his love for Lucie when he fulfills his vow and sacrifices his life to save Darnay, thus preserving the sacred family unit. In sacrificing himself, however, Carton also comes to save himself. Carton's sacrifice embodies Christ's statement that no man can gain his life unless first he loses it. In the novel's final scene, Dickens creates a vision of a person's full capacity to love selflessly. Carton's final words show his concern for Lucie, Darnay, and their daughter, as well as concern for the seamstress whom he befriends by holding her hand until the last moment.[123]

Critics have argued about the extent to which Carton's death is to be interpreted as a Christian sacrifice. Angus Wilson states that Carton's death is pagan because it is motivated by romantic love for Lucie.[124] However, Carton's sacrifice is not only for Lucie but for her entire family and friends. His death supersedes romantic love to become brotherly love, the love he comes to feel for Darnay and also for the seamstress. The final scenes break down boundaries of class and race as Carton joins hands with the lower class girl who is dying with aristocrats, and who is French while he is English, thereby again using Dickens' theme of universality and the common brotherhood of humanity.

Critics have overlooked the strongest evidence for reading Carton's sacrifice as being a Christian one and himself being a Christ-figure: his death at the guillotine. Earlier in the novel, Dickens states that the guillotine has come to replace the Christian cross as an object of worship during the French Revolution: "La Guillotine.... It was the sign of regeneration of the human race. It superseded the Cross. Models of it were worn on breasts from which the Cross was discarded, and it was bowed down to and believed in where the Cross was denied."[125] Consequently, if the guillotine has become the Cross, Carton's death at the guillotine is a symbol of Christ's crucifixion. Furthermore, Dickens here blends Christianity with the Gothic literary tradition, for the guillotine also represents Rosicrucianism; the guillotine is a red cross because it is bathed in its victims' blood. Carton's death by guillotine, therefore, is a Christian sacrifice by which he saves his loved ones from death, as well as saves his own soul so he can achieve eternal life in heaven. His death also assures for Carton a type of Rosicrucian immortality in the prolonged earthly existence of his name and memory because he foresees the Darnays naming their descendants after him.

Dickens' intention that Carton's sacrifice be interpreted as Christian is evidenced when Carton repeats Christ's words, "I am the Resurrection and the Life, saith the Lord: he that believeth in me, though he were dead, yet shall he live: and whosoever liveth and believeth in me shall never die."[126] Carton had been dead to life, but by his selfless love for others, he has been resurrected to eternal life. As Lyons notes, Dickens further portrays Carton as a Christ-figure when Carton comforts the seamstress, reminiscent of when Christ comforts the thief who is crucified with him.[127] Finally, like Christ, Carton has the gift of prophecy. This prophecy displays Dickens' theory of historical evolution:

> I see a beautiful city and a brilliant people rising from this abyss, and, in their struggles to be truly free, in their triumphs and defeats, through long years to come, I see the evil of this time and of the previous time of which this is a natural birth, gradually making expiation for itself and wearing out.[128]

Carton envisions the future of France and the good that can still arise from all the atrocities committed by the Reign of Terror, making the events of the present part of a historical process by which God brings about good for humanity despite transgression or original sin. Carton's vision reflects a positive Christian view of history that begins with Adam and Eve's transgression and ends with Christ's Second Coming, representing that good can come from evil. Consequently, as Goldberg points out, the novel reflects the shared historical viewpoint of Dickens and Carlyle of history as a "God written apocalypse,"[129] but for Dickens, the apocalypse results in the establishment of a new Eden upon the earth.

Carton also prophesies concerning the future of the Darnay family:

> I see the lives for which I lay down my life, peaceful, useful, prosperous and happy, in that England which I shall see no more. I see Her with a child upon her bosom, who bears my name. I see her father, aged and bent, but otherwise restored, and faithful to all men in his healing office, and at peace. I see the good old man, so long their friend, in ten years' time enriching them with all he has, and passing tranquilly to his reward.
>
> I see that I hold a sanctuary in their hearts, and in the hearts of their descendants, generations hence. I see her, an old woman, weeping for me on the anniversary of this day. I see her and her husband, their course done, lying side by side in their last earthly bed, and I know that each was not more honoured and held sacred in the other's soul, than I was in the souls of both.[130]

In this reflection, Carton realizes he has redeemed himself by loving and having that love returned both by the woman he loves and his rival for that love. Lyons remarks of this passage, "Carton, an outcast in the world, not unlike Christ Himself, accepts his fate of saving the new Adam and Eve willingly."[131] Carton envisions that he will be eternally remembered by Lucie and Darnay, the new Adam and Eve who will generate a new race. His memory will inspire them to teach their descendants about the love and honor he demonstrated. His sacrifice is so important in their memories that they will name their child after him.

> I see that child who lay upon her bosom and who bore my name, a man winning his way up in that path of life which once was mine. I see him winning it so well, that my name is made illustrious there by the light of his. I see the blots I threw upon it, faded away. I see him, foremost of just judges and honoured men, bringing a boy of my name, with a forehead that I know and golden hair, to this

place—then fair to look upon, with not a trace of this day's disfigurement—and I hear him tell the child my story, with a tender and faltering voice.[132]

This paragraph contains a complex number of symbolic images. It reflects Dickens' debt to *Zanoni* by providing a final image of a child, although for a different purpose than Bulwer-Lytton had used. Jack Lindsay argues that in *Zanoni* the child is the symbol of new life, while for Dickens it symbolizes the lovers' union.[133] However, the lovers are passed over in Carton's vision to make the child the final emphasis. Because the Darnays represent the new Adam and Eve, the child symbolizes the future human race. Lyons suggests that this child, named for Carton, represents "the new apostle who will 'preach' the 'gospel' of Carton's life."[134] This child will grow up and tell Carton's story to his own child, making him a type of disciple to Carton.

Consequently, Carton envisions his death as significantly influencing the future as Christ's death established the Christian Church. In addition, Carton imagines Darnay's son bearing his own name, and that son also naming his child after Carton. Carton focuses primarily upon the immortal life of his soul, but he also remains concerned with his earthly immortality as it will be carried on by the Darnay descendants named for him. David Marcus argues, therefore, that Carton secularizes the Christian immortality theme for one of earthly "continuity of generations."[135] While Zanoni lost his immortality through his sacrifice at the guillotine, Carton, through the Darnay child named for him, will achieve earthly immortality, reflecting his Rosicrucian life-extension. His death at the Rosicrucian, rosy cross of the guillotine gives him eternal salvation in heaven, but also a form of Rosicrucian life-extension upon earth. Furthermore, Carton's death to preserve the family ensures that he will be an eternal part of that family by the children named in his memory.

Following this unique blending of literary symbolism, Dickens closes the novel with Carton's famous lines: "It is a far, far better thing that I do, than I have ever done; it is a far, far better rest that I go to than I have ever known."[136] With these words, Carton is able to go to his "rest," a word whose connotation is the exact opposite of "wandering." Sidney Carton has been transformed from a Gothic wanderer to a savior and symbol of redemption. For Dickens, the transgressor can achieve not only eternal life in heaven, but his good deeds can also provide him with a form of earthly immortality.

Conclusion

Bulwer-Lytton's Zanoni uses his supernatural powers for the good of humanity, but in the end, the power of love makes him the victim of human evil. By comparison, Dumas' Cagliostro is a misguided character with supernatural powers who seeks to bring about good, but through questionable means. The result is a fruitless pursuit for change that reflects the saying that the more things change, the more they stay the same, for as Cagliostro is warned, if the French monarchy is overthrown, another tyrant will take its place. Dickens, without using the supernatural, is the most optimistic about the future, but he realizes it is not society but only the individual who can be redeemed. In the end, the Gothic wanderer, who is the victim of society, cannot save that society. He can only save himself, or those he loves, and in the process, he becomes a model for others of how they can also bring about the salvation of their souls, even at the expense of their physical wellbeing.

The French Revolution may have been the impetus for the explosion of Gothic novels in the 1790s, but by the mid-Victorian period, it was being depicted in historical and realistic ways. Through their efforts, French and British Gothic novelists shaped the perception of the French Revolution that countless readers hold today.

Chapter 7
The Road to *Dracula*
Polidori's French and British Imitators from Bérard to Stoker

"These things do not happen in reality, only in
French pulp novels, intended to appease an uncritical
audience's appetite for sensation."
— *Powers of Darkness*, the Swedish *Dracula*

To discuss all the nineteenth-century works of vampire fiction would be an overwhelming and probably impossible task. In France alone, approximately thirty-five vampire plays were produced, and several more were produced in Great Britain and the United States throughout the century.[1] Numerous vampire short stories also exist. In this chapter, I will focus on many of the significant and longer prose works—novels and plays—and a few short stories in French and in English that were inspired by Polidori's *The Vampyre* and ultimately led to the writing of Bram Stoker's *Dracula*.

Until recent years, most explorations of Dracula's literary origins have focused on the English texts, namely Polidori's *The Vampyre*, Rymer's *Varney the Vampire*, and Le Fanu's *Carmilla*. French vampire literature has been mostly ignored, although it is far richer and more prolific than British vampire literature. Many of these French works have been rediscovered and translated into English in the twenty-first century, and not a few have been held up as sources for *Dracula*. I contend that Stoker did read some of these vampire stories in French or in translation even though hard evidence does not exist for these influences. Regardless, these texts deserve more attention. They reflect the general development of the vampire figure in literature, and their treatments of that figure may have influenced Stoker on some level. While my ultimate goal is to discuss the influence of these works on *Dracula* at the end of this survey, it must be understood that these texts are marvelous works by their own merit and deserve to be appreciated as more than simply potential ur-texts for Stoker's work.

This chapter will be divided into three sections:

1. Polidori's *The Vampyre* and its imitators, most of which have characters named or directly based on Lord Ruthven.
2. Other vampire texts that were influenced by Polidori's story but do not closely follow it.
3. *Dracula* and how it was influenced by the Gothic works discussed throughout this book.

I will not discuss Caroline Lamb's *Glenarvon* (1816), which might be argued to be the first vampire novel, or *Varney the Vampire*, the 1840s English penny dreadful and perhaps the greatest vampire novel before *Dracula*, since I have discussed them in *The Gothic Wanderer: From Transgression to Redemption*. I will also avoid a full discussion of *Dracula*, which I also provided in *The Gothic Wanderer*, and instead focus on the possible influences of the works discussed in this book upon *Dracula*.

Polidori's *The Vampyre* and Its Imitators

In Chapter 1, I emphasized the incredible popularity of Polidori's *The Vampyre*, but I have saved discussion of the plot for now so it will be fresh in readers' minds as we explore its variations in later French, British, and even a couple of American works. It is worth noting that in later editions, Polidori changed the name Ruthven to Strongmore, no doubt to remove the negative connotations in relation to Lord Byron, but by then the secret was out. I will retain the name Ruthven in my discussion since it was the original name and the one Polidori's imitators played off.

Polidori's story opens with a young English gentleman named Aubrey. He is an orphan who shares an inheritance with his sister. When he enters London society, Aubrey meets and befriends Lord Ruthven, a charismatic man who invites him on a continental tour; unknown to Aubrey, Ruthven is fleeing his creditors. During their sojourn on the continent, Aubrey gets to know Ruthven better and gradually realizes he is of bad moral character. Aubrey writes letters back to England to inquire about Ruthven and receives confirmation of his misgivings. Eventually, the two friends part, but not before Aubrey interferes when Ruthven tries to take advantage of a young woman about to be married.

Aubrey then travels to Greece where he meets the beautiful Ianthe. She soon after falls victim to a vampire, and Aubrey becomes ill immediately after. Aubrey wakes to find Ruthven caring for him. Ruthven is repentant and their relationship is mended. Soon after, Ruthven is attacked by bandits and wounded. As he lays dying, Ruthven asks Aubrey to "swear that for a year and a day you will not impart your knowledge of my crimes or death to any living being, in any way, whatever may happen, or whatever you may see."[2] As soon as Aubrey agrees, Ruthven dies.

Aubrey goes to bed, but in the morning, he returns to take care of the corpse, only to find it gone. He learns it was conveyed by robbers to the pinnacle of a neighboring mountain because of a promise they had given Ruthven. Aubrey, astonished, goes to the mountain pinnacle, but he finds no trace of the corpse. (Aubrey does not realize at this point that Ruthven is a vampire or that vampires can be revived by moonlight, which is why Ruthven wanted his body placed on the mountain where the moonlight would strike him.)

Aubrey returns to England, where he finds himself haunted by Ruthven's apparition. When Aubrey falls ill again, he is cared for by his sister until she becomes engaged to the Earl of Marsden. Aubrey does not meet the groom until the wedding day; he then realizes Marsden and Ruthven are the same person. Aubrey then wants to break his oath to reveal Ruthven's crimes, but Ruthven warns him that if he does, his sister will not be married and she will be dishonored, the implication being that she has already had sexual relations with Ruthven. Aubrey's rage becomes so great that he bursts a blood vessel and is conveyed to bed. Meanwhile, the marriage ceremony takes place. When Aubrey wakes, he reveals what he knows to his sister's guardians, but by then, it is too late. Ruthven has disappeared, and "Aubrey's sister had glutted the thirst of a VAMPYRE!"[3]

Polidori considered writing a sequel to his story because of its popularity, but his early death in 1821 at age twenty-six prevented him. Instead, French author Cyprien Bérard would write a sequel before Polidori was even dead. However, it would be Charles Nodier's play, based on Polidori's story, that would cement Lord Ruthven's place in literature. Notably, Ruthven is not a blood drinker in Polidori's work, but Bérard's work will establish blood drinking as the predominant vampire trait.

Cyprien Bérard's *Lord Ruthwen ou les vampires*

Because *The Vampyre* was misattributed as a work by Lord Byron, Pierre-François Ladvocat would publish the story under Byron's name in France. Ladvocat would also publish Cyprien Bérard's sequel titled *Lord Ruthwen ou les vampires*. Charles Nodier, who worked for Ladvocat and later wrote the play version of Polidori's story, would provide the introduction to Bérard's book, causing some misattribution of the story to him.[4]

Bérard and Nodier's work would cement the popularity of vampire literature in France, where it would be more popular than in Great Britain. This popularity may reflect the embracing by the French of the vampire figure as an aristocrat who preys on people, a metaphor for how the upper classes had preyed upon the French people prior to the French Revolution. That the vampire was equated with Lord Byron, and thus, with nobility, only strengthened this connection. The monarchy was restored in France after the fall of Napoleon in 1815, so the rise of vampire fiction in the years that followed served as a suitable metaphor for aristocracy and continuing debates over whether France would be a monarchy or a republic.

While scholars have not been overly kind to Bérard's story, it is significant because it determined what elements of Polidori's story would become standards of vampire lore. As Brian Stableford states, "Thanks to Polidori, Nodier and Bérard—and also, albeit indirectly, to Lord Byron—later writers had a pattern of established clichés to guide them in their efforts (or, of course, conscientiously to avoid) and to give them and their publishers confidence in the acceptability of such narratives."[5] While no one can claim Bérard's novel is great literature, it is an entertaining story and far more involved than Polidori's significantly shorter work. Bérard employs typical Gothic techniques, including the story-in-a-story format that the Gothic had long used and adapted from *The Arabian Nights*. Most, but not all, of the stories in Bérard's novel relate to the main vampire tale, so I will only summarize the primary plot. Notably, Bérard spells Ruthven's name as Ruthwen. Later, Nodier would change it in his play to Rutwen.

"Part I: The Story of Bettina and Léonti" begins in Venice where the beautiful Bettina loves a young man named Léonti. When a fete is held, a stranger arrives and so does Elmoda, a fortune teller. Elmoda predicts that Bettina will soon die with her blood drained. Elmoda is about to reveal that the vampire is already present and who he is when the stranger stops her. He then gives a discourse on vampires and claims to have seen one. He tells Léonti the only way to save Bettina is to abduct her since her father opposes their marriage. The stranger even offers

Léonti a position in the Scottish army. However, the stranger is manipulating events so he can have Bettina for himself. Léonti ends up being arrested by Venetian soldiers for signing up with the Scottish army, which is seen as treason to the state. Meanwhile, Elmoda is found dead, and then Bettina dies. Once out of prison, Léonti searches for the stranger. When he meets Aubrey from Polidori's novel, they share notes, which convinces Aubrey that the stranger who killed Bettina is the Lord Ruthwen who killed his sister. The two new friends become determined to find Ruthwen and get revenge for how he has killed Aubrey's sister and Bettina.

"Part II: The Pursuit of Lord Ruthwen" shows the two new friends traveling about and learning of possible vampire incidents, one of which turns out to have been faked as a joke. When they reach Naples, they learn that Ruthwen was involved in the death of a woman there. Bettina's apparition appears now to Léonti, urging him on to defeat Ruthwen. Next, Aubrey and Léonti hear the story of a Moravian woman who was betrayed by her lover and died. She then returned from the grave and pursued him—this is believed to be the first story of a female vampire in French literature. (Geraldine in Coleridge's 1816 poem "Christabel" predates it in English.) It is then confirmed that Bettina is now a vampire, but Léonti insists that if she returned to life, it would be to protect and help him. Léonti and Aubrey befriend an Arab named Nadoor Ali. Bettina appears and tells them she rose from the grave as a vampire, but an angel came to protect her in a dream and told her she can't be reunited with Léonti until Ruthwen is returned to the tomb. Next, Nadoor Ali shares his story about a lost love, but he is interrupted before the story can be finished.

"Part III: The Duke of Modena's Minister" begins with the three friends being summoned to the Duke of Modena's court. A Lord Seymour (who will turn out to be Ruthwen) has insinuated himself into the Duke's court and become his prime minister. Lord Seymour tells a story of a vampire in Baghdad in the time of

Haroun al-Rashid. Then the Duke's palace catches on fire—a fire probably set by Seymour. Seymour saves the Duke and wants for his reward the hand of the Duke's daughter, Eleanora. However, Eleanora loves a soldier named Albini, who rescued her from the fire. Regardless, a wedding is held for Eleanora and Seymour. At the wedding, Albini confronts Seymour. Aubrey, Léonti, and Nadoor Ali all declare they recognize Seymour as being Ruthwen, who hurt the women they loved. They are arrested and Albini condemned to death. Eleanora now agrees to marry Seymour/Ruthwen if he will save Albini from death. Bettina appears from the grave and confirms that Seymour is a vampire. She then falls and dies. The vampire hunters rush in and Léonti plunges a blade into Ruthwen's breast. Ruthwen dies and is buried, but in the days that follow, many women begin dying, so he is dug up. When it is seen that life is still on his lips, he is destroyed by having red-hot irons applied to his heart and eyes.

The story concludes with Bérard stating that he has found a manuscript that Ruthwen left about his early life and he may publish it if there is sufficient interest. Apparently, there was not since the work was never published and perhaps never written.

Regardless, *Lord Ruthwen ou les vampires* is interesting since Ruthwen is audacious enough to tell tales of vampires, which may well be stories about himself. He also dies in this version, but he manages to return without being revived by moonlight. The moonlight revival would be popular in subsequent vampire works despite its omission here. Overall, the novel is entertaining, and even the stories irrelevant to the main plot are enjoyable. It is really surprising the book was not more popular. One can only imagine what an origin story for Lord Ruthwen might have been like had Bérard written one.

Critic Kevin Dodd states that the story is important because it created several vampire tropes, including the daughter/sister coerced to marry a vampire, a warning from spirits to the intended victim, and the use of Roman Catholicism, as seen by Bettina being a kind of Virgin Mary to Ruthwen's Satan. Dodd notes Bérard's story is the only Ruthwen narrative in which an "unquestionably good vampire" opposes Ruthwen. "She feeds on no one and is genuinely altruistic."[6] Stableford, in a similar vein, refers to Bettina as an "anti-vampire," also stating she is the first of the "seductive female revenants, which appear in such works as Étienne-Léon de Lamothe-Langon's *La Vampire, ou la Vierge de Hongrie* (1825), Théophile Gautier's "La Morte amoureuse" (1836; tr. as "Clarimonde"), Pierre-Alexis Ponson du Terrail's *La Baronne trépassée* (1852), and Paul Féval's *La Vampire* (1856). I will explore all of these works after completing the discussion of works directly serving as variations of the Lord Ruthven story. Finally, I find it noteworthy that the story reflects a band of men who have all loved women who were victimized by the vampire and who come together to hunt down and kill him. We will not see such a band of male vampire hunters again until *Dracula*.

Charles Nodier's *The Vampire*

Charles Nodier (1780-1844) was the perfect author to popularize the vampire figure in French literature. He had previously published several Gothic novels, including *Les Proscrits* (*The Proscribed*, 1802) and *Le Peintre de Salzbourg* (*The Painter of Salzbourg,* 1803).[7] Besides adapting Polidori's play, he would go on to adapt other British works, including *Bertram ou le Pirate* (1822), based on the play *Bertram, or The Castle of St. Aldobrand* by British Gothic novelist Charles Maturin and *Le Monstre et le Magicien* (1826), adapted from an English play based on Mary Shelley's *Frankenstein*.[8]

Nodier's decision to turn Polidori's story into a play is not surprising given that Nodier had previously lived in Ljubljana, Slovenia, where he collected local vampire legends. He even claimed to have met a vampire.[9]

Nodier begins his play *The Vampire* (1820) halfway into Polidori's story. Sir Aubrey is home with his sister Malvina. She is to marry Count Marsden, the older brother of Aubrey's best friend, Ruthven, who has died. In the prologue, Ituriel, angel of the moon, speaks to Oscar, a "genius" or spirit and the protector of marriage, who is watching over Malvina. Malvina has taken refuge in a grotto. Oscar has followed her to protect her from vampires. When a vampire appears, Oscar drives it off.

In Act I, Malvina has been found and brought home safely, but she says she feels uneasy and that she saw ghosts rise up from open tombs in the grotto. She puts these fears aside to prepare for her marriage to Marsden. Aubrey has never met Marsden, but he feels a bond to his friend's brother. However, when Marsden arrives, he turns out to be Ruthven. Ruthven says his older brother has died so he has succeeded to the title. Aubrey is surprised that Ruthven is alive since he had left him for dead. (Like in Polidori's story, Ruthven has obviously been revived by moonlight.) Ruthven says before he and Malvina can marry, he must visit Castle Marsden. Malvina recognizes Ruthven as the man she saw in the cemetery, but she feels attracted to him regardless.

In Act II, Ruthven and Aubrey travel to Castle Marsden where they attend the wedding of Ruthven's servant, Edgar, to Lovette. Oscar, dressed as a bard, appears and sings a song of warning to the bride, but to no avail. Ruthven decides to attack Lovette, only to be shot by Edgar. Aubrey, unaware of the reason for Edgar's actions, obeys Ruthven's final wish to have his body placed in the moonlight and not to let anyone know what has happened to him for twelve hours.

In Act III, Malvina prepares for her marriage since she does not yet know Ruthven is dead. Her servant Brigitte asks a monk—Oscar in disguise—to read the future. He warns her that Malvina is in danger. Ruthven now arrives. He tells Malvina they must marry and leave immediately because the king is trying to force him to marry someone he does not love. His real reason is to get the marriage ceremony over before Aubrey is free to speak without breaking his oath. Aubrey, on seeing Ruthven, tries to speak but is reminded of his oath. Aubrey is now believed to be mad and is dragged off, but he escapes and manages to forestall the ceremony until 1 a.m. strikes and he is free to speak. Once Aubrey speaks, the shades of Ruthven's past victims appear and pursue him. Then he is struck by lightning, which destroys him.

The play is dramatic and interesting enough, even if it does not move far from Polidori's story. Dodd points out that it is ironic that the moon, which fraternizes with Oscar who is trying to protect Malvina, is also the one reviving Ruthven. The play would become the primary influence on the vampire literature that followed, with Polidori's story being more of an indirect influence.[10]

J. R. Planché's *The Vampire* and *Der Vampyr*

James Robinson Planché's *The Vampire, or The Bride of the Isles* (1820) is basically a rewrite of Nodier's play into English. The plot is very similar with a few variations.

The scene opens in Scotland with a prologue titled "Introductory Vision," in which Margaret, daughter of Ronald, Lord of the Isles, has sought shelter from a storm in the Cave of Fingal. As Margaret sleeps, a dialogue ensues between two spirits, Unda and Ariel, about how Margaret is to marry the Earl of Marsden. She has never met him, but he is the brother of her father's late friend Lord Ruthven. Unknown to Margaret, he is also a vampire, so the spirits wish to protect her. An interesting aspect of the spirits' discussion is that a vampire is not a dead person come back to life, but rather a dead person whose body has been taken over by a wicked soul.

> *Unda.* Thou knowest, Ariel, that wicked souls
> Are, for wise purposes, permitted oft
> To enter the dead forms of other men,
> Assume their speech, their habits, and their knowledge,
> And thus roam o'er the earth; but subject still
> At stated periods, to a dreadful tribute.

In addition, we learn that vampires can only survive if they not only have blood, but the blood of a virgin/maiden, and they can only have that blood if they marry her.

> *Ariel.* Ay, they must wed some fair and virtuous maiden,
> Whom they do after kill, and from her veins
> Drain eagerly the purple stream of life;
> Which horrid draught alone hath pow'r to save them
> From swift extermination.

The spirits share that Marsden's life of terror will end if he does not marry Margaret tomorrow. To protect her, the spirits cause Margaret to dream of Marsden and realize his evil nature.

In Act I, Margaret has been found and restored to her father, Lord Ronald. The servants celebrate her return home, and one servant, McSwill, tells a tale of how years before a Lady Blanch married a Scottish nobleman and they entered the grotto where Margaret had sought refuge. Later, the bride was found covered in blood with teeth marks at her throat while the groom was never seen again. We are also given more specifics about what a vampire must do to survive. McSwill then repeats that it is necessary for a vampire to marry a virgin, and only after the marriage can he have her blood:

> these horrible spirits, called vampires, kill and suck the blood of beautiful young maidens, whom they are obliged to marry before they can destroy. And they do say that such is the condition of their existence, that if, at stated periods, they should fail to obtain a virgin bride, whose life-blood may sustain them, they would instantly perish.

Margaret is hesitant to marry Marsden, but her father reminds her that he is the brother of his friend Lord Ruthven. Lord Ronald grew to respect Ruthven when he found his dying son being cared for by Ruthven in Athens. Unfortunately, soon after Ruthven was attacked by assassins. His last request was to place his body in the moonlight. Ronald did so and departed for safety's sake, but upon returning later, he found the body gone. Regardless, he assumes Ruthven is dead.

Earl Marsden now arrives and, of course, turns out to be Lord Ruthven, having succeeded to his brother's estate and title. Margaret instantly recognizes him as the phantom from her dream, but she feels compelled to obey her father and marry him. The wedding is to be the next day, but Ruthven's time is running short, so he insists on it being that night, claiming he has to go to London tomorrow and the king is pressuring him to marry another, so he wants to present Margaret as his bride before he can be forced into another marriage. Margaret and her father agree to have the wedding that evening.

Ruthven then gives a soliloquy, which provides the first moment in vampire fiction when a vampire gains a bit of sympathy from the reader/audience by showing regret for his actions. He states:

> Demon as I am, that walks the earth to slaughter and devour! The little that remains of heart within this wizard frame, sustained alone by human blood, shrinks from the appalling act of planting misery in the bosom of this veteran chieftain. Still must the fearful sacrifice be made, and suddenly, for the approaching night will find my wretched frame exhausted—and darkness—worse than death—annihilation is my lot! Margaret! unhappy maid! thou art my destined prey! thy blood must feed a vampire's life, and prove the food of his disgusting banquet.

That same evening, a servant, Robert, is to marry his beloved Effie. Ruthven attends the wedding, which takes place before his own. Ruthven, regretting that he must hurt Margaret, decides to make Effie his victim, saying, "Should I surprise her heart, as by my gifted spell I may, the tribute that prolongs existence may be paid and Margaret may (at least awhile) be spared."

When Ruthven tries to seduce Effie, she pleads that she can only love Robert, but Ruthven tries to carry her off regardless.

Robert pursues them and shoots Ruthven. Lord Ronald arrives in time once again to promise Ruthven that he will place his body in the moonlight and not say a word about his death until after midnight.

In Act II, Ruthven returns to the castle to marry Margaret. Lord Ronald is surprised he is alive. He has also learned from Robert that Ruthven tried to abduct Effie, so he is now against Margaret marrying Ruthven. However, Ruthven reminds Lord Ronald of his oath not to speak of his death until after midnight. When Ronald tries to persuade his daughter to postpone the wedding until after midnight, Ruthven calls him a madman. A scuffle ensues that manages to delay the wedding long enough for midnight to come. Suddenly, it is too late for Ruthven. A lightning bolt strikes him dead.

The play itself is not so very extraordinary other than for its having a momentarily sympathetic vampire. An anonymous version of the play borrowing from Planché and titled *The Bride of the Isles* was later produced that year, which I will skip over. Then in 1821, a German adaptation of Nodier's play, titled *Der Vampyr*, led to Henrick Marschner's opera of the same name in 1828.* This work inspired Planché to write his own *Der Vampyr*, a loose translation of the opera that allowed him to rewrite the play the way he had originally wanted.

In his *The Recollections and Reflections of J. R. Planché*, Planché describes how Nodier's play was historically inaccurate and that it was wrong to set it in Scotland, where the vampire superstition never existed. He remarks that this setting reflected "the usual recklessness of French dramatists." In writing the 1820 play, he wanted to change the setting to somewhere in Eastern Europe like Hungary, but Samuel Arnold, the producer, rejected this idea.[11]

---

* A production of Marschner's opera is available at YouTube https://www.youtube.com/watch?v=pBqYcaU7YEI. It was filmed on March 25, 2022. Although it takes a few liberties, including introducing the characters of Lord Byron and the Wandering Jew, and it modernizes a bit—there is an automobile—it is a spectacular production that helps us better understand what vampire plays were like in the early nineteenth century. Accessed May 1, 2022.

In 1829, Planché convinced Arnold to produce the version he had wanted to write. He borrowed the German opera's music and wrote a new libretto. The play was set in Hungary and the Carpathians, which Planché claimed had a vampire tradition, and he believed it improved tremendously upon the earlier version.[12]

Der Vampyr[*] opens with the Lord of Evil, Eblis, telling the vampire, Malika, he has thirty-one days to kill a victim if he wishes to live for a year. When Malika tries to elope with a young lady named Ianthe and attacks her, she screams. She is rescued and Malika is wounded. As Malika lays dying, a Hungarian officer named Alexis finds him. Malika had saved Alexis' life in Palestine, so he agrees to Malika's wish to swear his silence for thirty days and move him into the moonlight. Malika is restored to life after Alexis leaves.

Malika then spends thirty days crossing the Carpathian Mountains to reach the Castle of Kassova, where he had previously arranged to marry the lord of the castle's daughter, Henrika. However, Henrika has just been reunited with her beloved, who turns out to be Alexis.

Malika, now calling himself Mavrocordo, arrives at the castle. When he hears of a peasant wedding, he attends and seduces Liska from her bridegroom Wenzel. Alexis tries to interfere but is reminded of his oath. When Mavrocordo again pesters Liska, he is shot, presumably by Wenzel. Mavrocordo falls from his wound, but moonlight surrounds the place where he falls, so his body quickly disappears.

Mavrocordo soon after shows up to wed Henrika. She does not want to marry him, but he and her father force her to go through with the ceremony. I am uncertain how the play ends, but it is said to follow the plot of Marschner's opera, so I would assume that Alexis breaks his oath and stops the wedding long enough for Mavrocordo to fail to meet his deadline and be struck by lightning.

---

[*] No printed version seems to exist of Planché's *Der Vampyr*, so I have relied here upon the discussion of the play by Kevin Dodd who consulted the manuscript in the British Library (Dodd p. 194).

What is interesting about *Der Vampyr* besides how it heightens the drama through the use of opera music[13] is that it is the first work set in the Carpathians, nearly seventy years before *Dracula*. (And we will see more works associated with the Carpathians before we discuss *Dracula*.) Planché can be commended for moving the story from Scotland to Hungary and the Carpathians, but as we will see, French author Lamothe-Langon would beat him in creating a Hungarian connection in his novel *The Virgin Vampire* (1825). That said, had Planché not helped disassociate the vampire legend from Scotland, not only may we have never had *Dracula*, but Romania today might not be dealing with countless tourists who view their country as a sort of Gothic Disneyland — a situation good for the Romanian economy but perhaps poor for their image.

Alexandre Dumas' *The Vampire*

Numerous other dramatic versions of Polidori's novel exist as listed in Chapter 1, but the next significant treatment in French literature was Dumas' play in 1851. It is also more original and detailed than Nodier's or other versions, changing the storyline but retaining many of the basic vampire elements.

Dumas' decision to write this play really began when he came to Paris at age twenty-one and saw his first play, which happened to be Nodier's *The Vampire*. In his memoirs, Dumas filled five chapters in describing the difficulty he had getting into the theatre and how he sat next to an elderly gentleman who was reading an antique cookbook; the gentleman turned out to be none other than Nodier. The two held a conversation on cuisine, travel, Roman history, and vampires. Nodier then told Dumas that in Illyria (Spalatro) he had seen a vampire. As a result of this chance meeting and Dumas being enthralled with the play, he became Nodier's protegé and joined his circle of Romantics.[14] According to Richard Switzer, in writing his own play, Dumas (or perhaps Maquet, who was Dumas' frequent collaborator) studied all previous incarnations of Ruthven and synthesized them together.[15] While Maquet's role in Dumas' work is considerable, Dumas' attendance at Nodier's play and his references to Ruthven in *The Count of Monte Cristo* and the vampire story he included in *The Thousand and One Ghosts* (discussed later in this chapter), both of which predate his vampire play, suggest that Dumas was well-versed in vampire literature.

Act I of Dumas' *The Vampire* opens in an inn where a wedding is taking place. A servant at the inn, Lazare, is dismissed because the groom, who is marrying the innkeeper's daughter, does not like that Lazare has flirted with her. As Lazare leaves, he meets a woman named Juana who asks him to accompany her to the nearby castle where she is to meet her lover in secret, but Lazare refuses because the castle is haunted. Meanwhile, a group of travelers is turned away from the inn because it is full. Gilbert, the leader of the party, is approached by Juana, who asks him to go to the castle with her, to which he agrees. We are also introduced to a Moorish lady, Ziska, who is staying at the inn, but her role in the story is not yet clear.

Act II finds Ziska at the castle before the others and now appearing young and beautiful. In time, she will be revealed to be a spirit or "ghoul" and in love with Gilbert. When Gilbert and his party arrive at the castle, Ziska hides from them. Gilbert says he does not fear ghosts, but he believes the castle may be inhabited by bandits who have spread rumors of ghosts to protect their hideout. Gilbert also mentions how he grew up in a room with an enchanted tapestry depicting the fairy Melusine, and that she used to rock him in his cradle. Another traveler tells a story of how he once visited the home of a Jewish family that was visited by a vampire. As the traveler begins to describe how the vampire entered the house, Lord Ruthven enters. Although everyone is surprised to see him, they accept his story that he has also come for shelter since there was no room at the inn. Lazare has come with him, having overcome his fear that the castle is haunted because of Ruthven's generous payment. Lazare tells the story of the castle. There were three brothers, each of whom had a castle. The brother who owned the castle they are currently in killed his brothers so he could inherit their castles. After their deaths, the brothers haunted him. The murderous brother had three sons so each one could inherit a castle. When he traveled with each son to the castle the son was to inherit, the son would die until all three sons were dead. When the murderous father then died, the castle was inherited by a cousin, Don Luis, who turns out to be Juana's lover. Don Luis has asked Juana to meet him at the castle. However, Lazare reveals that each time an heir enters the castle, he dies. Soon after the story is finished, Don Luis is found dead. Then Juana is heard screaming in her room. Gilbert rushes to her, only to find Ruthven coming out of the room. As Juana dies, Gilbert attacks and mortally wounds Ruthven, assuming he assaulted her. Ruthven, however, claims he had only gone to Juana's rescue and arrived before Gilbert. Feeling guilty over his rash actions, Gilbert agrees to Ruthven's wish to leave his body exposed to the moon. Once Ruthven's body is left in the moonlight, everyone leaves. Ruthven then rises, deploys wings, and flies away.

In Act III, Gilbert has returned to his home in Brittany. His sister, Helen, is waiting for his return so she can marry Baron de Marsden. Lazare has now become Gilbert's servant. He arrives before Gilbert to let Helen know her brother is coming, but he also says he saw a masked man on the road, which makes Helen fear for Gilbert's safety. When Gilbert arrives, he says that he was attacked, but a woman (we'll later learn it is Ziska) saved him. Helen then tells Gilbert she is to marry Marsden. Gilbert tells her he now loves a girl named Antonia. Of course, when Marsden arrives for the wedding, he turns out to be Ruthven. Gilbert is astonished that Ruthven is alive, but Ruthven explains the wound wasn't mortal and he has inherited his older brother's title so he is now Marsden. Ruthven then works some magic on Gilbert, who begins choking. Ziska tells Gilbert to sleep in the chamber with the enchanted tapestry to recover. While Gilbert sleeps, Melusine steps out from the tapestry and reveals to Gilbert that Ruthven is a vampire. She asks his ancestors to protect him.

In Act IV, Ruthven tells Lazare he'll give him a guinea every time he agrees with him to ensure Lazare will not reveal his secrets. Ruthven tells Helen that Gilbert's belief that someone wants to kill him is a sign of madness. Gilbert confronts Ruthven, saying he knows he's a vampire and needs the blood of two virgins every year. Ruthven now demands Ziska appear, then reminds her that because they are both supernatural beings, they are forbidden to betray each other to humans. She assures him she did not reveal that he was a vampire; she just told Gilbert to sleep in the tapestry room. Ruthven and Helen now marry. Then Lazare reveals to Helen that Gilbert is not mad; she explains that he witnessed how Ruthven killed Juana, and then how Ruthven died but was revived. Helen begins to fear Ruthven. Gilbert appears to say Ruthven chained him but he broke free. Gilbert and Ruthven fight and Helen dies in the melee, but in the end, Gilbert succeeds in throwing Ruthven over the balcony and burying his body under a rock.

In Act V, Antonia is awaiting Gilbert's arrival in Circassia because after Helen died, Gilbert refused to live in Europe. Ziska now appears to Gilbert, revealing to him that she loves him and consequently hates Antonia. A ship is seen foundering at sea. Ruthven is on the ship and manages to make it to shore. When Lazare sees him climbing over the terrace, he throws Ruthven into the sea, but that only stops Ruthven momentarily. Meanwhile, Gilbert begs Ziska to protect Antonia from Ruthven. She refuses. Then he says he and Antonia will die together. Because Ziska loves Gilbert, she does not want him to die, so she decides she won't let Antonia die either. Antonia then breaks the rule not to betray another supernatural being by telling Gilbert he cannot kill Ruthven with just a sword; instead, a priest must bless the sword. She reveals she will die for betraying Ruthven, but Gilbert will then know who truly loved him. Gilbert gets the sword blessed and confronts Ruthven. He asks Ruthven to repent, but Ruthven refuses, so Gilbert chases him with the sword to a graveyard and then buries the sword into Ruthven's chest. The play ends with Juana and Helen descending from the sky with angels to take Ziska off to heaven while wishing Gilbert and Antonia happiness.

The role of religion is significant in the play. The sword becomes a holy sword to defeat the vampire and predates the use of holy water and crosses that will be used in later works. Also important is there is no oath to prevent the hero from revealing the vampire's identity. Roxana Stuart also notes that Dumas' play is darker than previous plays because the vampire succeeds and comes back, and Dumas adds the revenge element to the vampire's nature.[16]

Dion Boucicault's *The Vampire* and *The Phantom*

Dion Boucicault (1820-1890) is a significant person in the history of Gothic literature because of his long career in the theater and the many authors he knew and may have influenced, including Dickens and Stoker. In Chapter 6, I mentioned that Boucicault wrote a dramatization of Dumas' *Le Chevalier de Maison-Rouge* titled *Geneviève; or the Reign of Terror*, which may have influenced Dickens in writing *A Tale of Two Cities*. He also adapted Dumas' play *The Corsican Brothers* and wrote or adapted numerous other works. Toward the end of his life, he was involved with Bram Stoker through his work with Sir Henry Irving. Stoker references him several times in *Personal Reminiscences of Henry Irving*. When Boucicault died, *The New York Times* called him "the most conspicuous English dramatist of the 19th century."[17]

Boucicault's play *The Vampire* (1852) was a rewrite of Dumas' play of the same name but with many alterations. It is set near Raby Castle in 1660 just after Charles II's restoration. Raby Castle is in ruins and allegedly haunted. A young woman named Lucy arrives at an inn seeking assistance. She was to meet her lover Roland there, but she learns he has gone to Raby Castle. She goes to the castle with others from the inn. Once at the castle, conversation ensues about vampires. Then Alan Raby, under the alias Gervase Rookwood, arrives dressed like a Puritan and claiming he has come to the castle to take shelter from the storm. Soon after, Roland is found dead in the castle. Meanwhile, Lucy is sleeping. Suddenly, she screams, and when the others go to assist her, they find Raby coming from his room. One of the characters, thinking Raby assaulted her, shoots Raby, but before Raby dies, he claims he only came to her assistance. He gets the person who killed him to agree to leave his body in the moonlight, which restores him to life.

A hundred years later, Raby is still alive and must feed on a virgin who is one of his descendants. Once again, the scene is at Raby Castle. The heir, Edgar, returns with his friend Gervase Rookwood, who saved his life. Rookwood quickly becomes enamored of Edgar's sister Alice, and she becomes like a bird fascinated by a serpent when she is near him. After getting Alice to confess her love for him, Rookwood/Raby leaves her in the castle's portrait room, which contains pictures of his past victims who are also his and Alice's relatives. The subjects of the portraits cannot rest because Raby's blood is still in them, and if he succeeds with his next victim, they will be cursed for another century. They step out of their portraits to warn Alice of her danger. Regardless, in the end, Raby feeds on Alice before escaping the castle.

Next, the play jumps ahead to 1860. This time, an heir named Charles returns to Raby Castle to find Ada, his beloved, secluded in the castle and under the power of Gervase Rookwood. Rookwood/Raby is planning to leave England with her, but the family attorney finds proof that Rookwood is Raby, which means he must be a vampire. Charles then pursues Raby to Lucy's grave. Before Raby can escape, Lucy's hand drags him into the tomb and the play ends.[18]

The play is interesting for several reasons, including how the vampire returns every hundred years and that he must always victimize a family member. The introduction of a character named Lucy suggests that Stoker may have borrowed the name from this play for Lucy Westenra in his novel. The portrait gallery is also interesting and adapted from the figures in the tapestry coming to life in Dumas' play. Vampires are still restored by moonlight in this play. The name of Rookwood is no doubt borrowed from William Harrison Ainsworth's novel. The name Raby is also surprising. While the play is definitely influenced by the earlier Ruthven plays, the name Ruthven is ignored here. However, when the play toured America, Boucicault temporarily changed the vampire's name to Sir Alan Ruthven, Lord of Lochiel, and returned it to its Scottish setting.[19] As in other plays, the female victims are mesmerized by the vampire. Finally, the manner of Raby's death is different from in any of the other plays. Also significant is that Raby was the first vampire on stage to sport a black cape,[20] which would become a standard element for vampires from that date on.

The play was not a critical success, but Boucicault remained interested in it and revised it several times, even renaming it *The Phantom* in 1856 and shortening it to two acts. Part of his enthusiasm for the play may have been that it was his debut as a leading actor; the role of Alan Raby had been written for Charles Kean, but when Kean turned down the role, Boucicault chose to play it himself. *The Phantom*'s first act is similar to that of *The Vampire*. The second act includes the 1760 plot, though set in 1750. Boucicault does not bring the play up to the near future of 1860. Perhaps most significant is that we have our first student of vampirism in Dr. Rees, who replaces the attorney from the earlier play. Dr. Rees is the literary ancestor of Professor Van Helsing in *Dracula*. Dr. Rees, through reading a book on necromancy by Dr. Dee, learns a vampire can be killed by fire or a bullet. Eventually, Edgar, the heir to Raby Castle, succeeds in shooting Raby. But Raby falls in the moonlight, so while the other characters leave the site of his death, Dr. Rees remains to see if the moonlight will revive him. When Raby begins to revive, Dr. Rees ends his life by casting his body into the abyss. One final difference between the plays is that in *The Phantom*, the vampire has made "a compact with the fiend"[21] to revive him from death, which brings in the Faust legend.

The Phantom would have a long run in New York and have revivals in New York and Chicago. It was one of the first plays about the supernatural performed in the United States.[22] (Not the first vampire play, however, which was probably Smyth Upton's 1845 *The Last of the Vampires* as I noted in Chapter 1.) Drama historian Roxana Stuart suggests that the American public may have equated Raby with the stereotypical bloodsucking landlord, and this, in turn, opened the door for the popularity of Dracula, also perceived as a landlord figure, in America.[23] Boucicault may well be said to have brought the vampire figure back to English-speaking theater-goers. Others who had tried to do so had not had such extreme success.

Jules Dornay's *Douglas Le Vampire*

Vampires remained popular enough in France that, in 1865, Jules Dornay yet again resurrected Lord Ruthven, but he renamed him Douglas in his play *Douglas Le Vampire*. Despite the vampire character's new name, it is clear Douglas is modeled on Ruthven. Both are Scottish names after all.

Dornay also added some new aspects to the story. The setting is Edinburgh in 1648. Sir William Clifford is gambling away his money, but he is not concerned because he believes he is about to inherit the fortune of the late Lord Douglas. Notably, the gambling theme was previously used in Polidori's original story. Sir William is a distant relative of Lord Douglas, but no other relatives are known to exist. Lord Douglas had a daughter named Lucy (a name likely taken from Boucicault's play) who ran away with a man from Moldavia, and they went to live in his native land. They are both now dead, but it's believed Lucy had a son, though the child's whereabouts are unknown. On the off chance the child survived and could be found, Lord Douglas stipulated a two-month wait for his will to be settled.

The play opens with the two months set to expire on the next day. Of course, the true heir shows up in time. He makes his entrance dressed like a wraith at a party Sir William holds the night before to celebrate his inheritance. Guests at the party joke that the man dressed as a wraith is really a vampire. Maxwell, a young man in love with Anna, Sir William's daughter, speculates on vampires by stating that: "The Slav, Greek, and Romanian populations of the principalities of the Danube, Greece, Hungary, Poland all report this superstition, and who knows if there's not a grain of truth in these tales."[24] Interestingly, as Romanian *Dracula* scholar Cristina Artenie has argued and I learned personally in visiting the country, Romania has no native tradition of vampires, so this may be the first mention of Romania associated with vampires—earlier mentions of the Carpathians in Planché's play aside—which was, of course, cemented as an association once *Dracula* was published.

When the wraith begins to talk about beliefs in vampires, a thug named Dick Thorn, intent on killing him at Sir William's bequest, confronts him, accusing him of mocking him by trying to get him to believe in vampires. Dick then runs the stranger through, and Maxwell, who is a doctor, has the stranger carried off. The scene now shifts to Maxwell's lab. Maxwell decides that since vampires are real, he won't revive the stranger. However, Anna arrives to tell Maxwell how her father is against their marriage. Maxwell then, determined on revenge, pulls back the curtain to let the moon revive Douglas and repay his wrongs with the blood of men. His plan backfires when the first woman Douglas sees is Maxwell's sister, Fanny. Maxwell then realizes he has allowed the Devil's work to begin.

In Act II, Lord Douglas' will is about to be read. However, at the stroke of midnight, when the wait for Lord Douglas' grandson will have ended, the rightful Lord Douglas appears. Sir William is horrified that Douglas is still alive, but Douglas says he will make things right so that if Sir William can't inherit the fortune, his grandchildren can by Douglas marrying Anna.

Maxwell is horrified by this. When he claims that Douglas is a monster, everyone thinks he has gone mad (a plot twist that goes back to Nodier's play).

In Act III, the wedding of two other characters, Betsy and Tom, takes place. When Douglas tells Betsy he loves her—because he is in need of virgin blood—she is terrified. Maxwell then appears and shoots Douglas, who flees, trying to reach moonlight before he will die.

In Act IV, Maxwell follows Douglas to stake him before he revives, but he is too late. Meanwhile, Fanny tells Anna she cannot marry Douglas because she is herself in love with him. Fanny, however, is only seeking to protect Anna. She agrees to take Anna's place at the wedding to Douglas. Douglas then comes to claim his bride and sends Sir William a letter saying they are leaving that evening on the brig *Inferno*.

Act V takes place on the ship. Douglas knows that if he doesn't get a virgin's blood within the hour, he will have to return to the grave and then be limited to emerging only one hour per night. When he tries to attack Fanny, thinking she is Anna, she reveals her identity and tries to stab him, but he threatens to mesmerize her. By this point, Maxwell and Tom have boarded the ship. Douglas tries to use Fanny's body as a shield to protect himself from their bullets, but then a lightning bolt strikes Douglas and he is destroyed. The characters thank God for his death.

The lightning bolt goes back to Nodier's play. The revival by moonlight goes back to Polidori. Eliminated again is the oath that keeps the vampire's identity a secret. Also absent is any dispute at the wedding ceremony.

What is new and fresh, as Dodd points out, is that this is the first time a character intentionally revives the vampire, thinking the vampire will carry out his own wishes. Furthermore, it is the first time the victim, Fanny, actively fights back.[25] Also, the battle on the ship is interesting since a ship will later play a major role in *Dracula* to get the vampire to England, whereas here it is used to help the vampire escape.

Maxwell is perhaps the play's most intriguing character since he is a doctor and chooses to revive the vampire. One can't help wondering if he was inspired by Victor Frankenstein, another doctor who revives the dead only to find he cannot control what he revives.

The references to Romania and Moldavia are also new, at least in French literature—Moldavia was a province of Romania in 1865. Moldavia and Wallachia had joined together in 1859 to become Romania. Transylvania, home to Dracula, would not become part of Romania until the end of World War I; it belonged to the Austro-Hungarian Empire at the time of Dornay's play.

However, as other scholars have noted, a German story, "The Mysterious Stranger," had previously been set in Transylvania and the Carpathians. It was published in 1854 in English as an unauthorized translation of Karl von Wachsmann's "Der Fremde" ("The Stranger"), first published in his collection *Erzählungen und Novellen* (1844). Scholars have suggested Bram Stoker read this story and was inspired to set Castle Dracula in Transylvania as a result. I am not sure that theory is completely accurate, but it is possible the story was read by other authors, perhaps even Dornay, who adapted the setting in their works so that Wachsmann's story eventually but indirectly influenced Stoker. I will discuss "The Mysterious Stranger" in more detail later when I discuss vampire short stories that may have influenced *Dracula*. We will also see the Carpathians mentioned in other works that predate *Dracula* in the discussion that follows.

Douglas Le Vampire is the last serious play that uses the Ruthven story as its plot basis. However, vampires would never go out of fashion. One last play deserves mention before we turn to how the vampire was treated in novels and short stories by French and British authors.

Gilbert and Sullivan's *Ruddigore*

By the late nineteenth century, Lord Ruthven had become so well-known that he easily lent himself to spoofs. The most notable comical play that uses the Ruthven plot and the only one that still enjoys some popularity today is Gilbert and Sullivan's *Ruddigore; or The Witch's Curse*, first produced in 1887.

Given that Gilbert and Sullivan were British authors, it is natural they were most influenced by Boucicault's play as evidenced by their borrowing of the scene of ancestors emerging from portraits, which is the most famous and memorable scene from *Ruddigore*.[26] Ironically, the play contains no vampires, though some literary and drama historians have mistakenly described the ancestors as vampires.

Rather than discuss the play's various revisions from its conception through the first few decades of its existence, I refer readers to Roxana Stuart's *Stage Blood*. Today, the version performed is that from 1920. At least two productions of the play in recent years can be viewed at YouTube at the time of this writing, as well as excerpts from several other productions. Despite the play's comic nature, these productions are the closest we may ever get to seeing what Victorian Gothic melodrama may have been like. Because of *Ruddigore*'s subject matter, it is my favorite of Gilbert and Sullivan's operettas. The song "When the Night Wind Howls" is itself a masterpiece of Gothic music. The play may be more appreciated today by lovers of Gothic literature than operetta enthusiasts. I will offer here a plot summary that highlights the play's more Gothic elements.

Act I is set in Cornwall. Rose Maybud is the prettiest girl in the village, but the men are too shy to court her. A group of professional bridesmaids are sad that no marriages are taking place. They complain about the situation to Rose's aunt, Dame Hannah, asking if she will ever marry. Dame Hannah says she has vowed to remain single ever since she broke her engagement to Sir Roderic Murgatroyd, one of the evil baronets of Ruddigore. She did not learn his true identity until the day they were to be married.

Dame Hannah then tells the bridesmaids about the Ruddigore family curse. Centuries before, Sir Rupert Murgatroyd, the first baronet, burned a witch at the stake. Before she died, she cursed all the future Baronets of Ruddigore. The curse requires that the current baronet commit a crime every day or he will perish in agony. Since then, every baronet has been evil, trying to prevent a horrible death, but eventually, each one has no longer been able to commit a daily crime and died in anguish. This curse in the play obviously resembles Faustian pacts and the vampire's need to haunt or prey on his own family since it is an ancestral curse. However, the ancestors are not vampires, only reluctant criminals.

Dame Hannah now asks her niece, Rose, whether she will ever marry. Rose says all the men are too shy and etiquette says she cannot speak to a man unless she is first spoken to. Finally, a farmer named Robin Oakapple finds the courage to approach Rose, claiming he is seeking her advice on behalf of a friend who is in love, but the conversation goes nowhere.

Robin has a servant, Adam, who arrives after Rose has left. Because Adam addresses Robin as Sir Ruthven Murgatroyd, we learn that Robin fled his inheritance twenty years ago to avoid the family curse. After some plot twists concerning Robin's friend Richard, who almost ends up marrying Rose, Rose and Robin come together and she agrees to marry him.

At this point, Mad Margaret appears, having been driven mad by her love for Sir Despard Murgatroyd, the current bad baronet and younger brother to Ruthven/Robin, who inherited the baronetcy after his brother's disappearance. Margaret wishes to warn Rose that Sir Despard plans to carry her off to fulfill his necessary crime for the day. They leave the scene just before Sir Despard arrives. Sir Despard turns out to dislike having to commit the crimes required by the curse. He always commits his daily crime early in the morning to get it over with, and then he does good deeds the rest of the day to compensate. While in the village, Sir Despard learns his brother Ruthven is still alive and about to marry Rose. He is elated because he can now return the baronetcy to his brother.

Sir Despard interrupts Rose and Robin's wedding and reveals that Robin is his elder brother Ruthven and the rightful heir to the baronetcy. Rose is horrified by the revelation and decides to marry Despard instead, but he refuses her because he plans to marry Mad Margaret. Rose then decides she will marry Richard since he's the only other man available. Meanwhile, Robin now resigns himself to taking up his rightful role as Sir Ruthven Murgatroyd. To this point, the play is more comical than Gothic, but the second act makes up for it.

Act II opens at Ruddigore Castle where Sir Ruthven is trying to adapt to the evil life he must lead. His servant Adam suggests several evil deeds he might do, but Ruthven tries to get off by doing things that are rude rather than evil. Ruthven's failure to commit true evil crimes now causes his ancestors' ghosts to become involved. The curse means they must ensure their successors commit a daily crime or they will be forced to torture him to death. The ancestors emerge from their family portraits to review the bad deeds Ruthven has so far committed, deeds that are laughable like not paying his income tax (which no one pays anyway), forging his own will, and disinheriting his unborn son. Ruthven's late uncle Sir Roderic orders him to carry off a lady or perish in horrible agony, and then the ghosts all reveal to him the kinds of agonies he will suffer if he does not comply. Ruthven finally agrees to abduct a young lady and gives Adam orders to carry out the act.

Not all the family wants Ruthven to carry on the curse, however. Despard and Margaret visit and urge Ruthven to give up his life of crime. At their urging, Ruthven resolves to defy his ancestors. Meanwhile, Adam has abducted a woman, who turns out to be Dame Hannah. She is a formidable opponent, causing Ruthven to cry out to Sir Roderic for his help. When Sir Roderic appears and recognizes his former fiancée, he asks Ruthven to leave him and Dame Hannah in private. The two former lovers then have a special moment before Ruthven returns to reveal his intentions. He states that not committing a daily crime is equal, according to the curse, to suicide, but suicide itself is considered a crime. Therefore, none of his ancestors should have ever died because they committed suicide. The revelation of this loophole sets Ruthven free of the curse. Rose, finding her lover is no longer evil, once more becomes engaged to him. Roderic returns to life and is able to marry Dame Hannah. Richard is left to settle for Zorah, one of the professional bridesmaids.

The play has a typical comical plot where all problems are resolved through technicalities. The ancestral curse, abductions, and ancestral ghosts are the play's major Gothic elements. In the original ending, all the ghosts came back to life, but William S. Gilbert revised the ending after the premiere so that only Sir Roderic returns to life. Since *Ruddigore* is best known for the ancestral portraits coming to life, it is unlikely anyone today sees the play without knowing this event will happen, yet it is still an eerie moment that gives us a hint of the Gothic melodrama of its dramatic precursors.

Bram Stoker almost definitely knew *Ruddigore*. William S. Gilbert was good friends with Stoker's wife, Florence, and sent her tickets for *Ruddigore*, so Bram likely attended with her.[27] Stoker probably had the play in the back of his mind as he wrote *Dracula*, although Stoker's plot is far more serious. Stoker's more immediate dramatic influence must have been Boucicault's play, which was a literary descendant of Polidori's story. Therefore, we have a direct line of influence from Polidori to Nodier to Dumas to Boucicault to Gilbert and Sullivan and to Stoker. While we cannot know if Ruthven might have enjoyed future variations of his character on the stage had *Dracula* not been published, it is fair to say that *Dracula*'s success finally drove the stake through Lord Ruthven's popularity.

Other Vampire Texts Between *The Vampyre* and *Dracula*

As stated at the beginning of this chapter, in most studies of *Dracula* in English, the vampire works cited as sources for or at least predating *Dracula* are always Polidori's *The Vampyre*, Rymer's *Varney the Vampire*, and Le Fanu's *Carmilla*. Critics have almost always ignored the rich French tradition of the vampire, although the Ruthven plays are occasionally mentioned. Here I hope to remedy that shortcoming by exploring other major vampire works of fiction, both in French and English, not associated with Ruthven. Fortunately, in the twenty-first century, many of the French works that were previously obscure or at least unknown to English-speaking readers have now been translated into English and are readily available. I will also mention two American texts of significance.

Uriah Derick D'Arcy's "The Black Vampyre"

"The Black Vampyre, or a Tale of St. Domingo" is the first vampire story written and set in the Americas. Soon after, a short-lived play version of Polidori's *The Vampyre* was produced in New York City at the Pavilion Theatre in July 1819. The text of that play is no longer extant, but it must have been a loose adaption since the principal characters were Lord Ruthven, Aubrey, and a new character named Pedro.[28] By contrast, while Lord Ruthven does not appear as a character in the American short story "The Black Vampyre," Polidori's story is the obvious inspiration for it.

"The Black Vampyre" was written under the pseudonym Uriah Derick D'Arcy (critics still debate who the actual author was[29]) and intended as a burlesque of Polidori's story. It must have been quickly conceived since Polidori's *The Vampyre* was published April 1, 1819 and "The Black Vampyre" was published June 23 of the same year. In fact, its author states he wrote it in two afternoons. The story is set in Haiti, which changed its name from Saint-Domingue in 1804 after it became a free country. However, US newspapers continued to call the country Saint-Domingue into the 1820s.[30]

According to critic Andrew Barger, "The Black Vampyre" is the first Black vampire story, first comedic vampire story, the first story to include a mulatto vampire, the first vampire story by an American author, and perhaps the first anti-slavery short story.[31] I would add that it is the first prose work to include a female vampire, something usually credited to Cyprien Bérard. Bérard still holds the honor of creating the first seductive female vampire. "The Black Vampyre" is also one of the first zombie stories since it blends Haitian Obeah practices that involved narcotics and spiritual healing with the vampire legend.[32] Finally, it is the first time in fiction that vampires are associated with punishment of colonizers or conquerors, which will be a theme in later novels such as Marie Nizet's *Le Capitaine Vampire* and Stoker's *Dracula*, as we will explore later.

While "The Black Vampyre" is an American story, its European influences are notable. The story begins with a passage from Lord Byron's poem "The Giaour" (1813). A giaour in Islam is an unbeliever or infidel. In Byron's poem, the giaour kills a Turkish harem master. The Ottoman narrator predicts the giaour will be punished by becoming a vampire and pursuing his family. The poem also takes up the cause for Greek independence from the Turks, a cause Byron would lose his life fighting in 1824. A similar fight for freedom is reflected in "The Black Vampyre," which is set in the years before Haiti's revolution. The poem also has several references to *The Arabian Nights*, a frequent influence on the period's Gothic literature. Among the references or allusions are the title character and his companion being referred to as "genii,"[33] the title character being dressed like a "Moorish prince,"[34] and a jeweled cavern that resembles "a vast hall of Arabian romance."[35]

Although "The Black Vampyre" is considered comedic, an intense seriousness underlies its bizarre events. It clearly was written as a polemic against slavery, a topic of great concern in the United States the year it was published because of debates over whether Missouri would enter the union as a free or slave state.[36]

To fully appreciate the story's message and Gothic elements, I will summarize it in full.

The story begins by stating it contains the family history of Mr. Anthony Gibbons. Gibbons' ancestors were Africans captured from Guinea and brought on a French ship to St. Domingo to be sold into slavery. They all died soon after except one little boy who was sold to Mr. Personne. The plot begins when Mr. Personne, unhappy with the boy, knocks out his brains, but the moon quickly revives him. Mr. Personne makes several more attempts to kill the boy, but each time, the moon revives him. Finally, Mr. Personne burns him, but before the boy dies, he tosses Mr. Personne into the fire with him. These attempts to kill what is obviously a vampire foreshadow what will come in *Varney the Vampire*, in which Varney repeatedly and unsuccessfully tries to kill himself. That said, the comedy here lies in the boy repeatedly coming back to life, though the scene doesn't stay funny for long.

Mr. Personne survives the fire but is badly burned. Bandaged but dying in his bed, he asks that his wife Euphemia come to him with their infant son. However, Euphemia discovers their son is missing; only his skin, hair, and nails are in his bed. Learning his son is probably dead is enough to kill Mr. Personne.

The narrative now jumps ahead sixteen years. Euphemia has remarried twice. (The text later contradicts itself by saying she had three more husbands.) While she is mourning the death of the last husband, she is approached by a tall Black man dressed like a Moorish Prince who leads by the hand a white boy named Zembo. Euphemia falls in love with the Prince and they marry, despite her chaplain trying to dissuade her.

At midnight, following the wedding, the Prince takes Euphemia to the graves of her departed husbands and her other children who have died. The Prince and Zembo dig up the grave of her son Spooner who died at age seven. Zembo then falls on Spooner's body like a hungry dog. Euphemia is horrified, but she is also surprised that her son's body looks fresh. The Prince uses blood from Spooner's heart to make a mixture in a goblet that he forces Euphemia to drink. Euphemia faints and wakes to find herself on Mr. Personne's grave. She feels cravings that make her realize she has become a vampire.

Mr. Personne now rises from the dead and he and Euphemia embrace. They catch each other up on what has happened in the last sixteen years since he died. She professes her love for him. The Prince then brings the other husbands back to life. Personne now threatens the Prince with a thigh bone, saying Euphemia is his wife alone. The Prince proposes a duel between the husbands, but Zembo puts stakes through the other husbands. Personne then wants to fight the Prince, but he refuses. He says instead Mr. Personne and Euphemia will sail to Europe as a family, apparently with Zembo, who turns out to be the baby who disappeared.

That this family of vampires is to be sent to Europe suggests the Prince seeks to revenge himself through them on the white race. However, before the family can leave for Europe, the Prince takes them into a bejeweled cavern that resembles something from *The Arabian Nights*. The cavern is also full of signs of "Negro witchcraft," including animal teeth, bones, and eggshells.[37]

Mr. Personne realizes the creatures in the cave are "GOULS." But there are also Vampyre monarchs, though it's not clear if these are the Personnes themselves or other creatures. A Vampyre Ball then takes place.

Next, the Prince shares that there are only two ways to kill vampires—with stakes or with a potion that will restore them to their former human existence. A group of soldiers now enters the cavern and kills all the creatures except for Mr. Personne and Euphemia, who drink the potion and become human again. Since Mr. Personne was dead sixteen years, he appears to be sixteen years younger than his wife, but she does not mind. When Zembo emerges from the cavern, he reveals that he told the soldiers to attack. Apparently, he turned against the Prince who raised him but kidnapped him from his parents. Obviously, he has always remained loyal to his white, slave-holding family. He is then baptized and renamed Barabbas.

As a final twist, as the story ends, we learn Euphemia gave birth to the Prince's mulatto son, and that Anthony Gibbons of the present day is that child's descendant. Gibbons now lives in New Jersey.

As bizarre as "The Black Vampyre" is, the violence Mr. Personne inflicts upon the negro child forcefully displays the wrongs of slavery and justifies a slave rebellion. The vengeance the Prince inflicts on the family is understandable, even if violence is morally wrong. That he might send the vampire family to Europe is momentarily terrifying as a way to wreak vengeance on the colonizers and all the white race. However, like most subversive Gothic texts, the story ends with the status quo restored.

Most interesting is that colonialism and slavery are at the heart of the vampire threat the family experiences. Later, another character from the West Indies with negro blood will become a vampire in Florence Marryat's *The Blood of the Vampire* (1897). *Dracula* also notably reflects a threat from a foreign land to Western Europeans. Romania, where *Dracula* is set, was treated like a colony by Britain at the time, even if technically it wasn't. Vampirism, therefore, is used to get revenge on Europeans trying to subject a foreign land.

Most of the following vampire stories we will explore make the vampire threat more local, although for the French, as seen in the Ruthven stories, Scotland was apparently foreign and exotic enough to be a vampire hotspot. However, the suggestion that the West Indies and other colonies are a threat to their European colonizers would recur by the end of the nineteenth century, making "The Black Vampyre" ahead of its time in many ways, although its influence on future vampire stories cannot be directly traced. Regardless, it was far-seeing.

Étienne-Léon de Lamothe-Langon's *The Virgin Vampire*

Étienne-Léon de Lamothe-Langon's *La Vampire, ou la Vierge de Hongrie* (1825), translated into English by Brian Stableford as *The*

Virgin Vampire, is the first work to have a female vampire as its main character and only the third depiction of a female vampire in fiction, after Euphemia in "The Black Vampyre" and Bettina in Bérard's *Lord Ruthwen ou les vampires*, as discussed earlier. In those works, both women are less evil creatures than true Gothic wanderers subjected to a fate they did not choose. While Bettina becomes a vampire, she uses her powers for good to track down the vampire who made her his victim. Euphemia is the wife of a slaveowner, but unlike her husband, she is not seen as contributing to the wrongs of slavery, so perhaps she does not deserve her fate. Lamothe-Langon's Alinska is more complicated. While she becomes an object of terror to the novel's other characters, once her backstory is revealed, the reader sympathizes with her.

The Virgin Vampire is set in France in the years following the Napoleonic Wars. Edouard Delmont, a colonel in Napoleon's army, has decided to leave Paris and relocate his family—his wife Hélène, son Eugène, and daughter Juliette—to a chateau near Toulouse. He tells his wife a change in their finances requires them to move, but the truth is he has received a demanding letter from Alinska, whom he had formerly promised to marry when he was stationed in Hungary with Napoleon's army. There they engaged in a blood pact promise, but when the army departed, Edouard decided to forget about Alinska and later married Hélène.

Not long after the Delmonts have arrived in the area of Toulouse, Edouard's sister's marriage problems cause him to visit his sister to try to get her to reconcile with her husband. While Edouard is away, Alinska moves into the neighborhood. Raoul, a former soldier who served under Edouard and is now a servant to the Delmonts, knows of Alinska's past relationship with Edouard, but no one else does. The local residents only think her reclusive behavior strange. When Raoul tries to confront Alinska about why she is pursuing Edouard, he is manhandled by her powerful servant. He then tries to write to Edouard to warn him of the danger, but his letters are inexplicably torn to pieces or become covered in blood. Eventually, Edouard's children and then Hélène befriend Alinska. When Alinska's house burns down and her servant dies in the fire, Hélène invites Alinska to seek shelter under her roof.

Edouard now returns home to find himself in an uncomfortable situation. Alinska confronts him about how he broke his vow to her, but he can do nothing to resolve the situation since he is married to Hélène. Then Edouard and Hélène's son Eugène becomes ill. Raoul, realizing Alinska is not quite human, looks through a keyhole one night when she is watching over the child and sees her sucking out Eugène's blood through his mouth. Raoul enters the room and shoots Alinska, but she manages to stab and kill him. She later claims the house was attacked by thieves, who killed Raoul, and the family believes her. Alinska recovers from her wounds, but Eugène dies.

Soon after, Hélène also begins to weaken. Edouard takes her away from Toulouse, but she feels the need to see Alinska again and calls her to her deathbed. Hélène asks Alinska to take care of her daughter Juliette after her death, which Alinska agrees to. Once Hélène dies, Alinska refuses to attend the funeral. She tells Edouard she cannot. Alinska tries to care for Juliette but finds herself repulsed by the girl, so Edouard sends Juliette off to boarding school.

By this point, neighbors report seeing Hélène and Eugène's ghosts entering the house. Edouard tries to recompense Alinska by offering to marry her, but she says she cannot be married by a priest. She finally agrees to a civil ceremony, but following that, Edouard brings her to a chapel where a priest awaits. Alinska now feels she must give in to her destiny. When Edouard removes her glove to put a ring on her finger, her hand is revealed to be that of a skeleton and her corrupted blood pours out of open wounds. The priest orders the demon to make itself known, but it is too late for Alinska has fallen to the floor as a corpse.

The novel's power does not come through in such a simple summary. We are repeatedly shown Alinska being antisocial, rejecting visitors, fleeing from priests, refusing to go to church, and lamenting her fate or making cryptic statements to the Delmont family about her past and how she cannot partake of happiness. The most dramatic of these statements comes when Alinska tells Edouard she cannot marry him in a church:

> Thus, making an effort, she cried: "No, Edouard, no, don't talk to me about a ceremony to which I once attached all the felicity of my existence. Can I be yours now, when I do not belong to myself? Besides, where are your pretentions taking you? Feeble child of humankind, what union are you proposing? Shall I prostrate myself at the foot of the altar that has rejected me? I've already told you—banished from the Lord's temples by a terrible malediction, I would not dare to cross the redoubtable threshold. You would believe it to be open to us, but I would see an exterminating angel there, which would escape your mortal sight. You love me, you say? Well, give me proof of it, by not importuning me again. I believe in your affection; that must suffice—it is not permissible for you to doubt mine.
>
> "And it's because it speaks so poignantly to me [sic] heart that I want to be sure of it. Cruel friend, recover now the entire exercise of your reason; don't forge phantoms. Even an incomplete suicide is doubtless a crime before the Divinity, but if there is no sin that repentance cannot efface, why should yours be pursued by an inflexible rigor?
>
> "That is how humans are! One is delirious every time one speaks of them of things they cannot understand, or tells them a truth that they cannot unveil. Do you not understand that the moment you expect to complete our common felicity would be that of our eternal separation? And that separation fills me with horror. Here, we can remain together; down there"—she lowered her voice as she continued—"would each take an opposite route. What will the priest say before whom I shall present myself?

"Will he possess the gift of divination? Will he know in R*** what sin your love caused you to commit in Hungary?

"Edouard, God marked the forehead of the fratricide Cain with a terrible mark; I bear an equally formidable sign on mine; you cannot see it, but he would perceive it, and then it would be necessary to say adieu to you forever, for there is here, as in Hungary, consecrated ground ever-ready to receive bodies that must dissolve."

"Poor girl! How I pity you! You're misled by the prejudices of your education; thus, by virtue of a chimerical dread, you oppose our common happiness. If you fear the rigors of the church, though, would you be equally afraid of a union consecrated by the civil authorities?"

"Oh, that wouldn't matter—no sacred hand would touch my own."[38]

Alinska's claim that she has a similar mark to that of Cain places her firmly in the role of Gothic wanderer. However, unlike most Gothic wanderers, she has not committed a true transgression but rather been transgressed against by her lover who deserted her, though one might argue that the pact she and Edouard made was based in pagan superstition and, therefore, a transgression against God. In Hungary when Edouard first fell in love with Alinska, he found that she remained virtuous, causing him to agree to the pact, as described below:

> The more he saw of Alinska, the more his affection for her increased. He took that to the extreme, and one evening, after an entire day spent in the most delightful pleasures, he pierced his arm with a sharp dagger, and in blood drawn from the slight wound he wrote a promise of marriage, which he confided to the loyalty of his friend. Impressed by this action, she hastened to do likewise. The double pact, according to the ancient custom of the country, was deposited for five nights under the stone of a sepulcher, and from then on, the engagement was ratified in Heaven.

> No one doubts, in Hungary, that by such an act, two lovers are irrevocably bound to one another; any union that is not contracted between the two of them cannot be happy. Eventually, a female virgin affianced in that fashion may rise from the tomb that covers her after her death, in order to torment, in the fashion of a Vampire, the perfidious man who has abandoned her. Delmont, a stranger to the land, was unaware of these superstitious details. He had no fear of the future, for it seemed to him to be impossible that he could ever forget Alinska.[39]

The text never makes clear what happened to Alinska after Edouard abandoned her. She apparently died and then rose from the grave as a vampire, though how she died is unclear. We may assume it was from a broken heart. Her punishment of becoming a vampire is unfair since she was abandoned by her lover, and she continually fights her vampiric urges while knowing she is cursed by God and will eventually suffer hellfire. As Brian Stableford points out, we cannot feel sympathy for Edouard since he abandoned her, but the real villain may be God, who creates such unjust punishment in the novel's world. Stableford remarks that Alinska herself is the instrument of God's Divine Wrath, and:

> Within the metaphysical schema of *La Vampire*, the question tentatively asked and left unanswered by Bérard, as to why God allows evildoing vampires to persecute the innocent, simply does not arise. Here, vampires are not evil, and any persecution that is going on is the work of God. The innocents drained of their blood are not victims at all, because—from God's viewpoint—death is merely a commutation of their sentence of life, and by taking them into Heaven sooner rather than later he is doing them a favor.[40]

Stableford goes on to state that:

> [Alinska's] eternal and irrevocable damnation is way over the top by reference to any conceivable scale of justice.

> If she is a monster, she is not a self-made monster; her monstrousness has been inflicted upon her. The only veritable and voluntary monster in the plot is the God who dictates the fates of Edouard, Alinska and their secondary victims: a vile individual who is not merely immune to sympathy for the objects of his implacable wrath, but also seems to be taking something of a sadistic delight in their torture, which inevitably overflows into the torment of the secondary victims of vampirism. One can hardly doubt that His Hell will be a horrid place to be, but one is surely bound to worry, too, about the quality of His Heaven.[41]

The remark is interesting in its questioning of God's righteousness, especially in relation to other French Gothic texts of the period like Quinet's *Ahasvérus* that we explored in Chapter 4. That Alinska does not choose to be a monster but has her monstrousness thrust upon her recalls the Monster in *Frankenstein*, which predates the novel by seven years. This sense of injustice from one's creator is used metaphorically in *Frankenstein* to question God's creation of man. Here Lamothe-Langon seems to be raising similar questions about the righteousness of God, although we cannot be sure how consciously he does so. Certainly, the modern reader cannot help but feel the injustice, but Lamothe-Langon may not have questioned it because to do so would unravel or deconstruct the world he created. Nevertheless, questioning God's justice was becoming a common theme in early nineteenth-century Gothic novels.

Also notable about *The Virgin Vampire* is the depiction of Eastern Europe. The description of Hungarians as superstitious reaches racist extremes in this novel. Such racism would carry on into other works I will discuss below with Eastern European settings, including Dumas' *The Thousand and One Ghosts*, Le Fanu's *Carmilla*, and Bram Stoker's *Dracula*. Raoul, when discussing his experiences in Hungary as a soldier, describes the country as follows:

> You know that Hungary is a vast country, extending from the extremity of Germany to the Turkish frontier. The people of its rural areas are only half-civilized; they are more closely related to beasts than to humans, properly speaking. They spend their lives in a kind of slavery, to which we would have difficulty becoming accustomed—but if they remain submissive to their masters while they're in this world, they take their revenge when they're covered with six feet of earth. Some of them, after being interred in their coffins and laid in the grave, rise up in the cold winter nights, with the assistance of the one that Monsieur le Curé calls the Devil, and return to earth, to the misfortune of the living.[42]

Striking here is the comparison of the people to beasts and slaves. Here is the racist seed of the dramatic scene in the Swedish *Powers of Darkness* where bestial creatures are submissive to Count Draculitz as I described in Chapter 5.

In his preface, Lamothe-Langon lists the vampire superstition as being native to "Hungary, Moravia, Epirus and the Greek islands." Romania and Transylvania are absent from this list but would soon join it in other vampire novels. Lamothe-Langon also comments upon the work of Dom Augustin Calmet, whose 1746 treatise on vampires, *Dissertations on the Apparitions of Angels, of Demons and of Spirits, and on Revenants or Vampires of Hungary, of Bohemia, of Moravia and of Silesia*, first popularized the idea of vampires and their association with Eastern Europe. Calmet would be a major source for many authors of vampire literature, but Lamothe-Langon appears to be the first novelist to connect the vampire with Eastern Europe.

One might also argue, given that the novel was written in the aftermath of the Napoleonic Wars, that the novel represents a discomfort with the conquest of much of Europe by Napoleon. The vampire comes from one of the countries Napoleon subjected, and it seeks revenge upon one of Napoleon's soldiers by following him home to destroy his family. In this respect, the novel has much in common with "The Black Vampyre."

The Virgin Vampire also shares with "The Black Vampyre" the idea that vampires exist metaphorically in our society and are everywhere. "The Black Vampyre" lists as vampires the dandies who bleed their fathers dry of money, traffickers in stocks, brokers, bank directors, and even plagiarists, the author finally concludes the list by asserting that he himself is a vampire[43] (perhaps because he has capitalized upon Polidori's vampire text to write his own). Similarly, Lamothe-Langon finds vampires everywhere, stating:

> Are not the insatiable conquerors who are always at war, exhausting their states in consequence, Vampires drunk on our purest blood? Do we not incessantly encounter men avid for our sweat, who always think that the burdens with which they overwhelm us are light? Do you think that those wretches who wander through towns and the countryside to constrain the popular will with the lure of gain or the fear of suspicion are not real Vampires? And the man who, placed at a high rank, finding virtue in his path, stifles it with embroidered garments or strangles it with a silken ribbon—should we not call him a Vampire?
>
> Do you think that the banker of a gambling house, where so many fortunes are swallowed up and such worthy reputations ruined, does not march in the foremost rank of Vampires? In the middle of Paris, in the busiest streets and the most obscure alleys, do we not find today, at night, Vampires who are sometimes adorned with all the charms of the beloved sex, no less possessed of depravity, avidity, vice and criminal inclination than their colleagues of the other world?
>
> Finally, does not one see Vampires everywhere, some in priestly vestments and others in judicial togas? They

can be seen wearing military uniform or administrative sashes. Their greatest concentration is to be found among tradesmen and entrepreneurs, the agents of the law and speculators, where they are present in large numbers; they can even be found in the ranks of physicians.

This may be the earliest reference in nineteenth-century literature to the priesthood as vampires. Certainly, Radcliffe's Schedoni and Sue's Rodin are priests with vampire-like qualities, and those who bleed people dry financially, people like the lawyer Vholes in Dickens' *Bleak House* (1853) or the financier Melmotte in Trollope's *The Way We Live Now* (1875), while not technically vampires, also have vampiric qualities. So, by 1825, the vampire metaphor being used to represent social injustices was well-established and would continue throughout the nineteenth century and into the modern day.

If Polidori's *The Vampyre* is the father of vampire literature, then we might call *The Virgin Vampire* the mother of it, for it would inspire many more female vampires and many more novels that would grapple with the theme of whether vampires could be redeemed.

Elizabeth Caroline Grey's "The Skeleton Count, or The Vampire Mistress"

"The Skeleton Count, or The Vampire Mistress" is a short story believed to have been first published in 1828. If so, it is one of the most fascinating of the early vampire texts, but controversy exists over its authenticity. First, let us review the plot and then I will discuss the controversy.

The story opens when Count Rodolph, who lives in Ravensburg Castle near Heidelberg, makes a pact with the devil so he can become proficient in alchemy. He wishes to restore people to life, which reflects a possible influence of *Frankenstein* upon the story. He begins by studying anatomy, and with the help of two resurrectionists, he acquires the body of a hanged man. Rodolph learns how to reanimate a corpse but also that he needs a special elixir to sustain its life. When he feels ready, he has his resurrectionists dig up the corpse of a newly dead young woman named Bertha. Rodolph places Bertha in a magical circle in his castle, uses a magic wand, utters cabalistic words, and brings her to life. She is not very responsive, however, until he gives her the restorative cordial. She then moves about like she has never died, but she has no memory of her past. She is like "an Eve" and adores him as her creator. He makes her mistress of his castle and they become lovers, but they do not marry. The count's servants are surprised by the sudden appearance of their new mistress.

The night after Bertha is restored to life, she leaves Rodolph's bed and goes into the village to satisfy her cravings, realizing she has somehow become a vampire because of the strange way she has been resurrected. She enters a cottage and sucks the blood of a young girl named Minna (perhaps a source for the name of Mina in Stoker's *Dracula*). This scene may be the first homoerotic scene in vampire fiction, recalling the possible vampirism of Geraldine and Christabel in Coleridge's 1816 poem "Christabel."

When Minna wakes, she shouts for help, causing her family to burst into the room. Bertha tries to escape, but Minna's father pursues her and shoots her. He sees her fall into the river and assumes she's dead, but the moon restores her. She returns to the castle and slips into Rodolph's bed without waking him.

Rodolph finds it strange during the day to note that Bertha does not eat or drink, not realizing she is a vampire. Meanwhile, the villagers worry Minna will become a vampire, but they believe Bertha was killed by the gunshot.

Rodolph now reveals his secret to Bertha, making her swear to keep it. Seven days have passed since he began his pact with the devil, meaning it is now time for him to fulfill his end of the bargain, which is that he will turn into a skeleton from sunset to sunrise. Bertha promises to keep his secret. She then witnesses his transformation into a skeleton. During the night, she returns to the village, this time sucking the blood of a young woman named Theresa.

Like Minna, Theresa wakes, screams, and scares off Bertha, but she also has recognized her as the recently dead Bertha and tells the villagers. After debating what to do, the villagers decide to dig up Bertha's coffin, only to find it empty, thus confirming she is the vampire. Meanwhile, the servants at the castle have revealed to the villagers that they have a new mistress who does not eat or drink. Realizing the vampire Bertha resides in the castle, the villagers attack it.

At first, the villagers get the upper hand in the attack. Bertha tries to tell Rodolph the attack is because they have learned he is practicing necromancy, but the villagers' cries soon inform Rodolph that they believe Bertha is a vampire. Rodolph thinks his transformation into a skeleton might scare them off, but after his transformation, while they are momentarily surprised, they still capture Bertha and burn down the castle. The villagers drag Bertha to her grave and rebury her with a stake through her heart. Later, one villager returns to the castle in time to see the skeleton turn back into Count Rodolph and enter the castle ruins. The story concludes by assuring us Minna and Theresa never turned into vampires.

The story is remarkable in many ways. First, it is the first vampire story by a female author. It follows what have already become established tropes of moonlight reviving vampires, first found in Polidori, and a stake killing a vampire, first found in Bérard. It has a count living in a castle on a hill, like Dracula will later do, and it shows villagers attacking the castle, reminiscent of the Universal horror films of the 1930s and 1940s. We also have a pact with Satan, alchemy, resurrection men, and the dead coming back to life. What more could a lover of the Gothic want?

However, the story seems more developed in some ways than other vampire stories of the time, perhaps containing too many Gothic elements of a later date to make it feel legitimate. The story was "rediscovered" in 1995 by Peter Haining, who published it that year in his *The Vampire Omnibus*. Haining claimed it was published in 1828 in the serial magazine *Casket*, which would make it the first "serial" vampire story. Haining said a collector brought him the only copy of the magazine that existed and he based the text on that copy. Haining died in 2007 and no copy of the magazine has been seen by anyone else. Furthermore, it is known that Haining created other hoaxes. He invented a fake biography for penny dreadful character Sweeney Todd so he could claim Todd was a historical person.[44] He also appears to have created two pseudo-historical incidents concerning the Victorian urban legend of Spring-Heeled Jack.[45]

Haining claimed Elizabeth Caroline Grey (1798-1869) was the story's author. Grey was a popular writer of silver fork and other types of novels, but her name never appeared on any penny dreadfuls. Since many penny dreadfuls were published anonymously, this may not be surprising. Grey began to be given attribution as the author to several such tales beginning in 1922 when Andrew De Ternant claimed she wrote penny dreadfuls in an article in *Notes & Queries*. Recent scholarship suggests Grey did not write penny dreadfuls at all and that De Ternant, like Haining, was not always trustworthy.[46] One additional point against the likelihood that the story dates to the early nineteenth century is the homoeroticism of the female vampire preying upon members of her own sex, which to this point is only seen in Coleridge's "Christabel" (1816) and not again until *Carmilla* (1871).

Whether Grey, Haining, or someone else wrote "The Skeleton Count, or The Vampire Mistress," it is an excellent story. But we must remain skeptical of its place in literary history and whether it had any influence on later nineteenth-century vampire texts.

Théophile Gautier's "Clarimonde"

In 1836, French author Théophile Gautier published the short story "Le Morte Amoreuse" in *Le Chronique de Paris*. The title translated would be "The Dead in Love," but it was published in English as "Clarimonde," being named after its female protagonist. In my opinion, it is a work ahead of its time both for its use of Gothic themes and its psychological exploration.

The story begins when a young priest, Romuald, is about to be ordained. At his ordination, he sees the beautiful Clarimonde and is immediately smitten with her. He develops strong erotic desires for her that threaten to make him reject becoming a priest. Here we can clearly see the influence of Matthew Lewis' *The Monk*. Then Romuald hears a voice promising him love that will be greater than anything he could experience in Paradise. Despite the temptation, Romuald finishes the ceremony. Afterwards, he receives a letter with just Clarimonde's name upon it.

Romuald is soon after stationed at a parish in the country where he feels trapped as a priest. One night, a man comes to him to tell him a woman is dying who wishes to see a priest. The woman turns out to be Clarimonde, but she is already dead when Romuald arrives. Unable to restrain himself, he leans over and kisses her. He is surprised when she returns the kiss. For a brief moment, she seems to return to life and tells him they will be reunited. Romuald then faints as he sees the breath leave Clarimonde's body.

Days later, Romuald awakes, thinking he has dreamt the experience, but then Clarimonde appears to him. This time, she does not look dead but alive, and she convinces him to go on a journey with her. They travel to Venice where they live together. At times, Romuald wakes and realizes he is dreaming, but soon the dreams begin to feel more real to him than his real life, and sometimes, he feels like he is a grandee who is having nightmares about living a life as a priest.

Eventually, Clarimonde becomes ill and Romuald fears for her life. Then Romuald accidentally cuts his finger. When Clarimonde sucks the blood from it and is restored to health, Romuald realizes she is a vampire, but in his dream state, he is unable to resist her.

Meanwhile, Abbé Serapion warns Romuald that his desires for Clarimonde are born of sin and that the devil is trying to lead him astray. To prove to Romuald the truth, Serapion takes him to Clarimonde's tomb where they find her corpse and a spot of blood at the corner of her mouth. Calling her a demon, Serapion sprinkles holy water on her corpse. She then crumbles to dust.

That night, Clarimonde appears to Romuald in a dream for the last time, admonishing him for how he has treated her and asking him what harm she truly did him.

The story concludes with Romuald regretting Clarimonde's loss, although he knows her destruction has saved his soul. He then warns the reader never to look at a woman because even just one glance can cause one to lose his soul.

While "Clarimonde" is not a long story, it contains several elements worth noting that seem like harbingers of later Gothic works.

For me, the story's most remarkable aspect is the extent to which Romuald enters into a dream world. Each night he seems to be living happily with Clarimonde to the point where the real world seems like a dream to him. No other nineteenth-century author used dreams to such a powerful extent until George du Maurier in *Peter Ibbetson* (1891) where the characters engage in lucid dreaming, even communicating with each other through their dreams.

Clarimonde's mesmeric eyes are also worth noting; they share the hypnotic abilities of the eyes of the Wandering Jew and other vampires. Romuald, on first seeing Clarimonde, describes her eyes as:

> sea-green eyes of unsustainable vivacity and brilliancy. What eyes! With a single flash they could have decided a man's destiny. They had a life, a limpidity, an ardour, a humid light which I have never seen in human eyes; they shot forth rays like arrows, which I could distinctly see enter my heart. I know not if the fire which illumined them came from heaven or from hell, but assuredly it came

from one or the other. That woman was either an angel or a demon, perhaps both. Assuredly she never sprang from the flank of Eve, our common mother.[47]

The reference to Eve is interesting since Eve is usually the transgressor of Eden who brought sin to mankind, but Clarimonde is distanced here from her, clarifying that she is not human even before she dies, which suggests she was already a vampire when Romuald first saw her. Given that he also hears a voice, she may have telepathic powers and have purposely arranged for him to be brought to her when she is dying so she could suck his blood.

Perhaps most interesting is how once Romuald is in Clarimonde's power, he feels like he has two identities and is living two separate existences. He is almost like Dr. Jekyll feeling he is powerless to break the control one of his identities has over him, and he is even unsure which is his real identity. He states:

> From that night my nature seemed in some sort to have become halved, and there were two men within me, neither of whom knew the other. At one moment I believed myself a priest who dreamed nightly that he was a gentleman, at another that I was a gentleman who dreamed he was a priest. I could no longer distinguish the dream from the reality, nor could I discover where the reality began or where ended the dream. The exquisite young lord and libertine railed at the priest, the priest loathed the dissolute habits of the young lord. Two spirals entangled and confounded the one with the other, yet never touching….[48]

Romuald eventually realizes he must kill one or the other of the men or kill both because so terrible an existence cannot be otherwise endured.

Clarimonde's death scene is exquisitely described and plays upon the Eastern European belief that when the soul leaves the body, it takes the form of a butterfly. After Romuald kisses her, we are told, "The last remaining leaf of the white rose [which Clarimonde is holding] for a moment palpitated at the extremity of the stalk like a butterfly's wing, then it detached itself and flew forth through the open casement, bearing with it the soul of Clarimonde."[49] This detail is fascinating because it suggests Gautier may have had some knowledge of the Eastern European vampire tradition. The dead, and vampires particularly, were said to have a butterfly fly out of their mouths when they died, thus releasing their souls. Examples of this Eastern European myth can be found in Milovan Glisic's 1880 Serbian vampire novel *After Ninety Years* and James Lyon's 2013 novel *Kiss of the Butterfly*.

Finally, the story is significant because the vampire is destroyed through the use of holy water, a Catholic weapon against vampires. I believe it is the first use of holy water to defeat a vampire in literature and one of the earliest uses of a Catholic weapon, later to be joined by crucifixes and Eucharistic wafers in *Dracula*.

"Clarimonde" would go on to influence French works like Paul Féval's *The Vampire Countess* and directly or indirectly British works like *Carmilla* and *Dracula*. Today, "Clarimonde" is far from a household name—*Dracula* gets all the press—but Gautier's innovative additions to vampire fiction make it prophetic of the direction such literature would eventually take.

Alexandre Dumas' *The Thousand and One Ghosts*

In 1849, Dumas published a curious book named *Les mille et un fantômes* (*The Thousand and One Ghosts*), modeled on *The Thousand and One Nights* (*The Arabian Nights*). The premise is that a group of characters, including Dumas himself, come together to tell some strange stories. Despite the title, the stories do not concern ghosts or phantoms, but mostly speculate on whether the heads of decapitated people remain alive and capable of speech for several minutes after death. Rather than a thousand stories in the book, there are perhaps half a dozen depending on how you count them. Dumas may have planned to expand the book but never did.

The final story, which takes up four of the book's fifteen chapters, is told by a pale lady, who reveals her experiences with vampires in the Carpathians. These chapters have often been published separately in English under the title *The Pale Lady*. That title has made some critics, who have obviously not read the book, assume the title character is the vampire. Actually, she is not a vampire, but rather pale because a vampire has sucked her blood.

This vampire story is rather an anomaly among other vampire works of the period. It predates Dumas' *The Vampire* by two years, showing Dumas was already interested in vampire literature. However, it is not aligned with the Lord Ruthven tradition or that of female vampires. It was also written with the assistance of Paul Bocage (1824-1887), a French novelist and playwright who sometimes collaborated with Dumas.

The story is set in the Carpathians, which suggests Dumas may have known J. R. Planché's 1829 play *Der Vampyr* since that was the first work to associate the Carpathians with vampires. The story's pale lady, Hedwig, is the narrator. Hedwig's father is a Polish lord involved in the 1825 struggle between the Poles and Russians.

When all hope appears lost for the Poles, the teenage Hedwig is sent by her father for safety to the Monastery of Sahastro in the Carpathians. By this point, Hedwig's brothers have died and she knows the Russians will kill her father when they lay siege to his castle. On the way to the monastery, Hedwig avoids the Russians, but her company is attacked by Moldavian brigands. Hedwig faints during the attack, and when she wakes, she finds she has been captured. She has been taken to a castle where she is the guest of its owner, Gregoriska. He lives with his mother, Smerande. Smerande once had an affair, so she also has an illegitimate son, Kostaki. Both brothers fall in love with Hedwig, but she favors Gregoriska. Smerande, however, supports Kostaki's efforts. After Kostaki declares his love to Hedwig, he warns her he will kill her before he will let her be another's.

After it is confirmed that Hedwig's father is dead, Gregoriska and Hedwig make plans to elope. He sells some of his land so they can leave the castle and live elsewhere. One day, when Gregoriska leaves to make preparations, Kostaki follows him. Hedwig fears a confrontation between the brothers. When Gregoriska returns, he says he knows nothing of Kostaki's whereabouts, but he has blood on him. Then Kostaki's horse returns alone. Eventually, Kostaki's body is found and it is discovered he was run through by a sword. Smerande makes Gregoriska swear that he will avenge his brother's death in one of the story's most dramatic moments:

> "Go ahead and swear, Gregoriska, swear, on pain of my curse—do you hear me, my son? Swear that the murderer will die, that you will not leave a single stone of his house still standing; that his mother, his children, his brothers and his wife or his betrothed will perish at your hand. Swear, and as you swear, call down on you the wrath of Heaven if you fail to observe this sacred oath. If you fail to observe this sacred oath, then doom yourself to misery, the execration of your friends and your mother's curse."
>
> Gregoriska stretched forth his hand over the corpse.
>
> "I swear that the murderer will die," he said.
>
> At this strange oath, whose true meaning only I and the dead man perhaps could understand, I saw, or thought I saw, a dreadful and marvellous sight. The corpse's eyes opened and stared at me, more alive than I had ever seen them, and, as if the two rays they emitted had been palpable, I felt what seemed like two red-hot irons plunging into my heart.[50]

Hedwig fears Gregoriska killed Kostaki, but she has bigger problems. Smerande has continually tried to force Kostaki's suit, frequently telling Hedwig, "Kostaki loves you." Now that Kostaki is dead, Smerande continues to say the same thing, using present tense as if Kostaki is still alive. She also gives Hedwig widow's weeds to wear. At night, Hedwig feels like an insect bit her, and she becomes weak and pale. Finally, she confesses to Gregoriska that she fears she is being attacked by a vampire (presumably Kostaki).

Gregoriska and Hedwig marry, and then he tells her his plan to capture and destroy the vampire. He has her lie in bed with a branch of boxwood (a type of evergreen) that has been consecrated by a priest and is still wet with holy water. (Dumas here clearly borrowed from Gautier, who first used holy water to fight vampires.) Hedwig places this talisman to her lips while she awaits the vampire while Gregoriska conceals himself.

Kostaki, the vampire, now enters:

> Then I distinctly heard the noise of those slow and deliberate footsteps echoing on the stairs and coming up to my door.
>
> Then my door slowly opened, quite noiselessly, as if pushed open by a supernatural force, and then….
>
> I saw Kostaki, as pale as I had seen him on the litter; his long black hair, falling loosely to his shoulders, was dripping with blood; he was wearing his usual clothes, but his shirt was cut away at his breast and revealed a bleeding wound. Everything about him was dead and corpselike… his flesh, his clothes, his gait…only his eyes, those terrible eyes, were alive.[51]

As Kostaki and Hedwig stare at one another, Gregoriska emerges from his hiding place behind the wooden stalls, "looking like the exterminating angel, holding his sword."[52] He stops to make the sign of the cross. He demands Kostaki answer his questions, which results in Kostaki's confession that Gregoriska did not kill him but rather he ran onto Gregoriska's sword. Gregoriska orders him to his tomb, but he refuses unless Hedwig will go with him. Gregoriska then takes his consecrated sword and presses it to Kostaki's raw wound, forcing him to retreat.

The retreat takes an hour as Gregoriska forces Kostaki back to the tomb, his eyes flashing all the way. Hedwig follows to watch the proceedings.

Once they reach the tomb, Gregoriska tells Kostaki to repent, but he refuses, so Gregoriska plunges his sword into Kostaki, destroying him. Gregoriska then instructs Hedwig to take a handful of the earth that has been saturated with Kostaki's blood to put on her vampire bite to protect her. Hedwig now hopes to enjoy married life, but Gregoriska tells her that his battle with death will cause his own death. She kisses Gregoriska goodbye as he dies beside his brother.

The story ends with Smerande telling Hedwig that her family, the Bronkovans, have been cursed to the third and fourth generation because one of them killed a priest, but now the curse is over. She says she will leave all her fortune to Hedwig when she dies. Hedwig then travels to France to live, stating that her health returned and "the only mark I bear of this event is the deathly pallor that accompanies to the grave every creature that has suffered a vampire's kiss."[53]

The story is the first in which a vampire haunts his family across generations, predating Boucicault's plays in which the vampire returns every century to attack his family members. Despite that similarity, the story does not seem to have had a major influence on the expansion of vampire lore. However, it paved the way for Dumas' greater achievement in his play *The Vampire*.

George W. M. Reynolds' *The Necromancer*

George W. M. Reynolds' *The Necromancer* was serialized in *Reynolds's Miscellany* from December 27, 1851 to July 31, 1852. Although it does not contain a vampire, I am including it in this discussion because it was clearly influenced by earlier depictions of Lord Ruthven, plus it uses the Faust legend, which Reynolds had previously used in the novel named for that character, as we saw in Chapter 5. Despite the lack of an actual vampire in the novel, the main character's situation is similar to that of other vampire characters we have explored. Furthermore, while Reynolds does not use the name Ruthven in this novel, he must have been familiar with the Lord Ruthven vampire tradition since in his earlier novel *May Middleton* (1854-6), there is a General Ruthven with a daughter Josephine Ruthven, and in *Kenneth, a Romance of the Highlands* (1851), there is Sir Alberic Ruthven of Stirling Castle.[54] None of these characters are vampires but the use of the name suggests Reynolds was capitalizing upon its popularity. That said, it is a legitimate Scottish surname dating back to the Middle Ages.

The necromancer of the title is Lord Danvers, a man who has made a pact with Satan to obtain several incredible powers, including perpetual youth and the ability to change his appearance. In exchange, he must, over the course of 150 years, convince six women to elope and marry him, thus allowing Satan to take their souls. Danvers began his pact in 1390, but the novel opens in 1510 when he has acquired the soul of Clara Manners, his fifth victim. The story then jumps ahead six years. We are not fully let into Danvers' secret until the end of the novel, but it is clear from the beginning that he has supernatural powers and is up to no good.

Each of Danvers' victims has family members who have sworn to gain their revenge on him for what he did to the women he abducted from their families. What these people do not know is that Danvers is one person and not several generations of men. He has the ability to change his age and appearance, and he has taken on numerous first names.

The novel's major plot concerns Musidora, a young woman with a secret she will not reveal that has made her more quiet and hard than she was in her youth. At this time, King Henry VIII is unhappy with his wife, Katherine of Aragon, and it is believed he will divorce her and find a new wife. Musidora's relatives convince her father to have her visit them since they live near Greenwich Palace. Although they are in disgrace with the king, they believe Musidora is so beautiful that King Henry will fall in love with her and then they will be restored to their former positions at court. Things go precisely as planned, and soon Musidora has agreed to marry Henry. A secret wedding is held in which Henry produces a document from the Pope testifying to the annulment of his previous marriage and his ability to marry again. A violent storm erupts as soon as the marriage is over, and before long, all is revealed, including that Danvers has been impersonating Henry VIII.

As these events develop, the novel intersperses the tales of Danvers' five previous victims, as told by their relatives or descendants. These stories become rather tedious since it's clear Danvers will convince the maiden to elope with him each time, and the repetitive stories slow down the action, but they do explain each family's reasons for revenge.

Eventually, Musidora escapes from Danvers' clutches and marries her cousin. Many years then go by. Meanwhile, St. Louis, a relative of one of the other victims, who is in the king's favor, is visited by his ancestress in a dream and told to go to the Holy Land. There he meets the father of another victim. The man warns St. Louis that Danvers' time to finish his contract with Satan is running out, and St. Louis must stop Danvers from capturing his last victim. The old man gives St. Louis a crucifix to aid him in his efforts.

St. Louis returns to England and, with Musidora's help, goes to Danvers' castle on the Isle of Wight where Danvers is about to abduct his last victim. Musidora prevents him by using the crucifix to open the castle doors so she can make her way to Danvers and Marian, his latest proposed victim, who turns out to be Musidora and Danvers' daughter (the long kept secret of Musidora's youth). Horrified to learn he has nearly destroyed his own child, Danvers repents. Musidora then prays for him as Satan comes to take him, but her prayers are fruitless. The other souls of the victimized women are released and sent to heaven, but Danvers goes to hell with Satan.

The novel is rather long, but has plenty of excitement and Gothic trappings. Scholar Dick Collins suggests the novel was influenced by Eugène Sue's *The Wandering Jew* (1846) and Charles Maturin's *Melmoth the Wanderer* (1820).⁵⁵ The novel's generations bent on revenge may have been inspired by Sue's use of generations of families with secrets in *The Wandering Jew*. Melmoth's need to seduce young maidens might also be an inspiration, although the vampire stories we have explored seem a more likely influence. Other typical Gothic trappings include the incest plot, where a father nearly abducts his daughter—a plot that hearkens back at least as far as Mrs. Radcliffe's *The Romance of the Forest* (1791)—and nearly kills his daughter, which occurs first in Mrs. Radcliffe's *The Italian* (1797). The ghost that haunts the family—in this case, St. Louis' ancestor appearing to him in a dream—can be traced back to Matthew Lewis' *The Monk* (1795) where Raymond is haunted by the Bleeding Nun. Collins cites several other sources for the novel, including William Harrison Ainsworth's *Auriol, or The Elixir of Life,** a Rosicrucian novel; both Ainsworth and Reynolds' novels are concerned with acquiring extended life, as are most Rosicrucian novels. In both novels a man will attain eternal life if he can provide the Devil with the souls of virgins who gave him their virginity out of love.⁵⁶ Another possible source Collins cites is Captain Marryat's *The Phantom Ship* (1839), in which Captain Vanderdecken must sail the Seven Seas until Doomsday unless he can find a woman who will die for love for him.⁵⁷

For me, the Ainsworth story that seems more directly related to *The Necromancer* is "The Spectre Bride," which I discussed in Chapter 3. There the Wandering Jew character must acquire a million victims and cast them into hell, but he is destined to enter hell himself in the end. Like Ainsworth's character, Danvers is compelled to collect victims whether he wishes to or not. All of these works are possible influences, and Reynolds may well have

---

* For more on *Auriol, or The Elixir of Life*, see my blog post https://thegothicwanderer.wordpress.com/2015/10/31/auriol-or-the-elixir-of-life-ainsworths-rosicrucian-and-faustian-novel/.

been indirectly influenced by them; such plots of previous books he had read might have been subconsciously floating in his brain rather than his directly copying their plots.

Perhaps most interesting is the role of the crucifix in the novel. Earlier, Reynolds had used a crucifix in *Wagner the Wehr-Wolf* for the title character to hold off Satan, but here it has the power to open locked doors behind which hides Satan's servant. One has to wonder if Stoker drew inspiration for the use of the crucifix in *Dracula* from Reynolds' uses of it. Another possible influence on *Dracula* is how Danvers drives his own coach, allowing him to cover incredible distances in impossibly quick times. In one particularly dramatic scene, Danvers promises to take Clara Manners' father to her at his castle; they arrive in just hours when the journey should have taken considerably longer. The scene reminds one of Jonathan Harker's coach ride to Dracula's castle; while that journey does not defy the barriers of time, both are filled with mystical atmosphere.

Certainly, *The Necromancer* is a much overlooked Gothic novel that deserves a key place in the history of Gothic literature, both for its use of previous Gothic literature and its likely influence on Stoker and other Gothic novelists. As I stated before, as a master of the Gothic, Reynolds deserves far more recognition than he has received.

Angelo de Sorr's *The Vampires of London*

Originally titled *Le Vampire* and published in 1852, this satiric novel by French novelist Angelo de Sorr (pseudonym of Ludovic Sclafer, 1822-1881) is a sign that the reading public was again growing tired of the Gothic. While at times the novel takes the Gothic seriously, at other times it is clearly written in a tongue-in-cheek manner. Indeed, we might call it the first postmodern vampire novel because of the way the narrator continually inserts himself into the text to make metafiction remarks such as that he is only following, not creating the characters. It's not even really clear if the novel contains a vampire or the term is only used metaphorically to describe how people prey upon one another.

The story largely resembles in tone, when being serious, that of Féval's *Les Mystères de Londres* with a convoluted plot and characters who have various identities and disguises. The novel's antihero, Horatio Mackinguss, is somewhat reminiscent of Féval's Rio Santo, but without any noble purpose amid the destruction he creates.

Like most Gothic novels, the plot is too complicated to summarize in full so I will hit only highlights. The story opens in an inn in a small town in France where Horatio Mackinguss, the second son of a Scottish lord, and Robert de Rolleboise, a Frenchman, are dining. Then Monsieur le Vicomte de Saint-Loubès arrives. While the narrator has no problem interjecting his remarks about the process of writing a novel into the narrative, he also uses Saint-Loubès as a voice of parody. The men tell tales of strange events, causing Saint-Loubès to complain about the boredom of being in a romantic inn where no doubt something romantic or dramatic will happen and how dull that all is. By this point, French Romanticism was on a decline and the comments reflect the overuse of its literary elements.

Of course, something dramatic does soon happen. Horatio Mackinguss goes upstairs, and soon after, gunshots are heard, causing Saint-Loubès to deplore how he's now stuck in some Romantic adventure. It turns out that Horatio's dog had previously been bit and was rabid, but only now have the rabies developed enough that he has attacked his master. The gunshot came from Horatio shooting his dog. Horatio was bit by the rabid dog, but a doctor cauterizes the wound so it won't be infected and Horatio appears to be fine. More than a year will pass before the novel ends, and only near the end will Horatio become rabid. (Rabies usually develops in two to eight weeks but in rare cases can develop as quickly as ten days or as slowly as two years, so Sorr's depiction of rabies is not beyond the realm of belief.[58])

In time, Horatio marries Olivia, the second daughter of the Duke of Firstland. Most of the novel from this point is set in London among fashionable British society or at the Castle of the Falls in Scotland, which is allegedly haunted by vampires. The Scottish setting reflects the earlier Ruthven plays set in Scotland, a country the French thought just as exotic as Transylvania. Olivia has an older half-sister, Ophelia, who is a sort of doppelgänger to her. Ophelia's mom died soon after she was born and her father married again to Olivia's mother. Olivia's mother always hated Ophelia and eventually tried to kill her by hanging her, but she botched the attempt and ended up hanging herself. Ophelia then fled, unwilling to reveal to her father that his wife had tried to kill his daughter. Olivia wants to make sure her sister doesn't return, so she visits a Jew in London who can help her. Olivia does not know that Antares is really Edgard, Horatio's brother, in disguise. Such switched identities are common in the novel. Olivia also hides her identity when she goes to visit Antares by dressing as a man.

The plot is somewhat pointless. In the end, Ophelia marries Robert and all ends happily for them while Horatio dies of rabies. Horatio bites Olivia before he dies, and she jumps out of a window, presumably to her death. Then Edgard realizes he has rabies also—it's not clear how he got it—and kills himself. In the closing scene, Ophelia and Robert read in the newspaper that a minor character, Lodore, has been hung in London for being a vampire, but it's not clear if we are to take this literally or not since Lodore has not exhibited much vampire behavior in the novel other than sinking into a graveyard, which benefits the resurrection man by letting him know where the most recent dead bodies have been buried. Certainly, Lodore is less of a vampire than other characters like Horatio, who prey on others.

The narrator rushes to the ending, claiming he forgot about Saint-Loubès for a while, but now Saint-Loubès shows up to remark how he was having a nice ordinary trip without any extraordinary landscapes and no one telling him old legends, only to complain that he has once again gotten caught up in a Romantic storyline at the novel's very end.

One of the novel's most interesting scenes is when Lodore gains power over Robert and convinces him to pretend to be the dead brother of Amadeus, who is supposed to marry Olivia. Robert pretends not only to be the dead brother but a vampire. He terrorizes Amadeus but tells him he doesn't want his blood; he wants his reason. As a result, Amadeus goes insane and ends up in an asylum. One wonders if Stoker knew the novel given that the main character goes insane because of a vampire pursuing him—it relates to both Harker and Renfield's situations, but also recalls the earlier Ruthven tales where Aubrey is thought insane for declaring Ruthven is a vampire.

The narrator's tone makes it clear we are not to take the novel too seriously, to the point of degrading the very literary genre in which the novel is written. In Chapter 5, in describing Robert, we are told:

> Robert also possessed a certain mental illness that imaginative souls will doubtless appreciate. Rolleboise was one of those young heads imbued with an exaggerated literature in which passions are twisted and tormented to the utmost stab of pain. By virtue of plunging his heart into illusions, he had become one of those imaginary lovers who dream of an excessive sentiment, cataleptic delights and impossible joys: one of those illuminated minds who take seriously the mad ideas of intoxicated poets, absorbing them avidly and trustingly, and then seeking bravely to make them a palpable reality, to make the sunbeam concrete. His mind was saturated to the point of indigestion with all that crazy literature of the nineteenth century. He had sated himself with so many fantasies and novels that he had come, by a thousand hallucinatory gradations, to believe in them.[59]

Robert's romantic delusions lead him to pursuing Madame de Lormont, even though she is married, but eventually, he comes to his senses, and while he is susceptible to Lodore's powers, in the end, he is the closest thing the novel has to a hero since he's almost the only man left standing and he ends up happily married.

While *The Vampires of London* tries not to take itself too seriously, allowing the narrator to interrupt for a few short paragraphs now and then, these interruptions are so infrequent that the reader almost forgets the story is a parody of the Gothic and gets caught up in the Romantic melodrama as if we are to take it seriously. That the novel has this kind of power over the reader transforms it into the vampire mesmerizing us, and when the narrator breaks the spell, we find ourselves laughing that like Robert, we can let "all that crazy literature of the nineteenth century" cause our imaginations to run away with us. Once we know the vampire is hanged and the novel is over, we can safely return to reality before we go insane like Amadeus.

If Jane Austen had been French, male, and lived a few decades later, *The Vampires of London* may well have been the Gothic parody she would have written instead of *Northanger Abbey*. However, I think she would have personally disapproved of Sorr. We can get an idea of what he was like from one incident in his life. Just before he finished the novel, Sorr went hiking in the Pyrenees and fell into a precipice. His body was not found but the *Universal Monitor* announced his death and two friends wrote obituaries for him. Sorr then reappeared and admitted the announcement of his death was a hoax concocted by the Marquis Laurent de Villedeuil, director of *Le Soleil*, a newspaper Sorr collaborated with. Sorr hadn't denied the news because he hoped it would have a positive effect on the novel's sales.[60]

Given Sorr's ability to resurrect himself in this way, I'm sure he would be pleased to know his novel has been resurrected with an English translation by Brian Stableford in recent years. Its biting humor should delight many modern readers.

Pierre-Alexis Ponson du Terrail's Vampire Novels

While Sorr chose in *The Vampires of London* to parody the Gothic, the genre was far from dead. Readers, however, were tending toward wanting less of the supernatural being real in their fiction, so a revival of Mrs. Radcliffe's explanations for supernatural events resulted.[61] Pierre-Alexis Ponson du Terrail was up to the task of writing novels that were almost the film noir of his day, taking readers on a wild ride through seemingly inexplicable plots filled with supernatural events that in the end he would explain away.

In his introduction to Ponson du Terrail's *The Vampire and the Devil's Son*, translator Brian Stableford remarks, "nothing succeeds like excess," and nothing could be truer of Ponson du Terrail's methods. A writer of feuilletons like Dumas and Féval, Ponson du Terrail wrote in a slapdash fashion, not taking the time to revise; consequently his sentence structure often leaves something to be desired. Given that he produced 2.5 million words a year and was often writing five serials simultaneously, this failure to revise is understandable, if not desirable.[62] Fortunately, Stableford's translations of Ponson du Terrail's novels are exceedingly readable, and *The Immortal Woman* I count among my favorite Gothic novels.

Ponson du Terrail's two vampire novels, *The Vampire and the Devil's Son* (*La Baronne Trépassée*, 1852) and *The Immortal Woman* (*La Femme Immortelle*, 1869), both create incredible supernatural events that are eventually explained. Besides Radcliffe's influence, the vampire themes were likely inspired by the popularity of Dumas' *The Vampire*. Both novels also reflect the female vampire tradition with female vampires tormenting the male protagonists. Since Ponson du Terrail's vampires bite people's necks, Gautier's "Clarimonde" is another possible influence. Neck bites would not become a standard vampire element until *Carmilla* and *Dracula*. Because Ponson du Terrail also explain the marks, the stories are as much detective fiction as vampire hunter fiction.[63] However, if the reader did not know a rational explanation would be coming, they might well believe the supernatural events are intended to be real as they follow the maze of otherwise inexplicable happenings. I will summarize the main points of each novel's plot and how Ponson du Terrail uses the supernatural.

The Vampire and the Devil's Son

In *The Vampire and the Devil's Son,* the main character, Baron Hector de Nossac, is about to marry Héléné, a woman he does not love, for her money. (Her name is likely no accident and pays homage to Lamothe-Langon's *The Virgin Vampire*.) However, the baron has made a promise to his mistress that he will come to her for twenty-four hours at any time, and she makes him fulfill this promise immediately after his wedding. When Héléné learns of her husband's infidelity, she decides to punish him. He is led to believe she has died of grief over his infidelities, and the reader is also kept in the dark, thinking she has died. Since the baron only wanted her money, this is not a problem except that she left a will stipulating that if he does not remarry within two years, her fortune will revert to her family.

The baron now embarks on a string of supernatural adventures. After embroiling himself in a battle in which he rescues King Stanislaus of Poland, he ends up traveling through the forest in Germany where he comes to the castle of the Black Huntsman. This strange being quickly convinces the baron he is the son of the Devil after the baron undergoes some seemingly supernatural experiences in the castle. The Black Huntsman has several sons and a daughter, and the baron agrees to marry the daughter. That night, the baron wakes to find a phantom standing over him. She turns out to be a vampire who gets into bed with him and sucks his blood, which he finds enjoyable.

In the morning, the baron's host reveals that he is not really the supernatural Black Huntsman but the Graf von Holdengrasburg. The baron begins to question his sanity, thinking he's dreaming since everything supernatural from the night before has now been explained to him, except how he got the bite marks on his neck.

The plot becomes more and more complicated as one event after another causes the baron to question his sanity. Eventually, he leaves the castle, but even then, he keeps seeing young women, including Gretchen, the Black Huntsman's daughter, who resemble his dead wife. He falls in love with each woman, thinking she is his dead wife and wondering if he is going mad. Finally, he has Heléné's body exhumed to convince himself she is dead. The sight of her decayed body makes him realize she is.

Then the baron attends a masked ball, hoping to find a new wife so he can retain Heléné's fortune. At the ball, he meets a masked woman who agrees to marry him. He tells her he is dying from all he has experienced, but by marrying him, she will become rich. He just can't love her because he only ever loved his wife. The masked woman now reveals that she is Heléné. She was not dead. She passed off her dead sister's body as her own to test him. Now that he has confessed she is the only woman he has truly loved, she will return to him as his wife.

The plot is convoluted, at times confusing, and of course, unbelievable, yet Ponson explains it all away in a manner that the reader is willing to buy. Even with the explanations given, we are required to suspend our disbelief. As Stableford points out, it's hard to believe Heléné would go to the trouble of disguising herself as a ghost and wandering about her husband's room for hours every night for months.[64]

Regardless of the faults that a closer analysis reveals, the novel is ultimately satisfying; the reader is not disappointed to discover the vampires were not real and is happy for the happy ending. The novel may be one of the first to depict a character gaslighting another, leading to the baron questioning his sanity. In the process, it raises interesting questions about what madness is. Certainly, the supernatural exists on the border of madness since it is not natural but supernatural, and therefore, not usually a part of reality. It is no accident that from Polidori to Stoker we encounter a series of characters who are insane or at least believed to be so by others and sometimes even by themselves.

The Immortal Woman

Ponson du Terrail's *The Immortal Woman* is structured on a similar premise of gaslighting a character. However, this time the alleged supernatural being is not trying to win a husband's love but to exact revenge on an enemy. Ponson du Terrail draws on elements of vampire and Rosicrucian novels as well as *The Arabian Nights'* story-in-a-story structure to create an elaborate mystery with all the excitement of a Dumas novel.

The novel opens when the Marquis de la Roche-Maubert is invited to a dinner at the table of the French Regent, Philippe d'Orleans, about the year 1715. At the dinner, people discuss how the Chevalier d'Esparron has mysteriously disappeared. He was invited by letter to a rendezvous with a woman. Later, a pinprick was seen on his neck. Then he was seen getting into a boat with a woman wearing a mask. He has not been seen since.

The marquis, who is seventy, shares that he had a similar experience in his youth. When he was nineteen, he received a letter inviting him to meet a young woman in a boat. A hood was placed over his head to prevent him from seeing where they were going. She took him to her boudoir where she removed his mask and he saw how beautiful she was. They spent many days together until he realized she was a vampire. She told him she was a hundred years old and had known Henry IV. Her mother had come to France with Queen Marie de Medici and was burned as a witch. Her mother asked her to avenge her, and she could not die or grow old until the revenge was carried out, which would happen when the great-grandson of the man who had betrayed her was killed. She had known many lovers, but she told the marquis she loved only him and would break her promise to revenge her mother if he so wished. He decided the little bit of blood she needed from him to remain youthful was not a large sacrifice and agreed to stay with her.

However, once the vampire got all the blood she needed, she expelled the marquis from her life. He then discovered she was collecting blood from other young men. Eventually, he learned she was not a vampire but a witch in search of the philosopher's stone. To create gold, she needed blood as an ingredient. In time, she was arrested and burned as a witch. As she died, she cried out that she was immortal.

Soon after the witch's death, a man saw an old woman with a black goat go into the witch's house. He followed her and found inside the house thirty men dancing who all had pinpricks on their necks. They were the witch's past victims. The old woman then poured out the ashes of the woman who was burnt, at which point, the man fainted. When he woke, he saw the beautiful woman who had been burnt and she told him she was immortal.

At this point, the marquis' story is interrupted by the entry of d'Esparron, who confirms he has been with a beautiful woman, but she is no vampire. The marquis says he would have protested the same when he was young, but because of the similarity of d'Esparron's experience to his, the marquis decides to get to the bottom of the mystery. In time, he meets the woman d'Esparron has been involved with and learns her name is Janine. The marquis declares his love for her, believing she is the witch from his past, but she tells him he is foolish and interfering in her plans. Before he knows it, the marquis finds himself imprisoned.

Meanwhile, Janine and d'Esparron reveal to the Regent that they are planning revenge on the Margrave Prince of Lansbourg-Nassau who was previously responsible for Janine being burnt at the stake. As the novel progresses, we learn Janine is not immortal but the niece of the woman who was burned. Her mother had pretended to be her sister after she was burnt, and now Janine, who resembles her aunt and mother, is taking up the challenge of revenge on the family. While all these explanations rationalize the novel's supernatural events, the supernatural element persists because Janine dreams of her mother urging her on to revenge.

Her mother even appears like a phantom to her, which crosses the line of reality into the supernatural.

Throughout, the novel keeps the reader in suspense and longing to know whether the marquis will escape and the margrave be punished. I won't reveal the ending since it is not directly related to our interest in the supernatural. However, the novel makes it easy to understand why Ponson du Terrail was so popular in his day.

Ponson du Terrail did have his detractors. The Comte Auguste Villiers de l'Isle Adam mocked him in his satirical novella *Claire Lenoir* (1867). It features an anti-hero named Tribulat Bonhomet, supposedly an archetype of bourgeois crassness who waxes lyrical on the virtues of the unnamed but easily recognizable Ponson du Terrail. Praise from the anti-hero implies Ponson du Terrail was not a good writer.[65] That said, I find *Claire Lenoir* and just about everything else Villiers de l'Isle Adam wrote practically unreadable, so his opinions hold little merit for me. By comparison, Prosper Mérimée, in an 1865 letter to Stendhal, praised Ponson du Terrail, stating, "There is but one man of genius at present, and that is Ponson du Terrail. Have you read any of his serials? No one handles crime and murder like him. I am delighted by them."[66]

Ponson du Terrail would write a third novel with a vampire component, *L'Auberge de la Rue des Enfants Rouges* (*The Inn in the Street of the Red Children*) (1876). Unfortunately, this work has not yet been translated into English.

Despite his fabulous Gothic plots, today Ponson du Terrail is best known for creating the character Rocambole, a traveler who has fantastic adventures. He appears in nine books by Ponson du Terrail, including *Les Misères de Londres* (*The Miseries of London*), a clear play on Sue and the city mysteries genre. However, Ponson du Terrail's work deserves far more recognition beyond Rocambole.

Léon Gozlan's *The Vampire of the Val-de-Grâce*

Léon Gozlan's 1861 novel *The Vampire of the Val-de-Grâce* continues the treatment Ponson du Terrail began of vampires being metaphorical and the supernatural being unreal and explainable. The novel was published with two other stories in *Le Faubourg mystérieux* (*The Mysterious Neighborhood*) in 1861 in two volumes. The first volume contained the story "Encore une âme vendue au diable" ("Another Soul Sold to the Devil"), followed by *The Vampire of the Val-de- Grâce*, which is novel length. The second volume contained the story "La Folle du no. 16" ("The Madwoman in No. 16") and the short story "Le Portefeuille de maroquin noir" ("The Black Morocco-Leather Wallet").[67] Brian Stableford's 2012 translation for Black Coat Press contains only the two stories in the first volume.

Given that the Faust compact with the Devil is a common theme in the Gothic, it's worth noting that "Another Soul Sold to the Devil" is a Faust-like story of a painter who does not get the respect he believes he deserves, so he sells his soul to the devil in exchange for artistic acclaim. After becoming famous and rich, marrying, and then having his wife cheat on him, he wakes in a garret to find himself still poor and unacclaimed, but he begins to work hard to achieve artistic stature. The story concludes by saying that the only devil is our imagination. In a similar manner, the supernatural events in *The Vampire of the Val-de-Grâce* will ultimately be explained.

The Vampire of the Val-de-Grâce opens in 1849 when Dr. Kanali arrives in Paris with his wife and daughter, Marthe, during a cholera epidemic. Eventually, we get the family's backstory. Dr. Kanali has adopted the surname of his wife's father, the famous Dr. Salomon Kanali, a chemist who also studied alchemy and experimented in embalming, believing it was the first step to resurrection. Hints of *Frankenstein* exist here. Dr. Salomon Kanali had found the secret recipe of the historical Dutch anatomist Frederik Ruysch (1638-1731) for embalming and making the dead appear younger. Dr. Salomon Kanali was eventually accused of murdering a man he tried to resurrect, but he managed to escape imprisonment.

Dr. Salomon Kanali then fell in love with a young Hungarian woman who was supposed to marry the Graf von Markfeld. The Graf is pale but youthful, signaling right away to the reader that he is a vampire, and that he already has had two youthful wives die supports that argument. When he goes to marry the young woman, his hand is as cold as ice and she is warned by a woman at the ceremony that she's about to marry a vampire. Her brother then fights and kills the Graf, who turns out to be Bem Strombold, a vampire who keeps returning to life under new identities. Because her brother does not drive a stake through Strombold's stomach (oddly, not the heart), he continues to cause trouble. Meanwhile, the young lady marries Salomon Kanali.

Dr. and Mrs. Kanali have a daughter who grows up believing in resurrection and vampires like her Hungarian mother. She falls in love with her father's pupil, Hermann von Rosenthal, but he dies before they can marry. Then she has a dream about him. At her and her mother's request, Dr. Salomon Kanali agrees to resurrect Hermann so he can marry the young woman, but he finds Hermann's tomb empty. The daughter, not believing him, goes to the tomb, finds Hermann's body there, and thinks her father has lied to her. Her father then goes with her to the tomb, but they are seen and realize they better flee to Italy or they will be arrested for body-snatching. Dr. Salomon Kanali dies soon after, leaving all his manuscripts with his daughter.

The daughter then meets an actor whom she agrees to marry if he will take the Kanali name. He consents and becomes the second Dr. Kanali. He leaves the stage to pursue the science of his deceased father-in-law. The couple have a daughter, Marthe, and move to Paris where they live at a hospital, bringing us up to when the novel opened.

At the hospital, Marthe falls in love with her father's assistant, Cesar Casaneuve. When Cesar accidentally causes a fire in the hospital, people believe the hospital's staff is intentionally burning cholera victims and they become outraged. While it is soon revealed the fire was an accident, both Cesar and Dr. Kanali's family are asked to leave the hospital. The doctor then dismisses Cesar from his service.

Dr. Kanali and his family now take up residence at another sanitorium. Cesar, however, continues to love Marthe and refuses to give up on her. Eventually, Cesar becomes ill and dies. Marthe is devastated, but soon the Kanalis and the narrator (a male attendant at the hospital named Morel) discover she is secretly meeting with a soldier, who turns out to be Cesar. Madame Kanali now believes Cesar is a vampire and the resurrected Bem Strombold (aka the Graf aka Hermann de Rosenthal), who has been persecuting her family for three generations. This belief is interesting given that Gothic plots are family plots and the vampire, like an ancestral ghost, has persecuted grandmother, mother, and daughter. (For this reason, Kevin Dodd sees the story as influenced by the Ruthven vampire stories.[68] Similarly, Boucicault's Alan Raby haunts his family over generations.) Cesar is confronted and cast from the garden, but he vows he will return to abduct Marthe.

For five successive days, Cesar manages somehow to get inside the sanitarium walls and leave notes for Marthe that pledge his love and count down the days until they can be together. Because Morel and the Kanalis cannot explain how Cesar is entering the sanitarium, Madame Kanali's belief is strengthened that Cesar is a vampire. Morel, however, thinks Cesar is sneaking in by pretending to be one of the other attendants or in a cart. Morel and the Kanalis decide to hide and await Cesar on the night he plans to abduct Marthe. They overhear him tell her how he has kept managing to get inside. He tried and failed to do it the way Morel thought the only plausible explanation. Instead, given how bad the cholera has been, he has hidden in coffins and waited for the death-carriages that come every night to carry off the dead. The carriages are left unattended long enough for him to sneak into them to be transported in and out. He has made this daring move five successive nights, on one occasion nearly being disposed of as one of the dead. When he asks Marthe to escape with him in this manner, she agrees.

Before the couple can elope, Dr. Kanali comes out of hiding to give them his blessing. He states he will be proud to have a son-in-law so brave as to risk his life in such a way for love of his daughter. The novel ends on this happy note with any belief that Cesar could be a vampire put to rest. However, the novel never explains the vampire stories surrounding the Graf or Hermann.

Hiding in a coffin as a plot device may be original to the novel. Notably, a year later in 1862, Victor Hugo published *Les Misérables*. In Part Two, Chapter 8 of *Les Misérables*, Jean Valjean hides in a coffin so he can get out of the convent he previously entered by climbing over a wall. Valjean is nearly buried alive before he is rescued by the gardener Fauchelevent, who helped him plot the exit. Of course, the buried alive theme was around earlier as noted in Dickens' *A Tale of Two Cities* and his sources, but Hugo and Gozlan are the only authors I know to use the coffin device. While Hugo's manuscripts would need to be consulted to determine if he wrote his scene before *The Vampire of the Val-de-Grâce* was published or if he borrowed it from Gozlan, it is likely a coincidence. We know Hugo had plans for convent scenes based on his notes from 1847, and in May 1860 he made notes to "shift the convent" and made revisions to the scenes in January 1861.[69] Consequently, it seems unlikely an influence exist since Hugo probably didn't read Gozlan's novel in January of the year it was published, if he read it at all. The coincidence, however, speaks to how popular resurrection themes were at the time since both Gozlan and Hugo have their characters hide in coffins to make escapes.

Paul Féval's Vampire Novels

Given Rio Santo's many vampire-like characteristics in *Les Mystères de Londres*, it is no surprise that Paul Féval would turn his pen to writing vampire stories. The works I will discuss here were written in the 1860s and 1870s, but Féval's interest in vampires probably dated at least to the 1840s since vampire elements are clearly in *Les Mystères de Londres*. It has also been claimed Féval wrote a play titled *Le fils Vampire*, but this is likely due to a literary scholar misremembering the title of his book *Le Fils de Diable*, as theatre scholar Roxana Stuart discusses in *Stage Blood*.[70]

Féval would write three vampire works: *The Vampire Countess* (serialized in 1855 and published in book form in 1865), *Knightshade* (*Le Chevalier Ténèbre*, 1860), and *Vampire City* (*La Ville-Vampire*, 1874). These works show a knowledge of the vampire tradition and the works of Mrs. Radcliffe. They may well have influenced Bram Stoker, as I will explore.

The Vampire Countess

Féval's first treatment of vampires is an improvement, in my opinion, on his treatment of the Wandering Jew legend in *The Wandering Jew's Daughter*, discussed in Chapter 4. While Féval parodies the Wandering Jew, with *The Vampire Countess*, he is trying to write a serious Gothic novel. Some comic elements do make it into the novel, but Féval retains a sincere Gothic atmosphere. Only later in *Vampire City*, his final vampire work, would he fall into parody.

Still, *The Vampire Countess* is flawed from a lack of tight plotting—a fault of writing for serialization. It is also difficult to follow because it is a sequel to his earlier novel *La Chambre des Amours* (*The Love Nest*, 1866), which has not been translated into English but was the work that preceded it when it was republished in 1866 as part of his collection *Drames de la Mort* (*Dramas of Death*). Consequently, readers miss out on understanding fully the main characters and their relationships to each other. As with

The Wandering Jew's Daughter, it reads almost like a fragment of what could have been a great book. Only about one-third of the way through this roughly 300-page book does the story become really fascinating.

Furthermore, while the novel is mostly serious, as Stableford points out, Féval can't decide from the opening whether to take his vampire theme seriously.[71] He states that vampires are being talked about in Paris, largely because of some bodies found in the Seine, but he also introduces the metaphor that Paris itself is the real vampire, sucking the life out of people. Then he suggests Paris' problem is not real vampires but crime.

Regardless, the vampire countess is a very real supernatural being in the book. Still, she is not the typical vampire; there is no bloodsucking in the novel. Instead, the countess tears off the scalps of young women and wears them as her own hair, which makes her youthful again for a short time. Perhaps Féval knew of Elizabeth Báthory (1560-1614), the infamous Hungarian countess who liked to bathe in the blood of young virgins, believing it would help her to retain her youth. Certainly, plenty of other instances of efforts to be young exist in Gothic fiction, in line with the Rosicrucian quest for the elixir of life, so Féval would have had plenty of inspiration.

The countess is also very sexual, more so than any earlier literary female vampires. While she masquerades as Countess Marcian de Gregoryi, she is really Addhema, a legendary vampiress whose male vampire lover is Szandor. Szandor will only "kiss" her if she brings him large sums of money. Stableford points out that the French word *baiser*, which he translates as "kiss," can also mean "organism" in French.[72] The novel's final scene depicts Addhema and Szandor in the throes of their passion before Addhema plunges a red-hot iron through his heart and then hers—a murder-suicide. It is quite a sexual and disturbing scene.

Much more of *The Vampire Countess* is confusing, not necessarily logical, and fascinating. While Addhema passes herself off in France as the Countess Marcian de Gregoryi, she also at one point claims to be Lila, whom she says is the countess' sister. Lila seduces the main character René and tells him the story of Addhema. She does this because, according to Féval, a vampiress cannot have a lover unless she first tells him she is a vampiress. Lila gets around this by telling René the story but not clarifying that she is the vampiress. Later, René dreams that Lila turns into the countess, but when he wakes, it's not clear whether he ever was with Lila. This dream or hallucination is part of Féval's intentional blending of reality and the supernatural to keep the reader and characters questioning whether vampires are real, as well as Féval's own inability to be sincere about his vampire fiction.

The novel is set when Napoleon was First Consul, and Féval pulls Napoleon into the plot. One of the men the countess marries ends up accusing Napoleon of being her lover and challenging him; of course, Napoleon comes out on top. Later, the countess claims Napoleon has given her a letter so military men will do her bidding. In truth, she has a forged document. She also appears to be plotting to overturn Napoleon and is in league with the Brotherhood of Virtue. None of these political activities are completely clear in the novel—least clear is why the countess is politically motivated at all since politics cannot serve her purpose to stay young or achieve the money to pay Szandor for the kisses she craves.

Altogether, *The Vampire Countess* is a strange novel, much of it feeling like filler that Féval wrote to complete his required page-count for serialization since he wasn't sure yet where the plot was going. It is far from a perfect or even a truly powerful Gothic novel save perhaps for the final scene where Addhema kills Szandor and then herself. Féval lacks the intensity or sincerity of Eugène Sue or James Malcolm Rymer, which kept him from being a first rate Gothic novelist. That said, *The Vampire Countess* is an interesting novel for its historical place in vampire fiction and for being the most serious of Féval's vampire novels.

Knightshade

Féval's novella *Knightshade* (*Le Chevalier Ténèbre*, 1860) tells the story of two brothers named Ténèbre. One is a vampire and the other an oupire. Vampires drink blood while oupires eat human flesh.

The novella opens at a party. Baron von Altheimer is entertaining his guests with a story about the brothers. The baron tells how the brothers impersonated gypsies to get inside Prince Jacobi's home where they abducted his daughter, Lenore, for a ransom. The irony is the baron is one of the brothers, and his brother is also at the party disguised as a clergyman. In fact, the brothers are masters of impersonation. As part of his ruse, the baron claims his goal is to capture the brothers to bring them to justice.

In time, a young marquis who was at the party discovers the secret and begins to hunt down the brothers. In the process, he falls in love with Lenore. With Prince Jacobi's help, the brothers' resting place is discovered. According to Féval, the brothers must return to their graves once a year. If their hearts are burned with a red-hot iron, then the world can be rid of them. (This rule for killing a vampire—and oupire—is Féval's invention.) Although the two brothers end up killed, the story concludes by telling us their criminal activities continue, suggesting they have somehow risen from the grave.

Brian Stableford suggests that Féval never quite wanted to give full credit to the supernatural, so he leaves the reader wondering whether the brothers were vampires or they were just using vampirism as a ruse to confuse people and carry out their crimes.[73] Here Féval is in keeping with his contemporaries Sorr, Ponson du Terrail, and Gozlan. Stableford also notes that Féval is writing an early form of metafiction here where characters tell tales in which they include themselves. The novel itself references Antoine Galland, translator of *The Arabian Nights* into French, and Stableford refers to the novel as using "the Galland formula" of inserting stories within stories, although Galland did not himself create the framing device; it is original to *The Arabian Nights*. Stableford also says the novella is an example of the "Féval formula," which explains the supernatural as resulting from a criminal enterprise.[74]

The novella has a confusing narrative, just like in *The Vampire Countess*, *The Wandering Jew's Daughter*, and even *Les Mystères de Londres*, that makes you feel like you're reading a fragment or rough draft of an unfinished novel, or just a bad translation. The fault largely lies with Féval's inability to take his topics seriously, which makes him unable to reach the emotional depth other authors achieve to tie together their narratives.

One additional note of interest regarding *Knightshade* is that Lenore has a small pet dog named Mina. Did Bram Stoker borrow the dog's name for his heroine in *Dracula*?

Vampire City

Vampire City (*La Ville-Vampire*, 1875) is the most successful of Féval's vampire works. While it is a parody, it is clear in its intention, and therefore, lacks many of the faults of *The Vampire Countess* and *Knightshade*. The purpose of *Vampire City* is to parody Mrs. Radcliffe's novels and the Gothic. Stableford suggests it is the first real Gothic parody novel, although I would argue that Thomas Love Peacock's *Nightmare Abbey* (1818) and Jane Austen's *Northanger Abbey* (1818) are both earlier parodies, as is Angelo de Sorr's *The Vampires of London* (1852). And as Stableford points out, even the first Gothic novel, Horace Walpole's *The Castle of Otranto* (1764), can hardly be taken seriously.[75]

Regardless, Féval's parody surpasses anything prior to it. I agree with Stableford that it is a novel far ahead of its time and may be the first horror-comedy hybrid,[76] which is what the Gothic has largely devolved to in our own time. Because here Féval is clear in his intentions, his lack of sincerity is not grating but amusing.

Like many Gothic novels, *Vampire City* has a frame. Unlike other Gothic novels, however, the author writes himself into the novel. Féval begins by complaining about how the English are pirating his novels. Then a female friend named Milady (obviously fictional and perhaps a tribute to Dumas' character in *The Three Musketeers*) tells him she knows where he can get a wonderful story to write about. She takes him to England where he meets the ninety-seven-year-old cousin of Mrs. Radcliffe, who tells him a story about Mrs. Radcliffe that explains why she was so fascinated with the Gothic.

Féval refers to Radcliffe as Anna or *She* throughout the novel. Stableford compares Anna to the more recent character of Buffy the Vampire Slayer,[77] and not without merit since Anna ends up pursuing and helping to destroy a vampire. However, while Stableford states "Stoker certainly never read Féval,"[78] I am not so certain. Féval's depiction of Anna as a vampire hunter also foreshadows the male vampire hunters in *Dracula*. Féval was aware that very little was known about the details of Mrs. Radcliffe's life, so he felt she was fair game to fictionalize as he chose. In fact, he draws upon Sir Walter Scott's short biography of her in *Lives of the Novelists* for the few details known about her at the time.

The story begins when Anna Ward is about to marry William Radcliffe (her husband in real life). However, she leaves her home and bridegroom the morning of her wedding because she receives a letter from Ned, her cousin Cornelia's fiancé, that Cornelia has been abducted on the continent.

The abductor turns out to be a vampire named Monsieur Goetzi. Anna and a servant head to the continent. They first find Ned at an inn where he has been attacked by Goetzi and is lingering near death. They also meet a woman named Polly, who has partially become a vampire herself because Goetzi attacked her. She is his first victim, so she has a special connection to him. She says that only she can help kill him, which must be done by inserting a key in his breast at a specific hour when he is weak. (Féval makes up such rules about vampires throughout the novel, obviously going for exaggerated humor, but it is interesting that like in Bérard's novel and later in *Dracula*, the vampire's victim is also able to bring about his destruction.)

Goetzi eludes the vampire hunters again and again—partly because all of his victims become part of him in a sense, and they can even seem to double for him or at least serve his purposes. At one point, Goetzi escapes by crossing water and brings all his doubles or companions with him. They all enter inside of him, and then he lays flat on the water and floats on his back, feet forward, to his destination.

After traveling across Europe, Anna and her companions finally make it to Vampire City where all the vampires reside. They get inside the city and manage to cut out Goetzi's heart. Then the other vampires wake and begin to pursue them. Eventually, the vampire hunters are saved by celestial music that scares off the vampires. But the music is not created by angels but the godlike Arthur, a young nobleman whose true identity Anna's cousin says she cannot reveal. The celestial music is the result of Arthur playing a lute as he rides by. He is completely oblivious to how he has saved Anna and her companions. (At the very end, it is revealed that the godlike Arthur was really the young Duke of Wellington.)

Such humor pervades the entire novel, and much of it is directed at Radcliffe. For example, here is how Anna is described when about to leave on her rescue mission:

> Although she had not yet composed any of her admirable works, she already possessed the brilliant and noble style which Sir Walter Scott was to praise to the skies in his biography. Indeed, she could not help exclaiming: "Goodbye, dear refuge. Happy shelter of my adolescence, adieu! Verdant countryside, proud hills, woodlands full of trees and mystery, shall I ever see you again?"[79]

The reader familiar with Radcliffe cannot help laughing out loud because Radcliffe's heroines do talk in such affected style, although Radcliffe's seriousness makes it feel Romantic rather than absurd and the reader willingly enters into her Romanticized world.

In several places, Féval tries to use Radcliffe's method of introducing supernatural events and then providing a realistic explanation for them. In the following passage, he explains how at the crucial moment, a supernatural event, such as the characters falling into a pit that suddenly opens in the ground, is possible.

> The earth suddenly opened up to engulf them, thus confirming the presentments of our Anna.
>
> If you balk at believing in the instantaneous formation of a deep pit, I will freely confess that the personal opinion of our Anna was that a cave-in had already taken place, caused by the high tides of the new moon. The principal charm of a narrative like ours is its realism. And besides, in making further progress we shall encounter more than enough hyperphysical incidents.
>
> *She* was fond of that word—which could, I suppose, be rendered "supernatural."[80]

I have searched Radcliffe's novels and found no use of "hyperphysical" in them, though perhaps Féval meant another word lost in translation. Regardless, the intent is to parody Radcliffe, and it succeeds well in that aim. I am rarely one to laugh out loud when reading, but Féval made me do so many times.

Another fine example of how Féval gives mock rational explanations for the supernatural comes at the end when Anna has gotten herself into a very sticky situation, only to wake up to find it was all a dream and it is her wedding day. Féval, via Anna's cousin, assures us it wasn't all a dream because after she married, Anna went to the continent where she discovered the places she had visited and she experienced many other events that seemed to coincide with her dream—perhaps a sign that she had the second sight or was prophetic.

Ultimately, *Vampire City* was ahead of its time in its ability to mock the Gothic. It is surprising it has been overlooked for so long and Féval's fame has largely resided instead upon his Black Coats crime novels.

Finally, again we must ask: Did Stoker read Féval? As stated earlier, Stableford says no and notes that while Le Fanu's *Carmilla* (1871-2) did influence *Dracula*, Le Fanu also probably never read Féval so there is not even an indirect influence. However, Stableford says that Féval, Le Fanu, and Stoker all read *Dissertations sur les Apparitions des Esprits, et sur les Vampires* (1746) by Dom Augustin Calmet, which clearly was a huge influence on vampire fiction, so it is not surprising if there are some similarities in their works.

I agree some similarities could be due to Calmet, but I think the similarities between *Dracula* and *Vampire City* can't be wholly coincidental. I do believe Stoker could read French, and I already mentioned he may have borrowed the name Mina from the pet dog of that name in *Knightshade*. More specifically, Mina's relationship to Dracula may have its seeds in Polly's relationship with Goetzi. Throughout the novel, Polly is both longing to destroy Goetzi to get revenge and sympathizing with him. In earlier vampire works, female victims have only sought to revenge themselves on the vampire. Parody aside, Féval is the first author to make the victim feel sympathy for the vampire and also feel conflicted about her role in bringing about his destruction. Similarly, Mina Harker understands that Dracula's power over her is so great that she avoids learning everything the men know from fear she will betray them and use it to help Dracula. In both cases, this sympathy results from the vampire's hold upon his female victim, and Féval is the first author to employ sympathy as a plot device in this manner. Polly even goes so far as to become Goetzi once his actual body is destroyed. Nowhere does a vampire have another character serve as almost a double for him before *Vampire City*, and nowhere again does it occur until *Dracula*. I think Stoker may have read the novel and, setting aside its humor, realized its dramatic possibilities.

Another similarity between the novels is the use of animals. Neither Polidori's vampire, nor Varney the Vampire, nor Carmilla, nor any of the other pre-Stoker vampires appear to have doubles or control over animals who serve them. In *Vampire City*, however, the vampires often have dogs, bats, and other creatures serving them. In *Dracula*, the vampire not only has control over such creatures but can turn into them.

Furthermore, many literary critics have written about homosexual elements in vampire literature and particularly in *Dracula*. Stoker never goes so far as to allow Dracula to attack a male character, thus creating a homoerotic scene, but in Féval when the vampires awaken in Vampire City, they are described as "The men of considerable stature, but for the most part effeminate; the females, by contrast, were both tall and bold."[81] These sound like typical twenty-first-century stereotypes of effeminate gay men and butch lesbians. Stoker may have borrowed from Féval this sense of sexual perversion or gender confusion among vampires, something that, in truth, may have been inspired by the bisexual Lord Byron.

Finally, is it a coincidence that Arthur is the hero and savior in *Vampire City* and that there is an Arthur Holmwood among the male heroes in *Dracula*? Furthermore, he is the "Honorable" Arthur Holmwood who eventually becomes Lord Godalming, while Féval's Arthur turns out to be the future Duke of Wellington, and is himself "Honorable" as the third son of an earl in his youth when he appears as a character in *Vampire City*.

We may never know whether Stoker read Féval, and to some extent it does not matter. To say Stoker drew from Féval may in some ways limit Stoker's genius. To say Féval influenced Stoker may make it seem like Féval's work is inferior to Stoker's. It may be a detrimental argument for both their sakes. That said, one cannot help wondering, and I do not believe either author is more or less important if the line of influence exists. Both authors made significant contributions to vampire literature and deserve to be acknowledged and appreciated for it.

Joseph Sheridan Le Fanu's *Carmilla*

After so many French vampire novels throughout the nineteenth century, and a quarter of a century after the publication of *Varney the Vampire*, the vampire returned to British literature through the hands of Irish author Joseph Sheridan Le Fanu. His novella *Carmilla* was serialized in 1871 and then published in 1872 in his short story collection *In a Glass Darkly*. Today, *Carmilla* is the best-known British vampire story after *Dracula* and is well-known to have influenced it. Le Fanu set the story in Styria, which caused Stoker to consider setting his novel there, as evidenced by "Dracula's Guest," a chapter taken from an earlier draft of *Dracula,* in which an unnamed Englishman (presumably Jonathan Harker) visits Styria and encounters the tomb of a female vampire countess. Hmm, we've encountered female vampires several times now, but only one female vampire countess—Féval's Marcian de Gregoryi. Coincidence?

Carmilla always seemed like an odd duck to me beside the other three major British nineteenth-century vampire stories— Polidori's *The Vampyre, Varney the Vampire,* and *Dracula*—all of which have male vampire protagonists. In fact, there are no definite female vampires in British fiction before Carmilla, while there are plenty in French vampire fiction. Therefore, it makes sense to see the novel as part of the French vampire tradition.

The only likely British source for *Carmilla* of a female vampire is Geraldine in Coleridge's fragmented poem "Christabel" (1816). Coleridge's intentions with "Christabel" have never been solved since he left the poem incomplete, although many critics have argued that Geraldine is a vampire.* The poem's basic plot is that Christabel is in the forest praying for the safety of her departed lover. She comes upon a young maiden, Geraldine, tied to a tree. Geraldine claims to have been abducted by bandits. Christabel brings Geraldine home, and during the night, they sleep in the same bed. The ghost of Christabel's dead mother tries to protect her daughter, but Geraldine scares her off. The next morning, Christabel introduces Geraldine to her father, who realizes Geraldine is the daughter of an old friend, and he plans to take her home to her father. The fragment breaks off there. Critics have ever since discussed the poem's symbolism, whether Geraldine is a lamia/vampire or Christabel's lover in disguise, and the possible lesbianism.

The plot of *Carmilla* has many similarities to "Christabel." Le Fanu's story opens with Laura, the narrator, as a young lady living with her father in a home not far from the ruins of Karnstein Castle. Laura's father is English, but her deceased mother is from Styria and a descendant of the Karnstein family, although no one of that name is still alive. A carriage accident near Laura's home results in Carmilla, one of the passengers, being hurt. Carmilla's mother says she has urgent business and must depart immediately, but Carmilla is unable to travel so she is left with Laura and her father for three months. During this time, Laura and Carmilla become close friends, but Laura also slowly becomes ill. Meanwhile, Laura's father has some family portraits restored, one of which shows Mircalla Karnstein, a relative of Laura's mother. Laura notices how Mircalla resembles Carmilla, and Carmilla remarks that she is also descended from the Karnstein family, making the two young ladies cousins of some degree. After all, Gothic plots are family plots.

---

* This argument was made extensively in Arthur Nethercot's *The Road to Tryermaine* (1939). That said I have always been reluctant to believe Geraldine was simply a vampire. For my own interpretation of the poem, see my article "'Christabel': Coleridge's Conflict between Christianity and Celtic Pantheism." *Michigan Academician*. 27.4 (1995): 493-501.

As Laura grows weaker, the family is visited by a general who is an old friend of Laura's father. He is grief-stricken because his niece and ward recently died after being preyed upon by a vampire named Mircalla. Soon it is revealed that Mircalla and Carmilla are the same person. To save Laura's life, the general goes to the ruins of Karnstein Castle, and with the help of a baron, locates Mircalla's tomb and destroys her.

The similarities between "Christabel" and *Carmilla* are fairly obvious:

- In both works, a strange young woman is invited to stay with the family.
- Carmilla professes love for Laura, speaking like a lover to her while Geraldine takes Christabel to her bosom.
- Laura's mother is dead like Christabel's.
- Both Carmilla and Geraldine sense their victim's mother's ghost and shoo her off.

However, while Carmilla preys upon Laura as a vampire, it is unclear what Geraldine does to Christabel at night, nor does Christabel appear pale or drained afterward. Of course, Coleridge may have shown Christabel weakening if he had continued the poem. Christabel is described twice as in a "dizzy trance"[82] suggesting the vampire's mesmerism since Geraldine has "a serpent's eye."[83] Clearly, Le Fanu was building upon Coleridge's outline, even though he changed the story's setting from medieval England to Styria.

Carmilla satisfies as a vampire story based on its simple plot, but what adds depth to Carmilla's character is she may be an unwilling vampire and it's questionable just how responsible she is for her actions. Yes, Carmilla's strange remarks to Laura can be read to have the deeper meaning that she intends to prey upon Laura. For example, she tells Laura, "You are mine, you shall be mine, you and I are one for ever."[84] And when Laura questions her about the things she keeps secret, Carmilla states:

> The time is very near when you shall know everything. You will think me cruel, very selfish, but love is always selfish; the more ardent the more selfish. How jealous I am you cannot know. You must come with me, loving me,—to death; or else hate me and still come with me, and hating me through death and after.[85]

These statements suggest Carmilla is fully aware that she plans to kill Laura, to drain her of her blood, as she apparently did to the general's niece.

In other instances, however, Carmilla seems unaware of her actions or at least unable to explain them. Early in the novella, we are told Laura experienced a strange dream as a child in which she saw a female crawl out from her bed and bite her. The reader is obviously intended to see this as a foreshadowing of Carmilla later being in Laura's life. When Laura then meets Carmilla, Carmilla remarks that she recognizes Laura from a dream of her own, stating:

> I was a child, about six years old, and I awoke from a confused and troubled dream, and found myself in a room, unlike my nursery, wainscoted clumsily in some dark wood, and with cupboards and bedsteads, and chairs, and benches placed about it. The beds were, I thought, all empty, and the room itself without anyone but myself in it; and I, after looking about me for some time, and admiring especially an iron candlestick, with two branches, which I should certainly know again, crept under one of the beds to reach the window; but as I got from under the bed, I heard some one crying; and looking up, while I was still upon my knees, I saw you—most assuredly you—as I see you now; a beautiful young lady, with golden hair and large blue eyes, and lips—your lips—you, as you are here. Your looks won me; I climbed on the bed and put my arms about you, and I think we both fell asleep. I was aroused by a

scream; you were sitting up screaming. I was frightened, and slipped down upon the ground, and, it seemed to me, lost consciousness for a moment; and when I came to myself, I was again in my nursery at home. Your face I have never forgotten since. I could not be misled by mere resemblance. You are the lady whom I then saw.[86]

This implies that Carmilla is as astonished and confused about her dreams as Laura is. Carmilla may be faking her confusion, but why would she even admit to having had such a dream and then act confused by it? Plus, Laura does not recount her experience until after Carmilla relates hers, so Carmilla is not just playing off some fancy she has created after hearing Laura's story.

Later, the general states that the Karnsteins were a "bad family" with "blood-stained annals,"[87] but we are never told what they did that made them bad. Instead, we eventually learn Mircalla was the Countess of Karnstein and has been dead for more than a century. The baron who assists the general in locating Mircalla's tomb shares why confusion exists about the location of her tomb. A Moravian man had located and destroyed a vampire who had been tormenting the villagers. This same man was originally from Styria and had loved Mircalla. However, another man had committed suicide, which caused him to become a vampire. After the vampire visited Mircalla, she ended up dying. The man who loved her then had her tomb moved from fear people would suspect she also became a vampire and then they would disturb her rest. The irony is Mircalla did become a vampire—but not through any fault of her own, so we can feel some sympathy for her. Le Fanu was not interested in following the French tradition of having the female vampire seek revenge on the vampire who turned her. Instead, he simply let her become a lesbian vampire preying on innocent girls, although given that a man had loved her, we can assume she was heterosexual before she died.

Carmilla remains an odd story in the field of vampire literature. Carmilla is not a typical female vampire in the French tradition, yet some sympathy for her exists like in that tradition. Le Fanu hints at reasons to feel sympathy for her, but he never develops the reasons. Even after Carmilla's destruction, Laura appears to be frightened whenever she thinks of her. Similarly, Le Fanu's story haunted readers, including Bram Stoker, who would build upon it to create his own vampire masterpiece.

Marie Nizet's *Captain Vampire*

Marie Nizet's *Le Capitaine Vampire* (*Captain Vampire*, 1879) is a recently rediscovered vampire novel that has received some attention as a possible influence on *Dracula*. Like many other nineteenth-century vampire novels, it has been marketed by its twenty-first century publisher, Black Coat Press, as predating *Dracula*. This implies the general reading public thinks *Dracula* the first vampire novel, making all earlier vampire works like novelty items, which to some extent they are. Critics are divided on whether *Captain Vampire* did influence *Dracula*, but again, a literary work's value is not solely dependent on whether it influenced a more popular or superior later literary work. While I do not feel *Captain Vampire* as remarkable a novel as other critics have claimed, it is a worthy achievement based on its own merits.

The author of *Captain Vampire*, Marie Nizet (1859-1922), was not French but Belgian. She traveled as a young woman to Paris to study where she befriended Romanian emigrants. They inspired her interest in Romania and her outrage at Russia's efforts to dominate the country. In *Captain Vampire* and also in her poetry, she depicts how the Romanian soldiers allied with the Russians were mistreated in the Russo-Turkish War of 1877-8. Nizet published the novel in Paris in 1879 when she was twenty. Notably, she is the first female author of vampire fiction (unless we count the controversial Elizabeth Caroline Grey), and her young age warrants comparison to Mary Shelley, who wrote *Frankenstein* when she was eighteen. Unlike Shelley's novel, Nizet's was forgotten not long after it was published. It was only rediscovered by Romanian scholar Radu Florescu in his search for possible sources for *Dracula*. A later scholar, Matei Cazacu, appended a reprint of Nizet's novella to his own compound biography (in French) of Dracula (Vlad Țepeș), in which he speculated that the novel may have influenced Stoker.[88]

Before discussing the novel's merits and possible influence on *Dracula*, I will provide a plot summary. I will say I was disappointed in the novel's overall shortness and the simplicity of its plot.

Captain Vampire begins by introducing us to a group of Romanian characters, the primary ones being a young man named Ioan and Mariora, the girl he loves. It is May 1877 and the Romanians have joined the Russians to fight the Turks. The Russians treat the Romanians as second-class citizens, as is made apparent when the Russian officer Boris Liatoukine makes his appearance. Boris is known among his own soldiers as "Captain Vampire," even though he is now a colonel, because of events that happened when he was a captain. At that time, he was so disliked by the men under him that while away from camp, a group of them attacked him, stripped him naked, poured water on him, and left him to freeze in winter. When the men returned to camp, they were surprised to find him there before them, fully dressed and not at all chilled. Other rumors say that Captain Vampire has had two wives, both of whom died with red marks on their necks. Furthermore, he has a powerful gaze no one can withstand.

When Captain Vampire appears among the Romanians, he is so discourteous that Ioan grabs ahold of him in anger while the captain is still on his horse. Captain Vampire then drags Ioan behind him on his horse, causing Ioan to vow revenge. Little does Ioan know he'll end up serving under his enemy.

Mariora and Ioan become engaged before he goes off to war, and he gives her a copper ring. After Ioan has left for war, Mariora finds herself alone on the road when she meets Captain Vampire. He quickly mesmerizes her with his eyes so that she cannot depart. What happens next is not depicted, but it is hinted that Captain Vampire has his way with Mariora, though she later denies it.

During the war, the Russians continue to mistreat the Romanians who serve under them. After they torment Relia, one of Ioan's friends, Ioan confronts Captain Vampire about the abuse. Captain Vampire simply mocks him by showing him the copper ring he gave Mariora. Ioan is shocked by this turn of events. Captain Vampire then has Ioan and Relia lashed for their insolence.

The army now arrives at Gravitza Redoubt, which they plan to conquer. The Russians use the Romanians as fodder by sending them to fight first. When Relia is wounded during the battle, Ioan carries him to safety. Along the way, he tries to get help from various Russians for his friend, but they all refuse. When Relia dies, Ioan goes ballistic. He finds Captain Vampire, shoots and stabs him, and leaves a dagger from his father in the body. Ioan also removes the copper ring he gave Mariora from Captain Vampire's finger and puts it on his own.

Wounded, Ioan soon ends up in the hospital where he begins to hallucinate or be delirious. He dreams that Captain Vampire steals his ring. When he wakes, Ioan finds that the ring is gone, but he reasons someone in the hospital must have stolen it.

Once out of the hospital, Ioan returns home. He finds Mariora and, in a rage, accuses her of being Captain Vampire's mistress. She denies it, assuring him that nothing happened between her and the captain. The lovers reconcile and decide to marry.

The day before the wedding, a Russian soldier arrives with a gift for them—it turns out to be the copper ring and the dagger Ioan had left in Captain Vampire's body. Soon after, while visiting a church in preparation for their wedding, Ioan and Mariora see Captain Vampire. Of course, Ioan is shocked, thinking he had killed him. (This may be the only scene of possible influence on *Dracula*, resembling when Jonathan Harker is shocked to see a younger version of Count Dracula in London.)

The epilogue tells us that Ioan and Mariora marry and he becomes a prosperous landowner. Captain Vampire marries again, only to have his wife die soon after. After that, he continues to be insolent in the drawing rooms of St. Petersburg, but no woman is willing to marry him now that he has buried three wives. He is promoted to general, but rumors continue that he died and only his living corpse is now seen walking. Furthermore, anyone who tries to find out more about him ends up dead.

Captain Vampire has been called an anti-war novel, although it is less against war itself than against the Russians and how they treated the Romanians. While Captain Vampire is the primary vampire figure in the novel, Russia is also treated like a vampire. Historically, Romania had agreed to allow the Russians to travel through its territory to attack the Turks. Nizet describes this event as the Russians "descending like locusts upon the magnificent country of Rumania, which had been surrendered to them as prey."[89] Nizet leaves it vague as to whether Captain Vampire is really a vampire or just the subject of rumors. Translator Brian Stableford suggests that Ioan's imagination is active and he may actually have hallucinated the entire murder of Captain Vampire. It is also possible, according to Stableford, that Mariora is not honest with Ioan about what happened between her and Captain Vampire. The novel certainly has some holes, and the nineteen-year-old Nizet may simply not have been up to the task of creating a more seamless plot.[90] I agree with Stableford on all these points.

As for whether the novel influenced *Dracula*, the evidence seems minimal. One of the most interesting points is the novel's Romanian setting. While earlier vampire novels have referenced Romania in relation to vampires, this is the first to be set there, the Carpathians aside. Jules Verne's *The Carpathian Castle*, discussed below, is also set in Romania, and it is more likely Stoker was familiar with that work, though perhaps Verne read and was influenced by Nizet's novel, thus creating an indirect influence on Stoker. All that said, Stoker set his novel in Transylvania, not Romania. At the time Nizet, Verne, and Stoker wrote their novels, Transylvania was not a part of Romania but of the Austro-Hungarian Empire. It would only become part of Romania at the end of World War I.

Matei Cazacu's argument for *Captain Vampire*'s influence on *Dracula* relies on parallels he sees between the novels, namely that the main character is a male aristocrat, he possesses hypnotic powers, and he attacks the hero's fiancée.[91] However, as Brian Stableford points out, these similarities between the novels are equally similarities with Polidori's original story and that of his successors, and it is far more likely Stoker was influenced directly by Polidori or perhaps Dumas' play than by Nizet.[92]

However, British Gothic scholar Marie Mulvey-Roberts makes some good arguments for the possibility that Stoker would have read the novel. First off, he likely had a reading knowledge of French, especially since his parents moved to France in 1872, and we know he traveled there often.[93] Consequently, his picking up a copy of the novel in France when it was published is possible. Mulvey-Roberts also elaborates on a second argument Cazacu makes that Stoker's brother had served as a physician in the Turkish army that fought in Bulgaria during the Russo-Turkish war, suggesting this connection may have attracted Stoker to the book.[94] George Stoker published a book in 1878 about his experiences titled *With 'The Unspeakables;' or Two Years' Campaigning in European and Asiatic Turkey*. Stoker himself discusses his brother's exploits in his book *Personal Reminiscences of Henry Irving*. Mulvey-Roberts suggests George Stoker's knowledge of the Balkans may have been a resource to Stoker in writing both novels he set in Eastern Europe, *Dracula* and *The Lady of the Shroud*. Furthermore, Stoker would have been sympathetic to Nizet's negative depiction of the Russians since at the time Russia was a threat to British imperialism in the Balkans.[95]

Until the 1970s, scholars largely dismissed *Dracula* as just a scary vampire story, but today *Dracula* is often interpreted as commentary on late nineteenth-century British imperialism.

Dracula is racist in its treatment of Transylvania, which was treated almost like a British colony in its day, and like Romania, part of the breadbasket of Europe due to its fine grain that was imported to Britain and elsewhere.[96] Consequently, the land was desirable to the British and the Russians. It is not a stretch to compare Romania to India or British colonies in Africa for how Great Britain treated it. (Ironically, today Ukraine is known as the breadbasket of Europe, and at the time of this writing, has its own Russian Captain Vampire invading it.)

While colonialism benefited the British people, many were uncomfortable with mistreatment of foreign peoples or the influence those people might have on their own citizens who served as soldiers. A fear of reverse colonization resulted, if not literally, in the negative effects British citizens might bring back home to Britain. This fear is apparent in several Victorian novels, usually in subtle ways—*Jane Eyre*'s madwoman in the attic, Bertha Rochester, reflects this since she comes from the colonies. Similarly, in H. Rider Haggard's *She*, the male characters fear the supernaturally power Ayesha might come to Britain. Stoker takes on this theme with *Dracula* where a main character from a (practically) colonized land, Romania/Transylvania, decides to colonize Britain. This sense that Romania is a colony and the victim of imperialism is first suggested in fiction in Nizet's novel, even if the imperialists there are Russian rather than British.

While I do not think Stoker was heavily influenced by Nizet's novel in creating his plot or developing his main character, he was well aware of the situation in the Balkans at the time of Nizet's novel and may have been influenced by the same situation that inspired Nizet to take up her pen. Perhaps he read *Captain Vampire* when it was first published and it simmered in the back of his mind, consciously or subconsciously influencing him as he wrote *Dracula*. We may never know the answer, and no hard evidence exists that Stoker read the novel, but it remains a possibility.

Regardless of any influences *Captain Vampire* had on Stoker or anyone else, it is a significant work in vampire literature for its

Romanian setting and its depiction of vampirism in relation to war and colonialism.

Anonymous' *The Vampire: or, Detective Brand's Greatest Case*

The anonymously written American dime novel *The Vampire: or, Detective Brand's Greatest Case* (1885) was only recently rediscovered and republished in 2022 by scholars Gary D. Rhodes and John Edgar Browning. While they have declared it America's first vampire novel, the possibility exists that its author was British. It was sold as No. 161 in the Old Cap Collier Library series produced by Munro's Publishing House. The title page lists it as "By the Author of "Star", "Harley Mayne," etc." By looking at earlier publications in the series, Rhodes and Browning discovered that "Star" was "By the Author of The Scotland Yard Detective" and that novel, No. 36 in the series, was credited to Hawley Smart. Rhodes and Browning suggest Hawley Smart may be Captain Hawley Smart (1833-1893) a British army officer who turned author.[97] However, it is unclear why Smart, the author of numerous novels published under his own name, would choose to publish an anonymous novel in another country. If it is America's first vampire novel, it seems odd an Englishman would have written it, plus the author would have been very familiar with the novel's setting of New York City.

The Vampire is far from great literature, but it provides many interesting elements that reflect the development of vampire lore in the decades leading up to *Dracula*. Modern readers will be hard-pressed not to think of Batman right from the start since the opening sentence is "Gotham is puzzled." Gotham is the city where the *Batman* comics are set, and although the comics traditionally suggest the city is located in New Jersey,[98] the term was first used as a nickname for New York City, beginning in 1807 when Washington Irving used it in his satirical periodical *Salamagundi*.[99] Numerous geographical references in the novel make it clear the setting is New York City.

The story begins when a policeman finds a rich man dead on the street. It is one in a series of recent similar murders. The policeman looks up to see a man in a black cape and hat that make him resemble a bird or vampire when he stretches out his arms. Later, the same mysterious man abducts a young woman named Helena from a ship arriving in New York. The man's identity is unknown, so he is frequently referred to by descriptive names in the novel, such as "the vampire" or "the assassin." In a couple of instances, the murderer even disguises himself as a woman. He makes remarks to the woman he abducts about how he will drain her blood to increase his life, which reflects blood transfusion themes and also the idea that other people's blood and youth can provide an elixir of life. In time, the man is revealed to be Victor Lee, a wealthy young man who hopes to marry into high society. Once Detective Brand captures him, Lee states that he is cursed by a madness that sometimes comes over him and he fears it will eventually completely control him. This madness theme predates Stevenson's *Strange Case of Dr. Jekyll and Mr. Hyde*, which would be published in 1886. Although Lee does not use a potion that brings on his madness as happens for Dr. Jekyll, the effects of his madness are largely the same. In killing his victims, he also likes to prick them in the neck to fool people into believing they were bitten by a vampire.

Lee says his madness began when he learned the truth of his birth. Born in the United States, he did not know his parents, but he was raised in Europe under the impression that he belonged to a wealthy Creole family. When he returned as a young man to the United States to claim his estates, he discovered he was penniless and the child of a quadroon slave. This knowledge drove him mad, and since then, he has preyed upon men like a wild beast. Lee's repulsion of his African blood reflects the obvious racism of the time. Later, we will see similar racism about African blood in Florence Marryat's *The Blood of the Vampire*. Plus, we saw such racial concerns in "The Black Vampyre."

After telling his story, Lee kills himself before Brand can arrest him. He does so by pressing a button on a ring that injects poison into his finger. He says the ring belonged to the Borgias.

The anonymous author tells a compelling story, but leaves a gaping hole in the plot. I suspect the author began writing without having yet decided who the murderer would be. Consequently, though Lee turns out to be the killer, he was earlier depicted as being on the wharf with his friend Morgan May to meet Helena when she arrived in New York, so it is impossible he could have abducted her. Even though Lee arrives late and does not see the abduction, he does not have the time to return to the wharf after the abduction because we later learn the boat capsized and he was found washed up on shore by a fisherman and his wife who took care of him for several days. This plot hole doesn't hurt the enjoyment of reading the story, but it does make the conclusion fall flat.

Rhodes and Browning describe the novel as a missing link in how vampires were perceived in America. They note that Polidori's story was known in America, but *Varney the Vampire* was never published there and *Carmilla* not until later. However, as we have seen vampire plays like Smyth Upton's *The Last of the Vampires* (1845) and Boucicault's *The Phantom* (1856) were known in the United States, plus Edgar Allan Poe wrote stories that seem to contain vampires, including "Berenice" and "Morella," both published in 1835, so vampire literature was definitely known in the United States. Rhodes and Browning also discuss how the novel rationalizes the supernatural, stating it began a new kind of vampire fiction and that it reflects an American trait to prefer realism. They cite Charles Brockden Brown's *Wieland* (1798) as an early example of the supernatural being explained in American literature.[100] These arguments may be true in terms of American preferences, but they ignore that Brown was writing in the tradition of Mrs. Radcliffe, and that French vampire literature, written in the same strain, had been explaining away the supernatural for decades, as we have seen in the works of Ponson du Terrail and others. While Rhodes and Browning seem to think later British vampire works wouldn't have influenced the story, I think the use of the name Helena might suggest the author knew Lamothe-Langon's *The Virgin Vampire* or Ponson du Terrail's *The Vampire and the Devil's Son* since both contain characters named Hélène. If so, the author may also have adopted the rational explanations for the novel from the latter's work.

Whoever its author and whatever its influences, *The Vampire* is a fascinating story of madness, secret identities, and crime in a large city. It owes as much to the city mysteries genre as to vampire literature in its treatment of crime in a large city, and it reflects that American literature followed the trends of British and French literature in its treatment of vampires. Perhaps Bram Stoker even read a copy of the novel while touring the United States with Henry Irving, though any direct influence on *Dracula* seems unlikely. It does, however, raise the question of what other nineteenth-century vampire fiction in America may yet be waiting to be rediscovered.

Jules Verne's *The Carpathian Castle*

Jules Verne's *Le Château des Carpathes* (*The Carpathian Castle*, 1892) is another novel that has been suggested as a source for *Dracula*, primarily because it is set in the Carpathians. It was not the first vampire novel or play set there, as we have seen, and it is not even a vampire novel, which made me dismissive of it on a first reading, but a closer reading reveals several similarities to *Dracula* that make it plausible as an influence on Stoker. Verne's works were translated into English almost immediately, so Stoker would have had easy access to it, probably in both languages.

The plot is not complicated and centers around a belief that a castle is haunted, but while Stoker allows the supernatural to be real in his work, Verne is of the school of Mrs. Radcliffe, providing explanations for supposedly supernatural events. In fact, the novel opens with the following statement:

> This story is not fantastic; it is simply romantic and nobody would think of classing it as legendary.
>
> Moreover, nobody would invent legends at the close of this practical and positive nineteenth century, not even in Transylvania, where the Carpathian scenery lends itself so naturally to all sorts of supernatural imaginings. But it is well to note that Transylvania is still much attached to the superstitions of the early ages.[101]

Later in this chapter, I will discuss how Stoker probably read Eric Stenbock's short story "The Sad Story of a Vampire" and changed his setting from Styria to Transylvania because of that story's opening lines. I think Stoker may have also read the opening of Verne's novel and decided to prove Verne wrong by inventing the legend of Dracula and setting it in Transylvania. Of course, we know Stoker started writing *Dracula* as early as 1890, but the Transylvanian setting and how Stoker chose to treat his story as supernatural in opposition to Verne's intention is hard to ignore.

There is little else between the two works that are similar. Despite some critics arguing that Verne's Carpathian Castle resembles Dracula's Castle, the castles really aren't similar. I will briefly summarize Verne's novel to dispel any myths about similarities and then point out where there are some legitimate comparisons that might reflect influence.

The story begins when a Jewish peddler sells a telescope to a farmer in the village of Werst. The nearby castle is believed abandoned by its owner Baron Rodolphe de Gortz until the farmer looks through the telescope and sees smoke rising from the castle. This discovery results in discussions at the inn about the situation and two townspeople deciding to try to reach the castle. This scene at the inn may well have been inspired by the inn in Dumas' *The Vampire* that results in his characters also going to the vampire's castle. The two characters who try to reach the castle meet several obstacles that they interpret as supernatural efforts to stop them, and consequently, they never get inside the castle.

Then Count Franz de Télek stops at the inn as he passes through town and hears the stories about the castle, including that it belonged to Baron Rodolphe de Gortz. The villagers have not seen the baron in twenty years, and since he left, the castle's beech-tree has lost one of its main branches every year. Eighteen branches have fallen, leaving only three now, and when the last falls, it is believed the castle will be destroyed. This superstition is interesting because it suggests Verne may have read Ainsworth's *Rookwood* in which the baronet dies whenever a bough falls from a tree. The villagers believe the baron must be dead, but Télek saw him just five years before in Italy; in fact, at the time, they were rivals for the affections of the beautiful Italian prima donna La Stilla. When La Stilla died, the baron blamed the count for her death.

The count decides to investigate the castle and has several strange experiences that rather remind one of the marquis' quest in Ponson du Terrail's *The Immortal Woman*, although the plotting is not as elaborate. Primarily, Télek is surprised when he hears La Stilla singing inside and even more surprised when he sees her image. Is she alive, or is she dead and haunting the castle? In the end, Télek discovers that the baron and the inventor Orfanik are living in the castle and through listening devices, holographs, and phonographs, they have created the impression among the villagers that the castle is haunted. Verne sets the novel a few years into the future at the very end of the nineteenth century to make the novel's technology seem plausible given it will likely evolve by then. In the end, the count realizes he has only heard a recording of Stilla's voice and viewed a holographic image. The climax comes when the castle is destroyed in an electric explosion.

The castle's destruction might be a sign that Stoker knew the novel. In the original manuscript of *Dracula*, Dracula's castle is also destroyed. Stoker wrote, then later crossed out, "From where we stood it seemed as though the one fierce volcano burst had satisfied the need of nature and that the castle and the structure of the hill had sunk again into the void."[102] Later, Stoker decided to leave the castle intact so the Harkers and their friends could visit it again years later. Possibly, Stoker changed the ending because he did not want to be seen as copying *The Carpathian Castle*, although he could just as easily have borrowed the idea of the castle's destruction from Poe's "The Fall of the House of Usher," in which the house splits into two and sinks into a lake. Really, there is nothing terribly original about the destruction of a haunted (or allegedly haunted) house or castle. Thornfield burns down in *Jane Eyre*, and there are countless other examples. That said, Stoker biographer Paul Murray notes that in *The Lair of the White Worm* (1911), Stoker does have a house destroyed by electricity, so it is possible Stoker knew Verne's novel.

Scholar Raj Shah also suggests Stoker read the novel based on the fact that both novels are very much interested in mechanical reproduction. The recording and holographic images in Verne's novel are mechanical reproductions of reality. Similarly, in *Dracula*, the characters continually reproduce the realistic events in mechanical means—Seward using his phonograph and Mina her typewriter.[103] The novel's influence on *Dracula* then is not in the depiction of vampires or other typical Gothic elements so much as the use of technology.

In addition, I think Stoker may have borrowed some of the concept of Dracula's ancestry from Verne's novel. Verne describes the Barons of Gortz in a manner not unlike how Dracula speaks of his own family. Verne states:

> The barons of Gortz had been lords of the country from time immemorial. They were involved in all the wars which ensanguined the Transylvanian fields; they fought against the Hungarians, the Saxons, the Szeklers; their name figures in the "cantices" and "doines," which perpetuate the memory of these disastrous times. For their motto they had the famous Wallachian proverb, *Da pe*

maorte, "Give unto death;" and they gave: they poured out their blood for the cause of independence, the blood which came to them from their ancestors, the Romans.[104]

Verne goes on to describe how, despite the Romanians' devotion and sacrifice, the people became oppressed, but have never despaired of shaking off their yoke for "The Roumanian does not know how to perish."[105] And then we are told that Baron Rodolphe is the last of his line.

Compare these statements to Dracula's words when describing his past:

> "We Szekelys have a right to be proud, for in our veins flows the blood of many brave races who fought as the lion fights, for lordship. Here, in the whirlpool of European races, the Ugric tribe bore down from Iceland the fighting spirit which Thor and Wodin gave them, which their Berserkers displayed to such fell intent on the seaboards of Europe, ay, and of Asia and Africa too, till the peoples thought that the were-wolves themselves had come. Here, too, when they came, they found the Huns, whose warlike fury had swept the earth like a living flame, till the dying peoples held that in their veins ran the blood of those old witches, who, expelled from Scythia had mated with the devils in the desert. Fools, fools! What devil or what witch was ever so great as Attila, whose blood is in these veins?" He held up his arms. "Is it a wonder that we were a conquering race; that we were proud; that when the Magyar, the Lombard, the Avar, the Bulgar, or the Turk poured his thousands on our frontiers, we drove them back? Is it strange that when Arpad and his legions swept through the Hungarian fatherland he found us here when he reached the frontier; that the Honfoglalas was completed there? And when the Hungarian flood swept eastward, the Szekelys were claimed as kindred by the victorious Magyars, and to us for centuries was

trusted the guarding of the frontier of Turkey-land; ay, and more than that, endless duty of the frontier guard, for, as the Turks say, 'water sleeps, and enemy is sleepless.' Who more gladly than we throughout the Four Nations received the 'bloody sword,' or at its warlike call flocked quicker to the standard of the King? When was redeemed that great shame of my nation, the shame of Cassova, when the flags of the Wallach and the Magyar went down beneath the Crescent? Who was it but one of my own race who as Voivode crossed the Danube and beat the Turk on his own ground? This was a Dracula indeed! Woe was it that his own unworthy brother, when he had fallen, sold his people to the Turk and brought the shame of slavery on them! Was it not this Dracula, indeed, who inspired that other of his race who in a later age again and again brought his forces over the great river into Turkey-land; who, when he was beaten back, came again, and again, and again, though he had to come alone from the bloody field where his troops were being slaughtered, since he knew that he alone could ultimately triumph! They said that he thought only of himself. Bah! what good are peasants without a leader? Where ends the war without a brain and heart to conduct it? Again, when, after the battle of Mohács, we threw off the Hungarian yoke, we of the Dracula blood were amongst their leaders, for our spirit would not brook that we were not free. Ah, young sir, the Szekelys—and the Dracula as their heart's blood, their brains, and their swords—can boast a record that mushroom growths like the Hapsburgs and the Romanoffs can never reach. The warlike days are over. Blood is too precious a thing in these days of dishonourable peace; and the glories of the great races are as a tale that is told."[106]

Stoker's passage is far more elaborate than Verne's, and also more dramatic since it is in Dracula's voice, but the same sense of pride in Romania/Transylvania's past lies in the words. Similarly, like Rodolphe, Dracula is the last of his race.

Even without vampires, *The Carpathian Castle* may well have inspired Stoker in selecting the location for his novel, the backstory of Dracula, and the use of technology to further the plot. Stoker also takes the superstition of Verne's peasants and turns their fears into reality in his novel, creating a truly supernatural tale.

Florence Marryat's *The Blood of the Vampire*

Florence Marryat's *The Blood of the Vampire* (1897) was published later in the same year as *Dracula* so it is unlikely it influenced or was influenced by *Dracula*. However, I have included it as an example of how the only female British author of nineteenth-century vampire fiction (again excepting the controversial Elizabeth Caroline Grey) treated the vampire theme. Interestingly, it took a female author—the daughter of Captain Marryat no less—to depict a female vampire in a completely sympathetic manner. The novel also draws on racial themes like earlier American vampire stories.

The novel begins in Belgium where Harriet Brandt is a guest at a summer resort. There she meets two Englishwomen, Margaret Pullen and Elinor Leyte. Margaret's husband, Colonel Pullen, is the older brother of Elinor's fiancé. Elinor is snobbish and not interested in befriending Harriet, but Margaret likes Harriet and takes her under her wing. Harriet reveals to the women that she is from Jamaica, where she grew up in a convent after her parents died. Prior to that, she lived on a plantation. She says outlandish things about how she misses the overseer who would let her whip the slaves when they were lazy. Now that she is of age, Harriet has used her inheritance to move to Europe.

Harriet begins spending time with Margaret and is fond of her baby. Margaret, however, is cautious about letting Harriet hold the baby, and soon Margaret is uncomfortable being around

Harriet altogether. At one point Harriet touches her, which makes Margaret feel drained of energy, and she begs Harriet to let go. Harriet seems oblivious to her effect upon people.

Also at the resort is the Baroness Gobelli, who is considered rather ridiculous by the resort's other visitors. She claims to have good social connections, but she is vulgar by continually bragging about them. She also claims to have communication with supernatural, invisible beings, and she is not above threatening to use them to wreak vengeance on those who offend her. Her husband, the baron, acts submissive to her, as does her nineteen-year-old son from a previous marriage, Bobby Bates. Baroness Gobelli also befriends Harriet, inviting her to visit her in England.

Meanwhile, Harriet spends more time with Margaret and her child until the child becomes severely ill. When Doctor Phillips examines the child, he cannot determine what is causing its illness. However, he recognizes Harriet's surname and says he knew her father. Then he reveals her family story to Margaret. Meanwhile, Ralph, Elinor's fiancé, visits the resort. He begins to fall in love with Harriet. Doctor Phillips warns Ralph to stay away from Harriet, but Ralph says he's no longer sure he wants to marry Elinor. Eventually, the baby dies and the season ends, so Harriet leaves. She travels to Brussels where Ralph is supposed to join her, but he does not. Then she travels to England with the Gobellis.

In England, Baroness Gobelli returns to her career of helping famous people with her spiritual powers, leaving Harriet to entertain herself, which she does by spending time with Bobby. When Bobby becomes ill, the baroness accuses Harriet of being cursed with both negro and vampire blood.

Harriet, becoming concerned she is causing those she loves to become ill because she is somehow draining their strength, seeks out Dr. Phillips to learn what he knows about her family. He tells Harriet her father was a doctor who performed experiments on his patients in a Swiss hospital that eventually expelled him. Dr. Phillips had also worked in the hospital, but he did not associate with her father. Later, Harriet's father moved to Jamaica, where he set up a private lab and experimented on the negroes, who finally revolted; they murdered Harriet's parents and burned down their house. The doctor tells Harriet her parents were never married, and her mother was a "fiend." She was a "fat, flabby half-caste" with "her sensual mouth, her greedy eyes, her low forehead and half-formed brain, and her lust for blood."[107] Harriet's grandmother had been a slave; she was bit by a vampire bat while pregnant, which caused Harriet's mother's blood lust.

Dr. Phillips advises Harriet never to marry because of her past and his belief that her negro blood makes her unfit for society. By this point, Harriet has still been having some intercourse with Ralph, but he now decides he can't marry her and have "piebald" children.[108] Eventually, Bobby dies from having spent so much time with Harriet.

In the meantime, Harriet has met Anthony Pennell, a young socialist and Margaret's cousin. He sympathizes with Harriet and does not care about her family background. Harriet begins to doubt the truth of the doctor's stories about her parentage. She also rejects the idea that she could be causing the deaths of those she loves; she thinks the stories were just made up to separate her from Ralph. She decides she cannot really hurt Anthony by loving him.

Anthony and Harriet marry, and for a short time they are happy, but we are told that "the savage in her was *not* tamed."[109] Eventually, Anthony starts to feel unwell, and then he dies in his sleep. Harriet, distraught, is comforted by a nun and considers entering a convent, but instead poisons herself. In her will, she leaves everything to Margaret. Enclosed in the will, Margaret finds a scrap of paper written by Harriet that reads: "Do not think more unkindly of me than you can help. My parents have made me unfit to live. Let me go to a world where the curse of heredity which they laid upon me may be mercifully wiped out."[110]

The novel is curious, both for being sympathetic to its ill-fated heroine, and yet racist in its depiction of her. It was immediately compared to *Dracula* by reviewers. In January 1898, a review in *The Speaker* claimed it was part of a "wave of imitations by inferior writers."[111] One has to wonder what these other alleged imitations were that appeared so quickly after *Dracula*. If they exist, further research needs to be done to find them, assuming they are actual vampire works. Since Marryat's novel was published so soon after *Dracula*, it is unlikely she was trying to imitate it. I have been unable to locate the novel's exact publication date, but *Dracula* was published on May 26, 1897, so Marryat would have only had seven months at most to read *Dracula*, write her own novel, and get it published, if she was trying to capitalize on *Dracula*'s success. That seems unlikely. Nor is there anything similar about the two novels.

The same review in *The Speaker* complained of the novel's sensationalism in terms of Harriet's illegitimate birth and her being the daughter of a mad scientist and a "voluptuous Creole slave."[112] These complaints are justified, but without these elements, there would be no novel. It is interesting that once again, the vampire threat comes from the West Indies, like it did in "The Black Vampyre." Also interesting are Harriet's father's experiments. We are not told exactly what the experiments were, but they involved "vivisection" practiced on animals, and Doctor Phillips states:

> in addition to his terrible experiments upon animals — experiments which he performed simply for his own gratification and for no use that he made of them in treating his fellow creatures — he had been known to decoy diseased and old natives into his laboratory, after which they were never seen again, and it was the digging up of human bones on the plantation, which finally roused the negroes to such a pitch of indignation that they rose en masse....[113]

The suggestion here may be that Harriet's father performed experiments that mixed human and animal elements, so that if the novel was influenced by any other recent work, most likely it was H. G. Wells' *The Island of Dr. Moreau* (1896). Like Harriet's father, Moreau is driven from his native country for experimenting on animals, goes to a distant land to continue his experiments, and is eventually destroyed by the people/creatures he experiments upon. Also interesting in relation to the novel's experiments is its similarities to the Swedish *Powers of Darkness*. In that novel, Count Draculitz presides over a group of creatures who appear to be half-beast, half-man. All three works play with ideas of evolution and hybrids.

Another influence on *The Blood of the Vampire* may be *Frankenstein*. Perhaps it is no coincidence that Harriet's father, like Victor Frankenstein, begins his experiments in Switzerland. Like the Monster, Harriet is not responsible for her parentage—creation—but she feels herself the victim of it. Both Harriet and the Monster are mistreated by humans. However, Marryat's novel is gentler in tone than *Frankenstein*. Shelley's Monster seeks revenge by destroying those his creator loves. Harriet's creators are dead, and rather than seek revenge on those who spurn her, she kills herself to prevent others she may love from dying.

The novel is also revolutionary because Harriet preys on members of both sexes, even if she does so unintentionally. Margaret does not die, but she feels Harriet sapping her energy. Margaret's baby, who does die, is female. Bobby and Anthony are male. The difference, however, between Harriet and Count Dracula is that she is an energy vampire. She does not bite people on the neck or suck their blood. She just drains their energy. That said, her grandmother was bit by a vampire bat. Marryat may have chosen to avoid the sexual connotations of vampirism in the novel, but they are implied, suggesting a bisexual component.

Of course, we have seen lesbianism in *Carmilla*. In that novel, however, we have simply one woman preying upon another. In *The Blood of the Vampire*, we have another case of reverse colonization where a character from the colonies comes to Western Europe to prey upon the oppressors, specifically British subjects, regardless of sex. We cannot say for sure whether Marryat read *Carmilla*, but it is likely she was aware of it or the earlier French vampire texts, especially Lamothe-Langon's, or the vampire plays in which female vampires are treated sympathetically. As we have seen, Carmilla at least acts like she is unaware of her vampirism or confused by it, while at the same time, she seems intent on making Laura be with her. Harriet similarly is unaware of her vampirism until enough bodies accumulate that she can no longer deny it.

One has to wonder what the fate of *The Blood of the Vampire* would have been if *Dracula* had not been published at almost the same time, thus obscuring it. Would the female vampire tradition have received a boost to creating more female vampires? There are very few female vampire characters in *Dracula*'s wake. Or would the novel have faded into total obscurity? An argument can be made that it is only remembered today because *Dracula*'s popularity has caused other vampire texts to be explored. In either case, it is fascinating that Stoker and Marryat, writing within the same tradition, had such completely different visions of what a vampire novel should be.

Vampire Short Stories

Before I conclude this book by discussing *Dracula*, it is worth mentioning a few shorter vampire works. It is impossible to discuss all of them, and my focus has been primarily on how French and British Gothic influenced each other, but I will note a few short stories, one French, three British, one American, and one originally German but pirated and translated into British, that have been suggested as possible influences on Bram Stoker's masterpiece.

Karl von Wachsmann's "The Mysterious Stranger"

The most noteworthy short story that may have influenced

Dracula is "The Mysterious Stranger," a German story translated into English in 1854. The original version is Karl von Wachsmann's story "Der Fremde" ("The Stranger"), published in his 1844 collection *Erzählungen und Novellen*. The English translation was first published in *Chambers Repository of Instructive and Amusing Tracts* with attribution to the author.[114] In 2019, scholars Katy Brundan, Melanie Jones, and Benjamin Mier-Cruz proposed that Stoker chose the Carpathians for *Dracula*'s setting because he read this story. They state:

> But he [Stoker] stumbled instead upon an anonymous vampire tale set in Transylvania, which helped redirect the novel's setting toward eastern Europe. Like *Dracula*, "The Mysterious Stranger" (1854) features an older, aristocratic vampire with "piercing" grey eyes and a sallow complexion who lives in a castle in the wolf-infested Carpathians (14). The very anonymity of 'The Mysterious Stranger' seems to have invited borrowing, which Stoker promptly did. The tale's exact origins eluded researchers for decades, but we now know it is an unauthorized translation of Karl von Wachsmann's *Der Fremde* (*The Stranger*), first published in his collection *Erzählungen und Novellen* (1844).
>
> In closely modelling the early portion of *Dracula* on an anonymous, pirated translation of a German story, Stoker created new textual life from a translated text whose ties to the original author had been severed. This example demonstrates how nineteenth-century mass culture's parasitic consumption—a mirror of the vampire's own insatiable appetite—depended in part on translational practices. Stoker's unauthorized reproduction makes him complicit in the archive's suppression of the German author responsible for many details of Dracula's character, from the vampire's "repulsive" but magnetic manner to his waving the wolf pack away with a hand ("Mysterious Stranger" 14).[115]

Yes, the similarities are there, but overall, I feel this argument rather weak. Two characters having "piercing" eyes is hardly enough to claim influence. As we have seen, countless Wandering Jews, vampires, and other characters throughout nineteenth-century literature have hypnotic, piercing, or mesmerizing eyes. A sallow or pale complexion is also common to most vampires in literature—Stoker could have found such details in several of the earlier vampire stories we have explored. The Carpathian setting was nothing new to vampire stories, even in 1844 when Karl von Wachsmann wrote his story since Planché used the same setting in his 1829 play *Der Vampyr*. Dumas also used it in *The Thousand and One Ghosts*, and as we just saw, Jules Verne set his vampire novel there. All of these sources seem to have been more easily accessible to Stoker than Wachsmann's story even in its English translation. Furthermore, while Brundan, Jones, and Mier-Cruz say Stoker "stumbled upon" the story, we don't know for certain that he ever saw it. That leaves only the wolves as a significant similarity that could show influence. I will summarize the story before drawing further conclusions since it is the only story discussed here that has not been anthologized numerous times.*

The story begins when Count Fahnenberg, an Austrian nobleman, is traveling to an estate he recently acquired in the Carpathians. He is accompanied by his nephew Franz, his daughter Franziska, and her friend Bertha. Franz appears to be romantically interested in Franziska, but she confides to Bertha that he is too effeminate for her. By contrast, Bertha is engaged to Woislaw, a military man, who is heroic and admirable in Franziska's eyes. Woislaw is away fighting in the Turkish war, while Franz has refused to go.

On their way to the count's new estate, they fear being attacked by wolves whom they can hear crying in the distance, so they take shelter in some ruins said to be haunted. As the

---

* The full text of "The Mysterious Stranger" can be found online at https://souo.fandom.com/wiki/Full_Text:_Mysterious_Stranger.

wolves grow closer, a stranger appears and, by a gesture, sends off the wolves. The rescued do not learn the stranger's name.

When they arrive at the count's mansion, the party learns from the locals that the ruins they took shelter in are those of Klatka Castle, whose last lord was Azzo von Klatka, a despotic tyrant who was hanged by the peasants he had oppressed.

When the count's party returns to visit the ruins, they again meet the stranger who saved them. They thank him for his help and the count invites him to visit them. Although the stranger seems to be a hermit and is rather sullen, he agrees to visit them at a later date.

Eventually, the stranger becomes a regular visitor and shows interest in Franziska. She likes the stranger, who reveals his name is Azzo (a hint he is the nobleman who was hung). Franz, however, sees the stranger as a rival. Then, Franziska falls ill and begins having a strange dream in which Azzo comes in a mist, kisses her throat, and then vanishes in a mist. The next morning, Franziska's neck is red with blood. No one can explain her illness or the dream.

Then Bertha's fiancé, Woislaw, arrives from the war with the Turks. He has lost a hand in the war and had a new one made of gold, which is very strong. He recognizes Franziska's symptoms as the result of a vampire attack and attributes them to the stranger, but he keeps his conclusions to himself. When the stranger next visits, Franz challenges him to a duel. In a tense scene, Azzo picks up Franz like he was a baby, but Woislaw intervenes and makes him drop Franz through the great physical strength of his golden hand. Azzo, thinking Woislaw's strength is supernatural, calls him "blood-brother," apparently believing Woislaw is a vampire like himself.

Woislaw now visits the ruins and finds Azzo sleeping in his tomb. Woislaw nails Azzo's coffin shut and leaves a packet of nails on top of it. Then he brings Franziska there and tells her she must drive the three nails (stakes) through it. After she does so, he says liquid will flow from the coffin. She must dip her fingers in the blood and smear it on the scratch at her throat.

Only after Franziska does all this and begins to heal does Woislaw reveal that Azzo was a vampire; Woislaw knows this from a past experience with one. He says a vampire must be destroyed by the one who has been afflicted by him, which is why Franziska had to kill Azzo. The story ends happily with a double wedding between Franziska and Franz, and Woislaw and Bertha.

While "The Mysterious Stranger" does have similarities to *Dracula*, especially in the vampire having control over wolves, the story being set in the Carpathians, and the vampire appearing in a mist and disappearing, as well as it seeming to be like a dream, there is also much that is strange about it—primarily the insistence that the victim is the one who must kill the vampire. Perhaps if Stoker was influenced by the story, he decided to change this element of vampire lore since that would require both Lucy and Mina to kill the vampire. Why he would make such a change could be an entire article in itself, disputing whether it was to increase the action of the plot not to have Lucy kill Dracula, or whether it was considered too unfeminine for a woman to commit such an act of violence. Although we have seen women in earlier works be the victims of vampires and even seek revenge on the vampires, we have not seen female characters resort to violence against a vampire to this point.

Given that the story is German, we also must wonder whether Von Wachsmann knew Polidori's story—it seems unlikely he did not since it was translated into many languages. He may have also been aware of other vampire works that predate his own, in French or perhaps German. Unfortunately, little is known about him in the English-speaking world other than that he lived from 1787 to 1862 and was part of the German literary Romantic Movement. Only the French and German versions of Wikipedia have entries for him, and they reveal little about him or his works.[116] "The Mysterious Stranger" may be his only work that was translated into English. There were other vampire works in

German that are beyond the exploration of this book,* but the story likely was influenced directly or indirectly by Polidori. Whether it influenced Stoker remains questionable.

William Gilbert's "The Last Lords of Gardonal"

"The Last Lords of Gardonal" is mainly of interest because its author, William Gilbert, was the father of William S. Gilbert of Gilbert and Sullivan, which may help explain the famous duo's decision to write *Ruddigore*. The story was originally included in Gilbert's 1867 collection of tales about Innominato (meaning Nameless), a wizard who lived in the fourteenth century and used his powers to help people. The full work was titled *The Wizard of the Mountain*.

In the story, an evil baron named Conrad mistreats the local residents. He falls in love with a local girl named Teresa, but her father refuses to let Conrad wed her. Regardless, Conrad persecutes her until the girl dies. Conrad then visits Innominato, who agrees to help him. Innominato brings Teresa to him, but she is now a corpse-like bride, though she looks beautiful. When Conrad realizes she is a vampire, he tries to escape from her, but she sucks all his blood and he dies.

Stoker very likely knew this story given that he and his wife were friendly with William S. Gilbert. That said, there are no real similarities between it and *Dracula* other than that they both contain a vampire.

Guy de Maupassant's "The Horla"

"The Horla" may be the most interesting story discussed here. Written by Guy de Maupassant, one of the most famous of French short story authors, "The Horla" was originally a very short story published in 1886 that was expanded the next year.

In the original version, the story is set in a sanitarium run by Dr. Marrande. A thin corpse-like man who is a patient in the

---

* For an exploration of German vampire literature, see Heide Crawford's *The Origins of the Literary Vampire*.

sanitarium tells a story of how he was a well-to do and happy person until a year ago when he began to feel an uneasiness. Then one night he began to feel like something was eating at his mouth. He begins to get thinner and is convinced something is entering his room at night. He does experiments, such as leaving water in the room, to see if it will disappear, which it does. Obviously, the invisible creature he now believes is haunting him drank it. He names the creature "The Horla," though he is not sure why he chooses that name. (In French, the term comes from hors là, which means outside or beyond.[117]) Eventually, he goes to the asylum and begs to be allowed to remain there. After Dr. Marrande hears his story, he goes to the man's house and finds that three of his neighbors are similarly infected. The story ends with a report of invisible vampires coming from Brazil. The man afflicted realizes he saw a Brazilian ship pass by his house, which is on the water's edge, just before he began to be afflicted. He predicts that a new race now exists on the earth that will eventually multiply to the point of replacing humans.

Maupassant revised and expanded the story to about three times its original length, incorporating additional material he had previously published.[118] The expanded version basically tells the same story with some added details. It is written in diary format and there is no mention of the narrator being in a madhouse. Included in it is a tale of a woman who when hypnotized does things she does not intend to do; the narrator says her behavior is similar to how the Horla imposes his will on humans. The narrator tries to destroy the Horla by burning down his house, but he only succeeds in killing his servants whom he forgot were in the house. In the end, he realizes the Horla will triumph and he plans suicide. The threat again comes from Brazil, but this time we are told the ship came down the Seine.

The story is interesting because, as in earlier works we've explored, a type of reverse colonialism is suggested—a threat from a foreign country colonized by a European power, although Maupassant's choice of Brazil is odd since it wasn't a French colony; perhaps he simply chose it as an exotic location. While the invisible creatures have vampire-like qualities, the story seems more akin to the strange stories of H. P. Lovecraft than most vampire works. I don't see any real connection to *Dracula*, other than that the vampire threat comes from a foreign land and an insane asylum is involved. It's possible Stoker was influenced to create Renfield and Dr. Seward's sanitorium from the story, but we have seen so many insane asylums in Gothic literature already, such as in Eugène Sue's *The Wandering Jew*, and characters who have gone mad or been accused of being mad as early as Charles Nodier's *The Vampire*, that a direct influence by this story seems unlikely. The story's only other possible resemblance to *Dracula* is that the extended version uses a diary format like much of *Dracula*, but it is known Stoker was inspired by Collins' *The Woman in White* in this respect.

Not surprisingly, H. P. Lovecraft in *Supernatural Horror in Literature* (1927) said Maupassant's story was "perhaps without peer in its particular department." It is also believed to have inspired Lovecraft's famous story "The Call of Cthulhu," which features a creature able to influence minds, a creature destined to conquer humanity.[119]

Personally, I prefer the shorter version, thinking it more dramatic and horrifying because it is more concise.

Julian Hawthorne's "Ken's Mystery"

Julian Hawthorne, son of American author Nathaniel Hawthorne, knew Bram Stoker and visited him in Ireland, so his story "Ken's Mystery" is far more likely to have been an influence on Stoker. It is the only vampire story set in Ireland in this period, and since Stoker was Irish, that may be a reason for it to stand out as a possible source. Hawthorne visited Ireland about 1877 to soak up local folklore to inspire the story, at which time he must have first met Stoker.[120] They would know each other for many years, and Stoker lists Hawthorne among those who would attend First Night dinners at the Lyceum where he was employed in his *Personal Reminiscences of Henry Irving*.[121] "Ken's Mystery" would be published in Hawthorne's 1888 collection *David Poindexter's Disappearance*.[122]

The story is told by a nameless narrator who is the friend of the main character, Ken. Ken is a wealthy American who visited Europe and met a girl from New York there to whom he became engaged. However, the engagement was broken without anyone knowing the reason. When the narrator visits Ken, he notes his friend seems deranged. Finally, Ken reveals that he's been in Ireland. He shows the narrator a banjo that the narrator gave to him just the year before, which was brand new then but is now rotting. Ken explains this strange occurrence by saying the banjo existed in the sixteenth century so it is old enough to rot. Ken then explains how this is possible.

While in Ireland, Ken heard a tale of a girl stolen on her wedding night by vampires. Then one night, as he walked back to where he was staying, he came upon a woman in a hooded cloak. She told him he was at the grave of Ethelind Fionguala, known as Elsie, the woman who allegedly was abducted by vampires. The hooded woman got Ken to play the banjo while they walked, and eventually, he felt compelled to give her a ring he wore.

After they parted, Ken entered his residence, only to find a woman's hand reaching toward him. She was dressed like a bride and had cold hands. She kissed him and got him to eat and drink. She also had an elfish smile. He noticed she wore the ring he gave to the hooded woman, suggesting they are the same woman. As time passed, while he played the banjo for her, she grew ruddy while he grew pale.

Then one day, Ken woke in a decaying room holding a decaying banjo. He felt pale and haggard and like he would never get over the chill.

The woman may be a vampire, but I would consider the story a borderline vampire tale and closer to a fairy tale. It seems more inspired by Celtic mythology and the legend of La Belle Dame

Sans Merci, the beautiful woman without pity who takes lovers with her to fairyland, then abandons them, only for them to find years have passed. The story owes more inspiration to John Keats' poem on the subject than to most vampire literature. Yes, the man grows pale while the woman grows ruddy in Hawthorne's story, but similarly, the knight in Keats' "La Belle Dame Sans Merci" is also "palely" and "haggard."

I am certain Stoker knew the story, but other than the power the female vampires have over Jonathan Harker in *Dracula*, there are few similarities.

Eric Stenbock's "The Sad Story of a Vampire"

Eric Stenbock (1860-1895) was a Swedish count and the grandson of a Manchester, England cotton tycoon. Consequently, he attended Oxford, lived largely in England, and became well known in British literary circles. His story "The Sad Story of a Vampire" (1894) opens in a format that implies it is a parody, and the title suggests we are to feel sorry for the vampire, but beneath the humor lies one of the most disturbing vampire stories we have explored in this book. Not only is it the first we have encountered in which a male vampire preys upon another male, but the male prey is a boy, suggesting it is a tale of homosexuality, pederasty, and child molestation.

The story is clearly influenced by J. S. Le Fanu's *Carmilla*. The narrator is a young girl named Carmela, and the story opens with the humorous line, "Vampire stories are generally located in Styria; mine is also."[123] We are then told Styria is not at all romantic. Carmela operates an asylum for stray animals. She says the reason she does so is the result of a vampire who visited their home after arriving not in a romantic carriage but on a railway train.

Carmela lives with her father and brother Gabriel. Their mother died when they were little. Gabriel is a strange boy who seems to be at one with nature. Carmela says he is "praeterhuman,"[124] more human than animal and, consequently, animals flock to him. She thinks this is partly due to their mother having been a member of the gipsy race. The suggestion here is that Gabriel is part animal, part man, rather like Count Draculitz's gypsy and bestial relatives in the Swedish *Powers of Darkness*.

One day, the children's father brings home Count Vardalek, a Hungarian who had missed his train. The children's father has offered Count Vardalek shelter for the night. When Gabriel sees Count Vardalek, he looks like a "bird fascinated by a serpent."[125] The count looks "worn and wearied,"[126] but he goes upstairs, as does Gabriel, and when the count returns, he looks younger and less pale. Of course, he is preying upon Gabriel. And, of course, he ends up staying with the family for an extended period. The children's father likes the count because he can understand mystical books the father cannot.

In time, Gabriel grows ill. Then Count Vardalek goes to Trieste. When he returns, he looks pale while Gabriel seems to have regained some strength. Vardalek greets Gabriel with a kiss on the lips and soon regains his color. Then in the most dramatic scene, Carmela spies on the vampire and hears him talking to Gabriel, who is in a kind of trance. He says to Gabriel:

> "My darling, I fain would spare thee: but thy life is my life, and I must live, I who would rather die. Will God not have any mercy on me? Oh! Oh! life; oh, the torture of life!" Here he struck one agonized and strange chord, then continued playing softly, "O, Gabriel, my beloved! my life, yes life—oh, why life? I am sure this is but a little that I demand of thee. Sorely thy superabundance of life can spare little to one who is already dead. No, stay," he said now almost harshly, "what must be, must be!"[127]

This language is clearly inspired by Carmilla's speech to Laura about how Laura belongs to her, and also how Carmilla herself feels like she does not quite understand her actions. Count Vardalek knows what he is doing to Gabriel, but he clearly regrets it and cannot help himself.

Eventually, Gabriel is so drained of blood that he is on his deathbed. Vardalek demands a priest be called for before it is too late to give Gabriel last rites. Vardalek then disappears from the house before the priest arrives, and he is never seen again. Gabriel dies and his father soon after dies from grief. Carmela is left to honor her brother's memory by opening a home for stray cats and dogs.

The story definitely has its humor. It also is largely predictable, but it is equally shocking that the victim is a young boy preyed upon by another male. At one point, the father mentions a little drummer boy he knew and Vardalek's pupils dilate, suggesting he is sexually excited at the thought of another boy and clearly has a fetish for them.

The name Vardalek in the story is likely a version of vourdalak, a word that first appears in Russian author Alexander Sergeyevich Pushkin's work and is a distortion of several words that refer to vampires or werewolves in Slavic and Balkan folklore. The word was used perhaps most famously in Russian author Aleksey Konstantinovich Tolstoy's Gothic novella "The Family of the Vourdalak" (1839), also titled in English as "The Curse of the Vourdalak," which was interestingly written in French and not translated into Russian or published until 1884.[128] I suspect Stenbock knew Tolstoy's story and was inspired by it since it includes a traveler and a child who dies, but the traveler ends up the victim of vampires rather than the vampire himself. Furthermore, Tolstoy likely was influenced by Polidori's *The Vampyre*, which was translated into Russian in 1828. The influence is apparent in that like Polidori, Tolstoy places his vampire in upper class society.[129]

I doubt Stoker knew Tolstoy's novella, but it is very likely he knew Stenbock's short story. In fact, the story's opening line might have been reason enough for Stoker to change his mind about setting his story in Styria. Stoker may even have known Stenbock since Stenbock published most of his books in the 1890s and died young due to his drug and alcohol addiction.

Stenbock was homosexual, and his literary executor, More Adey, also homosexual, was a member of Oscar Wilde's circle and testified at his trial.[130] Consequently, given Stoker's well-known connections with the Wilde family, it is likely he knew both Adey and Stenbock.

Mary E. Braddon's "Good Lady Ducayne"

"Good Lady Ducayne" (1896) may well have influenced Stoker since he knew Mary E. Braddon, best known for her sensational novel *Lady Audley's Secret* (1862). The primary connection between this story and *Dracula* are the blood transfusions performed.

It is a simple story of a young woman named Bella Rolleston who works for an employment agency. Through the agency, she secures a position as lady's companion to Lady Ducayne, who has had little success with her companions; they all eventually become weak and die, but she is pleased with Bella, who is young and strong.

Bella travels to Italy with Lady Ducayne and Dr. Parravinci, who looks after her since she is an invalid. In time, Bella starts having strange dreams and feels like mosquitos are biting her arms. It turns out Dr. Parravinci is drugging Bella and then draining her blood to give to Lady Ducayne to keep her alive. In fact, such blood transfusions have kept her alive for a long time, which explains why her past companions have died and she has made it to age ninety-five.

Meanwhile, Bella has befriended a brother and sister. The brother, Herbert, develops feelings for her and eventually realizes why she is becoming ill. When he confronts Lady Ducayne, she decides she no longer wants to undergo the doctor's strange experiments to keep her alive anyway. She gives Bella a gift of money and Bella goes off to marry Herbert.

Stoker may have gotten the idea of blood transfusions from Braddon's story. (Notably, the blood transfusions in *Dracula* would have killed Lucy in real life and probably would have killed Lady Ducayne also since no understanding of blood types existed at the time.) Braddon wrote a letter of praise to Stoker after *Dracula* was published. In it, she said, "We will talk of it more anon! when I have soberly read and meditated thereupon. I have done my humdrum little story of transfusion in the Good Lady Ducayne—but your 'bloofer lady'..."[131] Although complimenting Stoker, Braddon must have wondered if he borrowed the blood transfusion idea from her. It seems highly possible.

Bram Stoker's *Dracula*

And so, we finally arrive at *Dracula*. Perhaps no greater work of Gothic literature exists in any language. Certainly, none, except maybe *Frankenstein*, has been more influential. The significance of Stoker's vampire is aptly summed up by vampire drama scholar Roxana Stuart:

> Lord Ruthven was killed many times onstage, but only Count Dracula could keep him in the grave. Dracula is one of those creations that transcends the work in which it is presented—one of Jung's archetypal patterns of the subconscious and a powerful poetic image of Freud's "primal hoarder." Dracula possesses tremendous cunning, grace, strength, the ability to revert to animal form and fly through the air, an aristocratic manner, an ironic sense of humor, a commanding presence, a contempt for mankind, and a hypnotic power over women. He far surpasses Ruthven in his egotism and ambition—he seems to be planning world domination. He is one of the great fictional creations of Victorian literature.[132]

I would go further to say he is one of the greatest fictional creations of world literature. Few characters have enjoyed so much attention. The novel has been translated into multiple languages and sold millions of copies. It has never been out of print.[133] In addition, the numerous film versions, comic books, and other Dracula-related merchandise make it hard to imagine anyone does not have at least some idea of who or what Dracula is, even if that concept is far from Stoker's own.

I will not go into great detail with analysis of the novel or give a thorough plot summary since I can't imagine anyone would read this book who has not already read *Dracula*, probably multiple times. What I will discuss here is how *Dracula* is a culmination of the French and British Gothic traditions that I have explored throughout this book. I contest that Stoker was influenced by both traditions, and whether he consciously drew from or even read every text I have suggested as containing a possible influence, the ideas and Gothic elements he drew upon were clearly in the air in Victorian England.

That is not to suggest Stoker was not original or even ingenious in writing *Dracula*. Stoker's ability to assemble all these Gothic elements into a new form and create new levels of terror, depth, and fascination for his readers is what has made *Dracula* into immortal literature and caused almost every other novel mentioned in this book to dwell in its shadows, known to hardly anyone other than literary scholars, historians, and a few true Gothic enthusiasts.

Before I analyze the various Gothic elements Stoker used in *Dracula*, I will provide a brief look at Stoker's connections to the French language and French literature and his role as an Irishman. This will give us an idea of how both influenced the creation of *Dracula*.

Stoker's French Connections

It is my belief that Stoker could read French well enough to do so with little real effort, or at the very least, that he read in translation many of the French novels I've discussed in this book. Stoker stated he only knew a "smattering" of French, but it is far easier to read than speak a foreign language, and he would have needed to speak enough French to get by on his many visits to France.

In 1872, Stoker's parents moved to France because it was less expensive to live there.[134] They later moved to Switzerland where French is also spoken. After his father died abroad, his mom and sister Mathilde moved to Naples in 1876 before returning to Dublin in 1880. During these years, Stoker is known to have been in Paris in 1874 and also in 1878 on trips to visit his family.[135] In 1889, Mathilde would marry Charles Petitjean, a Frenchman she had met while living abroad.[136] Furthermore, Bram and Florence Stoker hired a French tutor/governess for their son Noel, who consequently spoke such good French that when he was in France, he was mistaken for a Frenchman.[137] Florence is also known to have attended a production of *Hamlet* in France, so she could likely speak the language.[138]

Consequently, Stoker was surrounded by people who spoke French so it is hard to imagine he could not speak and read it himself, and his only reference to his ability to speak French is likely made out of modesty. That reference appears in *Personal Reminiscences of Henry Irving* where he states:

> There came also three other Frenchmen of literary note Jules Clery, Jacques Normand and the great critic Francisque Sarcey. There was a marked scarcity of language between us as none of the Frenchmen spoke in those days a word of English, and neither Irving nor I knew more than a smattering of French. We got on well, however, and managed to exchange ideas in the manner usual to people who want to talk with each other.[139]

I suspect Stoker is being both humorous and modest here since he obviously knew enough French to carry on a conversation. Therefore, I think it likely Stoker could have also read French literature in the original language, although most of the works I will mention as possible influences on him would have been translated into English in his time.

Stoker's Irish Influences

Despite his French connections, Stoker was first and foremost an Irishman. Although he was living in London and working with Henry Irving when he wrote *Dracula*, I believe his Irish roots also profoundly affected his creation of *Dracula*. Many critics have written about Ireland's role in Stoker's novels, seeing Count Dracula as symbolic of English landlords in Ireland. While I think these readings into the novel may go too far, we cannot doubt that Stoker was heavily influenced by Irish literature and sympathetic to the plight of the Irish.

For those reasons, I also think Stoker would have been drawn to Paul Féval's *Les Mystères de Londres* because its protagonist, the Marquis de Rio Santo, is an Irishman trying to free Ireland from British rule and, indeed, bring down the entire British Empire. Similarly, Count Dracula tries to destroy or conquer England. As previously noted, Féval's *Les Mystères de Londres* was serialized in France from 1842-4 and published in an abridged English translation in 1847. While the novel was not popular in England, probably because of its anti-British content, Irish readers may have sympathized with it, and I think it likely since Féval also wrote vampire novels that Stoker would have been aware of it. While the English translation was severely abridged, if Stoker read the full French version, it may have influenced him to an even greater extent than I've suggested here.

As an Irishman, Stoker may have viewed Rio Santo's cause more favorably than most. However, Stoker disliked the Fenians who sought to create an Irish republic through violence. He thought Home Rule should come about through ameliorative means,[140] so he would not have approved of Rio Santo's methods. But given his interest in vampires, Stoker may well have been fascinated by Rio Santo's vampire-like qualities.

Lady Caroline Lamb's *Glenarvon* (1816) is another novel with a vampire-like hero that is about the fight for Irish freedom. Consequently, it is possible it may have inspired Stoker in writing

Dracula or even Féval in writing *Les Mystères de Londres*.

Despite belief in Home Rule rather than Irish independence, Stoker had plenty of connections to those who sought to win Irish freedom. In 1798, a French army had landed in Mayo not far from Sligo where Stoker's mother Charlotte had lived. The French were intending to help the Irish insurgents begin a republic like France had recently done. Charlotte identified one of the insurgents, George Blake, who was captured and hanged, as her mother's brother, making him Stoker's great-uncle.[141] In Stoker's boyhood, in 1858, the Irish Republican Brotherhood was founded, which led to the 1867 uprising in Ireland. Florence Stoker's father was made an honorary lieutenant colonel of the brotherhood.[142]

Stoker was also good friends with the Wilde family. In fact, Florence Stoker had originally been engaged to Oscar Wilde before deciding to marry Stoker. Stoker was part of the literary circles of Lady Jane Wilde, Oscar Wilde's mother. Lady Wilde wrote extensively about Irish myths and legends, but she also wrote republican material for the patriot newspaper *The Nation*. One of her pieces was used to charge her editor with sedition.[143]

In addition, one of Stoker's childhood friends, Valentine Blake Dillion, became a lawyer for the Land League and defended Charles Stewart Parnell, leader of the Irish Party and Land League, after he was arrested in 1880.[144] An 1885 *Punch* cartoon depicted the Irish National League, successor to the Land League, as a vampire bat with the head of Charles Parnell. The Irish National League's goals were moderate agrarianism and Home Rule with electoral functions. It was autocratic with Parnell holding immense authority and direct parliamentary control.[145] That the league was seen as resembling a vampire reflects how the English saw it as preying upon them. Like Count Dracula, the Irish National League reflected a foreign/Irish threat to England. All of these examples suggest that the efforts for Irish independence would have been constantly brought to Stoker's attention even if he did not agree with them.

Nor can we underestimate the influence of Irish literature upon Stoker. Not only did he likely read the major Irish authors, but he had connections to several of them. Besides knowing Lady Wilde and Oscar Wilde, he attended Trinity College where he was friends with the grandson of Charles Maturin, author of *Melmoth the Wanderer*.[146] Furthermore, Oscar Wilde was Maturin's great-nephew by marriage; Lady Wilde's mother was a sister to Maturin's wife.[147] Stoker likely knew not only Maturin's *Melmoth the Wanderer*, but probably Maturin's earlier novels *The Wild Irish Boy* (1808) and *The Milesian Chief* (1812), which critic Robert Miles states reflect Maturin's Irish Nationalism beliefs and are "attempts at imagining an Irish romance of natural becoming."[148] It is unknown if Stoker ever crossed paths with J. S. Le Fanu, but it seems very likely. He did know one, if not two of Le Fanu's sons.[149] Also, Wilkie Collins, whom Stoker probably did not know personally but whose *The Woman in White* would be a major influence upon *Dracula*'s structure, was the grandson of an Irish writer, William Collins.[150] Stoker also would have known the writings of Fitzjames O'Brien, whose short story "What Was It?" (1859) contains a malevolent, invisible creature, which may have influenced Guy de Maupassant's story "The Horla."[151] Plus, Florence Stoker had a collection of Maria Edgeworth's novels,[152] most of which are set in Ireland and contain themes like the criticism of Anglo-Irish landlords who mishandle their estates, including *Castle Rackrent* (1800) and *The Absentee* (1812), while other novels like *Belinda* (1801) contain Gothic elements.

Given this rich tradition of Irish Gothic literature, it can be no accident that Stoker's early novels featured Irish characters and treated Irish themes. His first novel, *The Primrose Path* (1875), concerns a man who leaves Ireland and goes to work in London where, thinking his wife is unfaithful, he murders her. Such a plot is not that different from Féval's *Les Mystères de Londres* where the family moves to London, only to have the daughter seduced by an Englishman and the son seek revenge for his sister's shame.

Stoker's second novel, *The Snake's Pass* (1885), is fully set in Ireland and full of Gothic elements.

Biographer Paul Murray suggests that Stoker may have gotten the idea from Lady Wilde to use Irish superstitions and legends and transport them to Transylvania in *Dracula*. Lady Wilde drew attention in her works to parallels between Transylvanian and Irish legends, referring to Emily Gerard's book *The Land Beyond the Forest*, and stating that many Transylvanian legends "will be found identical with the Irish." She lists examples, including the belief that the dead are sometimes allowed to visit their living relatives.[153] Lady Wilde began publishing her multi-volume work *Ancient Legends* in 1888, which works perfectly with the timing of *Dracula*, which Stoker began working on in 1890.[154] Murray notes the phrase "Children of the Night," which Count Dracula uses, appears in Lady Wilde's book, as does the concept of the Prince of Darkness.[155]* While Lady Wilde's influence on Stoker is very probable, it should be noted the phrase "Prince of Darkness" does not exist in *Dracula* and seems to be a phrase to reference Dracula added later by filmmakers. Furthermore, it was first used in English in Milton's *Paradise Lost* and is a translation of the Latin *princeps tenebrarum*, which occurs in the fourth century *Acts of Pilate*, so it is not original to Lady Wilde.[156] Regardless, the passage in Lady Wilde's book is interesting because it reads much like a vampire story. It occurs in the Introduction and states:

> There is also a belief that every seven years the fairies are obliged to deliver up a victim to the Evil One, and to save their own people they try to abduct some beautiful young mortal girl, and her they hand over to the Prince of Darkness.[157]

---

* The phrase "Children of the Night" appears in Lady Wilde's chapter "Our Ancient Capital" in Ancient Legends. In *Dracula*, Dracula speaks it in Chapter 2, p. 45. Wilde uses the phrase to refer to the descendants of Japeth while Stoker uses it to refer to the howling of wolves.

This act of the fairies is much like that of Lord Danvers in *The Necromancer* or Lord Ruthwen in Planché's *Der Vampyr* in which victims must be delivered in exchange for the vampire or immortal character to maintain its own existence.

While reading *Dracula* as a story about an Anglo-Irish landlord preying upon the Irish may be going too far, Stoker's Irish background would have certainly made him sympathetic toward anyone oppressed by the more powerful. At the same time, he also drew upon literary depictions of nobles oppressing the common people, examples of which can be found in Mrs. Radcliffe's *The Romance of the Forest* (1791) and Dickens' *A Tale of Two Cities* (1859). But if Stoker drew upon such literary sources, it was likely because as an Irishman living in an Englishman's world, he may well have felt like an outsider among foreigners and could relate to the oppressed of all cultures.

I will now turn to *Dracula* to explore the many elements in it derived, whether consciously or unconsciously by Stoker, from the rich British and French Gothic traditions we have explored throughout this book.

Dracula's Setting

Stoker may have originally intended to set part of *Dracula* in Styria given the reference to the Countess Dolingen of Styria in "Dracula's Guest." This work was originally thought to be the opening chapter of the novel that Stoker cut, due to Florence Stoker's statement that it was "an hitherto unpublished episode from *Dracula*. It was originally excised owing to the length of the book."[158] Florence Stoker published it as the title story in a short story collection in 1914 after Stoker's death. She probably did so to help the collection sell better. Today, scholars believe "Dracula's Guest" was actually cut from an earlier draft and not simply a cut chapter from the final version of *Dracula* we have today. To what extent Florence Stoker was aware of her husband's overall process and the number of drafts of *Dracula* is unknown.

"Dracula's Guest" tells of an unnamed Englishman, presumably Jonathan Harker, who encounters the tomb of an alleged vampire in a village near Munich. Her marble tomb has a large iron stake driven through it, suggesting she was staked like a vampire would be. The inscription on the tomb reads "COUNTESS DOLINGEN OF GRATZ/IN STYRIA/SOUGHT AND FOUND DEATH/1801."[159] However, the grave is in a village outside Munich, which is a good two hundred miles from Styria. How the countess ended up near Munich is never explained.

Better evidence that Stoker may have originally intended to set the story in Styria comes from his notes for the novel. One note states "Letter to Aaronson from Count ___ Styria asking to come or send trustworthy law[yer] who does not speak German."[160] This suggests the Count himself would have resided in Styria.

Critics have suggested Stoker created the Styria connection because he was inspired by *Carmilla*. He may even have sought to express his inspirational debt to Le Fanu.[161] That Stoker later changed the setting to Transylvania may reflect that he felt the setting's connection to *Carmilla* was too obvious or bordered on plagiarism, and Stenbock's opening line to his vampire short story about how all vampire tales are set in Styria may have also influenced Stoker's decision. That Countess Dolingen plays no role in the final version of *Dracula* also may reflect that Stoker was inspired by Féval, who created the first vampire countess, but Stoker decided he had to be more original and not copy another author.

Whatever Stoker originally intended in relation to Styria and vampire countesses, it is clear the intention was always for Jonathan Harker to travel to Eastern Europe to meet Count Dracula. The Transylvania setting, especially the references to the Carpathian Mountains, also reflects debts to earlier vampire works, but those works were not as well known in Great Britain nor as recent as *Carmilla*. As we have seen, Planché was the first to set his play *Der Vampyr* in the Carpathians, and Dumas' vampire story in *The Thousand and One Ghosts* and his play *The Vampire* were also set there. Later, "The Mysterious Stranger" and Verne's novella *The Carpathian Castle* would use the same setting, showing that Stoker was in no way original in his choice of location. As I previously stated, it may well be Stoker saw Verne's statement that no one would invent legends in Transylvania as a challenge that inspired his choice.

Dracula's Castle also has literary origins. Scholars Haining and Tremayne have discussed Stoker's visits to Cruden Bay in Scotland and how he was inspired by New Slains Castle in creating Dracula's Castle.[162] In fact, an octagonal room in New Slains Castle may have inspired the octagonal room in Dracula's Castle.[163] What is interesting about this possible influence is that Scottish castles are linked with vampires in the earliest vampire works, including Polidori's *The Vampyre*. Could Stoker have gone to Scotland for inspiration because he knew of the Scottish vampire literary tradition? Also notable is the ancestral portrait gallery in New Slains Castle. Since we know W. S. Gilbert sent Florence Stoker tickets to *Ruddigore*,[164] it's possible Stoker saw the operetta and was inspired by it to create the portrait gallery in Count Draculitz's castle if, indeed, *Powers of Darkness* reflects an earlier version of *Dracula* that Stoker wrote. However, no mention of a portrait gallery or ancestral portraits or paintings of any kind are in the castle in *Dracula* itself. Of course, ancestral portraits appear in numerous Gothic novels, including *Melmoth the Wanderer*, and most aristocratic families would have had them, so it would stand to reason a proud aristocrat like Count Dracula would have portraits of his ancestors.

Harker's Coach Ride

In *Dracula*, Harker is met by a coachman of great strength who takes him to the castle. Again, Stoker may have borrowed from others in this depiction. In Reynolds' *The Necromancer*, we learn that Lord Danvers drives his own coach, which allows him to cover incredible distances in impossibly quick times. In one particularly dramatic scene, he drives Clara Manners' father to his castle; they arrive in just hours when the journey should have taken considerably longer.

The supernatural coach ride is also equated with death in Irish mythology. When a person is dying, the cry of the Banshee is heard and then the Death Coach arrives to carry off the dead person.[165] In both cases, such supernatural coachmen are able to overcome the barriers of time and geography. In *Dracula*, when the mysterious coach arrives, the coachman's comments result in a passenger in the other coach quoting a line from "Lenore," translated as "For the dead travel fast."[166] Harker enters the coach and soon finds himself on a mysterious ride in which it seems like the same ground is being traversed over and over until midnight. Mysterious blue flames appear and the driver must scare off wolves before they finally arrive at the castle. None of the strangeness of the coach ride is ever explained in the novel. Regardless, it creates a superstitious atmosphere that associates the coach with the Irish Death Coach and a hint that Harker may be crossing the boundaries between worlds to arrive at the castle.

Count Dracula's Characteristics

The character of Count Dracula himself also reflects a hodgepodge of literary Gothic elements embodied in one character. His notable characteristics all have their origins in earlier Gothic works. The way Stoker brought them together is what makes his villain so threatening and memorable. Dracula's characteristics include:

1. Being a noble who seduces women
2. Being a vampire, specifically a blood drinker
3. Making a pact with the devil
4. Having mesmeric eyes
5. Being a master of disguise
6. Having the ability to shapeshift into a bat and wolf

7. Having a scar on his forehead
8. Dressing in black
9. Climbing walls/defying gravity
10. Possessing superhuman strength
11. Having a three-syllable name
12. Having a proud and ancient ancestry.

Let us briefly examine each characteristic and its sources.

1. **Being a noble who seduces women:** Gothic literature is filled with nobles who use their position to hurt others. One of the first is the Marquis de Montalt in Radcliffe's *The Romance of the Forest*. This nobleman murdered the heroine Adeline's father and he pursues her, attempting to seduce her. Of course, Lord Ruthven is also a nobleman who seduces women. Another example is the Marquis de St. Evremonde in Dickens' *A Tale of Two Cities* who, with his brother, raped Madame Defarge's sister and killed her brother. In Paul Féval's *Les Mystères de Londres*, the Marquis de Rio Santo also seduces women. Noblemen's crimes against women relate to the idea of *droit de seigneur*—that a lord had the right to sleep with a woman before she wed her husband if the husband and wife were his vassals. Consequently, being a seducer of women is closely tied to the concept of nobility. In addition, while Dracula seduces women for their blood, lost is the concept from earlier vampire plays like Marschner's *Der Vampyr* that his life extension is dependent upon bringing new victims to hell. In that play, Ruthwen must seduce three women every year. That Dracula has three female vampires in his castle may reflect a vestige of this concept.

2. **Being a vampire/blood drinker:** As a vampire, Dracula is the heir to all the literary vampire works we have explored in this chapter directly or indirectly. Polidori's Lord Ruthven only seduced women, but Bérard made Lord

Ruthven a blood drinker. Ever since, vampirism has been associated with blood drinking.

3. **Making a pact with the devil:** Like many of the Gothic characters we have explored, including Reynolds' Faust and Lord Danvers in *The Necromancer*, Dracula has made a pact with the devil. In Chapter 18 of *Dracula*, Professor Van Helsing, quoting his friend Arminius, states:

> The Draculas were, says Arminius, a great and noble race, though now and again were scions who were held by their coevals to have had dealings with the Evil One. They learned his secrets in the Scholomance, amongst the mountains over Lake Hermanstadt, where the devil claims the tenth scholar as his due.[167]

Furthermore, Stoker biographer Paul Murray notes that Stoker begins capitalizing personal pronouns for Count Dracula as the novel progresses, which equates him with God or the Antichrist.[168] For example, when Dracula is on the *Demeter*, the captain in his log, not quite knowing what is afflicting his ship, calls him a "fiend or monster" and then refers to him as "He—It!"[169]

4. **Having mesmeric eyes:** Mesmeric eyes and the ability to hypnotize and control someone's will go back to the Wandering Jew. The number of characters in Gothic literature with this ability are legion and include Lewis' Wandering Jew, Coleridge's Ancient Mariner, Maturin's Melmoth the Wanderer, George du Maurier's Svengali, and even Matthew Arnold's Scholar-Gipsy.

5. **Being a master of disguise:** Dracula is a true master of disguise not only because once he begins his blood drinking he is able to appear younger, but because of his ability to shapeshift. As early as the Ruthven plays, the vampire is a master of disguise. Several of the plays depict Ruthven supposedly dying, then reappearing as the Earl of Marsden, believed to be his brother, or not

revealing immediately that he and the earl are now the same person because he has succeeded to the title. Later, in the city mysteries novels, we have Prince Rodophe, masquerading as a common man in Paris in *The Mysteries of Paris*, and the Marquis de Rio Santo in Féval's *Les Mystères de Londres* reversing this by being a commoner masquerading as a nobleman—a poor Irishman who changes his identity by being a Portuguese nobleman. Similarly, Dumas' Count of Monte Cristo begins as Edmond Dantès, but masquerades not only as the count, but also as Lord Wilmore and Abbé Busani. Later, we have women also masquerading as someone else; for example, Heléné who haunts her husband the baron in Ponson du Terrail's *The Vampire and the Devil's Son*.

6. **Having the ability to shapeshift into a bat and wolf:** Shapeshifting may seem like something more original to *Dracula*, but Dracula's ability to change into both a bat and a wolf have their precedents in earlier works. Tales of werewolf transformation in Gothic novels date back to Captain Marryat's *The Phantom Ship* (1839) and include George W. M. Reynolds' *Wagner the Wehr-Wolf* (1846-7) and Dumas' *Le Meneur de loups* (*The Wolf Leader*, 1857). As for bat precedents, in Dumas' 1851 play, Lord Ruthven sprouts wings and flies off, which equates him with a bat or bat-like creature. The first vampire film, *The Haunted Castle* (1896), directed by the first film director, the Frenchman George Méliès, also depicts a bat transforming into a man. Later, the vampire is driven off with a large crucifix.*

---

* This film can be viewed at YouTube at https://www.youtube.com/watch?v=OPmKaz3Quzo. It is questionable whether Stoker saw it, but it reflects that the idea of a man turning into a bat or vice-versa was already part of vampire elements before *Dracula* was published. Kevin Dodd goes into great detail on the relation of vampires and bats in his chapter "'Blood Suckers Most Cruel:' The Vampire and the Bat in and before *Dracula*" in *The Tale of the Living Vampyre: New Directions in Vampire Studies*. p. 86-105.

7. **Having a scar on his forehead:** Dracula's scar is the result of Jonathan Harker striking him with a shovel while he is in his coffin. The scar is itself a sign of being damned or cursed and goes back to the mark of Cain in the Bible. The Wandering Jew, beginning with Lewis' *The Monk*, has a cross on his forehead. Similarly, Féval's Rio Santo has a scar on his forehead.

8. **Dressing in black:** Critics have suggested that Stoker depicted Dracula as wearing a black cape because of performances by Henry Irving in which he wore a black cape. However, nowhere in the novel is a black cape mentioned. Too often popular images of Dracula from films and stage plays interfere with close attention to the novel's text. The cape was added later in stage and film versions. However, Dracula is described as being dressed in all black when he first welcomes Jonathan Harker into the castle and later when he is found seducing Mina. Regardless of Dracula's failure to wear a cape, Raby was the first vampire to sport one in Boucicault's *The Vampire*. In *The Vampire; or, Detective Brand's First Case*, the vampire figure also wears a cape and when he grabs it and stretches out his arms, it makes him appear like a bat—a scene that would be replayed in countless Dracula films. Prior to both of these literary precedents, there was the Victorian urban legend of Spring-Heeled Jack, who wore a vampire-like cape and was able to leap to great heights and distances—hence the suggestion his heels had springs to bounce from. Reports of Spring-Heeled Jack first appeared in the *London Times* on January 9, 1838.[170] A penny-dreadful, *Spring-Heeled Jack: The Terror of London*, was serialized in 1867. Furthermore, among the many letters police received when investigating the Jack the Ripper murders was one dated October 4, 1888 that was signed Spring-Heeled Jack.[171] Plus, we saw earlier in *Notre-Dame de Paris* that when Frollo tries to rescue Esmeralda by boat, he is

disguised by a hood and long robe so Esmeralda does not recognize him. He is there described as being "like a spectre in the dark. His hood, still lowered, had the effect of a kind of mask, and each time he opened his arms as he rowed, with the wide black sleeves hanging down, they looked like two huge batwings."[172] Cape or not, it is interesting that Dracula wears all black and once Lucy becomes a vampire, she is known in the newspapers as "The Woman in Black" which may signify her connection to Dracula. Eighteen-Bisang and Miller also suggest that this phrase would have been recognized by Victorian readers as a pun on Wilkie Collins' *The Woman in White*.[173] If so, Stoker likely was paying homage to Collins' novel, to which he owed a debt for *Dracula*'s narrative structure.

9. **Climbing walls/defying gravity:** Jonathan Harker is surprised when he looks out a window of the castle to see the Count climbing up the side of the wall, but Dracula's behavior has a precedent in Quasimodo who also climbs the façade of Notre-Dame.

10. **Possessing superhuman strength:** Dracula and vampires in general have incredible strength. Van Helsing remarks of Dracula, "in many ways the UnDead are strong. He have always the strength in his hand of twenty men."[174] Incredible strength is also common among Gothic characters. Hugo's Quasimodo has superhuman strength. Sue's Prince Rodolphe is incredibly strong, and so is Hugo's Jean Valjean. In "The Mysterious Stranger," when the colonel exhibits great strength because of his golden arm, the vampire assumes the colonel is also a vampire. Consequently, Stoker also drew this characteristic from his predecessors.

11. **Having a three-syllable name:** Paul Murray suggests that Croly's *Salathiel* may have influenced Stoker. Albert Power elaborates on this possibility by noting that both

Dracula and Salathiel have three-syllable names with the stress falling on the first syllable, and each novel has its main character's name as the title of the book.[175] I feel this argument a bit weak given that Stoker did not decide on his novel's title until just before publication, originally calling it *The Undead*. But regardless, as Power states, both Dracula and Salathiel are doomed to unwanted immortality because of a great sin, each is a powerful warrior, and each is denied rest.[176]

12. **Having a proud and ancient ancestry:** As previously noted, Verne gives a noble ancestry to the owner of his allegedly haunted castle in *The Carpathian Castle*. Stoker expands on this, having Dracula himself tell of his ancestry in dramatic fashion.

All of these characteristics of Count Dracula suggest that Stoker was well-versed in both the British and French Gothic traditions and drew upon them in creating his formidable villain. Other critics such as Stoker biographer Barbara Belford have suggested that Sir Henry Irving was the inspiration for Dracula, even titling her book *Bram Stoker and the Man Who Was Dracula*, the "man" referenced being Irving. She describes a tense or hostile relationship between them or at least repressed frustration on Stoker's part toward his employer. While biographer Paul Murray agrees that Irving may have physically been a model for Dracula because of his looks and height, he feels the idea that Irving was the model for Dracula is unlikely and his Gothic roles, particularly Faust, were more likely the inspiration.[177]

I have to agree with Murray. Stoker's depiction of Irving in *Personal Reminiscences of Henry Irving* is hardly anything but affectionate and complimentary. Granted, Stoker was writing a book for public consumption that he wanted to sell, which meant he was capitalizing upon his relationship with Irving to sell books, but if Stoker resented Irving, it is unlikely he would have been so glowing in his descriptions of his former employer. I don't know how anyone who reads Stoker's biography of Irving could possibly believe in the antagonism some critics have claimed existed between Stoker and Irving to create an explanation for Dracula's creation. As Murray states, the only case for Irving being a source for Dracula is that they were both tall, had dramatic personalities, and were largely nocturnal. Stoker's descriptions of Irving do not compare him to anything supernatural, and the allegation that Stoker felt himself exploited by the actor is lacking in evidence.[178]

Laurence Irving, Henry Irving's grandson, claims the relationship soured in later years and that Stoker's idolatry of Irving and his "emotional impetuosity" "handicapped him in dealing with Irving's business affairs in a forthright and sensible manner."[179] But this may just be supposition on Laurence Irving's part and does not reflect the type of deep animosity, conscious or subconscious, that Belford claims makes Henry Irving the model for Dracula. Personally, I believe the creation of Dracula's character can be best explained in the elements that already existed in the Gothic tradition. Stoker was a master in drawing together these characteristics to create his archvillain.

Harker's Imprisonment and Encounter with Female Vampires

The imprisonment of Jonathan Harker in Castle Dracula also has precedent in earlier vampire novels. As early as Léonti in Bérard's *Lord Ruthwen ou les vampires,* men are imprisoned to stop them from thwarting a vampire. Others are declared insane or placed in insane asylums. In the Swedish *Powers of Darkness,* Dr. Seward becomes a prisoner in his own insane asylum.

The most dramatic scene of Harker's imprisonment in the castle comes when he meets the three female vampires. Their power over him puts him into a stupor where he is barely conscious of what is happening. Stoker may have been inspired in creating this scene by Chapter 31 of *The Count of Monte Cristo,* in which Franz visits the count and is served hashish. He then falls asleep and dreams of making love to three female statues in the count's residence. The statues represent the courtesans Phryne, Cleopatra, and Messalina. The scene's eroticism is as intense as the scene between Jonathan and the female vampires. And while the women Franz dreams of are statues, they still belong to the count just like the female vampires belong to Count Dracula.

Stoker's female vampires, however, do stand out from earlier female vampires. Excepting for Carmilla, earlier female vampires were reluctant in their roles. Stoker's do not express any regret for their desire to seduce or feast upon Jonathan Harker. Haining and Tremayne argue that Stoker's female vampires may reflect Irish legends of beautiful young women who lure strong men to their doom and suck the blood out of them.[180] As we have seen, Julian Hawthorne likely drew upon such traditions in creating his seductive female vampire/Belle Dame Sans Merci figure in "Ken's Mystery." Dracula's female vampires may well belong to this same mythical tradition, though Stoker probably knew the French female vampire tradition as well.

The most notable suggestion that Stoker knew the French female vampire tradition is reflected in Mina Harker's behavior after she is forced to suck Dracula's blood. Mina then becomes both the servant of Dracula and one bent on revenge against him, much like the female vampires in the Lord Ruthven plays and stories, beginning with Bettina in Bérard's *Lord Ruthwen ou les vampires*. I will explore this aspect of Mina's behavior in more detail below.

Another notable aspect of Jonathan's imprisonment is that he tries to escape by communicating with the gypsies who work for Dracula, only to have them betray him by surrendering his letters to the Count. Gypsies are frequent throughout Gothic literature, including Esmeralda in *Notre-Dame de Paris* and the characters in Ainsworth's *Rookwood*. However, their connection to vampires first appears in Stenbock's short story in which the boy Gabriel and his sister Carmella have a mother with gypsy blood. Gabriel is easily seduced by the vampire Vardaluk, which may suggest in the story that those of gypsy blood are subject to a vampire's powers. Of course, gypsies commonly reside in Transylvania and their historical role as outcasts and their refusal to assimilate would naturally make them more prone to fall under the control of a powerful lord like Dracula, one whom they might see as a protector but also as someone to fear and obey.

Dracula's Migration to England

While Harker remains imprisoned in the castle, Dracula begins his journey to London. Stoker may have been inspired by vampire drama in creating this journey. In Dornay's *Douglas Le Vampire*, the vampire tries to escape by ship from those in pursuit of him. Stoker has Dracula travel both to and from England by ship, presumably because he would have more free rein on a ship than trying to make the journey by train across the continent. Dumas' *The Vampire* may also have influenced Stoker. In Act V, a ship is seen foundering at sea. Soon after, Lord Ruthven makes his way over the balcony, obviously having arrived on the foundering ship.

Dracula's murder of everyone aboard the *Demeter* on the way to England may reflect a tradition of ghost ships that could go back to Coleridge's "The Ancient Mariner," which Stoker quotes in *Dracula*. Another literary source is Captain Vanderdecken as depicted in Frederick Marryat's *The Phantom Ship* (1839), Richard Wagner's opera *The Flying Dutchman* (1843), and W. G. Wills' play *Vanderdecken*, the last of which Irving performed in before Stoker began working for him in 1878. Stoker was at the performance, and because the play was too long, afterwards, he helped Irving trim it down.[181] In the Flying Dutchman stories, Captain Vanderdecken (or the Dutchman in Wagner's opera) is cursed to sail the seas for all eternity and usually operates the ship alone. In *Dracula*, the captain of the *Demeter* leaves a log describing how all of his crew has died before he himself also dies. The *Demeter* arrives in England without any crew. Stoker biographer David Skal also suggests this scene could have a source in the Irish "coffin ships" of the famine years, in which the passengers arrived dead.[182] Yet another literary source may be *Varney the Vampire* with its ship disaster and storms at sea.[183]

Dracula's desire to settle in England is due to his believing there are more resources there—more victims for him to feed upon. While this reason may be logical, Stoker also chose England and London specifically for most of the action because he is drawing upon the city mysteries genre; the characters find Lucy's illness and the other events to be a mystery that must be solved. London becomes the primary location for the hunt for Dracula as the characters discover his various secret locations for hiding his coffins. Surprisingly, despite Dracula's blood thirst, Stoker does not suggest Dracula preys upon anyone in England other than Lucy and then Mina. However, once Lucy becomes a vampire, she begins preying upon children, adding to the mystery feeling as the newspapers and police try to solve the case of the "bloofer lady." Such crimes reflect the way crime appeared random and difficult to explain or prevent in urban cities.

In *Images of Fear*, Martin Tropp theorizes that the characters of Frankenstein's Monster, Dr. Jekyll and Mr. Hyde, and Count Dracula added a new urban form of terror to modern life and Gothic literature. Tropp states, "Random purposeless violence is the ultimate horror of the city in the twentieth century, a horror made possible by urban anonymity and the loss of community."[184] This statement is true of these novels in their own time, and helps to explain why they have remained so popular in our own, although Frankenstein's Monster does not really visit an urban setting. Stoker takes the city mysteries genre a step further here because while Féval and Reynolds allow the reader ultimately to understand even the most inexplicable crimes in their novels, removing all traces of the supernatural, the crimes committed in *Dracula* all result from vampires—supernatural beings—who cannot be explained away rationally.

Dracula's Adversaries

Once Dracula arrives in England and makes Lucy his first victim, he sets in motion a chain of events that will ultimately bring about his own demise. That happens because Lucy has a large number of friends ready to go to extremes first to protect her and then to avenge her death. In creating this circle of friends, Stoker again may have drawn upon several previous French and British texts. The band of men seeking to protect or avenge the women they love goes back as far as Bérard's novel in which Aubrey, Léonti, and Nadoor Ali band together to defeat Ruthwen. Not only as a group but individually, Dracula's adversaries reflect possible influences from earlier Gothic works.

- **Lucy Westenra:** Excepting for Mina (see below), Lucy is the most likely character to have been inspired by earlier vampire texts. The name Lucy first appears in vampire literature in Boucicault's *The Vampire* where Lucy is the first victim of the vampire. Later, Lucy's hand drags the vampire down to his grave. In Dornay's *Douglas Le Vampire*, the name again appears, having likely been taken from Boucicault's play. Here Lucy does not appear as a character, but we learn she eloped to Moldavia with another man, who is the father of her son, and that son is heir to the family fortune. Stoker knew Boucicault[185] and likely knew his play *The Vampire*. Stoker may have also known Dornay's play. Another possibility is that Stoker was inspired by the name of Lucie Manette in *A Tale of Two Cities*. This may seem like more of a stretch since Dickens' novel has no vampires in it, but as I will show below, *Dracula* has a very similar ending to *A Tale of Two Cities* that suggests a probable influence.
- **Honorable Arthur Holmwood/Lord Godalming:** Arthur may also have his origins in previous vampire works. Interestingly, in the manuscript Stoker delivered to his publisher, which survives, the names of Van

Helsing, Renfield, and Arthur Holmwood are not included. Blank spaces were left for inserting names, which was done after the novel was typed.[186] In any case, I think it likely Stoker was influenced by Féval's *Vampire City* in choosing the name Arthur. In *Vampire City*, the Duke of Wellington appears as a character. The duke's first name was Arthur and like Arthur Holmwood, he would have had the honorific "Honorable" before his name as the son of a lord. Both the duke and Arthur Holmwood would become lords upon their father's deaths, Holmwood becoming Lord Godalming during the novel's events.

- **Quincey Morris:** Quincey is the only major character in *Dracula* without a precedent in previous vampire literature. This is not surprising given he is American. Other critics have explored who or what may have inspired his creation, including the possibility that he was modeled on Colonel William F. Cody, "Buffalo Bill," whom Stoker knew through Cody's friendship with Irving.[187] Suggestions have also been made that Morris, who is at times incompetent at shooting and lets Dracula escape, may have originally been intended as an ally of Dracula, even perhaps a secret vampire.[188]

- **Dr. John Seward:** Dr. Seward does not have a namesake in vampire literature, but we have seen numerous depictions in Gothic novels of insane or allegedly insane characters and insane asylums that could have inspired his creation. In *The Count of Monte Cristo*, Dantès, disguised as Abbé Busani, feeds Villefort incredible stories, including that the Count has bought a house to open a lunatic asylum.[189] Similarly, Dracula, another count like Monte Cristo, takes an interest in an insane asylum, buying property next door to one. Adrienne in *The Wandering Jew* is held prisoner in a lunatic asylum. Similarly, we know Stoker was heavily influenced by

Wilkie Collins' *The Woman in White*, in which Laura Fairlie is also locked up in an insane asylum. In addition, Edward Bulwer-Lytton famously had his wife Rosina locked up in an insane asylum. Any of these stories could have influenced Stoker to create Dr. Seward and his asylum.

- **Dr. Abraham Van Helsing:** Van Helsing is one in a series of vampire hunters in Gothic literature, beginning with the trio who search for Lord Ruthwen in Bérard's novel. In Boucicault's *The Vampire*, an attorney studies vampires and through his efforts learns how Raby can be destroyed. In Boucicault's revision to that play, *The Phantom*, the attorney became Dr. Rees, thus making him the first doctor who is a vampire hunter. In Féval's *Vampire City*, Mrs. Radcliffe becomes a vampire hunter. She is what might almost be considered the first professional vampire hunter in Gothic fiction. Critics have suggested that Stoker modeled Van Helsing upon Arminius Vambery, one of the foremost authorities on vampires in his day, whom Stoker met. After all, in the novel Van Helsing refers three times to "Arminius"[190] as a source of information on vampires. Stoker may well have been inspired by Vambery in creating Van Helsing, but he was not the sole inspiration. There were plenty of precedents already in vampire literature. Plus, we must wonder why Stoker gave his own first name of Abraham in its full form to his vampire hunter.

Also, notably, the characters use technology to preserve their actions as a record. Mina uses her typewriter and Dr. Seward uses a phonograph. As Raj Shah suggests, Stoker may have borrowed this use of modern technology from Verne, who also uses technology in *The Carpathian Castle*. However, Verne's characters use it to make others superstitious while Stoker's characters use it to fight superstition that has become reality.

Renfield and Insanity

As an insane character, Renfield has plenty of Gothic predecessors. Numerous times characters who attempt to thwart the vampire by breaking their oath are accused of madness or insanity. While women are more apt to end up in an insane asylum in literature than men—above I mentioned Adrienne in *The Wandering Jew* and Laura in *The Woman in White*—there are plenty of male characters who do so.

In Dumas' play, Ruthven accuses Gilbert of being mad and paranoid that someone wants to kill him. Maupassant's narrator in "The Horla" also ends up in an insane asylum. In Sorr's *The Vampires of London*, Lodore gains power over Robert and convinces him to pretend to be the dead brother of Amadeus, who is supposed to marry Olivia. Under this pretense, Robert sets about terrorizing Amadeus, but he tells Amadeus he doesn't want his blood; he wants his reason. As a result, Amadeus goes insane and ends up in an asylum. One wonders if Stoker knew *The Vampires of London* given that the main character goes insane because of a vampire pursuing him, just as Harker nearly goes mad.

Certainly, the link between madness and horror is strong in Gothic fiction, horror often leading to madness, so it is not surprising that Stoker included a madman and the theme of madness in his novel.

Blood Transfusions and Blood-Drinking

The fight to destroy Dracula begins as a fight to save Lucy's life while the characters still do not know the cause of her illness. The first act in this fight is the blood transfusions she is given to replace the blood mysteriously being drained from her. While much attention has been paid by critics to the fact that the blood transfusions would have killed Lucy in real life because blood types were not understood at the time, Stoker was more interested in how the blood being sucked from Lucy affected the Count's health and vitality.

Early on, Stoker decided Dracula's blood drinking would allow him to grow younger, reversing his aging process.[191] The most likely source for this idea is Mary Braddon's story "Good Lady Ducayne" in which an old woman siphons a younger woman's blood to keep herself alive. However, the idea exists earlier in Léon Gozlan's *The Vampire of the Val-de-Grâce* where embalming is seen as a way to attain youth or prolong life. In that novel, Dr. Salomon Kanali, a chemist, studies alchemy and experiments in embalming as a step toward resurrection. This does not appear to be injecting funereal fluids into the body but other chemicals to restore life. In *Dracula*, chemicals are replaced with blood to preserve life. Dracula's ability to regenerate himself and grow younger makes him all the more formidable.

Oaths

In Chapter 25 of *Dracula*, the men all swear an oath. Stoker uses the scene to reverse how oaths were used in earlier vampire works. Beginning with Polidori's *The Vampyre*, the vampire character makes another character swear an oath not to reveal his death or the circumstances surrounding it.

The swearing of an oath appears in several other vampire works, including Nodier's play. In fact, oaths are a staple of Gothic literature. In *The Mysteries of Udolpho*, Emily swears an oath to her father on his deathbed that she will destroy papers containing family secrets without reading them. In *Melmoth the Wanderer*, Melmoth asks an English clergyman to conceal the fact of his death. In *Varney the Vampire*, a sexton swears to Varney that he will not reveal that he is a vampire, but Varney remarks no such oath is needed because the sexton will stay silent from fear for his life.

By comparison, the oath in *Dracula* is not one to maintain secrecy. It is sworn to Mina as a promise to kill her before she can fully turn into a vampire. It ties the male characters together in a bond similar to that shared by members of a secret society or by crusader knights fighting evil. In fact, Van Helsing likens them to crusader knights, saying, "we go out as the old knights of the Cross to redeem."[192]

Catholicism

Just as with the use of oaths, Stoker reinfuses new life into the Gothic depiction of Catholicism. Most British Gothic novels may be termed anti-Catholic in their depictions of the Catholic Church and its beliefs and actions. France, being largely Catholic, made French authors less prone to depict the Catholic Church as evil, although exceptions exist, such as in the novels of Eugène Sue.

Critics have often remarked upon how Stoker goes against the grain of British Gothic novels in turning Catholicism or at least Catholic holy objects into a means to fight evil, but neither is this without precedent in the Gothic tradition, even if Stoker takes it farther than previous authors. Stoker as an Irishman, though not a Catholic, probably knew more Catholics than most Englishmen and would have been more open-minded to them. Furthermore, in 1904, Florence Stoker converted to Catholicism, which suggests overall goodwill toward Catholics in the Stoker household much earlier, such as at the time of the writing of *Dracula*.

The use of holy objects dates back at least to the works of Dumas. In *The Thousand and One Ghosts*, Gregoriska protects herself by using a "blessed palm frond still wet with holy water."[193] Blessed palms have fallen out of fashion, but holy water remains popular in vampire fiction and films to this day, although notably Stoker does not use it in *Dracula*. Also in *The Thousand and One Ghosts*, Gregoriska makes the sign of the cross to protect herself before addressing her vampire brother-in-law. In Dumas' play *The Vampire*, Gilbert has a blessed sword that he drives through Ruthven's chest. In time, this sword would evolve into the popular stake that Stoker and his countless successors have used to kill their vampires.

George W. M. Reynolds in *Wagner, the Wehr-Wolf* has the title character use a crucifix to scare off Satan. Later, in *The Necromancer*, Reynolds' characters use a crucifix to open the doors of Lord Danvers' Castle so they may enter. Stoker's characters also use crucifixes as well as non-holy items like garlic to fight Dracula.

Perhaps the most interesting Catholic item used, however, is the sacred wafer that Van Helsing applies to Mina's forehead. As previously mentioned, Stoker may have been inspired to have a sacred wafer placed on Mina's forehead by an anecdote about George Croly, the author of *Salathiel*. When writing, Croly would stick an adhesive wafer to his forehead to show that he was not to be disturbed. When the wafer leaves a burn mark on Mina's forehead, Stoker is drawing upon the legend of the Wandering Jew who has a cross on his forehead, as depicted in Lewis' *The Monk* and other works. Similarly, Rio Santo has a mysterious scar on his forehead in Paul Féval's *Les Mystères de Londres*. All these marks are literary descendants of the biblical mark of Cain. God places the mark on Cain's forehead to show he is protected, but it also is a reminder that he murdered his brother and is cursed. Similarly, the Wandering Jew and related characters are cursed. In *Dracula*, Van Helsing presses the wafer to Mina's forehead to protect her, but it proclaims she is cursed like Cain because it burns her flesh. She immediately falls to her knees, seeing the burn as a sign that she is unclean; she believes she must bear the mark of shame upon her forehead until Judgment Day.

Mina and the Second Sight

While Mina is unclean as Dracula's victim, she also becomes the means for defeating him. One of the most astonishing supernatural aspects of *Dracula* is that Mina can communicate with her vampire lover, sensing his movements or reading his thoughts, which allows her to communicate his actions to the men. This power of telepathy or second sight has no precedence in British Gothic literature to my knowledge, but it is prevalent in French Gothic literature.

As we have seen, the female victims of vampires become vampires themselves in the early French Ruthven stories, and yet those female vampires, rather than being in league with their vampire seducers, strive to fight against them. The first example is Bettina in Bérard's novel *Lord Ruthwen*. However, the use of the second sight also occurs in Dumas' *The Mesmerist's Victim*. In that novel, Gilbert hypnotizes Andrée so he can learn the whereabouts of their son Sebastian. While Andrée does not know where Sebastian is, in the trance, she is able to see things usually beyond human ability. Similarly, Balsamo earlier in the Marie Antoinette novels was able to put his wife Lorenza in a trance to learn information. What makes the scene with Andrée stand out, however, and plausible as a possible source for Stoker, is that once in the trance, Andrée realizes Sebastian has had an accident and been rescued by a "vampire" doctor. Dumas used second sight or remote viewing in other novels such as *Urbain Grandier* (1841) and *The Corsican Brothers* (1844), any of which Stoker may have known. Indeed, Henry Irving acted in the play version of *The Corsican Brothers*, written by Dion Boucicault and first performed in 1852.[194] Irving's production at the Lyceum in 1880 included Stoker in the cast as an extra, the only time Stoker is ever known to have performed.[195]

Nor can we overlook the character of Polly in Féval's *Vampire City*. Polly becomes part-vampire herself after the vampire Goetzi attacks her. As his first victim, Polly has a special connection with Goetzi and declares to the other characters that she is the only one who can help kill him—oddly by inserting a key in his breast at a specific hour when he is weak. The relationship between Polly and Goetzi is interesting because, like that between Mina and Dracula, it is a mix of sympathy for the vampire and a longing to destroy him. Féval was the first author to make the vampire's female victim feel sympathy for him. Polly's connection to Goetzi is so strong that she becomes him once his body is destroyed. Nowhere in vampire literature before *Vampire City* is the female victim a type of double or complement to the vampire, and it does not happen again until *Dracula*. It seems unlikely this is a coincidence.

Even Mina's very name may have been inspired by Féval since a dog named Mina is in his novella *Knightshade*. There is also a Minna in "The Skeleton Count or the Vampire Mistress" attributed to Elizabeth Caroline Grey, but as previously discussed, this work may be a forgery and even if it is a legitimate early Gothic work, its obscurity makes it unlikely Stoker read it.

Dracula's Death and Aftermath

Stoker is to be commended for the suspense he creates in the final scenes as the characters pursue Dracula to Transylvania, but even this transcontinental pursuit of a vampire was first used in Féval's *Vampire City*. Furthermore, Dracula's death scene bears a striking resemblance to that of the Marquis de Rio Santo in Féval's *Les Mystères de Londres*.

As previously stated, Rio Santo's death scene in the moonlight makes one wonder if Féval is not suggesting the marquis has vampire-like qualities. As Rio Santo dies, the moon falls upon his body so that Mary McFarlane, leaning over his body, can see the final expression on his face.

> The moon had ascended to such a height, that its rays fell full upon the features of the dead.
> The mouth appeared to have closed with a serene smile—that dreaming, happy smile, so full of mysterious joys, which so often played upon the lips of the Marquis de Rio Santo, when he withdrew his thoughts from the world around him, and communed with himself.[196]

We are told that the moonlight, breeze, splendors of the night, and Mary kneeling over him and praying all mean "no death bed scene could be more tranquil or more beautiful."[197]

Compare the death scene of Count Dracula, which Mina relates:

> But, on the instant, came the sweep and flash of Jonathan's great knife. I shrieked as I saw it shear through the throat. Whilst at the same moment Mr. Morris's bowie knife plunged into the heart.
>
> It was like a miracle, but before our very eyes, and almost in the drawing of a breath, the whole body crumbled into dust and passed from our sight.
>
> I shall be glad as long as I live that even in that moment of final dissolution, there was in the face a look of peace, such as I never could have imagined might have rested there.[198]

Dracula finds peace in being freed from the vampirism and extended life that now appear to have tormented him, perhaps making him act unnaturally or against his will; similarly, Rio Santo may have felt forced to behave in unnatural ways due to the vengeance that consumed him.

Dracula quickly moves to its conclusion once the Count is dead. Quincey Morris dies right after Dracula from the wound he got in the battle, but as he dies, he is happy to see that Mina's forehead is once again "stainless" because Dracula is dead. The novel concludes with a scene set seven years after Dracula's death. The final section is written by Jonathan Harker, and the focus is upon his and Mina's son Quincey. Jonathan writes:

> It is an added joy to Mina and to me that our boy's birthday is the same day as that on which Quincey Morris died. His mother holds, I know, the secret belief that some of our brave friend's spirit has passed into him. His bundle of names links all our little band of men together. But we call him Quincey.[199]

The group of vampire hunters has traveled to Transylvania to see the castle again and is now discussing their past adventures when Van Helsing says, with the child Quincey on his knee:

"We want no proofs. We ask none to believe us! This boy will some day know what a brave and gallant woman his mother is. Already he knows her sweetness and loving care. Later on he will understand how some men so loved her, that they did dare much for her sake."[200]

Quincey's existence at the end of the novel is symbolic. *Dracula* scholars Robert Eighteen-Bisang and Elizabeth Miller state:

> The Harkers have been blessed with a son "whose bundle of names links all our little band of men together." They call him "Quincey." Everyone who tried to prolong their life by unnatural means is dead, but our heroes have been granted natural forms of immortality with the birth of a child and by having their stories told and retold by people all over the world for years to come.[201]

Eighteen-Bisang and Miller make two important points here: 1) the child provides a kind of immortality for the other characters, and 2) the telling of the characters' story will ensure their immortality. Both points are worth exploring for a moment, including because they reflect the possible influence of *A Tale of Two Cities* upon Stoker. We know Stoker was familiar with Dickens' novel since he arranged when Henry Irving was ill for Martin Harvey to produce the play *The Only Way*, a version of *A Tale of Two Cities*.[202] Irving was also friends with Dickens' children and Dickens himself praised Irving's performances.[203]

Quincey Harker is named for all those who fought against Dracula but mostly for Quincey Morris. Quincey Morris dies a sacrificial death just like Sidney Carton in *A Tale of Two Cities*, and like Carton, he is remembered for it. Carton envisions that one day Charles and Lucie Darnay will name a child for him. He states: "I see Her with a child upon her bosom, who bears my name."[204] Carton also knows his story will be told for generations, saying, "I see that I hold a sanctuary in their hearts, and in the hearts of their descendants, generations hence."[205] The same is true for Quincey Morris, who will not be forgotten because of the child named for him, and indeed, all the characters will be remembered through having their names bestowed on the child.

However, Quincey Harker also reflects another type of immortality for the characters. As critic Mark Hennelly notes, while Quincey Harker is born on the date of Quincey Morris' death, he is also born on the anniversary of Dracula's death, so the story that will be remembered is not only that of the protagonists but equally the story of Dracula.[206] Furthermore, Hennelly points out that because Mina drank Dracula's blood, it has entered into her veins and she may have passed it on to her son.[207] Van Helsing had said earlier that "great men and good women"[208] have sprung from Dracula's loins, and Mina's son may now be regarded as one of them, making the young Quincey the physical manifestation of the good that Dracula had to contribute. Hennelly states that the child is symbolic of the forbidden knowledge Dracula possessed and which, as Harker wished earlier, has now been preserved, although unexpectedly in Harker's own child.[209] Even more significant, as Clive Leatherdale observes:

> He [Quincey] is linked to the band of Dracula's adversaries in more than just their names: he also has their blood. Worse, he has that of Dracula flowing through his veins. His mother has sucked the blood of Dracula, who had previously sucked that of Lucy, who had already received transfusions from Seward, Van Helsing, and Holmwood. The only blood not in the boy is that of Quincey Morris, his nominal 'father,' for Lucy died before she could transmit his blood to Dracula.[210]

It is hard to imagine Stoker did not intend this symbolic blood transfusion into Quincey Harker. Hennelly observes that the child's shared names suggest he is representative of all the branches of society and both the East and West for he is American, British, Dutch, Transylvanian, upper and middle class combined.[211] Quincey's shared blood supports such a reading. Furthermore, because Dracula had lived for centuries, he provides the young Quincey with a link to the ancient past, making him an Everyman figure who carries on the traditions of the past into the twentieth century for the future of the entire human race. All of the good blood in the young Quincey is sure to predominate over any evil taints in Dracula's blood, and Van Helsing's earlier statement that from Dracula's loins sprung "great men and good women"[212] suggests that the young Quincey is a symbol of hope. While Dracula is never allowed to speak for himself in the novel—the few words he says are presented to us in the other characters' documents—he may have had the last word by his blood being passed on to Quincey. Ultimately, Dracula's redemption includes his role as the vessel through which all the blood, and consequently the bravery and goodness of his adversaries, is inherited by Quincey; therefore, while Dracula may represent the past, he indirectly helps to create hope for the future.

Stoker's novel has been criticized for being racist and xenophobic in its treatment of Eastern European cultures—even more so is the Swedish *Powers of Darkness*, at the end of which no Quincey Harker is born. But despite the novel's faults, and acknowledging that Stoker was a product of his time, one has to wonder how intentionally Stoker blends all the good and the bad into Quincey Harker; is Stoker suggesting that in the end we are all human and have our contributions to make regardless of our race, culture, or ethnic background?

With *Dracula*, the great nineteenth-century Gothic tradition ends on a note of hope, despite the horrors that the twentieth century would soon bring about—horrors that neither Stoker nor any of the authors we have explored here could have ever envisioned. Even Jules Verne would have been shocked by the atrocities of war and how advanced technologies would be used to wreak calamities upon humanity, creating a new kind of Gothic literature closely related to science fiction.

But more to our purpose here, in *Dracula* we have the culmination of the British and French Gothic literature traditions. *Dracula* is to Gothic literature what Quincey Harker represents to the other characters. *Dracula* is a story brought to life through metaphorical blood transfusions given by Lord Ruthven, the Wandering Jew, historical fiction, Mrs. Radcliffe, Dumas, Dickens, Féval, and a host of other literary figures and sources. It is as if all of the Gothic's previous characters gave their blood to create *Dracula*, and though many of their names have been forgotten, they live on in Stoker's pages.

Dracula received little critical appreciation until the 1970s, but today it garners tremendous interest from scholars. While I applaud the postcolonial interpretations it has recently received and the refining of biographical interpretations of Stoker's life, I strongly feel *Dracula* cannot be fully understood without treating it in the context of the Gothic tradition from which it sprung, a tradition as much French as British. As Quincey Harker himself represents, *Dracula* and the Gothic transcend national boundaries. There is no pure British Gothic tradition and no pure French Gothic tradition. Instead, there is a human Gothic tradition, for what is human existence if not in many ways a Gothic experience, full of fear, horror, mysteries, secrets, murder, lies, regret, grief, forgiveness, redemption, and the eternal struggle to find meaning and elusive happiness?

Afterword

"Without translation, I would be limited to the borders of my own country. The translator is my most important ally. He introduces me to the world."

— Italo Calvino

I HOPE I HAVE MADE A COMPELLING ARGUMENT that French and British Gothic authors of the nineteenth century were influenced to lesser or greater degrees by each other. What astounds me is that so few literary scholars have commented on this influence, usually limiting their comments to individual authors. *Vampire Grooms and Spectre Brides* hopefully shows that Gothic inspiration crossed the English Channel frequently and significantly.

Of course, part of why this level of influence has been ignored or even been unknown is due to language barriers. Here in the United States, few people are bilingual, much less multilingual. In Europe, speaking multiple languages is more common, but even so, few readers seek out the literature of nations beyond their own. Furthermore, many of the most influential Gothic texts have become difficult to find or forgotten. Only in the last few decades has any real *Dracula* scholarship arisen. The Gothic has always been alive, but the study of it has often been marginalized because the Gothic has been treated as a bastard child to real literature—a secret to be kept hidden away. Fortunately, publishers like Valancourt Books and Black Coat Press and translators like Brian Stableford have brought many forgotten Gothic texts in both English and French into the limelight.

The need to explore the literature of other nations and languages to understand our own has also been made apparent in recent years with the discovery that what was thought to be a simple translation into Icelandic of *Dracula* was really a rewriting or earlier version of the novel. That discovery led to the revelation that the Icelandic version was only an abridgement of the Swedish version, which is dramatically different from Stoker's original. The jury is still out on whether the variations are solely the work of the translator or result from an earlier version of Stoker's text that has not been discovered.

Also noteworthy is that the Gothic has frequently crossed cultural barriers. While Dracula is a terror to the English in Stoker's novel, the Turkish translation/adaptation by Ali Riza Seyfioglu, known as *Dracula in Istanbul*, treats him as the traditional enemy of the Turkish people. Only in recent decades have scholars begun to theorize that Stoker based Count Dracula upon Vlad Țepeș, but the 1928 Turkish version made that explicit long before literary scholars discovered it.

Furthermore, in *European Gothic*, a collection of essays about how the Gothic was made popular throughout Europe and the influences of different nations' versions of the Gothic on one another, the point is made by several contributors that the Gothic was largely a product of the process of translation, and those translations, which were often revisions or rewrites of the original texts, influenced how the Gothic developed in the languages into which the works were translated. Consequently, as Terry Hale states "many of the conventions which we associate with the British Gothic novel today arose as a by-product of the translation process."[1]

Clearly, much more exploration needs to be done of how Gothic literature has been translated and how it has influenced various cultures. Most specifically, more work needs to be done on the influences of French and British and probably also German Gothic literature upon each other. We know the three are closely connected although few scholars have explored the subjects in depth. And what about other languages and literatures' influences? Dutch author Multatuli references Eugène Sue's *The Wandering Jew* in *Max Havelaar*. Hans Christian Andersen wrote plays based upon Sir Walter Scott's novels, and the influence of Polidori's *The Vampyre* deserves far more exploration upon other European literatures. While good translators will always be needed, the power of tools like Google Translate, which allowed me to read all of *Isaac Laquedem* in English, will make other nations' literatures more easily available to us.

Furthermore, while I have focused on nineteenth-century Gothic, the influence goes well beyond into the twentieth and twenty-first centuries. In *European Gothic*, an essay by Jerrold E. Hogle explores how Gaston Leroux's *Le Fantôme de l'Opéra* (*The Phantom of the Opera*, 1908) was heavily influenced by American and British Gothic texts. In the same book, Avril Horner discusses the influence of French Gothic upon American author Djuna Barnes' novel *Nightwood* (1936). There are countless other examples.

Who knows what may result from this greater access to world literature due to increased translations? What Gothic works remain to be discovered by English-reading audiences? What Gothic works remain to be created by authors inspired by French vampire novels that were not accessible twenty years ago? Perhaps the spread of vampirism has only just begun. While Dracula failed in his mission to conquer England, Stoker, aided by translators, is conquering the world and Dracula's French and English literary ancestors will haunt the nations in his wake. The Gothic nightmare continues, and it is unlikely the world will awaken from it any time soon.

Acknowledgments

This book was a mammoth project and could not have been completed without the assistance and feedback of several people. I wish to thank the following in no particular order:

Elizabeth Kingsley for providing me with a copy of Paul Féval's *Les Mystères de Londres*.

Robert Burke for sharing my interest in Gothic literature and sending me or informing me of many Gothic works I might have otherwise overlooked.

Diana Deluca and Roslyn Hurley for reading early drafts of this book.

Jenifer Brady for her excellent proofreading skills.

Brian Stableford, without whose translations of many of the French Gothic works discussed here (see the bibliography for just how many), I never would have been able to write this book or even have been introduced so thoroughly to the wonders of French Gothic literature.

All the other translators of French novels into English.

Valancourt Books for publishing some of the more obscure English Gothic novels, including George W. M. Reynolds' *The Mysteries of London*.

The Dumas Society for providing complete texts of Dumas' novels on its website.

Google Translate for its incredible translation services.

Wikipedia, which despite its faults, is an amazing resource and often the starting point for further exploration. The French version was particularly helpful for this book.

Will Trimble for not only commissioning a translation of the Swedish *Powers of Darkness*, but for giving me the honor of an early read of the translation and the opportunity to write an introductory essay for it.

Greg Casperson, Ellen Moody, and Rory O'Farrell for research assistance in locating several books and articles.

Larry Alexander for his layout expertise, cover design, patience, and continual support of all my book projects.

Inna Vjuzhanina for her wonderful artwork for the cover. She is incredibly talented and I am especially pleased to support a Ukrainian artist during the Russian invasion of her country. Please check out her work at: www.innavjuzhanina.com.

My previous readers, especially of *The Gothic Wanderer*. Their interest encouraged me to write this second book on Gothic literature.

Bibliography

Primary Sources

Ainsworth, William Harrison. *Rookwood*. 1834. Philadelphia, PA: The Rittenhouse Press, n.d. Kindle edition.

Ainsworth, William Harrison. *Sir John Chiverton*. 1826. London: John Ebers. n.p.: Reprint Creative Media Partners, n.d.

Ainsworth, William Harrison. "The Spectre Bride." 1821. https://en.wikisource.org/wiki/The_Spectre_Bride. Accessed November 24, 2021.

Ainsworth, William Harrison. *The Tower of London*. 1840. In *The Greatest Novels of William Harrison Ainsworth (Illustrated Edition)*. n.p.: e-artnow, 2019. Kindle edition.

Anonymous. "The Mysterious Stranger." 1854. Translation of Karl Von Wachsmann's story *"Der Fremde"* ("The Stranger," 1844). Text available at https://souo.fandom.com/wiki/Full_Text:_Mysterious_Stranger. Accessed April 24, 2022.

Anonymous. *The Vampire; or, Detective Brand's Greatest Case*. 1885. Chicago, IL: Strangers from Nowhere Press, 2022.

Bérard, Cyprien. *The Vampire Lord Ruthwen*. Trans. Brian Stableford. Encino, CA: Black Coat Press, 2011. Kindle edition.

Bulwer-Lytton, Edward. *Zanoni*. 1842. Boston: Estes and Lauriat, 1892. Vol. 18 of *Bulwer's Novels Edition Deluxe*. 32 Vols.

Bulwer-Lytton, Edward. *Zanoni*. 1842. n.p.: A Public Domain Book, n.d. Kindle edition.

Boucicault, Dion. *The Phantom: A Drama in Two Acts*. New York, NY: Samuel French, 1857. Online at https://babel.hathitrust.org/cgi/pt?id=hvd.32044050957604&view=1up&seq=5&skin=2021. Accessed May 1, 2022.

Braddon, Mary Elizabeth. "Good Lady Ducayne." 1896. *Vampire Tales: The Big Collection*. n.p.: Dark Chaos, 2019. p. 318-48. Kindle edition.

Brontë, Emily. *Wuthering Heights*. 1847. New York, NY: Bantam, 1983.

Burgan, William M. "Masonic Symbolism in *The Moonstone* and *The Mystery of Edwin Drood*." *Dickens Studies Annual: Essays on Victorian Fiction*. 16 (1987): 257-303.

Burnett, Frances Hodgson. *Little Lord Fauntleroy*. In *The Frances Hodgson Burnett MEGAPACK ®: 40 Classic Works*. n.p.: Wildside Press, 2014. Kindle edition.

Burney, Fanny. *The Wanderer; or, Female Difficulties*. 1814. Oxford, Gr. Brit.: Oxford UP, 1991.

Carlyle, Thomas. *The French Revolution: A History*. 1837. New York, NY: Modern Library, 2002.

Coleridge, Samuel Taylor. "Christabel." 1816. *The Portable Coleridge*. Ed. I. A. Richards. New York, NY: Viking Press, 1970. 105-27.

Collins, Wilkie. *The Moonstone*. New York, NY: Pyramid Books, 1973.

Croly, George. *Salathiel the Immortal, a History*. 1828. London, Gr. Brit.: Henry Colburn, 1855. Miami, FL: HardPress, 2017. Kindle edition.

D'Arcy, Uriah Derick. "The Black Vampyre, a Legend of St. Domingo." 1819. Edinburgh, Gr. Brit.: Gothic World Literature Editions, 2020. Kindle edition.

Dickens, Charles. *A Tale of Two Cities*. 1859. New York, NY: Bantam, 1983.

Dickens, Charles. *The Letters of Charles Dickens*. London, Gr. Brit.: MacMillan and Co., 1909.

Dornay, Jules. *Douglas Le Vampire*. (*Douglas the Vampire*). 1865. Trans. Frank J. Morlock. In *Lord Ruthven Begins*. Encino, CA: Black Coat Press, 2010. Kindle edition.

Dumas, Alexandre. *Celebrated Crimes*. 1839-1841. In *Alexandre Dumas: Collection of 34 Classic Works with analysis and historical background (Annotated and Illustrated)*. n.p.: Annotated Classics, n.d. Kindle edition.

Dumas, Alexandre. *The Count of Monte Cristo*. 1845. Trans. Robin Buss. London, Gr. Brit.: Penguin Books, 2003. Kindle edition.

Dumas, Alexandre. "Prologue." *Isaac Laquedem: A Tale of the Wandering Jew*. 1853. Trans. Paul Terence Matthias Jackson and Cécile Césarini-Jackson. Whately, MA: Noumena Press, 2020. Pdf.

Dumas, Alexandre. *Isaac Laquedem*. 1853. French Edition. n.p.: Editions Norph-Nop, 2011. Kindle edition.

Dumas, Alexandre. *Isaac Laquedem*. 1853. Published at www.dumaspere.com. Translated by Google Translate. Accessed December 15, 2022.

Dumas, Alexandre. *Joseph Balsamo*. 1846-8. n.p.: Hawthorne Classics, 2020. Kindle edition.

Dumas, Alexandre. *The Hero of the People*. 1853. Trans. Henry Llewellyn Williams. New York, NY: J. S. Ogilvie Publishing Company, 1892. Kindle edition.

Dumas, Alexandre. *The Knight of Maison-Rouge*. 1845. Trans. Julie Rose. New York, NY: Modern Library, 2003. Kindle edition.

Dumas, Alexandre. *The Mesmerist's Victim (Annotated)*. 1848. Trans. Henry Llewellyn Williams. New York, NY: J. S. Ogilvie, 1892. Reprint. Kindle edition.

Dumas, Alexandre. *The Countess of Charny*. 1853-5. n.p.: Otbebookpublishing, n.d. Kindle edition.

Dumas, Alexandre. *The Thousand and One Ghosts*. 1849. Trans. Andrew Brown. Richmond, Gr. Brit.: Alma Classics, 2018. Kindle edition.

Dumas, Alexandre. *The Royal Life Guard*. 1853-5. In *Alexandre Dumas: Collection of 34 Classic Works with analysis and historical background (Annotated and Illustrated)*. n.p.: Annotated Classics, n.d. Kindle edition.

Dumas, Alexandre. *The Queen's Necklace*. 1859-60. In *Alexandre Dumas: Collection of 34 Classic Works with analysis and historical background (Annotated and Illustrated)*. n.p.: Annotated Classics, n.d. Kindle edition.

Dumas, Alexandre. *Storming the Bastille: (Six Years Later)*. 1853. n.p.: n.p., n.d. Kindle edition.

Dumas, Alexandre. *The Wolf Leader*. 1857. Trans. Alfred Allinson. n.p.: n.p., n.d. Kindle edition.

Dumas, Alexandre. *The Vampire*. 1851. Trans. Frank J. Morlock. In *The Return of Lord Ruthven*. Encino, CA: Black Coat Press, 2004. Kindle edition.

Edgeworth, Maria. *Harrington*. 1817. Miami, FL: HardPress, 2017. Kindle edition.

Féval, Paul. *Gentlemen of the Night*. 1848. In *Gentlemen of the Night, Captain Phantom: Two Stage Plays by Paul Féval*. Trans. Frank J. Morlock. Encino, CA: Black Coat Press, 2007. Kindle edition.

Féval, Paul. *Knightshade*. 1860 serial, 1875 book. Trans. Brian Stableford. Encino, CA: Black Coat Press, 2003. Kindle edition.

Féval, Paul. *The Mysteries of London; or Revelations of the British Metropolis*. 1844. Trans. R. Stephenson. London, Gr. Brit.: J. S. Pratt, 1847. Abridged. http://www.archive.org/details/mysteriesoflondo00step. Accessed October 23, 2021.

Féval, Paul. *Vampire City*. 1875. Trans. Brian Stableford. Encino, CA: Black Coat Press, 2003. Kindle edition.

Féval, Paul. *The Vampire Countess*. 1865. Trans. Brian Stableford. Encino, CA: Black Coat Press, 2003. Kindle edition.

Féval, Paul. *The Wandering Jew's Daughter*. 1878. Trans. Brian Stableford. Encino, CA: Black Coat Press, 2005.

Gautier, Théophile. "Clarimonde." 1836. Trans. Lafcadio Hearn. 1909. n.p.: Public Domain Book, n.d. Kindle edition.

Gilbert, William. "The Last Lords of Gardonal." 1867. *Vampire Tales: The Big Collection*. n.p.: Dark Chaos, 2019. p. 94-117. Kindle edition.

Glisic, Milovan. *After Ninety Years: The Story of Serbian Vampire Sava Savanovic*. 1880. Trans. James Lyon. n.p.: CreateSpace, 2015.

Godwin, William. *St. Leon*. 1799. New York: Oxford UP, 1994.

Gozlan, Léon. *The Vampire of the Val-de-Grâce*. 1861. Trans. Brian Stableford. Encino, CA: Black Coat Press, 2012. Kindle edition.

Grey, Elizabeth Caroline. *The Skeleton Count, or The Vampire Mistress*. 1828. n.p.: Snazz eBooks, 2012. Kindle edition.

Haggard, H. Rider. *She*. 1887. *The Works of H. Rider Haggard*. Roslyn, NY: Black's Readers Service Company, 1928. p. 173-354.

Hawthorne, Julian. "Ken's Mystery." 1888. *Vampire Tales: The Big Collection*. n.p.: Dark Chaos, 2019. p. 196-208. Kindle edition.

Hugo, Victor. *Les Misérables*. 1862. Trans. Christine Donougher. n.p.: Penguin, 2013. Kindle edition.

Hugo, Victor. *Mary Tudor (Marie Tudor)*. 1833. In *The Greatest Works of Victor Hugo*. n.p.: e-artnow, 2019.

Hugo, Victor. *Notre-Dame de Paris*. 1831. Trans. Alban Krailsheimer. Oxford, Gr. Brit.: Oxford UP, 1999. Kindle edition.

Keats, John. "La Belle Dame Sans Merci." 1820. *English Romantic Writers*. Ed. David Perkins. New York: Harcourt Brace Jovanovich, 1967. p. 1181-2.

Lamb, Lady Caroline. *Glenarvon*. 1816. London, Gr. Brit.: J. M. Dent, 1995.

Lamothe-Langon, Étienne-Léon de. *The Mysterious Hermit of the Tomb*. 1816. Trans. Brian Stableford. Encino, CA: Black Coat Press, 2018.

Lamothe-Langon, Étienne-Léon de. *The Virgin Vampire*. 1825. Trans. Brian Stableford. Encino, CA: Black Coat Press, 2011.

Le Fanu, J. S. *Carmilla*. In *In a Glass Darkly*. Vol. 3. 1872. Kindle edition.

Lyon, James. *Kiss of the Butterfly*. n.p.: CreateSpace, 2013.

Lewis, Matthew. *The Monk*. 1795. New York: Oxford UP, 1980.

Marryat, Florence. *The Blood of the Vampire*. 1897. n.p.: Xingu, 2020. Kindle edition.

Marryat, Frederick. *The Phantom Ship*. 1839. London, Gr. Brit.: n.p., 1896. Public Domain Book. Kindle edition.

Maturin, Charles. *Melmoth the Wanderer*. 1820. New York: Oxford UP, 1989.

Maupassant, Guy de. "The Horla." 1887. *Vampire Tales: The Big Collection*. n.p.: Dark Chaos, 2019. p. 190-5. Kindle edition.

Maupassant, Guy de. "The Horla." 1887. *Weird Fiction in France: A Showcase Anthology of Its Origins and Development.* Trans. Brian Stableford. Encino, CA: Black Coat Press, 2020. p. 652-703. Kindle edition.

Milton, John. *Paradise Lost.* 1667. *John Milton: Complete Poems and Prose.* Ed. Merritt Y. Hughes. New York: Macmillan, 1957. p. 207-469.

Multatuli. *Max Havelaar; or, The Coffee Auctions of the Dutch Trading Company.* 1860. New York, NY: New York Review Book, 2019.

Nizet, Marie. *Le Capitaine Vampire.* (*Captain Vampire*). 1879. Trans. Brian Stableford. Encino, CA: Black Coat Press, 2007. Kindle edition.

Nodier, Charles. *The Vampire.* 1821. Trans. Frank J. Morlock. In *Lord Ruthven the Vampyre.* Encino, CA: Black Coat Press, 2004. Kindle edition.

Planché, J. R. *The Vampire Or, The Bride Of The Isles: A Romantic Melo-Drama.* London, Gr. Brit.: John Cumberland, n.d. Text online: http://www.forgottenfutures.com/game/ff6/vampire.htm. Accessed April 28, 2022.

Polidori, John. *The Vampyre.* 1819. In *The Vampyre and Ernestus Berchtold: or, The Modern Oedipus.* 1819. *Collected Fiction of John William Polidori.* Toronto, Canada: U of Toronto P, 1994. p. 33-49.

Ponson du Terrail, Pierre-Alexis. *The Immortal Woman.* 1869. Trans. Brian Stableford. Encino, CA: Black Coat Press, 2013. Kindle edition.

Ponson du Terrail, Pierre-Alexis. *The Vampire and the Devil's Son.* 1852. Trans. Brian Stableford. n.p.: Black Coat Press, 2007. Kindle edition.

Quinet, Edgar. *Ahasuerus.* 1834. Trans. Brian Stableford. Encino, CA: Black Coat Press, 2013. Kindle edition.

Radcliffe, Ann. *The Italian.* 1797. Oxford, Gr. Brit.: Oxford UP, 1987.

Radcliffe, Ann. *The Mysteries of Udolpho.* 1794. Oxford, Gr. Brit.: Oxford UP, 1988.

Radcliffe, Ann. *The Romance of the Forest.* 1791. Oxford, Gr. Brit.: Oxford UP, 1986.

Radcliffe, Mary Anne. *Manfrone, or The One-Handed Monk*. 1809. Kansas City, MO: Valancourt Books, 2007.

Reynolds, George W. M. *Faust: A Romance of the Secret Tribunals*. 1846. London, Gr. Brit: John Dicks, n.d. Reprint by the British Library.

Reynolds, George W. M. *The Modern Literature of France*. 1839. London, Gr. Brit.: George Henderson, 1839. Vol. 1. Google Books pdf.

Reynolds, George W. M. *The Modern Literature of France*. 1839. 2 vols. London, Gr. Brit.: George Henderson, 1839. Vol. 2. Miami, FL: HardPress. Kindle edition.

Reynolds, George W. M. *The Mysteries of London*. 1845-6. Vol. 1. Richmond, VA: Valancourt Books, 2013.

Reynolds, George W. M. *The Mysteries of London*. 1845-6. Vol. 2. Richmond, VA: Valancourt Books, 2015.

Reynolds, George W. M. *The Necromancer: A Romance*. 1852. Richmond, VA: Valancourt Books, 2007. Kindle edition.

Reynolds, George W. M. *Wagner, the Wehr-Wolf*. New York: Hurst and Company, n.d. A Public Domain Book. Kindle edition.

Rymer, James Malcolm. *The Black Monk*. 1844. Richmond, VA: Valancourt Books, 2014.

Rymer, James Malcolm or Thomas Peckett Prest. *Varney the Vampire or, The Feast of Blood*. 1847. New York: Dover, 1972. 2 Vols.

Sade, Marquis de. "An Essay on Novels." *The Crimes of Love*. 1800. New York, NY: Oxford UP, 2005. p. 3-20.

Sade, Marquis de. *Justine*. 1791. New York, NY: Book-of-the-Month Club, 1993.

Scott, Sir Walter. *Anne of Geierstein*. 1829. In Waverley Novels, Vol. 7. New York: Collier Publisher, n.d. p. 235-472.

Scott, Sir Walter. *Ivanhoe*. 1819. In Waverley Novels, Vol. 3. New York: Collier Publisher, n.d. p. 1-218.

Scott, Sir Walter. *Quentin Durward*. 1823. In Waverley Novels, Vol. 6. New York: Collier Publisher, n.d. p. 140-274.

Scott, Sir Walter. *Lives of the Novelists*. "Mrs. Ann Radcliffe." Ed. Marciano Guerrero. n.p.: n.p., 2013. p. 150-94. Kindle edition.

Scribe, Eugène and Mélesville. *Being Lord Ruthven*. (orig. title *The Vampire*) Trans. Frank J. Morlock. In *Lord Ruthven the Vampyre*. Encino, CA: Black Coat Press, 2004. Kindle edition.

Seyfioglu, Ali Riza. *Dracula in Istanbul*. 1928. n.p.: Neon Harbor, 2017.

Shelley, Mary Wollstonecraft. *Frankenstein*. 1818. New York: Scholastic, 1969.

Shelley, Percy. *Prometheus Unbound: A Lyrical Drama*. 1820. *English Romantic Writers*. Ed. David Perkins. New York: Harcourt Brace Jovanovich, 1967. p. 980-1019.

Sorr, Angelo de. *The Vampires of London*. 1852. Trans. Brian Stableford. Encino, CA: Black Coat Press, 2014.

Stenbock, Eric. "The Sad Story of a Vampire." 1894. *Vampire Tales: The Big Collection*. n.p.: Dark Chaos, 2019. p. 312-6. Kindle edition.

Stoker, Bram. *Dracula: The Postcolonial Edition*. 1897. Ed. Cristina Artenie. Montreal, Canada: Universitas Press, 2016.

Stoker, Bram. "Dracula's Guest." In *Bram Stoker's Dracula Omnibus*. Edison, NJ: Chartwell Books, 1992. p. 430-41.

Stoker, Bram. *Lair of the White Worm*. 1911. In *Bram Stoker's Dracula Omnibus*. Edison, NJ: Chartwell Books, 1992. p. 309-426.

Stoker, Bram. *Powers of Darkness: the wild translation of Dracula from turn-of-the-century Sweden*. Swedish adaptation by A—e. Ed. W. Trimble. Trans. Anna Berglund. n.p.: n.p., 2022. Kindle edition.

Stoker, Bram and Valdimar Asmundsson. *Powers of Darkness: The Lost Version of Dracula*. Trans. Hans Corneel de Roos. New York and London: Overlook Duckworth Press, 2017.

Stoker, Bram. *Personal Reminiscences of Henry Irving*. 1906. In *The Collected Works of Bram Stoker*. n.p.: Delphi Classics, 2014. Kindle edition.

Stoker, Bram. *Famous Impostors*. 1910. n.p.: e-artnow, 2021. Kindle edition.

Sue, Eugène. *The Iron Trevet, or Jocelyn the Champion.* Trans. Daniel De Leon. In *The Mysteries of the People: History of a Proletarian Family Across the Ages.* n.p.: Otbebookpublishing, 2018. p. 2223-2525. Kindle edition.

Sue, Eugène. *The Mysteries of Paris.* 1842-3. Trans. Carolyn Betensky and Jonathan Loesberg. New York, NY: Penguin, 2015.

Sue, Eugène. *The Pocket Bible or Christian the Printer.* Trans. Daniel De Leon. In *The Mysteries of the People: History of a Proletarian Family Across the Ages.* n.p.: Otbebookpublishing, 2018. p. 2845-3431. Kindle edition.

Sue, Eugène. *The Sword of Honor.* Trans. Solon De Leon. In *The Mysteries of the People: History of a Proletarian Family Across the Ages.* n.p.: Otbebookpublishing, 2018. p. 3891-4525. Kindle edition.

Sue, Eugène. *The Wandering Jew.* e-artnow, 2020. Kindle edition. Trans. unknown but same as the W. L. Allison edition. New York, circa 1869-92.

Tolstoy, Alexei. "The Curse of the Vourdalak." *Vampire Tales: The Big Collection.* n.p.: Dark Chaos, 2019. p. 70-85. Kindle edition.

Trollope, Anthony. *Barchester Towers.* 1857. New York, NY: Bantam Books, 1959.

Trollope, Anthony. *The Small House at Allington.* 1864. n.p.: Musaicum Books, 2017. Kindle edition.

Trollope, Anthony. *The Way We Live Now.* 1875. *The Second Anthony Trollope's Collected Works.* n.p.: James Books, 2016. Kindle edition.

Verne, Jules. *The Carpathian Castle.* 1892. New York, NY: Ace Books, 1963.

Verne, Jules. *The Mysterious Island.* 1875. Orinda, CA: SeaWolf Press, 2022.

Verne, Jules. *Twenty Thousand Leagues Under the Sea.* 1870. Trans. I. O. Evans. London, Gr. Brit.: Octopus Books, 1980.

Villiers de l'Isle-Adam, Jean-Marie-Mathias-Philippe-Auguste. *Claire Lenoir.* 1867. *Weird Fiction in France: A Showcase Anthology of Its Origins and Development.* Trans. Brian

Stableford. Encino, CA: Black Coat Press, 2020. p. 420-578. Kindle edition.

Wallace, Lew. *Ben-Hur*. 1880. London, Gr. Brit: Dean & Son, n.d.

Wallace, Lew. "Introductory Letter." *Tarry Thou Till I Come or Salathiel, The Wandering Jew* by George Croly. New York & London: Funk & Wagnalls Company, 1901. https://www.gutenberg.org/cache/epub/56750/pg56750-images.html. Accessed November 11, 2021.

Wallace, Lew. *The Prince of India*. New York: Harper and Brothers, 1893. 2 vols.

Walpole, Horace. *The Castle of Otranto*. 1764. *The English Novel Before the Nineteenth Century*. Eds. Annette Brown Hopkins and Helen Sard Hughes. Boston: Ginn, 1915. p. 483-577.

Wells, H. G. *The Island of Dr. Moreau*. 1896. New York: Tor, 1996.

Wilde, Lady. *Ancient Legends Mystic Charms & Superstitions of Ireland*. 1888. LONDON, Gr. Brit.: Chatto & Windus, 1919. https://www.gutenberg.org/files/61436/61436-h/61436-h.htm. Accessed May 14, 2022.

Secondary Sources

Andersen, Jens. *Hans Christian Andersen*. Trans. Tiina Nunnaly. New York: Overlook Duckworth, 2005.

Anderson, George K. *The Legend of the Wandering Jew*. Providence, RI: Brown UP, 1965.

Andrews, S. G. "Shelley, Medwin, and The Wandering Jew." *Keats-Shelley Journal*. 20 (1971): 78-86.

Artenie, Cristina. *Dracula: A Study of Editorial Practices*. Montreal, Canada: Universitas Press, 2016.

Artenie, Cristina. Ed. *Dracula: The Postcolonial Edition* by Bram Stoker. Montreal, Canada: Universitas Press, 2016.

Artenie, Cristina. *Dracula Invades England*. Montreal, Canada: Universitas Press, 2015.

Atkinson, Juliette. "The London Library and the Circulation of French Fiction in the 1840s." *Information & Culture: A Journal of History*. 48:4 (2013): 391-418. https://muse.jhu.edu/article/523365. Accessed February 6, 2022.

Baehr, Carl. "11 Short Streets with Curious Names." November 17, 2020. https://urbanmilwaukee.com/2020/11/17/city-streets-11-short-streets-with-curious-names/. Accessed August 9, 2021.

Belford, Barbara. *Bram Stoker and the Man Who Was Dracula*. Cambridge, MA: De Capo Press, 2002.

Bellos, David. *The Novel of the Century: The Extraordinary Adventure of* Les Misérables. New York, NY: Farrar, Straus and Giroux, 2017.

Berghorn, Rickard. "Dracula's Way to Sweden: A Unique Version of Stoker's Novel." *Weird Webzine: Fantasy and Surreality*. http://weirdwebzine.com/draculitz.html. Accessed August 19, 2020. Site no longer active.

Birkhead, Edith. *The Tale of Terror: A Study of the Gothic Romance*. 1921. New York: Russell and Russell, 1963.

Blumberg, Jane. *Mary Shelley's Early Novels*. Iowa City, IA: U of Iowa P, 1993.

Brooks, Peter. "Foreword." *The Mysteries of Paris* by Eugène Sue. New York, NY: 2015. p. xiii-xv.

Brundan, Katy, Melanie Jones, and Benjamin Mier-Cruz. "Dracula or Draculitz?: Translation Forgery and Bram Stoker's 'Lost Version' of *Dracula*." *Victorian Review*. 45.2 (2019): 293-306.

Buss, Robin. "A Note on the Text." In *The Count of Monte Cristo* by Alexandre Dumas. Trans. Robin Buss. n.p.: Penguin Books, n.d. Kindle edition.

Buss, Robin. "Notes." In *The Count of Monte Cristo* by Alexandre Dumas. Trans. Robin Buss. n.p.: Penguin Books, n.d. Kindle edition.

Campbell, James L. *Edward Bulwer-Lytton*. Boston: Twayne, 1986.

Carver, Stephen. "The Design of Romance: *Rookwood*, Scott, and the Gothic." Blog post January 16, 2013. https://ainsworthandfriends.wordpress.com/2013/01/16/the-design-of-romance-rookwood-scott-and-the-gothic/. Accessed October 22, 2021.

Carver, Stephen. *The Man Who Outsold Dickens: The Life and Work of W. H. Ainsworth.* Barnsley, Gr. Brit.: 2020.

Chevasco, Berry. "Lost in Translation: The Relationship between Eugène Sue's *Les Mystères de Paris* and G. W. M. Reynolds's *The Mysteries of London*." *G. W. M. Reynolds: Nineteenth Century Fiction, Politics, and the Press*. New York, NY: Routledge, 2016. p. 135-48.

Chevasco, Berry Palmer. *Mysterymania: The Reception of Eugène Sue in Britain, 1838-1860*. Frankfurt: Peter Lang, 2003.

Chevasco, Berry Palmer. *The Reception of Eugène Sue in Britain, 1838-1860*. Dissertation. University College London. 2000.

Collins, Dick. "George William McArthur Reynolds: A Biographical Sketch." In *The Necromancer: A Romance* by George W. M. Reynolds. Richmond, VA: Valancourt Books, 2007. Kindle edition.

Collins, Dick. "Afterword." In *The Necromancer: A Romance* by George W. M. Reynolds. Richmond, VA: Valancourt Books, 2007. Kindle edition.

Cornwell, Neil. "European Gothic and Nineteenth-Century Russian Literature." *European Gothic: A Spirited Exchange 1760-1960*. Ed. Avril Horner. Manchester, Gr. Brit.: Manchester UP, 2002. p. 104-27.

Coward, David. "Introduction." *The Crimes of Love* by the Marquis de Sade. New York, NY: Oxford UP, 2005. p. vii-xxxi.

Crawford, Heide. *The Origins of the Literary Vampire*. Lanham, MD: Rowman and Littlefield, 2016.

Dargan, E. Preston. "Scott and the French Romantics." *PMLA*. 49.2 (June 1934): 599-629.

Davidson, Arthur F. *Alexandre Dumas: His Life and Works*. 1902. Reprint. n.p.: Perfect-Life Biographies, 2017. Kindle edition.

Day, William Patrick. *In the Circles of Fear and Desire: A Study of Gothic Fantasy*. Chicago: U of Chicago P, 1985.

De Roos, Hans C. "Introduction: *Makt Myrkranna*: The Forgotten Book." In *Powers of Darkness: The Lost Version of Dracula*. New York: Overlook Duckworth, 2017. p. 13-43.

Devonshire, M. G. *The English Novel in France, 1830-1870*. 1929. New York, NY: Octagon Books, 1967. Internet archive.

https://archive.org/details/englishnovelinfr0000devo/. Accessed July 3, 2022.

Dobrée, Bonamy. "Introduction." *The Mysteries of Udolpho* by Ann Radcliffe. Oxford, Gr. Brit.: Oxford UP, 1988.

Dodd, Kevin. "Plot Variations in the Nineteenth-Century Story of Lord Ruthven, Pt. 1." *Journal of Vampire Studies*. 1.2 (2020): 19-43.

Dodd, Kevin. "Plot Variations in the Nineteenth-Century Story of Lord Ruthven, Pt. 2." *Journal of Vampire Studies.* 1.2 (2021): 192-209.

Dodd, Kevin. "'Blood Suckers Most Cruel:' The Vampire and the Bat in and before Dracula." *The Tale of the Living Vampyre: New Directions in Vampire Studie*s. Montreal, Canada: Universitas Press, 2021. p. 86-105.

Eigner, Edwin M. "Charles Darnay and Revolutionary Identity." *Dickens Studies Annual: Essays on Victorian Fiction*. 12 (1983): 147-59.

Eighteen-Bisang, Robert and Elizabeth Miller. *Drafts of Dracula*. n.p.: Tellwell Talent, 2019. Kindle edition.

Ellis, Kate Ferguson. *The Contested Castle: Gothic Novels and the Subversion of Domestic Ideology*. Urbana: U of Illinois P, 1989.

The Examiner. "Review of 'Notre-Dame: A Tale of the Ancien Regime.'" *Nineteenth-Century Literature Criticism*. Ed. Janet Mullane and Robert Thomas Wilson. Vol. 21. Gale, 1989. *Gale Literature Resource Center*. https://link.gale.com/apps/doc/H1420014838/LitRC?u=viva_gmu&sid=LitRC&xid=09faa4a9. Accessed May 26, 2020. Originally published in *The Examiner*, no. 1334, August 25, 1833. p. 533-4.

Flibbert, Joseph T. "Dickens and the French Debate over Realism: 1838-1856." *Comparative Literature*. 23.1 (1971): 18-31.

Forster, John. *The Life of Charles Dickens*. London, Gr. Brit.: Cecil Palmer, 1872-4. Full text online at http://victorian-studies.net/CD-Forster.html. Accessed July 28, 2022.

Franklin, Wayne. *James Fenimore Cooper: The Early Years*. New Haven, CT: Yale UP, 2007.

Gaull, Marilyn. *English Romanticism: The Human Context*. New York, NY: W. W. Norton, 1988.

Glen, Heather. "Introduction." *Tales of Angria* by Charlotte Brontë. London, Gr. Brit.: Penguin, 2006. p. xi-lii.

Goldberg, Michael. *Carlyle and Dickens*. Athens: U of Georgia P, 1972.

Grosskurth, Phyllis. *Byron: The Flawed Angel*. Boston: Houghton Mifflin, 1997.

Haggis, Donald. "The Popularity of Scott's Novels in France and Balzac's Illusions perdues." *J. European Studies*. XV (1985): 21-29.

Haining, Peter and Peter Tremayne. *The Un-Dead: The Legend of Bram Stoker and Dracula*. London: Constable, 1997.

Hale, Terry. "Translation in Distress: Cultural Misappropriation and the Construction of the Gothic. *European Gothic: A Spirited Exchange 1760-1960*. Ed. Avril Horner. Manchester, Gr. Brit.: Manchester UP, 2002. p. 17-38.

Hogle, Jerrold E. "The Gothic Crosses the Channel: Abjection and Revelation in *Le Fantôme de l'Opéra*." *European Gothic: A Spirited Exchange 1760-1960*. Ed. Avril Horner. Manchester, Gr. Brit.: Manchester UP, 2002. p. 204-29.

Holley, William Bradley. *Fantastic Encounters: Identity, Belief and the Supernatural in Works by Paul Féval*. Dissertation. University Of Alabama, 2011. https://ir.ua.edu/bitstream/handle/123456789/1308/file_1.pdf?sequence=1&isAllowed=y. Accessed March 19, 2022.

Hornback, Bert G. *"Noah's Arkitecture": A Study of Dickens's Mythology*. Athens: Ohio UP, 1972.

Horner, Avril. "A Detour of Filthiness: French Fiction and Djuna Barnes's *Nightwood*." *European Gothic: A Spirited Exchange 1760-1960*. Ed. Avril Horner. Manchester, Gr. Brit.: Manchester UP, 2002. p. 230-51.

Horner, Avril Ed. *European Gothic: A Spirited Exchange 1760-1960*. Manchester, Gr. Brit.: Manchester UP, 2002.

Horner, Avril. "Introduction." *European Gothic: A Spirited Exchange 1760-1960*. Ed. Avril Horner. Manchester, Gr. Brit.: Manchester UP, 2002. p. 1-16.

Humpherys, Anne and Louis James, eds. *G. W. M. Reynolds: Nineteenth Century Fiction, Politics, and the Press*. New York, NY: Routledge, 2016.

Humpherys, Anne and Louis James. "Introduction." *G. W. M. Reynolds: Nineteenth Century Fiction, Politics, and the Press*. New York, NY: Routledge, 2016. p. 1-16.

Hurwitz, S. "Ahasver, the Eternal Wanderer: Psychological Aspects." *The Wandering Jew: Essays in the Interpretation of a Christian Legend*. Eds. Galit Hasan-Rokem and Alan Dundes. Bloomington, IN: Indiana UP, 1986. p. 210-26.

Isaac-Edersheim, E. "Ahasver: A Mythic Image of the Jew." *The Wandering Jew: Essays in the Interpretation of a Christian Legend*. Eds. Galit Hasan-Rokem and Alan Dundes. Bloomington, IN: Indiana UP, 1986. p. 195-210.

James, Louis. "Time, Politics and the Symbolic Imagination in Reynolds's Social Melodrama." *G. W. M. Reynolds: Nineteenth Century Fiction, Politics, and the Press*. New York, NY: Routledge, 2016. p. 181-200.

James, Sara. "G. W. M. Reynolds and the Modern Literature of France." *G. W. M. Reynolds: Nineteenth Century Fiction, Politics, and the Press*. New York, NY: Routledge, 2016. p. 19-32.

Johnson, Edgar. *Charles Dickens: His Tragedy and Triumph*. 2 vols. New York, NY: Simon & Schuster, 1952.

Johnson, Edgar. *Sir Walter Scott: The Great Unknown*. 2 vols. New York, NY: MacMillan, 1970.

Jordan, Alexander Hugh. "A Latter-Day Mystery: Thomas Carlyle and Eugène Sue." *Victorian Literature and Culture*. 45.3 (2017): 493-508. DOI: https://doi.org/10.1017/S106015031700002X Published online by Cambridge University Press: August 25, 2017. https://www.cambridge.org/core/journals/victorian-literature-and-culture/article/latterday-mystery-thomas-carlyle-and-eugene-sue/9B4A5D1075CFFC32F0C1E60C150A2EA8. Accessed February 6, 2022.

Kester, Monica. "The Ironic History of 'It Was a Dark and Stormy Night.'" https://historyofyesterday.com/the-ironic-history-of-it-was-a-dark-stormy-night-7762242724db. Accessed February 2, 2022.

Knight, Stephen. *G. W. M. Reynolds and His Fiction: The Man Who Outsold Dickens*. New York, NY: Routledge, 2019.

Knight, Stephen. *The Mysteries of the Cities: Urban Crime Fiction in the Nineteenth Century*. Jefferson, NC: McFarland & Company, 2012.

Krailsheimer, Alban. "Introduction." 1993. *Notre-Dame de Paris* by Victor Hugo. Oxford, Gr. Brit.: Oxford UP, 1999. p. vii-xxiv. Kindle edition.

Lanone, Catherine. "Verging on the Gothic: Melmoth's Journey to France." *European Gothic: A Spirited Exchange 1760-1960*. Ed. Avril Horner. Manchester, Gr. Brit.: Manchester UP, 2002. p. 71-83.

Lindsay, Jack. *Charles Dickens*. New York, NY: Philosophical Library, 1950.

Lofficier, Jean-Marc. "Introduction." In *Lord Ruthven Begins*. Encino, CA: Black Coat Press, 2010. Kindle edition.

Lofficier, Jean-Marc and Randy. *Shadowmen: Heroes and Villains of French Pulp Fiction*. Encino, CA: Black Coat Press, 2003.

Looser, Devoney. "'Her Later Works Happily Forgotten': Rewriting Frances Burney and Old Age." *Eighteenth-Century Life*. 37.3 (2013): 1-28.

Ludlam, Harry. *A Biography of Dracula: The Life Story of Bram Stoker*. London, Gr. Brit.: Foulsham, 1962.

Lycett, Andrew. *Wilkie Collins: A Life of Sensation*. London, Gr. Brit.: Windmill Books, 2014.

Lyons, Shawn R. "Fact and Fiction: The French Revolution in the Works of Charles Dickens and Frances Burney." Thesis. U of Alaska at Anchorage, 1995.

Lytton, Earl of. *The Life of Edward Bulwer First Lord Lytton*. London, Gr. Brit.: MacMillan, 1913. 2 vols.

Macdonald, D. L. *Poor Polidori: A Critical Biography of the Author of* The Vampyre. Toronto, Canada: U of Toronto P, 1991.

Macdonald, D. L. and Kathleen Scherf. "Introduction." *The Vampyre and Ernestus Berchtold: or, The Modern Oedipus.* 1819. *Collected Fiction of John William Polidori.* Toronto, Canada: U of Toronto P, 1994. p. 1-29.

Manning, Robert Douglas. "Eugène Sue." In *The Wandering Jew (and the Wandering Jewess).* Canada: SALE, 2013.

Marcus, David D. "The Carlylean Vision of *A Tale of Two Cities.*" *Studies in the Novel.* 8 (1976): 56-68.

Matthews, John. *The Mystery of Spring-Heeled Jack: From Victorian Legend to Steampunk Hero.* Rochester, VT: Destiny Books, 2016.

Maxwell, Richard. "Appendix III: Dickens and His Sources." In *A Tale of Two Cities* by Charles Dickens. New York: Penguin, 2003. p. 399-443.

Maxwell, Richard. "Introduction." In *A Tale of Two Cities* by Charles Dickens. New York, NY: Penguin, 2003. p. ix-xxxiii.

McMorran, Will. "The Marquis de Sade in English, 1800-1850." *The Modern Language Review.* 112.3 (2017): 549-66.

Miles, Robert. "Europhobia: The Catholic Other in Horace Walpole and Charles Maturin." *European Gothic: A Spirited Exchange 1760-1960.* Ed. Avril Horner. Manchester, Gr. Brit.: Manchester UP, 2002. p. 84-103.

Morlock, Frank J. "Introduction." In *Gentlemen of the Night, Captain Phantom: Two Stage Plays by Paul Féval.* Trans. Frank J. Morlock. Encino, CA: Black Coat Press, 2007. Kindle edition.

Morlock, Frank J. "Introduction: The Birth of Modern Vampirism." In *Lord Ruthven the Vampyre.* Encino, CA: Black Coat Press, 2004. Kindle edition.

Morlock, Frank J. "Introduction: The Dark Side of Alexandre Dumas." In *The Return of Lord Ruthven.* Encino, CA: Black Coat Press, 2004. Kindle edition.

Mulvey-Roberts, Marie. *Dangerous Bodies: Historicising the Gothic Corporeal.* Manchester, Gr. Brit.: Manchester UP, 2016.

Murray, Paul. *From the Shadow of Dracula: A Life of Bram Stoker.* Dublin, Ireland: Fitz-Press, 2016.

Myerson, Joel. "Poe's Manuscript Review of 'The Wandering Jew.'" *Studies in the American Renaissance.* (1991): 201-11. https://www.jstor.org/stable/30227608?seq=1. Accessed March 29, 2022.

Nelson, Harland S. "Shadow and Substance in *A Tale of Two Cities.*" *The Dickensian.* 84:2.415 (1988): 96-106.

Nethercot, Arthur C. *The Road to Tryermaine: A Study of the History, Background, and Purposes of Coleridge's "Christabel".* 1939. Westport, CT: Greenwood Press, 1967.

The New American Bible. New York: Thomas Nelson, 1971.

Oddie, William. *Dickens and Carlyle: The Question of Influence.* London, Gr. Brit.: Centenary, 1972.

Partridge, Eric. *The French Romantics' Knowledge of English Literature (1820-1848).* Paris, France: Libraire Ancienne Édouard Champion, 1924.

Paulson, Ronald. *Representations of Revolution (1789-1820).* New Haven, CT: Yale UP, 1983.

Plasma, Panton. "On the Spectacle and History of The Black Vampyre." In *"The Black Vampyre, a Legend of St. Domingo" by Uriah Derick D'Arcy.* Edinburgh, Gr. Brit.: Gothic World Literature Editions, 2020. p. 11-24. Kindle edition.

Power, Albert. "Who Marvels at the Mysteries of the Moon." *The Green Book: Writings on Irish Gothic, Supernatural and Fantastic Literature.* 14 (Samhain 2019): 7-21. Swan River Press. https://www.jstor.org/stable/10.2307/48573143. Accessed July 3, 2022.

Prawer, S. S. *Karl Marx and World Literature.* London, Gr. Brit.: Oxford UP, 1976.

Punter, David. *The Literature of Terror: A History of Gothic Fictions from 1765 to the present day.* New York, NY: Longman, 1980.

Rhodes, Gary D. and John Edgar Browning. "About the Book." In *The Vampire; or, Detective Brand's Greatest Case.* Chicago, IL: Strangers from Nowhere Press, 2022. p. 5-6.

Rhodes, Gary D. and John Edgar Browning. "About the Author." In *The Vampire; or, Detective Brand's Greatest Case.* Chicago, IL: Strangers from Nowhere Press, 2022. p. 7-8.

Rhodes, Gary D. and John Edgar Browning. "America's First Vampire Novel and the Supernatural as Artifice." In *The Vampire; or, Detective Brand's Greatest Case*. Chicago, IL: Strangers from Nowhere Press, 2022. p. 243-66.

Robb, Graham. *Victor Hugo: A Biography*. New York, NY: W. W. Norton, 1998.

Roberts, Marie. *Gothic Immortals: The Fiction of the Brotherhood of the Rosy Cross*. London, Gr. Brit.: Routledge, 1990.

Rogers, Samuel. *Balzac and the Novel*. n.p.: Octagon Books, 1969.

Ross, Michael. *Alexandre Dumas*. Gr. Brit.: New Abbot, 1981.

Senf, Carol. *The Vampire in Nineteenth Century English Literature*. Bowling Green, OH: Bowling Green State U Popular P, 1988.

Shah, Raj. "Counterfeit Castles: The Age of Mechanical Reproduction in Bram Stoker's *Dracula* and Jules Verne's *Le Château des Carpathes*." *Texas Studies in Literature and Language*. 56.4 (2014): 428-71.

Shannon, Mary L. "Introduction." *The Mysteries of London* by George W. M. Reynolds. Vol. 2. Richmond, VA: Valancourt Books, 2015. p. v-x.

Simpson, Samuel James. "Beyond 'Monk' Lewis." Thesis. University of York, January 2017. White Rose eTheses Online. https://etheses.whiterose.ac.uk/17458/. Accessed September 26, 2021.

Skal, David J. *Something in the Blood: The Untold Story of Bram Stoker the Man Who Wrote Dracula*. New York, NY: Liveright, 2016.

Soubigou, Gilles. "Dickens's Illustrations: France and Other Countries." In *The Reception of Charles Dickens in Europe*. Ed. Michael Hollington. London, Gr. Brit.: A&C Black, 2013. p. 154-67.

Stableford, Brian. "Afterword." In *Captain Vampire* by Marie Nizet. 1879. Trans. Brian Stableford. Encino, CA: Black Coat Press, 2007. Kindle edition.

Stableford, Brian. "Afterword." In *The Immortal Woman* by Pierre-Alexis Ponson du Terrail. Encino, CA: Black Coat Press, 2013. Kindle edition.

Stableford, Brian. "Afterword." In *The Vampire and the Devil's Son* by Pierre-Alexis Ponson du Terrail. Encino, CA: Black Coat Press, 2007. Kindle edition.

Stableford, Brian. "Afterword." In *The Wandering Jew's Daughter* by Paul Féval. Encino, CA: Black Coat Press, 2005.

Stableford, Brian. "Afterword." In *Vampire City* by Paul Féval. Encino, CA: Black Coat Press, 2003. Kindle edition.

Stableford, Brian. "Afterword: A Brief Note on the Theodicy of *La Vampire*." In *The Virgin Vampire* by Étienne-Léon de Lamothe-Langon. Encino, CA: Black Coat Press, 2011.

Stableford, Brian. "Afterword: Nineteenth-Century Vampire Fiction Before and After *The Vampire Countess*, with Some Further Observations on Hesitations and Inconsistencies in the Text." In *The Vampire Countess* by Paul Féval. Encino, CA: Black Coat Press, 2003. Kindle edition.

Stableford, Brian. "Introduction." In *Ahasuerus* by Edgar Quinet. Encino, CA: Black Coat Press, 2013. Kindle edition.

Stableford, Brian. "Introduction." In *Captain Vampire* by Marie Nizet. Encino, CA: Black Coat Press, 2007. Kindle edition.

Stableford, Brian. "Introduction." In *The Immortal Woman* by Pierre-Alexis Ponson du Terrail. Encino, CA: Black Coat Press, 2013. Kindle edition.

Stableford, Brian. "Introduction." In *The Mysterious Hermit of the Tomb* by Étienne-Léon de Lamothe-Langon. Encino, CA: Black Coat Press, 2018.

Stableford, Brian. "Introduction." In *The Parisian Jungle, Book One: The Engraved Armband* by Paul Féval. Encino, CA: Black Coat Press, 2008. Kindle edition.

Stableford, Brian. "Introduction." In *The Vampire and the Devil's Son* by Pierre-Alexis Ponson du Terrail. Encino, CA: Black Coat Press, 2007. Kindle edition.

Stableford, Brian. "Introduction." In *The Vampire of the Val-de-Grâce* by Léon Gozlan. Trans. Brian Stableford. Encino, CA: Black Coat Press, 2012.

Stableford, Brian. "Introduction." In *The Vampire Lord Ruthwen* by Cyprien Bérard. Encino, CA: Black Coat Press, 2011. Kindle edition.

Stableford, Brian. "Introduction." In *The Wandering Jew's Daughter* by Paul Féval. Encino, CA: Black Coat Press, 2005.

Stableford, Brian. "Introduction." In *Vampire City* by Paul Féval. Encino, CA: Black Coat Press, 2003. Kindle edition.

Stableford, Brian. "Introduction." In *Weird Fiction in France: A Showcase Anthology of Its Origins and Development*. Trans. Brian Stableford. Encino, CA: Black Coat Press, 2020. Kindle edition.

Stableford, Brian. "Notes." In *The Vampire Countess* by Paul Féval. Encino, CA: Black Coat Press, 2003. Kindle edition.

Stowell, Robert. "Brontë Borrowings: Charlotte Brontë and *Ivanhoe*, Emily Brontë and *The Count of Monte Cristo*." *Brontë Society Transactions*. 21.6 (1996): 249-251. https://www.encyclopedia.com/arts/educational-magazines/count-monte-cristo. Accessed November 10, 2021.

Taylor, Antony. "'Some Little or Contemptible War upon her Hands': *Reynolds's Newspaper* and Empire." *G. W. M. Reynolds: Nineteenth Century Fiction, Politics, and the Press*. New York, NY: Routledge, 2016. p. 99-120.

Tennyson, G. B. *Sartor Called Resartus: The Genesis, Structure, and Style of Thomas Carlyle's First Major Work*. Princeton, NJ: Princeton UP, 1966.

Tichelaar, Tyler R. "'Christabel': Coleridge's Conflict between Christianity and Celtic Pantheism." *Michigan Academician*. 27.4 (1995): 493-501.

Tichelaar, Tyler R. *The Gothic Wanderer: From Transgression to Redemption, Gothic Literature from 1794-present*. Ann Arbor, MI: Modern History Press, 2012.

Tichelaar, Tyler R. "Romania and Racism in the Swedish *Dracula*." In *Powers of Darkness: the wild translation of Dracula from turn-of-the-century Sweden*. Swedish adaptation by A—e. Ed. W. Trimble. Trans. Anna Berglund. n.p.: n.p., 2022. Kindle edition.

Timko, Michael. "Splendid Impressions and Picturesque Means: Dickens, Carlyle, and the French Revolution." *Dickens Studies Annual: Essays on Victorian Fiction*. 12 (1983): 177-95.

Tombs, Robert. "Introduction." In *Les Misérables* (*The Wretched*) by Victor Hugo. New York: Penguin Books, 2013. Kindle edition.

Townshend, Dale. "On the Authorship of *Manfrone*." In *Manfrone, or The One-Handed Monk* by Mary Anne Radcliffe. Kansas City, MO: Valancourt Books, 2007. p. 265-96.

Twitchell, James B. *The Living Dead: A Study of the Vampire in Romantic Literature*. Durham, NC: Duke UP, 1981.

Walz, Robin. "The Crime Factory: The Missed Fortunes of Paul Féval's *Les Habits Noirs*." *Proceedings of the Western Society for French History*. 37 (2009): 205-19.

Warren, Louis S. "Buffalo Bill Meets Dracula: William F. Cody, Bram Stoker, and the Frontiers of Racial Decay." *The American Historical Review*. 107.4 (2002): 1124-57.

Williams, Anne. *Art of Darkness: The Poetics of Gothic*. Chicago, IL: U of Chicago P, 1995.

Wilson, Angus. *The World of Charles Dickens*. New York: Viking, 1970.

Wolff, Robert Lee. *Strange Stories and Other Explorations in Victorian Fiction*. Boston, MA: Gambit, 1971.

Worth, George. *William Harrison Ainsworth*. New York, NY: Twayne Publishers, 1972.

Wright, Angela. "European Disruptions of the Idealized Woman: Matthew Lewis's *The Monk* and the Marquis de Sade's *La Nouvelle Justine*." *European Gothic: A Spirited Exchange 1760-1960*. Ed. Avril Horner. Manchester, Gr. Brit.: Manchester UP, 2002. p. 39-54.

Zatlin, Linda Gertner. *The Nineteenth Century Anglo-Jewish Novel*. Boston, MA: Twayne, 1981.

Films

Dracula, Dead and Loving It. Dir. Mel Brooks. Gaumont, Brooksfilms, and Castle Rock Entertainment, 1995. Starring Leslie Nielsen.

Bram Stoker's Dracula. Dir. Francis Ford Coppola. American Zoetrope and Osiris Films, 1992. Starring Gary Oldman,

Winona Ryder, Keanu Reeves, and Anthony Hopkins.
The Haunted Castle. Dir. George Méliès. 1896. Available at YouTube.
Tower of London. Dir. Rowland V. Lee. Universal Pictures, 1939. Starring Boris Karloff and Basil Rathbone.
Tower of London. Dir. Roger Corman. Admiral Pictures, 1962. Starring Vincent Price and Michael Cate.

Websites of Interest

Websites are too numerous to list, especially since multiple pages at Wikipedia and French Wikipedia were consulted in writing this book. Please consult the endnotes for specific website addresses.

My blog can be found at:

GothicWanderer.com and

thegothicwanderer.wordpress.com.

Endnotes

Introduction

1. Collins, Wilkie p. 359.
2. Trollope, *The Small House*, p. 281.
3. Trollope, *Barchester Towers*, p. 424.
4. Braddon p. 324.
5. Quoted in Atkinson p. 21-2.
6. Horner, "Introduction," p. 1.
7. Reynolds, *Modern Literature*, Vol 1. p. iv.
8. Jordan.
9. Hale p. 31.

Chapter 1 Vampire Invasion

1. Macdonald and Scherf p. 22.
2. Stableford, "Introduction," *Vampire City*.
3. Dobrée p. v.
4. Dobrée p. v.
5. Féval, "Prologue," *Vampire City*.
6. Partridge p. 42.
7. Partridge p. 100.
8. Wright p. 40.
9. Sade p. 13.
10. Sade p. 13.
11. Sade p. 13.
12. Coward p. 27.
13. https://en.wikipedia.org/wiki/Matthew_Lewis_(writer). Accessed September 26, 2021.
14. Simpson p. 9-10.
15. Reynolds, *Modern Literature*, Vol. 1. p. 83.
16. Stableford, "Introduction," *The Mysterious Hermit*, p. 15.
17. Reynolds, *Modern Literature*, Vol. 1. p. 112.
18. Reynolds, *Modern Literature*, Vol. 1. p. 113.
19. Lofficier, *Shadowmen*, p. 7-8.
20. Reynolds, *Modern Literature*, Vol. 1. p. 238.
21. Lanone p. 75.
22. Rogers p. 21.
23. Reynolds, *Modern Literature*, Vol. 1. p. 29.
24. Lofficier, *Shadowmen*, p. 73.
25. Johnson, *Sir Walter Scott*, p. 972.
26. Franklin p. 248-51.
27. Andersen p. 598.
28. Multatuli p. 163.
29. https://en.wikipedia.org/wiki/Waverly,_Tioga_County,_New_York. Accessed September 2, 2021.
30. Baehr.
31. https://en.wikipedia.org/wiki/Walter_Scott. Accessed September 16, 2021.
32. https://en.wikipedia.org/wiki/Walter_Scott. Accessed September 16, 2021.
33. Prawer p. 386.
34. Johnson, *Sir Walter Scott*, p. 1001.
35. Johnson, *Sir Walter Scott*, p. 1001-3.
36. Dargan p. 601.
37. Partridge p. 120.
38. Haggis p. 21.
39. Dargan p. 603.
40. Dargan p. 605.
41. Dargan p. 620-1.
42. Ross p. 51, 76, 146.
43. Haggis p. 21.
44. Dargan p. 614-5.

45. Haggis p. 28.
46. Haggis p. 29, n. 7.
47. Haggis p. 27-8.
48. Quoted in Haggis p. 29, n. 6.
49. Dargan p. 619.
50. Dargan p. 605.
51. Dargan p. 607.
52. Dargan p. 610.
53. Partridge p. 259-61.
54. Partridge p. 134-5.
55. Partridge p. 141.
56. Partridge p. 198.
57. Partridge p. 271.
58. Partridge p. 240.
59. Partridge p. 271.
60. Partridge p. 271.
61. Lamb p. 123.
62. Gaull p. 250.
63. Twitchell p. 104.
64. Twitchell p. 75.
65. Stableford, "Introduction," *The Vampire Lord Ruthwen*.
66. Grosskurth p. 343.
67. Twitchell p. 107.
68. Stableford, "Introduction," *The Vampire Lord Ruthwen*.
69. Macdonald p. 192-6.
70. Punter p. 119.
71. Macdonald p. 201.
72. Polidori p. 37.
73. Punter p. 118.
74. Roberts p. 96.
75. Macdonald p. 136.
76. Macdonald p. 192.
77. Macdonald p. 193.
78. Macdonald p. 193.
79. Macdonald p. 171.

Chapter 2 Historicizing the Gothic and Gothicizing History

1. Looser p. 1.
2. Scott, *Ivanhoe*, p. 40.
3. Scott, *Ivanhoe*, p. 217.
4. Robb p. 101.
5. Robb p. 101.
6. Robb p. 101.
7. Reynolds, *Modern Literature*, "Chapter 1: Victor Hugo," Vol. 2.
8. Reynolds, *Modern Literature*, "Chapter 1: Victor Hugo," Vol. 2.
9. Hugo, *Les Misérables*, Book X, Chapter 5.
10. Partridge p. 267.
11. Partridge p. 267.
12. *The Examiner* p. 533.
13. Reynolds, *Modern Literature*, "Chapter 1: Victor Hugo," Vol. 2.
14. Dargan p. 610-12.
15. Krailsheimer.
16. Krailsheimer.
17. Robb p. 119-20.
18. Hugo, *Notre-Dame de Paris*, Book 5, Chapter 2.
19. Hugo, *Notre-Dame de Paris*, Book 7, Chapter 4.
20. Hugo, *Notre-Dame de Paris*, Book 4, Chapter 5.
21. Hugo, *Notre-Dame de Paris*, Book 5, Chapter 1.
22. Hugo, *Notre-Dame de Paris*, Book 9, Chapter 1.
23. Hugo, *Notre-Dame de Paris*, Book 9, Chapter 6.
24. Hugo, *Notre-Dame de Paris*, Book 11, Chapter 1.
25. Krailsheimer.
26. Hugo, *Notre-Dame de Paris*, Book 11, Chapter 1.
27. Hugo, *Notre-Dame de Paris*, Book 11, Chapter 3.
28. Hugo, *Notre-Dame de Paris*, Book 2, Chapter 3.
29. https://en.wikipedia.org/wiki/Shtriga. Accessed August 7, 2020.

30. Hugo, *Notre-Dame de Paris*, Book 4, Chapter 1.
31. Zatlin p. 135n.
32. Hugo, *Notre-Dame de Paris*, Book 4, Chapter 3.
33. Hugo, *Notre-Dame de Paris*, Book 4, Chapter 5.
34. Hugo, *Notre-Dame de Paris*, Book 11, Chapter 2.
35. Krailsheimer.
36. Johnson, *Sir Walter Scott*, p. 1000.
37. Carver, *The Man Who Outsold Dickens*, p. 39.
38. Williams p. 22-3.
39. Carver, blog post. https://ainsworthandfriends.wordpress.com/2013/01/16/the-design-of-romance-rookwood-scott-and-the-gothic/. Accessed November 7, 2021.
40. Carver, blog post. https://ainsworthandfriends.wordpress.com/2013/01/16/the-design-of-romance-rookwood-scott-and-the-gothic/. Accessed November 7, 2021.
41. Carver, *The Man Who Outsold Dickens*, p. 58.
42. Glen p. xxii.
43. Glen p. xxiii.
44. Burnett, Chapter 9.
45. Carver, *The Man Who Outsold Dickens*, p. 119, 129.
46. Carver, *The Man Who Outsold Dickens*, p. 143.
47. Carver, *The Man Who Outsold Dickens*, p. 181.
48. Wikipedia. https://en.wikipedia.org/wiki/The_Tower_of_London_(novel). Accessed September 15, 2021.
49. Ainsworth, *The Tower of London*, Preface.
50. Ainsworth, *The Tower of London*, Preface.
51. Carver, *The Man Who Outsold Dickens*, p. 129-30.
52. Worth p. 71-3.
53. Hugo, *Notre-Dame de Paris*, Book V, Chapter 2.
54. Ainsworth, *The Tower of London*, Part I, Chapter 3.
55. Carver, *The Man Who Outsold Dickens*, p. 119.
56. Carver, *The Man Who Outsold Dickens*, p. 125.
57. Carver, *The Man Who Outsold Dickens*, p. 125.
58. Carver, *The Man Who Outsold Dickens*, p. 125.
59. Worth p. 63-4.
60. Carver, *The Man Who Outsold Dickens*, p. 121.
61. Ainsworth, *The Tower of London*, Part I, Chapter 1.
62. Robb p. 101.
63. Ainsworth, *The Tower of London*, Part II, Chapter 20.
64. Ainsworth, *The Tower of London*, Part II, Chapter 29.
65. Ainsworth, *The Tower of London*, Part II, Chapter 42.

Chapter 3 City Mysteries

1. Sue, *The Mysteries of Paris*, p. 856.
2. Sue, *The Mysteries of Paris*, p. 384-5.
3. Flibbert p. 18.
4. Flibbert p. 19.
5. Flibbert p. 26.
6. Partridge p. 287.
7. Knight, *The Mysteries of the Cities*, Chapter 1.
8. Partridge p. 128.
9. Brooks p. xiii.
10. Brooks p. xiii.

11. Brooks p. xiii.
12. https://en.wikipedia.org/wiki/The_Mysteries_of_Paris. Accessed November 3, 2021.
13. Brooks p. xiii; https://en.wikipedia.org/wiki/The_Mysteries_of_Paris. Accessed November 3, 2021.
14. https://fr.wikipedia.org/wiki/Les_Myst%C3%A8res_de_Londres. Accessed November 8, 2021. Translation from Microsoft Translator Online.
15. Lofficier, *Shadowmen*, p. 8.
16. Betensky and Loesberg, p. 57n, 645n.
17. Sue, *The Mysteries of Paris*, p. 5.
18. Knight, *The Mysteries of the Cities*, Chapter 1 and footnote 40.
19. Sue, *The Mysteries of Paris*, p. 41.
20. https://fr.wikipedia.org/wiki/Les_Myst%C3%A8res_de_Londres. Accessed November 8, 2021; Walz p. 210. Walz says December 20, 1832 for the beginning serialization of the novel, but this is surely a typo for 1842.
21. Quoted in Knight, *The Mysteries of the Cities*, Chapter 3.
22. Knight, *The Mysteries of the Cities*, Chapter 3.
23. Morlock, "Introduction," *The Gentlemen of the Night, Captain Phantom*; Knight, *The Mysteries of the Cities*, Chapter 3, footnote 6.
24. Knight, *The Mysteries of the Cities*, Chapter 3.
25. Féval, *Les Mystères de Londres*, p. 434.
26. Knight, *The Mysteries of the Cities*, Chapter 3.
27. Féval, *Les Mystères de Londres*, p. 447.
28. Knight, *The Mysteries of the Cities*, Chapter 3.
29. Féval, *Les Mystères de Londres*, p. 374.
30. Féval, *Les Mystères de Londres*, p. 468.
31. Féval, *Les Mystères de Londres*, p. 508.
32. Féval, *Les Mystères de Londres*, p. 508-9.
33. Féval, *Les Mystères de Londres*, p. 509.
34. Stoker, *Dracula*, p. 364.
35. Féval, *Les Mystères de Londres*, p. 409.
36. https://en.wikipedia.org/wiki/Burke_and_Hare_murders. Accessed November 3, 2021.
37. Morlock, "Introduction," *The Gentlemen of the Night, Captain Phantom*.
38. Lofficier, *Shadowmen*, p. 124.
39. https://fr.wikipedia.org/wiki/La_Quittance_de_minuit. Accessed March 19, 2022.
40. Lofficier, *Shadowmen*, p. 237.
41. Morlock, "Introduction," *The Gentlemen of the Night, Captain Phantom*.
42. https://en.wikipedia.org/wiki/Twenty_Thousand_Leagues_Under_the_Seas#English_translations; https://en.wikipedia.org/wiki/The_Mysterious_Island#Publication_history_in_English. Accessed August 26, 2022.
43. Collins, Dick, "George William MacArthur Reynolds: A Biographical Sketch"; Knight, *G. W. M. Reynolds and His Fiction*, p. 1.
44. Collins, Dick, "George William MacArthur Reynolds: A

45. Collins, Dick, "George William MacArthur Reynolds: A Biographical Sketch."
46. https://en.wikipedia.org/wiki/George_W._M._Reynolds. Accessed November 7, 2021.
47. Reynolds, *Modern Literature*, Vol. 1. p. 218-9.
48. Reynolds, *Modern Literature*, Vol 2. Chapter 1.
49. Collins, Dick, "George William MacArthur Reynolds: A Biographical Sketch."
50. James, Sara. p. 21.
51. Knight, *George W. M. Reynolds and His Fiction*, p. 19.
52. https://en.wikipedia.org/wiki/The_Body_Snatcher. Accessed November 7, 2021.
53. Reynolds, *Modern Literature*, Vol 2. Chapter 3.
54. https://en.wikipedia.org/wiki/Bandiera_brothers. Accessed November 7, 2021.
55. https://theculturetrip.com/europe/united-kingdom/articles/there-were-eight-assassination-attempts-on-queen-victoria/. Accessed November 20, 2021.
56. Reynolds, *The Mysteries of London*, Vol. 2, p. 1133-4.
57. Shannon p. ix-x.
58. Knight, *The Mysteries of the Cities*, Chapter 2.
59. Knight, *The Mysteries of the Cities*, Chapters 1 and 2.
60. Humpherys and James, "Introduction," p. 3.
61. Knight, *The Mysteries of the Cities*, Chapter 2.
62. Chevasco, "Lost in Translation," p. 139, 146.
63. https://en.wikipedia.org/wiki/The_Mysteries_of_Paris. Accessed November 3, 2021.
64. https://fr.wikipedia.org/wiki/Les_Myst%C3%A8res_de_Londres. Accessed November 8, 2021.
65. Lofficier, *Shadowmen*, p. 8.
66. Buss, "A Note on the Text."
67. Buss, "Notes," Chapter XIV, footnote 2.
68. Dumas, *Count of Monte Cristo*, p. 152.
69. Dumas, *Count of Monte Cristo*, p. 412.
70. Dumas, *Count of Monte Cristo*, p. 354.
71. Dumas, *Count of Monte Cristo*, p. 373.
72. Dumas, *Count of Monte Cristo*, p. 322.
73. Dumas, *Count of Monte Cristo*, p. 413.
74. Dumas, *Count of Monte Cristo*, p. 475.
75. Dumas, *Count of Monte Cristo*, p. 477.
76. Dumas, *Count of Monte Cristo*, p. 1043.
77. Dumas, *Count of Monte Cristo*, p. 1079.
78. Stowell p. 249-51.
79. https://en.wikipedia.org/wiki/Ben-Hur:_A_Tale_of_the_Christ#Characters. Accessed November 10, 2021.
80. Stableford, "Introduction," *The Parisian Jungle*.

Chapter 4 Wandering Jews

1. Zatlin p. 135n.
2. Hurwitz p. 222; Tennyson p. 201.
3. Tennyson p. 212.
4. Isaac-Edersheim p. 190, 198.

5. Isaac-Edersheim p. 197.
6. Isaac-Edersheim p. 196.
7. Roberts p. 208.
8. Roberts p. 74.
9. Roberts p. 75.
10. Tennyson p. 202.
11. Roberts p. 74.
12. Anderson p. 168-73.
13. Roberts p. 78.
14. Roberts p. 75.
15. Anderson p. 177.
16. Andrews p. 85.
17. Anderson p. 179.
18. Lewis p. 168.
19. Lewis p. 169-70.
20. Lewis p. 172.
21. Lewis p. 176.
22. Day p. 38.
23. Anderson p. 180.
24. Radcliffe, *The Italian*, p. 35.
25. Carver, *The Man Who Outsold Dickens*, p. 12.
26. https://en.wikisource.org/wiki/The_Spectre_Bride. Accessed November 24, 2021.
27. https://en.wikisource.org/wiki/The_Spectre_Bride. Accessed November 24, 2021.
28. https://en.wikisource.org/wiki/The_Spectre_Bride. Accessed November 24, 2021.
29. https://en.wikisource.org/wiki/The_Spectre_Bride. Accessed November 24, 2021.
30. https://en.wikisource.org/wiki/The_Spectre_Bride. Accessed November 24, 2021.
31. Power p. 14.
32. Power p. 14.
33. Croly p. 1.
34. Croly p. 25.
35. Croly p. 43.
36. Croly p. 43.
37. Croly p. 232.
38. Croly p. 326-7.
39. https://en.wikipedia.org/wiki/Flying_Dutchman#Origins. Accessed November 13, 2021.
40. Croly p. 447.
41. Croly p. 459.
42. Crowley p. 179.
43. Croly p. 462-3.
44. Croly p. 467.
45. Croly p. 469.
46. Croly, *Salathiel*, 1901 Funk & Wagnall edition. p. 532-5. Available at https://www.gutenberg.org/cache/epub/56750/pg56750-images.html. Accessed November 12, 2021.
47. Croly p. 172-3.
48. Power p. 7-8.
49. Power p. 16.
50. Anderson p. 189-90.
51. Murray p. 184-5.
52. Stoker, *Famous Impostors*, Chapter 3: The Wandering Jew.
53. Stoker, *Dracula*, p. 291-2.
54. Power p. 21.
55. https://en.wikipedia.org/wiki/Ben-Hur:_A_Tale_of_the_Christ. Accessed November 14, 2021.
56. Power p. 7.
57. Stableford, "Introduction," *The Wandering Jew's Daughter*, p. 34.
28. https://en.wikipedia.org/wiki/Edgar_Quinet. Accessed November 14, 2021.
59. Quinet, *Ahasvérus*, "The Second Day: The Passion, II."
60. Quinet, *Ahasvérus*, "The Second Day: The Passion, VII."
61. Quinet, *Ahasvérus*, "The Third Day, XIII."
62. Quinet, *Ahasvérus*, "The Third

Day, XIX."
63. Quinet, *Ahasvérus*, "The Fourth Day, XIII."
64. https://en.wikipedia.org/wiki/Edgar_Quinet. Accessed November 16, 2021; Stableford, "Introduction," *Ahasvérus*.
65. Stableford, "Introduction," *Ahasvérus*.
66. Stableford, "Introduction," *Ahasvérus*.
67. Anderson p. 201.
68. Manning, "Eugène Sue."
69. Anderson p. 232.
70. Anderson p. 235. Anderson cites what was then an unpublished manuscript review in the Henry E. Huntington Library, San Marino, California. The review was published in 1991 by Joel Myerson in "Poe's Manuscript Review of 'The Wandering Jew.'" *Studies in the American Renaissance*. (1991): 201-11.
71. Sue, *The Wandering Jew*, p. 156-7.
72. Sue, *The Wandering Jew*, p. 6.
73. Sue, *The Wandering Jew*, p. 158.
74. Sue, *The Wandering Jew*, p. 1367, 1378, 1381.
75. https://en.wikipedia.org/wiki/The_Wandering_Jew_(Sue_novel). Accessed December 11, 2021.
76. Tombs p. xiv.
77. Sue, *The Wandering Jew*, p. 241.
78. Sue, *The Wandering Jew*, p. 1472.
79. Sue, *The Wandering Jew*, p. 1484.
80. Sue, *The Wandering Jew*, p. 1506.
81. https://en.wikipedia.org/wiki/The_Wandering_Jew_(Sue_novel). Accessed December 11, 2021.
82. Sue, *The Wandering Jew*, p. 130.
83. Sue, *The Wandering Jew*, p. 131-2.
84. Sue, *The Wandering Jew*, p. 1220.
85. Sue, *The Wandering Jew*, p. 695.
86. Sue, *The Wandering Jew*, p. 1306-7.
87. Sue, *The Wandering Jew*, p. 140.
88. Sue, *The Wandering Jew*, p. 725.
89. Sue, *The Wandering Jew*, p. 861.
90. Chevasco, *The Reception of the Fiction of Eugène Sue in Britain, 1838-1860*, p. 33.
91. https://encyclopedia2.thefreedictionary.com/Marie-Joseph-Eugene+Sue. Accessed June 16, 2022.
92. Manning, "Eugène Sue."
93. https://fr.wikipedia.org/wiki/Le_Juif_errant_(opéra). Accessed December 11, 2021.
94. https://en.wikipedia.org/wiki/Le_Juif_errant_(opera). https://fr.wikipedia.org/wiki/Le_Juif_errant_(opéra). Accessed December 11, 2021.
95. Multatuli p. 236.
96. Stoker, *Famous Impostors*, Chapter 3: The Wandering Jew.
97. Ludlam p. 97.
98. Lycett p. 193-202.
99. Taylor p. 105.
100. Stableford, "Introduction," *Ahasvérus*.
101. http://www.dumaspere.com/pages/bibliotheque/chapitre.php?lid=r25&cid=42. Accessed December 15, 2021.
102. Dumas, Prologue to *Isaac Laquedem*, p. 73.
103. Dumas, Prologue to *Isaac Laquedem*, p. 91.
104. Dumas, Prologue to *Isaac Laquedem*, p. 95.
105. Dumas, Prologue to *Isaac Laquedem*, p. 96.

106. Anderson p. 263.
107. Anderson p. 263.
108. http://www.dumaspere.com/pages/dictionnaire/isaac_laquedem.html. Accessed December 17, 2021.
109. http://www.dumaspere.com/pages/dictionnaire/isaac_laquedem.html. Accessed December 17, 2021.
110. Davidson, Chapter 8.
111. Stableford, "Introduction," *The Wandering Jew's Daughter*, p. 12.
112. Stableford, Back Cover Text of *The Wandering Jew's Daughter*.
113. Féval, *The Wandering Jew's Daughter*, p. 202.
114. Stableford "Introduction," *The Wandering Jew's Daughter*, p. 8.
115. Stableford, "Introduction," *The Wandering Jew's Daughter*, p. 7.

Chapter 5 Secret Societies

1. qtd. in Paulson p. 223.
2. qtd. in Paulson p. 223.
3. Paulson p. 24.
4. Paulson p. 241.
5. Macdonald p. 192.
6. Macdonald p. 191.
7. Paulson p. 241.
8. Blumberg p. 49.
9. Blumberg p. 51.
10. https://en.wikipedia.org/wiki/Vehmic_court#Origin. Accessed December 23, 2021.
11. Scott, *Anne of Geierstein*, p. 362-3.
12. Scott, *Anne of Geierstein*, p. 364.
13. Scott, *Anne of Geierstein*, p. 367.
14. Scott, *Anne of Geierstein*, p. 367.
15. https://en.wikipedia.org/wiki/George_W._M._Reynolds#Novels. Accessed December 23, 2021.
16. https://en.wikipedia.org/wiki/George_W._M._Reynolds#Novels. Accessed December 23, 2021.
17. James, Louis. p. 190.
18. Reynolds, *Wagner, the Wehr-Wolf*, Chapter 53.
19. Reynolds, *Wagner, the Wehr-Wolf*, Chapter 58.
20. De Roos p. 35-6.
21. Berghorn p. 15.
22. https://en.wikipedia.org/wiki/Hermetic_Order_of_the_Golden_Dawn. Accessed January 16, 2022.
23. https://en.wikipedia.org/wiki/Cipher_Manuscripts. Accessed January 20, 2022.
24. Stuart p. 325.
25. *Powers of Darkness*, Part I, Harker's Journal, the 21st.
26. *Powers of Darkness*, Part I, Harker's Journal, the 25th.
27. *Powers of Darkness*, Part III, Chapter 2.
28. *Powers of Darkness*, Part III, Chapter 2.
29. *Powers of Darkness*, Afterword.
30. Berghorn cited at https://en.wikipedia.org/wiki/Powers_of_Darkness#The_Swedish_Count_as_a_Social_Darwinist. Accessed January 22, 2022.
31. See *Personal Reminiscences of Sir Henry Irving*, Chapter 38.
32. Murray p. 49.
33. Féval, *Les Mystères de Londres*, p. 447.

Chapter 6 The French Revolution Revised

1. Murray p. 183-4.
2. https://exhibits.lib.byu.edu/

literaryworlds/lytton.html. Accessed January 30, 2022.
3. https://en.wikipedia.org/wiki/Edward_Bulwer-Lytton#cite_note-47. Accessed January 31, 2022.
4. https://fr.wikipedia.org/wiki/Zanoni. Accessed January 31, 2022.
5. "Introduction." *Zanoni*. p. 4. Kindle edition.
6. https://biography.yourdictionary.com/edward-bulwer-lytton. Accessed January 30, 2022.
7. Bulwer-Lytton p. xiv-xv; Campbell p. 115.
8. Bulwer-Lytton p. 255.
9. Birkhead p. 80.
10. Bulwer-Lytton p. 176.
11. Bulwer-Lytton p. xiv.
12. Campbell p. 115.
13. Campbell p. 116.
14. Wolff p. 185, 207.
15. Bulwer-Lytton p. 192.
16. Bulwer-Lytton p. 195.
17. Bulwer-Lytton p. 243.
18. Bulwer-Lytton p. 243.
19. Bulwer-Lytton p. 243.
20. Bulwer-Lytton p. 243.
21. Bulwer-Lytton p. 272.
22. Bulwer-Lytton p. 272.
23. Bulwer-Lytton p. 376.
24. Bulwer-Lytton p. 377.
25. Wolff p. 226.
26. Bulwer-Lytton p. 298.
27. Bulwer-Lytton p. 341-2.
28. Bulwer-Lytton p. 393.
29. Bulwer-Lytton p. 419.
30. Punter p. 172.
31. Roberts p. 181.
32. Campbell p. 114; Roberts p. 179.
33. Lytton, *Life*, p. 35.
34. Partridge p. 128.
35. Devonshire p. 264.
36. Kester.
37. Ross p. 196.
38. Carlyle p. 301.
39. Davidson, Chapter 8.
40. https://en.wikipedia.org/wiki/Alexandre_Dumas#The_Marie_Antoinette_romances. Accessed August 28, 2021.
41. https://en.wikipedia.org/wiki/The_Queen%27s_Necklace. Accessed August 28, 2021.
42. Lofficier, *Shadowmen*, p. 152.
43. Morlock, "Introduction: The Dark Side of Alexandre Dumas."
44. Dumas, *The Storming of the Bastille*, Chapter 10.
45. Dickens, *A Tale of Two Cities*, p. 13.
46. Forster, Book 9, Chapter 2.
47. Dumas, *The Storming of the Bastille*, Chapter 13.
48. Dumas, *The Storming of the Bastille*, Chapter 14.
49. Dumas, *The Hero of the People*, Chapter 15.
50. Dumas, *The Hero of the People*, Chapter 15.
51. Dumas, *The Hero of the People*, Chapter 30.
52. Dumas, *The Royal Life Guard*, Chapter 27.
53. Soubigou p. 159.
54. Johnson, *Charles Dickens*, p. 537.
55. Johnson, *Charles Dickens*, p. 537.
56. Soubigou p. 159.
57. Johnson, *Charles Dickens*, p. 611-2.
58. Johnson, *Charles Dickens*, p. 612.
59. February 4, 1863 letter to French actor Charles Fechter. *The Letters*

of *Charles Dickens* p. 554. (Earlier Dickens had told Fechter he'd be happy to meet Féval in a November 4, 1862 letter.)
60. Dumas, *The Countess of Charny*, Chapter 32.
61. https://fr.wikipedia.org/wiki/Complot_de_l%27%C5%93illet. Accessed August 29, 2021.
62. https://en.wikipedia.org/wiki/Le_Chevalier_de_Maison-Rouge. Accessed August 29, 2021.
63. Carlyle p. 580.
64. Dumas, *Le Chevalier de Maison-Rouge*, Chapter 16.
65. Dumas, *Le Chevalier de Maison-Rouge*, Chapter 51.
66. Dumas, *Le Chevalier de Maison-Rouge*, Chapter 54.
67. Dumas, *Le Chevalier de Maison-Rouge*, Chapter 56.
68. Maxwell, "Appendix III," p. 435.
69. http://www.dumaspere.com/pages/dictionnaire/chevalier_maison_rouge_th.html. Accessed September 5, 2021.
70. Maxwell, "Appendix III," p. 440.
71. https://en.wikipedia.org/wiki/Benjamin_Nottingham_Webster. Accessed September 5, 2021.
72. Devonshire p. 322.
73. Jordan. https://www.cambridge.org/core/journals/victorian-literature-and-culture/article/latterday-mystery-thomas-carlyle-and-eugene-sue/9B4A5D1075CFFC32F0C1E60C150A2EA8#en6.
74. Maxwell, "Introduction," p. xiii, xxxi.
75. Maxwell, "Introduction," p. xiii.
76. Maxwell, "Introduction," p. xvi-xvii.
77. Maxwell, "Appendix III," p. 418-421.
78. Maxwell, "Introduction," p. xvii.
79. Maxwell, "Appendix III," p. 430-1.
80. Maxwell, "Introduction," p. xxv.
81. Maxwell, "Appendix III," p. 431.
82. Maxwell, "Appendix III," p. 437.
83. Dickens, *A Tale of Two Cities*, p. 205.
84. Dickens, *A Tale of Two Cities*, p. 351.
85. Sue, *The Sword of Honor*, p. 3916.
86. Sue, *The Sword of Honor*, p. 3921.
87. Nelson p. 96-106.
88. Dickens, *A Tale of Two Cities*, p. 1.
89. Hornback p. 87-8.
90. Hornback p. 121.
91. Hornback p. 122.
92. Marcus p. 58.
93. Goldberg p. 116-7.
94. Hornback p. 119.
95. Lyons p. 84.
96. Oddie p. 81n.
97. Dickens, *A Tale of Two Cities*, p. 35.
98. Dickens, *A Tale of Two Cities*, p. 256.
99. Dickens, *A Tale of Two Cities*, p. 36.
100. Dickens, *A Tale of Two Cities*, p. 89.
101. Carlyle p. 167-8.
102. Oddie p. 81n.
103. Dickens, *A Tale of Two Cities*, p. 11.
104. Dickens, *A Tale of Two Cities*, p. 11.
105. Dickens, *A Tale of Two Cities*, p. 12.
106. Dickens, *A Tale of Two Cities*, p. 11.
107. Milton, XI, lines 330-1.
108. Hornback p. 122.

109. Dickens, *A Tale of Two Cities*, p. 253.
110. Dickens, *A Tale of Two Cities*, p. v.
111. Goldberg p. 118.
112. Dickens, *A Tale of Two Cities*, p. 305.
113. Dickens, *A Tale of Two Cities*, p. 310.
114. Burgan p. 295.
115. Burgan p. 257-8.
116. Eigner p. 151.
117. Eigner p. 155.
118. Dickens, *A Tale of Two Cities*, p. 82.
119. Dickens, *A Tale of Two Cities*, p. 138.
120. Dickens, *A Tale of Two Cities*, p. 138.
121. Dickens, *A Tale of Two Cities*, p. 140-1.
122. Marcus p. 65.
123. Timko p. 193.
124. Wilson p. 267.
125. Dickens, *A Tale of Two Cities*, p. 255.
126. Dickens, *A Tale of Two Cities*, p. 351.
127. Lyons p. 49.
128. Dickens, *A Tale of Two Cities*, p. 352.
129. Goldberg p. 123-4.
130. Dickens, *A Tale of Two Cities*, p. 352.
131. Lyons p. 49.
132. Dickens, *A Tale of Two Cities*, p. 352.
133. Lindsay p. 365.
134. Lyons p. 50.
135. Marcus p. 61.
136. Dickens, *A Tale of Two Cities*, p. 352.

Chapter 7 The Road to *Dracula*

1. Stuart p. 3.
2. Polidori p. 43.
3. Polidori p. 49.
4. Stableford, "Introduction," *The Vampire Lord Ruthwen*.
5. Stableford, "Introduction," *The Vampire Lord Ruthwen*.
6. Dodd, "Plot Variations, Part I," p. 28.
7. Morlock, "Introduction: The Birth of Modern Vampirism."
8. https://en.wikipedia.org/wiki/Charles_Nodier. Accessed September 13, 2021.
9. Robb p. 118.
10. Dodd, "Plot Variations, Part I," p. 30.
11. https://en.wikipedia.org/wiki/The_Vampire_(play). Accessed April 30, 2022.
12. https://en.wikipedia.org/wiki/The_Vampire_(play). Accessed April 30, 2022.
13. Stuart p. 118.
14. Stuart p. 134-5.
15. Stuart p. 136.
16. Stuart p. 138.
17. https://en.wikipedia.org/wiki/Dion_Boucicault#Life_and_career. Accessed April 7, 2022.
18. Plot summary of *The Vampire* adapted from Dodd, "Plot Variations," p. 200-1.
19. Stuart p. 149.
20. Eighteen-Bisang and Miller p. 248, 258.
21. Boucicault p. 9.
22. https://en.wikipedia.org/wiki/The_Phantom_(play). Accessed April 8, 2022.
23. Stuart p. 154.
24. Dornay, Act I, Scene I.

25. Dodd, "Plot Variations, Part II," p. 205-6.
26. Eighteen-Bisang and Miller p. 251.
27. Murray p. 125.
28. Rhodes and Browning p. 245.
29. https://en.wikipedia.org/wiki/The_Black_Vampyre:_A_Legend_of_St._Domingo. Accessed March 26, 2022.
30. Plasma p. 11-2.
31. Plasma p. 22.
32. Plasma p. 18.
33. D'Arcy p. 44.
34. D'Arcy p. 40.
35. D'Arcy p. 54.
36. Plasma p. 16.
37. D'Arcy p. 54.
38. Lamothe-Langon, *The Virgin Vampire*, Chapter 23.
39. Lamothe-Langon, *The Virgin Vampire*, Chapter 10.
40. Stableford, "Afterword: A Brief Note on the Theodicy of *La Vampire*."
41. Stableford, "Afterword: A Brief Note on the Theodicy of *La Vampire*."
42. Lamothe-Langon, *The Virgin Vampire*, Chapter 8.
43. D'Arcy p. 65-8.
44. https://en.wikipedia.org/wiki/Elizabeth_Caroline_Grey#The_Skeleton_Count,_or_The_Vampire_Mistress. Accessed March 27, 2022.
45. Matthews p. 56-7.
46. Matthews p. 56-7.
47. Gautier p. 5-6.
48. Gautier p. 28.
49. Gautier p. 21.
50. Dumas, *The Thousand and One Ghosts*, p. 185-6.
51. Dumas, *The Thousand and One Ghosts*, p. 195-6.
52. Dumas, *The Thousand and One Ghosts*, p. 197-98.
53. Dumas, *The Thousand and One Ghosts*, p. 203.
54. Knight, *G. W. M. Reynolds and His Fiction*, p. 167, 181.
55. Collins, Dick, "Afterword."
56. Collins, Dick, "Afterword."
57. Collins, Dick, "Afterword."
58. Canadian Centre for Occupational Health and Safety. https://www.ccohs.ca/oshanswers/diseases/rabies.html. Accessed June 25, 2022.
59. Sorr, Chapter 5.
60. https://fr.wikipedia.org/wiki/Angelo_de_Sorr. Accessed June 25, 2022.
61. Stableford, "Introduction," *The Immortal Woman*.
62. Stableford, "Introduction," *The Vampire and the Devil's Son*.
63. Stableford, "Introduction," *The Vampire and the Devil's Son*.
64. Stableford, "Afterword," *The Vampire and the Devil's Son*.
65. Stableford, "Introduction," *The Vampire and the Devil's Son*.
66. Stableford, "Introduction," *The Vampire and the Devil's Son*. The passage is on pages 465-6 of *Claire Lenoir* which can be found in the bibliography.
67. Stableford, "Introduction," *The Vampire of the Val-de-Grâce*.
68. Dodd, "Plot Variations, Part II," p. 203-4.
69. Bellos p. 183.
70. Stuart p. 343, n. 23.
71. Stableford, "Afterword," *The Vampire Countess*.
72. Stableford, "Notes," *The Vampire*

73. *Countess*, n. 102.
74. Stableford, "Introduction," *Knightshade*.
74. Stableford, "Introduction," *Knightshade*.
75. Stableford, "Introduction," *Vampire City*.
76. Stableford, "Introduction," *Vampire City*.
77. Stableford, "Introduction," *Vampire City*.
78. Stableford, "Afterword," *Vampire City*.
79. Féval, *Vampire City*, Chapter 2.
80. Féval, *Vampire City*, Chapter 3.
81. Féval, *Vampire City*, Chapter 12.
82. Coleridge, lines 589 and 607.
83. Coleridge, line 585.
84. Le Fanu, Chapter 4.
85. Le Fanu, Chapter 6.
86. Le Fanu, Chapter 3.
87. Le Fanu, Chapter 13.
88. Stableford, "Introduction," *Captain Vampire*.
89. Nizet, Chapter 1.
90. Stableford, "Afterword," *Captain Vampire*.
91. Stableford, "Afterword," *Captain Vampire*.
92. Stableford, "Afterword," *Captain Vampire*.
93. Mulvey-Roberts p. 182.
94. Stableford, "Afterword," *Captain Vampire*.
95. Mulvey-Roberts p. 184-5.
96. Artenie, *Dracula Invades England*, p. 59-76.
97. Rhodes and Browning, "About the Book," p. 5-6; and "About the Author," p. 7-8.
98. https://en.wikipedia.org/wiki/Gotham_City. Accessed April 23, 2022.
99. https://en.wiktionary.org/wiki/Gotham. Accessed April 23, 2022.
100. Rhodes and Browning, "America's First Vampire Novel," p. 249-51.
101. Verne, *The Carpathian Castle*, p. 9.
102. Eighteen-Bisang and Miller p. 210.
103. Shah p. 428-71.
104. Verne, *The Carpathian Castle*, p. 24.
105. Verne, *The Carpathian Castle*, p. 25.
106. Stoker, *Dracula*, p. 56-63.
107. Marryat, Florence p. 89.
108. Marryat, Florence p. 183.
109. Marryat, Florence p. 231.
110. Marryat, Florence p. 240.
111. https://en.wikipedia.org/wiki/The_Blood_of_the_Vampire#Contemporary_reception. Accessed April 24, 2022.
112. https://en.wikipedia.org/wiki/The_Blood_of_the_Vampire#Contemporary_reception. Accessed April 24, 2022.
113. Marryat, Florence p. 100.
114. "The Mysterious Stranger." *Chambers Repository of Instructive and Amusing Tracts.* 8.62 (1854): 1-32.
115. Brundan et al. p. 297.
116. https://fr.wikipedia.org/wiki/Karl_Adolf_von_Wachsmann._https://de.wikipedia.org/wiki/Karl_Adolf_von_Wachsmann. Accessed April 25, 2022.
117. Stableford, *Weird Fiction in France*, n. 71.
118. Stableford, "The Horla Introduction," *Weird Fiction in France*, p. 652.

[119] https://en.wikipedia.org/wiki/The_Horla. Accessed June 24, 2022.
[120] Haining and Tremayne p. 98.
[121] Stoker, *Personal Reminiscences of Henry Irving*, Chapter 34.
[122] Haining and Tremayne p. 98.
[123] Stenbock p. 312.
[124] Stenbock p. 313.
[125] Stenbock p. 314.
[126] Stenbock p. 314.
[127] Stenbock p. 316.
[128] https://en.wikipedia.org/wiki/The_Family_of_the_Vourdalak#Plot_summary. Accessed August 12, 2022.
[129] Cornwell p. 119.
[130] Skal p. 310. https://en.wikipedia.org/wiki/Eric_Stenbock; https://en.wikipedia.org/wiki/More_Adey. Both websites accessed April 28, 2022.
[131] Quoted in Haining and Tremayne p. 96.
[132] Stuart p. 181-2.
[133] Warren p. 1125.
[134] Haining and Tremayne p. 62; Mulvey-Roberts p. 182.
[135] Haining and Tremayne p. 88, 99.
[136] Murray p. 104.
[137] Murray p. 106.
[138] Murray p. 106.
[139] Stoker, *Personal Reminiscences*, Chapter 14.
[140] Murray p. 49; Stoker, *Personal Reminiscences of Sir Henry Irving*, Chapter 38.
[141] Haining and Tremayne p. 45.
[142] Haining and Tremayne p. 104.
[143] Haining and Tremayne p. 65.
[144] Haining and Tremayne p. 48.
[145] https://en.wikipedia.org/wiki/Charles_Stewart_Parnell. Accessed May 15, 2022.
[146] Haining and Tremayne p. 54.
[147] https://en.wikipedia.org/wiki/Charles_Maturin. Accessed September 11, 2022.
[148] Miles p. 90.
[149] Haining and Tremayne p. 84.
[150] Haining and Tremayne p. 135.
[151] Haining and Tremayne p. 36.
[152] Haining and Tremayne p. 179.
[153] Lady Wilde, *Ancient Legends*, "The Ancient Mysteries," https://www.gutenberg.org/files/61436/61436-h/61436-h.htm.
[154] Eighteen-Bisang and Miller p. 18.
[155] Murray p. 187.
[156] https://en.wikipedia.org/wiki/Prince_of_Darkness_(Satan). Accessed July 10, 2022.
[157] Lady Wilde, *Ancient Legends*, "Introduction," https://www.gutenberg.org/files/61436/61436-h/61436-h.htm.
[158] Stoker, "Dracula's Guest," p. 430.
[159] Stoker, "Dracula's Guest," p. 436.
[160] Eighteen-Bisang and Miller p. 39.
[161] Haining and Tremayne p. 19.
[162] Haining and Tremayne p. 144-59.
[163] https://en.wikipedia.org/wiki/New_Slains_Castle, citing Shepherd, Mike. *When Brave Men Shudder: The Scottish Origins of Dracula*. Wild Wolf Publishing, 2018.
[164] Murray p. 125.
[165] https://en.wikipedia.org/wiki/Death_Coach. Accessed June 30, 2022.
[166] Stoker, *Dracula*, p. 36.

167 Stoker, *Dracula*, p. 246-7.
168 Murray p. 185.
169 Stoker, *Dracula*, p. 113.
170 Matthews p. 6.
171 Matthews p. 1.
172 Hugo, *Notre-Dame de Paris*, Book 11, Chapter 1.
173 Eighteen-Bisang and Miller p. 258.
174 Stoker p. 213.
175 Power p. 21.
176 Power p. 21.
177 Murray p. 172-5.
178 Murray p. 169-70.
179 Quoted in Murray p. 191.
180 Haining and Tremayne p. 73.
181 Belford p. 80-1.
182 Skal p. 184.
183 Skal p. 184.
184 Tropp, *Images of Fear*, p. 130. Quoted in Eighteen-Bisang and Miller, *Drafts of Dracula*, p. 229-30.
185 Murray p. 54.
186 Haining and Tremayne p. 171.
187 Stoker, *Personal Reminiscences*, Chapter 59; Warren, "Buffalo Bill Meets Dracula."
188 Warren p. 1129, 1149.
189 Dumas, *Count of Monte Cristo*, p. 655.
190 Stoker, *Dracula*, p. 246 twice; p. 296.
191 Haining and Tremayne p. 172.
192 Stoker, *Dracula*, p. 312.
193 Dumas, *The Thousand and One Ghosts*, p. 193.
194 Belford p. 130.
195 Skal p. 219; Stoker, *Personal Reminiscences*, Chapter 15.
196 Féval, *Les Mystères de Londres*, p. 508-9.
197 Féval, *Les Mystères de Londres*, p. 509.
198 Stoker, *Dracula*, p. 364.
199 Stoker, *Dracula*, p. 365.
200 Stoker, *Dracula*, p. 365.
201 Eighteen-Bisang and Miller p. 243.
202 Stoker, *Personal Reminiscences*, Chapter 74.
203 Stoker, *Personal Reminiscences*, Chapter 26.
204 Dickens, *A Tale of Two Cities*, p. 352.
204 Dickens, *A Tale of Two Cities*, p. 352.
206 Hennelly p. 90.
207 Hennelly p. 89.
208 Stoker, *Dracula*, p. 247.
209 Hennelly p. 90.
210 Quoted in Senf, *Vampire*, p. 70.
211 Hennelly p. 90.
212 Stoker, *Dracula*, p. 247.

Afterword

1 Hale p. 17.

Index

Book titles are listed under the names of their authors with the exception of those with anonymous authors. French titles are primarily listed by their English title.

A

Adam and Eve, 158, 219, 244, 256, 297-9
Adey, More, 420
Ainsworth, William Harrison, vii, ix, x, 25, 29, 35, 50-69, 73, 92, 103, 128-31, 279, 321, 357, 399, 439
  Ainsworth's Magazine, 58, 105
  Auriol, or The Elixir of Life, 357
  The Combat of the Thirty (trans.), 59
  Crotchet Castle, 29, 63-4
  Guy Fawkes, 62-3
  Old Saint Paul's, 73
  Rookwood, ix, 25, 51-8, 321, 399, 439
  Sir John Chiverton, 50
  "The Spectre Bride," vii, 128-131, 357
  The Tower of London, 35, 51, 57-69, 279
American Civil War, 12
Anti-Catholicism, 5, 61-3, 68, 172, 178, 191, 220, 447
Apocalypse, 248, 297
Arabian Nights, The, 109, 113, 305, 331, 333, 350, 366, 376-7
Austen, Jane,
  Northanger Abbey, ix, 9n, 362, 377

B

Ballantyne, James, 10
Balzac, Honoré de, 9, 14-5, 38, 54, 93, 143
  Le Dernier Chouan, 14
  L'Héritière de Birague, 9
  Melmoth Reconciled, 143n
  The Human Comedy, 14
Barnes, Djuna
  Nightwood, 459
Bastille, 38, 66, 74, 112, 253, 263-5, 278-9, 281-3, 286-90, 293
Báthory, Elizabeth, 374
Batman, 33, 75-6, 79, 394
Beauchamais, Prince Eugène, 173
Bérard, Cyprien
  Lord Ruthwen ou les vampires, 19, 23, 304-8, 331, 335, 339, 345, 379, 432, 438-9, 442, 444, 449
Berry, Duchesse de, 14
Bible, The, 21, 45, 185, 435
Blake, William, 153
Blake, George, 425
Blanc, Louis, 271
Blood transfusions, 227, 395, 420-1, 445-6, 453, 455
Bocage, Paul, 74, 351
Bonaparte, Josephine, 173
Bonaparte, Napoleon, 13, 84, 106, 165, 186, 250, 260, 267, 269, 305, 335, 341, 375
Borgias, The, 107, 209-11, 396
Boucicault, Dion, 25-6, 267, 275-6, 319-22, 326, 329, 354, 371, 396, 435, 442, 444, 449
  The Corsican Brothers, 267, 275n, 319, 449
  Geneviève; or the Reign of Terror, 275-6, 319

~ 503 ~

The Phantom, 25-6, 321-2, 354, 396, 444

The Vampire, 25-6, 319-22, 326, 329, 354, 371, 435, 442, 444

Braddon, Mary Elizabeth, iii, 420-1

"Good Lady Ducayne," iii, 420-1, 446

Lady Audley's Secret, iii-iv, 99, 420

Bride of the Isles, The (1820, anonymous), 23, 313

British Empire, 80-1, 83-4, 87, 91, 234-5, 424

Brontë, Charlotte, 56-7

Jane Eyre, 56, 147, 151, 393, 400

Tales of Angria, 56

Brontë, Emily, 56-7, 115

Wuthering Heights, 56-7, 115

Brown, Charles Brockden

Wieland, 396

Buffy the Vampire Slayer, 378

Bulwer-Lytton, Edward, 43n, 66, 103, 176, 196, 236-49, 251, 259, 261, 266, 269, 276, 280, 284, 289, 299, 300, 444, 512, 514

Paul Clifford, 238

The Haunted and the Haunters, 239

The Parisians, 239

Zanoni, 43n, 66, 196, 236-49, 251, 261, 266, 270, 276, 283-4, 293-4, 299, 300

Zicci, 239

Burke and Hare, 89, 97

Burnett, Frances Hodgson

Little Lord Fauntleroy, 57-8, 69

Burney, Fanny

The Wanderer, or Female Difficulties, 30-2

Byron, Lord, 1-2, 16, 18-20, 23, 109-10, 147, 173, 216, 303-5, 313n, 331, 382

Don Juan, 216

"The Giaour," 331

Manfred, 109

as literary vampire source, 1-2, 18-20, 109-10, 303-5, 313n, 382

Byronic hero, 11, 18-9, 21, 109

C

Cagliostro, 109, 231, 251, 253, 259, 261-70, 272, 300

Caine, Hal, 175

Calmet, Dom Augustin, 341, 381

Calvino, Italo, 457

Captain Vanderdecken, 357, 440

Carlyle, Thomas, vi, 249, 251, 274, 276-7, 279-80, 285, 288, 297

The French Revolution: A History, 251, 274, 276, 280, 288, 297

Sartor Resartus, 251n

Carmouche, Pierre-Frédéric-Adolphe, 23-4

Carpathian Mountains, 24, 314-5, 323, 325, 351, 391, 397-8, 403, 409-10, 412, 429

Catholicism (see also Anti-Catholicism), 5-6, 21, 49, 51-2, 61-8, 82, 159, 160, 166, 171-2, 178, 191-2, 220, 230, 258, 307, 350, 447-8

Charles X, 40

Chateaubriand, François-René de, 271

Christianity 41, 49-50, 78, 93, 116, 119-21, 124, 127, 159, 171, 173, 177, 181-2, 185, 187-8, 194, 196, 199, 219-20, 229-30, 240-2, 246, 283-4, 296-7, 299, 384n

Christie, Agatha, 72

City Mysteries, viii, 27, 71-117, 161, 238, 277-8, 368, 397, 434, 441

Clairmont, Claire, 2

Cleopatra, 110, 184, 186, 262, 439

Colburn, Henry, 18, 139

Cody, William F. "Buffalo Bill," 443

Coleridge, Samuel Taylor
  "Christabel," 31, 306, 344, 346, 383-5
  "The Rime of the Ancient Mariner," 127, 136, 433, 440
Collins, Wilkie
  The Moonstone, iii
  The Frozen Deep, 280
  The Woman in White, 99, 176, 415, 426, 436, 444
Comte de Saint-Germain, 109
Conspiracy theories, 108, 117, 193-4, 196-7, 238, 269
Cooper, James Fenimore, 11, 13, 17, 73
  The Pilot, 73
Cousin de Grainville, Jean-Baptiste
  The Last Man, 153
Creation, The (biblical), 154, 168, 185-6, 285, 289, 340
Croly, George, 131-53, 159, 187, 448
  Marston, 131
  Salathiel, 131-53, 159, 174, 436
Cruikshank, George, 35, 60, 65

D

D'Arcy, Uriah Derick
  "The Black Vampyre," 22-3, 330-5, 342, 395, 406
Defauconpret, Auguste, 13
Der Vampyr (Lindpaintner & Heigel), 24
Der Vampyr (Lyser), 24
Der Vampyr (Marschner & Wohlbrück), 24, 26, 313, 432
Der Vampyr (Planché), 24, 310-5, 351, 410, 428-9
Der Vampyr (Ritter), 24
Dickens, Charles, iv, x, 50, 57, 66, 72-3, 75, 77, 80, 89, 92, 94, 96, 99, 103-4, 112, 196, 236-8, 249, 251, 264-5, 269-300, 319, 343, 372, 428, 432, 442, 452, 455
  Bleak House, 99, 104, 278, 343
  The Cricket on the Hearth, 276
  Master Humphrey's Clock, 94
  The Mystery of Edwin Drood, 292
  Oliver Twist, 75
  Our Mutual Friend, 99, 278
  The Pickwick Papers, 94
  A Tale of Two Cities, 66, 88, 96, 104, 112, 116, 147, 196, 237-8, 249, 251, 264-5, 270-300, 319, 372, 428, 432, 442, 452
    The Only Way (play of *A Tale of Two Cities*), 452
Dillion, Valentine Blake, 425
Dornay, Jules
  Douglas Le Vampire, 26, 322-5, 440, 442
Doyle, Arthur Conan, 72, 224
Duke of Wellington, Arthur Wellesley, 379, 382, 443
Dumas, Alexandre, iii, viii, x, 9, 12, 14-7, 25-6, 54-6, 66, 72, 91, 93-4, 103-17, 160, 167, 179-88, 190-1, 197, 211, 215, 231n, 236-8, 249-80, 300, 315-9, 321, 329, 340, 350-4, 363, 366, 378, 392, 398, 410, 429, 434, 440, 445, 447, 449, 455, 461
  Andrée de Taverney (see *The Mesmerist's Victim*)
  Ange Pitou (see *The Storming of the Bastille*)
  Angèline, 94
  The Castle of Eppstein, 9
  Celebrated Crimes, 215
  Le Chevalier de Maison-Rouge, 253, 263, 269-76, 279, 319
  Christine, 271

The Corsican Brothers, 262, 267, 275n, 319, 449

The Count of Monte Cristo, 56, 59, 66, 72, 89, 91, 105-17, 171, 180, 187, 278, 316, 434, 438, 443

The Countess de Charny, 253, 268-70, 272

Henri III et sa cour, 17

The Hero of the People, 253, 262-3, 265-8

Isaac Laquedem, 179-88, 190, 211, 459

Joseph Balsamo, 251-61, 270

The Man in the Iron Mask, 278-9

Mes Mémoires, 17

The Mesmerist's Victim, 253, 261-2, 266, 449

The Mouth of Hell, 9

The Pale Lady (see *The Thousand and One Ghosts*)

The Queen's Necklace, 253, 262-3

The Royal Life Guard, 253, 268

The Storming of the Bastille, 263-5

Souvenirs de 1830 à 1842, 17

The Thousand and One Ghosts, 316, 340, 350-4, 410, 429, 447

The Three Musketeers, 186-7, 249, 378

The Vampire, 25, 315-9, 351, 354, 363, 398, 429, 440, 447

Le Vicomte de Bragelonne, 279

The Wolf Leader, 434

Urbain Grandier, 262, 449

E

Edgeworth, Maria, 31, 426
  The Absentee, 426
  Belinda, 426
  Castle Rackrent, 426
  Harrington, 31
Edinburgh, 12, 89, 322

Existentialism, 36, 41-2, 49, 55

F

Faber, Henry, 18
Fantasmagoriana, 2
Faust, Johann Georg, 207n
Faustian pact (see also Satanic pact), 25, 48, 111, 327
Felix (French opera), 7
Féval, Paul, i, viii, x, 4, 6, 56, 72, 74, 80-91, 96-8, 100, 105-6, 108-9, 115-7, 119, 160, 188-92, 196, 233-5, 271, 278, 308, 350, 359, 363, 373-83, 424-6, 429, 432, 434-5, 441, 443-4, 448-50, 455
  Bel Demonio, 90
  Les Compagnons du Silence, 90
  Dramas of Death, 373
  Les Habits Noirs (The Black Coats), 90, 381
  Jean Diable, 90
  Jerusalem Street, 90
  Knightshade, 373, 376-7, 381, 450
  The Love Nest, 373
  Les Mystères de Londres, i, 56, 80-91, 96, 98, 105-6, 115-7, 196, 233-5, 278, 359, 373, 377, 424-6, 432, 434-5, 448, 450-1
  The Mysteries of London, or The Gentlemen of the Night (play), 89-90
  Le Quittance de Minuit (The Midnight Rent), 90-1
  Vampire City, x, 4, 373, 377-83, 443-4, 449, 450
  The Vampire Countess, 350, 373-5, 377, 383, 397, 429
  The Wandering Jew's Daughter, 119, 188-92, 373-4, 377
  The White Wolf, 105
Fitzball, Edmund
  The Flying Dutchman: or the Phantom Ship, 136
Fitzgerald, F. Scott

The Great Gatsby, 116
Flood, The (biblical), 285
Flying Dutchman, 136, 176, 440
Follies-Dramatiques, 5
Forster, John, 271, 277
Franco-Prussian War, 180
Freemasons, 21, 108, 194, 224, 292
French Revolution, vii-viii, 5-7, 13, 21, 29, 65-6, 71, 108, 157, 160, 177-8, 190, 193-6, 231n, 236-300, 305

G

Galitzin, Princess, 13
Galland, Antoine, 376
Garden of Eden, 215-6, 244, 246, 285, 295, 297, 349
Gautier, Théophile, 16, 271, 308, 346-50, 353, 363
    "Clarimonde," 308, 346-50, 353, 363
Gavarni, 5
Genlis, Madame de, 16
George III, 178
Gerard, Emily
    The Land Beyond the Forest, 427
German literature, vii, 2, 22, 24, 54-5, 123, 313-4, 325, 408-13, 459
Gilbert and Sullivan
    Ruddigore, 22, 26, 325-9, 413, 430
Gilbert, William
    "The Last Lords of Gardonal," 413
    The Wizard of the Mountain, 413
Gilbert, W. S., 430
Glasgow, 12
Glisic, Milovan
    After Ninety Years, 350
Godwin, William
    St. Leon, 43n, 109, 127, 239-41, 248
Goethe, Johann Wolfgang von, 19, 123, 207
    Faust, 207

Sorrows of Young Werther, 123
Gotham, 394
Gozlan, Léon
    "Another Soul Sold to the Devil," 369
    "The Black Morocco-Leather Wallet," 369
    "The Madwoman in No. 16"
    The Mysterious Neighborhood, 369
    The Vampire of the Val-de-Grâce, 26, 369-72, 446
Granville, Lord, 13
Grey, Elizabeth Caroline
    "The Skeleton Count, or The Vampire Mistress," 343-6, 388, 403, 450
Guillotine, 65, 190, 194, 246-7, 262, 266-7, 269-70, 273-6, 283, 294, 296-7, 299

H

Haggard, H. Rider
    She, 233, 393
Haining, Peter (and literary fraud), 345-6
Harvey, Martin, 452
Hawthorne, Julian, 415-7, 439
    David Poindexter's Disappearance, 416
    "Ken's Mystery," 415-7, 439
Hawthorne, Nathaniel, 415
Heigel, Cäsar Max
    Der Vampyr, 24
Henry VIII, 64-5, 355-6
Hermetic Order of the Golden Dawn, 224
Hoffman, E. T. A., 54
Holy Vehme, 198, 200, 202-10
Home Rule (Ireland), 235, 424-5
Hugo, Victor, ix-x, 9, 12, 14-6, 35-51, 54-55, 57-62, 65, 68, 72, 78-9, 93, 103-4,

116, 159, 163, 165n, 169, 185, 193, 250, 271, 279, 372, 436
  The Demon Dwarf (*Hans of Iceland* trans), 35
  Hans of Iceland, 35, 65
  Hernani, 38
  Les Misérables, 36, 78-9, 116, 163, 169, 193, 372, 436
  Marie Tudor, 55, 58-9
  Notre-Dame de Paris, i, ix, 9, 15-6, 35-51, 54-5, 59-62, 65, 68, 106, 165n, 169, 250, 279, 435-6, 439
Hungary (Austro-Hungarian Empire), 101, 313-5, 323, 325, 335, 338-41, 392
Hypnotism (see also Mesmerism), 21, 79, 107, 109, 176n, 252, 266, 348, 392, 410, 414, 421, 433, 449

I

Illuminati, 194
Inquisition, 5, 32, 66-7, 169, 200, 217, 219-20, 246, 266n
Insanity (see also Madness), 65, 101, 165, 176, 231, 233, 361-2, 366, 415, 438, 443-5
Irish Death Coach, 431
Irish National League, 425
Irving, Laurence, 438
Irving, Sir Henry, 175-6, 267, 319, 397, 423-4, 435, 437-8, 440, 443, 449, 452
Irving, Washington, 128, 394
  "The Specter Bridegroom," 128

J

James, G. P. R.
  The Jacquereie, or the Lady and the Page, 279
Janin, Jules
  "The Orphan," 97
Jesuits, 52, 160, 163-4, 166-73, 177-8, 196

Jones, John Paul, 254
Jouffroy, Achille de, 23-4

K

Karloff, Boris, 69
Keats, John
  "La Belle Dame Sans Merci," 417
Kempis, Thomas à
  The Imitation of Christ, 171
Kock, Paul de
  La Barbier de Paris, 9

L

Laclos, Pierre Ambroise François Choderlos de
  Les Liaisons Dangereuses, 13
Ladvocat, Pierre-François, 19, 304
Lafayette, Madame de
  La Princesse de Clèves, 10
Lake Geneva, 2
Lamartine, Alphonse de, 93, 159, 271
Lamb, Lady Caroline
  Glenarvon, 1, 17-18, 302, 424
Lamothe-Langon, Étienne-Léon de
  The Mysterious Hermit of the Tomb, 8
  The Virgin Vampire, 308, 315, 334-43, 364, 397, 408
Le Fanu, Joseph Sheridan, 426
  Carmilla, 301, 330, 340, 346, 350, 363, 381-8, 396, 407-8, 417-8, 429, 439
  In a Glass Darkly, 383
Lecroix, Paul, 54
Lee, Sophia
  The Recess, 10, 64
Leroux, Gaston
  The Phantom of the Opera, 45, 459
Lewis, Matthew,
  The Monk, v, viii-ix, 3, 5-8, 36, 54, 120, 123-8, 152, 165n, 347, 357, 433, 435, 448

Lindpaintner, Peter Joseph von,
  Der Vampyr, 24
London Library, vi
Lord Ruthven depictions, vii, 1, 18-27, 36, 82, 86, 103, 109-10, 128, 130, 188, 195, 235, 302-13, 316-9, 321-2, 325-30, 334-5, 351, 354-5, 360-1, 371, 421, 428, 432-4, 438-40, 442, 444-5, 447, 449, 455
Louis XVI, 176n, 259, 263, 265-6, 269, 272, 279, 287-8
Lovecraft, H. P., 415
Lyon, James
  Kiss of the Butterfly, 350
Lyser, Johann Peter
  Der Vampyr, 24

M

Macready, William, 271
Madness (see also Insanity), 8, 43, 46, 50, 78, 107, 113, 213, 225, 231, 286-7, 310, 318, 324, 327-8, 361, 365, 395, 397, 415, 445
Maquet, Auguste, 25-6, 315-6
Mark of Cain, 45-6, 83, 124, 133, 145, 181-3, 235, 291-2, 338, 435, 448
Marlowe, Christopher
  Doctor Faustus, 207
Marryat, Captain Frederick, 403
  The Naval Officer, 73
  The Phantom Ship, 136, 357, 434, 440
Marryat, Florence
  The Blood of the Vampire, 334, 395, 403-8
Marschner, Heinrich
  Der Vampyr, 24, 26, 313-4, 432
Martineau, Harriet, 248
Marx, Karl, 12, 173
Mathias, Thomas James
  The Pursuits of Literature, 237
Maturin, Charles, 8, 54, 426

Bertram, 308
Melmoth the Wanderer, ix, 32, 66, 127, 143-4, 195, 200, 215, 220, 239-40, 246, 248, 357, 426, 430, 433, 446
The Milesian Chief, 426
The Wild Irish Boy, 426
Maupassant, Guy de
  "The Horla," 413-5, 426, 445
Maurier, George du
  Peter Ibbetson, 348
  Trilby, 107, 433
Méliès, George
  The Haunted Castle, 434
Mérimée, Prosper, 15, 93, 368
  Chronique du Reègne de Charles IX, 15
  Mateo Falcone, 93
Mesmerism (see also Hypnotism), 23, 79, 98, 107, 147, 176n, 252, 261-2, 264, 266, 268, 321, 324, 348, 362, 385, 389, 410, 431, 433, 449
Michelet, Jules, 160-1
Milton, John, 147
  Paradise Lost, 196, 245, 285, 287, 289, 427
Mirbel, Madame de, 13
Moncrieff, W. T.
  The Vampire, 23
Mount Vesuvius, 210-1
Multatuli (Edward Douwes Dekker)
  Max Havelaar, 11, 174, 459

N

Napoleon Bonaparte (see Bonaparte, Napoleon)
Napoleon III (Louis Napoleon), 180, 185, 188, 270, 273
Napoleonic Wars, v, 84, 121, 131, 163, 335, 341
Naturalism, 49
New Slains Castle, 430

New York City, 12, 74, 257, 322, 330, 394-6, 416
Newgate, 85
Newgate novels, 51, 55, 238
Nizet, Marie
  Captain Vampire, 331, 388-94
Noah's Ark, 209-10
Nodier, Charles, v, 13-5, 23-4, 35, 47, 93, 304-5, 308-10, 315-6, 324, 329, 415, 446
  Bertram ou le Pirate, 308
  Le Monstre et le Magicien, 308
  Le Peintre de Salzbourg, 308
  Les Proscrits, 308
  The Vampire, 23-4, 47, 308-10, 313, 315-6, 324, 329, 415, 446

O

O'Brien, Fitzjames
  "What Was It?", 426
O'Connell, Daniel, 82, 90-1
Oaths, 12, 21, 24, 38, 129, 136, 195, 204-5, 304, 309, 313-4, 319, 324, 349, 352, 445-7
One Thousand and One Nights (see *Arabian Nights*)
Orléanist Conspiracy, 223

P

Paccard, Jean-Edme, 5
Parnell, Charles, 425
Peacock, Thomas Love
  Nightmare Abbey, ix, 377
Philips, Watt
  The Dead Heart, 280
Planché, James Robinson
  The Recollections and Reflections of J. R. Planché, 313
  The Vampire, or The Bride of the Isles, 23, 310-13
  Der Vampyr, 24, 310-5, 323, 351, 410, 428-9
Poe, Edgar Allan, 162
  "Berenice," 396
  "The Fall of the House of Usher," 400
  "Morella," 396
Polidori, John
  The Vampyre, v, vii, 1-2, 10, 17-23, 27, 29, 36, 72, 86, 109, 195, 235, 301-6, 308-10, 315, 322, 324, 329-30, 342-3, 345, 365, 382-3, 392, 396, 412-3, 419, 430, 432, 446, 459
Ponson du Terrail, Pierre-Alexis, 8, 91, 308, 363-9, 376, 397, 399, 434
  Rocambole (character), 91, 368
  The Immortal Woman, 363, 366-8, 399
  The Inn in the Street of the Red Children, 368
  The Miseries of London, 91, 368
  The Vampire and the Devil's Son (La Baronne trépassée), 363-6, 397, 434
Porter, Jane, 115
  The Scottish Chiefs, 10, 32
Powers of Darkness (Icelandic *Makt Myrkranna*), 221-2, 458
Powers of Darkness (Swedish *Mörkrets Makter*), viii, 197, 221-36, 301, 341, 407, 418, 430, 438, 454, 458
Price, Vincent, 69
Protestantism, 5, 61-3, 65, 67-8, 82, 164, 171, 177
Pushkin, Alexander Sergeyevich, 419

Q

Quinet, Edgar, 172, 180, 187
  Ahasvérus, 152-62, 340
  Génie des religion (The Genius of Religions), 160
  Des Jésuites, 160-1
  Tablets of the Wandering Jew, 153

R

Racism, 174, 183, 223, 260, 340-1, 393, 395, 405, 454

Radcliffe, Mrs. (Ann), v, viii-ix, 1-10, 16, 27, 32, 36, 40, 50-1, 53-4, 57-8, 66, 72, 101, 127, 165n, 195, 199-201, 278, 343, 357, 363, 373, 377-80, 396-7, 428, 432, 444, 455

   The Castles of Athlin and Dunbayne, 3

   The Italian, 3, 5, 32, 36, 66, 127, 165n, 200, 343, 357

   The Mysteries of Udolpho, 1, 3-5, 9, 29, 101, 195, 278, 446

   The Romance of the Forest, 3, 6, 40, 199, 278, 357, 428, 432

   A Sicilian Romance, 3

Radcliffe, Mary Anne

   Manfrone, or The One-Handed Monk, 8n

Redemption, 11, 75-8, 96-7, 99-100, 102, 106, 115, 119, 121, 158, 163, 168, 187, 210-1, 215, 218-9, 239, 244-5, 283-300, 343, 402, 447, 454-5

Reims Cathedral, 40

Reynolds, George W. M., i, v-vi, viii, x, 7-9, 25-6, 35, 37, 57, 72, 74, 80-1, 88-9, 91-105, 117, 177-9, 197, 207-220, 278, 354-8, 430, 433-4, 441, 448

   The Baroness, 94

   The Errors of the Christian Religion Exposed, 93

   Faust: A Romance of the Secret Tribunals, 25, 103, 197, 207-12, 218, 354, 433

   The French Self Instructor, 94

   Kenneth, a Romance of the Highlands, 355

   Master Timothy's Bookcase, 94

   May Middleton, 355

   The Modern Literature of France, v, 7, 35, 93, 97, 105

   The Mysteries of London, i, 72, 74, 80-1, 88-9, 92-105, 207-8, 211, 278

   The Mysteries of the Court of London, 81, 103, 177-9

   The Necromancer, 25-6, 103, 207, 354-8, 428, 430, 433, 448

   The Parricide, 94

   Pickwick Abroad, 94

   Pickwick Married, 94

   Robert Macaire, 94

   Wagner, the Wehr-Wolf, 103, 197, 207, 211-20, 358, 434, 448

   The Youthful Impostor, 94

Ricard, Auguste, 93

Richardson, Samuel

   Clarissa, 77

   Sir Charles Grandison, 32

Ritter, Heinrich Ludwig

   Der Vampyr, 24

Robespierre, Maximilien, 247-8, 260, 269

Robin Hood, 34, 105

Romania, 222-3, 233, 315, 323, 325, 334, 341, 388-94, 401, 403, 512, 514

Romantic myth of consciousness, 245

Romanticism, iv-v, 5, 10, 11n, 13, 35, 38-41, 73, 115, 123, 126, 152, 191, 196, 245, 249, 285, 315, 359, 361-2, 379-80, 398, 412, 417

Rosencreutz, Christian, 42, 212, 217-8, 220

Rosicrucians, 21, 32, 42, 43n, 107-8, 110, 123, 194-6, 212, 217-8, 224, 239-42, 248, 250, 261, 267, 270, 283-300, 357, 366, 374

Rousseau, Jean Jacques, 259-61, 267

   Le Contrat Social, 259

Russo-Turkish War, 388, 392

Rymer, James Malcolm

   The Black Monk, 33-4

   Varney the Vampire, 11n, 195, 210-1,

218, 301-2, 330, 332, 375, 382-3, 396, 441, 446

S

Sade, Marquis de, 6-8, 31, 165n
   Crimes of Love, 7
   An Essay on Novels, 6-7
   Justine, 6-8, 31, 165n
Sand, George, iii, vi, 93
Sartre, Jean-Paul, 41
Satanic pact (see also Faustian pact), 11, 209
Sauval, Henri
   Histoire et recherches des antiquités de la ville de Paris, 42
Schiller, Friedrich, 16
Scotland, viii, 11, 31, 89, 306, 310-1, 313, 315, 321, 334, 360, 394, 430
Scott, Sir Walter, iii-iv, 3-4, 10-7, 27, 29-40, 50-1, 53-5, 57-8, 63-4, 72, 115, 136, 142-3, 177, 179, 197-207, 210, 250, 276, 378-9, 459
   The Abbot, 39
   Anne of Geierstein, 10, 30, 197-207, 210
   The Black Dwarf, 35
   The Bride of Lammermoor, 11
   The Fortunes of Nigel, 39
   Guy Mannering, 13
   Ivanhoe, 10-4, 16-7, 30-5, 38, 72, 87, 147, 177, 179
   Kenilworth, 11-2
   Lives of the Novelists, 10, 378
   Old Mortality, 14-5
   Peveril of the Peak, 37
   Quentin Durward, 12, 14, 16, 36, 38-40
   Waverley, 10-1, 14-5, 37
   Waverley Novels, 14-6, 39
   Woodstock, 10, 12
   Places named for Scott, 12

Sir Walter Scott Monument (Edinburgh), 12
Scribe, Eugène, 22, 24, 173, 271
   Le Vampire, 22, 24
Second Coming, 30, 292, 297
Second sight, 262, 266-7, 380, 448-9
Secret societies, 21, 27, 117, 163, 171-3, 193-236, 238, 254, 261, 269-70, 447
Seyfioglu, Ali Riza
   Dracula in Istanbul, 458
Shakespeare, William, 16-7, 64, 115, 147, 202
   Hamlet, 423
   Henry VI, 202
Shelley, Mary, ix, 2, 29, 199, 308, 388, 407
   Frankenstein, ix, 2, 11, 29, 88, 195-6, 199, 308, 325, 340, 343, 369, 388, 407, 421, 441
Shelley, Percy Bysshe, 2
   Prometheus Unbound, 153, 158
Shoberl, Frederic, ix, 35
Smart, Hawley, 394
Smith, Albert
   The Marchioness of Brinvilliers, 279
Smith, J. F.
   The Substance and the Shadow, 279, 283
Socialism, 73, 78, 117, 173, 178, 405
Society of Jesus (see Jesuits)
Sorr, Angelo de
   The Vampires of London, 358-63, 376-7, 445
Soulié, Frédéric, 8-9, 93
   The Two Cadavers, 8
   The Devil's Memoirs, 8-9
Spring-Heeled Jack, 346, 435
Stenbock, Eric
   "The Sad Story of a Vampire," 398, 417-20, 429, 439

Stendhal, 16, 368
Stevenson, Robert Louis
  "The Body Snatcher," 96-7
  Strange Case of Dr. Jekyll and Mr. Hyde, 349, 395, 441
Stoker, Bram, viii, 2, 24-5, 87, 110-1, 144-6, 153, 174-6, 221-4, 230-6, 267, 301-2, 319-20, 325, 329, 358, 361, 365, 373, 377-8, 381-3, 388-9, 391-3, 397-403, 408-10, 412-3, 415, 417, 419-55, 458-9
  Dracula, viii-ix, 2, 24-5, 27, 48, 86-7, 89, 107, 110-1, 116, 119, 131, 144-6, 152-3, 175-6, 190, 195, 197, 221-33, 235-6, 266-7, 301-3, 305, 307-9, 311, 313, 315, 317, 319-25, 327, 329-31, 333-5, 337, 339-41, 343-5, 347, 349-51, 353, 355, 357-9, 361, 363, 365, 367, 369, 371, 373, 375, 377-83, 385, 387-395, 397-403, 405-13, 415, 417, 419-55, 457-9
  "Dracula's Guest," 383, 428-9
  Famous Impostors, 144-5, 174-5, 231n
  The Lady of the Shroud, 392
  The Lair of the White Worm, 400
  Personal Reminiscences of Henry Irving, 319, 392, 416, 423, 437
  Powers of Darkness (see separate entries)
  The Primrose Path, 426
  The Snake's Pass, 427
  comments on *Salathiel*, 144-6
  comments on Sue's *The Wandering Jew*, 174-6
  and French, 381-2, 422-3
  and Irish influences, 424-8
Stoker, Florence, 329, 423, 425-6, 428, 430, 447
Stoker, George, 392
Styria, 383-5, 387, 398, 417, 419, 428-9
Sue, Eugène, iii, vi, viii, x, 15, 52, 71-80, 89-90, 92-3, 100, 103-5, 113, 116-7, 145, 153, 160-80, 187, 190-1, 196, 230, 238, 271, 276-81, 283, 343, 357, 368, 375, 415, 436, 447, 459
  Jean Cavalier, 15
  Kernock le Pirate, 73
  The Mysteries of Paris, 71-79, 104-5, 113, 163, 169, 173, 175, 177-8, 277, 434
  The Mysteries of the People, 73, 177-9, 187, 238, 279-80
    The Iron Trevet, or Jocelyn the Champion, 279
    The Pocket Bible, 177
    The Sword of Honor, 178, 280
  The Wandering Jew, x, 52, 73, 153, 160-78, 196, 230, 357, 415, 443, 445, 459
Superman, 33, 79
Swedenborg, Emanuel, 107, 254

T

Tales of the Dead (see *Fantasmagoriana*)
Tarzan, 79
Thackeray, William Makepeace, 1, 104
  Pendennis, iv
  Rebecca and Rowena, 11
  Vanity Fair, 104
Tower of London, The (films), 69
Theatre Doyen, 5
Thierry, Augustin, 14
Thompson, Richard
  The Mysteries of Old St. Paul's, 73
Tieck, Johann Ludwig, 54
Tolstoy, Aleksey Konstantinovich
  "The Family of the Vourdalak" ("The Curse of the Vourdalak"), 419
Tolstoy, Leo
  War and Peace, 16

Tower of Babel, 108
Transylvania, 227, 232, 325, 341, 360, 391-3, 398, 400, 403, 409, 427, 429-30, 440, 450-1, 453, 512
Trollope, Anthony, iii, 80, 103
　Barchester Towers, iii
　The Small House at Allington, iii
　The Way We Live Now, 116, 343
Trollope, Frances, 80
Twain, Mark, 12
　A Connecticut Yankee in King Arthur's Court, 12
　The Adventures of Huckleberry Finn, 12
　Life on the Mississippi, 12

U

Upton, Smyth
　The Last of the Vampires, 25, 322, 396

V

Vambery, Arminius, 444
Vampire: or, Detective Brand's Greatest Case, The (anonymous), 394-7, 435
Verne, Jules, viii, 91, 391-2, 397-403, 410, 430, 437, 444, 454
　The Carpathian Castle, 391, 397-403, 430, 437, 444
　The Mysterious Island, 91
　Twenty Thousand Leagues Under the Sea, 91
Villiers de l'Isle-Adam, Comte de
　Claire Lenoir, 368
Volcanoes, 122, 137, 182, 210-1, 400

W

Wachsmann, Karl von
　"Der Fremde" ("The Mysterious Stranger"), 325, 408-13, 430, 436
Wagner, Richard
　The Flying Dutchman, 136, 440

Wallace, Lew, 115-6, 147-52, 153, 173-4
　Ben-Hur, 115-6, 147, 151
　The Prince of India, 116, 151-3, 173-4
　comments on *Salathiel*, 147-52
Walpole, Horace, 9, 51, 54
　The Castle of Otranto, viii, 29, 377
Wandering Jew (depictions of), 21, 27, 30-2, 34, 45, 79, 83, 107, 109, 111-3, 116, 119-92, 287, 291-2, 313n, 348, 357, 373, 410, 433, 435, 448, 455
Webster, Benjamin, 276, 280
Wells, H. G.
　The Island of Dr. Moreau, 407
Wilde, Lady Jane, 425-7
　Ancient Legends, 427
Wilde, Oscar, 420, 425-6
Wills, W. G.
　Vanderdecken, 440
Wohlbrück, Wilhelm August, 24
Wood, Mrs. Henry
　East Lynne, 99

Y

Yeats, William Butler, 224

Z

Zahed, Éliphas Lévi, 239
Zola, Émile, 41
　The Mysteries of Marseilles, 74

516 *Vampire Grooms and Spectre Brides*

Discovering Dracula at the Vlad Țepeș birthplace, Sighișoara, Romania

In search of Zanoni and a good cup of tea at Bulwer-Lytton's Knebworth House, England

Bram Stoker refuses to give up his secrets at Hotel Castel Dracula, Transylvania

About the Author

TYLER R. TICHELAAR has a PhD in Literature from Western Michigan University and Bachelor and Master's Degrees in English from Northern Michigan University. He is the owner of Marquette Fiction, his own publishing company, and of Superior Book Productions, a professional editing, proofreading, and book layout company. He has served as president and vice president of the Upper Peninsula Publishers and Authors Association, has been a book reviewer for Reader Views, *Marquette Monthly*, and UP Book Review, and regularly blogs about Gothic and Arthurian literature and Upper Michigan history.

Tyler published his first novel *Iron Pioneers: The Marquette Trilogy, Book One* in 2006. Since then he has published twenty-two titles. In 2009, Tyler won first place in the historical fiction category in the Reader Views Literary Awards for his novel *Narrow Lives*. He has since sponsored that contest, offering the Tyler R. Tichelaar Award for Historical Fiction. In 2011, Tyler was awarded the Marquette County Outstanding Writer Award, and the same year, he received the Barb Kelly Award for Historical Preservation for his efforts to promote Marquette history. In 2014, his play *Willpower* was produced by the Marquette Regional History Center, with the assistance of a grant from the Michigan Humanities Council. Tyler has twice been nominated for the Pushcart Prize for his short stories. In 2021, his biography of

Ojibwa Chief Charles Kawbawgam, titled *Kawbawgam: The Chief, The Legend, The Man*, was named a UP Notable Book.

A lifelong love for Gothic literature led Tyler to write his doctoral dissertation on nineteenth-century British Gothic literature. It was published in an expanded form in 2012 as *The Gothic Wanderer: From Transgression to Redemption* by Modern History Press. *Vampire Grooms and Spectre Brides: The Marriage of French and British Gothic Literature* is a companion work to his earlier book. Tyler has presented papers on Gothic and Arthurian literature at the Michigan Academy of Arts and Sciences, the Bulwer-Lytton Conference, and the Medieval Studies Conference. He also taught composition and literature at Northern Michigan University, Western Michigan University, and Clemson University before becoming self-employed as an author and editor.

In his spare time, Tyler enjoys reading Gothic and many other types of literature, living in beautiful Upper Michigan, walking along Lake Superior, doing jigsaw puzzles, and traveling to historical and Gothic places like Bulwer-Lytton's Knebworth House, Notre-Dame de Paris, the Tower of London, and Bran Castle in Romania. He plans to write many more books.

Visit Tyler at:

www.GothicWanderer.com

www.MarquetteFiction.com

www.ChildrenofArthur.com

Books by Tyler R. Tichelaar

Nonfiction

The Gothic Wanderer: From Transgression to Redemption, 1794-Present

Vampire Grooms and Spectre Brides: The Marriage of French and British Gothic Literature, 1789-1897

King Arthur's Children: A Study in Fiction and Tradition

The Nomad Editor: Living the Lifestyle You Want, Doing Work You Love

My Marquette: Explore the Queen City of the North, Its History, People, and Places

Haunted Marquette: Ghost Stories from the Queen City of the North

Kawbawgam: The Chief, The Legend, The Man

Creating a Local Historical Book: Fiction and Nonfiction Genres

Historical Fiction

Iron Pioneers: The Marquette Trilogy, Book One

The Queen City: The Marquette Trilogy, Book Two

Superior Heritage: The Marquette Trilogy, Book Three

Narrow Lives: A Novel

The Only Thing That Lasts: A Novel
Spirit of the North: A Paranormal Romance
The Best Place: A Novel
When Teddy Came to Town: A Novel

Historical Fantasy

Arthur's Legacy: The Children of Arthur, Book One
Melusine's Gift: The Children of Arthur, Book Two
Ogier's Prayer: The Children of Arthur, Book Three
Lilith's Love: The Children of Arthur, Book Four
Arthur's Bosom: The Children of Arthur, Book Five

Drama

Willpower: An Original Play About Marquette's Ossified Man

www.ingramcontent.com/pod-product-compliance
Lightning Source LLC
Chambersburg PA
CBHW070519010526
44118CB00012B/1028